Lion of Jordan

Lion of Jordan

The Life of King Hussein in War and Peace

Avi Shlaim

Alfred A. Knopf　New York, 2008

THIS IS A BORZOI BOOK PUBLISHED BY ALFRED A. KNOPF AND
ALFRED A. KNOPF CANADA

Copyright © 2007 by Avi Shlaim

All rights reserved. Published in the United States by Alfred A. Knopf,
a division of Random House, Inc., New York, and in Canada by Alfred A. Knopf Canada,
a division of Random House of Canada Limited, Toronto.

www.aaknopf.com

www.randomhouse.ca

Originally published in the United Kingdom by Allen Lane, Penguin Books Ltd.,
London in 2007.

Knopf, Borzoi Books, and the colophon are registered trademarks of Random House, Inc.
Knopf Canada and the colophon are trademarks of Knopf Canada.

Library of Congress Cataloging-in-Publication Data

Shlaim, Avi.

Lion of Jordan : the life of King Hussein in war and peace / Avi Shlaim.—1st US ed.

p.   cm.

Includes bibliographical references and index.

ISBN 978-1-4000-4305-7

1. Hussein, King of Jordan, 1935–1999. 2. Jordan—Politics and government—1952–1999.
3. Arab–Israeli conflict—1993—Peace. I. Title.

DS154.54.S54 2008

956.9504'3092—dc22

[B]   2008021804

Manufactured in the United States of America

FIRST UNITED STATES EDITION

TO GWYN

Contents

Maps

Illustrations

Preface

This preface is written with a mixture of satisfaction and sadness: satisfaction at having completed a big book but a tinge of sadness at having to put it to bed and losing the chance to further revise or add to it. Gibbon compared the finishing of a book to saying the final farewell to a very old and dear friend. I feel somewhat the same way about this one, a much more modest book than his. I have been working on it for the last seven years, and it is difficult to imagine life without it.

This is not the book I set out to write, and it is three times longer than I had envisaged. As I was on leave for three out of the past seven years, I cannot plead that I did not have the time to write a short book. My original plan was to write a monograph, *King Hussein and the Quest for Peace in the Middle East*, with the emphasis on his diplomacy in the aftermath of the June 1967 War. But, as I did the research for this study in diplomatic history, I became fascinated by the personality of the PLK, or "plucky little king," as he was often referred to in the West. The book acquired a life of its own and gradually developed, almost without my making a conscious decision, into a full-scale biography.

A. J. P. Taylor once said that every historian should write a biography, if only to discover how different this is from the writing of history. My own academic discipline is International Relations, and I am well aware that writing with reference to one individual is not in the best tradition of social science research. Yet, in this particular instance, given the king's dominant position within his own country and his highly personalized, not to say idiosyncratic, style of conducting foreign policy, it is the only sensible approach. International Relations is primarily the study of conflict and conflict resolution, of war and peace, and King Hussein's entire career, as the subtitle to this biography indicates, revolved round waging war and making peace.

One makes peace with one's enemies, not with one's friends. With Jordan and Israel, however, the dichotomy between war and peace is less clear-cut than in most other cases. They have been aptly described as "the best of enemies." The triangular relationship between Jordan, Israel and the Palestinians is difficult to analyse. But it is as vital to understanding the past as it is crucial in determining the final shape of the peace settlement in the Middle East. Jordan was a pivotal actor in the peace process that got under way in the aftermath of the June 1967 War. Whereas the literature on Israel and the Palestinians is very extensive, little has been written on Jordan. One of the main aims of this book is to fill the gap by providing an account of King Hussein's role in the search for peace in the Middle East, with particular emphasis on his involvement in the Palestinian question and on his secret contacts with Israel, which culminated in the signature of a peace treaty in 1994.

This book represents a natural development of my academic work over the last three decades. My training has been both in history and in the social sciences, and I like to think that I combine the skills of an International Relations generalist with those of a Middle East area specialist. The earlier book that is most directly relevant to the present project is *Collusion Across the Jordan: King Abdullah, the Zionist Movement, and the Partition of Palestine* (1988). There I challenge many of the myths that have come to surround the birth of the State of Israel and the 1948 Arab–Israeli War, most notably the myth that Arab intransigence alone was responsible for the political deadlock that persisted for three decades after the guns fell silent. In contrast to the conventional view of the Arab–Israeli conflict as a simple bipolar affair, I dwelt on the special relationship between King Abdullah of Jordan (the grandfather of King Hussein) and the Zionist movement, and on the interest that the Hashemites and the Zionists shared in containing Palestinian nationalism. The central thesis advanced is that, in November 1947, the Hashemite ruler of Transjordan and the Jewish Agency reached a tacit agreement to divide up mandatory Palestine among themselves and to help abort the birth of an independent Palestinian state, and that this agreement laid the foundations for continuing collaboration in the aftermath of the war—until Abdullah's assassination by a Palestinian nationalist in 1951.

The other book that is intimately connected with the present one is *The Iron Wall: Israel and the Arab World* (2000). That work extends my revisionist critique of Israeli foreign policy from 1948 to 1998, in other words, to the first fifty years of statehood. Among the themes covered are seven Arab–Israeli wars and all the major diplomatic initiatives to settle the Arab–Israeli dispute. It is not a comprehensive history of the Arab–Israeli conflict but a detailed study of one actor: Israel. Jordan features but no more prominently than any of the neighbouring Arab states or the Palestinians. The main theme of *The Iron Wall* is that since 1948 Israel has been too ready to use military force and remarkably reluctant to engage in meaningful diplomacy to resolve its dispute with the Arabs. From 1967 Israel had ample opportunities to trade land for peace in accordance with UN Resolution 242, the cornerstone of nearly all international plans to resolve the conflict. But, with the exception of the peace treaties with Egypt in 1979 and with Jordan in 1994, Israel preferred land to peace with its neighbours. Israel did sign the Oslo Accord with the PLO in 1993 but began to renege on this historic compromise with the other principal party to the conflict following the return to power of the Likud three years later. The blind spot that Israeli leaders have always had in dealing with Palestinian nationalism persists down to the current day.

The present book examines the Arab–Israeli conflict and many of the same attempts to resolve it peacefully, but this time not from an Israeli perspective but from a Jordanian one, or, more specifically, from the perspective of Jordan's principal decision-maker: Hussein bin Talal. It explores the four main circles of Hussein's foreign policy: Israel, the Palestinians, the Arab world and the Great Powers. Special attention is devoted to the persistent tension in Hussein's foreign policy between the commitment to Arab nationalism and the desire to reach a modus vivendi with Israel. The key to understanding all four strands of his foreign policy, it will be argued, was the survival of the Hashemite dynasty in Jordan. This was the overarching aim; everything else flowed from it.

The first part covers the colonial context for the emergence of modern Jordan, the Hashemite legacy, Hussein's childhood, the making of a king and the early years of his reign. But the bulk of the book deals with the period after 1967, and, more specifically, with Hussein's efforts to recover the West Bank and East Jerusalem. It was in this context that Hussein repeatedly offered full peace in return for full withdrawal but encountered relentless Israeli expansionism. This is where the covert contacts with Israel's leaders fitted into the broader framework of his foreign policy. The first meeting across the battle lines was in fact held as early as 1963. The initiative for the meeting came from the Jordanian monarch, who followed in the footsteps of his grandfather. Each sought a peaceful solution to the conflict, each broke the Arab taboo on direct contact with the enemy, and each was described by his own supporters as the king of realism. But for Hussein the great watershed was 1967. It was only after the loss of the West Bank and East Jerusalem that his back channel to Tel Aviv assumed critical importance.

The list of prominent Israeli politicians who met secretly with Hussein before 1994 included Golda Meir, Yigal Allon, Moshe Dayan, Abba Eban, Shimon Peres, Itzhak Rabin and Itzhak Shamir. The list of Hussein's secret meetings with Israeli officials printed at the end of this book is probably incomplete, but it gives an idea of the scope and intensity of the extraordinary dialogue between two parties that remained formally at war with one another, and lends substance to the description "the best of enemies." It captures the essence of a unique adversarial partnership.

My primary aim in writing this book has been to provide an account of Hussein's long reign and to make it as detailed, accurate, readable and interesting as possible. I hope it will also help the reader make sense of nearly half a century of tangled and tortuous Middle Eastern history. It attempts to break new ground in a number of ways. First, it provides information that is not currently available on a crucial aspect of the diplomacy surrounding the Arab–Israeli conflict. Second, and more importantly, it challenges the conventional view that Israel faced a monolithic and implacably hostile Arab world and the related myth of Arab intransigence. Third, whereas much of the literature on the Middle East peace process is written by American and Israeli scholars and focuses on the roles of the United States and Israel, this book focuses on the role of one of the major Arab actors. Like Britain in the post-war era, King Hussein constantly strove to "punch above his weight." His influence in regional affairs was much greater than one might reasonably expect from the ruler of an impecunious and insignificant desert kingdom. He was also a master of the art of political survival. Against all odds, he remained on the Hashemite throne for forty-six years, from 1953 until his death from natural causes in 1999.

Historians of the recent past need lucky breaks; mine was that Hussein very trustingly gave me an interview on the most sensitive of subjects: his clandestine relationship with Israel. The interview took place on 3 December 1996 at Hussein's residence in Britain, Buckhurst Park. It lasted two hours, was recorded and later transcribed. This was one of the rare occasions when Hussein spoke on the record about his meetings with Israeli leaders prior to the establishment of diplomatic relations between the two countries. The interview explains a good deal of his thinking about Israel and individual Israeli leaders, about his troubled relations with the PLO and with other Arab rulers, and about the major stages in his struggle for peace. After the king's death, I published an edited version of this interview: "His Royal Shyness: King Hussein and Israel" (*New York Review of Books*, 15 July 1999). The complete transcript of this interview runs to thirty-six pages, and it served as a major source for this biography.

At the meeting at Buckhurst Park, I indicated to King Hussein that after finishing the book on Israel's foreign policy, I planned to write a book about him, and he gave me every encouragement. He invited me to visit him in Amman and volunteered to share with me his notes on the meetings that I found so fascinating. But I was too slow: he fell ill, and I lost my chance. Despite missing the opportunity for further privileged access to Hussein and his papers, I did not abandon the idea of writing a book about him. But, as with any contemporary history project, this one presented me with problems as well as opportunities. The main problem has been that of access to the relevant official documents; it is particularly acute in this case because Jordan has no proper national archive. My answer has been to make the most of the primary sources I could access rather than lament the ones I could not, on the principle that it is better to light a candle than to curse the darkness. The main opportunity has been to get the first-hand testimony of people who were involved in the events that I have written about. Interviews are, of course, notoriously fallible in some respects, but for a project such as this one they are also indispensable.

Because King Hussein had allowed me to interview him and told me so much, many members of his family and of his inner circle helped me with this book after his death. At the end is a list of seventy-six interviews that I conducted with Jordanians who served Hussein in one capacity or another; it includes his younger brother Hassan, his sister Basma, his eldest son and heir, Abdullah II, his cousin Zaid bin Shaker, Talal bin Muhammad, his nephew and national security adviser, prime ministers, senior officials, diplomats and soldiers. These interviews with policy-makers of the Hussein era are often revealing and illuminating; they provide much colour, they help to bring the story to life, and they fill in many gaps. They are used here not as a substitute for the written sources but as a supplement to them. I have found that conducting so many interviews has enabled me to take some kind of meta-position, to balance different narratives, and to make allowances for personal and political agendas.

One interviewee deserves a special mention: Major-General Ali Shukri, who served as the director of King Hussein's Private Office from 1976 until 1998. General Shukri was one of the king's closest aides and confidants: he was entrusted with many sensitive missions; he set up and attended many of the secret meetings with the Israelis; and he accompanied Hussein on sixty-one visits to Baghdad between 1980 and the Gulf crisis of 1990. General Shukri's help to me included sixteen long interviews, countless conversations, the checking of facts and introductions to other key officials. The interviews contain detailed information, deep insight into the late king and his policies, and a number of startling revelations, including an attempt by Hussein to arrange a meeting between Saddam Hussein and Itzhak Rabin, a secret meeting he sponsored on a Jordanian air base between Saddam Hussein and Hafiz al-Asad of Syria, the attempt to broker an "Arab solution" to the Gulf crisis, a crucial meeting with Itzhak Shamir in Britain twelve days before the outbreak of the 1991 Gulf War, and a Syrian plan to assassinate the king and his brother after he signed the peace treaty with Israel.

Any biography is bound to raise the question of the biographer's attitude towards his subject. It seems to me that a certain degree of sympathy for one's subject is essential to a successful biography. As will become clear to any perceptive reader of this book, I certainly felt such sympathy towards Hussein, who appeared to combine humility with humanity and exceptionally gracious manners. I knew him only slightly, but, on the few occasions when we did meet, he invariably came across as an open-minded and sincere individual, and as a decent human being. My sympathy with him as a person was enhanced by the discovery that his efforts to work out a peaceful solution to the conflict in the Middle East met, for the most part, with ignorance and indifference on the part of the top American policy-makers and dishonesty and deviousness on the part of the Israeli ones.

On the other hand, it was much more difficult to reconcile my sympathy for the king with a similar sense of solidarity with the Palestinians, the real victims of the Zionist project. Although I admired Hussein, I did not adopt his perspective on the Palestinians who made up more than half of the population of his kingdom. Nevertheless, concentration on the king has inevitably been at the expense of providing a richer account of the Palestinian struggle for independence and statehood. In dealing with Hussein, I had to maintain a delicate balance: I valued the personal contact with my subject and the help he extended to me, but at the same time I had to be careful that my work did not topple over into hagiography. I set out to write an honest, scholarly and critical book on the life and times of Hussein bin Talal. Whether I have been successful is not for me but for the reader to judge.

AT VARIOUS STAGES in the long journey that will end with the publication of this book, I received support from institutions and individuals that it is my pleasure to acknowledge. My greatest debt is to the British Academy for awarding me a three-year research professorship in 2003–6 and for the research grant that accompanied it. The professorship freed me from my teaching and administrative duties at the University of Oxford, while the grant enabled me to travel, to visit archives and to employ research assistants. Without the generous support of the British Academy this book could not have been written. My other debt is to the United States Institute of Peace for a generous research grant in 2001–2 that enabled me to employ Adiba Mango as a full-time research assistant and to make several extended visits to Jordan.

The Middle East Centre at St. Antony's College provided a most congenial work environment. My greatest debt is to Eugene Rogan, the director of the centre and one of my closest friends, for his advice, support and encouragement since the inception of this project. Eugene is working on a history of the Arabs, and our regular meetings to read and critique each other's work provided a welcome break from the isolation chamber of book-writing. His expertise in Jordanian history was an added bonus. Mastan Ebtehaj, the librarian, and Debbie Usher, the archivist, dealt with all my requests promptly, efficiently and with good cheer.

A number of friends read the first draft of this book, corrected mistakes and gave me the benefit of their opinion. Adiba Mango, Christopher Prentice and Charles Tripp went over the entire manuscript with great care and made extremely helpful suggestions for improving it. Sir Mark Allen read and suggested revisions to the chapter on the Gulf War. Randa Habib commented on the final chapter and contributed additional information on the change of the succession, on which she is a leading expert. I am very much in the debt of all these friends.

During different phases of work on this project, I enjoyed the support of three very able and dedicated research assistants: Adiba Mango, Shachar Nativ and Noa Schonmann. In addition to collecting material and transcribing tapes, they rendered invaluable assistance as IT advisers, administrators, editors and proofreaders. Nezam Bagherzade, while still at school, volunteered to help me with research in the Public Record Office in Kew, with very fruitful results. Zehavit Ohana helped me with the archival research in Israel.

Two collections of private papers merit a special mention. Philip Geyelin, a distinguished American journalist, worked for many years on a biography of King Hussein but sadly died without completing it. My colleagues and I are grateful to his wife, Sherry Geyelin, and to his daughter, Mary-Sherman Willis, for depositing his papers and his unfinished manuscript in the Middle East Centre Archive. Dr. Yaacov Herzog was the Israeli official most intimately involved in setting up and maintaining the back channel to Amman. I am grateful to his daughter Shira Herzog for giving me access to the meticulous and copious records he kept of the secret meetings from 1963 to 1970. This is the first time a writer has drawn upon these papers as a source for a book in English, and they are a real treasure trove.

A large number of friends have helped me in various ways. They include, in alphabetical order, Ze'ev Drory, Miriam Eshkol, Randa Habib, Foulath Hadid, Mustafa Hamarneh, Donald Lamm, Roger Louis, Avi Raz, Tom Segev, Avraham Sela, Moshe Shemesh, Asher Susser, the late Mreiwad Tall and Tariq Tall. The individuals I interviewed, both Jordanians and others, are listed at the end of the book. Some of these interviews go back to 1981–82, when I spent a sabbatical year in Israel doing research for *Collusion Across the Jordan*. Other interviews are with British and American officials who served in Jordan. I am grateful to all the people on this long list for sparing the time to see me, for answering my questions and for putting up with what sometimes turned into vigorous cross-examination.

My thanks go to the staff at Penguin Books and especially to Stuart Proffitt for his wise direction, superb editing and unfailing support and encouragement. His assistant, Phillip Birch, was very helpful in many different ways. Donna Poppy edited the typescript intelligently, imaginatively and with meticulous attention to detail. Cecilia Mackay was a dynamic, resourceful and inspired picture researcher. Mike Shand drew the maps; Auriol Griffith-Jones compiled the index; and Richard Duguid skilfully supervised the entire production process.

Finally I wish to thank my wife, Gwyn Daniel, for continuing to be interested in my work after thirty-three years of marriage, for many stimulating conversations, incisive criticism, perceptive comments and encouragement throughout many seasons. But for her insistence on taking out the jokes and the clichés, this book would have been even longer!

Avi Shlaim
Oxford
August 2007

Lion of Jordan

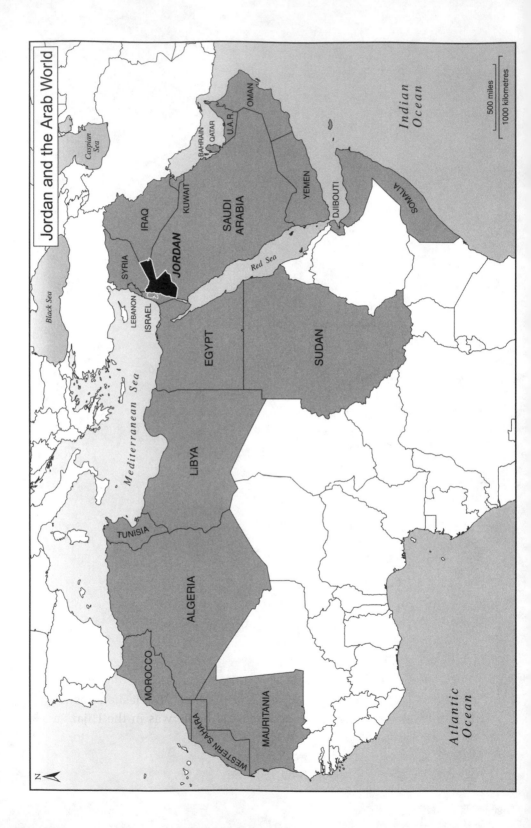

Jordan and the Arab World

1. The Hashemite Heritage

King Hussein of Jordan was a man of slight build who possessed a powerful personality and immense political stature. He was in every respect except the physical a towering figure whose courage helped to earn him the popular title "Lion of Jordan." Hussein bin Talal was born on 14 November 1935 in Amman. He ruled over Jordan as an absolute monarch from 1953, when he was only seventeen years old, until his death in 1999 at the age of sixty-three. Throughout his long reign Jordan was in the eye of the storm of Middle Eastern politics, constantly caught up in the turmoil and violence of the region, and Hussein himself emerged as a major player in regional and international politics. He was also a leading actor in the Arab–Israeli conflict, one of the most bitter, protracted and intractable of modern times. Hussein's cardinal objective was the stability and survival of the Hashemite monarchy in Jordan, and in this he was successful against all the odds. His other major objective was to find a peaceful solution to the Arab–Israeli conflict, but in this his record is much more controversial. Hussein's supporters see him as a man who consistently pursued a strategy of peace and ultimately succeeded in bridging the historic gulf by concluding a peace treaty with Israel. His critics take a radically different view of his legacy of accommodation with Israel, seeing it as a surrender and a betrayal of the Palestinians. In a region where the past is so powerful and ever-present, the question of whether Jordan's rulers have betrayed or championed the Palestinians has been at the heart of a heated, ongoing dispute. It is one of the tasks of this book to explore the realities behind these two positions thoroughly for the first time.

Whatever opinion one takes of Hussein, the starting point for understanding his foreign policy is the Hashemite legacy. The Hashemites are an aristocratic Arab family whose ancestral home was in the Hijaz in the western part of the Arabian Peninsula, along the Red Sea littoral. They are descendants of the prophet Muhammad through his daughter

Fatima, whose husband Ali was fourth of the caliphs. The family took its name from Hashem, the great-grandfather of the prophet and a prominent member of the Kureish tribe. The Hashemites were religious, rather than temporal, leaders, the guardians of the Muslim holy places in Mecca and Medina during the centuries of Ottoman rule. The title "sharif of Mecca" passed to the next in line within the family. In Arabic the adjective "sharif" means distinguished, eminent, illustrious or noble, and the title "sharif" is reserved for the descendants of the prophet.

In the early twentieth century, however, the Hashemites sought to translate their noble lineage into political power and gradually assumed the leadership of an Arab nationalist bid for freedom from the Ottoman Empire. The break between the Hashemites and their fellow Muslim overlords in Istanbul began with the Young Turks' Revolution of 1908. The Young Turks were a group of officers, officials and intellectuals who ruled the Ottoman Empire from the time of the revolution until the end of the First World War. The shift they brought about in the ideology of the ramshackle empire from Islam to Turkish nationalism displeased and disturbed the Hashemites. The decision of the Young Turks to join the war on the side of Germany then created an opportunity for a Hashemite alliance with Britain in accordance with the Arab adage "My enemy's enemy is my friend." This dramatic *renversement des alliances* transformed the Hashemites from Arab aristocracy into actors on the international stage.

Hussein bin Ali (1852–1931) was an unlikely candidate to lead a nationalist Arab revolt against Ottoman rule. He was fifty-five by the time he was appointed sharif of Mecca in 1908. His main concern was to secure his own position and that of his family, and he was robust in resisting Ottoman attempts to encroach on their traditional authority. There is no evidence to suggest that he was attracted to the ideas of Arab nationalism before the war: on the contrary, by temperament and upbringing he was a conservative and inclined to view nationalist ideology as an unwelcome innovation, inconsistent with the principles of Islam. Nor was the Hijaz a particularly fertile ground for the growth of nationalism. A traditional society, bound by religious and tribal identities, it was short on the kind of intellectuals and radical army officers who are normally to be found in the vanguard of nationalist movements.[1]

Hussein bin Ali had four sons: Ali, Abdullah, Faisal and Zaid. The two middle sons were more politically ambitious than the other two and they played a major part in persuading their father to assume the leadership of the Arab Revolt. Faisal was the principal commander of the Arab Army, and his association with the legendary T. E. Lawrence ("Lawrence of Arabia") helped to spread his fame beyond Arabia. Abdullah, however, was the chief architect, planner, schemer and driving force behind the revolt. As Faisal himself confided to Lawrence, his liaison officer and the most renowned chronicler of "the revolt in the desert," the idea of an Arab uprising against the Turks was first conceived by Abdullah. As a small boy Abdullah had acquired the nickname "Ajlan"—"the hurried one"—and he remained true to this name for the rest of his life.

A profound faith that the Hashemites were destined to rule over the entire Arab world inspired Abdullah throughout a long and eventful political career that started in the Hijaz and later saw him amir of Transjordan and finally king of Jordan. Born in Mecca in 1880, Abdullah received his education and his military training in Istanbul and in the Hijaz. Between 1912 and 1914 he was the deputy for Mecca in the Ottoman parliament, where he promoted his father's interests with energy and enthusiasm. It was during this period that Abdullah was exposed to ideas of Arab nationalism and began to link his father's desire for autonomy in the Hijaz to the broader and more radical ideas of Arab emancipation from Ottoman rule. In February 1914 Abdullah returned to Mecca by way of Cairo, where he met Lord Kitchener, the British minister plenipotentiary, and tentatively explored the possibility of support in the event of an uprising against the Ottomans. Soon after his return home, Abdullah became his father's political adviser and foreign minister.

It was only gradually, and under constant prodding from Abdullah, that the conservative sharif of Mecca raised his sights from the idea of home rule in his corner of Arabia inside the Ottoman Empire to complete independence for all its Arab provinces from Yemen to Syria. While Abdullah became convinced of the necessity to break up the empire at the beginning of 1914, Hussein would become a separatist only after he had tried and failed to attain his limited political objectives within the framework of the Ottoman Empire. A further difference, one of ideology, separated father from son: Hussein's idea of nationalism was based on the traditional concept of tribal and family unity whereas Abdullah's was based on the theory of Arab pre-eminence among Muslims. Whatever the source of their aspirations or their ultimate aims, the indigent rulers of the Hijaz province had to have the backing of a great power to have any chance of success in mounting an open rebellion against the mighty Ottoman Empire. That power could only be the British Empire, which had its own designs on Arabia. This posed a problem. The guardian of the Muslim holy places in Mecca could not easily bring himself to embrace a Christian power in his struggle against fellow Muslims. Divided counsels within his own family did nothing to ease his predicament. Faisal emphasized the risks and pleaded for caution; Abdullah wanted to play for high stakes and urged his father to raise the standard of an Arab revolt. Hussein warily plotted a middle course: he continued to negotiate with the Turks while making secret overtures to the British. Turkish rejection of his demands for a hereditary monarchy in the Hijaz made him tilt further in the direction of Britain. The outbreak of war in August 1914 made the British more receptive to these overtures, and to Abdullah fell the task of weaving together the threads of this unholy alliance against the Sublime Porte.

Between July 1915 and March 1916 a number of letters were exchanged between Hussein and Sir Henry McMahon, the British high commissioner in Egypt, discussing the terms under which Hussein would ally himself with the British. In his first note Hussein, speaking in the name of "the Arab nation," demanded British recognition of Arab independence in all of the Arabian peninsula and the area covered by present-day Syria, Lebanon, Jordan, Israel and part of Iraq. To this claim, which reflected Abdullah's grandiose territorial ambitions, was added a request for British approval of a proclamation of an Arab caliphate of Islam. Britain accepted these principles but could not agree with Hussein's definition of the area claimed for Arab independence. In his note of 24 October 1915 McMahon excluded certain areas: "The districts of Mersin and Alexandretta and portions of Syria lying to the west of the districts of Damascus, Homs, Hama and Aleppo cannot be said to be purely Arab, and must on that account be excepted from the proposed delimitation." After a year of desultory negotiations, Hussein undertook to join the Allies by mounting a rebellion against the Ottomans. The correspondence, conducted in Arabic, was shrouded in ambiguity, vagueness and deliberate obscurity. It reveals a continuous thread of evasive pledges by Britain and opaqueness, if not obtuseness, on the part of Hussein. It is difficult to tell how much Hussein was moved by dynastic interests and the desire to extend the power of his family and how much by the wish to represent the Arabs in their pursuit of independence. It is clear, however, that his dream was to found an independent Hashemite kingdom on the ruins of the Ottoman Empire. The British failed to spell out the difference between Hussein's ambition and the extent of their commitments. In particular, the McMahon–Hussein correspondence was imprecise as to whether Palestine was to be included in the area designated by Britain for Arab independence. Conflicting interpretations of this omission were to plague Anglo–Arab relations after the war.[2]

In the spring of 1916 Hussein proclaimed what is often called the Great Arab Revolt, which holds pride of place in the chronicles of the Arab nationalist movement. It is seen as the dawn of a new age, as the first serious Arab bid for independence and unity. Some scholars, however, have questioned the link between the revolt and Arab nationalism. They point out that the original terms on which the revolt was launched had little to do with Arab nationalism.[3] Islam, according to this view, featured much more prominently than nationalism in its original aims. All nationalist movements dwell on the past, and in the case of the Arabs the past was necessarily Islamic. William Cleveland has categorically asserted that the revolt "was proclaimed in the name of preserving Islam, not in the name of Arabism or the Arab nation."[4]

In diplomatic terms, however, as its origins make clear beyond doubt, the Arab Revolt was in essence an Anglo–Hashemite plot. Britain financed the revolt as well as supplying arms, provisions, direct artillery support and experts in desert warfare, among whom was T. E. Lawrence. Lawrence did more than any other man to glorify the revolt and to advertise its military successes. He also surrounded it with a romantic aura by portraying it as the product of a natural affinity between the British and the Arabs, or at least the "real" Arabs, the nomads of the Arabian Desert.[5] The French, on the other hand, took a cynical view of the Arab Revolt from start to finish, dismissing it as British imperialism in Arab headgear.

The Hashemites promised much more than they were able to deliver. After Hussein's proclamation, only a disappointingly small number of

Syrian and Iraqi nationalists flocked to the sharifian banner. Many Syrian notables dissociated themselves from what they saw as treason. The Iraqis had their own leaders; and the Iraqi Shia were particularly apprehensive about the prospect of a Sunni sharif and an outsider taking over their country. (The Sunnis are the leading sect within Islam and strict followers of the teaching of the prophet Muhammad. They differ from the minority Shia sect in doctrine, ritual, law, theology and religious organization.) The Lebanese Christians saw no advantage in exchanging the old Islamic Empire based in Istanbul for a new Islamic Empire, or caliphate, based in the Hijaz. The Egyptians were more hostile than all the others to the idea of separation from the Ottoman Empire and to being ruled from the backward Hijaz. Even in Arabia itself, popular support for the rebellion was nowhere near as enthusiastic or widespread as the British had been led to expect. The Arabian Bedouin and tribesmen who made up the rank and file of the sharifian army were more attracted to British gold than they were to nationalist ideology.

The usual grand narrative of the Arab Revolt, based on T. E. Lawrence's classic accounts, greatly exaggerates not only its spontaneity, size and scope but also its military value. The first phase was confined to the Hijaz, where Mecca, Taif and Jedda fell in rapid succession to the rebel forces consisting of Hijazi Bedouins commanded by the sharif's four sons, Ali, Abdullah, Faisal and Zaid. Three of these groups laid siege to Medina and were tied down there until the end of the war, contributing to the war effort largely by sabotaging the Hijaz Railway, the main Turkish supply route to Medina. Only Faisal's unit assisted the British offensive in Palestine and Syria, and, on 1 October 1918, entered Damascus first and hoisted the Arab flag.

The entry of the Ottoman Empire into the First World War on the side of the Central Powers hastened its final dissolution, and by the time the war ended it had lost its Arab provinces. After the end of the war, the Hashemite princes who headed "the revolt in the desert" became the leading spokesmen for the Arab national cause at the 1919 Versailles peace conference and in the settlement following the dismemberment of the Ottoman Empire. For their contribution to the Allied war effort against the Turks, Britain had promised, or half promised, to support Arab independence. But the territorial limits governing this promise had been left so ineptly and obscurely defined in the McMahon–Hussein correspondence that a long and bitter wrangle ensued between the two sides—especially over the disposition of Palestine.

Another major uncertainty surrounded the regime and institutions to be installed in the Arab areas that were indisputably marked for independence. Should this independence take the form of a united kingdom, a federation or an alliance between independent states? Was Britain committed only to the recognition of Arab independence or also to Hashemite rule over these areas? One searches in vain for answers or even clues to these questions in the McMahon–Hussein correspondence. Sharif Hussein himself regarded Arab unity as synonymous with his own kingship and as an empty phrase unless so regarded; it meant little to him except as a means to personal aggrandizement. He aspired to head a united Arab kingdom consisting of the Arabian peninsula, Greater Syria and Iraq, with his sons acting as viceroys, and such was his impatience that within four months of the outbreak of the revolt he proclaimed himself "King of the Arab Countries." At first the British refused to recognize him, and, when they eventually did so, it was only as king of the Hijaz.

The task of fashioning a new political order in the Middle East following the collapse of the Ottoman Empire was further complicated by other commitments undertaken by the British government after the initiation of its clandestine exchanges with the sharif of Mecca. The first was an agreement signed in secret by Britain and France in May 1916 and named after its chief negotiators, Sir Mark Sykes and Charles François George Picot. Under the terms of the Sykes–Picot Agreement, the whole Fertile Crescent, comprising modern Syria, Lebanon, Iraq, Jordan and Palestine, was divided into British and French spheres of influence. Syria and Lebanon were in the French sphere of influence, while Iraq, Jordan, and Palestine fell into the British sphere. Each sphere was in turn divided into two zones, one to be placed under direct British or French rule and the other turned into semi-independent Arab states or a confederation of states. France and Britain were to supply advisers and enjoy economic privileges in the Arab states that would emerge within their respective spheres. In short, this was an agreement, in the event of an Allied victory, to divide the spoils of war without any reference to the wishes of the local inhabitants.

Were Britain's promises to the sharif of Mecca compatible with those they made to the French? Elie Kedourie has argued that the Sykes–

Picot Agreement did not violate the commitments contained in the McMahon–Hussein correspondence because the latter were so vague and qualified.[6] T. E. Lawrence, who was involved at the sharp end in Britain's wartime diplomacy, was much less charitable. According to him, "Sir Henry [McMahon] was England's right-hand man in the Middle East till the Arab Revolt was an established event. Sir Mark Sykes was the left hand: and if the Foreign Office had kept itself and its hands mutually informed our reputation for honesty would not have suffered as it did."[7]

Another promise made by the British government during the war was to support the establishment of a national home for the Jewish people in Palestine. Unlike the promise to Hussein and the Sykes–Picot Agreement, the Balfour Declaration was not a secret but a public pledge. On 2 November 1917 Arthur Balfour, Britain's secretary of state for foreign affairs, issued the following statement:

His Majesty's Government view with favour the establishment in Palestine of a national home for the Jewish people, and will use their best endeavours to facilitate the achievement of this object, it being clearly understood that nothing shall be done which may prejudice the civil and religious rights of existing non-Jewish communities in Palestine, or the rights and political status enjoyed by Jews in any other country.

Was Britain's promise to the Zionists compatible with its earlier promise to the sharif of Mecca? Again, there is a vast scholarly literature on the subject. One Israeli historian has denied that Palestine was a twice-promised land and concluded that the charges of fraudulence and deception levelled against the British after the war are largely groundless.[8] Groundless or not, these charges acquired the status of dogma not only in the eyes of Arab nationalists but, much more surprisingly, in the eyes of most British officials as well.[9] My own view is that the Balfour Declaration was one of the worst mistakes in British foreign policy in the first half of the twentieth century. It involved a monumental injustice to the Palestine Arabs and sowed the seeds of a never-ending conflict in the Middle East.

In the case of Hussein bin Ali, who was proclaimed and recognized in October 1916 as king of the Hijaz, it is necessary to distinguish clearly between the initial response to the Balfour Declaration and the subsequent attitude. When news of the declaration reached Hussein, he was greatly disturbed by it and asked Britain to clarify its meaning. Whitehall met this request by the dispatch of Commander D. G. Hogarth, one of the heads of the Arab Bureau in Cairo, who arrived in Jedda in the first week of January 1918 for a series of interviews with King Hussein. "Hogarth's Message," as it came to be known, reaffirmed the Allies' determination that "the Arab race shall be given full opportunity of once again forming a nation in the world." So far as Palestine was concerned, Britain was "determined that no people shall be subject to another." Britain noted and supported the aspiration of the Jews to return to Palestine but only in so far as this was compatible with "the freedom of the existing population, both economic and political."[10]

Hogarth's Message is crucial for understanding King Hussein's attitude to the Balfour Declaration. Following the meetings in Jedda, Hussein thought that he had Britain's assurance that the settlement of the Jews in Palestine would not conflict with Arab independence in that country. This explains his initial silence in public and his private efforts to allay the anxieties of his sons. Hussein had great respect for the Jews, seeing them, in keeping with the Koran, as "the People of the Book," as monotheists with a prophetic scripture. He was not opposed to the settlement of Jews in Palestine and even welcomed it on religious and on humanitarian grounds. He was, however, emphatically opposed to a Zionist takeover of the area. Hogarth gave him a solemn pledge that Britain would respect not only the economic but also the political freedom of the Arab population. When Britain subsequently refused to recognize Arab independence in Palestine, Hussein felt betrayed and accused Britain of breach of faith.[11]

If the disenchantment of Hussein and his sons with Britain was gradual, the hostility of the Arab nationalists towards Britain on account of the Balfour Declaration was immediate and unremitting.[12] The Sykes–Picot Agreement and the Balfour Declaration became the two basic points of reference in all the Arab nationalist discourse that followed—enduring symbols of the cynicism and selfishness of the Western powers, of their disregard for Arab rights, of their sinister design to keep the Arabs divided and weak, and, worst of all, of their support for the Zionist intruders into Palestine. Zionism itself came to be considered not as the national liberation movement of the Jews but as an outpost of European imperialism in the Middle East.

The Versailles peace conference liberated the Arabs from Turkish control but ensnared them in a more complex diplomatic web spun by rivalries of the Great Powers and the baffling array of pledges that those powers had made in their eagerness to inherit the Ottoman Empire. Faisal, who had formed a temporary administration in Syria, attended the peace conference in Paris as the envoy of the king of the Hijaz. By temperament inclined to moderation and compromise, Faisal was enjoined by his authoritarian and now crotchety old father to insist on nothing less than complete independence.[13]

Faisal possessed more than a touch of the romantic aura, gentle melancholy, physical grace and perfect manners that many upper-class Englishmen found irresistibly attractive. But he was out of his depth in the world of Great Power diplomacy, and he left the conference empty-handed to face a rapidly deteriorating situation in Syria. Faisal tried to pursue a middle-of-the-road policy regarding the French, the troubles in Iraq and the Palestinian Arabs' complaints against the Jews. But a clash with the French was made inevitable by the inflexibility of his Syrian nationalist supporters and by their insistence on a completely independent kingdom of Greater Syria, embracing Transjordan and Lebanon. A fervently nationalistic Arab–Syrian Congress, meeting in Damascus in March 1920, crowned Faisal as king of Syria. Faisal hesitantly accepted the crown, thereby simultaneously embarrassing the British and antagonizing the French, who refused to recognize him.

Brushing aside Arab nationalist claims, in April 1920 the Supreme Council of the Peace Conference proceeded to the Italian Riviera resort of San Remo to make the final decisions regarding the Ottoman Empire. They agreed to detach the Arabic-speaking parts of the empire and to divide them between Britain and France. Iraq, Transjordan and Palestine were placed under the "mandatory authority" of Britain; Lebanon and Syria under the "mandatory authority" of France. These mandates were to be administered on behalf of the League of Nations, the Palestine mandate in accordance with the Balfour Declaration. Under the terms of the mandates, these territories were all destined for eventual independence. But, as shortly became clear, the promise was little more than window-dressing, a cloak for European colonialism. In all but name, this was a victors' peace.

The French demanded complete control over Syria, and Faisal was willing to come to terms with them, but his Syrian followers deflected him from the course of compromise. In July 1920 French troops marched from Beirut to Damascus, banished Faisal and took over the government of the country. The French prime minister declared that Syria henceforth would be held by France: "The whole of it, and forever."[14] The ease with which regime change in Damascus was accomplished seemed to support the French suspicion that Arab nationalism was a British invention designed to cheat France out of its claim to Syria.[15] Thus was created the modern state of Syria, under French rule, and on the ruins of the dream of a united Arab kingdom led by the Hashemites. Many later developments in Middle East politics have their origins in the events that unravelled in Damascus between 1918 and 1920, including the abiding mistrust of the French towards British intentions and policies in this part of the world, and the grudge nursed by Syrian nationalists against the Western powers for broken promises, bad faith and betrayal. The Hashemites constantly harked back to their short-lived kingdom in Damascus and based on it their various expansionist plans for Greater Syria; the fact that they allied themselves with Britain in order to further their dynastic ambitions accounts for the estrangement and mutual suspicion between themselves and the more radical Arab nationalists.

When the Syrian Congress elected Faisal to the throne of Syria in March 1920, it also nominated Abdullah to the throne of Iraq. But he received no encouragement from the British to seek that particular throne. Casting about for a principality to make his own, Abdullah turned his attention to the mountainous country lying east of the Jordan that nominally formed part of the British mandate for Palestine but in practice had been left to its own devices and had degenerated into brigandage and lawlessness. No troops had been left to hold this barren territory, only a handful of British political advisers who were instructed to set up ad hoc administrative centres.

It was to this territory that Abdullah set off from Medina, with his father's blessing, at the head of a small force of nearly 2,000 men. In November 1920 he arrived in Ma'an and proclaimed his intention to march on Damascus and to drive out the French aggressors. The British representative in Ma'an, Captain Alec Kirkbride, having received no instructions on how to deal with this unlikely contingency, decided to welcome the Arabian prince in the name of something he called the National Government of Moab. Abdullah expressed the hope that the young Englishman would stay and give him his support and advice in the difficult days that lay ahead. "By the way," he added with a twinkle in his eye, "has the National Government of Moab ever been recognized internationally?" Kirkbride replied graciously, "I am not quite sure of its international status. I feel, however, that the question is largely of an academic nature now that Your Highness is here."[16]

In March 1921 Abdullah arrived in Amman and set up his headquarters, still with the declared intention of raising a larger force to mount an invasion of Syria from the south. Abdullah's arrival in Transjordan threw into disarray a conference being held in Cairo by Winston Churchill, the British colonial secretary, to discuss Middle Eastern affairs. Churchill had already promised the throne of Iraq to Faisal as a consolation prize for the loss of Syria. This offer was part of his favoured "sharifian policy" of forming a number of small states in Arabia and the Fertile Crescent, all headed by members of the sharif's family and of course under British influence and guidance. Abdullah's bold march into Transjordan, and his well-advertised plan of fighting to regain Damascus threatened this policy. Although such a move would have been doomed to failure, it could embroil the British in further difficulties with their suspicious French allies—and besides, Transjordan was needed by them as a link between Palestine and Iraq.

The initial impulse of the eminent experts assembled in Cairo was to eject the upstart out of Transjordan, by force if necessary, and to administer the area directly. But on further reflection it was decided to accept the fait accompli and let Abdullah stay in Transjordan as the representative of the British government. Sir Herbert Samuel, the Jewish high commissioner for Palestine, doubted Abdullah's ability to check anti-French and anti-Zionist activities in the area, but Churchill stressed the importance of securing the goodwill of the king of the Hijaz and his sons. T. E. Lawrence, Churchill's adviser on Arab affairs, claimed that Abdullah was better qualified for the task than the other candidates by reason of his position, lineage and very considerable power, for better or for worse, over the tribesmen. Lawrence was convinced that anti-Zionist sentiment would wane, and that Transjordan could be turned into a safety valve by appointing a ruler on whom Britain could bring pressure to bear to check anti-Zionist agitation. The ideal, said Lawrence, would be "a person who was not too powerful, and who was not an inhabitant of Transjordan, but who relied on His Majesty's Government for the retention of his office."[17] In other words, the British were looking for a pliant client who could be entrusted to govern the vacant lot east of the Jordan River on their behalf.

Britain was simply too busy setting up an administration in Palestine proper, west of the Jordan River, to bother with the remote and undeveloped areas that lay to the east of the river. Moreover, these areas were meant to serve as a reserve of land for use in the resettlement of Arabs once the national home for the Jews in Palestine had become an accomplished fact. There was no intention at this stage of turning the territory east of the river into an independent Arab state.[18]

At a hastily arranged meeting in Jerusalem in late March 1921, Churchill himself, with the eager assistance and encouragement of Lawrence, therefore offered Abdullah the Amirate of Transjordan, comprising the territory between the Jordan River and the Arab Desert to the east. The condition was that Abdullah renounce his avowed intention of attempting to conquer Syria and recognize the British mandate over Transjordan as part of the Palestine mandate. Abdullah, relieved to be quit of a military adventure with an extremely doubtful outcome, accepted both conditions without argument. In return for Abdullah's undertaking to forswear and prevent any belligerent acts against the French in Syria, Churchill promised to try to persuade them to restore Arab government there, this time with Abdullah at its head. Abdullah's suggestion that he should be made king of Palestine as well as of Transjordan was declined by Churchill on the grounds that it conflicted with British commitment to a Jewish national home.

Abdullah had to settle for a temporary arrangement, lasting six months, within the framework of the Palestine mandate and under the supervision of the high commissioner, who would appoint a British adviser in Amman to help the amir to set up a central administration. During this period, the amir was to receive from the British government a monthly subsidy of £5,000 to enable him to recruit a local force for the preservation of order in Transjordan. Thus, by the stroke of a pen on a sunny Sunday afternoon, as he was later to boast, Churchill created the Amirate of Transjordan.

In April 1921 a government was formed in Transjordan. The initial six months were full of problems, as Abdullah, who was extravagant and absurdly generous towards his friends, squandered his allowances, while the country was swarming with Syrians bent on taking up arms against the French. Abdullah's inability to run the country efficiently raised doubts about his value to Britain. Nevertheless, towards the end of the year the temporary arrangement was given permanence when the British government formally recognized "the existence of an independent government under the rule of His Excellency the Amir Abdullah Ibn Hussein," subject to the establishment of a constitutional regime and the conclusion of an agreement that would enable Britain to fulfil its international obligations.

This was the first step down a new road in British policy: the separation of Transjordan from Palestine. The second was taken in 1922, when Britain, in the face of strong Zionist opposition, obtained the necessary approval from the League of Nations to exclude the territory of Transjordan from the provisions of the Palestine mandate relating to the Jewish national home. In May 1923 the British government granted Transjordan its independence, with Abdullah as ruler and with St. John Philby as chief representative, administering a £150,000 grant-in-aid. It was largely Abdullah's own failure to fulfil the condition of constitutional government that prolonged the dependent status of Transjordan. Another reason for the delay was the progressive deterioration in the relations between the British and Abdullah's illustrious father. At the Cairo conference, in March 1921, some of the post-war problems in the Middle East had been settled to the satisfaction of at least some of the parties concerned: Churchill got his "economy with honour"; Faisal got the throne of Iraq; and Abdullah got the Amirate of Transjordan. Iraq and Transjordan became the two main pillars of Britain's informal empire in the Middle East. Churchill candidly explained the advantages to Britain of ruling the Middle East through the Hashemite family:

A strong argument in favour of Sherifian policy was that it enabled His Majesty's Government to bring pressure to bear on one Arab sphere in order to attain their ends in another. If Faisal knew that not only his father's subsidy and the protection of the Holy Places from Wahabi attack, but also the position of his brother in Trans-Jordan was dependent upon his own good behaviour, he would be much easier to deal with. The same argument applied, mutatis mutandis, to King Hussein and Amir Abdallah.[19]

That summer Colonel Lawrence was sent to Jedda to tie up some loose ends, only to discover that the grand sharif himself had become the greatest obstacle to the consolidation of Britain's sharifian policy.

Lawrence offered a formal treaty of alliance that secured the Kingdom of the Hijaz against aggression and guaranteed indefinite continuation of the handsome subsidy paid annually to Hussein since 1917. But the old man, embittered by what he regarded as British bad faith and betrayal, refused to sign and angrily rejected the conditions stating that he should recognize the mandate system and condone the Balfour Declaration.

The subsequent ending of the British subsidy and the removal of British protection left the king of the Hijaz exposed to the mercies of his great rival, Sultan Abd al-Aziz ibn Saud of the Najd in Eastern Arabia. Only British diplomatic pressure and the payment of a subsidy to Ibn Saud had kept the rivalry between the two Arabian rulers dormant during the First World War. After the war an inevitable trial of strength developed between the king, who assumed that his sponsorship of the Arab Revolt entitled him to political authority over his neighbours, and the chieftain, whose determination revived the Wahhabi movement. The Wahhabiyya, named after Muhammad bin Abdul Wahhab, was an ultra-conservative Sunni Muslim movement that arose in the Arabian Peninsula in the second half of the eighteenth century. Ibn Saud turned the Wahhabi movement into an effective military force.

The first serious clash occurred on 21 May 1919 in Turaba, on the eastern border of the Hijaz, when Ibn Saud's forces almost totally obliterated a large Hashemite army commanded by Abdullah. The wild Wahhabi warriors, the Ikhwan, crept up at night on Abdullah's unguarded camp and killed many of the men in their beds. Thirty-five of his personal guard died fighting at the door of his tent. Abdullah himself escaped in his night clothes with the taunts of *shurayif* ("little sharif") ringing in his ears, wounded in body and pride. Moreover, as his biographer has observed:

The battle at Turaba was a turning point in Abdullah's life and in the history of Arabia. From that time on, Husayn and his sons were on the defensive while Ibn Saud grew inexorably more powerful . . . Abdullah's Arabian ambitions died at Turaba as well. The reverberations of the dreadful rout echoed throughout Arabia, diminishing his stature and his family's prestige. In a single night his dreams of an Arabian empire had turned to nightmares.[20]

More defeats were to follow. In March 1924, after the Turkish National Assembly abolished the caliphate, Hussein proclaimed himself caliph. Characteristically, this was a unilateral move for which he had not obtained the agreement of any other Islamic leaders. It was also a misjudgement of his own power and position. For Ibn Saud and his Wahhabi followers, it was the last straw. The decisive battle began in September 1924, when the Ikhwan mounted an offensive that Hussein could not withstand. After they captured Taif, Hussein abdicated in favour of his eldest son, Ali, hoping to save the Kingdom of the Hijaz for his family. But Ali too was overthrown and banished from the Hijaz a year later. In October 1924, Ibn Saud captured Mecca, and Hussein escaped to Aqaba. From Aqaba, Hussein was taken by a British naval vessel to Cyprus, where he lived in exile until his death in 1931.

The Hijaz became part of Saudi Arabia. Ibn Saud inflicted on Hussein and his eldest son the crowning humiliation of seeing him assume the administration of the holy places in Mecca and Medina. Thus, with the loss of the two most sacred sites of Islam, the Hashemite claim to leadership of the Muslim world disintegrated, as did the dream of a mighty Hashemite empire. And, by a cruel historic irony, it was in its own ancestral home that the Hashemite dynasty sustained the most monumental and shattering of defeats.

Hussein's eclipse gave a dramatic illustration of the immense power wielded by Britain in shaping the fortunes of the Arab nations and their rulers. The political shape of the region did not evolve naturally but was largely the product of British design tailored to fit Britain's own imperial needs. It was not the Syrians who expelled Faisal nor was it the Iraqis who raised him to the throne in their own countries. Abdullah could not have gained power in Transjordan without Britain's approval, and had he tried to do so in defiance of Britain he would not have survived for very long. Ibn Saud was not invited by the Hijazis to their country but rather he was enabled by British-supplied arms to enter and conquer their land. And just as the withdrawal of British support paved the way to the decline and fall of the Hashemite kingdom in the Hijaz, so it was British protection, and only British protection, that could preserve the Hashemite crown in Transjordan.

Ibn Saud was not content with his victory over Hussein. Driven by political ambition to expand his own realm and by the religious zeal of the Wahhabi reform movement, he turned northwards with the intent of completing the destruction of the house of Hashem. Abdullah's incorporation of the provinces of Ma'an and Aqaba, which formerly belonged to the Kingdom of the Hijaz, into the Amirate of Transjordan exacerbated the poor relations between the two rival dynasties. In August 1924 Wahhabi forces crossed the border into Transjordan, and had it not been for an RAF squadron from Jerusalem and a detachment of British armoured cars that furiously mowed down Ibn Saud's column of camel riders, Abdullah undoubtedly would have met the same fate as his father.

Ibn Saud did not abandon his designs on Transjordan, and the conflict continued to smoulder, with occasional forays across the border and tribal clashes. The 1928 treaty, which recognized Transjordan's independence but left finance and foreign affairs under British control, was signed at the time when Wahhabi raids were increasing. It was just as well for Abdullah that the British also undertook to defend the borders of the amirate, because this time the Wahhabis, fired by the fervour to sweep away all corruption and restore their pristine and puritanical brand of Islam, advanced upon Amman itself. Once again it was only the swift and forceful intervention of the RAF, this time assisted by the Arab Legion, that repelled the invasion and kept the amir on his throne in Amman. The Arab Legion (Al-Jaish al-Arabi) was a military formation created in Transjordan in 1920 by the British to maintain internal law and order. It was financed by Britain and commanded by British officers, underlining the local ruler's dependence on his colonial masters.

The principality that Abdullah had carved out for himself and from which he was in danger of being ejected was a political anomaly and a geographical nonsense. It had no obvious *raison d'être* and was indeed of such little political significance that the European powers, in their generally acquisitive wartime diplomacy, tended to overlook it as an unimportant corner of Syria. The status of this territory had remained indistinct until Abdullah's arrival. The Amirate of Transjordan was then created by the famous stroke of Churchill's pen, in mitigation of the sense of guilt the British felt towards the sharif, and in the hope of securing a modicum of stability and order east of the Jordan River at the lowest possible cost to their exchequer.

The borders of the new principality did not correspond to any particular historic, cultural or geographical unit. Bounded by the valley of the Yarmouk on the north, by the Arabian Desert on the east, by the Jordan River, the Dead Sea and Wadi Araba on the west, it had no outlet to the sea until Abdullah grabbed Ma'an and Aqaba from the expiring Kingdom of the Hijaz. Effectively, Transjordan was a strip of cultivable land 270 kilometres long with a width tapering from 80 kilometres in the north to almost nothing in the south, and flanked by a great deal of desert; it possessed some 230,000 inhabitants, one railway line and hardly any roads, no industrial resources and no revenue except for a modest British subsidy. The capital and largest town of this backward amirate was Amman—a drab and dusty place that could not even boast a glorious past. It was perhaps not altogether inappropriate that such a place should serve as the capital of this provincial backwater. And it was in a modest palace on the eastern hill overlooking Amman that Amir Abdullah settled down, "loyally and comfortably," as Churchill had hoped, with two official wives and a beautiful concubine.

But Transjordan was a very insubstantial principality for so ambitious a prince. The contrast between the barren and insignificant patch of territory assigned to him to administer on behalf of the British mandatory power and Abdullah's own heart's desire could hardly have been greater. Proud of his provenance, he was moved by an unshakeable faith that the true destiny of the Arabs lay in unity under Hashemite rule. From his father, Abdullah inherited the belief in Arab greatness, the yearning to revive the glories of the Islamic past and the vision of a mighty Hashemite empire and caliphate. But he did not inherit either the sanctimonious self-righteousness or the quixotic obstinacy that had brought his father's kingdom crashing down in flames.

Among Arab politicians Abdullah was never a popular or trusted figure. In his own way he was an ardent Arab nationalist, but the authoritarianism that marked his approach to the affairs of state and the confidence he exuded of being marked out by destiny to lead the Arab world to independence did not endear him to other Arabs, especially when they happened to be fellow kings or rulers in their own right.

Given his pride in his heritage, the faith that he himself was destined to play a commanding role, his penchant for playing for high stakes and the vaulting ambition he had nursed since his youth, it was inevitable that Abdullah would regard Transjordan as only the beginning, not the end, of his political career. "Much too big a cock for so small a dunghill" was Lord Curzon's comment on Abdullah in September 1921. Another contemporary described him as "a falcon trapped in a canary's cage, longing to break out, to realize his dreams and passions of being a great Arab leader; but there he was, pinned up in the cage of Transjordan by the British." Abdullah spent the rest of his life in a sustained attempt to project his political presence and influence beyond the borders of Transjordan. Behind this attempt lay not merely a personal sense of destiny and grievance but a statesmanlike appreciation that Transjordan needed a regional role if it was ever to become independent of Britain.

To this end Abdullah looked in all directions, but his greatest ambition was Greater Syria—Syria in its historical, or "natural," dimensions, encompassing Palestine, Transjordan and Lebanon. Abdullah aspired to realize this vision of Greater Syria with its capital in Damascus, the hereditary seat of the Umayyad caliphate, and with himself as king and overlord. He consistently maintained that Transjordan was only the southern part of Syria, and that his presence there was just a prelude to the attainment of complete Arab liberation, in the pursuit of which his family had sacrificed the Hijaz. The motto he adopted was: "All Syria to come under the leadership of a scion of the House of Hashem; Transjordan was the first step." The cherished notion of a great Arab empire that eluded the father would thus be realized by the son.

In the early years of Abdullah's rule, frustrated Syrian nationalists and enemies of the French mandate descended on Amman in droves. Some found their way into Abdullah's embryonic administration, while others, more militant and bent on pursuing their struggle against the French, even mounted raids across the border. With Faisal keeping a low profile in Baghdad, and Hussein fighting a rearguard battle until 1924 in his remote corner of Arabia, Abdullah emerged as a leading champion of Arab unity, and Amman became a focal point for Arab nationalist politics. But the initial euphoria evaporated rapidly, and with the passage of time the gulf between his idea of Arab unity—based on Islam, autocracy and the preservation of the old social order—and the younger nationalists' conception of unity—based on attaining liberation from foreign rule, and freedom and social reform at home—grew wider and resulted in mutual disenchantment.

Abdullah's tendency to assume that what was good for the Hashemites was good for the Arabs did not gain him many friends abroad. He began to focus more narrowly on his dynastic and personal interests at the expense of the broader political ideals. After the loss of the Hijaz to Ibn Saud and the expansion of his domain down to the Gulf of Aqaba, Abdullah settled down patiently to await opportunities for promoting his Greater Syria scheme. This was modified following the death in 1933 of his brother Faisal. From that point on he was to toy with various ideas for merging Iraq with Greater Syria, possibly in a federation of the Fertile Crescent of which he, as the oldest member of the Hashemite family and the only surviving leader of the Arab Revolt, would be the natural ruler.

Abdullah worked industriously, if rather fitfully, to propagate the idea of Greater Syria, always harking back to Faisal's lost kingdom, which should revert to him, just as Faisal's lineal heirs should succeed to the throne of Iraq. He assiduously cultivated a following in Syria itself and managed to enlist the support of some of the conservative elements there: the Ulama (religious scholars), the small landlords and the tribal shaikhs scattered around the country. Among Abdullah's most prominent supporters were Abd al-Rahman Shahbandar, the nationalist politician, and Sultan al-Atrash, the Druze leader from Jabal al-Druze in south-eastern Syria. (The Druze are an Arabic-speaking national–religious minority in Syria, Lebanon and Israel. Their sect is a branch of Shia Islam whose origins go back to the eleventh century.)

A not insignificant number of Syrians retained their monarchist sentiments, and after Faisal's death in 1933 pinned their hopes on his aspiring older brother. But as long as the French remained in Syria and Lebanon, Abdullah had little chance of success, for the French regarded the Greater Syria movement as an unwitting stalking horse, and Abdullah as a direct instrument of sinister British plots to undermine their own position in the area. In actual fact the British had never encouraged Abdullah to pursue his claims to Greater Syria; after the departure of the French in 1946, when Abdullah's expansionist plans were directed perforce against his Arab neighbours, they actively tried to discourage him. In March 1946, under the terms of a new treaty, Britain granted Transjordan formal independence; Abdullah assumed the title of "king," and the name of the country was changed from the Amirate of Transjordan to the Hashemite Kingdom of Jordan. Formal independence, however, was not matched by real independence.

Caught up in Great Power rivalries and in the cut and thrust of inter-Arab politics, the Greater Syria scheme ran for decades as a leitmotif in the affairs of the Middle East, provoking suspicion, antagonism and outright hostility towards Abdullah. Attack on it came from every corner of the Arab world. The Lebanese emphatically refused to become absorbed in a unitary Muslim state. The republicans in Syria, who had struggled for so long to achieve independence from the Ottomans and the French, were not about to surrender their hard-won gains by turning their country over to Hashemite rule. They also felt that if there were to be a Greater Syria, they were better equipped to lead it than the upstart from the Hijaz, and that its core and political centre of gravity should be Syria itself rather than backward Transjordan. Syria, after all, believed itself to be the beating heart of Arab nationalism. The Hashemites of Iraq and the nationalist politicians around them thought that their country was the natural leader of the Arab world; they devised their own plans for a federation under their leadership and gave Abdullah little support. The Saudis naturally opposed any plan that might strengthen the Hashemites and were determined not to let Abdullah extend his power outside Transjordan, lest he be tempted to try to reconquer the Hijaz. The Egyptians added their opposition to the concept of a Greater Syria, seeing the Hashemite bloc as the principal rival for their own hegemony in the Arab world. By trying to impose himself as the champion of Arab unity, Abdullah thus ended up antagonizing the majority of Arab nationalists both inside and outside the boundaries of Greater Syria. The nationalists came to see him as the lackey and tool of British imperialism in the Middle East; they perceived his expansionist plans as a threat to the independence of the other Arab states in the region; and they were critical of his accommodating attitude towards Zionism and the Jews in Palestine.

Without abandoning his larger goal, from the late 1930s onwards Abdullah gradually began to turn his thoughts and energy to Palestine. Palestine was only one of the four parts into which "natural Syria" had been divided, and a small one at that. But for Abdullah it had importance out of all proportion to its small size. To want to rule over Palestine was not for him a vacuous ambition, nor was it an accident that at the very first meeting with Churchill he asked to be entrusted with its administration. Transjordan and Palestine were bound together by a complex network of political and family ties, trade relations and routes of communication stretching back to the very distant past. Transjordan needed the capital, the markets, the trained manpower and an outlet to the Mediterranean Sea that only Palestine could provide.

This unity was severed by the British decision in 1922 to exclude

Transjordan from the area available to the Jewish national home. Imperial self-interest, rather than respect for the rights of the local communities, lay behind this decision. Geopolitics and grand strategy were the controlling considerations in separating Transjordan from western Palestine. Transjordan was needed as a buffer in the south between Saudi Arabia on the one hand and Egypt and Palestine on the other; it could also serve as a buffer to contain France in the north. Both Ottoman and Faisali Syria had extended down to Transjordan. Now a sharper line was drawn between the British and the French spheres of interest in the Levant.

The internal division of the Palestine mandate met with both strong Zionist opposition and resentment from Abdullah. True, Abdullah had formally recognized the British mandate over the whole of Palestine and the Balfour Declaration—something his father had resisted to the bitter end—but he felt that he had had no real choice in the matter. To Abdullah's way of thinking, gaining control over Palestine thus represented both an important end in itself and a possible means to a still larger long-term objective. The British attitude, here as always, was an important factor in Abdullah's calculations. He believed that the British would not look with the same disfavour on his plans for Palestine as they had always displayed towards his Greater Syria scheme. The other two elements that had to be taken into consideration were the Palestine Arabs and the Jews. Accordingly, Abdullah's policy for furthering his design on Palestine operated in three distinct but overlapping circles: the British; the Palestine Arabs; and the Jews. In all three, he used the same method—personal diplomacy.

Of all the political friendships cultivated by Abdullah, the most controversial, the least well understood by fellow Arabs and the most damaging to his reputation was his friendship with the Zionists. No other aspect of his policy provoked such intense suspicion, stirred such strong passions or brought him so much opprobrium. Abdullah's motives for seeking such an understanding were indeed complex, but they can be reduced to two basic and seemingly inconsistent factors: his fear of Zionism and his perception of the opportunity it offered him to realize his own goals in Palestine.

Abdullah may not have fully understood the ideas that propelled the Zionists to strive so relentlessly for a state of their own, but he recognized a going concern when he saw one. A newcomer though he was to the affairs of Palestine, he read the situation of the Jews there, and the politics of his Arab kinsmen, with remarkable clarity. Whereas the latter indulged in facile optimism and hopes of an easy victory until overtaken by the disaster of 1948, he never underestimated the power, skill and commitment that activated Jewish nationalism in Palestine. Realizing that Zionism could not be destroyed or ignored, his strategy was attuned to circumventing it and preventing a head-on collision. But he was also shrewd enough to see at an early stage that Zionism's force, if rightly channelled, could turn out to be not a barrier but a help in fulfilling his ambition of a Greater Transjordan: Jewish enmity could only weaken his chances of being accepted by the world as the ruler of Palestine, but Jewish acquiescence, especially if it could be purchased at the price of autonomy under his rule, might pave the way to a Greater Transjordan, incorporating part, or possibly all, of the Holy Land.

In his personal dealings with the Zionists, Abdullah was not hampered by any racist prejudice. Hatred of the Jews did not burn in his heart, and he stood above the fanatic anti-Jewish prejudices harboured by some Arabs. His unbiased and pragmatic attitude towards the Jews, while not unique, did stand in marked contrast to the anti-Semitism of the majority of Arabs. Respect for the Jews, the People of the Book, was in fact for the Hashemites a family tradition, consistent with the teachings of the Koran. Abdullah's father refused to condone the Balfour Declaration not out of blind anti-Zionism but because it did not safeguard the civil and religious rights of the Arabs, and disregarded what he perceived as their inalienable political and economic rights in Palestine. He was not opposed to letting the Jews live in peace beside Muslims in the Holy Land on the clear understanding that all the legitimate rights of the Muslims would be respected.

Abdullah was not the first member of his family to hold exploratory talks with Zionist leaders. In January 1919 his brother Faisal initialled an agreement with the moderate Zionist leader Chaim Weizmann, one he was unable to ratify because of the strength of Arab opposition. Soon after he got his principality, Abdullah embarked on a tangled relationship with the Zionists that was to last until the end of his life. To his early contacts with the Zionists Abdullah brought the self-confidence and flexibility in dealing with minorities that he had acquired under the Ottoman regime. His view of the Jews as fabulously wealthy and skilled in the ways of the modern world also went back to his time in

Istanbul, where he had first met Jewish physicians, merchants and financiers. The Zionist leaders for their part could not fail to be impressed by the moderation and pragmatism of their new neighbour to the east, and their policy in consequence acquired a pro-Hashemite orientation at a very early stage.

The first meeting between Abdullah and Weizmann took place in London in 1922. Abdullah offered to support the Balfour Declaration if the Zionists accepted him as the ruler of Palestine and used their influence with the British authorities to procure this appointment for him. The offer was politely brushed aside, but the traffic between the Zionists and the amir had begun. The basic solution, which Abdullah advanced at different times and in ever-changing forms, was a "Semitic kingdom" embracing both Palestine and Transjordan, in which Arabs and Jews could live as of right and as equals, with himself as their hereditary monarch. It is worth noting that none of these forms allowed for Jews living abroad to have an automatic right to come to Palestine: immigration controls of some sort were to be imposed to ensure Arab preponderance and to keep the Jews to a minority status in this "Semitic kingdom."

There was never any chance of Abdullah's offer of autonomy within a larger kingdom being acceptable to the official leadership of the Yishuv, the pre-independence Jewish community in Palestine. The official leaders of the Zionist movement aspired to an independent Jewish state, and the offer of a limited autonomy under Arab rule fell far short of their expectations and was indeed incompatible with the basic goal of their movement. They wanted good relations with Abdullah, but they had no wish to be his subjects. This was the view of the Labour Zionists who dominated the political institutions of the Yishuv; further to the right were Ze'ev Jabotinsky's Revisionist Zionists, who not only spurned any idea of subservience to an Arab ruler but were never reconciled to the partition of mandatory Palestine and continued to include the East Bank of the Jordan in their ambitious blueprint for a Jewish state.

Abdullah's contacts with the mainstream Zionists continued almost without a break until his death in July 1951.[21] They assumed particular importance during the critical phase in the struggle for Palestine following Britain's announcement, in February 1947, of its decision to relinquish the mandate. On 29 November 1947 the UN General Assembly voted to replace the British mandate in Palestine with two states, one Arab and one Jewish. The Jewish Agency accepted the UN partition plan because it endorsed the Jewish claim to independence and statehood. The Arab League and the Palestinian leaders rejected it as immoral, illegal and impractical, and they went to war to nullify it. The passage of the partition resolution by the UN was thus both an international charter of legitimacy for the establishment of a Jewish state and the signal for the outbreak of a vicious war in Palestine.

The First Arab–Israeli War is usually treated as one war. Israelis call it the War of Independence, whereas Arabs call it Al-Nakbah, or "The Catastrophe." In fact, it could be considered two wars in that it had two distinct phases, each with a different character and, on the Arab side, each with different participants. The first phase lasted from 29 November 1947, when the UN passed the partition resolution, until 14 May 1948, when the British mandate expired and the State of Israel was proclaimed. The second phase lasted from the invasion of Palestine by the regular armies of the Arab states on 15 May 1948 until the termination of hostilities on 7 January 1949. The first and unofficial phase of the war was between the Jewish and Arab communities in Palestine, and it ended in triumph for the Jews and tragedy for the Palestinians. The second and official phase of the war involved the regular armies of the neighbouring Arab states, and it ended with an Israeli victory and a comprehensive Arab defeat.

Most of the literature on the First Arab–Israeli War relates to the official, or inter-state, phase that began with the invasion of Palestine by the armies of seven Arab states upon expiry of the British mandate. In many respects, however, the unofficial phase of the war was more important, and more fateful, in its consequences. The first phase was, essentially, a civil war between the local communities. It was during this phase that the irregular Palestinian military forces were defeated, Palestinian society was pulverized and the largest wave of refugees was set in motion. It was only after the collapse of Palestinian resistance that the neighbouring Arab states committed their own regular forces to the battle.

King Abdullah's hope was to effect a peaceful partition of Palestine between himself and the Jewish Agency, and to isolate his great rival, Hajj Amin al-Husseini, the leader of the Palestinian national movement. The political agendas of the two rivals were incompatible. The

Mufti rejected categorically any idea of Jewish statehood and staked a claim to a unitary Arab state over the whole of Palestine. Abdullah was prepared to accommodate a Jewish state, provided it allowed him to make himself master of the Arab part of Palestine. The British secretly backed Abdullah's bid to incorporate the Arab part of Palestine into his kingdom because he was their client, whereas the Mufti was a renegade who had supported Nazi Germany in the Second World War. In British eyes a Palestinian state was synonymous with a Mufti state. They there-fore colluded with Abdullah in aborting the birth of a Palestinian state but at the same time urged him not to cross the borders of the Jewish state as defined by the UN and to avoid a direct collision with the Jew-ish forces.

Abdullah had a secret meeting with Golda Meyerson (later Meir) of the Jewish Agency in Naharayim, by the Jordan River, on 17 November 1947. Here they reached a preliminary agreement to coordinate their diplomatic and military strategies, to forestall the Mufti and to en-deavour to prevent the other Arab states from intervening directly in Palestine.[22] Twelve days later, on 29 November, the United Nations pro-nounced its verdict in favour of dividing the area of the British mandate into two states. This made it possible to solidify the tentative under-standing reached at Naharayim. In return for Abdullah's promise not to enter the area assigned by the UN to the Jewish state, the Jewish Agency agreed to the annexation by Transjordan of most of the area earmarked for the Arab state. Precise borders were not drawn, and Jerusalem was not even discussed, as under the UN plan it was to remain a *corpus sep-aratum* under international control.

Abdullah's hope of a peaceful partition was dashed by the escalation of fighting in Palestine. The collapse of Palestinian society and the birth of the Palestinian refugee problem generated intense popular pressure on the Arab governments, and especially that of Transjordan, to send their armies to Palestine to check the Jewish military offensive. Abdul-lah was unable to withstand this pressure. The flood of refugees reach-ing Transjordan pushed the Arab Legion towards greater participation in the affairs of Palestine. The tacit agreement that Abdullah had reached with the Jewish Agency enabled him to pose as the protector of the Arabs in Palestine, while keeping his army out of the areas that the UN had earmarked for the Jewish state. This balancing act, however, became increasingly difficult to maintain. Suspecting Abdullah of col-

laboration with the Zionists, the anti-Hashemite states in the Arab
League began to lean towards intervention with regular armies in Palestine, if only to curb Abdullah's territorial ambition and stall his bid for
hegemony in the region. On 30 April 1948 the Political Committee of
the Arab League decided that all the Arab states must prepare their
armies for the invasion of Palestine on 15 May, the day after the expiry
of the British mandate. Under pressure from Transjordan and Iraq,
Abdullah was appointed as commander-in-chief of the invading
forces.[23]

To the Jewish leaders it looked as if Abdullah was about to throw in
his lot with the rest of the Arab world. So Golda Meir was sent on
10 May on a secret mission to Amman to warn the king against doing
so. Abdullah looked depressed and nervous. Meir flatly rejected his
offer of autonomy for the Jewish territories under his crown and
insisted that they adhere to their original plan for an independent Jewish state and the annexation of the Arab part to Transjordan. Abdullah
did not deny that this was what had been agreed, but the situation in
Palestine had changed radically, he explained, and now that he was
one of five he had no choice but to join with the other Arab states in the
invasion of Palestine. Meir was adamant: if Abdullah was going back
on their agreement and if he wanted war, then they would meet after
the war and after the Jewish state had been established. The meeting
ended on a frosty note, but Abdullah's parting words to Ezra Danin,
who accompanied and translated for Meir, were a plea not to break off
contact, come what may.[24]

In Zionist historiography the meeting of 10 May is usually presented
as proof of the unreliability of Israel's only friend among the Arabs and
as confirmation that Israel stood alone against an all-out offensive by a
united Arab world. Meir herself helped to propagate the view that
Abdullah broke his word to her; that the meeting ended in total disagreement; and that they parted as enemies.[25] The king's explanation of
the constraints that forced him to intervene was seized upon as evidence of treachery and betrayal on his part. In essence, the Zionist
charge against Abdullah is that when the moment of truth arrived, he
revoked his pledge not to attack the Jewish state and threw in his lot
with the rest of the Arab world.[26] This helped to sustain the legend that
the outbreak of war was a carefully orchestrated all-Arab invasion plan
directed at strangling the Jewish state at birth.

The truth about the second Abdullah–Meir meeting is rather more nuanced than this self-serving Zionist account would have us believe. Abdullah had not entirely betrayed the agreement, nor was he entirely loyal to it, but something in between. Even Meir's own account of her mission, given to her colleagues on the Provisional State Council shortly after her return from Amman, was nowhere near as unsympathetic or unflattering as the account she included much later in her memoirs. From her own contemporary report on her mission, a number of important points emerge. First, Abdullah did not go back on his word; he only stressed that circumstances had changed. Second, Abdullah did not say he wanted war; it was Meir who threatened him with dire consequences in the event of war. Third, they did not part as enemies. On the contrary, Abdullah seemed anxious to maintain contact with the Jewish side even after the outbreak of hostilities. Abdullah needed to send his army across the Jordan River in order to gain control over the Arab part of Palestine contiguous with his kingdom. He did not say anything about attacking the Jewish forces on their own territory. The distinction was a subtle one, and Meir was not renowned for her subtlety.

Part of the problem was that Abdullah had to pretend to be going along with the other members of the Arab League who had unanimously rejected the UN partition plan and were bitterly opposed to the establishment of a Jewish state. What is more, the military experts of the Arab League had worked out a unified plan for invasion, one that was all the more dangerous for having been geared to the real capabilities of the regular Arab armies rather than to the wild rhetoric about throwing the Jews into the sea. But the forces actually made available by the Arab states for the campaign in Palestine were well below the level demanded by the Military Committee of the Arab League. Moreover, Abdullah wrecked the invasion plan by making last-minute changes. His objective in ordering his army across the Jordan River was not to prevent the establishment of a Jewish state but to make a bid for the Arab part of Palestine. Abdullah never wanted the other Arab armies to intervene in Palestine. Their plan was to prevent partition; his plan was to effect partition. His plan assumed and even required a Jewish presence in Palestine, although his preference was for Jewish autonomy under his crown. By concentrating his forces on the West Bank, Abdullah intended to eliminate once and for all any possibility of an independent Palestinian state and to present his Arab partners with annexation as a fait accompli. In the course of the war for Palestine there were some bitter clashes between the Arab Legion and the Israel Defence Force (IDF), especially in and around Jerusalem. But by the end all the invading Arab armies had been repelled and only the Arab Legion held its ground in central Palestine.

Thus there are two rival versions of Jordan's conduct in the First Arab–Israeli War: the loyalist version and the Arab nationalist one. The loyalist version maintains that Abdullah acted in accordance with the wishes of the Palestinians both in sending the Arab Legion into Palestine in 1948 and in uniting the West Bank with the Hashemite Kingdom of Jordan in 1950. The Arab nationalist version portrays Abdullah as a greedy villain whose collaboration with the Jews led to the Arab defeat in the 1948 war and to the enlargement of his kingdom at the expense of the Palestinians.[27]

The principal weakness of the loyalist narrative lies in its failure to make any mention of Abdullah's secret dealings with the Jewish Agency in the lead-up to the Palestine war. My own version of events is set out in my book *Collusion Across the Jordan* and is close to the Arab nationalist narrative in as much as it stresses the importance of this secret diplomacy in determining the course and outcome of the First Arab–Israeli War. The main thesis advanced in my book is that in November 1947 Abdullah reached a tacit agreement with the Jewish Agency to divide Palestine between themselves following the termination of the British mandate, and that this laid the foundations for mutual restraint during the 1948 war and for continued collaboration in the aftermath of that war.

The thesis of "Collusion Across the Jordan" has been hotly denied by some Israeli scholars.[28] This thesis contradicts the traditional, heroic, moralistic version of the emergence of the State of Israel and of the 1948 war. It also challenges the conventional view of the Arab–Israeli conflict as a simple bipolar affair in which a monolithic and implacably hostile Arab world is pitted against the Jews. It suggests that the Arab rulers were deeply divided among themselves on how to deal with the Zionist challenge and that one of them favoured accommodation rather than confrontation and had indeed reached an understanding with the Jews on the partition of Palestine. The evidence for this comes mainly from official Israeli documents, and it is far too extensive to reproduce here. But one piece of evidence is worth quoting at length because it is particularly incisive and illuminating: the testimony of Yaacov Shimoni, a senior official in the Jewish Agency, who was directly involved in the contacts with Abdullah. In an interview with the present author, Shimoni emphatically maintained that, despite Abdullah's evasions, the understanding with him

was entirely clear in its general spirit. We would agree to the conquest of the Arab part of Palestine by Abdullah. We would not stand in his way. We would not help him, would not seize it and hand it over to him. He would have to take it by his own means and stratagems but we would not disturb him. He, for his part, would not prevent us from establishing the State of Israel, from dividing the country, taking our share and establishing a state in it. Now his vagueness, his ambiguity, consisted of declining to write anything, to draft anything, which would bind him. To this he did not agree. But to the end, until the last minute, and if I am not mistaken even during his last talk with Golda [on 10 May 1948], he always said again and again: "Perhaps you would settle for less than complete independence and statehood, after all; under my sovereignty or within a common framework with me, you would receive full autonomy or a Jewish canton, not a totally separate one but under the roof of the Hashemite crown." This he did try to raise every now and again and, of course, always met with a blank wall. We told him we were talking about complete, full, and total independence and are not prepared to discuss anything else. And to this he seemed resigned but without ever saying: "OK, an independent state." He did not say that, he did not commit himself, he was not precise. But such was the spirit of the agreement and it was totally unambiguous.

Incidentally, the agreement included a provision that if Abdullah succeeded in capturing Syria, and realized his dream of Greater Syria—something we did not think he had the power to do—we would not disturb him. We did not believe either in the strength of his faction in Syria. But the agreement included a provision that if he does accomplish it, we would not stand in his way.

But regarding the Arab part of Palestine, we did think it was serious and that he had every chance of taking it, all the more so since the Arabs of Palestine, with their official leadership, did not want to establish a state at all. That meant that we were not interfering with anybody. It was they who refused. Had they accepted a state, we might not have entered into the conspiracy. I do not know. But the fact was that they refused, so there was a complete power vacuum here and we agreed that he will go in and take the Arab part, provided he consented to the establishment of our state and to a joint declaration that there will be peaceful relations between us and him after the dust had settled. That was the spirit of the agreement. A text did not exist.[29]

Shimoni uses the word "conspiracy," which is even stronger than "collusion." On the other hand, unlike the Arab nationalists, he does not lay all the blame for the Arab defeat at Abdullah's door. In particular, Shimoni draws attention to the part that the Palestinians themselves played in the loss of Palestine. Abdullah, in fact, offered the Palestinians his protection, but they rejected it. They put their trust in the Arab League, which failed them. True, after being spurned by the Palestinians, Abdullah proceeded to play a part in aborting the United Nations partition resolution of 29 November 1947 that called for the establishment of two states, one Palestinian and one Jewish. But since the Arab League, the Arab states and the Palestinians all categorically rejected the partition plan, they were hardly entitled to complain. There was, as Shimoni points out, a complete power vacuum on the Arab side. To be sure, there was a great deal of rhetoric coming from the Arab side on the liberation of Palestine. Rhetoric, however, as the Palestinians were to discover to their cost, was not much use on the battlefield.

Abdullah was not alone in pursuing a dynastic agenda. All the Arab participants in the 1948 war were propelled by narrow national interests while pretending to serve the common cause. The difference was that Abdullah was alone among the Arab leaders in possessing a realistic appreciation of the balance of forces in 1948. Because of his realism, he was more successful in achieving his objectives than they were. But it was the inability of the Arab leaders as a group to coordinate their diplomatic and military strategies that was in no small measure responsible for the catastrophic defeat that they suffered at the hands of the infant Jewish state. Inter-Arab conflict is the untold story of the war for Palestine.[30]

Only two parties emerged as winners from the Palestine war: Jordan and Israel. Jordan managed to defend the West Bank and East Jerusalem, and to incorporate them into its territory. Israel succeeded in extending its territory considerably beyond the UN partition borders. Egypt was soundly defeated in Palestine, but it did hold on to the Gaza Strip along the Mediterranean coast. The losers were the Palestinians.

Having rejected the partition of Palestine, they were left with no part of Palestine at all, and the name Palestine was wiped off the map.[31] Over 700,000 Palestinians became refugees and over half of that number ended up in Jordan, drastically changing the demographic balance of the kingdom.

The Palestinians called Abdullah a traitor. He sold them down the river, they said. Yet, if Abdullah had not sent his army into Palestine upon expiry of the British mandate, it is likely that the whole of Palestine would have been occupied by Israel and an even larger number of Palestinians turned into refugees. There is thus at least a case to be made for viewing Abdullah not as a traitor but as a saviour of the Palestinians.[32] The Palestinian retort is that Abdullah preserved a part of Palestine from being swallowed up by Israel, only in order to swallow it up in Jordan. Some arguments never end.

After the guns fell silent, Israel signed armistice agreements with all its neighbours: Egypt, Lebanon, Jordan and Syria. The Israel–Jordan armistice agreement was signed on 3 April 1949. The armistice demarcation line between Jordan and Israel, including the division of Jerusalem, was the product of secret negotiations between Abdullah and the Israelis. Jerusalem, the scene of some of the fiercest and bloodiest fighting of the entire war, was quietly partitioned between the two sides along the ceasefire line in order to pre-empt the United Nations' move to turn it into an international city. The Arab states that had rejected the UN partition plan of November 1947 now ironically became enthusiastic proponents of a UN regime for the Holy City. Abdullah understood that his Arab rivals were out to deprive him of the most glittering prize he had won in the war. So he and the Israelis bypassed the UN and partitioned Jerusalem between themselves in a remarkable display of the common interests that set them apart from the rest of the Arab world.

Even after the yielding of some territory under duress, Abdullah emerged as the most successful Arab participant from the First Arab–Israeli War. That "falcon trapped in a canary's cage" at long last succeeded in breaking out and expanding his exiguous dominion. He not only held on to the Old City and East Jerusalem but also acquired additional land on the West Bank of the Jordan River. His Arab detractors denounced Abdullah as a traitor and a quisling, and at least one British official described him as "a born land-grabber." No saint, Abdullah bin Hussein. Yet those who sit in judgement upon him should recall that after the Arab rejection of the UN partition plan, the war for Palestine degenerated into a general land-grab, and the real distinction was not between saints and sinners but between more successful and less successful land-grabbers. Only the Palestinians did not figure in this equation. They were the real losers in that war.

In Abdullah's defence it can be argued that he saved what he could from the dismal wreck of Arab Palestine. This is more than can be said for his detractors. With his extraordinary sense of realism, his practice in war and peace of the art of the possible, his willingness to look beyond ideological and religious differences, and his penchant for the sly, saving bargain, he was typical of a Middle Eastern political culture that was to be blown away by the politics of zeal, with ruinous results for the Arab world in the Palestine war and its aftermath.

The end of the war brought no respite from the endemic inter-Arab rivalries. Unable to close ranks in the face of the bitter consequences of defeat, the Arabs indulged in mutual recrimination and the search for scapegoats, which further weakened their position in the diplomatic negotiations that followed the end of hostilities. Abdullah was singled out for the most vituperative attacks because he had accepted partition, because he was willing to trade on Palestinian rights and because he was widely suspected of being in cahoots with the Jews against his Arab kinsmen. Though he had done well out of the war in terms of territory, Abdullah was thus doomed to spend the closing years of his reign in bitter conflict with his fellow Arabs. In Palestine he met his triumph and his nemesis.

Undeterred by the hostile propaganda and the shrill charges of treason levelled against him, Abdullah pressed on with the incorporation of the West Bank into his realm. "Union" between the two banks of the Jordan was formally proclaimed in April 1950. The Palestinians for the most part resigned themselves to annexation by Jordan, if only to avert the threat of being overrun by the Israeli Army. They were so demoralized, divided and helpless that the idea of an independent Palestinian state was no more than a pipe-dream, and the union of the two banks of Jordan was the most sensible course of action open to them. Yet Abdullah's claim to the West Bank was rejected by all the other members of the Arab League. It was recognized officially only by Britain and Pakistan, and privately by Israel.

Abdullah wanted to secure his enlarged kingdom by concluding a peace settlement with Israel, and for a while he pursued both aims simultaneously. His negotiations for an overall settlement with Israel were protracted and tortuous, but they appeared to be on the verge of a dramatic breakthrough in February 1950 when the "Draft Agreement between Israel and Jordan" was initialled. At this point Abdullah realistically estimated that he could not simultaneously defy the Arab League on both the peace talks and the annexation, so he suspended the talks with Israel in order to go forward with the union of the two banks. The suspension was meant to be temporary, but the attempt to sign a peace treaty, though subsequently renewed, never regained its momentum. In retrospect it is clear that the suspension of the talks constituted a massive and irreversible defeat in Abdullah's quest for peace, marking the end of serious Arab–Israeli peace negotiations until Egyptian President Anwar Sadat's visit to Jerusalem in 1977. Abdullah himself continued his talks with the Israelis almost literally until his dying day.

Two principal reasons account for the failure of the peace negotiations: Israel's strength and Abdullah's weakness. Abdullah displayed considerable courage in swimming against the powerful current of Arab hostility towards the State of Israel. The Israelis unquestionably wanted a settlement with Abdullah and even offered him an outlet to the Mediterranean with a narrow corridor, 50 to 100 metres wide, under Jordanian sovereignty, as well as various economic concessions. But this was not enough. The king needed to recover sufficient lost territory to justify the making of peace with Israel in the eyes of the Arab world. The Israelis felt that a corridor of the width he required would jeopardize their security. They were not prepared to relinquish any significant area of Palestine or to allow the return of the Palestinian refugees in order to attain peace. They wanted peace, but as the victors they were under no pressure to pay the price for it.

David Ben-Gurion, Israel's first prime minister, was a striking example of these contradictory impulses. Peace with the Arabs was something he desired, but it was not an urgent need or a priority. In an interview with Kenneth Bilby, the correspondent of the *New York Herald Tribune*, Ben-Gurion succinctly summed up his contradictory position: "I am prepared to get up in the middle of the night in order to sign a peace agreement—but I am not in a hurry and I can wait ten years. We are under no pressure whatsoever."[33] Ben-Gurion had especially serious doubts about the desirability of a final peace settlement with Jordan. He gave several reasons. First, Jordan was not a natural or stable political entity but a regime based on one man who could die any minute and who was entirely dependent on Britain. Second, a political settlement with Jordan was liable to get in the way of a settlement with Egypt, the most important of the Arab states. Third, an accord with Abdullah without peace with Egypt could not end Israel's isolation in Asia, Africa and Europe. Fourth, such an accord would reinforce Britain's hold in the surrounding area. Fifth, Ben-Gurion did not want to commit himself to the existing border with Jordan, which he called "ridiculous." In other words, he wanted to leave open the possibility of territorial expansion at Jordan's expense.[34] This lack of commitment to a political settlement with Jordan was a major factor in the failure of the talks.

The other principal reason for the failure of the peace talks was Abdullah's weakness, or what the Israeli Arabists termed "the sinking of Abdullah's regime." By adding the West Bank and its inhabitants to his kingdom, Abdullah helped to unleash forces that ended up eroding his previously absolute personal rule. In the new political constellation created by the union, he could no longer lay down the law in the arbitrary fashion to which he was accustomed but had to take account of public opinion, of the feelings of his Palestinian subjects, of parliament and above all of the growing opposition among his own ministers to his policy of accommodation with Israel. The anti-peace faction in the Jordanian government, bolstered by the popular anti-Israeli groundswell and pan-Arab opposition to negotiations with Israel, ultimately prevailed. Although the king's personal commitment to peace was unaffected by the new setting, his ability to give practical expression to it was seriously diminished.

In the last week of his life Abdullah seemed to have a premonition of his imminent death. On 15 July 1951 Riad al-Sulh, the former prime minister of Lebanon, was assassinated while on a visit to Jordan. In the aftermath of the assassination, the atmosphere in Jordan reeked of resentment, inflamed passions and fears of further violence. Reports of plots against the life of the monarch added to the anxieties of the Jordanian authorities and led them to step up security precautions. Abdullah's aides pleaded with him not to go to Jerusalem for Friday prayers, but he was adamant. Abdullah's fifteen-year-old grandson, Hussein, was to accompany him on what turned out to be his last journey. Hussein remembered that as they discussed the visit to Jerusalem the sense of foreboding was so strong that even his grandfather—a man not given to unnecessary alarm—seemed to have a premonition of disaster.

On Friday, 20 July 1951, Abdullah went to pray at the Al-Aqsa Mosque in the Old City of Jerusalem, accompanied by his grandson Hussein and an Arab Legion bodyguard. They entered the vast courtyard surrounding the Muslim Holy Places just before noon. First Abdullah visited the tomb of his father and then proceeded to the entrance of the Great Mosque, where the Koran was being recited to about 2,000 worshippers. As he stepped across the threshold, the old shaikh of the mosque, a venerable ecclesiastic with a long white beard, came forward to kiss his hand. The king's guard fell back, and, as they did so, a young Palestinian nationalist stepped out from behind the massive door of the mosque, pressed a pistol to the king's ear and fired a solitary shot, which killed him instantly. The king fell forward and his turban rolled away across the marble pavement.

On hearing the news of Abdullah's assassination, Ben-Gurion's first thought was to seize the opportunity to capture Jordanian territory. He asked his military advisers to prepare a plan for the capture of the West Bank.[35] This was abandoned, but Abdullah's assassination did cause something of a change in Ben-Gurion's thinking. Until 1951 he had accepted the territorial status quo and done nothing to disturb it. Once Abdullah was removed, his own commitment to the status quo began to waver, and he indulged in dreams of territorial expansion. The murder also made him more pessimistic about the prospects of peace with the rest of the Arab world. He concluded that peace with the Arabs could not be attained by negotiation; instead they would have to be deterred, coerced and intimidated. Abdullah's murder was thus a critical episode in the history of Israeli–Arab relations.

From the Jordanian perspective, the founder of the kingdom failed to crown his contacts with the State of Israel with a peace treaty or to normalize relations between the two states. A formal and comprehensive peace settlement with Israel was beyond his power. The legacy that he left behind was complex and contradictory. He was a full-blooded Hashemite, but the Hashemites operated at two distinct levels: ideology and pragmatism. Ideologically, they were deeply committed to Arab nationalism. Indeed, they claimed to be the trail-blazers of the Arab awakening. The Arab Revolt was the great foundation myth of the Arab national movement, and they were the driving force behind that revolt. Pragmatically, however, the Hashemites relied heavily on outside powers to counter their isolation and to bolster their weak position within the region.

The founder of the Hashemite Kingdom of Jordan had been dealt a particularly poor hand. He was given a desert kingdom with very meagre resources, no prestigious past and a very uncertain future. He consequently felt compelled to resort to politics, diplomacy and alliances. During the First World War he and his family forged an alliance with Great Britain and after it he developed a special relationship with the rising economic and political force in the region, the Zionist movement. Engagement with the Zionists served his dynastic interests, but for that very reason it also undermined his credentials as an Arab nationalist. Although alliances with foreign powers strengthened the position of the Hashemites regionally and internationally they also laid them open to the charge of serving other people's interests, of being clients and, even worse, collaborators. Abdullah was much more strongly identified in the public eye with pragmatism than with ideology. He saw himself as an Arab patriot, but he was, in the final analysis, the king of realism. This mixed legacy is crucial for understanding Jordanian foreign policy during the brief interregnum of his son Talal and the long reign of his grandson Hussein.

2. Murder of a Mentor

The murder of his beloved grandfather at the entrance to the Al-Aqsa Mosque was one of the most traumatic events in Hussein's life and a decisive influence in moulding his character and outlook. The memory of it seared itself on the mind of the young prince, and gave him his first taste of the perils and pitfalls of monarchical politics. In his autobiography Hussein underscores its centrality: "I have decided to start these memoirs with the murder of my grandfather, since he, of all men, had the most profound influence on my life. So, too, had the manner of his death."[1]

Nothing in Hussein's earlier life had prepared him for this terrible tragedy. He was born in Amman on 14 November 1935, and during his early years his family lived simply but happily. His father, Prince Talal, was Abdullah's eldest son and heir apparent. Born in 1909 in the Hijaz, Talal was educated in Britain at the royal military academy at Sandhurst. On his return from England, Talal became an officer in the British-commanded Jordanian Army, or the Arab Legion, as it was called. But two periods of attachment to British infantry regiments stationed in Palestine bred in Talal resentment and rebelliousness against the British masters of his country, an attitude that brought his military career to an inglorious end.

Talal's marriage to his cousin Sharifa Zain bint Jamil (1916–94), who was herself of Hashemite ancestry, and the birth of their first son gave him the benefit of a settled family life. They lived on Jebel Amman, one of the capital's seven hills, in a modest five-roomed villa set in a small plot of land. Although Talal was crown prince, his salary from the state was modest, leading them to live fairly frugally. Zain was a remarkable person: well educated, fluent in four languages, highly intelligent and with a modern outlook on life in what was a traditional, male-dominated society. She displayed towards her son constant affection and gave him a great deal of encouragement and guidance while

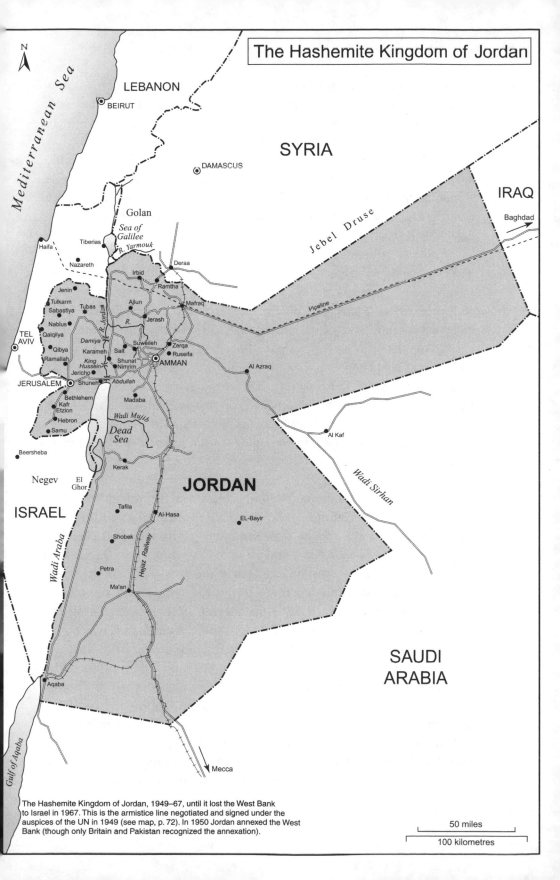

N

The Hashemite Kingdom of Jordan

Mediterranean Sea

LEBANON
⊙ BEIRUT

SYRIA

⊙ DAMASCUS

IRAQ

Baghdad →

Golan

Sea of Galilee

Tiberias

R. Yarmouk

Haifa

Nazareth

Deraa

Irbid

Ramtha

Jebel Druse

Jenin

Ajlun

Mafraq

Tulkarm

Sabastiya

Tubas

R.

Jerash

Pipeline

Nablus

Qalqilya

R. Jordan

Suweileh

Zerqa

Damiya

Karameh

Salt

Ruseifa

TEL
AVIV ⊙

Qibya

Ramallah

King Hussein

Shunat
Nimrim

⊙ AMMAN

Al Azraq

Jericho

Abdullah

JERUSALEM ⊙

Shuneh

Bethlehem

Madaba

Kafr
Etzion

Wadi Mujib

Al Kaf

Hebron

Dead Sea

Samu

Wadi Sirhan

Beersheba

Kerak

Negev

El
Ghor

JORDAN

ISRAEL

Tafila

Al-Hasa

EL-Bayir

Wadi Araba

Shobek

Hejaz Railway

Petra

Ma'an

SAUDI
ARABIA

Aqaba

Gulf of Aqaba

↓ Mecca

The Hashemite Kingdom of Jordan, 1949–67, until it lost the West Bank
to Israel in 1967. This is the armistice line negotiated and signed under the
auspices of the UN in 1949 (see map, p. 72). In 1950 Jordan annexed the West
Bank (though only Britain and Pakistan recognized the annexation).

50 miles

100 kilometres

avoiding the pomp and protocol that usually go with royalty. Talal too was a devoted husband and a loving father, but he showed increasing signs of the mental illness that was eventually diagnosed by Arab and European experts as schizophrenia.

Whether Talal was born with the seeds of mental illness is difficult to say, but there can be no doubt that his troubled and acrimonious relationship with his father seriously aggravated his condition. In his memoirs Hussein candidly admitted that his grandfather and father never got on well together:

The two men were separated by different lives and different ages, and their differences were exacerbated by opportunists. Worst of all, my grandfather never really realized until the end of his life how deeply afflicted my father was. He could not conceive that a man at times gentle and sensible, but at other times very ill, was not being just awkward or difficult. My grandfather was so healthy and tough he could not appreciate what illness was. We in the family knew. We watched our father with loving care, but my grandfather, who lived partly in the heroic past, saw him from outside. He had wanted a brave, intrepid, Bedouin son to carry on the great tradition of the Arab Revolt, and was incapable of accepting an invalid in place of his dream. It was the bitterest disappointment of his life.[2]

Apart from temperamental incompatibility and the generational gap, father and son were completely at odds with one another in their attitude towards Britain and its representatives in Jordan. Abdullah was one of Britain's closest friends and allies in the Middle East. In the Arab world he was widely regarded as a stooge and lackey of British imperialism. In fact, Abdullah felt that he and his family had been badly betrayed by the British and he privately nursed grievances against them. But he also recognized his dependence on them and was consequently determined to preserve their friendship at any cost. Talal, on the other hand, bitterly resented British interference in the affairs of his country and saw no reason to conceal his resentment. He had many public clashes with British representatives, and these enhanced his popular reputation as a Jordanian patriot and an Arab nationalist.

Britain's two most senior representatives in Jordan were General John Bagot Glubb, who was generally referred to by his honorific title of Glubb Pasha, and Alec Kirkbride. Glubb was a British Army officer who joined the Arab Legion in 1930 and rose to the position of commander-in-chief. Although he served the Hashemites under contract, rather than on secondment from the British Army, in the eyes of the nationalists he was the symbol of Britain's imperial domination in Jordan. Alec Kirkbride lived in Jordan with only short breaks from 1918 onwards for a total of thirty-three years. From 1927 to 1938 he was assistant British resident; from 1939 to 1946 British resident; and from 1946 to 1951 minister plenipotentiary. Kirkbride was a shrewd and experienced politician, a robust character and the real *eminence grise* of Jordanian politics. A colonial pro-consul would have been a more fitting description of Kirkbride's role than any of his official titles. He called his memoirs *From the Wings: Amman Memoirs 1947–1951*, whereas in fact he was at the centre of the political scene, very close to the monarch. Glubb and Kirkbride treated Abdullah with the utmost courtesy and genuine affection, but they were the effective power behind the throne, and their influence over him was all the more effective for being exercised in a subtle and indirect way.

Both men, in their memoirs, pooh-poohed the idea that Talal was anti-British. Glubb claims that never in his life did he meet with more kindness and consideration than he did from Talal. Glubb notes that in Syria, Egypt and Palestine Talal was depicted as a noble patriot who had quarrelled with his father because Abdullah was a British tool. But he dismisses this view as pure fiction. The lack of sympathy between the two men, according to Glubb, was domestic.[3] In a similar vein, Kirkbride writes that Talal did not differ from his father with regard to the policy that should be pursued in relation to Britain.[4] Yet Kirkbride himself had described Prince Talal in a 1939 cable to London as "intemperate in his habits, untrustworthy and, at heart, deeply anti-British."[5] The most plausible explanation for this discrepancy is that the memoirs are self-serving, designed to protect Britain's reputation.

Strong evidence of Talal's anti-British sentiments comes from his cousin, Prince Raad bin Zaid, the lord chamberlain of Jordan. Raad made a clear distinction between the younger generation of Hashemites—Talal and his cousin Ghazi, who was the king of Iraq from 1933 to 1939—and their fathers:

Prince Talal's and Prince Ghazi's sentiments were very anti-British. They saw eye-to-eye regarding the British. They were angry with the British for the following reasons. First, for the way that the British treated their grandfather when Sharif Hussein declined to sign the Versailles Peace Treaty and refused to accept the Balfour Declaration. Second, because the British did not fulfil the McMahon promise that Syria, Lebanon, and Palestine will be free. Third, for the way the British treated, humiliated, and banished Sharif Hussein into exile in Cyprus. There was humiliation to his person . . . He died a disappointed man. He felt that he was let down. At the beginning he had high regard and trust in the British and in the French but this was not to be. These are the underlying reasons for Talal's and Ghazi's anti-British sentiment. Abdullah and Faisal, being in a position of leadership, had to go along with the consequences of Versailles, which was not of their doing. They had to plan for the time when changes could be made and mandates removed, as happened in Iraq in 1932 and much later, in 1946, when Jordan gained independence.[6]

The endless disagreements between Talal and Abdullah were not confined to high policy but extended to domestic matters as well, including the education of Hussein. Hussein went to no fewer than six different schools in Amman. He loved being in the company of other boys and wanted to be treated as one of them, without any special privileges. But, although he made many friends, none was really close. In his memoirs he suggests that "Perhaps this was because I changed schools so often. Opposing forces always seemed to be tugging at my education. I would be comfortably installed in one school, then my grandfather—who, to say the least of it, had a domineering character— would decide that I needed special tuition in religion, so back to the house I would go for extra private lessons. Then my father would decide that I needed more tuition in Arabic and I would have to change again."[7]

To round off his secondary education, Hussein was sent to Victoria College in Alexandria, a prestigious but spartan English public school with an excellent combination of English and Arabic. Despite its public school ethos, the college had a highly cosmopolitan atmosphere on account of its mixed student body, which included Armenians, Jews and the sons of well-to-do Arabs as well as the sons of British officials serving in the Middle East. Hussein's grandfather paid his fees, as his parents could not afford them. The polyglot group of students welcomed Hussein to the school, and he adjusted to the new environment without any difficulty. A whole new world opened up for him—football, cricket, books and companionship. In his memoirs he recalled the long dormitory that he shared with about thirty other boys, the cold showers every morning, the uniform of grey flannels and blue blazers. His two years at Victoria were among the happiest of his life. It was also a formative experience in as much as he was able not only to survive academically but to do well, gain self-respect and grow in terms of self-reliance. In addition to the normal curriculum, Hussein took courses in Arabic and religion, always the subjects that his grandfather looked at first when scrutinizing his reports. During his last term at Victoria, Hussein got a good report and won a medal in fencing. His grandfather was so pleased with this achievement that he gave him the honorary rank of captain in the Arab Legion and an officer's uniform to go with it.[8]

During his two years at Victoria College, Hussein's closest friend was his cousin Zaid bin Shaker, who was fifteen months older. Scion of a prominent sharifian family, Zaid went on to serve as ADC to the king, chief of staff, chief of the royal court and prime minister. Shaker felt that he and his cousin had "as perfect a relationship as two men can have."[9] Hussein used to say to Zaid, "We are one soul in two bodies."[10] Zaid Rifa'i, another future Jordanian prime minister, was also a contemporary at the college. Other lifelong friends from this period included the Saudi brothers of Hashemite stock, Ghassan and Ghazi Shaker. During his time at Alexandria, Hussein first set eyes on the girl who was to become his third wife many years later, in 1972. Alia Toukan came from a prominent Palestinian family from Nablus. She was born in Egypt in 1948. Her father, Baha Uddin Toukan, was the Jordanian ambassador to Egypt, and Hussein was a frequent visitor at the ambassador's residence in Cairo. Alia was one year old when Hussein first met her, and he used to play with her. In 1951, when her father was appointed ambassador to Turkey, her family moved to Ankara.

It was during the long vacations that Hussein grew closer to his grandfather, who considered school holidays as an opportunity to study harder. Abdullah saw in Hussein a more promising keeper of the Hashemite flame than his two sons, so he took him in hand and started to groom him. The daily routine is described by Hussein in his memoirs. He would get to the palace by 6:30 a.m. A room was reserved as a school room and a tutor appointed to give Hussein Arabic lessons. But Abdullah would invariably start the day's work himself and leave detailed instructions for the teacher. In the course of the morning

Abdullah would sometimes barge in like a school inspector to check on the pupil and to cross-examine the teacher.

Some days grandfather and grandson shared a modest breakfast around 8:30 a.m.—Bedouin coffee flavoured with cardamom and some flat cakes of bread without butter or jam. Abdullah believed that one worked better on a half-empty stomach. When lessons were over, Hussein would go to his grandfather's office and quietly watch him at work. Occasionally, Hussein would be invited to act as an interpreter, for though Abdullah understood English, he could not speak it. Most days Hussein would return to the palace before evening prayers and dine with his grandfather, who talked at length about the problems and pitfalls of kingship and about the intricate politics of the Arab world. A recurrent theme in these soliloquies was Abdullah's disappointment with the British and the French. He felt that he had been a leading figure in the struggle for Arab independence but that he was also the victim of duplicity. Nor did Abdullah conceal from Hussein his disappointment with his two sons, Talal and Naif. Only in retrospect did it dawn on Hussein why his grandfather lavished so much affection on him towards the end of his life: he had become the son that Abdullah had always wanted.[11]

Abdullah, a Bedouin at heart, loved the desert so much that he staked a tent in the palace grounds in Amman for passing the time in a more relaxed manner. In the cool of the evening he would often recline there on silken cushions and hold court to his friends and other notables. It was in this tent that Hussein spent many evenings listening to the advice and wisdom of the grandfather he revered so much. One moment, however, three days before the visit to Jerusalem remained firmly inscribed in Hussein's memory and had a powerful impact on him for the rest of his life. They were sitting and talking when Abdullah turned to him for no reason that he could fathom and said to him in a gentle voice,

"I want you to make me a promise." I said, "Of course sir, what is it?" He said, "I have lived in this nation, I have loved it all my life, and I have worked for its greatness. I love these people. I hope you realize that some day you will have to assume responsibility. I don't know what the future will bring but please promise me that you will never despair and that you will never let my work go unfinished. I look to you to see that my work is not lost." Without understanding what I was saying, I said, "Of course I do, sir," and that Friday he was gone. It was that promise, probably more than anything else, that kept me going through all the years that have followed. As a Hashemite and as his descendant, I personally promised him, without knowing much of what I was saying, to do my best.[12]

The significance of this private exchange was publicly acknowledged by Hussein forty years later, after his first brush with cancer. In a televised address to his countrymen on his return to Amman in November 1992, after cancer surgery at the Mayo Clinic in the United States, he explained that he would be making regular visits to the clinic for check-ups to confirm that he had been cured. Hussein went on to say that the "life of an enlightened people and a vibrant nation cannot be measured by the life of an individual." He was ever mindful, he continued,

of the legacy of my grandfather, the founder of this Kingdom, who had said to me that he perceived his life as a link in a continuous chain of those who served our [Arab] nation and that he expected me to be a new and strong link in that same chain. He had singled me out as a young member of his family and a youth from Amman and Jordan. In passing on his legacy, he—God rest his soul—changed this young man's life. Even now I recall the moment when I vowed to God and to myself that I would follow in his footsteps and in those of his fathers and grandfathers for the good of our beloved people and the future of our great [Arab] nation.[13]

On the day of the murder, at Abdullah's insistence, Hussein wore his brand-new uniform, with its Jordanian Star First Class, his reward for winning the school fencing prize, proudly fastened over his heart. The atmosphere on the way to the Al-Aqsa Mosque was highly charged. Walking behind his grandfather, Hussein saw the assailant emerge from behind the door and fire the shot that killed Abdullah instantly. Hussein lunged towards the man, saw him point his squat black gun at him, heard the shot and reeled as he felt the shock on his chest. The assassin continued to fire right and left, until he was killed by the royal bodyguard. Later Hussein discovered that the bullet had hit the medal on his chest and ricocheted off. He had no doubt that his grandfather's insistence that he wear the uniform saved his life.

Though Abdullah's influence on Hussein's life was profound, it was his death that taught him the ultimate lesson. The murder was the first time that violence had touched Hussein personally, and on that terrible day, by his own account, he learned much, even if he did not immediately realize it. He learned the unimportance of death: that when you have to die, you die, for it is God's judgment, and only by not fearing death do you find inner peace. Belief in fate encouraged him to give of his utmost in the brief span allotted to him on earth. It also encouraged him to live with courage and to abide by his principles, regardless of the difficulties he faced, so that when the time came for him to lose his life, he would at least have done his best. "These beliefs," he said, summing up, "have helped me greatly to bear the loss of my grandfather, and later have served me well in moments of crisis and danger. Without doubt, it was the death of my grandfather that made me clarify my philosophy of life for the first time."[14]

The death of his grandfather also taught Hussein to distrust and even despise politicians and to put his faith in simple soldiers. In the midst of the mayhem, he noticed that most of his grandfather's so-called friends were fleeing in every direction: "I can see now, these men of dignity and high estate, doubled up, cloaked figures scattering like bent old terrified women. That picture, far more than the face of the assassin, has remained with me ever since as a constant reminder of the frailty of political devotion."[15] Only the soldiers stood their ground, protected him and gave him sincere sympathy and support. This went for British soldiers as well. General Glubb reacted swiftly the moment he heard the news by sending a separate aircraft to whisk Hussein back to safety in Amman. On the tarmac at the airport on the outskirts of Jerusalem, a man in air force uniform approached the sedated, shell-shocked boy. Very shyly he said in a thick Scottish accent, "Come with me, sir. I'll look after you." The man led the boy to a twin-engine plane, a Dove, and invited him to squeeze into the co-pilot's seat next to him. He then revved up the motors, and they flew back to Amman. The man was Wing-Commander Jock Dalgleish of the Royal Air Force. Two years later Dalgleish would teach Hussein to fly. The next day Hussein carried a gun for the first time in his life.[16]

One question that has continued to puzzle observers is: why did Abdullah disregard all the warnings and keep to his plan of Friday prayers in Jerusalem? One possible answer, which was long to remain a closely guarded secret, is that Abdullah had arranged to meet two

Israeli officials in Jerusalem the next day, Saturday, 21 July 1951. The two officials were Reuven Shiloah and Moshe Sasson, who was continuing the negotiations for a peace treaty that his father, Elias, had begun. At one of their first meetings, Moshe Sasson asked Abdullah, "Why do you want to make peace with Israel?" The king replied, "I want to make peace with Israel not because I have become a Zionist or care for Israel's welfare but because it is in the interest of my people. I am convinced that if we do not make peace with you, there will be another war, and another war, and another war, and another war, and we shall lose all these wars. Hence it is the supreme interest of the Arab nation to make peace with you."[17] The secret meeting fixed for the day after the Friday prayers at the Al-Aqsa Mosque was thus only one link in a long chain, part of a sustained effort to reach a peaceful settlement. It also shows that Abdullah maintained his contact with the Zionists almost without a break, and in the face of all the opposition and hazards involved, from the creation of the Amirate of Transjordan in 1921 almost until his dying day.

In official Israeli circles the reaction to Abdullah's assassination was one of profound shock and concern for the future. He was seen as the closest thing to a friend that Israel possessed among the Arab leaders. No one felt the blow more acutely than Elias Sasson, the diplomat of Lebanese extraction who knew how to offer and elicit sympathy, and with whom he had held countless meetings. Sasson described Abdullah's disappearance from the political scene as a grave loss to Jordan, to the Arab world, to the Western world and to Israel. As he wrote to his superiors,

King Abdullah was the only Arab statesman who showed an understanding for our national renewal, a sincere desire to come to a settlement with us, and a realistic attitude to most of our demands and arguments . . . King Abdullah, despite being an Arab nationalist and a Muslim zealot, knew how to look with an open and penetrating eye on events . . . He also served as the trumpet announcing these changes to the members of his nation and religion wherever they might be, in a pleasant, moderate, and logical tone. We as well as some of the Arabs and foreigners are going to feel for a long time to come his absence, and to regret more than a little his removal from our midst.[18]

The Zionist leaders were acutely aware that in their relations with their neighbour to the east they depended almost entirely on one individual, and they regretted that it proved impossible to develop normal state-to-state relations even after both countries had attained formal independence. But for the most part they accepted this exclusive link with the royal court as an unfortunate fact of life. Abdullah, for all his limitations, was a sincere friend and a genuine man of peace. David Ben-Gurion, the founder of the State of Israel and its first prime minister, emphasized Abdullah's uniqueness among Arab rulers in a consultation on Arab policy held after the Egyptian Free Officers' Revolution of July 1952. "We did have one man," recalled Ben-Gurion, "about whom we knew that he wanted peace with Israel, and we tried to negotiate with him, but the British interfered, until a bullet came and put an end to business. With the removal of the Abdullah factor, the whole matter was finished."[19]

While giving credit where credit was due, Ben-Gurion misrepresented Israel's position in the aftermath of the 1948 war. In the first place, Abdullah was not the only Arab ruler who wanted peace with Israel. Husni Za'im, following his military coup in Syria in March 1949, openly stated his ambition to be the first Arab leader to make peace with Israel and called for high-level talks, but Ben-Gurion refused to meet him.[20] Ben-Gurion also declined all of Abdullah's requests for a face-to-face meeting. So the claim that there was no one to talk to on the Arab side is simply not true. Moreover, one of the reasons for the failure of the negotiations with both Za'im and Abdullah was Ben-Gurion's insistence that peace be based on the status quo, with only minor territorial adjustments and no return of Palestinian refugees. None the less, the death of Abdullah did mark a turning point in Ben-Gurion's thinking: he finally gave up any hope of a voluntary agreement with the Arabs and reverted to the old and seriously flawed premise that force is the only language that the Arabs understand.

Unlike Ben-Gurion, Mendel Cohen had a great deal of direct contact with King Abdullah and was able to observe him and the politics of the royal court at close quarters. Cohen was a first-rate Jewish carpenter who was employed by the royal court in Amman for ten years; his job was to refurbish and furnish the houses of the amir, his wives, his children and his aides. In 1980 Cohen published in Hebrew a book of memoirs entitled *At the Court of King Abdullah*. The book gives a fascinating account of the king, his two sons and the crisis for the succession following the murder at the mosque. One point that emerges clearly from the book is Abdullah's genuine respect and admiration for the Jews. There is also an account of the deep estrangement between Abdullah and his eldest son, Talal, the result, in part, of very different attitudes towards the Jews. Talal objected to the employment of Jews at the royal court and supported the Arab League's economic boycott of the State of Israel. On one occasion, Talal expounded to Cohen the reasons for his view that there could be no accommodation between the Arabs and the Jews in the Middle East. "The Jews," said Talal "are rich, shrewd, educated, and they have culture and unlimited capability. The Arabs, by contrast, are poor, simple, and lacking in education. Any contact between Jews and Arabs is therefore bound, in the end, to be for the benefit of the strong and to the detriment of the weak."[21]

According to Cohen, Abdullah thought his second son, Naif, was also an unsuitable successor, but when he went abroad he usually appointed Naif as regent. Naif, however, never played an independent role. He was a puppet in the hands of the prime minister and the British representatives. The two brothers struck Cohen as totally different: whereas Talal held firm views and expressed them forcefully, Naif was weak, flabby, uneducated, phlegmatic and susceptible to external influences. Abdullah regarded him as the better son because he did not criticize, challenge or defy him. Whereas Talal was openly hostile to the British, Naif was not. Similarly, Naif had a more positive attitude to the Jews than his elder brother. Naif struck up a friendship with Cohen and made frequent visits to his home and his workshop in Jerusalem. Cohen was not surprised that so many politicians preferred Naif to Talal following the murder of their father. These supporters, according to the well-informed Jewish carpenter, expected Naif to be a mere puppet, while real power remained in the hands of the government.[22]

In Jordan, the death of the founder provoked a frenetic spate of political intrigues, dynastic rivalries and jockeying for power. A large number of Abdullah's top officials were of Palestinian extraction. Samir Rifa'i, a Palestinian from Safed, resigned as prime minister a few days after the trial and execution of the murderers, to be replaced by Tawfiq Abul Huda, a Palestinian from Acre. The politicians were deeply divided among themselves as to what course they should follow, and this exacerbated the power vacuum at the centre. The real authority behind the scenes, however, was Alec Kirkbride. It should come as no surprise, therefore, to learn that the British continued to exercise control over the country even after the grant of formal independence in 1946. Kirkbride and Glubb Pasha together played a critical part in resolving the crisis of the succession in favour of Prince Talal and ultimately his son Hussein.

At the time of Abdullah's death, Talal, the forty-one-year-old crown prince, was receiving treatment for mental illness in Switzerland. The Jordanian constitution of 7 December 1946, in its English version, unambiguously designated Talal, the first-born son of the founder of the dynasty, as successor. But an error in the Arabic translation made it possible to argue that if Talal did not succeed to the throne, his half-brother Naif would be next in line of succession. Mohammed Shureiki, the current chief of the royal court, seized on this discrepancy to argue that since Talal would never be mentally fit for the job, Naif should be proclaimed king without further ado.[23] There was no shortage of opportunists to follow Shureiki's lead. In fact, the majority of Jordanian politicians initially inclined towards Naif. It is not too cynical to suggest that some of the politicians who flocked to Naif's banner did so in the knowledge that he was feeble and docile, and therefore easy to manipulate; what they were after was a puppet king. In any case, as his half-brother was out of the country, Naif was appointed regent in July and remained in that post until 5 September 1951. The regency council consisted of Ibrahim Hashem, Suleiman Toukan and Abdul Rahman Rusheidat, with the Amira Zain as chairman.

Naif's credentials for kingship were far from compelling. In the first place, his mother was the great-granddaughter of the Ottoman sultan Abdel Aziz, and he himself had had a period of service with the Turkish Army. More importantly, he was poorly educated, ill informed, inept and incompetent. He did not seem to have inherited any of his father's quick intelligence, political capacity or zest for life. Naif was generally considered to be a nonentity. One British observer described him as "a very dull and ineffective creature." Kirkbride too had a very low opinion of him. In 1948 he reported to the Foreign Office that Naif was involved in smuggling, black-marketeering and other forms of corruption; he dismissed him as a "bonehead" who did not "appear to possess sufficient intelligence to play any political role, either good or bad."[24]

In 1951 most Jordanians assumed that Kirkbride favoured Naif on account of Talal's well-advertised anti-British sentiments. Indeed, many believed that there was nothing wrong with Talal and that the wily British fabricated the story about his madness in order to get him out of the way. In fact, in 1951 Kirkbride was not in favour of Naif's becoming king, not only because of his doubts about his capabilities but also because his accession would have been attributed by many Arabs to a Machiavellian plot on the part of the British government to exclude their enemy Talal.[25]

The solution worked out between Kirkbride, Abul Huda and some of the elder statesmen was to bring Talal back from Switzerland to Amman and to put him on the throne but in the clear expectation that he would not be able to reign for long. It was also hoped that once Talal became king, there would be no further doubt about Hussein's right to succeed his father.[26] In short, Talal's role was to keep the throne warm for his son. Hussein's mother, the Amira Zain, fully supported this plan and worked to the best of her considerable ability to realize it. Zain was a strong-minded and determined woman with a full share of the Hashemite sense of realism. She knew that her husband was mentally unstable and erratic, and that he could not reign for very long, but she hoped to sustain him in power just long enough to enable their son to succeed. In other words, for her too Talal was just a stopgap.

Despite this secret consensus in favour of Talal, his path to the throne was far from smooth. Settling the succession was not a purely Jordanian affair; it was complicated by Arab intrigues and by a particularly clumsy intervention by the Iraqi branch of the Hashemite dynasty. Despair of his two sons had apparently driven Abdullah to begin secret discussions about a Jordanian–Iraqi federation, though no concrete decision had emerged from these talks. Abdullah's sudden demise provided the Iraqis with an opportunity to try to revive this dormant plan. A high-level Iraqi delegation arrived in Amman for the funeral, headed by the regent, Abd al-Ilah, Prime Minister Nuri as-Said and Foreign Minister Saleh Jaber. Nuri launched his bid for union between the two countries under the Iraqi crown even before the king's body had been laid to rest. He also interfered in the internal power struggle in Jordan, backing the claims of Naif against those of Talal. But, having found no senior Jordanian figures willing to take up the idea of a federation, Nuri and his compatriots were forced to drop it.[27]

When news of the plan to bring back Talal reached Naif and his supporters, they stepped up their efforts to capture the throne. The air in

Amman was thick with rumours of plots and conspiracies. In his memoirs Kirkbride mentioned reports circulated from various quarters of
plans to murder the young Amir Hussein. Even though these were not
taken too seriously, he and his mother were given a guard of Bedouin
troops as a precaution.[28] Naif sent soldiers to surround the house of
Zain and Hussein, placing them under "protective custody." Kirkbride's wife, who was genuinely fond of Talal and Zain, came to the rescue. She sent Zain a note smuggled inside a bouquet of flowers, urging
her to come to the British Embassy. The problem was how to get there.
The resourceful Zain grabbed the washer-woman, locked her in the
wood shed in the garden and borrowed her clothes. Zain then left the
house from the servants' quarter with her face covered. She made her
way to the British Embassy, met the Kirkbrides and confirmed them in
their view that her husband was the right choice.[29]

The political crisis was compounded by divisions within the army.
The 10th Infantry Regiment, a quasi-Praetorian Guard, was commanded by Habis Majali, who threw in his lot with Naif. The 10th
enjoyed such a high degree of autonomy that Glubb could not be sure
its officers would obey his orders in the event of a showdown with the
pretender to the throne. It also possessed six-pounder anti-tank guns
and some armoured cars—a serious deterrent to an assault on the
palace. Glubb decided to put the officers to the test by ordering the guns
and the armour to be transferred to Mafraq, about forty miles north-east
of the capital, ostensibly for training purposes. In the event, Glubb's
order was meekly obeyed and the plot, if it was a plot, quickly collapsed. Naif moved with his family to Beirut, Mohammed Shureiki
left his post at the royal court and the 10th Infantry Regiment was
disbanded.[30]

The way was now clear to bring Talal back from his nursing home in
Geneva. He was flown to Amman aboard an Arab Legion aircraft on
6 September 1951, welcomed at the airport by a guard of honour and a
strong detachment of armoured cars, and conveyed in a cavalcade to
the parliament building to take the oath of office. He was invested as
king before the assembled members of both the upper and lower houses
of parliament and the diplomatic corps, of which Kirkbride was the
doyen. Three days later Hussein bin Talal was officially named crown
prince. Talal's formal accession to the throne marked the end of an era
in the history of Jordan. In the words of one observer, it "proved to be

the 'crowning' act in the transition of power from Abdullah to a group of men whose understanding of the twin pillars of the Hashemite monarchy—survival and endurance—was no less than his own."[31]

Talal himself survived on the throne barely a year. His kingship was essentially an interregnum between the long reign of his father and the even longer reign of his eldest son. Talal's most significant achievement was the inauguration, on 1 January 1952, of "The Constitution of the Hashemite Kingdom of Jordan," which replaced the 1946 constitution. The new constitution reflected Talal's pan-Arabism, describing the Hashemite Kingdom of Jordan as an independent sovereign Arab state and the people of Jordan as "part of the Arab Nation." Islam was the religion of the state and Arabic its official language. The system of government was described as "parliamentary with a hereditary monarchy." The nation was said to be the source of all power, but in actuality the palace had real power and parliament only the semblance of it.

In Talal's constitution, legislative power was vested in the king and the National Assembly, which was comprised of the Senate and the Chamber of Deputies. Executive power was vested in the king, to exercise through his ministers or directly through royal decree. The king was the head of state and the supreme commander of the armed forces; he ratified the laws and promulgated them; he declared war, concluded peace and ratified international treaties and agreements; and he issued orders for holding elections to the Chamber of Deputies. The Council of Ministers, consisting of the prime minister and his ministers, was entrusted with administering the affairs of state, internal and external; it was collectively responsible before the Chamber of Deputies for its policies. The chamber could force the resignation of the council by passing a motion of no confidence. But, under the constitution, ultimate power rested in the hands of the king. It was the king who hired and fired prime ministers, ministers and senators, and it was he who had the sole prerogative to adjourn, prorogue or dissolve the Chamber of Deputies or the Senate. Talal's constitution was an improvement on his father's, but it was far removed from any modern notion of a constitutional monarchy. In a constitutional monarchy the monarch reigns but does not rule; in the Jordanian system of government the monarch both reigns and rules.

Talal's return to Jordan freed Hussein to resume his education. His own preference was to return to Victoria College. But Egypt's antagonistic attitude towards Jordan, and the presence there of individuals who had aided and abetted the murderers of King Abdullah, made it an unsafe place for the new heir to the throne. The same old guard, both Jordanian and British, who had defeated Naif and brought back Talal now decided to send Hussein to Harrow in England, followed by an abbreviated training course at the military academy at Sandhurst. Talal had also been to both Harrow and Sandhurst, and emerged from them with an anti-British bias. Greater care was therefore taken with Hussein's schooling to ensure that this pattern did not repeat itself; he was to develop a more positive attitude towards the host country.

At Harrow, Hussein was at first unhappy and longed to be back at Victoria College. At Victoria there was a good social mix, a lively social life and a cosmopolitan atmosphere, whereas at Harrow most of the boys were from upper-class English families, discipline was strict, and the teachers were sticklers for protocol. At Victoria they spoke English at a leisurely pace; at Harrow "everybody seemed to gabble at double speed." At Victoria Hussein's main subjects had centred around the Arabic language; at Harrow his best subjects were history and English literature. When he arrived at Harrow, Faisal, his cousin, friend and heir apparent to the Iraqi Hashemite throne, was already there. Hussein and Faisal were the only boys who did not have surnames. Their snobbish classmates, unable to call them by their given names, rarely called them anything at all.

On the one hand, Hussein was at a psychological disadvantage at this quintessentially English public school. On the other, he felt himself to be "a man among boys" because of the teachings of his grandfather, his position at home and all he had been through.[32] Hussein's housemaster at Harrow gave the following appraisal: "A determined fellow but limited in his academic ability. I would not say he was a success at Harrow, but we did what we could to equip him for the scramble we knew would face him when he returned to the Middle East."[33] The report perhaps says as much about the institution as about the pupil.

Hussein's royal status did set him apart from the other boys. A string of journalists from the Middle East came to the school to interview him and Faisal, giving them a handy excuse for missing lessons. Things gradually improved. Hussein learned to play rugby and enjoyed the game enormously. He was allowed more leave than the other boys and often went to London for weekends. Fawzi Mulki, the young Jordanian ambassador, was very kind and indulgent towards him. Hussein also got a driving licence, and a friend of his father's gave him his first motor-car, a sky-blue Rover. This was the beginning of his love of fast cars, and he soon developed a taste for ever bigger and better ones.

For the summer holidays Hussein went to Geneva to join his mother, two brothers and sister. On 12 August 1952, when the others were out, a hotel page came in with a large envelope on a silver platter. Hussein did not need to open it to know that his days as a schoolboy had ended, as the envelope was addressed to "His Majesty, King Hussein." Inside was a letter from the prime minister, informing him that his father had abdicated and that he was now king of Jordan. Hussein, like the rest of his family, was aware that his father's mental illness had grown more serious in the months since he had ascended the throne, but news of the abdication was no less distressing for having been expected. The decision had been taken by the two houses of parliament, and Hussein's presence in Jordan was required as soon as possible. The previous day the prime minister, Tawfiq Abul Huda, had reported to the two houses that Talal was no longer fit to exercise his constitutional powers. He then submitted reports on the monarch's health made by two foreign and three Jordanian doctors. The constitution included a provision that if any Jordanian king was incapacitated by mental illness, parliament had the power to depose him and to transfer the royal prerogatives to his heir. Thus, at the age of seventeen, Hussein became the king of Jordan. His first act was to compose a cable to the prime minister, advising him that he would return as soon as possible and that he would be honoured to serve his country and the Arab world to the best of his ability.[34] The deposed king was sent to a sanatorium in Turkey, where he stayed in less than splendid isolation until his death in 1972.

The abdication of Talal was an embarrassing episode in the history of the Hashemite dynasty and a painful experience for all his children. Hussein often talked about his grandfather as a mentor and role model but rarely mentioned his father. The precise nature of his illness was never made public, and this fed suspicions not only of the British and the politicians who removed Talal but of the role played by members of his own family. Prince Hassan, Hussein's younger brother, was only five years old at the time but in later life he was assailed by mounting doubts regarding the diagnosis of Talal: not everything that was said about his father rang true to him. Hassan also thought that the treatment meted out to Talal, even by his nearest and dearest, was unjustifiably cruel:

My father exuded an ethos of patriotism which, in a funny way, my mother and my brother worked together to do "damage control" to because . . . they felt that he was an "unguided missile." The only way to control him was to neutralize him. Effectively, they put him behind bars for 20 years . . . My feeling is that my father was misdiagnosed. Maybe he was bipolar, but he was not schizophrenic. The strange thing is that I have never seen his medical papers. They were not given to me by my brother. For some reason he didn't want me or my sister to have these papers. And I feel that my father's diagnosis was not scientific.[35]

Hussein's flight back home in 1952 was an emotional one: he had left Jordan as a prince and he was now returning as a king. At the airport he inspected the guard of honour and shook hands with the country's leaders. Among them was Glubb Pasha fingering his beads in the Arab manner. If the official welcome home was stiff and formal, the rejoicing of the crowds that lined up the streets was spontaneous and frenzied. The people knew very little about their new king, but there was a huge reservoir of sympathy and affection for him following the murder of his grandfather and the abdication of his popular father. For Hussein, who had been an innocent bystander until now, this was an exhilarating experience: the people were not only cheering but sending out messages of sympathy and encouragement to the boy of seventeen suddenly made king.[36]

Hussein could not assume his constitutional powers until he reached the age of eighteen (or just under eighteen, as his age was determined by the Islamic calendar). So a regency council of three—the prime minister and the presidents of the upper and lower houses of parliament—was appointed to exercise them until then. This was the royal equivalent of a gap year for a college student, and Hussein's was both instructive and enjoyable. He went on a three-week tour of the country, visiting every major city and town, and scores of villages; he paid courtesy calls to numerous Bedouin shaikhs and chieftains. Another part of Hussein's grooming for the succession consisted of military training. His uncle, Sharif Nasser bin Jamil, had grown up in Iraq and attended the Baghdad Military Academy. When Zain became queen, she brought her younger brother over to Jordan, and he too became a force in Jordanian politics. Sharif Nasser was insistent that his nephew should receive military training at Sandhurst. Glubb Pasha also welcomed the idea and arranged with the War Office that his protégé should have a special, shortened course, cramming the normal curriculum into six months. Hussein was overjoyed at the prospect.

Hussein reported for duty at Sandhurst on 9 September 1952. Officer Cadet King Hussein of the Royal Military Academy, Sandhurst, was allotted Room 109, Inkerman Company, the Old College. Officials at the Foreign Office monitored Hussein's training and took steps to ensure that he "profited not only in his military instruction" but also from exposure to "aspects of British life." Sandhurst's commandant was encouraged to strike a balance between cushioning Hussein from the "rigour of Sandhurst" and avoiding an excess of "privileged treatment" that could, in the long run, "backfire" against both Hussein and Britain.[37]

Looking back on his days at Sandhurst, Hussein thought that in many ways they were the most formative of his life. At Harrow he had been treated as a boy; at Sandhurst as a man. He was given a choice between the soft option and the hard way, and with evident pride he chose the hard way. He also found the studies more interesting than at Harrow. "We Arabs are a martial race," he wrote in his memoirs, "so perhaps I took easily to the tough life of a cadet." He appreciated the discipline, and he liked the atmosphere and especially the team spirit at Sandhurst. Because his tour was short, he had extra spells of drills and marching, took part in night assaults across rough country, learned to fire modern weapons and did his utmost to grasp the essentials of military science. Hussein's academic performance, however, was as undistinguished as it had been at Harrow. "He did not seem to care much for the more academic side of the syllabus," according to his company commander, Major David Horsfield, "but shone to advantage in the practical part—drill, tactics, rifle shooting and mechanical engineering."[38]

At Sandhurst, Hussein, like most other cadets, worked hard and played hard. For although the training pushed them to the limit of their physical and mental endurance, off duty they could relax and enjoy themselves. Hussein's pleasures included a Lincoln convertible that he drove at startlingly high speed and riding a motorcycle. There were also frequent visits to London at weekends to sample the high life. Fawzi al-

Mulki again took charge of Hussein's extracurricular education, introducing him to young Jordanian officers who were in the United Kingdom for training. Mulki also took pains to ensure that the cadet-king enjoyed himself, for example, by going to parties at which he could meet attractive young women.

After Sandhurst's passing out parade, a month-long, cross-country tour of England, Wales and Scotland was organized for the fresh graduate by the Foreign Office. At the end of the tour he went to London to prepare for his flight home and the start of a new life. Hussein's British minders were evidently pleased with the result. Britain's educational establishment, as one biographer has put it, had "produced a leader it could be proud of; he had all the qualities that Harrow and Sandhurst were built to foster—courage, resolution, enterprise, a measure of self-assertiveness, a good practical judgement and the best public school manners."[39] About the good manners there could never be any doubt. For the rest of his life, Hussein addressed men of quite ordinary station—including academics like the present writer and newspaper reporters—as "sir." The "self-assertiveness" took a little longer to manifest itself.

3. The Making of a King

Hussein was seventeen years old when he assumed his constitutional prerogatives as the King of Jordan. On 2 May 1953, his eighteenth birthday according to the Islamic lunar calendar, he took the oath of office in the parliament building in Amman as the first step in his inauguration as king. The city was colourfully decorated, with flags flying everywhere, and large crowds gathered in the streets to cheer their new king. On the same day Hussein's cousin Faisal, his senior by six months, ascended the throne in Baghdad. Hussein wore his ceremonial uniform, and his car was escorted by cavalry of the Royal Guard on its way from the Basman Palace to parliament. It was the most momentous day of his life. Outwardly he tried to convey a sense of composure but inwardly he was assailed by self-doubt and an overwhelming sense of duty, with his mother's advice ringing in his ear: never to let power go to his head.[1]

The cheering of the crowds in the streets masked widespread national anxiety. From the outside, Jordan looked like a cheerful little country, but it was also an anxious one. The assassination of Abdullah, its founder, plunged the kingdom into crisis, confusion and power struggles. Hussein ascended the throne in circumstances that were deeply uncertain, and because he was so young and inexperienced he himself was part of that uncertainty. It was only natural for people to wonder whether the boy-king would be able to hold the country together. A cloud of doubt hung over Jordan, and it was to remain for a long time.

Queen Zain provided one element of continuity. She was a strong-willed and politically astute Hashemite with an intense commitment to the ideals and interests of her family, and was by far the most influential informal member of the Jordanian political establishment. Fluent in French, Zain assiduously promoted the interests of the Hashemite dynasty in her contacts with foreign diplomats. Selwyn Lloyd, the

British foreign secretary, dubbed her "the Metternich of the Arab world." She regarded the British as the principal protectors of the monarchy and referred to them as "the neighbours" because their embassy adjoined the royal compound. The Egyptians, on the other hand, were a hostile and subversive force. After 1953 Talal ceased to play any part in Jordanian politics. Zain, however, continued to play a very influential part behind the scenes after her eldest son ascended the throne: guide, confidante and counsellor, as well as mother to the king.

For the first year or two after becoming king, Hussein lived in the Basman Palace. It was too large and formal for his taste, so he moved to a small villa of his own in Al-Hummar in the royal compound north-west of Amman. The Basman Palace continued to house the royal court, with offices for Hussein and those who worked with him. It also contained a large dining room for official ceremonies and banquets. Zain continued to live in the Zahran Palace with her three younger children: Muhammad, who was thirteen, Hassan, who was five, and Basma, who was two. Princess Basma recollected that family life was very close, regardless of the amount of time that Hussein spent with them: "When he became king, I was barely three years old. At that time, for me and for my brothers he was really a father figure, particularly to me, because I was so young then that I have no early recollections of my father. It was my brother who filled that role. He continued to fill that role for the rest of my life. But on top of that he became my very close friend. He really was a hero for me."

Hussein was also a major figure in the life of his younger brother Hassan, who was sent at the age of ten to Summerfields Preparatory School and then to Harrow. Hassan would return to Amman every holiday and often joined Hussein on his trips abroad. For the middle brother, Prince Muhammad, Hussein was a father figure and a hero, as he was for their sister. Muhammad inherited their father's charm, kindness and gracious manners, as well as his psychological fragility. Princess Basma noted the special relationship that evolved between her siblings:

Prince Muhammad and His late Majesty had gone through a lot together as children. Prince Hassan and I were that much younger. The two elder brothers shared a lot of childhood experiences, memories and difficult times. They always maintained a very close relationship. He was also very protective of Prince Muhammad, accepted him and supported him in whatever he wanted to do. He was much more flexible with him than he was with anybody else. Prince Muhammad was totally devoted to him.

Princess Basma found it astonishing that, despite all the pressures on Hussein in the early years of his reign, he always managed to stay in such close touch with his family and to fulfil his filial duties:

He always had time. And when he came to my mother's house it was a wonderful relationship. His ties with her were extremely special. They were based on a lot of mutual respect. He was her eldest son and obviously she had huge concerns, worries and anxieties as a mother. But at the same time, the reflection to us was that while he was her son, he was also head of the family and king. So, whereas his love for her was very obvious and clear, it was mutually reciprocated by a lot of dignity and respect in the way she responded to him. Things were very simple, traditional but informal. All of us knew that when he was at home with his mother and younger siblings, it was family. He could probably really relax and be himself.[2]

As a young king Hussein had to work with men who were much older than himself, such as Abul Huda, Glubb and Kirkbride. Hussein did, however, form around him a small circle of friends and confidants who were closer to him in age and in outlook. Two of these friends were also officers in the Arab Legion. Perhaps the most influential was Hussein's maternal uncle, Sharif Nasser bin Jamil, a captain in the Arab Legion who became his ADC. Sharif Nasser's father, Sharif Jamil, was an Iraqi Hashemite. His sister Zain, who was much older than he was and very indulgent towards him, brought him over to Jordan during the crisis of the succession to help her protect her eldest son. Sharif Nasser was a good field officer and a figure of strength in the vulnerable royal family. But he was also a dissolute and corrupt man, and ultimately a destructive force. He used army Land Rovers to smuggle hashish from Syria to Jordan. He was big and burly, with blue eyes and a prodigious strength; often he came across as a bully and a thug. His rivals feared rather than respected him. Despite his hashish smuggling activities, he became firmly ensconced in the palace. Within the inner circle there, Sharif Nasser lobbied against Glubb Pasha and quickly emerged as a strong advocate of a proactive national security policy and of seizing the initiative in regional politics.[3]

Another member of the inner circle was Hussein's cousin and close friend from Victoria College, Sharif Zaid bin Shaker, who was now a lieutenant in the Arab Legion. The three of them, as Hussein later described it, had "formed a trio—you could perhaps have described us, by comparison with the more conservative, traditional elements of the family, as being the wild bunch—I mean, what we really most enjoyed was going out, travelling around the country, visiting the armed forces whenever possible, seeing the people as they really were, natural, unaffected."[4]

A third person who exerted considerable influence on the impressionable young monarch was Major Ali Abu Nuwar. Born in Salt to a Circassian mother, he was commissioned as an artillery officer in 1946 and served as a lieutenant in the First Arab–Israeli War in 1948. After the war he was sent for training to Britain's staff college at Camberley. Hussein's relationship with Ali Abu Nuwar is difficult to reconstruct but essential for understanding some of the most important episodes of the mid 1950s. The Arab defeat in the Palestine war discredited the old order and radicalized army officers, leading to the coup by Colonel Husni Za'im in Syria in 1949 and to the Free Officers' Revolution in Egypt in 1952. The Ba'th Party in Syria expounded a militant Arab nationalist ideology and attracted some supporters in Jordan. These supporters, led by Shahir Abu Shahut and Mahmud Ma'ayta, formed the Secret Organization of Jordanian Officers with the aim of liberating the Jordanian Army from the influence of the British and establishing military unity with Syria. Under the impact of the revolution in Egypt, the still secret organization changed its name to the Movement of Free Jordanian Officers. By the time King Talal's reign was over, these nationalist officers were a force to be reckoned with.[5]

Ali Abu Nuwar was not a founding member of the movement but when approached he completely identified with its aims. On his return to Jordan in 1950, he emerged as one of the most outspoken critics of British control over the Arab Legion. Glubb was generally suspicious of officers from urban areas because, on the whole, they had a higher level of education than officers from the rural areas, and because they were more politically conscious and more receptive to left-wing ideas. Glubb was wedded to the existing order and determined to keep politics out of his little army. During Talal's reign, Glubb suspected Abu Nuwar of conspiring against the British, so he exiled him to Paris as a military attaché. Hussein first met Abu Nuwar in 1953 during a stop in Paris on his way back to Jordan to succeed his father to the throne. According to Abu Nuwar, Hussein was receptive to his nationalist ideas and to his suggestions for freeing Jordan from British control. In August that year the young king visited London and invited Abu Nuwar and a number of other Jordanian officers to a party held at the embassy in his honour. Although he was an outsider, Abu Nuwar presented himself to Hussein as a senior member of the Free Officers. He also informed Hussein that the aim of the group was to "Arabize" the Jordanian Army. Hussein was impressed and asked to meet some of the other members of the group. After his return to Amman, Hussein repeatedly asked Glubb to transfer Abu Nuwar back to Jordan, but Glubb kept stalling. In the end, Hussein overruled Glubb and appointed Abu Nuwar as a senior ADC in November 1955.[6]

From the beginning of his reign Hussein took a close interest in the affairs of the Arab Legion; he got to know some of its radical young officers, and he was attracted to their nationalist agenda. His time for the first two months was almost entirely taken up with the receiving and paying of official visits, followed by a trip to London and a long holiday in Europe. Gradually, he began to make his presence felt in the political arena, expressing opposition, for example, to frequent changes of government. His chief interest, however, remained the armed services, leading him to follow closely all branches of military activity. He learned to fly but submitted to his government's desire that he should not fly solo.[7] Sharif Zaid bin Shaker testified that "His Majesty loved the army and the military. His happiest days were those he spent with his army." But it was not simply a matter of personal preferences: "The underlying conception of Jordan's security was to make sure that the army is well equipped and well trained."[8]

On social and economic matters Hussein had only half-formed ideas, which had begun to germinate when he attended Victoria College in Egypt. "I was impressed in the period when I was a student there," Hussein later recalled, "by the gaps that existed between the people in power and ordinary people. I didn't like that at all. In fact, it might have steered me towards having more leftist tendencies in terms of the idea of greater sharing and equality amongst human beings. Maybe now when I think back on it, it is really a question of human rights, much more than a political ideology, that I felt was missing then and I think is still missing in many parts of the Arab world."[9]

Hussein's choice for the first prime minister of his reign reflected these incipient liberal-populist ideas. Three days after ascending the throne, he accepted the resignation of Tawfiq Abul Huda and appointed in his place Dr. Fawzi al-Mulki, who had been his friend and confidant while studying at Harrow and at Sandhurst. Aged forty-one, Mulki was Jordan's first native-born prime minister and a representative of a new breed of politicians. He was born in Irbid to parents who had originally come from Syria, and studied veterinary medicine at the American University of Beirut and at the University of Edinburgh before embarking on a successful career in the diplomatic service of his country. As a student in Britain, Mulki came to admire the democratic system of government, with its political and civil liberties, the independence of the judiciary and the British model of constitutional monarchy. His plans to introduce liberal reforms and to increase political participation were backed by the king. What Mulki lacked was a power base in Jordan, although this may have commended Mulki to the queen mother. According to one observer, for Zain "there was political advantage in having as a premier a relatively weak political outsider who could not easily overwhelm and suffocate her son."[10]

King Hussein's letter of appointment instructed Mulki to pursue liberal reforms at home and Arab unity abroad. Mulki formed a coalition government that included some of the opposition parties; his style was based on consultation and compromise. But he turned out to be such a weak and ineffectual leader that people joked that there were ten prime ministers and one minister in his cabinet. Despite his weakness, Mulki had some success in implementing a progressive agenda in his first six months in power. He released political prisoners, lifted restrictions on the freedom of the press, revised the defence regulations and passed legislation guaranteeing freedom of speech. He also increased the power of parliament by enabling it to pass a vote of no confidence in the executive by a simple majority instead of by two thirds of the votes cast. Yet the democratic experiment over which he presided was not an unqualified success. Mulki became a victim of the revolution of rising expectations that he himself had helped to unleash. The concessions he made to parliament and the press only whetted their appetite for more.

The press took advantage of the lifting of censorship to launch virulent attacks on individual members of the royal family and on the Western powers. The communists and the Ba'thists exploited the new climate of freedom to engage in subversive activities, to incite the public against the monarchy and even to call for its overthrow in favour of a republic. New newspapers were started by the opposition groups with the help of funding from the enemies of the Hashemites in the Arab world. The staple diet on which these papers fed their readers consisted of tirades against the Hashemite throne and its imperialist backers. The result was growing political instability that provided the more conservative law-and-order elements in the political establishment with a stick with which to beat the government. As so often in history, the most dangerous moment for an autocratic regime is precisely when it begins to reform itself.

In foreign affairs Hussein enjoined his prime minister to promote Arab unity. In this respect too Hussein was closer to his father than to his grandfather. Abdullah had been a great proponent of Arab unity, but he tended to equate it with Hashemite hegemony. This contributed to the division of the Arab world into a Hashemite bloc consisting of Jordan and Iraq and an anti-Hashemite bloc led by Egypt and Saudi Arabia. As we have seen, Abdullah was also a territorial expansionist who dreamed about the reconquest of his ancestral home in the Hijaz and the establishment of Greater Syria. Talal abandoned these ambitions. His foreign policy was aimed at bringing Jordan into line with Saudi Arabia, Egypt and Syria and was thus directed against Britain and Iraq.

On becoming king, Hussein adopted a policy of keeping on good terms with all the Arab states, while resisting the tendency on the part of the Iraqi government to claim a privileged position in Jordan's affairs. There was also a marked improvement in Jordanian–British relations following Talal's abdication. Hussein was Jordan's first native-born king. To his nephew Talal bin Muhammad this point was crucial: "Although he was an Arab, in the good sense of the word, he was also a Jordanian. Jordan was his home. He had no sentimental attachment to the Hijaz. Jordan was the land that he loved, and Jordanians were the people that he loved."[11]

The most difficult problem that Hussein and his government had to deal with—partly domestic, partly foreign and at both levels hellishly complicated—was that of Palestine. Its root cause was the Zionist displacement of the Palestine Arabs, culminating in the Nakbah of 1948. Palestine was lost and, as already mentioned, more than 700,000 Palestinians became refugees. They were dispersed throughout all the neighbouring Arab countries, but 450,000 ended up in Jordan, which did more than any other Arab state to help them resettle and integrate with the rest of society. Self-interest was one of the motives behind this relatively benevolent policy. The refugees in Jordan wanted to preserve their separate Palestinian identity, but this ran counter to Abdullah's policy of "Jordanization." His expansionist agenda compelled him to extend to the Palestinians normal citizenship rights.[12] But the refugees were a great burden on the weak Jordanian economy; it simply did not have the financial resources to cope with a humanitarian tragedy on such a vast scale. As a consequence, the bulk of the displaced Palestinians continued to live in refugee camps in conditions of appalling poverty and misery, which bred political extremism with a deep hatred of Israel and of the Western powers, and constituted an easy recruiting ground for the various pan-Arab, leftist and Islamist parties.[13] The Palestinians thus became an important factor in domestic Jordanian politics.

Another consequence of 1948 was that Palestinian refugees began to cross the armistice lines into what was now Israel. When the armistice agreements were signed, many Palestinians innocently believed that they would be allowed to go back to their homes. Even when their return was blocked by Israel, some persisted in their attempts to cross the lines. Israeli spokesmen claimed that Palestinian infiltration into its territory was aided and abetted by the Arab governments following the defeat of their regular armies on the battlefield; and that it was a form of undeclared guerrilla warfare designed to weaken and even destroy the infant Jewish state. Israel, on the other hand, was portrayed as the innocent victim of Arab provocations and aggression while its own policy of military reprisals was depicted as a legitimate form of self-defence.

In an important book entitled *Israel's Border Wars* Israeli historian Benny Morris has challenged this conventional view at three critical points: the character and causes of infiltration; the attitude of the Arab governments towards this phenomenon; and the motives and consequences of the Israeli response. On the basis of painstaking archival evidence, Morris has concluded that infiltration into Israel was a direct consequence of the displacement and dispossession of over 700,000 Palestinians in the course of the Palestine war and that the motives behind it were largely economic and social, rather than political. Many of the infiltrators were Palestinian refugees whose reasons for crossing the border included looking for relatives, returning to their homes, recovering possessions, tending to their fields, collecting their crops and, occasionally, exacting revenge. Some were thieves and smugglers; some were involved in the hashish convoys; and some were nomadic Bedouins, more accustomed to grazing rights than to state borders. There were terrorist actions and politically motivated raids, such as those organized by Hajj Amin al-Husseini, the ex-Mufti, and financed by Saudi Arabia, but they did not amount to very much. In the period 1949–56 as a whole, 90 percent or more of all infiltrations, in Morris's estimate, were motivated by economic and social concerns.[14]

Morris has also shown that the governments of the neighbouring Arab states were opposed to the cross-border forays into Israel for most of the period under discussion. Arab governments were caught on the horns of a dilemma: if they openly intervened to stop infiltration, they risked alienating their own passionately pro-Palestinian publics; if they were seen to condone infiltration, they risked clashes with the Israeli Army and the possible loss of more territory. Each government dealt with this problem in its own way and with varying degrees of success. Jordan had the longest and most complicated border with Israel, with the largest number of civilians on both sides. The upshot was numerous cases of infiltration and an increasingly brutal Israeli policy of military retaliation that took the form of ground raids against villages in the West Bank, beginning in January 1951.

One of the most serious problems that Hussein had to grapple with after ascending the throne was the tension and violence along Jordan's border with its aggressive western neighbour. Hussein inherited from his grandfather an attitude of moderation towards the Zionists, but he was also aware that the Palestinians blamed his grandfather for betraying their cause and that this was the reason given for his assassination. Hussein put up a spirited defence of his grandfather in a foreword he wrote for Abdullah's second autobiographical volume, *My Memoirs Completed: "Al Takmilah."* He sharply contrasted his grandfather's realism with the lack of realism of his critics:

Let me set the record straight, clearly and categorically. No country in the world likes to be partitioned, and Palestine is no exception. King Abdullah . . . was, in his innermost soul, as opposed to the alienation of any part of Palestine as anyone else. But to him, moral judgement and personal beliefs were an exercise in futility, unless backed by viable and adequate power, in the broad meaning of the term.

He had perceived the Zionist iceberg and its dimensions, while others had seen only its tip. He makes reference to it in the Takmilah. His tactics and strategy were therefore attuned to circumventing and minimizing the possible consequences of a head-on collision. Others saw only the tip, and their responses were over-confidence, inflexibility and outright complacency.[15]

This foreword, however, was written in 1978. It does not reflect any of the doubts and uncertainties that Hussein experienced on assuming responsibility for his country and its problems. In 1996, when I asked him what were his initial impressions and thoughts about Israel when he ascended the throne in 1953, he said:

My initial thoughts and impressions were ones of not knowing very much of what actually the Israelis and their leadership thought of or had in mind regarding the future of our region. At the same time it was a period of violence. There had apparently been from time to time some incursions over the long ceasefire line. We had the longest line, longer than all the Arab ceasefire lines with Israel put together. And Israel's responses were extremely severe, extremely devastating, with attacks on villages, on police posts and on civilians along the long ceasefire line. Obviously, I was not very happy with that and it caused us a great deal of difficulty in terms of the internal scene in Jordan.

Egypt's attitude towards us was another problem, especially given the rise of Gamal Abdel Nasser as the leader of the Arab world. Jordan was placed in the position of the conspirator or the betrayer, and this was the perpetual thrust of the Egyptian propaganda machine. So that undermined even further the situation within Jordan itself. The Palestinians looked towards Egypt as the major power in the area and treated whatever was said there as the gospel truth. The Israeli raids worsened the situation in Jordan. They showed us as being incompetent and unable to defend our territory. And the Israeli attacks continued, although we had done everything that we could to prevent infiltration and to prevent access to Israel.

So this was the atmosphere in which I lived my first years, plus the loss of my grandfather, which was another factor. I knew that he had tried his best for peace and that he had not achieved it. But I did not have any details. When I assumed responsibility, I looked for papers to do with my grandfather's reign, but unfortunately no documents were found. So I didn't have any idea as to what exactly had happened. But gradually there was more and more of a feeling that, for whatever reason, we had a neighbour, a people who were close to us historically, whom circumstances in the world had forced into our region. The dilemma was how to avoid mutual destruction and how to find a way of living together once again and not to continue to pay the high price, which was not fair on either side. That was in fact what went on in my mind at that time, apart from thoughts on how to strengthen my country.[16]

Hussein's chief military adviser, Glubb Pasha, had been doing everything in his power to curb infiltration into Israel, to eschew violence and to cooperate with the Israeli authorities in maintaining security along the common border. Glubb's constant refrain to anyone who would listen was that the Arab Legion was doing its level best to maintain a peaceful border with Israel. Israel's response was that the Jordanian authorities were aiding and abetting border violations, and that they alone must be held responsible for the progressive breakdown of the armistice regime. These charges were contradicted not simply by Glubb's declarations but by the constructive and cooperative attitude displayed by all the Jordanian representatives within the Jordanian–Israeli Mixed Armistice Commission (MAC) in dealing with the problems that kept cropping up. The Mixed Armistice Commission was established after the conclusion of the armistice agreement in 1949. It consisted of Jordanian and Israeli military representatives and a UN chairman whose task was to deal with all aspects of border security.

Secret Jordanian military documents captured by the Israeli Army during the June War of 1967 have proved conclusively that Glubb's version of Jordanian policy was correct and that the Israeli version was utterly false. They reveal strenuous efforts on the part of the Jordanian civilian and military authorities in general and on the part of Glubb in particular to prevent civilians from crossing the line. For example, a document of 2 July 1952 shows that Glubb attended a meeting with district commanders that was devoted to the problem of infiltration. He estimated that if they adopted strict measures they should be able to prevent 85 percent of the incidents from taking place. He urged them to make greater efforts, show more vigilance and monitor more closely the behaviour of the police chiefs in their district. Glubb gave three reasons for this policy. First and foremost, curbing infiltration was necessary for

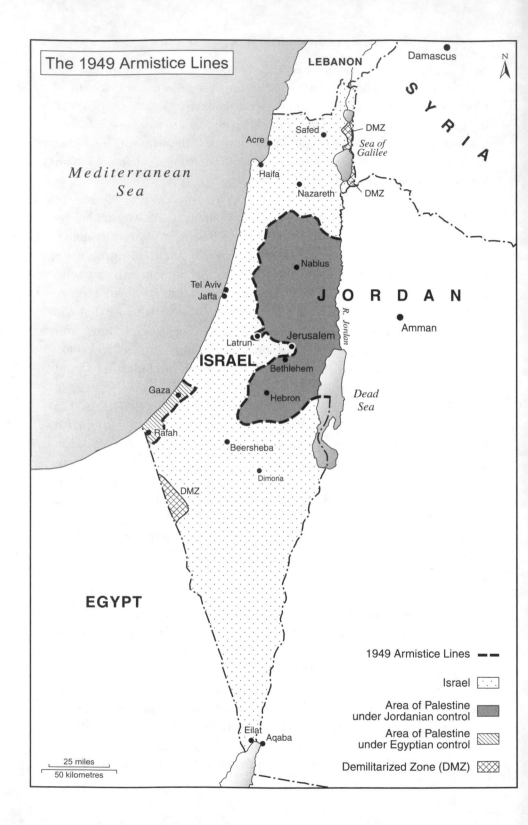

The 1949 Armistice Lines

LEBANON

Damascus

N

S Y R I A

Acre

Safed

DMZ

Sea of Galilee

Mediterranean Sea

Haifa

Nazareth

DMZ

Nablus

Tel Aviv
Jaffa

J O R D A N

R. Jordan

Amman

Latrun

Jerusalem

ISRAEL

Bethlehem

Gaza

Hebron

Dead Sea

Rafah

Beersheba

DMZ

Dimona

EGYPT

1949 Armistice Lines

Israel

Area of Palestine
under Jordanian control

Area of Palestine
under Egyptian control

Demilitarized Zone (DMZ)

Eilat
Aqaba

25 miles
50 kilometres

Jordan's sake, not for Israel's sake. Second, the Jews gained much more from confiscation in the Arab areas than the infiltrators gained from stealing from the Jewish area. Third, there was real fear of revenge being exacted by Jewish units inside Jordan.[17] This document and numerous others like it demonstrate beyond any doubt the high priority given to the border problem at the highest levels of the Jordanian government and armed forces.

The Israeli policy of military retaliation against West Bank villages continued despite all the messages and signals coming from the Jordanian side. The largest and most notorious of these raids was directed against the village of Qibya on the night of 14–15 October 1953. The attack followed the murder of an Israeli mother and her two children by infiltrators who had crossed the armistice line near Qibya. At the meeting of the MAC on 15 October the Jordanian representative denounced the murder, promised full cooperation in tracking down the perpetrators and conveyed Glubb's request to Israel to refrain from retaliation. The request was ignored and swift retribution followed.

The attack on Qibya was carried out by Unit 101, a small commando unit designed to give a sharp edge to the policy of reprisals and commanded by an unusually aggressive, ambitious and devious young major, Ariel ("Arik") Sharon. On this, as on many subsequent occasions, Sharon exceeded his orders. The village was reduced to a pile of rubble: 45 houses were blown up, the village school was destroyed and 69 civilians, two thirds of whom were women and children, were killed. Sharon and his men claimed that they believed all the inhabitants had run away and that they had no idea that anyone was hiding inside the houses. The UN observer who inspected the scene reached a different conclusion: "One story was repeated time after time: the bullet-splintered door, the body sprawled across the threshold, indicating that the inhabitants had been forced by heavy fire to stay inside until their homes were blown up over them."[18] Glubb was appalled to learn that the Israeli soldiers had fired at anyone who attempted to leave their house and that they threw incendiary bombs as well before withdrawing.[19]

The principal perpetrator of the massacre, however, remained unrepentant. Sharon was well pleased with his handiwork. He thought the operation did a power of good to IDF morale, and in his memoirs he claimed that David Ben-Gurion, the prime minister and minister of defence, even congratulated him on this operation. Ben-Gurion, according to Sharon, said to him that what mattered was not what was said about Qibya around the world but its impact in their region: "This is going to give us the possibility of living here."[20] Not all Israelis shared Ben-Gurion's positive verdict on the murdering of innocent civilians in their sleep. In some quarters in the IDF Sharon became known as "the murderer of Qibya."

At a cabinet meeting on 18 October, Moshe Sharett, the foreign minister, who had been horrified by the scale and brutality of the operation, proposed an official statement expressing regret about the action and its consequences. Ben-Gurion was against admitting that the IDF had carried out the action and proposed issuing a statement to say that it was the irate Israeli villagers who had taken the law into their own hands. The majority of the ministers supported Ben-Gurion, and it was decided that he should draft the statement. In a radio broadcast the following day Ben-Gurion gave the official version. He denied any IDF involvement; he placed responsibility for the action on the villagers, who were said to have been provoked beyond endurance; and he expressed the government's regret that innocent people had been killed.[21] This was to be one of Ben-Gurion's most blatant lies for what he saw as the good of his country.

The massacre unleashed a storm of international protest against Israel. Sending regular armed forces across an international border, without the intention of triggering a full-scale war, was a tactic that at the time distinguished Israel from all other countries; no other state acted in this way. Disturbing though this was, the world was even more shocked by the fact that soldiers murdered civilians in cold blood. The Israeli claim that the infiltrators were sponsored by the Arab Legion was utterly baseless. When in January 1954 Arye Eilan, an official in the Israeli Foreign Ministry, asked Yehoshafat Harkabi, the deputy director of military intelligence, for some clear documentary proof of the Arab Legion's complicity, Harkabi answered that "no proof could be given because no proof existed." Harkabi added that, having personally made a detailed study of the subject, he had arrived at the conclusion that "Jordanians and especially the Legion were doing their best to prevent infiltration, which was a natural, decentralized and sporadic movement." To this plainly stated message Eilan reacted by insisting that, whatever the truth of the matter, as Israel's leaders had repeatedly gone on record asserting Jordanian official complicity, Israeli spokesmen could not but continue to press the same point. As he put it, "if Jordanian complicity is a lie, we have to keep on lying. If there are no proofs, we have to fabricate them."[22] Israeli brutality was thus fully matched by Israeli mendacity.

The Qibya raid triggered serious civilian unrest inside Jordan and provoked street demonstrations on both the East and the West banks. There was a public explosion of anger at the government for its failure to protect the civilian population in the border area and to repel Israeli aggression. There were also manifestations of hostility towards Britain, whose reliability as an ally was loudly called into question. Opposition parties went on the offensive in parliament, with one group of deputies issuing calls to court martial Glubb, to dismiss the army's entire British officer corps and to tear up the Anglo–Jordanian defence treaty. One charge against the British officers was that they failed to dispatch an Arab Legion unit posted near by to the rescue of Qibya. Another was that they kept the legion short of ammunition.

Hussein was also dissatisfied with the British officers' performance. His source of information was Natheer al-Rasheed, a young man from the town of Salt and a member of the Movement of Free Jordanian Officers. At the time of the attack on Qibya, Rasheed was commanding an anti-tank unit on the West Bank. His unit indeed did not have adequate stocks of ammunition, and Rasheed did not think much of the British plans for the defence of the border area. Rasheed contacted the king, who received him in the royal palace, along with one of his ADCs, to hear what he had to say. The following day Hussein went to the army headquarters to call on Glubb. The officer in charge of army ammunition was at the meeting. This officer, who was also from Salt, told Rasheed that the king gave Glubb "a very hard time" over the amount of ammunition supplied by Britain to the army.[23] The British commander in the West Bank and the local battalion commander were dismissed immediately after the meeting.

The consequences of the Qibya massacre reflected the growth of nationalism in Jordan. Fawzi Mulki distanced himself from Britain and moved closer to the Arab states. He underlined the gravity of the Israeli threat to Jordan to the Political Committee of the Arab League, which met in Amman on 21 October and responded by passing a series of resolutions to rebuild Qibya at the Arab League's expense, to supply arms and ammunition to the border villages, and to make a contribution of

£2 million to the Jordanian National Guard. These commitments were not wholly fulfilled, but by creating the illusion of an "Arab option," they added weight to the opposition's case for cutting off all connections with the British and thereby increased the pressure on Hussein to do so.[24]

Qibya was the first, indirect encounter between Hussein and Sharon. It was followed by many more, both direct and indirect, none of them amicable. It was also a landmark in the making of the king. After Qibya, Hussein became more a prime mover than an onlooker on the political stage. He began to inject himself more and more forcefully into the affairs of state, to meet alone with foreign diplomats and to move beyond the expression of opinions to the issuing of orders to his ministers. This more assertive style reflected growing personal self-confidence on the one hand and disillusion with parliamentary democracy on the other. Hussein later suggested that this early political experiment failed because he and Mulki tried to move too quickly. But it was not at all clear how Hussein himself envisioned the development of Jordanian institutions.[25] Mulki was not a reliable instrument. Under his ministry "liberty turned into licence."[26] He was unable to control the press, parliament or even his own ministers. In May 1954 Hussein decided to dismiss him. As one scholar has observed, "That the protégé would finally sack the mentor was an important turning-point in Hussein's own political development."[27] By sacking Mulki, Hussein also put an end to the liberal experiment and reverted to the older style of Hashemite autocracy.

4. The Baghdad Pact Fiasco

The hiring and firing of prime ministers was a habit that Hussein acquired early on in his reign. On becoming king he announced his opposition to frequent changes of government but his adherence to this principle was short-lived. Fawzi Mulki lasted only a year in power, from May 1953 to May 1954. His replacement, Tawfiq Abul Huda, also lasted a year, from May 1954 until May 1955. Thereafter the pace of change quickened, with three further cabinet reshuffles before the end of the year. Frequent changes of prime minister became a permanent feature of Hussein's reign. The choice of an individual to form a government was usually connected with a policy that the king wanted to pursue at the time. Thus, if the king wanted to promote better relations with Iraq, he would choose a candidate with pro-Iraqi credentials. Prime ministers were also used to serve a second purpose, that of "shock absorbers." Dumping a prime minister was a way of dissociating the king from a policy that had become unpopular and of appeasing the public. Practice made the king more adept at playing this game. If there was a guiding principle, it was to protect the interests of the Hashemite dynasty.

Domestic politics were closely connected with regional politics. Everything in the Arab world was judged by the touchstone of Palestine and Israel, and it is on this that Jordan, or rather the Hashemite dynasty, was regarded with the greatest suspicion. The Hashemites were still seen as Britain's clients, planted in Jordan to divide the Arab world and to cooperate with the Zionists against the Palestinians. Abdullah was denounced as a traitor to the Arab cause and as a collaborator with the Jews. It was widely believed that the Hashemite family had abandoned the struggle for Palestine and that it might be willing to recognize the State of Israel in return for control over the territory to the east of Israel. This was the prevalent view in the Arab world among the intellectuals as well as the masses. Jordan's efforts to rehabilitate the Palestinian refugees did nothing to allay these fears. Public opinion in the Arab world sided with the Palestinians in Jordan against the regime. Consequently, Hashemites were thrown on the defensive. What is more, because of the centrality of the Palestine question in Arab public discourse, the entire Jordanian political system became susceptible to propaganda and pressures from its neighbouring Arab states.

The year 1955 was a crucial one in the history of Jordan and of the Arab world. It was the year of the Baghdad Pact, a Western attempt to organize the Middle East into a defensive alliance to block Soviet advances. Jordan became the cockpit of two cold wars that were going on simultaneously: the global cold war between East and West, and the regional cold war between President Gamal Abdel Nasser of Egypt and his rivals.

The Baghdad Pact was the unofficial name for the defence treaty concluded between Iraq and Turkey on 24 February 1955. It had its origins in Western fears of Soviet aggression and was part of a global strategy of containment. It had been preceded by an agreement between Turkey and Pakistan, and by bilateral military aid agreements between the United States and these three countries. Britain, Pakistan and Iran joined the pact in 1955. America was expected to join but it changed its mind, leaving Britain in the lurch. Although America participated in a number of committees and provided most of the funding, it did not formally join the pact. The upshot was a rather odd organization that ended by dividing the Arab world. Basically, the pact pledged military aid in the event of communist aggression against a fellow member, but the organization had little military power, and, in any case, only two of its members bordered on the Soviet Union. For most of them the main incentive for joining was to curry favour with Britain and the United States. With Iraq as the only Arab member, the organization could not boast of a strong link to the Arab world. To remedy this deficiency, all the existing members embarked on a drive to recruit more Arab members. Jordan was a prime target both because of its close links with Britain and its dynastic links with Iraq.

Nuri as-Said, Iraq's perennial prime minister, argued forcefully for Arab participation in the Western-sponsored Pact of Mutual Cooperation. He was a staunch friend of Britain and an equally staunch enemy of the Soviet Union. He viewed Zionism and communism as serious threats to the security of Iraq and the entire Arab world. But, like the rest of the Iraqi ruling elite, he regarded the Soviet threat as the greater and more immediate one. He ruled out Iraqi collaboration with the Soviets for fear that it would end in complete subordination to the Kremlin. Collaboration with the West, by contrast, was presented by Said as natural and in line with the covenant of the Arab League, provided agreement could be reached on the Suez base and Palestine issues.[1] For Said the region's progress and destiny lay in close alliance with the West.

Gamal Abdel Nasser was the leading proponent of a purely Arab collective security scheme under the Arab League. For him, the real threat to the security of Egypt and the Arab world lay in Israel, not in the faraway Soviet Union. In world politics he preferred the Arab world to pursue, under Egypt's leadership, an independent, non-aligned policy between the Western and the Eastern blocs. When the Baghdad Pact was announced, Nasser regarded it as a conspiracy between Britain and Iraq, and as a betrayal of Arab interests by the Iraqi premier. Nasser immediately denounced the pact for introducing great power rivalries into the Middle East, dividing and weakening the Arabs, and threatening to encircle Egypt. It was, Nasser felt, a Western device designed to perpetuate colonial control over the Arab world just as the Arab world was asserting its independence and autonomy. On both the ideological and the political planes, the pact thus represented a challenge to Nasser's bid for Egyptian hegemony in the Arab world. He therefore unleashed a violent propaganda campaign over the airwaves against Iraq and Nuri as-Said. The Egyptian radio station Sawt al-Arab, "The Voice of the Arabs," relentlessly pilloried Said as a traitor to the Arab cause and as the cat's-paw of Western imperialism. The war of words between Cairo and Baghdad went on for a few weeks and then died down.

In the spring Nasser and Sir Anthony Eden, who had recently succeeded Winston Churchill as prime minister, seemed to have reached an understanding through their ambassadors that Britain would not try to recruit additional Arab members to the pact, and, in return, Egypt would desist from propaganda against the pact in general and against Iraq in particular.[2] Sir Humphrey Trevelyan confirmed in his memoirs that his predecessor as ambassador to Cairo, on instructions from London, assured Nasser that no attempt would be made to secure the adherence to the pact of other Arab states. Nasser replied that he would not regard it as action hostile to Egyptian interests if other non-Arab states should join the initial members. As a result of this understanding, there was a lull in the war of words until the autumn.[3]

Egypt was not alone in opposing Arab participation in the pact. Saudi Arabia also took the line that Arab defence should be based on the Arab League Security Pact, which excluded membership of Western military organizations. It was therefore opposed to members of the Arab League joining the pact. There were other reasons as well. Saudi Arabia was on bad terms with Britain in the mid 1950s because it opposed Saudi claims with regard to border disputes, notably over the Buraimi Oasis. King Abd al-Aziz ibn Saud was therefore particularly opposed to Western defence plans that included his traditional rivals, the Hashemite kingdoms of Iraq and Jordan. He even perceived the pact as a threat to the existence of his kingdom, and this led him to join Egypt, a curious ideological bedfellow, in the struggle to prevent Jordan from joining the pact.[4]

Jordan's attitude towards the two emergent groups was described by the British ambassador as disappointingly timorous and indecisive:

Such was the preoccupation of the Jordan Government with the Palestine problem and Israel, and their unwillingness to take a definite line or to take any steps to educate and direct Jordan towards what they privately admitted was the best course for the country, that *faute de mieux* Jordan got caught up in the dangerous current of Arab neutrality. When the Iraqi–Turkish Treaty, which afterwards grew into the Baghdad Pact, was first announced, Jordan came dangerously near to toppling into the Egyptian camp. After recovering some degree of balance, however, when the dangers of that course were pointed out to them the Jordan Government adopted a policy of neutrality between Iraq and Egypt and claimed to be attempting to reconcile the two groups in the name of "Arab unity." Jordan's colours were firmly nailed to the fence.[5]

Hussein's initial instinct was to side with Nasser. He favoured the concept of "a northern tier" of defence against communist pressures. But, as he put it in his memoirs, "there was not much point in having a northern tier if people could step over it and build behind it."[6] Like Nasser, he believed in an autonomous Arab collective security pact, and, again like Nasser, he thought that the Baghdad Pact made no strategic sense because it was directed against the Soviet Union, whereas what the Arabs needed was a collective counterweight to Israel. With its policy of hard-hitting military reprisals against its Arab neighbours, Israel posed a problem to which the pact provided no answer. The cabinet headed by Tawfiq Abul Huda adopted a neutral position and lent its support to the king's efforts to help Egypt and Iraq come to a better understanding.

On 14 February 1955 Hussein made a visit to Baghdad, followed by another to Cairo. Iraqi–Jordanian rivalry is the unwritten part of the story of the struggle over the Baghdad Pact. Because of their common Hashemite dynasty, Radio Cairo increasingly linked the two countries in its attacks. "In fact," wrote Hussein in his memoirs, "Jordan and Iraq did not always see eye to eye. The Iraqi policy-making group considered themselves superior and rarely discussed matters with us."[7] Prince Talal, Hussein's nephew, was frank about the awkward relations between the two branches of the family:

Until Faisal II became king, there was a lot of tension between us. The Iraqis had a lot of money and they became Anglophiles and Westernized very quickly, while we had very little money even though we were the senior part of the family and remained much more Arab and Arabian. So they used to look at us as the poor country and we used to look at them as degenerates. But when Faisal II became king, the two branches of the family were brought back together. It is hard to remember how poor we were. I had an aunt who died because of pneumonia and the lack of heating and medicine. Our existence in Jordan was hand to mouth.[8]

Hussein's visit to Baghdad was frustrating and bore no fruit. He met his cousin and friend Faisal but found him virtually powerless. He tried to reason with Said but was firmly put in his place. Said's attitude was expressed in one sentence: "Sir, we are in the Baghdad Pact, that's that, and we are certainly not backing out of it."[9]

On his visit to Cairo, Hussein found Nasser in a much more flexible and reasonable frame of mind than his Iraqi rival. In his memoirs Hussein revealed that he had for a long time been impressed by Nasser: "I felt in those early days that he was a new element in the Arab world, an element that could bring about much needed reforms . . . The problems of the Arab world are almost always the fault of its leaders and politicians, not of the people, and so I had a lot of faith in Nasser and tried to support him as much as I could." Hussein asked Nasser about the Baghdad Pact, and he replied that the hasty way in which it was conceived, involving only one Arab country, had been most unwise. Now that the pact was a fait accompli, Nasser made it clear that it was not possible to remain friendly with Iraq. Hussein did not raise the possibility of Jordanian accession to the pact. Instead he asked Nasser why he insisted on keeping up his radio campaign against Jordan. Nasser feigned surprise and promised to look into the matter, but nothing was done.[10] Nasser's failure to halt the radio attacks on Jordan was taken by Hussein as proof of his duplicity. But on the critical issue of Jordanian accession to the pact, it was Eden who double-crossed Nasser and not Nasser who double-crossed Hussein.

The Foreign Office had a clear policy of neither encouraging nor discouraging Jordan's accession to the pact. This placed Hussein in a catch-22 situation. He wanted a revision of the Anglo–Jordanian treaty of 1948, especially in order to make the British subsidy payable to the Jordanian government instead of going into a special Arab Legion account that was under the direct control of Glubb. Britain replied that the time for treaty revision would come only when Jordan joined the Baghdad Pact. But the nationalist officers who most resented Britain's control of the finances of the Arab Legion were also the strongest opponents of Jordanian entry into the British-sponsored pact. A visit by Hussein to London in mid June provided no way out of this conundrum. Anthony Nutting, the minister of state at the Foreign Office, expressed the hope of early Jordanian accession. "The King replied that he was trying to avoid getting committed to either of the rival groups in the Arab world. He was trying to use his influence to bring them together. He made it plain that for these reasons an early decision by Jordan to accede to the Pact was unlikely."[11]

Said al-Mufti replaced Tawfiq Abul Huda as prime minister in May 1955 and, despite the change of government, the question of the pact remained on hold. Mufti, whose parents had fled from Czarist Russia, was a Circassian and a Hashemite loyalist with impeccable credentials. He was an independently wealthy landlord who, unusually for a Jordanian politician, was untarnished by the brush of corruption. Like many politicians from minority groups in Arab countries, he was a great supporter of Arab unity in word if not always in action. Mufti was a steady but unimaginative politician whom Hussein chose to form a new government because he was both popular and pliant. On the Baghdad Pact, Mufti had no strong sentiments one way or the other. Although several of his ministers were enthusiastic supporters of Jordanian accession, the cabinet itself had no collective position on the matter.

On 27 September 1955 Nasser announced a landmark Soviet–Egyptian arms deal, the so-called "czech" arms deal. Nasser first approached the Americans to sell them arms, but when they did not respond he turned to Moscow. Though Czechoslovakia negotiated and supplied some of the arms, the deal was principally with the Soviet Union. One of the reasons given by Nasser for his decision to buy arms from the Eastern bloc was the Baghdad Pact. As Hussein noted in his memoirs, a bombshell fell on the Arab world: "In an instant everything changed." The Czech arms deal dramatically increased Nasser's popular appeal throughout the Arab world and played a decisive part in turning Jordanian public opinion against the pact. "Hundreds of thousands of Jordanians, listening avidly to the propaganda on Radio Cairo, saw in Nasser a sort of mystical saviour . . . and their best bet for the future against Israel . . . he was the first Arab statesman to really throw off the shackles of the West." Hussein later admitted that he himself sympathized with that point of view to a great extent.[12]

Within the ranks of the Jordanian Army there was much excitement about Nasser's success in breaking the Western monopoly over the supply of arms to the Middle East. Politicians from all ends of the political spectrum praised Nasser's move. The Jordanian parliament cabled its congratulations to the Egyptian president, and Jordan's ambassador to Cairo described the deal as "the greatest Arab step in decades." Even the reticent Jordanian prime minister suppressed his suspicions of Russia and welcomed the move as a boost to Arab self-defence.[13] Radio Cairo intensified its propaganda with emotional appeals to the Jordanian people, calling on them to get rid of the British officers in the army and the king who was keeping Jordan as a tool of the West. The Czech arms deal, despite all the public praise it received in Jordan, was thus turned into a challenge to the legitimacy of the Hashemite dynasty. It also helped to turn Jordan into a major battleground in the cold war between the Arab radicals and the Arab moderates.

Nasser followed up the arms deal with the Eastern bloc by signing bilateral defence pacts with Syria and Saudi Arabia in October. By providing for a joint command of the armed forces of the three countries, these treaties created the beginning of an Arab counterweight to the Baghdad Pact. Jordan was now the missing link in the Arab front surrounding Israel, and the three countries offered Jordan a subsidy in an obvious attempt to lure it away from the British-led grouping. There were rumours that Britain was considering the withdrawal of its subsidy in the event of Jordan refusing to join the pact. The tripartite offer was intended to supplant British influence and to reassure Jordan that it would have an alternative source of income in case the British government withdrew its support.

Fearful of an increase in Nasser's power and Soviet influence in the Middle East, the Turks made a determined effort to persuade Hussein to join their pact with Iraq. Turkish President Çalal Bayar and Foreign Minister Fetim Zorlu arrived in Amman on 3 November and used every conceivable argument to convince the king and his ministers of the advantages of joining the pact. Membership, they said, would secure Turkey as an ally against Israel, it would secure Turkish assistance in countering any military threat from Syria, and it would speed up the revision of the treaty with Britain. Hussein replied that he understood the advantages of joining, but that Jordan needed economic aid as much as a military alliance. The visitors urged the king to write to the British government to explain his needs, and they promised to write at the same time to support his case.[14]

Hussein told the British ambassador, Charles Duke, that he was ready to join, provided Jordan received "the necessary backing" from Britain. On 16 November Hussein handed Duke a note explaining Jordan's difficulties and needs. Although the note did not say so explicitly, it implied that Jordan would consider joining the pact if its demands were met. Duke recommended to his government that Jordan's wavering should be ended with a firm commitment to treat it generously. Foreign Secretary Harold Macmillan wrote to Anthony Eden, "I very much fear that if we do not get Jordan into the Baghdad Pact, she will drift out of our control." Macmillan felt that Britain's prestige as a Middle Eastern power was being put to the test, and he persuaded his cabinet colleagues that Jordan's adherence was in Britain's interest. The Defence Committee accepted his recommendations and decided to send to Amman the chief of the imperial general staff, General Sir Gerald Templer. Templer's instructions were clear and simple: "Jordan must be made to join the pact."[15]

It was thought that the choice of a man of such exalted military rank as the bearer of the foreign secretary's views would appeal to Hussein's vanity. Templer was told that, according to Glubb, "the king fancies himself, in view of his Sandhurst background, as a military expert." Hence it was suggested that Templer might wish to adopt the line of "speaking as one soldier to another." Templer was also empowered to inform the king privately that Her Majesty's Government proposed to appoint him as an honorary air vice-marshal in the Royal Air Force once Jordan had joined the pact.[16] The wisdom of choosing Templer for this delicate diplomatic mission was open to doubt. He was a tough and incisive soldier who had made his name by crushing a communist insurgency in Malaya, but he was not noted for his patience or diplomatic skills. It was also a mistake to focus only on the king during the visit without trying to win over the government, parliament and public opinion.

On 6 December, General Templer arrived in Amman on a visit that lasted just over a week. At a series of meetings with the king and his officials, Templer tried hard to get a firm commitment from them to join the Baghdad Pact. Templer presented Britain's offer of money and arms to strengthen the Arab Legion and to meet Jordan's additional defence needs as a member of the pact. He also expressed readiness to replace the 1948 Anglo–Jordanian treaty by a special agreement under the pact, similar to that concluded with Iraq. The king was soon convinced of the advantages of joining. The cabinet, however, was deeply divided between East Bankers and the Palestinian ministers from the West Bank. The latter insisted that Egypt be consulted before any decision was made. Said Mufti, the prime minister, "never a strong man or one to take responsibility if he could avoid it, gave his Cabinet nothing of a lead in spite of the King's efforts to encourage him."[17] The sudden resignation of the four Palestinian ministers, who were generally believed to have been bribed to do so by the Egyptian government, deepened the crisis. Hussein was prepared to sign the Letter of Intent, which committed Jordan to the pact, himself, but Templer advised him against such a rash move. Templer realized that the king needed the endorsement of his ministers for a decision that was as critical as this one. But the cabinet was divided. Said Mufti lost his nerve and on 13 December hastened to the palace to tender his resignation. With the collapse of the government, the negotiations came to an abrupt end. The following morning Templer flew back to London to report on the failure of his mission. The offer he had brought with him turned out to be too little, too late.

Another reason for Templer's failure to move Jordan into the Baghdad Pact was the concerted campaign of propaganda and subversion unleashed by Egypt, Syria and Saudi Arabia. Egyptian and Syrian agents stepped up their support for the opposition parties. The Saudi Embassy in Amman disbursed lavish bribes to journalists and politicians who came out against Jordanian membership of the pact. Radio Cairo broadcast anti-Western tirades and denounced Jordan as the puppet of the imperialists. In his memoirs Hussein represented the Egyptian propaganda offensive as the betrayal of a promise by Nasser. He claimed that he had reported to Nasser about the progress of the talks with Templer and that he understood that Nasser had given him his blessing. Then suddenly everything changed. "I cannot recall another incident in history," wrote Hussein, "where a statesman has made such a volte-face. That was the end of Jordan and the Baghdad Pact. It was not the end of Nasser's double-crossing."[18] A more plausible explanation of Nasser's volte-face, however, is that he himself was double-crossed by the British government. As the British ambassador to Cairo candidly confessed, what he had been told by Whitehall to tell Nasser was not a fair statement of the purpose of the Templer mission.[19] Sir Humphrey Trevelyan had been instructed to say that General Templer's mission had not been to press Jordan to join the pact but to discuss the supply of arms.

Hussein's next move was to charge Hazza' al-Majali, the young and vigorous deputy prime minister and minister of the interior, with forming a government. Majali came from the southern town of Kerak from a family of tribal shaikhs. He was a staunch Hashemite loyalist and a man of courage who, unlike his predecessor, was not afraid to shoulder responsibility. On the external front, Majali was pro-British, close to Iraq and intent on forming a regional grouping against Nasserism with these two traditional allies. Majali had a high opinion of Glubb Pasha and shared his belief that the alliance with Britain was crucial to Jordan's national security and stability. The two men also believed that membership of the Baghdad Pact would bolster Jordan against the radical Arab challenge and help the kingdom defend its western border against attacks from Israel.[20]

Majali formed a government on 15 December with the publicly

declared object of taking Jordan into the pact. His closest ally at home was Wasfi al-Tall from the northern town of Irbid, who was to play a major part in Jordanian politics in the 1960s. Tall was appointed as director of the Department of Publications. He believed that the Arab world did not possess the intrinsic power to sustain a neutralist posture and advocated cooperation with the West against Arab radicalism.[21] He argued that the treaty with Britain restricted Jordan's freedom of action, whereas membership of the Baghdad Pact would increase its freedom and enhance its security. He also felt that Jordan had no chance against Israel if it stood alone and that the pact provided at least the potential for an Arab line-up against the enemy in their midst as well as the distant enemy to the north. Both Majali and Tall spoke clearly, forcefully and without any ambiguity in favour of Jordanian membership of the pact. According to Mreiwad al-Tall, Wasfi's younger brother, Hussein did not like strong men, preferring to surround himself with "yes men"; he brought in Majali only when he felt that his survival was at stake.[22]

The day after Majali formed his government, riots broke out in all the cities of the West Bank and in Amman, Salt and Irbid on the East Bank. These were the most serious to have taken place in Jordan's history. They were accompanied by anti-government demonstrations, the disruption of public services and attacks on Western embassies. The Ba'th Party and the communists were active in organizing the riots. But the unrest was also a manifestation of genuine anger and frustration on the part of the Palestinian population of Jordan. All sorts of rumours were circulated to inflame these fears—for example, that Jordan's accession to the Baghdad Pact would entail the indefinite shelving of the Palestine question and that Israel would later also become a member. In his memoirs Majali wrote that these rumours and lies were spread by opportunists with no morals and no conscience: "The most serious of the lies was that the negotiations with Templer were definitely leading to the loss of Palestine. Egypt and Saudi Arabia recruited their friends and agents; the communist agitators supported them in misleading the people; and the fantastic story of the loss of Palestine was repeated everywhere."[23]

When the crowds became violent, Majali decided to use the Arab Legion to quell the riots, and the king at first backed him. But the legion's performance was disappointing because it was a regular army with no training, no equipment and no plan for dealing with civil disturbances. At least fifteen people were killed and many more were arrested, but the country continued to teeter on the verge of anarchy. Some ministers were intimidated into resigning, and when Majali failed to find replacements for them, he went to the palace and tendered his own resignation after only five days in power. The king accepted both his resignation and his recommendation to dissolve parliament. Round one had been won by the opposition.

The king then called on Ibrahim Hashem, the elderly and respected president of the Senate, to form an interim government with the sole purpose of organizing fresh parliamentary elections. By 21 December, Hashem succeeded in forming a strong government that included three former prime ministers. But a group of deputies claimed that the king's action in dissolving parliament was illegal, and the High Court ruled that, for a minor technical reason, the decree dissolving parliament was indeed invalid. The court's ruling led the king to reconsider and to reverse his decision on holding elections. He had envisaged the elections as a referendum on Jordanian membership of the Baghdad Pact, but public opinion was moving in the opposite direction. More generally, Hussein's initial hope to restore his damaged reputation by an appeal to the people gave way to fears that elections would only strengthen the opposition and reinforce the neutralist tendency in the country's foreign policy. His decision to cancel the elections, however, provoked a second wave of riots that swept through the capital and the West Bank from 7 to 9 January 1956.

The riots and mob violence that erupted in January were both severe and disruptive. This time, however, the Arab Legion was much better prepared than it had been during the previous month. Prime Minister Hashem dithered. At first he told Glubb to take no action and to show no troops in the capital. But when the mobs broke into the Ministry of Agriculture, Hashem panicked and reversed his order to Glubb: "Disperse them at once! Open fire! They will burn down the city."[24] Hussein felt compelled to assume command because the country was now on the verge of collapse. "Now all hell had broken loose," he wrote in his memoirs. "Riots such as we had never seen before, led by the Communists again, disrupted the entire country. This time bands of fire-raisers started burning Government offices, private houses, foreign properties. I had no alternative but to call out the Legion, who with tear-gas and determination met force with force. I imposed a ten-day curfew on the country." Looking back on those days, he was convinced that the majority of ordinary Jordanians were profoundly grateful when the army appeared and that it saved the country.[25]

This judgement is open to question. The majority of the people were Palestinians, and the riots sprang from resentment of the king's cancellation of the elections and fear that his newly appointed government would again try to take the country into the Baghdad Pact. What the riots revealed was the deep animosity of the people towards the regime and its ties with the West. Hussein compounded his earlier mistakes by acting with such brutality. Using live fire against civilians was a distasteful task for the soldiers. When he ordered the army to fire into the crowds, Hussein damaged the reputation of both the army and the monarchy. He acted forcefully in his own dynastic interest, and for this he gained neither respect nor gratitude. On the contrary, his action alienated the people and deepened the rift between rulers and ruled. The age of "street politics" and mass protest had arrived. Palestinian refugees and ordinary Jordanians flexed their political muscles for the first time and found them strong. So they were unlikely to revert to their previous political apathy and acquiescence.

Richard Crossman, a fiery left-wing British MP, gave his Israeli hosts an interesting analysis of the recent events in Jordan. The riots there were much more serious, he said, than the British officials were prepared to admit. True, there was effective Egyptian propaganda and bribes were distributed on a generous scale, but these were not the underlying causes of the disturbances. What Crossman saw was a real revolt of the Palestinians against the attempt to push Jordan into the Baghdad Pact. Their fear was that membership of the pact would distract the attention of Jordanians from the one and only thing that preoccupied them, namely, the war with Israel. The slogan used by the demonstrators was: "They want to sell us out to the Jew!" Crossman was struck by the depth of the hatred that he witnessed in Jordan towards Israel. He believed that in the event of a clash between Israel and Egypt, the Jordanians would not stand idly by, and if Britain tried to prevent the army from getting involved, it would rebel against its British officers. In any case, he was certain that no government could possibly make another attempt to take the country into the pact.[26]

Following the suppression of the riots, Hussein called on Samir Rifa'i to form a new cabinet, and this was done on 9 January. Originally a Palestinian from Safad and a confidant of King Abdullah, Rifa'i was the strong man of the "Palace Politicians." He proclaimed martial law and imposed a curfew, but, to deflect popular anger against the regime, he forswore the Baghdad Pact and promised to work to strengthen Jordan's ties with the Arab states. Rifa'i also tried to pin responsibility for the Arab Legion's brutality during the riots on Glubb, so that the opprobrium would not fall on the king. Like many other Jordanian politicians, Rifa'i made Glubb take the responsibility in public for unpopular policies.

Glubb himself was a shrewd observer of the Jordanian scene, and he had a low opinion of Rifa'i, as he did of the great majority of the palace politicians. He was a strict and upright Christian, an officer and a gentleman, who never used his position to line his own pocket. Glubb was reactionary in his outlook and authoritarian in his methods, but in no way was he corrupt. He therefore found the corruption that plagued Jordanian politics deeply repugnant, though it was nothing unusual by Arab standards. Glubb held out the Arab Legion as a model of selfless dedication to public duty, and he resented criticism of it, especially when it came from politicians. In a top-secret letter dated 2 February 1956 to Sir Gerald Templer, Glubb gave his own perspective on the handling of the riots. He admitted that when the first wave of riots broke out in December, the army was unprepared, but he went on to claim that in the following fortnight it remedied the omissions. So when rioting recommenced in early January, it acted firmly to gain control of the situation:

However, we are still not happy. We [the army] thought that the suppression of the second lot of riots was our ideal opportunity to close down political parties and known subversive organizations, and have a firm Government on the lines of the present administration in Iraq. This we have failed to do. The New Government consists largely of the old type of politicians, most of them not above suspicion of taking money from the Saudis and the Egyptians.

During the disturbances the Arab Legion behaved extremely well. We tried to avoid British officers appearing too much in the suppression of the civil disturbances, especially as the Egyptians and the Communists made as much propaganda as they could to the effect that the Arab Legion was a "colonial" army and that the British were suppressing a national uprising. (The "Daily Herald" said the same!)[27]

The king was so alarmed by the second wave of rioting that he secretly approached both Britain and Iraq for political and military support without informing his new prime minister. He felt that the Arab Legion was fully extended, so he wanted an Iraqi division to be held ready to enter Jordan to help enforce martial law. London was asked to transmit his appeal for help to Baghdad, and the message was duly sent. The British cabinet also decided to fly two parachute battalions and a battalion of the Highland Light Infantry to Cyprus at once. The wing of the RAF Regiment in Habaniyya was alerted to fly from Iraq to Amman, and the armoured regiment in Aqaba was ordered to move closer to the capital.

No sooner had the British taken these precautions than an external military threat began to loom in the desert on Jordan's southern front. Hussein and the British received an intelligence report that a Saudi force, 1,500 to 2,000 strong, was moving towards the border. Anthony Eden promptly decided to inform the Saudi government that Britain was aware of these movements and to warn them that, in the event of aggression, it would help Jordan in accordance with the Anglo–Jordanian treaty. This warning had a salutary effect. The Saudi forces drew back from the border area, and the threat receded.[28]

The Iraqi response to Hussein's plea for help was favourable but also self-serving. Nuri Said promised all the help Iraq could give within its resources. He seized the chance to reduce his country's isolation in the Arab world, to strike a blow at Nasser and to gain more influence in Jordan. Nor was he oblivious to the new opportunity to realize his old ambition of a Hashemite union between Iraq and Jordan on Iraq's terms. On 12 January, Hussein, Glubb and Bahjat al-Talhouni, the chief of the royal court, flew secretly to Habaniyya to confer with the Iraqi leadership. Rifa'i and the queen mother were not informed. At the meeting the Iraqi leaders agreed to start military planning for a possible intervention in Jordan. Hussein was evidently determined to control the pace of events and not to rely on the politicians. As one historian has put it, "Although the direction was not particularly clear, the January events showed him intent on charting his own course."[29]

The struggle to take Jordan into the Baghdad Pact ended with a whimper. The riots gradually died down, there was a return to normal or near-normal conditions, and, as Richard Crossman had predicted, no government dared reopen the question of membership. Most historians agree that 1955 was a crucial year in the reign of King Hussein, but they differ as to why Jordan failed to join the British-led regional security pact. Some writers see the pact as an attempt to perpetuate colonial control of the region, which was defeated by the proponents of Arab autonomy led by Nasser. Others emphasize the internal dimension of the conflict that pitted the opposition parties and the street against the regime and ended with the triumph of the former. And others still hold with divisions within the Jordanian ruling elite.

Hussein was clearly a key player in the drama that ended in a fiasco. Regardless of the perspective taken of this eventful period in Jordan's history, the verdict on Hussein's performance is unflattering. Each view highlights a different set of misjudgements and mistakes. Hussein's most basic error was to opt for, after much hesitation and wavering, an alliance with the West against the Soviet Union, when the real enemy was Israel. This was compounded by his failure to counter effectively both Egypt's fierce propaganda campaign against the pact and Saudi subversion. Hussein also misjudged the national mood, underestimating the depth of popular anger against Israel and what were perceived as its Western sponsors. In addition, there was Hussein's failure to carry the ruling elite with him, evident from the rapid turnover of prime ministers. Last but not least was the ruthless manner in which he deployed the British-commanded Arab Legion to suppress popular protest against his policies. The Arab Legion emerged from the emergency as the only effective tool for dealing with internal challenges to the regime; but the question of who precisely controlled the legion consequently became a burning issue in the following weeks and months.

For Hussein, 1955 was an eventful year on the personal as well as the political front. Amid all the crises that convulsed the country, Hussein found time to court and marry Sharifa Dina Abdul Hamid, a distant cousin from the Egyptian branch of the Hashemite family. Dina was six years older than the royal groom: he was nineteen and she was twenty-five. Her lineage, like that of the groom, could be traced back to the prophet Muhammad, hence her birthright title of "*Al-Sharifa*." She was the great-grand-niece of Hussein, the sharif of Mecca, later the king of the Hijaz. Her father, Sharif Abdul Hamid al-Awn, moved to Egypt after the collapse of the Kingdom of the Hijaz in 1925. Through her mother, Dina, was connected to Egypt's Circassian elite. Like many children of the landed Arab aristocracy, she was sent to a boarding school in England, rounding off her education with a degree in English literature from Girton College, Cambridge, and a post-graduate diploma in social science from Bedford College, London. After her return home, she began to teach English literature and philosophy at the University of Cairo. She was a highly educated, sophisticated and emancipated young woman. In dynastic terms this was an excellent match. In cultural and intellectual terms, Hussein married way above his station. There was one other problem: Dina had strong Nasserist leanings.

Dina was a very beautiful woman, and very slight, no taller than Hussein. The main bond between them was their pride in their common Hashemite heritage. They had few shared interests apart from their love of dancing. They first met in London when Hussein was still a schoolboy at Harrow. As a cadet at Sandhurst, Hussein used to take Dina out to nightclubs and to parties. In Jordan and in Europe, Hussein was often photographed in the company of glamorous society girls. The rumour mill kept working and the flavour of the month kept changing. But during his visits to London after ascending the throne, he and Dina continued to meet. Queen Zain initially disapproved of the idea of marriage between them, but he was insistent. Prince Hassan, who was eight years old at the time, remembers his older brother stamping his feet in fury with their mother. Zain's main argument against the marriage was that Hussein was too young, but she also resented the woman in question. Hassan, looking back, felt that they were an odd couple: Dina was intelligent and cultivated, while Hussein was barely out of short trousers, with no social confidence. The tension in the family was palpable from the beginning: "My mother could see the dangers of both the timing of Hussein's marriage due to his youth and the age of the person he was to marry and the pitfalls that may have lain ahead. There is no doubt that she also felt threatened by an equally well-born, equally beautiful, equally intelligent woman within the family. So perhaps she did not help matters."[30]

Zain had to concede that Dina had impeccable Hashemite credentials as well as a good education and high social standing. Once she realized that her son could not be deflected, Zain bowed to the inevitable and took charge of the practical arrangements. Hussein's letter proposing marriage to Dina asked her for her help in preserving the Hashemite dynasty and in providing a focus for his people's loyalty. Dina accepted Hussein's proposal out of a sense of duty. "She was not in love with him," one of his biographers has written, "but believed he needed what she could give him."[31]

On 20 February 1955 Hussein went on an official visit to Egypt, at the end of which his engagement to Dina Abdul Hamid was announced. The royal wedding took place in the queen mother's palace in Amman on 19 April. Hussein signed the marriage contract in the presence of two witnesses: his cousin, King Faisal II of Iraq, and the cadi, or Islamic judge, of Amman. The guests sipped a celebratory glass of strawberry juice before stepping out to the balcony. Dina, who was wearing a grey and mauve dress and a chiffon scarf, waved regally to the cheering crowd. Farid al-Atrash, the Frank Sinatra of the Arab world, sang songs especially written for the occasion. "It felt as though a gust of fresh young air was sweeping through the palace, blowing away the feudal cobwebs."[32] The newlyweds set up house in Hussein's villa at Al-Hummar, called Darat al-Khair ("House of Goodness"). It looked like a perfect marriage.

The honeymoon of the royal couple took the form of a state visit to Spain. This was followed by a visit to the United Kingdom from 16 to 23 June as the guests of Her Majesty's Government, during which it was already apparent that the king and the queen were not on the happiest of terms—for which the king was generally blamed. At the end of the month they returned to Jordan, where a great deal of criticism was being voiced of the royal family, especially of the queen mother and her brother Sharif Nasser bin Jamil. Pamphlets attacking the royal family and the monarch were circulated for the first time. Hussein's known support for Jordan's entry into the Baghdad Pact also damaged his popularity and prestige.[33]

When Dina told Hussein that she was pregnant he was delighted. A baby girl was born on 13 February 1956, and they called her Alia. The arrival of their daughter led to a marked but temporary improvement in the relations between the parents. Dina performed the ceremonial duties of a queen: entertaining visiting dignitaries, hosting receptions and tea parties, visiting schools and hospitals, and doing charitable work. But she thought that she had been chosen to play a more substantive role in helping her husband to develop his country, and she behaved accordingly. It soon became clear that she was much more liberal in internal politics and much more interested in social issues than her husband. She was also thought to prefer the Palestinians of the

West Bank to the Jordanians of the East Bank. Zain was jealous of the prominent role in the affairs of state that her daughter-in-law was beginning to play and tried to confine her to routine palace duties. The birth of Alia made things worse because Dina resented her omnipresent and intrusive mother-in-law. Zain had strong views on the bringing up of children and took to complaining to her son about both the public and the private conduct of his wife. Zain was a woman of an indomitable will who jealously guarded her powers and prerogatives in the royal household. She represented tradition, whereas Dina represented modernity, and the relationship between them deteriorated very rapidly. Zain felt vindicated. She became a prime mover in bringing about the dissolution of the marriage. Hussein, the apprentice husband, was torn between the two assertive women in his life. He longed for simple companionship, and, when problems arose, he began to distance himself from his wife. Within eighteen months of the wedding, the marriage collapsed.

Not surprisingly, Hussein wanted to put his failed marriage behind him and move on. In his memoirs, he dwelt very briefly on this chapter in his life. His account consists of two terse and exceedingly uninformative paragraphs:

On 19 April 1955, I was married to Sharifa Dina Abdul Hamed, a distant cousin and a member of the Hashemite dynasty, who lived in Cairo. She was a highly intelligent woman with an MA degree at Cambridge, and a few years my senior. At first I was very hopeful that I could build a happy family life around this marriage, and when our baby daughter Alia was born I was overjoyed.

I have always wanted to share the fundamental happiness of the life of an ordinary man, but it was not to be—not then. The marriage was a failure. It was just one of those things that did not work out, despite all efforts; it was far better, and only fair to both of us, to end it. It was a sad and difficult period. There have been many criticisms about the divorce, but the basic principle of life is to live in the best way one can, honestly, regardless of people's opinions. It is better to meet such a crisis with courage and frankness. Eighteen months after our marriage we separated, and my ex-wife left for Cairo.[34]

In reality, Hussein's handling of the crisis in his first marriage displayed neither courage nor frankness, while his account of the divorce is highly economical with the truth. The official version, repeated by several of Hussein's British biographers, is that Dina went on holiday to Egypt in the autumn of 1956, leaving her baby daughter behind her, and that she did not return. In fact, she went to visit her father, who had been injured in a car accident, and she was not allowed to return. What the official version does not say is that Dina was not permitted to see her daughter, with one brief exception, for six years after the failure of the marriage.

Dina did not tell her side of the story until many years later and to the most improbable of chroniclers: two Israeli journalists, a husband and a wife. In 1986 Aharon and Amalia Barnea published in Hebrew a book that came out three years later in English under the title *Mine Enemy: The Moving, Hopeful Friendship of Two Couples—Israeli and Arab*.[35] The authors were the Israeli couple while the Arab couple were Dina and her second husband, Salah Ta'amari, a high-ranking member of the Fatah faction of the Palestine Liberation Organization and a lieutenant-colonel in the PLO's armed forces. Dina had always felt deep sympathy for the long-suffering Palestinian people, and as the short-lived queen of Jordan she developed a special affinity with the refugees among them. The Arab defeat in the June War of 1967 and Israel's occupation of the West Bank set in motion a second wave of refugees. The PLO guerrilla forces relocated to the East Bank of the Jordan to resume the armed struggle against Israel. Dina, who was then living in London, was outspoken in her support for the Palestinian cause. She opened a boutique to sell Palestinian handicrafts, the proceeds of which went to Fatah. At a reception for a visiting Fatah delegation in the summer of 1968 Dina met Salah Ta'amari, and two years later they got married.

Salah Ta'amari was twelve years younger than Dina. He was born in 1942 in Bethlehem, on what became the West Bank of the Hashemite Kingdom of Jordan. In 1955, when he was thirteen, Ta'amari took part in a demonstration in Bethlehem against Jordan's entry into the Baghdad Pact. He remembered well the spectacle of Jordanian soldiers opening fire on the demonstrators and killing four. Afterwards, the schools were closed for almost a year, increasing local resentment against the regime. Ta'amari studied at Ein Shams University in Cairo for a degree in English literature, and he did an MA thesis on T. S. Eliot. He also read widely about Jewish history, the Holocaust, Zionism and the State of Israel. His aim was to go back to Bethlehem to become a school-teacher. But when the PLO was formed in 1964 he joined Fatah and after the June War he could not go back. From 1967 he rose fast in the Fatah chain of command, to become coordinator of raids from the East Bank into the Israeli-occupied West Bank. During the confrontation between the Jordanian regime and the Palestinian guerrillas in September 1970, Dina's first and second husbands therefore fought on opposite sides. Having been defeated in Jordan, the guerrilla organizations regrouped in southern Lebanon to resume the armed struggle for the liberation of Palestine. In 1982 Israel invaded Lebanon, and Ta'amari was captured and taken prisoner. He was the highest-ranking Fatah commander to fall into Israel's hands. Aharon Barnea went to interview him for a radio programme.

This was the first of a series of meetings that grew into a friendship between the two men. As a special concession, the prisoner was allowed to pay a visit to Aharon Barnea at his home. Barnea was also instrumental in arranging a clandestine, conjugal visit for Dina with her husband in a beachfront hotel. Thus was born the unusual friendship between the two couples that cut across all the regional battle lines. The book that the Barneas wrote has only one chapter about Dina's first marriage, but it is a highly revealing one. Because the account of the marriage and its disintegration comes to us second-hand, its accuracy cannot be guaranteed, but it certainly has the ring of authenticity.

The most interesting part of Dina's account relates to the break-up of her marriage to Hussein. For a brief period following the birth of Alia, they succeeded in overcoming their troubles. But the rumours against her and the court intrigues persisted, until the king succumbed to the pressures on him. In the autumn of 1956, when Dina went to her father's bedside, she left six-month-old Alia in the care of Mrs. Greig, the British nanny, because Hussein refused to let her take the baby with her. When she called Hussein to make the arrangements for her return, she was in for a shock. He said, "I think you had better stay where you are, until the situation becomes more propitious." Dina's increasingly desperate pleas to Hussein to allow her to be reunited with her daughter all fell on deaf ears. When Alia was about nine months old, Hussein allegedly said to Dina, "If you think you and my enemies can use my daughter as a weapon against me, you are mistaken." He issued orders banning all communication between the queen and the court. In August 1957 Hussein sent word to Dina through the Jordanian ambassador to Cairo: as a twenty-eighth birthday present she would be

allowed to see Alia but only on neutral territory and under strict supervision. The meeting took place in a hotel in Istanbul. The party from
Amman included Alia, Mrs. Greig, several servants, three Circasssian
bodyguards and Queen Zain. Dina spent twenty-four hours with her
daughter, and then a messenger from Queen Zain came to tell her that
her time was up. Hussein subsequently charged his ambassador to
Cairo with the mission of serving Dina the divorce papers.

Dina had to wait nearly five years to see her daughter again. It was
not until Hussein got married for a second time, to the English girl who
became Princess Muna, that the unbelievably cruel royal ban was
lifted. It was Muna who persuaded Hussein to change his mind. Dina
was invited to stay at the palace to see her daughter and to begin a
series of regular meetings with her. Dina had had hardly any contact
with Hussein after her visit to Amman, but his conscience must have
troubled him. One day, many years after the reunion, he got word that
Dina was seriously ill in a London hospital. He asked to see her but she
refused. The next morning, as she was being wheeled to the operating
theatre, her carers diverted her bed to a small room. Her former husband was standing there. He uttered one sentence: "I am sorry." She felt
that she had no choice but to forgive him.[36]

Hussein's belated apology to his first wife indicates, above all, how
much he had learned in the intervening period. One should therefore
not be too harsh in judging his handling of either the political crisis or
his private life in 1955. At that time he was barely twenty years old. He
made serious mistakes, but they were the result of youth and inexperi-
ence in the face of unprecedented political upheavals. Political immaturity was more than matched by emotional immaturity: a callow youth
with a passion for dancing, he married a woman who was not just older
but considerably more mature, sophisticated and politically progressive than himself. He simply could not handle the relationship, and he
behaved abominably. But he was not inherently cruel or callous. He
was simply at the bottom of a steep learning curve.

5. The Dismissal of Glubb

The most spectacular event in Anglo–Jordanian relations in 1956 was the dismissal by royal edict of John Bagot Glubb from his position as commander-in-chief of the Arab Legion. Britain's pressure on Jordan to join the Baghdad Pact unleashed a powerful popular current of anti-British feelings that culminated in removal of the renowned British general. Glubb was an employee of the Jordanian government, and to this extent his dismissal was an internal Jordanian affair. But most Jordanians saw him as a British proconsul in Amman; most foreigners saw him as the real power behind the throne; and the Arab world saw him as the symbol of foreign control over the political and economic life of Jordan. Egypt and Syria, in particular, used Glubb's exalted position to taunt Jordan with being a British colony while they were free. By sacking Glubb, Hussein made a dramatic assertion, at the practical as well as the symbolic level, of his country's independence.

Personal relations between Hussein and Glubb had never been close or cordial. The gap in age between them was one problem. To the twenty-one-year-old king, the Englishman, who was now only a month off sixty, smacked too much of the Victorian era. There were other issues too. In the words of one British observer,

Hussein remained open to suggestions from the modernists and the reformers: and in particular he was sensitive, as a young king of pride and lofty breeding, to the insinuation that he was no more than a British toy, dancing to the batons of Glubb Pasha and the Foreign Office. It was obvious that Glubb was not the political master of Jordan, and had no pretensions to Kirkbride's role of grey eminence. His profession was soldiering, his responsibility was security, and on political matters he was not even consulted, let alone obeyed. Hussein had a skulking suspicion, though, that some other canards about Glubb were true: that he had in fact so hampered the Legion in Palestine that the war was lost; that he was outdated or defeatist in his thinking . . . Hussein was understandably overawed by Glubb, a soldier of long experience from his grandfather's generation, from whom he was separated by a great gulf of age and ingrained respect. As a young man of dashing tastes, he no doubt thought Glubb an old fuddy-duddy slow-coach, better at defence than offence. He was also often in the company of young, ambitious and politically conscious . . . Jordanian officers, jealous of British control of their Army, and covetous of senior commands; and he began to see that while in Jordanian eyes the Legion was an instrument of war against Israel, to the British War Office it was part of the West's defences against Russia. By 1955 Hussein had fostered a profound resentment of Glubb's dominating position, both commander and creator of the modern Arab Legion. His throne depended upon the surety of the Army, and it was galling to be dependent upon the skills of an elderly foreigner.[1]

The British failed to see any of this. During a visit to London in October 1955 Hussein tried to alert Foreign Office officials to the need to make changes in the command of the Arab Legion, but they did not take him seriously. Had they done so, they might have avoided the explosion that took place four months later.[2] Hussein's broad political reason for dismissing Glubb stemmed from his fear that if he did not place himself at the head of the nationalist movement, he would be overwhelmed by it.[3] But Hussein and Glubb also disagreed on two fundamental issues: the role of Arab officers in the Arab Legion and defence strategy. The Arab Legion was the single strongest national institution in Jordan, yet it was led by senior officers who could not ignore their loyalty to Britain. Hussein wanted to see a more rapid transfer of command and responsibility in the legion from British to Arab officers. Glubb dragged his feet. After months of patient negotiations, the British authorities finally agreed to submit a plan of Arabization that "in due course" would give more opportunities to Jordanian officers. Excitement at this minor victory turned into exasperation, however, when Hussein was informed that this meant that the Royal Engineers of the Arab Legion would have an Arab commander in 1985. This answer rankled with Hussein, especially as the question of when an Arab might command the armed forces of Jordan was not even mentioned.

The second issue on which the two men disagreed concerned the defence of the West Bank in the event of a war with Israel. Glubb proposed a conservative and cautious strategy of concentrating Jordan's slim forces on the defence of strategic high points and pulling them back at the outset of an attack from the West Bank to the East Bank. Hussein rejected this plan in favour of a more forward strategy. He argued that they should start their defence right on the 400-mile frontier and accept death with honour if they could not hold it. To his way of thinking, a purely defensive strategy could not possibly deter an enemy attack, though an offensive strategy might.

Behind these specific disagreements, wrote Hussein, lay the ghost of his grandfather. From his grandfather he had learned that all Arab peoples must be masters of their own affairs.[4] Here, however, the grandfather received more credit than he deserved. Although Abdullah was a proponent of Arab independence in theory, he was a client of Britain in practice. Whereas the idea of sacking Glubb would have been unthinkable to him, Hussein not only conceived it but carried it out. On the other hand, Hussein hardly mentioned the encouragement and support that he received from the Jordanian Free Officers to embark on this audacious undertaking. After all, his agenda was their agenda: to Arabize the Arab Legion. His early contacts with them went back to his days as a cadet at Sandhurst. One of their members, Ali Abu Nuwar, was constantly at the king's side following his appointment as ADC in November 1955, arguing for the removal of Glubb and a break with Britain. James Morris has painted a vivid portrait of the king and his ADC:

Hussein was not a very brilliant young man. Sometimes, when he appeared during these anxious months, his face looked old and creased, his eyes were tired, his body was tense and thin, and he seemed the very embodiment of a struggling conscience, of a man trying hard to do his best. Ali Abu Nuwar, on the other hand, was almost a parody of the evil counsellor: a saturnine, beak-nosed Iago, his eyebrows bushy, his moustache sneaky, his grin gleaming but forced, the sort of face you sometimes see, peering through silken draperies, in the shaded backgrounds of Japanese prints. This unsavoury partnership presently sparked an explosion.[5]

While Abu Nuwar was influential, a more important link between Hussein and the Free Officers was his cousin and childhood friend Zaid bin Shaker. During this period, Shaker was Hussein's closest confidant. This intimate relationship provoked jealousy on the part of Queen Zain and her brother Sharif Nasser. They tried to discredit Zaid by suggesting that he was a Ba'thist and by questioning his loyalty to the monarchy. But Zaid was completely devoted to the king and shared his aspirations for the country and for the Arab Legion.[6] The decision to dismiss Glubb belonged to the king alone, but it was made against a background of rising tension between the British commander-in-chief and the young nationalist officers. Things came to a head on 28 February 1956 when Hussein was presented by the prime minister with papers containing the names of those officers whom Glubb wanted dismissed from the army. Hussein was shocked: he knew and respected some of the officers on the list. The only fault of these men, as far as he could see, was that they were nationalistic and ambitious. Hussein threw the papers on the table. "Tell Glubb Pasha I refuse to sign them," he said angrily.[7]

In the evening of that day, a crucial meeting took place in Shaker's house; present were the king and five of the Free Officers, led by Shaher Abu Shahut and Mahmud Ma'ayta. There the king disclosed for the first time his plan to get rid of Glubb. Hussein asked the officers whether they were ready to move, and they replied without any hesitation that they were. Hussein then asked them whether they were sure they could pull it off, and again they replied positively, encouraging him to proceed.[8] At the end of the meeting Hussein gave the order to execute "Operation Dunlop." Speed and secrecy were of the essence. Three people in particular, Hussein instructed Shaker, had to be kept in ignorance. One was Bahjat Talhouni, the chief of the royal court, who, despite his poor English, was a client of the British and therefore likely to tip them off. Another was Queen Zain, who was expected to interfere with the plan because she saw Glubb and the British as the guarantors of the Hashemite throne. The third was Sharif Nasser, who was certain to tell the British and to try to foil the plot.[9]

Hussein also felt that Operation Dunlop had to be executed swiftly and decisively, so as to deny Glubb's allies the chance to rally to his support. The Arab Legion was divided into Bedouin regiments, recruited from the rural areas, and the Hadari regiments, recruited mostly from the urban areas. Glubb favoured the Bedouins because he thought they made better soldiers and were less interested in politics. He did a great deal to educate and train these Bedouin recruits and to help their families, and his bodyguard consisted of Bedouins from the areas bordering on Iraq and Saudi Arabia. They were fiercely loyal to him personally, and there was a real risk that they might try to stage a counter-coup to restore him. Various precautions were taken to ensure that this did not happen. Glubb's house was surrounded with armoured cars, his telephone lines were cut, and loyal troops were stationed on the way to the airport. The British officers were confined to their quarters, and their telephone lines were also severed.

The next morning, 1 March 1956, the king put on his uniform and drove to the office of the prime minister, followed by Land Rovers containing his escort of armed soldiers. Hussein slapped a handwritten piece of paper on the prime minister's desk, ordering the dismissal of Glubb and the relieving of several other senior British officers of their command. "These are my wishes," he said, "and I want them executed at once." Samir Rifa'i was stunned, but he realized that things had moved so far that the king could not back down.[10] Rifa'i summoned the cabinet at once and informed them of the royal edict. The ministers were equally stunned, but after some discussion they decided to carry out the king's orders. Falah Madadhah, the minister of the interior, was instrumental in bringing his colleagues to the point of decision. He pointed out to them that the soldiers they saw outside had been sent by the king to ensure that they exiled Glubb. Rifa'i then summoned the British ambassador, Charles Duke, to break the news to him. Rifa'i apologetically explained to the ambassador that the cabinet had not been consulted and that the royal order was an ultimatum. Although Rifa'i obeyed, he distanced himself and the cabinet from the affair by telling the ambassador that the king seemed to be going mad.[11]

At two o'clock Rifa'i summoned Glubb himself and, somewhat apologetically, gave him his marching orders. Glubb did not question the legality of the royal order, only the undignified haste with which it was being carried out. Rifa'i asked Glubb to leave the country by four. Glubb replied, "No, sir, I have lived here for twenty-six years and I cannot leave at two hours' notice." They compromised on seven o'clock the next morning. At the appointed hour Glubb was driven to the airport with full honours in the royal car but also under heavy armed guard. At the airport there was one of those curious scenes that abound in Britain's imperial history. The lord chamberlain handed Glubb a small gift from the king: a photograph of Hussein with the hand-written dedication "With our acknowledgements of the good services and untiring exertion, and with our best wishes for His Excellency Glubb

Pasha." It was an old Harrow school custom to give farewell photographs to your parting friends, and Hussein's good public-school
manners had not deserted him in the crisis. At a deeper level, however,
the deed was "a clang in the dirge for a dying empire."[12]

Despite the early warnings, Glubb's dismissal caught the British by
surprise, and they moved very swiftly to try to reverse it. Anthony Eden
was in a state of shock at the news and his reaction was almost hysterical. In the late afternoon of 1 March, at Eden's instruction, Duke went to
see the king to demand an explanation. The king began by telling the
ambassador that his action did not affect Jordan's long-standing friendship with Britain. Duke interjected that, on the contrary, it was a sharp
blow to this friendship. The king replied that it would not prove so in
the long run. He went on to complain about inadequate ammunition
stocks, deficiencies in the assignment of officers in the legion and
Glubb's failure to help him fight the Egyptian propaganda attacks. He
concluded by saying that he felt bound to do what he considered essential to preserve the honour of his kingdom.[13]

Eden was not satisfied with these explanations. They were no
excuse, he thought, for suddenly dismissing Glubb like a pilfering servant. He therefore instructed Duke to see the king again as soon as possible in order to deliver a message: that his action was inexplicable to
the British ministers, who had met that morning to discuss the events
in Jordan, and a severe blow to the confidence on which the good relations between their countries had been based. The king was urged to
take immediate action to remedy the situation.[14] To Hussein the message sounded like a threat. At one o'clock in the morning Duke called
the royal court and insisted on seeing the king, who had already gone to
bed. The meeting took place in the small study of the Basman Palace.
The atmosphere was demonstrably tense. Duke had in his hand a message from London. "I must advise you, sir," he said, "that Her Majesty's
Government feels that, unless you change your decision immediately
on this matter, unless Glubb Pasha is permitted to continue his work
here and we are given a chance to clear this whole matter up, the consequences could be very serious as far as you yourself, the monarchy"—
he hesitated—"and the whole future of Jordan is concerned."

The message from Eden angered Hussein because Glubb had been an
employee of the Jordanian government, not of the British government,
and in dismissing him he had merely exercised his constitutional pre-

rogative, as Glubb himself was the first to acknowledge. Hussein therefore rejected Duke's threat robustly and vehemently. In his memoirs he recorded his reaction: "I know my country, and I know my responsibilities. I am going to carry out what I believe to be right in the best way I can." Duke did not respond, so Hussein added, "I believe, Mr. Duke, that what I have done is for the good of my country and I am not going to alter my decision, regardless of any consequences. I would rather lose my life than change my mind. The monarchy belongs to the people, I belong to this country, and I know that I am doing this for the best, come what may."[15]

In the days that followed, Hussein and his officials repeatedly stressed to Duke that their policy remained unchanged and that they did not wish to mar the close and friendly relations between Jordan and Britain. They argued that Glubb's removal and the Arabization of the army did not constitute a departure from this policy. Hussein continued to view Britain as an ally and a true friend of Jordan.[16]

Public opinion in Britain was exercised not over the Jordanian decision but only over the manner of Glubb's dismissal. Public anger about what was seen as the shabby treatment of him was magnified by the romantic aura that surrounded him as a latter-day Lawrence of Arabia. Glubb himself, to his credit, took a more detached view of the whole affair. During a visit to Chequers, Glubb was the voice of tolerant realism. He advised Eden to make allowance for the young king, to be patient with Jordan and to do what he could to mend the damage to the relations between the two countries.[17] Sir Alec Kirkbride, another old Jordan hand, begged his colleagues in the Foreign Office not to overreact. In the end these counsels prevailed; the policy-makers in London swallowed their pride and took no punitive action. The British officers on secondment to the Arab Legion were withdrawn, but those, like Glubb, under contract to the Jordanian government were allowed to stay. The Anglo–Jordanian treaty remained in force, as did the British subsidy of about £12 million per year. Hussein's successful defiance of Britain's rulers enhanced his reputation as the Lion of Jordan.

Although the immediate crisis over "L'affaire Glubb" subsided, it inevitably had longer-term repercussions. Eden was convinced, on the basis of no evidence whatsoever, that Nasser had engineered the whole affair. For him Glubb's dismissal amounted to a resounding British diplomatic defeat at the hands of the Egyptian leader. Anthony Nutting, the minister of state for foreign affairs, later wrote that 1 March 1956 was the day Eden fatally resolved that "the Egyptian dictator" had to be toppled—that otherwise he would destroy Britain's position in the Middle East and his own position as the prime minister.[18] Glubb's dismissal may thus have had the unintended consequence of launching the paranoid British leader on the road that led to the Suez war eight months later.

In fact, Nasser knew nothing about the dismissal of Glubb until the Englishman left the country. The British foreign secretary, Selwyn Lloyd, was visiting Cairo and Dr. Mahmud Fawzi, the Egyptian foreign minister, hosted a dinner for him on 1 March. At the dinner President Nasser made some critical comments about Glubb, giving him as an example of the conservative forces in the Middle East who were out of touch with the progressive elements there. Lloyd was due to have a second meeting with Nasser at his home at nine o'clock the next morning. Just as Lloyd's car was drawing up in front of the house, Mohamed Heikal, Nasser's friend and confidant, called to report that Glubb had been fired. At first Nasser thought that Heikal was joking. It never occurred to him that the sacking was done on King Hussein's initiative. He assumed it had been a British move and that the timing was chosen as a gesture of goodwill to coincide with Lloyd's visit to Cairo. The subject came up at the beginning of the meeting and Nasser remarked, "It's good isn't it?" Lloyd went red in the face and demanded to know what was good about it. Nasser replied in all innocence that it showed that Britain at last understood that out-of-date figures like Glubb could no longer serve a useful purpose in the area. The look on his interlocutor's face made it clear to Nasser that they were talking at cross-purposes. After Lloyd left, Heikal called again. This time Nasser was laughing. "It's absurd," he said. "He thinks that we engineered the Glubb business, that we knew about it before the dinner started and that it was done deliberately to humiliate him."[19]

From Hussein's personal and from Jordan's national point of view, the removal of Glubb and of his senior aides was a masterly political stroke. The risks were enormous, including the possible downfall of the house of Hashem. But so was the prize for success. The ousting of the British officers powerfully boosted Hussein's popularity, and it gave his people a new sense of pride, a feeling that their army was now an Arab army that received its orders from its supreme Arab commander. As the

American ambassador to Amman noted, "The action has gone far toward removing Jordan's defensive position and inferiority complex vis-à-vis the Arab states. King is now hero and no longer puppet."[20] The twenty-one-year-old king had taken on the British Empire and won. The outburst of popular enthusiasm that followed was without precedent in the history of the Hashemite monarchy. In the words of one eyewitness, "From the drama of Glubb's dismissal King Hussein scored a brief brilliant triumph. The populace flocked to him. During three days [of] public celebration his hilltop palace in Amman was thronged about with joyful delegations from every corner of the land. The applause was tumultuous, delirious."[21] The crowds, "responsive to each breath of the political breeze, suddenly became passionately royalist."[22]

But the surge of popularity was less important than the fact of gaining control of the Arab Legion, identifying it as a national army and thus refuting the opposition charges against it.[23] Major-General Radi Innab, an elderly career officer, was immediately appointed by Hussein as chief of staff. Ali Abu Nuwar was promoted in one step from lieutenant-colonel to major-general, and, on 24 May, he took over from Radi Innab as chief of staff. The army's name was changed from the Arab Legion, a British designation, to the Jordanian Arab Army. Hussein had displayed great courage in securing control over the army, and, in so doing, also secured the loyalty and support of the nationalist Jordanian officers, which was to prove crucial for the survival of the Hashemite monarchy in the next two turbulent decades. In this respect he was much more far-sighted than his mother, who continued to regard the British as the guardians of the throne against the rising tide of Arab nationalism. But the move that brought Hussein so much popularity at home and in the Arab world also exposed him to danger from those who aided him in his move against Glubb.

For a while Hussein continued to bask in the after-glow of his successful coup. But the sudden departure of the British officers left a political, military and administrative vacuum that could not be filled easily. In his attempt to remedy this, Hussein had to experiment and inevitably he made some mistakes. The coup enhanced not only his self-confidence but also his innate propensity for taking risks. If before the fall of the British proconsul Hussein had suffered from lack of confidence, after the liberation he may have suffered from over-confidence. Hussein was basically an impetuous and unpredictable character, given to mood swings that sometimes translated into erratic behaviour and inconsistent policies. He was not a strategist who first charted a long-term course and then pursued it steadily and systematically; he tended to wait upon events, to rely on his intuition and sharp political instincts, and to make decisions on the hoof. There was also something of the gambler in him. Consequently his conduct of both domestic and foreign policy over the following year was not always consistent or coherent.

The main trend in Jordanian affairs in 1956 was the movement away from the influence of Britain and the progressive alignment with the views and policies of Egypt and Syria. This manifested itself in domestic politics as well as in external relations but especially in military affairs. It was sustained by the popular desire—fostered by Egyptian propaganda and example—to be free of Western influence; the ambitions of the nationalist officers eager for high command; and the aspiration of Hussein to cut a figure on the Arab stage. But the persistent deadlock over Palestine was perhaps the greatest single factor. On the one hand, Nasser's acquisition of arms from the Soviet bloc had enabled him to pose as the standard-bearer in the prospective reconquest of the "usurped homeland" and won over the Jordanian public to his side. On the other, the treaty with Britain was viewed by the Jordanian public as an anachronism because it gave them no protection against Israeli raids along the frontier and impeded any design for aggressive action.[24]

Jordan's continuing economic dependence on Britain inevitably restricted its freedom of action in foreign affairs. The most immediate problem was the British subsidy to the Arab Legion, which everyone expected would now be withdrawn. On 12 March, Egypt, Syria and Saudi Arabia volunteered to replace the British subsidy for ten years. Hussein knew that the offer was made with the aim of supplanting British influence, and he had his doubts about the reliability of his new allies. So he countered by accepting their offer only as an addition to the British subsidy. There were conflicting pressures at work. The British and the Americans encouraged Hussein to seek closer ties with Iraq. The nationalist officers encouraged him to move towards closer economic and military unity with Egypt and Syria. Hussein tried to prevent Jordan from being torn between the two blocs by a series of visits to Arab capitals. In his travels abroad, he enjoyed a warmer welcome in Cairo and Damascus than he did in Baghdad. The difficulty lay in translating promises into cash and summit communiqués into concrete action.

At home Hussein began to experiment with liberal ideas but his ultimate intentions were surrounded by uncertainty. At the end of May he got rid of Samir Rifa'i and replaced him with Said al-Mufti, who was described by the British ambassador as "a bibulous nonentity whose chief attribute was a desire to avoid responsibility and who was thus well fitted to occupy the role of non-governing Prime Minister for which he had been cast by the King." The king made the decision to dissolve parliament and hold free elections in the autumn on his own. After only a month in office Mufti was replaced by Ibrahim Hashem, "an elderly and enfeebled gentleman, who considered his only function to be to act strictly as a caretaker for the period of four months until the elections." During the interregnum, however, it was not at all clear that elections would be held. Many believed that the king might opt to suspend the constitution and establish an authoritarian regime with the support of the army rather than risk the emergence of an extremist parliament.[25]

During the summer attention shifted from domestic affairs to the rising tension along the border with Israel and to Britain's dispute with Egypt over the Suez Canal. Nasser's nationalization of the canal on 26 July sent shock waves throughout the Arab world. Hussein sent a telegram of congratulations to Nasser. Public opinion in Jordan overwhelmingly identified with Nasser in his struggle against the West, and opposition groups declared their strong support for his move. Nasser articulated the widely shared grievances against Britain and France, and inspired a sense of Arab pride and a feeling of popular participation in the campaign against their former colonial overlords. Given the intensity with which his people reacted to the crisis, Hussein had no choice but to join in the general Arab applause for Nasser. Whether Hussein liked it or not, the canal crisis thus ended up by providing a powerful boost to the domestic opposition parties in the lead-up to the general elections.

So did the rapidly deteriorating security situation along the border between Jordan and Israel. The renewed tension was caused by Palestinian refugees who went on murder and sabotage missions into Israel. Glubb's departure marked a turning point in this respect. Although

Glubb had had a strict and unswerving policy of doing everything possible to stop Palestinian infiltration across the armistice line, his successors were much more tolerant of infringements of the 1949 armistice agreement. According to an Israeli intelligence report, Egypt and Syria began to sponsor guerrilla activities from Jordan's territory in the autumn of 1955. These were clandestine because their organizers saw them not just as a means of hurting Israel but also as a way of destabilizing the Jordanian regime. In April 1956, after the departure of Glubb, the Jordanian authorities began to play a part in organizing these groups of irregulars, known as *fedayeen*, or "self-sacrificers," for terrorist attacks on Israel. The army assisted a group of about seventy fedayeen who had arrived from the Gaza Strip and also formed its own groups of irregulars along the border with Israel.[26]

The Israeli authorities insisted that Jordan was responsible for all hostile acts emanating from its territory, regardless of whether they were committed by regular or irregular forces. They used these acts to justify military reprisals on an ever-growing scale. Three separate attacks were launched by the IDF against Jordanian police stations in September, leaving 55 dead in their wake. On 10 October, in retaliation for the murder of two farmers, the IDF mounted a massive attack, with artillery and tanks, on the police station in Qalqilyah. The operation, which was commanded by Ariel Sharon, raised the level of casualties to a new height: 18 Israelis were killed and 68 wounded; 88 Jordanians were killed and 15 wounded. It was the most serious clash between Israel and the Arabs since the First Arab–Israeli War of 1948, and the end result of the Israeli policy of "an eye for an eyelash."

Hussein was distraught. He immediately invoked the Anglo–Jordanian treaty and asked for air support, but all he achieved was a British warning to Israel. He had to look for help in other directions. His previous appeals for military help from Iraq had been turned down. But on 11 October, the day after the Qalqilyah attack, Nuri as-Said, the Iraqi prime minister, decided to begin to transfer a division into Jordan four days later. The British chargé promptly notified Israel of the Iraqi decision and warned that his country would be obliged to side with Jordan in the event of Israeli aggression. The Israel government issued a public statement that Iraq's proposed move into Jordan constituted a direct threat to Israel's security. Hussein became alarmed at the danger of an imminent Israeli attack on his country. So on 15 October he asked that the division be held on the Iraqi side of the border but be readied to enter Jordan upon request. War between Israel and Jordan was avoided, but Jordan remained exposed and vulnerable.[27]

The Israelis hoped that Jordan would refrain from joining either Iraq or the Egyptian-led bloc. The British consul-general in Jerusalem emphasized to an Israeli official that the Iraqi Army posed no threat to Israel and that it would enter Jordan only to prevent the disintegration of the country.[28] From their other sources too the Israelis concluded that Iraq's main objective in sending troops would be to prevent Egypt from gaining control over Jordan, and at a later stage to make Jordan join the Baghdad Pact. What was not clear to the Israelis was for how long Jordan would be able to survive as an independent country between the two rival blocs. By preserving its freedom to react to Iraqi troop deployments in Jordan, Israel intended to signal to Hussein that he was running the risk of the destruction of the Hashemite Kingdom of Jordan.[29]

It was a warning that Hussein could not afford to ignore. The best option left to him was to turn to Egypt, Syria and Saudi Arabia for economic and military assistance to help Jordan cope with the threat from Israel. Accordingly, he initiated intensive contacts with these neighbouring Arab countries, and these led to closer coordination and unity. Small quantities of arms were obtained, as well as a financial contribution towards the maintenance of the National Guard.

The border war with Israel thus had a two-fold effect. First, it accelerated the trend in Jordan's foreign policy away from the reliance on Britain and Iraq and towards Egypt and Syria. Second, the border war radicalized further the opposition groups inside Jordan and prompted them to adopt an even more militant anti-Israeli and anti-imperialist stand in the lead-up to the general elections. Many of their candidates resorted to slogans about recovering "the usurped part of the homeland."[30]

The growing popular hostility towards Israel and the open calls by some of his Palestinian subjects for war on Israel, together with Israel's devastating military attacks, created serious internal problems for his regime. One was that the inhabitants of the border areas began to migrate to the cities to escape Israel's wrath. At a loss to know what to do, Hussein summoned Samir Rifa'i to seek his advice. Rifa'i recommended removing the National Guard from the border areas and replacing it with the army. He also suggested direct talks with the Israelis with the aim of reaching an informal agreement in the first instance. Rifa'i himself had had extensive first-hand experience of such talks as an aide to King Abdullah. He now suggested making contact with suitable Israelis whom he had met in the past. According to Israel's Jordanian informer, Hussein agreed and said he was prepared to accompany Rifa'i to a secret meeting with Israeli representatives in Europe or America or Iraq.[31]

There was no immediate follow-up to the suggestion of a face-to-face meeting with Israel, but Rifa'i planted the seed of what became one of the dominant ideas of Hussein's reign: dialogue across the battle lines. Already at this early stage it is possible to detect the beginning of an understanding on Hussein's part that Israel could be either his ultimate threat or his ultimate ally. The legacy of his grandfather pointed in the direction of a tacit alliance. King Abdullah had a closer understanding, based on a perception of common interests, and a more intimate political relationship with Israel than he did with any of his fellow Arab rulers. It was too soon for King Hussein at this stage in his career to follow in his grandfather's footsteps, but he was already reflecting on the advantages of contact and compromise with his belligerent Western neighbour.

In another private conversation earlier that year with Sir Alec Kirkbride, Hussein revealed a surprisingly moderate attitude towards Israel. He said he understood Israel's difficulty in taking back Palestinian refugees but thought that it ought to pay compensation to those who had left property behind—roughly 30 percent of the total. Hussein estimated that, if given a choice between compensation and repatriation, no more than 10 percent would opt for repatriation, and the majority of those would probably not stay there for more than six months. Hussein talked only about the refugee problem; he did not even mention the other key issue in the Arab–Israeli dispute—borders. But Kirkbride had the impression that Hussein, and those among his advisers who wanted Jordan to survive as an independent country, realized that this depended to a large extent on a settlement with Israel.[32] Hussein's emergence as an Arab nationalist was thus combined with traditional Hashemite moderation and pragmatism on the subject of the Jewish state.

6. The Liberal Experiment

The dismissal of Glubb was only the first of two exceptionally important decisions made by Hussein in 1956: the second was to hold free elections in the autumn. On the wisdom of holding the promised elections, Hussein's advisers were divided. The old guard warned that elections could risk the rise to power of the leftist, pro-Nasser parties, who would create instability and proceed to challenge the monarchy. In his memoirs Hussein explained the thinking that led him to disregard this warning and to come down on the side of reform and change:

I take full responsibility for that period of experiment. I had felt deeply that for too long Jordanian political leaders had relied on outside help, and it was only natural that these politicians should meet with bitter opposition from the younger, rising men of ambition, who, like myself, thought it was time to throw off external shackles.

I had decided, therefore, that younger and promising politicians and Army officers should have a chance to show their mettle. I realized that many were very leftist, but I felt that even so most of them must genuinely believe in the future of their country, and I wanted to see how they would react to responsibility.[1]

Jordan went to the polls on 21 October for the first truly free election in the history of the country. This was also the first election that was based more on political parties than on individuals. It did not follow, however, that the political parties had clear ideological positions or that the political process was essentially an inter-party contest. Everything in Jordanian politics revolved round money and patronage. The parties provided flexible frameworks to facilitate cooperation between individuals, especially at election time. There were also debates and divisions inside parties, especially on the left. Changing party for personal advantage was a common occurrence. The results were as follows:

Right-wing:	Islamic Liberation	1
	Muslim Brotherhood	4
Left-wing:	National Socialist	12
	National Front (Communist)	3
	Ba'th	2
Centre:	Independent	10
	Arab Constitutional	8

These results represent a remarkable victory for the left-wing opposition parties, who wanted to abrogate Jordan's treaty with Britain and to substitute for it military pacts with Egypt and Syria. The largest of these parties was the National Socialist Party (NSP). It captured 12 out of the 40 seats of the lower house, even though its leader, Suleiman Nabulsi, narrowly failed in his bid for a seat. Nabulsi (1910–76) was born in Salt and educated at the American University of Beirut, which, despite its name, was the intellectual stronghold of pan-Arabism. He went into politics at a relatively young age and gained a reputation as an outspoken critic of the monarchy and a fiery Arab nationalist. The party that he formed in 1954 aimed to liberate politics from the control of the palace, and to work for greater equality at home and Arab unity abroad. Nabulsi was an admirer of Nasser and the leader of the opposition to the king's bid to take Jordan into the Baghdad Pact. He was not a communist, but he wanted to distance Jordan from the conservative Arab states.

The question in everybody's mind was: how would the king react to the verdict of the electorate? After some serious reflection, the king decided to be relaxed and accept the situation. At that time he had to contend with external pressures: he was courting the radical Arab states, and he was seeking the support of his Palestinian subjects. Precisely because of his radical Arab pedigree, Nabulsi could be instrumental in achieving these ends. The king therefore invited him, as the leader of the largest party, to form a government. (Jordan's constitution did not require ministers to be members of parliament.) "Nabulsi was a leftist," Hussein noted, "but even so I felt he had to have his chance."[2] Hussein did this in the face of strong opposition from Zain. One contemporary observer saw Hussein's decision to bring Nabulsi and the National Socialists to power as the beginning of his rebellion against his mother: "She was a traditionalist and the king was toying with adventurous, liberal and nationalist ideas and people. Queen Zain had been ruling the country, telling Hussein whom to appoint to this and that post. She began to lose her power when Hussein started making his own decisions."[3] Whereas the decision to dismiss Glubb had been taken behind Zain's back, the appointment of Nabulsi was made in open defiance of her. It marked a further step in Hussein's political coming-of-age.

Even before Nabulsi assumed office, Hussein made another dramatic move to establish his credentials as an Arab nationalist. On 24 October he signed an agreement in Amman with Egypt and Syria, providing for a joint command of the armed forces of the three countries under the Egyptian commander-in-chief Major-General Abdel Hakim Amer. Amer and General Tawfiq Nizamuddin, the Syrian chief of staff, were guests of honour at the opening of the new parliament by the monarch the following day. Two days later Nabulsi was appointed prime minister, and he also assumed the foreign affairs portfolio. Hussein gave Nabulsi a free hand to form his own cabinet. The result was a coalition that included three independents, one communist and one member of the extremely pro-Syrian Ba'th Arab Socialist Party. Abdullah Rimawi, the leader of the Ba'th, was given the relatively humble post of minister of state for foreign affairs. But he was the most outspoken anti-royalist in the government and exercised disproportionate influence through his alliance with Nabulsi's more extreme ministers and with some of the Free Officers in the army. He openly proclaimed his opposition to Jordanian independence and called for its merger with Syria. He was reputed to make frequent trips to Damascus and to return with suitcases full of money.[4] Not a single Hashemite loyalist was included in the cabinet.

Failure to win a majority in the Chamber of Deputies weakened the position of the new prime minister and made it more difficult for him to impose his authority on his argumentative colleagues. Nevertheless, during his short period in power, Nabulsi acted as a relatively free agent. He interpreted the 1952 constitution literally and held himself responsible to parliament, not to the palace. His government, for the first time in Jordan's history, considered itself, rather than the king, as the principal decision-maker. The programme of the government reflected faithfully the electoral platforms of its constituent parts. The two main planks were to distance Jordan from Britain and to move closer to the radical Arab states. Hussein initially went along with this programme. The Amman pact for a unified military command fitted perfectly into this programme.

What the Jordanians did not know was that their conclusion of the new defence pact with Egypt coincided with a conspiracy between Britain, France and Israel to attack Egypt. Thus, on the eve of the Suez War, Jordan was in the curious position of having defence pacts with one of the villains as well as with the victim of what in Arab political discourse was usually referred to as *al-adwan al-thulathi*, or "the tripartite aggression." The timing of the Amman pact was singularly propitious for Israel. Israel's powerful propaganda machine was able to portray the military pact between its Arab neighbours to the north, east and south as a ring of steel justifying a pre-emptive attack. In reality, the Arab alliance was little more than a paper pact with no mechanism for creating an integrated command structure. In addition, Israel was trying to divert attention from its preparations to attack Egypt by deliberately raising the level of tension on the Jordanian front. The Amman pact contributed to the success of this strategic deception plan by focusing international attention on the Jordanian–Israeli conflict. More importantly, and to the evident satisfaction of the Israeli chief of staff, up to the last minute the general staffs of the Arab armies believed that Israel's intention was to march on Jordan.[5]

It was Anthony Eden, however, who got Britain into this hopeless tangle. The road to Suez began when the neurotic prime minister declared a personal war on Nasser following the dismissal of Glubb. Relations between Egypt and the West deteriorated further when America withdrew its offer to finance the building of the Aswan Dam. Nasser retaliated on 26 July 1956, the fourth anniversary of the Free Officers' Revolution, by announcing the nationalization of the Suez Canal—a potent symbol of Western colonial domination. Though not illegal, this action convinced Eden that force would have to be used to remove Nasser from power. Eden was adamant that Nasser must not be permitted to have "his thumb on our windpipe." Because Dwight D. Eisenhower was equally convinced that force must not be used, Eden resorted to the famous collusion with the Israelis and the French that paved the way to the tripartite attack on Egypt in October 1956. Israel got on the bandwagon of this colonial-style war at a later stage. The French were the match-makers between Britain and Israel. Like Eden, they saw the canal crisis as a replay of the 1930s, and, like him, they were determined that this time there must be no appeasement. They had another cause for complaint against "Hitler on the Nile," as they called President Nasser—his support for the Algerian rebels against the French Army. France's generals at that time had only three priorities—Algeria, Algeria and Algeria. They calculated that if Nasser could be put in his place, the Algerian rebellion would collapse. Although each country had its own motives, the aim that united them was to knock Nasser off his perch.

For Israel's leaders the overthrow of Nasser and the defeat of his army were the primary aims but Jordan featured in their thinking as a possible secondary target. Their view of Jordan was in a state of flux. With King Abdullah they had had a solid strategic partnership that had stood the test of time and brought rich rewards. Consequently, support for the survival of the Hashemite monarchy in Jordan became a basic tenet of Israeli defence policy. As a result of Hussein's apparent shift from the conservative to the radical Arab camp, however, this policy began to be reassessed. There were serious doubts about the capacity of the Hashemite Kingdom of Jordan to preserve its independence and territorial integrity against its covetous neighbours. At the same time, Israeli leaders were developing their own designs for territorial expansion at Jordan's expense. David Ben-Gurion recorded in his diary that Moshe Dayan, the chief of staff, was "in favour of reaching an agreement with the English regarding the whole of the Middle East, destroying Nasser and partitioning Jordan between us and Iraq."[6] This was completely outside the realm of possibility. Ben-Gurion, however, warmed to the idea and developed it into a comprehensive plan for a new political order in the Middle East. Although he admitted that this big plan might sound fantastic at first, he returned to it time and again in his diary and tried to sell it to his French co-conspirators in the course of plotting the attack on Egypt.

The tripartite collusion took place in a private villa in Sèvres on the outskirts of Paris from 22 to 24 October. At the first meeting with the

French leaders, before the arrival of Selwyn Lloyd, the reluctant British representative, Ben-Gurion presented his big plan for the reorganization of the Middle East to the French hosts. Jordan, he said, was not viable as an independent state and should therefore be divided. Iraq would get the East Bank in return for a promise to settle the Palestinian refugees there and to make peace with Israel, while the West Bank would be attached to Israel as a semi-autonomous region. Lebanon suffered from having a large Muslim population, which was concentrated in the south. The problem could be solved by Israel's expansion up to the Litani River, thereby helping to turn Lebanon into a more compact Christian state. The Suez Canal area should be given an international status, while the Straits of Tiran in the Gulf of Aqaba should come under Israeli control to ensure freedom of navigation. A prior condition for realizing this plan was the elimination of Nasser and the replacement of his regime with a pro-Western government that would also be prepared to make peace with Israel.[7]

Whether fantastic or not, this plan is highly revealing of Ben-Gurion's inner thoughts about Israel, the European powers and the Arab world. It revealed his craving for an alliance with the imperialist powers against the forces of Arab nationalism; it exposed an uninhibited desire to expand by force at the expense of his neighbours and to expand in every possible direction—north, east and south; and it exhibited a cavalier attitude towards the independence, sovereignty and territorial integrity of the Arab states in general and of Jordan in particular. Lebanon and Egypt were to lose some of their territory, and Jordan was to be snuffed out completely. A British official named Sir John Troutbeck once described King Abdullah as "a born land-grabber," but the term fitted Israel's founding father equally well. Far from Jordan threatening Israel's security, it was Ben-Gurion and his belligerent chief of staff who were plotting to dismember the Hashemite Kingdom of Jordan and to divide up the spoils with the Hashemites of Iraq.

The outcome of the secret deliberations in the suburban villa was recorded in a three-page document that came to be known as "The Protocol of Sèvres"; only the Israeli copy survived. This document constitutes the smoking gun of the conspiracy to attack Egypt. It makes the meeting at Sèvres the best-documented war plot in history. Most of its clauses detail the series of steps by which war was to be instigated: an Israeli strike against Egypt, an Anglo-French ultimatum to the combatants to withdraw from the Canal Zone and allied intervention following the inevitable Egyptian rejection of the ultimatum. Jordan, however, also features in the protocol. If Israel were to attack Jordan, Britain would have been obliged to go to Jordan's rescue under the terms of their treaty. For Eden this was the nightmare scenario. Article V tried to reconcile these conflicting commitments. Israel undertook not to attack Jordan during the period of operations against Egypt. But in the event of a Jordanian attack on Israel, Britain undertook not to come to the aid of Jordan.[8] The decks were now cleared for tripartite aggression against Egypt.

Israel launched its attack on the Egyptian forces in the Sinai Peninsula in the early hours of 29 October. Jordan was taken by complete surprise. A state of emergency was immediately declared. Hussein sent a telegram of support to Nasser. Hussein was nearly hysterical with anger and could hardly contain his rage. "During this crucial time," he said in a radio broadcast, "our nation is facing on the dear land of Egypt an unjust attack by the oppressive Zionism and tyrant Judaism, ally of evil and enemy of peace." General Amer, the commander-in-chief of the three armies, issued a mobilization order to the Syrian and Jordanian units associated with what came to be known as "Operation Beisan." The plan envisaged a rapid armoured thrust across Israel's most vulnerable point, its "wasp waist" from the West Bank to the Mediterranean. This was intended to relieve some of the pressure on the Egyptian forces in the south. Hussein pressed for the immediate execution of General Amer's order, but he met with resistance from Ali Abu Nuwar. The chief of staff considered it too risky to venture alone and counselled waiting until the arrival of the Syrian troops.[9]

Nabulsi had been prime minister for less than a week when called upon to face a crisis of the greatest magnitude. The king asked him to support Egypt by opening a second front against Israel. Although Nabulsi was "a leftist," to use the king's word, he refused a direct order from the king to launch a military offensive against Israel. The government was divided. Some of its members argued that opening a front in the war from the Jordanian side would lead to a break with the West and expose the country to the risk of invasion by the Jews. Others thought that it was necessary to consult with Syria and to contact Iraq in order to make a united stand.[10] These differences were bridged by a formula that said that Jordan's first duty to the Arab cause was to defend its own frontiers. Nabulsi himself came down on the side of caution. He was aware of Jordan's military weakness. He knew that the Jordanian troops were no match for the Israelis. He had his doubts about the reliability of the Syrians, and he was altogether opposed to the entry of Iraqi troops into Jordan. Finally, he also took seriously Britain's warning that it would not come to Jordan's aid if Jordan attacked Israel.

The memoirs of Anwar al-Khatib, the minister of public works in Nabulsi's government, throw additional light on the discussions of the cabinet and on the positions of the principal protagonists. He relates that Hussein was very eager to open a Jordanian front in order to relieve the pressure on the Egyptian Army. Hussein chaired a long meeting of the cabinet, accompanied by the new chief of staff, Abu Nuwar. The king opened the meeting by saying that they could not abandon Egypt to fight alone and that they had a duty to open a new front and to join in the fighting. The tone of his voice suggested that he was very determined. At this point Khatib asked the king to allow the chief of staff to give his assessment of the situation. Abu Nuwar began his survey with the following observations: "The Hebron district will fall into the hands of the enemy in the first twenty-four hours of the war because of the great difficulty of protecting it. After that the Nablus district will also fall. As for Jerusalem, we'll defend it to the last man and to the last drop of blood." After Abu Nuwar completed his survey, Khatib turned to the king and said, "Are we in a position to take on more refugees? Can we allow ourselves to lose more land after the loss of the land of Palestine? The picture presented to us by the commander of the army obliges us to behave sensibly and to wait. We all want to relieve the burden on Egypt, but our participation in this manner would only increase the load on Egypt and make it necessary for her to come to our aid while she herself is facing her ordeal." Nabulsi was torn by conflicting considerations: his sense of responsibility pointed in one direction, while his sense of solidarity inclined him towards participation in the struggle and in the fighting. The protracted deliberations ended with a decision to hold another meeting in the royal court to allow Salah Toukan, the minister of finance, to present an assessment by the Jordanian treasury and to consider whether it could bear the cost of war. This took place the following day, and when Toukan finished his report, the king looked crestfallen.[11]

The second stage of the war consisted of an Anglo-French attack on Egypt following its anticipated rejection of their ultimatum to withdraw from the canal. Collusion between the colonial powers and Israel was widely suspected at the time, and public opinion in Jordan was in a state of great agitation. Hussein was furious and thought he had been double-crossed by the British, as indeed he had, although the proof did not emerge until a decade later. Hussein sent a second telegram of support to Nasser. Charles Johnston, the new British ambassador to Amman, soon discovered that Hussein was "more resentful and distressed about our action over Suez than the most anti-British of his Ministers and subordinates."[12] In his fury, Hussein called Nasser and told him that he was ready to declare war on Israel. Nasser expressed his appreciation but declined the offer because he had already given his army the order to withdraw from Sinai. Hussein's anger was cooled only when Nasser begged him not to risk Jordan's army against overwhelming odds. The military position was hopeless, said Nasser, but he thought he might yet secure the withdrawal of the invading forces by diplomatic means.[13]

The desperate military situation led Nasser to countermand General Amer's initial order. On 1 November, while Egypt's airfields were being bombed by the allies, Amer issued new instructions to the Jordanian and Syrian chiefs of staff: "Halt the offensive preparations. Postpone Operation Beisan until further orders. Secure borders and prepare defenses against every possible invasion."[14] The majority of the ministers greeted the new order from Cairo with a sigh of relief. They had been under considerable strain since the outbreak of the crisis, with daily cabinet meetings, all of them dominated by the question of an eastern front. The ministers understood that the war between Israel and Egypt was now transformed into a much bigger one as a result of the intervention of Britain and France. Thus, according to Khatib's account, the cable from Cairo helped to calm the strained nerves and to settle the tense debate within Jordan.[15]

From his side of the hill, General Dayan noted that Jordan reinforced its defence system along the border with Israel and that every position that had formerly been manned by a company was now garrisoned by a battalion. "From the operational point of view, this move of Jordan is definitely defensive . . . It offers no sign of serious preparation for war."[16]

There is no way of knowing what might have happened had Hussein gone ahead and opened a second front against Israel. History does not reveal its alternatives. But it is arguable that Hussein's brave stand during the Suez crisis and his loyalty to Nasser greatly enhanced his credentials as an Arab nationalist, especially when compared with the more cautious approach of the leftist prime minister and chief of staff. Abu Nuwar claimed many years later that he had been ready to honour the terms of the new alliance with Egypt and Syria, and had prepared and positioned enough troops "to give the Israelis a very rough time." But "when Nasser said 'stop' and the King was urging me every minute to attack, I said 'no, Your Majesty, this would be suicide.' "[17] Hussein was young and impetuous, and he acted with a rush of sudden energy. He had the scent of battle in his nostrils and was bitterly disappointed by the attitude of his advisers. Prince Hassan recalls Hussein's frustration: "My brother wanted to make his own mark . . . he was thwarted by not having a confrontation in 1956."[18]

What the king did do was to invite the Syrian, Saudi and Iraqi governments to sent troops to reinforce Jordan's defences. In response to this request, a ragbag army of allies poured into Jordan, "each with different equipment, different methods, different orders and profoundly different motives."[19] The Syrian troops arrived on 4 November, but, to the great disappointment of the Jordanians, they were a disorderly mob, wholly unprepared for battle and probably more trouble than they were worth. The Saudi troops did not arrive until the fifteenth, long after the fighting had ended. The arrival of the Iraqis was the cause of the first row between the king and his prime minister. Nabulsi objected to the entry of Iraqi troops into Jordan on the grounds that Iraq was not a member of the Amman pact. The king made it clear to Nabulsi that the deployment of the Iraqi troops inside Jordan was a royal decision and that the cabinet had to accept it. Nabulsi replied that decisions of this kind were the prerogative of the cabinet, not the king. Nabulsi prevailed, and by the end of the month all the Iraqi troops had withdrawn from Jordan.[20]

With the British and French acceptance of the United Nations order for a ceasefire on 7 November, the Suez crisis subsided. The Jordanian government requested the withdrawal of all foreign troops, but only the Iraqis complied. Syrian and Saudi forces remained in the country after the military reasons for their presence had disappeared, creating the disturbing impression that they were simply positioning themselves to secure the best results in an eventual carve-up of Jordanian territory.[21] The Syrians soldiers continued to prove the most difficult of the foreign guests. According to one account, they started to bring their families, they took over the Jordan Army cantonment in Mafraq, and they gave the impression of intending to remain in the country permanently. Under the cover of Arab patriotism, they seemed to be preparing to grab what they could for themselves.[22] Whatever else it might have been, the Amman pact was not a serious threat to Israel's security.

The Suez War made a major change to the regional balance of power in the Middle East. America and Russia gradually replaced Britain and France as the dominant external players in the region. There were far-reaching consequences for Britain, for Jordan and for the relationship between the two. Suez marked the effective end of what Elizabeth Monroe called "Britain's moment in the Middle East." Britain alienated the Arab world by its aggression against Egypt and its collusion with France and Israel. A wave of anti-British feelings swept through the Arab world from North Africa to the Gulf.

One British diplomat suggested that the effects of the fiasco on ruling circles in Jordan were not as adverse as they were elsewhere in the Arab world. "To Jordanian eyes," he wrote, "Britain had often appeared in the past as a rather maddening nanny-figure in the Arab nursery. The Suez affair had proved that nanny was human after all and herself capable of the worst kind of naughtiness."[23] This assessment is amusing but unconvincing. The Jordanians took the Suez crisis much more seriously, and the damage to Britain's reputation there, both at the level of the political elite and at the level of the masses, was much deeper and more lasting than this flippant comment would suggest. One Arab history of Jordan in the twentieth century accurately describes the Suez War as one of the low points in its relations with Britain, comparable to the Palestine war. All Jordanians almost without exception, according to this history, regarded the tripartite aggression against Egypt as an aggression against themselves.[24]

There was an acute sense of betrayal at all levels of society, from the king downwards, and the political fallout from the war was impossible to contain. On 1 November parliament passed a resolution calling for the severance of diplomatic relations with France. Only the fear of bankruptcy deterred it from calling for a break in diplomatic relations with Britain too. On 20 November, however, parliament unanimously passed a resolution calling for the abrogation of the Anglo–Jordanian treaty and of an exchange of diplomatic representatives with Russia and China. The treaty was clearly doomed, but there was as yet no agreement on how to replace the subsidy it provided. Nabulsi wanted to delay the termination of the treaty until Arab funding could be secured. Hussein, on the other hand, wished to avoid dependence on Arab allies and made a determined bid to secure American financial support for Jordan. His aim was not Arab unity against the West but the replacement of one external patron and protector by another.

The first, secret approach to the Americans was made not by the king himself but by his chief of staff. On 9 November, Abu Nuwar requested from the American military attaché in Amman American economic and military aid to Jordan in "sufficient volume" to compensate for the imminent loss of British aid. If America put up the money and arms, Abu Nuwar said, communism would be prevented from dominating Jordan; he would dissolve parliament and take over the government: "I and the people of Jordan will follow US policies." He reiterated that he was strongly anti-communist, but he had to have aid; and if he did not get it from the United States, he would get it from the USSR.[25] Ten days later Hussein made a personal appeal for aid to the American ambassador, Lester Mallory. Mallory reported that "The two young men are changeable and impressionable." He was non-committal about aid and merely cautioned the "young men" about the dangers to Jordan of jumping from the frying pan into the fire.[26]

The American attitude towards the Hashemite Kingdom of Jordan up to this point had been one of benign neglect, seeing it as a British fiefdom, and in any case they were party to the widely held belief that King Hussein would not last on his throne for very long. He was therefore a potential liability rather than as an asset. A British diplomat recalled that the American assessment of Hussein during this period was "desperately negative." Hussein had been written off to the point that possible replacements were being discussed.[27]

Foreign Secretary Lloyd had his own doubts about Jordan's prospects of survival. He told John Foster Dulles, the US secretary of state, in December that the UK felt that the treaty with Jordan was of no further use and that "our money spent there is wasted, except that it may keep out worse money." Dulles asked, "What is the future of Jordan?" Lloyd replied, "I don't think it's got one." He then added, "Unless it becomes a little Satellite." He said he thought the king would go mad. Dulles was not especially alarmed at the prospect of Jordan becoming a Soviet satellite. He said that a non-contiguous satellite could be "pinched off" by the United States and the UK working together.[28] Worse was to follow later in the month. The British ambassador reported that, in Dulles's view, "the brutal fact was that Jordan had no justification as a state. This of course did not mean that now is the time to liquidate it."[29] Dulles could view the Middle East only through a cold war prism, and, consequently, he preferred to spend America's money on a country that might make a difference.

The British for their part were not only ready but eager to renegotiate their treaty with Jordan, not least because of budgetary constraints. After the dismissal of Glubb, the election of Nabulsi and the Suez débâcle, the subsidy had become a costly white elephant. The dilemma for the British was how to cut their losses without undermining the Hashemite state that they themselves had created in the aftermath of the First World War. The answer was to offer their ward up for adoption, and the most desirable candidate for parenthood was the United States of America. By a happy coincidence this was also the adoptive parent that Hussein had chosen for himself. Britain's and Hussein's efforts thus converged, without any coordination in trying to persuade the United States to assume the burden that Britain was about to shed. On 17 January 1957 the British ambassador spoke to Dulles and left him an *aide-mémoire* saying that Her Majesty's Government could not afford to continue indefinitely to give Jordan about £13 million a year and that it hoped the United States would be prepared to take over this commitment. The ambassador wished to point out that this was not a question of pulling a British chestnut out of the fire because no British chestnut was involved. Rather it was a matter for concern to the whole Western alliance that the Soviet Union might move into Jordan. Dulles immediately ruled out military assistance to Jordan, but he left open the possibility of economic assistance.[30]

For Hussein, time was running out. Washington's rejection of his urgent plea for aid in December came as a great disappointment. It left him no option but to go along with Nabulsi's efforts to find an Arab replacement for the British subsidy. Hussein went as the head of a ministerial delegation to Cairo, and, on 19 January, he signed an Arab solidarity agreement. Under its terms, Jordan was to receive £12.5 million per annum for ten years. Saudi Arabia and Egypt pledged £5 million per annum each, while Syria promised £2.5 million. The principal Jordanian protagonist of this agreement was Abdullah Rimawi, the Ba'thi minister of state for foreign affairs. Hussein expressed his deep gratitude to his three new patrons in public, but he was assailed by serious private doubts about their reliability. Britain reacted to the conclusion of the Arab solidarity agreement by requesting negotiations as soon as possible for termination of the Anglo–Jordanian treaty.

This was one of the low points of King Hussein's reign. For the first time since 1921, Jordan was to have no defence pact with a Western power. All the main pillars of strength of the Hashemite monarchy seemed to be crumbling—a Great Power guarantee, a united army and a loyal government. External threats compounded the problem. According to one Israeli source, British and American officials were talking frankly to the press about Jordan's vulnerability and lack of legitimacy in a manner that seemed calculated to prepare the ground for change. Against this background, the prospective visits of the Iraqi regent and of the Saudi monarch assumed particular significance because they represented the traditional contenders in the struggle for Jordan. The Israeli analyst considered it a real possibility that Jordan would be divided between Iraq and Saudi Arabia with the support of Britain and America.[31] The atmosphere of crisis was vividly captured by James Morris:

In the course of time King Hussein, now advancing into a stringy manhood, began to realize how unwelcome and how unfriendly were the jinns he had conjured . . . There were, of course, good arguments for the extinction of his monarchy and the absorption of Jordan in a wider Arab community: the State was unviable, the monarchy no longer commanded the loyalty of the majority, kings were out of date any way. Hashemite antecedents had lost their allure. Even the English, with their attachment to the regal and the nomadic, had lost interest in Jordan, and did not much care whether she sank, swam or blew the bubbles of desire. The Middle East surged with a yearning for unity and power, and to every Arab nationalist the useless little Jordanian monarchy seemed an irritating anachronism. The West, thwarted and divided by the Suez débâcle, was at the nadir of its prestige. Colonel Nasser, supported by the Russians, was rampant.[32]

The odds against the survival of the monarchy may have looked overwhelming but Hussein was not about to throw everything away. He was sustained by a firm belief in the manifest destiny of the Hashemite family that his grandfather had instilled in him. Nor did he stand alone in defence of the Hashemite regime. He received strong support and encouragement from his mother and uncle in what increasingly looked like a collective struggle for survival. Sharif Nasser persuaded his nephew to let him form a special Royal Guard contingent to safeguard the royal family.

Queen Zain, who had always seen the British as the protectors of the monarchy, worked behind the scenes to repair the damage of the Suez War. She extended a warm welcome to Charles Johnston, the new British ambassador, who found it extraordinarily difficult to establish any sort of close relationship with her son in the aftermath of Suez. In his memoirs, Johnston described Zain as a woman of charm, courage and considerable wit: "Listening to Her Majesty explaining the situation to me as she saw it, in her extremely outspoken and elegant Ottoman French, I had the impression all of a sudden that Britain and the West were not entirely friendless in the area."[33] Zain also played an important part in bringing about a rapprochement in Jordanian–Saudi relations, one based on a common recognition of the threat that fiery Arab nationalism posed to the conservative monarchies in the region. She prepared the ground for a meeting between her son and King Saud in Medina in mid January, at which the latter gave assurances of continuing financial support to the beleaguered monarchy. King Saud also offered to help Hussein in his efforts to rid his country of the influence of the Egyptian–communist agents.[34] Hussein could now begin "the slow process of piecing together the fragments of his regime."[35]

One factor that worked in favour of the palace was the division within the ranks of the government. The more radical among the ministers wanted to abolish the monarchy and turn Jordan into a republic, while the more moderate among them simply set their sights on moving Jordan closer to the radical Arab states and the Soviet Union. Nabulsi himself was all things to all men. He was an opportunist rather than an extremist, a demagogue rather than an ideologue. But he was not strong enough to control the different factions within his cabinet or to give a consistent lead. He favoured political union with the radical Arab states in the long term, but his more immediate goal was to transform

Jordan into a constitutional monarchy. "To this day," one observer has written, "the legacy of al-Nabulsi and the government he headed remains a symbol for both the best and the worst of Jordanian political life. To some, al-Nabulsi represents the promise of constitutional democracy and the rule of law; to others, al-Nabulsi is held up as the man who pandered to the jungle politics of the 'Street' and nearly presided over the very dismemberment of the kingdom. There are, in fact, elements of truth in both characterizations, for al-Nabulsi was a complex and perhaps confused man."[36]

Between January and April a series of clashes took place between Nabulsi and the king. The first was over the Eisenhower Doctrine, which was promulgated on 5 January and which aimed to fill the power vacuum created by the sharp decline of British and French influence. It offered American economic, political and military support to Middle Eastern states threatened by "International Communism." The Eisenhower Doctrine was welcomed by the king but denounced by the Foreign Affairs Committee of parliament and categorically rejected by the prime minister. Other clashes were provoked by the permission Nabulsi granted for the publication of a communist newspaper and by his invitation to the Russian news agency TASS to open an office in Amman. Hussein picked up Nabulsi's alleged sympathy for communism as the defining issue in the struggle between them. On 2 February, Hussein wrote a letter to Nabulsi and immediately issued it to the press. In it he spoke with great passion and intensity about his opposition to communism, warned against the dangers of communist infiltration and served notice of his determination to preserve Jordan's independence. The royal "we" rang loudly throughout the letter:

Imperialism, which is about to die in the Arab East, will be replaced by a new kind of imperialism. If we are enslaved by this, we shall never be able to escape or overthrow it. We perceive the danger of Communist infiltration within our Arab home as well as the danger of those who pretend to be Arab nationalists while they have nothing to do with Arabism. Our ranks must be free from corruption and intrigues. We will never allow our country to be the field for a cold war which may turn to a destructive hot war if the Arabs permit others to infiltrate their ranks. We firmly believe in the right of this country to live. Its foundations must be strong and built on the glories of the past and the hopes of the future. No gap must be left to allow the propaganda of Communism to ruin our country. These are our views which we convey to your Excellency as a citizen and as our Prime Minister.

The following day Nabulsi, Rimawi and Abu Nuwar asked for an audience with the king and tried to persuade him to tone down his letter. "Absolutely not!" he replied. "What I wrote is a directive on policy, not only for this Government but for any that follow."[37] The sting in the tail was not lost on the protesters, but the real purpose of the long missive was to attract Washington's attention. And in this respect the private-public letter met with instant success. The report from the US Embassy in Amman hailed the directive as the most important Jordanian political event in the previous few months, adding that it "publicly established his opposition to Communism and to alignment with the Western Camp," and that in view of "rapidly expanded Egyptian–Syrian–Communist influence here King's action involves him in critical battle with leftist elements which could result in loss of throne." Dulles instructed the ambassador in Amman to inform the king that "we are highly gratified at his recent public action in pointing out Communist menace." Lester Mallory, who had previously opposed additional aid to Jordan, now recommended that aid be granted if the king requested it under the Eisenhower Doctrine. The reason for the change was that "The battle is now joined. At least one champion is in the lists in [the] person [of] King Hussein."[38]

The royal assurances regarding Saudi financial backing and the prospect of American aid gave Hussein the confidence to proceed with the revision of the contractual relationship with Britain. The negotiations were conducted by the government, not by the palace. Both sides recognized that the treaty had outlived its usefulness. In the words of the British ambassador, "The Treaty régime sickened, lingered, sickened again and finally died when Glubb Pasha was expelled in March 1956. The agreed termination of the Treaty a year later was merely the delayed burial of a corpse."[39] The agreement terminating the 1948 Anglo–Jordanian treaty was signed by the British ambassador and the Jordanian prime minister in Amman on 13 March. In order to rid itself of a costly and largely obsolete commitment, Britain offered Jordan reasonable terms, and the two sides parted more or less amicably. The British were clearly demob happy. Jordanian conservatives, on the other hand, began to criticize Britain for leaving their country so soon.

An unexpected new variation on the old anti-British theme was "Beastly imperialists, *don't* go home." The British ambassador confessed in his memoirs that his side took advantage of the Arab aid agreement to extricate itself from its obligations, although it was obvious that Arab aid would not materialize on anything like the scale promised, if at all. The Jordanian government was left in the lurch. Its financial reserves were sufficient to pay the army until June or July but no longer. After that he expected chaos and confusion to follow and he was greatly relieved when this did not happen.[40]

Nabulsi and his left-wing colleagues had no such scruples. They claimed all the credit for liberating the country from the shackles of imperialism and sought to exploit their success in order to press further demands upon the king. Beyond disputes over specific issues, the king reached the conclusion that the programme of the government was incompatible with the survival of Hashemite rule over an independent kingdom of Jordan. He also began to suspect that he was the object of a conspiracy that involved extremist ministers, several senior officers in the army, Syria, Egypt and the Soviet Union. The major reform desired by the clique in power, it seemed to him, was to abolish the monarchy. Powerful propaganda, according to his account, spread the anti-royalist movement to left-wing sections of the army. Bribes were distributed lavishly, and the Soviets were promising arms to the army "once the traitor Hussein has gone." Soviet and Egyptian agents infiltrated the army and directed key men, including the chief of staff, who had been Hussein's close friend. Hussein received reports that Abu Nuwar was making regular visits to Damascus and holding meetings with the Soviet military attaché there. It was also reported that Rimawi and other ministers were driving to Damascus at night, especially after important cabinet meetings, and returning with suitcases full of money for themselves and to use as bribes.[41] No doubt some of these reports were inflated, and embellished further by Hussein in the retelling. Nevertheless, in the unhappy spring of 1957, the fate of the monarchy seemed to be hanging in the balance.

7. A Royal Coup

The year 1957 was critical in the reign of King Hussein. It was one of mounting internal opposition to the Hashemite monarchy and to Hussein himself. Nabulsi and his colleagues in the National Socialist Party saw Nasser as the stronger horse, and they backed him in the race against their own king. The Free Officers had pro-Nasser or pro-Syrian leanings, and some thought they could ease out the king by tactics of intimidation. Jordanian politics became polarized as both sides prepared for the inevitable crisis. The king began to gather support from the loyalists and the royalists on the right-wing of the political spectrum. He reckoned that in any showdown with the opposition, Ali Abu Nuwar's support would be crucial, but he was no longer confident that he would get it. So he pursued a strategy of improving his hold on the army and increasing the pressure on the government but without bringing matters to a head. Meanwhile, under the influence of Abdullah Rimawi, Nabulsi was abandoning his centrist position and veering sharply towards communism. His triumph over the termination of the treaty with Britain went to his head: he came to see himself as indispensable and his behaviour became increasingly confrontational. The American ambassador reported that Nabulsi "continues to build demagogic straw men and then claims that he had to march with them." Nabulsi seemed intent on destroying Jordan as presently constituted and throwing out the king in favour of a still undefined federation with Syria and Egypt. The king seemed determined to change the government as soon as possible, but he was uncertain how to bring this about. The ambassador concluded that the probability of some sort of a *coup de palais* was growing.[1]

In the event, the trial of strength was initiated by the government rather than the palace. On 2 April 1957 the government decided to establish diplomatic relations with the USSR. Moscow's strong support for Egypt against the tripartite aggression at Suez increased its popular-

ity in the Arab world. Staunchly anti-communist as he was, the king let
this decision stand so as not to bring matters to a head. The government
concluded that they had the king on the run and pressed their advantage further. On 7 April the government presented the king with a list of
royalist officials to be retired from the government. Dictating to the king
whom he should dismiss was a way of weakening and isolating him.
The list included the stalwart pro-monarchist Bahjat Tabbara, the director of the public security. The king reluctantly agreed to retire Tabbara
and to replace him with Mahmud al-Ma'ayta, a Free Officer. At this
point the government overplayed its hand. Subsequent evidence suggested to the British ambassador that this degree of haste was not
because of any special pressure from Russia or Egypt but because of the
faulty judgement of Rimawi, "the most dynamic member of the government and its evil genius." Rimawi developed close relations with Abu
Nuwar, who came to share some of his Ba'thist ideas. But, again in the
opinion of the British ambassador, Abu Nuwar was "an opportunist
without stability of character or principles," and even his associates in
the Nabulsi government did not seem to trust him altogether.[2]

On 8 April a strange incident took place. The First Armoured Car
Regiment, which was based in Zarqa, fifteen miles north of Amman,
took up positions outside the queen mother's palace and at other key
points on the outskirts of the capital. The regiment was commanded by
Captain Natheer Rasheed, who was a Free Officer, but it was made up
mostly of Bedouin troops who were fiercely loyal to the monarchy. The
exercise was named "Operation Hashim" as a tribute to the royal family. Rasheed claimed later that the operation was connected with a contingency plan to move troops from the East Bank to the West Bank in
the event of an Israeli invasion. It is hard to interpret it, however, as
anything but a tactic to intimidate the king. Old-guard royalists, including Bahjat Talhouni and Sharif Nasser, used the manoeuvre to warn the
king of an impending coup against him.[3] In his memoirs, the king
stated that when he heard the news, he was thunderstruck: "This could
only mean one thing—imminent danger to Jordan, a possible attack on
the Palace. Certainly it indicated that Abu Nuwar was plotting a military *coup*."[4] Hussein immediately summoned the chief of staff and
demanded an explanation. Abu Nuwar told him that it was an operation to check the vehicles entering and leaving Amman. Hussein suggested withdrawing the armoured cars back to their barracks; Abu

Nuwar readily agreed and left the room to carry out the order. In the British ambassador's retrospective judgement this incident seemed to represent "a half-baked attempt by the Government's supporters in the Army to put pressure on the King, possibly already with the intention of forcing him to abdicate."[5] At the time, however, Hussein was full of forebodings. "Now I was alone," he wrote. "Hour by hour the situation was deteriorating. I had few friends to help me and a Government openly hostile to me." The following day the armoured cars were withdrawn, but he knew that this might be only a respite.[6]

On 10 April the cabinet decided to dismiss another twenty-five officials, most trusted servants of the monarchy. The list included Bahjat Talhouni, the chief of the royal court and Hussein's right-hand man. For the king, this was the last straw; the time for action had come. By challenging so overtly the royal prerogative, the cabinet provided him with the perfect pretext to carry out the coup that he had been planning for some time. In the afternoon of the same day the king sent Talhouni to the cabinet with a written request for their resignations. Confident of their command of the situation and of their popular support in the country, Nabulsi and his colleagues complied. Had they not done so, Talhouni would have given them another letter in which they were dismissed outright. A few hours later Nabulsi arrived at the palace to tender his resignation. He was convinced that the king would be compelled to recall him on his own terms. The following three weeks were the most crucial period in the history of the modern Hashemite monarchy.[7]

Hussein had carried out his coup, but the situation remained dangerous and full of uncertainty. After all, he had just forced the resignation of the first democratically elected government in the country's history because he disagreed with its policies. This did not make him popular in the country. "The mob was testy, touchy and trigger-happy. The King never moved without a picked Bedouin escort, fierce and festooned. Jordan was on the very brink of a revolution, and many a political pundit picked up his newspaper that spring, stifled a nostalgic tear, sadly recalled an anecdote about Abdullah, and washed his hands of Jordan."[8]

That evening Hussein's uncle, Sharif Nasser bin Jamil, came to see him with other members of their family. Sharif Nasser was very worried about the grave turn of events, even though he did not know how close they were to a military revolt. The only two options he saw were abdication or fighting for survival. "I hate to say this to you, sir," he said, "but everything seems to be lost and the rumours and reports indicate that you are alone. Are you going to stand and fight or should we all pack our bags? Don't you think we ought to think about our families and their future and try to move them out of harm's way?" "I can't," Hussein told his uncle and the other family members. "I have to stay. You know I believe in what I am doing." The reason given by Hussein for this stand was that he understood the people of Jordan, trusted them and believed that when the crucial moment arrived he and his family would not necessarily lose. "No," he said to his uncle, "I cannot leave. You know that I believe in serving my country. I am going to stand and fight, whatever the consequences."[9]

Hussein was not in fact as isolated as he made out in his over-dramatized and transparently self-glorifying reconstruction of events. He had the backing of two foreign powers, America and Saudi Arabia. And dismissing a popular, democratically elected government is a strange way of serving one's country. In any case, the episode marked the end of Jordan's dalliance with Egypt and Syria and the beginning of closer cooperation with Saudi Arabia, where dynastic interests also reigned supreme. The Jordanian monarch was now free to take his place in what one British official termed "the Monarchistic Trade Union."[10] Saudi-Jordanian antagonism went back to Abd al-Aziz ibn Saud, the founder of Saudi Arabia who had defeated King Hussein of the Hijaz and forced him into exile. For the Hashemites this was the dynasty that had taken away their birth-right and their patrimony, and the antagonism between the two dynasties was therefore deep and bitter. Ibn Saud, however, died in 1953 and was succeeded by his son Saud ibn Abd al-Aziz. With new rulers in both countries it proved possible to reverse the historic antagonism between the two ruling families, and Saudi Arabia became an ally that helped Hussein secure his position.

A period of turmoil and instability ensued at home, with the National Socialists, Nabulsi's followers, torpedoing the king's attempts to form a new government under a moderate prime minister. On 13 April a confused and complicated sequence of events took place that most writers have treated as an abortive military coup. In Jordan's collective memory the "Zarqa Affair" conjures up conflicting images of disloyalty and treason, plots and conspiracies, royal courage and Bedouin bravery. It remains a highly contentious and controversial subject down to the present day. Every claim about this affair is hotly contested by one side or the other.

The official version of events maintains that Ali Abu Nuwar and the Free Officers, with the support of the Nabulsi faction, planned a military coup against the monarchy, but that the plot was foiled by loyalist elements in the army who tipped off the king and by the courage of the king in confronting the rebels head-on in Zarqa and suppressing the mutiny. This version is recounted in Hussein's autobiography in the chapter entitled "Zerka—The Final Round." According to this account, the first series of events unfolded on 8 April, when the First Armoured Car Regiment surrounded the capital. Just before Nabulsi resigned on 10 April, an open cable from Nasser was intercepted, urging the prime minister not to give in and to stay in his position. The second began on 13 April, when Hussein commissioned Said al-Mufti to form a royalist government after two other candidates had failed. Later in the day, however, Abu Nuwar and two of his colleagues summoned Mufti to the military barracks at Zarqa, half an hour's drive from Amman, and delivered through him an ultimatum to the king—appoint an acceptable government or the army would rebel. Abu Nuwar then drove to the palace and himself delivered the ultimatum. At this juncture a group of loyal officers arrived from Zarqa and warned the king that the units commanded by Natheer Rasheed and by Ma'an Abu Nuwar, a distant cousin of the chief of staff, would soon be ordered to move to Amman to surround the royal palace and arrest him. The informants pledged their loyalty to the king and returned to base. Another report reached Hussein that the troops in Zarqa were out of control, that there were rumours that he was dead, and that only his immediate presence could save the situation. Hussein and his uncle went to Zarqa at once, taking Ali Abu Nuwar with them. At Zarqa the loyalist troops kissed and mobbed the king, shouting, "Down with communism! Death to Abu Nuwar and all the traitors!" The evening ended with Ali Abu Nuwar breaking down, crying and begging for his life. The king allowed him to go to Damascus with his family and appointed General Ali al-Hiyari in his place.[11]

Ali Abu Nuwar always denied the charges of treachery. He claimed that he was the king's man all along, that his political rivals wanted to discredit him in the eyes of the king, and that, indeed, they tried to frame him. By his own account he was the "fall guy," the victim rather than the villain of the events of that day. He insisted that there was never any attempt at a coup against the king; it was the king who over-reacted to rumours of a plot and staged a pre-emptive coup himself. Ma'an Abu Nuwar, the commander of the predominantly Bedouin Princess Alia Brigade, denied with equal vehemence that he played any part in the alleged plot against the king. Ma'an Abu Nuwar's explana-tion was that he was mistakenly suspected because of his distant kin-ship with the chief of staff. Hiyari, the deputy chief of staff, denied altogether that there was any plot against the king, but he admitted that he and many other young officers had high-spirited ideas about Arab unity.[12] On the army side, Ali Abu Nuwar was clearly the key figure, and most observers continued to contest both his credibility and his competence. Miles Copeland, the CIA man who operated in the Middle East, wrote in his colourful book that Abu Nuwar "planned and actu-ally attempted a coup which held the prize for the clumsiest in modern history until the cup was passed on to King Constantine of Greece in 1968."[13]

Natheer Rasheed, another officer who was involved in the alleged plot, fled to Syria and was later pardoned by the king. He returned to Jordan in 1968, rejoined the army and was promoted to major-general and director of intelligence in 1970. He too denied the official version of the plan for a military coup and even went so far as to claim that what really took place was a royal coup against the Free Officers. Rasheed's testimony is full of previously undisclosed and fascinating details, and is therefore worth quoting at some length:

After the British left, I commanded the First Armoured Car Regiment. The role of that regiment was reconnaissance, and it was made up of mostly Bedouin elements who could hardly read and write.

On 13 April 1957 I decided to conduct a simple exercise around Amman to count the military hardware of that regiment. I was in the army headquarters receiving information from the squadron commanders. Bahjat Talhouni was chief of the royal court and he phoned His Majesty, informing him that a coup was taking place and that an armoured regiment was surrounding Amman. He asked His Majesty whether he knew anything about the situation. The king replied that he did not. The authorization had come from the army, which informed the minister of the interior, Abd al-Halim Nimr, who also came from Salt. But Nimr did not inform the prime minister, and the prime minister did not inform His Majesty. The prime minister said to His Majesty, "If you do not want me, you just have to tell me and I will resign. You do not have to use armoured cars against me." The king and the prime minister called in Ali Abu Nuwar. I knew nothing about what he was to tell the king. Ali Abu Nuwar told His Majesty that the army was angry, out of control, and unhappy with the director of the public security, Bahjat Tabbara. He suggested replacing him with a Ba'thi friend of his, Mahmud Ma'ayta. The king agreed.

I was called on the telephone to the royal palace by Ali Abu Nuwar's assistant, Ali Hiyari. He told me to pull back my regiment because His Majesty had agreed to replace the director of public security. I was surprised and refused to pull back my regiment. I told him that I was conducting a simple and agreed-upon exercise that I was going to complete. I told him that I was not interested in the nonsense that he and Ali Abu Nuwar were undertaking and never to mention my name in relation to it.

His Majesty then took a great step and made the coup against us. We were pushed out of the country . . . Zaid bin Shaker and some friends went to the infantry brigade in Khaw so he could get them to attack Zarqa, which is where we were located. A minor battle took place in Zarqa and a few soldiers were killed. His Majesty then toured the whole regiment and in no time they swore their allegiance to him . . . In April 1957, the king and Sharif Nasser stood together. Our royal family is not large in number. They all joined the king when he came to Zarqa and Khaw.

The king knew that the Free Officers were misbehaving, and he was right. He therefore took the initiative on 13 April to strike back. Ali Abu Nuwar did not have a plan for a coup. But he was an opportunistic and selfish man. He knew how to present himself and he spoke well, but he was a coward. I never respected him.

The whole episode took place because of the military exercise in April, the misinterpretation of the exercise by Ali Abu Nuwar and his men, and the ignorance of the prime minister for not informing His Majesty that the exercise was authorized by the army and agreed upon by the minister of the interior.

Following the episode, we were scattered. Some of us went to Syria and others to Egypt. A month after my arrival in Syria, I realized that the Ba'this in Jordan were well connected to the Ba'this in Syria. Akram Hourani, Salah Bitar and Michel Aflaq hosted a dinner for us in Damascus. They told us that we had made a mistake. We should have given His Majesty half a million Syrian liras and allowed him to flee Jordan. We knew from this meeting that there was a connection between them and Jordanian Ba'this. But the link between the Syrians and the Jordanian Free Officers was kept undercover, it was never announced in the open. We were the majority. Those who took Glubb Pasha from his house to the airport were from our side; they were not Ba'this. Adnan and Osama Kasim were with us. They were also dismissed from the army and we lived together in Syria in the same house.[14]

What emerges clearly from Natheer Rasheed's account is that the so-called conspirators were not united and had no agreed plan of action; that their moves were confused and ill coordinated; that the chief of staff was ineffectual, unreliable and pusillanimous; that the Syrian Ba'thists tried to use their secret allies in the Jordanian Army in order to topple the monarchy; and that the king exploited the crisis to stage a coup of his own to purge his opponents. What these various testimonies reveal in their different ways is a sorry tale of bungling and confusion, of miscommunication and misrepresentation—in short, a tragicomedy of errors. In a perceptive report to Whitehall, the British ambassador explained that Zarka "was no case of plot and counter-plot by two well-knit teams led respectively by masterminds. On the contrary, it was a confused triangular affair, a game of blind-man's-bluff with three contestants [Hussein, Nabulsi and Abu Nuwar] bumping into each other in the dark and none knowing clearly what was happening or what he ought to do next." In the ambassador's view, Hussein won because Abu Nuwar "proved himself still an amateur conspirator, while the king was moving towards professional status."[15]

No sooner had Hussein pre-empted and banished the nationalist officers who were charged with treason than an external threat began to loom on the horizon. On 14 April a brigade of some 3,000 Syrian troops that had been stationed in northern Jordan since the Suez crisis began to move towards Zarqa and Amman, apparently in support of the rebels. Hussein immediately moved troops to head off the Syrians. He also called President Shukri al-Quwatli to demand that the Syrian troops be withdrawn and to warn that any thrust south would be met by force. Quwatli promised to look into the matter, and shortly afterwards the troops were withdrawn and the threat subsided. During the crisis, King Saud ibn Abd al-Aziz came forward with an offer of help; for him the lesson of Suez was that Nasser was a greater danger to his kingdom

than the Hashemites. King Saud placed the two Saudi brigades en-
camped in the Jordan Valley at the disposal of Hussein, who contacted
them with a view to leading them against the Syrians if necessary. King
Saud also offered an immediate payment of £5 million as the Saudi
share of the Arab subsidy that had been promised in January. With Hussein's agreement, Iraq began to reinforce its troops on the border with
Jordan.

The Iraqi troop movements reassured Hussein but worried the
Israelis. Here America played a part. America's policy was to give Hussein the most effective support possible in his efforts to maintain the
independence and territorial integrity of Jordan without giving substance to the charges that he was acting at its instigation. In accordance
with this policy, America urged King Saud to render every assistance to
Hussein and to work effectively with the Iraqis. It also asked Israel to
take no action that might exacerbate the situation or hinder Hussein's
efforts to strengthen his position. Iraq gave assurances that its troop
movements were solely for the purpose of supporting Hussein. America passed on these assurances, at Iraq's request, to the Israelis. Israel
had mobilized its troops along the border in order to be prepared to take
advantage of a possible break-up of the Hashemite Kingdom of Jordan.
But in conversations with the Americans, the Israelis took the view that
the best chance for stability in the area lay in maintaining things in Jordan as they were. A kind of regional balance was thus created in favour
of the status quo. Each of the neighbouring states worked to preserve
the kingdom lest it might lose in the division of the spoils.[16]

The official version of the Zarqa Affair does not stand up to critical
scrutiny—not only because it is at odds with some of the facts that have
come to light since then but, more crucially, because it completely
ignores the role that the United States played behind the scenes. An
alternative interpretation sees the Zarqa Affair not as an attempt to
depose the king but as a royal coup, with strong American backing,
against a radical group of soldiers and politicians. One of the first writers to advance this theory was Erskine Childers, an Irish journalist and
novelist who reported his findings in the *Spectator* in 1959. According
to Childers, it was the king himself, aided and abetted by the Americans, who instigated the Zarqa rising through loyal Bedouin officers in
order to discredit the nationalists without ruining his own standing.
Childers dismisses the view, widely believed in the West at the time,

that the April crisis was masterminded in Cairo and implemented by Cairo Radio propaganda to support the plotters.

President Nasser told Childers that he wrote a letter to Nabulsi pleading with him "not to split Jordan between people and King" and that at the first sign of trouble he ordered Radio Cairo not to say a word against Hussein. This order was relaxed only after the king started to attack Egypt. At first Childers could scarcely credit what Nasser told him, but careful study of radio broadcasts confirmed it. The study also revealed that the "indirect aggression by radio" came from the West's "friends" during the whole month of April. Radio Baghdad kept up its attacks on Nabulsi throughout the crisis and alleged a connection between him and the Soviet ambassador in Israel. The day after Nabulsi's resignation, "indirect aggression" against Jordan came from Kol Israel's Arabic broadcast. The broadcast alleged that Nabulsi had been "assisted to power by Egyptian agents" and that he had wanted to turn Jordan into a Soviet base.[17]

The revisionist interpretation of the April crisis has been buttressed by further scholarly research. Lawrence Tal, in an exhaustive study of the relevant Arabic sources as well as recently declassified American and British documents, found substantial evidence of careful royalist planning for a coup against the radicals in the months before the April showdown. Tal also notes: that the military tribunals conducted later in the year failed to establish satisfactorily the guilt of the plotters, that no link was established between Abu Nuwar and Nabulsi, and that the plotters received only light sentences for their alleged crimes. Had the conspiracy cut as deeply as Hussein claimed, the plotters would have surely been dealt with more harshly and not rehabilitated so quickly by the regime. Finally, few of the former Jordanian officials (including royalists) interviewed by Tal believed the official version.[18] We may therefore confidently conclude that what took place on 13 April 1957 was not a military coup against the monarchy but the *coup de palais* that the American ambassador had predicted—and helped to engineer.

Zarqa was a defining episode in the personal story of Hussein bin Talal. It was the first serious test of his leadership because it involved not only anti-royalist politicians but the army—the mainstay of the regime. Many factors enabled Hussein to emerge on top but two were of paramount importance: his own personality and the loyalty of the Bedouin element in the army. At Zarqa he demonstrated the personal courage that was to be his hallmark for the rest of his reign. He acted swiftly and decisively to re-establish his authority despite the dangers involved in going to Zarqa in person. "By all accounts, the king did indeed risk his life by wading into the pandemonium . . . His bold action heartened loyalists and broke the spirit of any lingering rebels."[19] The other factor that worked to Hussein's advantage was the loyalty of the Bedouin soldiers and officers who formed the backbone of the mobile ground forces—infantry and armour—and tended to mistrust the townspeople who held the senior administrative posts and got involved in politics.[20] Hussein had been close to the Free Officers and they helped him to oust Glubb Pasha, but now they had outlived their usefulness and even posed a threat to the monarchy by their alignment with Nabulsi and his party. In the contest between the government and the palace, what mattered ultimately was not popularity in the country but control of the army. Sensing that he was beginning to lose that control to the Free Officers led by his erstwhile friend, Hussein staged his coup in order to purge the radical officers and make himself again master of his own troops.

A new government was successfully formed on 15 April by the independent, pro-Western Palestinian physician Dr. Hussein Fakhri al-Khalidi. Khalidi's cabinet consisted of royalist "notables" with the exception of Nabulsi, who agreed to join as minister for foreign affairs. Nabulsi's inclusion represented some sort of a reconciliation between his party and the palace. But the truce lasted just over a week. Two crises followed in rapid succession. On 20 April, after only four days in the post of chief of staff, Hiyari defected to Syria. In a press conference held in Damascus on the following day, he accused the king and palace officials of conspiring with "foreign military attachés," meaning American and British, against the independence of Jordan, its sovereignty and its ties with sister Arab countries. The thirty-two-year-old officer, who had been a Hussein favourite, also claimed that the royalist officials had fabricated the story of a military coup in order to oust their competitors from power, that the United States was behind a plan to discredit Nabulsi and his supporters, and that he himself had been ordered to "prepare the army against the people." General Hiyari's charges were countered with a curt official statement that he, like his predecessor, had "turned traitor to his king" and, in his turn, fled to Damascus.[21]

Two days after Hiyari left for Damascus, the political opposition in Jordan made a final bid for power. A National Congress of all the left-wing parties met in Nablus, including 23 lower house deputies and 200 opposition delegates. After a day of deliberations, the delegates adopted a breathtakingly bold anti-monarchist programme. The delegates demanded: (1) that the Khalidi government be replaced by a "popular government"; (2) that Sharif Nasser and Bahjat Talhouni be dismissed, and US Ambassador Lester Mallory and Military Attaché James Sweeney be expelled; (3) that all "nationalist officers" arrested in Zarqa be reinstated; (4) that Jordan unite with Egypt and Syria; and (5) that Jordan reject the Eisenhower Doctrine.[22] The "Patriotic Congress" reinforced its resolutions by calling for nationwide strikes and demonstrations. Demonstrations against the Eisenhower Doctrine and the Khalidi government took place the following day.

On being presented with this list of demands, Khalidi realized that his government did not command the support of parliament, and he went to the palace to tender his resignation. The departure of the loyalist government left the field to the king and the powerful opposition. One historian has argued that constitutionalism in Jordan was brought to an end not by the Zarqa Affair but by the Nationalist Congress. This congress is said to have convinced Hussein that "nothing but brute force applied at once—with minimal time allowed for preparation—could save him and the Hashemite state from disaster."[23] Hussein knew instinctively that he had to resist the Congress, but before doing so he sought explicit assurances of US backing. The American ambassador had predicted that if the Khalidi government fell, the alternatives would rapidly narrow down to a choice by the king of military rule or abdication, unless he was assassinated first. The king chose military government. On 24 April he sent an urgent message to John Foster Dulles through intelligence channels in which he said he proposed to take a strong line in Jordan, including martial law on the West Bank, suspension of constitutional rights, and a firm statement against Egyptian and Syrian activities in Jordan. In his message Hussein asked if he could count on US support if Israel or the Soviet Union intervened in the situation.

Dulles thought that America's interests would best be served by Hussein winning this fight. He immediately contacted President Eisenhower and told him that Hussein "has a program which is a good tough program and if it works it will be wonderful for us." The president agreed, and Dulles sent a message to Hussein, promising to warn Israel against any intervention, stating that an overt intervention by the Soviet Union would be viewed as a challenge under the Eisenhower Doctrine, and that, if requested by Jordan, they would intervene militarily. Eisenhower's press secretary announced that both the president and the secretary of state regarded "the independence and integrity of Jordan as vital."[24] This statement gave Jordan the distinction of being the first Middle Eastern country to receive support under the terms of the Eisenhower Doctrine and signalled America's commitment to underwrite the Hashemite Kingdom of Jordan. The following day the US Sixth Fleet, with marines aboard, was ordered to set sail for the eastern Mediterranean as a show of force to deter any outside intervention in Jordan.

On the night of 24–25 April, Hussein delivered his counter-stroke against the opposition. First, he convened in the palace a conclave of nearly all the Hashemite loyalists who had served his grandfather and held the kingdom together after the murder at the mosque. Queen Zain later told Charles Johnston that that night was almost the worst of the whole crisis. The king's men were reluctant to assume the responsibilities of office and recommended instead the formation of a military government. Queen Zain reportedly rounded on them and suggested that the ministers-to-be should not be allowed to leave the palace until they had taken the oath of office. "It was on this not altogether encouraging basis that the new government was eventually formed."[25] Once again, as in the pre-Nabulsi era, the palace was the main locus of decision-making in Jordan.

The new government was headed by Ibrahim Hashim, the elder statesman and staunch supporter of the dynasty, with Samir Rifa'i, the strong man of the right, as deputy prime minister and minister of foreign affairs. Abdel Monem Rifa'i, Samir's brother, was reappointed ambassador to the United States. Akif al-Fayez became minister for agriculture. It was the first time in the nation's history that a Bedouin was appointed to a cabinet post. Akif was the son of the chief of the Bani Sakhr "northern" tribes and was appointed in recognition of the role that the Bedouin community had played over the past few weeks.[26] Hussein emerged from the long night as the sole effective ruler of the country. The government was fervently royalist, pro-Saudi and pro-

American. During the same night it banned political parties, declared martial law and imposed a nationwide curfew. Overnight Jordan was transformed into a police state. Troops were deployed in the early hours to prevent the crowds from assembling and demonstrating as they had done against the Baghdad Pact. The result was described by the British ambassador: "On the morning of April 25th the streets of Amman were deserted except for large forces of troops and police. A number of the troops were Bedouin with blackened faces, a traditional measure designed to prevent recognition and family feuds in the event of bloodshed."[27] In a radio broadcast to the nation, Hussein went on the offensive. He accused the Nabulsi government of being soft on Israel and recalled that Nabulsi had prevented him from attacking Israel during its invasion of Egypt the previous year. Hussein denounced "international communism" as the root of Jordan's problems and charged that "the Communist Party here are the brothers of the Communist Party in Israel and receive instructions from them."

By defeating the challenge to the monarchy, Hussein gave the Hashemite Kingdom of Jordan a chance to survive. Before the royal coup Jordan was just a remnant of the age of European colonialism that was likely to be swept away by the nationalist tide sweeping through the region. But the crisis ended in such a way as to remove the question mark hanging over the country. The British ambassador was full of admiration for Hussein, describing his counter-stroke as decisive. In his annual report on 1957 the ambassador placed Hussein's actions in a longer-term historical perspective that stressed his debt to Britain:

The King's victory was complete. Seen in retrospect, it represents something which no one could have foreseen. The ramshackle Jordanian state, haphazardly formed by the union of two post-war vacuums—the "Transjordan" of 1918 and the "West Bank" of 1948—suddenly felt itself an entity and affirmed its will to live. The conspirators had wished it to be merged in a left-wing Syrian Republic. In defeating them, King Hussein had given "The Hashemite Kingdom of Jordan" for the first time a real meaning. For his victory he had to thank his British-trained army, and especially those elements in it from the Bedouin tribes whose loyalty to the Throne had been so laboriously won by Glubb Pasha in the 1930s. For the consolidation of his victory King Hussein had to thank a Government composed almost entirely of statesmen and administrators trained in the school of King Abdullah and the British Mandate.[28]

In his memoirs Charles Johnston wrote that King Hussein's determination saved him and his country three times in the course of a month: in the "armoured-car incident" of 8 April, in the Zarqa mutiny of 13 April and when threatened by the Syrian military on 14 April. Johnston added that, only just in time, the king struck a blow against the forces of extremism that was to prove decisive. As a result, Jordan felt a firm hand, which it had not known since the days of King Abdullah. At the end of the long night of 24–25 April, Hussein said to the chief of the royal court that he was exhausted and thought he would go to bed. Bahjat Talhouni replied respectfully that there was one more thing that His Majesty should do: he should kneel down, recite a verse of the Koran and give thanks to Allah for his grandfather, since without King Abdullah's training there would have been no ministers to carry on the government. The king did as Talhouni suggested and then retired and slept until late in the evening.[29]

Johnston, like most Western policy-makers, looked at events in Jordan from a cold war perspective. Watching their performance, he thought that the contest between America and Russia was like a bad game of lawn tennis, in which the only points scored were from the double faults of the other side. In this particular game, America made some initial mistakes but then wisely allowed the Russians to serve. The real winner was Jordan. The cold war rescued a country on the verge of bankruptcy: "It had produced out of nowhere an American paymaster to replace the British one who had said goodbye and the Arab one whose cheque had bounced. A year before, Jordan had been taking British money and Egyptian advice. By now she was taking American money and was not far from a disposition to take British advice once more." In their relationship to Jordan, Britain and the United States changed places: "It was now the US which bore the main burden of supporting this unviable country, and which was accordingly exposed to the full blast of Arab ingratitude."[30]

The Americans had no hesitation in assuming the burden that Britain had relinquished. John Foster Dulles, the arch cold warrior, regarded non-alignment in the cold war as an obsolete, immoral and impractical concept. He insisted that in the struggle between the forces of light against those of darkness every country should proclaim its allegiance, and that if you were not with them, you were against them. Hussein made a bold stand on the side of America against the Soviet

Union and international communism, and thus qualified in Dulles's eyes for support under the Eisenhower Doctrine. President Eisenhower told Dulles that the young king was certainly showing spunk and that he admired him for it. "Let's invite him over one of these days," said Eisenhower, "when the situation is less tense."[31]

Eisenhower's avuncular attitude ensured a prompt response to the young king's desperate appeal for aid. On 29 April the Eisenhower administration agreed to extend to Jordan $10 million in economic assistance to assure its "freedom" and to maintain its "economic and political stability." The speed with which the grant was made was without precedent. In late June this was followed by $10 million in military aid and $10 million in economic assistance. By now the total sum of American aid exceeded the annual British subsidy, and the American paymasters were much less strict about the way that their money was to be used than the British nanny had been. American aid was advanced with virtually no conditions attached. Moreover, to a far greater degree than the former paymaster, the Americans equated Jordan's security with the security of the king. America's toehold in Jordan depended from the beginning on the mortal existence of one man— Hussein. Yet the shift in American foreign policy was highly significant. The view of Jordan as an unviable state yielded to the assessment that it might survive against all the odds thanks to the courage and tenacity of its ruler. Jordan came to be seen for the first time as a strategic ally for America in the Middle East, but everything from that point hinged on the stability of the regime and the survival of the ruler.

Most observers assumed that American aid for Jordan began only after the withdrawal of British aid. In his annual survey of Jordan for 1957 Charles Johnston wrote: "Historically speaking the most important event of the year was the adoption of the Jordanian commitment by the United States. The termination of the Anglo–Jordanian Treaty in March, followed by King Hussein's courageous stand against Communism, seems to have forced the hand of the United States Government and left it with no alternative. American support, moral as well as financial, was an essential factor behind the regime's successes in stabilizing the situation."[32] As far as the State Department and the White House were concerned, this was indeed the true sequence of events. But CIA support for the king had begun before the termination of the treaty and even before the sacking of Glubb Pasha.

It is not possible to give a precise date for the first contact between Hussein and the CIA. Nor do we know which of them made the initial approach. The best guess is that the king took the initiative. However, some interesting details about the origins of the relationship emerge from a book by former CIA officer Wilbur Crane Eveland, *Ropes of Sand: America's Failure in the Middle East.* Eveland, whose patch covered Syria and Lebanon, went to help the CIA station in Amman after the dismissal of Glubb and his replacement with Ali Abu Nuwar. Eveland's main task was to assess the new army commander's attitude to the West. At that time the CIA had a young officer named Fred Latrash in contact with the king. Abu Nuwar requested a private chat with Eveland after he was introduced to him by an American journalist. Abu Nuwar's message was short and simple: he sought American help in freeing Jordan from dependence on British arms. When Eveland said he would report the request to Ambassador Lester Mallory, the general insisted that Mallory was too close to the British ambassador. The general urged Eveland to discuss this matter personally with the king, who was planning to visit Lebanon to drive in a sports-car rally. Eveland realized that Abu Nuwar was unaware of the CIA–Hussein liaison through Fred Latrash.[33]

A couple of months later Hussein arrived in a sleek silver Mercedes sports car to compete in the race in the Lebanese mountains. Abu Said, a Jordanian stringer for *Time* magazine, approached Eveland in the Saint George Hotel bar with an offer to arrange a meeting for him with the royal racing driver during his visit. That evening the concierge in Eveland's hotel greeted him with unusual formality. He handed the thirty-seven-year-old spook an envelope bearing the crest of the Jordanian Embassy and addressed to "His Excellency Mr. Wilbur Crane Eveland." Within there was a handwritten note advising him that the king would receive him in his suite at nine the next morning. There was a quality about the royal person that struck a chord with most Americans. Eveland's first impression was entirely favourable: "Hussein's erect bearing reflected both pride and the British military training he'd had before he'd been thrust onto the throne. Radio Cairo's appellation for him, 'Dwarf King,' bore no relation to Hussein's actual appearance. As for courage, few monarchs had been so tested. He'd been a boy when he saw his grandfather King Abdullah shot down, and later his father had cracked under mental pressure and been institutionalized in

Turkey. Finally, the odds on Hussein's survival were growing less attractive every day." Eveland opened the conversation by saying that in the past he had been involved in US military aid planning. Hussein expressed his own interest in obtaining the best equipment for his army, without regard to its source. "We expect soon to discuss this with your people," said Hussein, before turning to the Syrian situation, on which he was very well informed.[34]

In his report on the conversation, Eveland offered to serve as a channel of communications for the king during his frequent visits to Lebanon. Eveland's superiors, however, decided to put someone more senior on the case. The CIA was usually given "terminal cases" and told to do something about them. Jordan was not a terminal case, but there were doubts about its chances of survival. The choice fell on Kermit ("Kim") Roosevelt, the grandson of Theodore, who had achieved fame by organizing a coup in Iran in 1953 to overthrow the Mossadeq government and restore the shah. Roosevelt came up with a plan to bolster Hussein personally while the British continued to handle arms supplies. This was the start of a major programme to "beef up" Hussein and Jordan. Under the CIA's system of pseudonyms and cryptonyms, the first two letters designated the country in which the operation was located: "NO" stood for Jordan and "NORMAN" for King Hussein. Kim Roosevelt chose the code "NOBEEF" to stand for the programme to subsidize the king personally. For years this name covered what Eveland described as "the multi-million dollar payments" until someone stumbled on to the cryptonym and exposed it in the press.[35]

The exposure came in a sensational article by Bob Woodward stretched across the front page of the *Washington Post* on 18 February 1977 under the headline CIA PAID MILLIONS TO JORDAN'S KING HUSSEIN. The funnelling of the money to this Arab head of state was one of the most closely held and sensitive of all CIA covert operations, so the political class and the wider public were astonished. Woodward reported that for twenty years the CIA had made secret annual payments to King Hussein totalling millions of dollars, starting in 1957 under the Eisenhower administration. The initial payments apparently ran to millions of dollars, but they were sharply curtailed to $750,000 in 1976. Made under the codeword project name of "NOBEEF," they were usually delivered in cash to the king by the CIA station chief in Amman.

The CIA, reported Woodward, justified the direct cash payments by claiming that Hussein allowed the US intelligence agencies to operate freely in his strategically placed country. Hussein himself provided intelligence to the CIA and used its funds to make payments to other government officials who provided intelligence or cooperated with the CIA. Nevertheless, some CIA officials considered the payments no more than "bribes" and reported the matter to the Intelligence Oversight Board. Hussein himself, according to Woodward's sources, considered the payments simply as another form of US assistance. Within the CIA, "NOBEEF" was rated as one of its most successful operations, giving the United States great leverage and unusual access to the leader of a sovereign state.

Woodward told his readers that Hussein was only twenty-one when he first became a beneficiary of CIA funds: "It was a time when Jordan was virtually a ward of the United States and Hussein had little money to support his lifestyle, which earned him the reputation as a 'playboy prince'." Hussein has a well-publicized taste for sports cars and airplanes. As once previously reported, the CIA has provided Hussein with female companions. The agency also provided bodyguards for Hussein's children when they were abroad in school."[36] What the article implied was that Hussein was on the private payroll of the CIA; what it actually said was that the CIA was, in effect, running its own aid programme to Jordan free from any bureaucratic controls or congressional supervision. It also underlined the point that the money was given not to the Jordanian government but to the king, and in cash.

Woodward gave further details on the method of effecting the payments in material that he prepared but ultimately dropped from his book *Veil: The Secret Wars of the CIA 1981–1987*. This account was placed at the disposal of a fellow journalist, Philip Geyelin, who wrote the following in a sadly unfinished and unpublished book manuscript: "So the payments took the form of Jordanian dinars delivered in a plain envelope, never handed directly to Hussein. Rather it was unostentatiously placed on his desk in the course of a visit by the CIA station chief posted to the embassy. Any conventional transfer of funds to the Finance Ministry, or to any government department controlled by opposition appointees, would have been certain to expose Hussein to devastating charges of secret collaboration with the wicked imperialists; even a personal check would have left a paper trail, widening the risk of disclosure; any covert connection with Jordan had to be handled personally with Hussein, without formalities, in cash."[37] Ready cash was what the king needed and what the CIA provided. The acronym CIA stood for the Central Intelligence Agency, but in this case, as in so many others, it could equally have stood for Cash In Advance.

Bob Woodward's version of the Hussein–CIA relationship was challenged by a former CIA official who gave an altogether more benign account of the origins and nature of the relationship. The official stressed that in the early years of his reign, Hussein had no intelligence service. He used to pay people from his own pocket to tell him what was going on. CIA officials therefore decided to help the king to set up an intelligence service; they encouraged him, and provided training and a modest grant of 5,000 dinars a month as pocket money. This did not mean, claimed the official, that they were buying the king. The purpose of the payments was to help him gain information, especially on the army and the loyalty of its officers. Problems began when Hussein and his second wife, Muna, were divorced, and she brought her children to the United States. Although the secret service protected them at home, it had no resources to do so when they were at school. The State Department was reluctant to tell the king that they could not protect his children round the clock. So the CIA was persuaded to pick up the bill. It hired a private security company to protect Hussein's children at a cost of $700,000 to $800,000 per annum. Then Congress heard about the payments without knowing the background. There was an outcry, and the congressional committee cut off the funding.[38]

In Jordan too the press revelations excited intense interest and controversy. One of the most outspoken critics of the king and the American connection was Mreiwad al-Tall, a senior civil servant who worked in the palace in the early 1970s and strongly disliked what he saw there at first-hand, especially the corruption. Tall was a great admirer of Glubb Pasha and the British tradition of public service that he represented, giving him credit for building up an efficient administration in Jordan, for training a professional and disciplined army, for going to great lengths to educate the Bedouin recruits into the army and for being an honest, decent, incorruptible and faithful servant to Jordan. Hussein used to boast that it was he who had removed Glubb and to argue that only then did Jordan become a truly independent state. Tall claims that he told the king to his face that he did not buy this line and that he knew it was the Americans who were behind Glubb's removal.

Hussein allegedly just smiled, neither confirming nor denying the irreverent suggestion put to him.

Tall's version of Jordan's transition from British to American tutelage goes as follows:

Abrogating Jordan's treaty with Britain in 1956 under the Nabulsi government meant the exit of the British and the entry of the Americans. The main slogan of the Ba'thists, communists and Nasserites was to finish with the treaty. When Nabulsi delivered his speech in parliament announcing that his policy was to end the treaty, Britain readily agreed. The Americans immediately stepped in, replaced Britain and recruited Hussein. His code name was Big Beef. Part of the agreement with the Americans was that Hussein would allow the CIA to recruit any Jordanian to work for them. The CIA gave the king personally $3 million a year. The CIA station chief in Amman used to come with a briefcase to the palace once a month and hand over the money to Hussein. In total, the Americans provided Jordan with $21 million a year. The Americans bought the country. Jordan became a CIA asset until Jimmy Carter put an end to it in 1977, to the CIA payments to Hussein.

Tall bitterly regretted the departure of the British and what he saw as the takeover of his country by the crude and uncouth Americans. The British were efficient, reliable and dedicated to their protégé. "By contrast, the Americans played fast and loose with Jordan. Everything they touched here, they spoiled. They deliberately corrupted the country, making it easy for economic aid to find its way into private pockets. They not only tolerated but encouraged corruption. The Americans bought many officials and politicians in Jordan. If people were making money out of the system, they could hardly insist on high standards of public service or accountability. They became the clients of America. Hussein himself received money from the CIA starting in 1957. He set the example."[39]

The two main strands of Hussein's policy in the aftermath of the April crisis were repression at home and realignment abroad. The Americans enthusiastically approved of the former and actively supported the latter. The imposition of martial law on 24–25 April was a momentous step that transformed the entire political landscape, abruptly terminating the liberal experiment and blocking the road to democracy. Trade unions were disbanded, freedom of speech was curtailed, leftist publications were banned and the press was subjected to the most intrusive forms of supervision. The king destroyed all the checks and balances that had begun to emerge and concentrated all the power into his own hands. He ruled the country with the support of the army after a thorough purge of radicals and Arab nationalist officers. A Royal Guards regiment, with the best equipment and the most loyal elements in the army, was formed under the command of Sharif Nasser, and it was stationed in and around Amman. The cabinet was accountable to the king, not to parliament. Parliament was completely marginalized. It is therefore no exaggeration to speak, as Robert Satloff has done, of a "Hashemite restoration." "In the years after 1957," Satloff has rightly recorded,

neither government nor army was ever permitted to slide into opposition to the regime. Similarly, not parliament, democracy, or even some abstract and well-meaning notion of constitutionalism was ever again permitted to conflict with the royal "we" . . . In sum, after 1957, the contours of Hussein's monarchy bore a strong resemblance to the regime built up by Abdullah, Kirkbride, and Glubb in the years before the 1948 war. There were, of course, important differences . . . But the two eras of Hashemite history, pre-1948 and post-1957, were built on similar foundations and sustained on similar principles.[40]

Democracy was certainly not one of the principles of this Hashemite restoration. But before rushing to condemn Hussein for killing democracy in Jordan, we ought to place the events and the actors in the 1957 drama in their proper historical perspective. A number of questions suggest themselves to which there are no clear-cut answers even half a century later. Were Nabulsi and his colleagues responsible politicians with a sound programme for tackling the country's social and economic problems? Their supporters thought that they were, but their critics, not entirely without reason, saw them as a bunch of demagogues and loose cannons. What did the people of Jordan want above all at that time? This question is very difficult to answer. Some yearned for democracy and freedom; others placed security and stability above these values. If the monarchy had been overthrown, what would have replaced it? Again, it is impossible to say with any certainty except to note that the prevailing model in the Arab world at the time was not liberal democracy but military dictatorship. Egypt and Syria were military dictatorships and Iraq would become one following the Free Officers'

Revolution in 1958. A coup staged by the Free Officers in Jordan would have in all probability followed the same pattern.

To be sure, Hussein was an autocratic ruler, and his triumph over the opposition consolidated his autocracy. But he was more tolerant and more benign than most of the rulers who captured power in the Arab world in later years, especially in Syria and Iraq. His method of dealing with political opposition was not to cede power but to defend his prerogatives, to stand his ground and, whenever possible, to co-opt his opponents. All the officers who conspired against him in 1957 were subsequently forgiven, and allowed back to Jordan from their places in exile; they became loyal servants of the monarchy. The list included Ali Abu Nuwar, Ma'an Abu Nuwar, Ali Hiyari and Natheer Rasheed. Some of these men became *plus royaliste que le roi*. Forgiving and co-opting opponents became an enduring part of Jordan's political culture.

In foreign policy the main trend in the second half of 1957 was a realignment of forces in the Arab world, with Jordan drawing closer to the three pro-Western Arab states—Iraq, Saudi Arabia and Lebanon. Hussein kept in close contact with his fellow monarchs. In early June, King Saud visited Amman and later in the month Hussein led a ministerial delegation on a visit to Baghdad. One Saudi brigade remained in Jordan after the withdrawal of all the other foreign forces, as a token of Saudi Arabia's political and moral support for Hussein. Relations with Iraq also improved, despite the usual squabbles about the size of its subvention to Jordan. A conservative coalition began to emerge in the region as a counterweight to the Egyptian-led coalition. In November, Hussein began to float the idea of a confederation between Jordan and the neighbouring monarchies. He was vague about the details because this was essentially a political gesture "to steal the Arab unity bandwagon away from Egypt and Syria."[41]

Internal and external policies were closely interconnected. Having outmanoeuvred the internal opposition to his regime, Hussein was emboldened to embark on a more assertive regional policy. As we shall see, success in surviving the successive challenges to the monarchy at home rekindled old Hashemite ambitions of dominance in the Arab world. The British ambassador designated 1957 as the year of King Hussein. His Majesty, he wrote, knew where he was going:

It is significant that in his speeches he seldom refers to his grandfather, King Abdullah, but constantly to his great-grandfather, King Hussein of the Hijaz. He clearly sees himself as the heir, not of the Transjordanian Amir, but of the leader of the Arab Revolt. Despite the consolidation of his own power in Jordan, he envisages himself not as a static local sovereign, but as the dynamic leader of Arab unification. Unfortunately his impoverished Kingdom is ill-equipped to lead a movement in favour of Arab unity. True, it has certain affiliations with the Kingdom of Prussia in the period before German unification: the primitive virtues, the martial tradition, the unnaturally inflated army, the sandy wastes. But the sandbox of Europe had advantages which so far at least are lacking to the sandbox of the Levant: notably the strong state-structure, and the position of relative power among its neighbours.[42]

There was one other major impediment to the realization of Hussein's grandiose Hashemite ambition: his junior status as a client of Western imperialism, which undermined his legitimacy in the Arab world. Swapping a British patron for an American one did not resolve this underlying problem, to which in fact there was no solution. The Amirate of Transjordan had been created by Western imperialism, and it could not survive in a hostile environment without continuing Western support. King Hussein was fundamentally and structurally a client-king. The Arab Revolt was an illustrious Hashemite achievement, but for all practical purposes the Hashemite legacy that Hussein had inherited from his grandfather was one of continuing dependence on the West. Hussein had little prospect of holding on to his throne without outside help. That was why he took the precaution of lining up an American patron before his government ended the treaty relationship with Britain: he realized that even a short interval unaided could be fatal. There was thus never any real prospect of establishing for Jordan the kind of regional dominance to which Hussein began to aspire in the latter part of 1957. Events in Iraq in the following year were to reveal in the cruellest fashion the full extent of Jordan's weakness, vulnerability and dependence on Western protection. And it was only with great difficulty that Hussein himself managed to cling to his throne following the defenestration of the royal family in Baghdad.

8. The Year of Revolution

In 1958 a revolutionary tide was unleashed by pan-Arabism throughout the Middle East, and it seemed all but unstoppable, threatening to engulf pro-Western regimes like those of Iraq, Lebanon and Jordan. If in 1957 King Hussein concentrated on fending off internal challenges to his regime, in 1958 he desperately struggled for survival against much more powerful external challenges. On 1 February of that year the United Arab Republic (UAR) was established by the merger of Syria and Egypt. On 14 July a bloody military coup destroyed the monarchy in Iraq and transformed the country into a radical republic, which was expected to join the UAR. Jordan and Lebanon teetered on the brink of collapse. For a moment the enemies of Arab nationalism seemed to be on the run. Many observers thought that the countries allied to the West were about to fall one after the other. It was a revolutionary moment in the Middle East but in the end the revolution did not spread. With hindsight, 1958 had the potential to be a great turning point in Middle Eastern history, but history failed to turn.

The unification of Egypt and Syria into the UAR had two major effects. In the first place, it escalated the "Arab cold war," the contest that pitted the "revolutionary," pro-Soviet states of Egypt and Syria against the "reactionary," pro-Western states of Saudi Arabia, Lebanon, Iraq and Jordan.[1] Second, the birth of the union inspired great hopes among radicals that it would herald the realization of the pan-Arab dream. The conventional version assumes that the union was directed primarily against Israel, that it was forced on a reluctant Nasser by Syrian officers of the Ba'th Party in a move to head off their communist rivals, and that the United States was opposed to it, fearing it would strengthen the pro-Soviet camp in the Arab as well as the global cold wars.

Recent scholarship, however, has called all these assumptions into question. Elie Podeh, an Israeli historian, wrote a comprehensive and

well-documented revisionist account of the rise and fall of the United
Arab Republic that challenges the received wisdom on at least three
crucial counts. He shows that the Israeli threat played a negligible role
in the process that led to the formation of the union. In addition, he
rejects the notion that Nasser was compelled to enter the union by his
Syrian allies, arguing that Nasser intervened in Syria to gain a stronger
foothold against the Hashemites in Iraq and Jordan and that he initiated
secret contacts with America in order to secure its backing for his
move. In a message to John Foster Dulles, Nasser said that he had
become too deeply involved with the USSR and that he desired "true
neutrality." He also dangled the danger of a communist takeover in
Syria in order to justify his intervention in its domestic politics. Even
more arresting is Podeh's discovery that Dulles gave Nasser the "green
light" to operate in Syria and that he welcomed Egyptian action
designed to impede communist penetration there, provided it did not
harm American interests.[2]

The merger between Egypt and Syria gave Nasser a foothold in the
Fertile Crescent and a new base for the pursuit of his subversive activities. Not surprisingly, it caused great consternation in Baghdad and
Amman. Policy-makers in the two capitals saw the merger as a dire
threat to their interests and were disappointed by the American reaction. Crown Prince Abd al-Ilah's attempt to enlist American support for
an Iraqi operation in Syria was politely rejected. Hussein feared that
nearby Damascus would replace faraway Cairo as the main centre of
pan-Arab agitation. Both men were unaware that the formation of the
UAR dovetailed with America's regional interests and more specifically
with its desire to counter the communist danger in Syria.[3]

Hussein assumed the lead in organizing the Hashemite response to
the UAR challenge. This took the form of the short-lived union between
Jordan and Iraq. The idea was to pit a Hashemite model of unity against
the Nasserist model. Hussein had been exploring for some time
avenues of cooperation with other Arab countries that were opposed to
communism. The British ambassador observed that Hussein had an
idealistic attachment to the cause of Arab unity as such: "He saw himself as the principal heir of his great-grandfather, Hussein Ibn Ali, who
initiated the Arab Revolt against the Turks. King Hussein was indeed
quite possessive about the ideal of Arab unity; he regarded it as a sort
of Hashemite heirloom; and within the Hashemite family he seemed

to regard himself as the one pre-destined to carry on the task of his namesake."[4]

Hussein had hoped to attract Saudi Arabia into a tripartite union with Jordan and Iraq. Iraq supported Hussein's bid both in order to strengthen the anti-Nasser camp and in the hope that Saudi Arabia would share the burden of economic aid to Jordan. King Saud, however, was leery of a constitutional link with Iraq while it was a member of the Baghdad Pact. He also told the Jordanians that he was not in a position to pay them the £5,000,000 subsidy for 1958/9 that he had promised in signing the Arab solidarity agreement. With this rebuff from Riyadh, Hussein was forced to scale down his ambitions to a union between the two branches of the Hashemite family.

Baghdad's response to Hussein's urgent appeal was mixed. His cousin King Faisal II was nominally head of state, but real power lay in the hands of Nuri as-Said and Prince Abd al-Ilah, and both men had reservations. Said felt that Jordan would be an economic burden and a military liability in the event of a war with Israel. Abd al-Ilah regarded Jordan's large Palestinian population as a cause of instability that might spill over into Iraq. He said that "Hussein's trouble stemmed from the fact that 70 percent of his subjects were Palestinians with no loyalty to the throne; the balance of 30 percent were tribesmen who would sell their swords to the highest bidder."[5]

Abd al-Ilah was a nonentity who owed his elevated position in Iraq to an accident of birth rather than to any qualifications, talents or skills of his own. He was not particularly bright, not at all able, rather lazy and lacking in any social graces. He was born in the Hijaz to Sharif Ali bin Hussein, the eldest son of Hussein, the sharif of Mecca. Ali himself became king of the Hijaz in 1924, but a year later his kingdom was conquered by Ibn Saud. Abd al-Ilah moved to Baghdad with his father. In 1939 he became regent of Iraq on behalf of the infant King Faisal II after the death of his cousin King Ghazi. When Faisal ascended the throne in 1953, Abd al-Ilah became crown prince. By this time he had developed a taste for both power and its trappings, with a particular proclivity for plots and intrigues. He was never popular in Iraq, and his close association with the British counted against him among the masses. He and Nuri al-Said collaborated closely in promoting a pro-British agenda in Iraq. Said was the real mover and shaker and the supreme manipulator of Iraqi politics. He once told Glubb Pasha that a dog could not bark in

Baghdad without his hearing of it. In Abd al-Ilah, Said found a pliant figurehead who could hardly do anything on his own. The two were regarded by anti-Western Iraqis as the arch representatives of reaction and subservience to the foreigner.[6]

Hussein deeply disliked Abd al-Ilah and resented his arrogant and condescending manner. Hussein also blamed him for breaking the spirit of Faisal and preventing him from coming into his own as king. During the preliminary unity talks Faisal came to Amman without the crown prince, and everything went smoothly. Faisal and Hussein agreed to take it in turns to be head of the union. When the crown prince arrived, however, he strongly objected to this arrangement on the grounds that Iraq was the senior partner. Hussein felt humiliated but eventually agreed to let his cousin be the permanent head of the union.

Under the agreement, each country retained its separate national status, but they were required to pursue a common foreign policy and to place their armed forces under a joint command. The economies of the two members were also to be united, with Iraq contributing 80 percent and Jordan 20 percent to the budget of the union. A federal government was to be created and a legislative assembly elected by the existing houses of representatives of both countries, an equal number from each state. Baghdad and Amman were to alternate every six months as the union's capital.

The Arab Union was launched in a colourful ceremony in Amman on 14 February 1958. The entire Jordanian establishment was present as well as a large Iraqi delegation. The flag of the Arab Revolt—black, red, white and green—was unfurled for the second time to emphasize that it was the Hashemites, not the UAR, who were the keepers of the flame of Arab independence and unity. In a broadcast to the nation, Hussein proclaimed, "This is the happiest day of my life, a great day in Arab history. We are under one banner, the banner of Arabism which our great-grandfather, Hussein ibn Ali the Great, carried in the great Arab Revolt." Hussein boasted repeatedly that the Hashemite union was based on real equality, in contrast to the UAR, in which one partner was dominant and the other was subservient.[7] The brave rhetoric, however, concealed deep anxiety about the rising popularity throughout the Arab world of Nasser. The Arab Union was not so much a match for the UAR as a defensive response, a rearguard action. Even in Jordan itself the new union failed to capture the popular imagination. Iraq was still a member of the Baghdad Pact, which had provoked violent demonstrations in Jordan in 1955. On the West Bank the Palestinians were fervently pro-Nasser, and they believed his charges that Jordan had conspired with imperialism and world Zionism to betray them. By mid March, American policy-makers were aware that the West Bank Palestinians regarded the federation with Iraq as a step backward and that most Jordanians were convinced that they were in the wrong union.[8]

Nuri as-Said regarded Nasser and the UAR as the most serious threat to Iraq's position, a threat to which the union with Jordan provided puny defence. No sooner was the UAR formed than he started intriguing against Syria with the aim of detaching it from Egypt. His British allies, however, gave him no encouragement to pursue what they regarded as dangerously vague schemes. Nor did Said get any support for his idea of putting pressure on Kuwait to join the Arab Union so that it might share with Iraq the cost of propping up Jordan.[9] Damascus did not accord diplomatic recognition to the Arab Union and lost no time in attacking it over the airwaves, claiming it had uncovered a Hashemite-supported plot to undermine the government. It alleged that "imperialist and Zionist agents" had infiltrated Syria from Jordan and, in addition, that America had given $1 million to Sharif Nasser to arm and equip the Bedouin tribes in southern Syria. Jordan made it illegal to listen to Radio Damascus or Radio Cairo.[10] The propaganda war between the two unions continued, and, in March, Jordanian and Syrian troops clashed along the border.[11] Meanwhile, Said plotted to topple the republican regime in Damascus and to replace it with a monarchy headed by Abd al-Ilah. In mid June he visited London again and made another pitch for Anglo-American military intervention to bring down the Syrian government.[12] These intrigues, stemming from Said's pan-Arab ambition and the Syrian counter-plots, contributed indirectly to the military *coup d'état* that eventually brought down the Iraqi monarchy.

Hussein had advance warning of the conspiracies against the two branches of the Hashemite family. In Jordan a young officer with Nasserist links was arrested on suspicion of plotting to kill Hussein and his uncle Sharif Nasser. In the interrogation, Officer Cadet Ahmad Yusef al-Hiyari revealed that there was a UAR-instigated plan afoot to stage *coup d'états* simultaneously in Iraq and in Jordan in mid July. Hussein was also alerted by Israeli intelligence to a plot to use Egyptian agents to kill him and to seize power. The information was relayed by the Israeli military attaché in London to the Foreign Office with a request that they transmit it immediately to the Jordanian monarch.[13] Israel's move stemmed from a desire to preserve the Hashemite monarchy in Amman and to curb Nasser's influence in the Arab world. Hussein got his third tip-off from the CIA, who identified Lieutenant-Colonel Mahmud al-Rusan as the chief conspirator. Rusan was the Jordanian military attaché in Washington whose phone was tapped by the FBI. His co-conspirators were all nationalist Jordanian officers: his brothers Muhammad and Sadiq and Salih al-Shar'a. Rusan was also in contact with Colonel Mahmud al-Musa and through him with Abd al-Hamid Sarraj, a Syrian Army officer who was at that time the minister of the interior of the Northern Region of the UAR.[14] Hussein and his prime minister, Samir Rifa'i, reacted by arresting forty pro-Nasser officers "from cadet to colonel" and vowing that the Hashemites would not "act like lambs in the pen" to be eaten by the wolf at a time of its own choosing.[15]

Hussein telephoned Faisal immediately to warn him of the plot and to ask him to send urgently a trusted emissary to receive more details. Faisal thanked him and sent General Rafiq Arif, the commander-in-chief of the Arab Union forces, to Amman. Arif received a full briefing from the king, the prime minister and the chief of the royal court. Arif's reaction, however, was one of polite boredom. "Your Majesty," he said, "we are very thankful for your concern. I appreciate all your trouble, but I assure you the Iraqi Army is built on tradition. It is generally considered the best in the Middle East. It has not had the problems—nor the changes—your army has had, sir, in the past few years." He paused for breath. "I feel that it is rather we who should be concerned about Jordan, Your Majesty. This *coup* applies to your country, and it is you we are worried about. I beseech you to take care."[16] Arif was given precise information, and Hussein stressed to him that the plot they had uncovered within their armed forces was directly linked to a plot by Iraqi officers against the regime, but Arif simply repeated what he had already said: "You look after yourselves. Iraq is a very stable country, unlike Jordan. If there is any worry it is Jordan that should be worried."[17] Arif's own loyalty was not in question. But he completely rejected the possibility that the army was plotting against the regime.[18]

The Iraqi leadership in general looked down loftily on their Jordanian junior partner. But Hussein could not help thinking that Abd al-Ilah was partly responsible for the casual attitude shown by the Iraqi government to the warning they had received of the impending disaster.[19] In private Hussein was much more scathing about Abd al-Ilah than he was in his memoirs. Many years later Hussein told the director of his private office that Abd al-Ilah was so consumed by envy and ambition, and so desperate to be king, that he had plotted a quiet palace revolution with some army officers in order to remove young Faisal from the throne and take his place. In Hussein's judgement, Abd al-Ilah bore a large share of the responsibility for the court intrigues that culminated in the downfall of the monarchy.[20] Hussein kept his suspicions to himself because to air them in public would have been damaging to the reputation of the Hashemite dynasty.

The Hashemites were fighting the Nasserist challenge on several fronts. In Lebanon, UAR-supported domestic opposition groups were trying to bring down the pro-Western government of President Camille Chamoun. This had originated as a domestic crisis, a struggle for power between radicals and conservatives, rather than being instigated by the Soviets. But the American policy-makers viewed it through a cold-war lens and started to apply the Domino Theory which had first surfaced in South-East Asia, to the Middle East. The theory highlighted the danger of geo-strategic chain reactions in the event of one friendly state falling into the hands of the opposite camp. Hussein needed no geo-strategic theories to grasp that he would be the first domino to fall if a Nasserist regime were to rise to power in Lebanon. He and Samir Rifa'i impressed upon the Americans that if this came to pass, Nasser would emerge in the eyes of the Arab world as the victor, which would encourage the malcontents in Jordan, Iraq, Kuwait and Saudi Arabia to overthrow the existing regimes. With the situation in Lebanon rapidly deteriorating, Hussein asked his Iraqi allies to send troops to Jordan to provide protection against Syria. In response to this appeal, Said decided to send an Iraqi brigade to Jordan. The date for the move was set for 13 July.[21]

Ironically, the Iraqi move to protect Jordan provided the Iraqi Free Officers with the perfect opportunity to mount their own *coup d'état* at home. The leaders were Brigadier Abd al-Karim Qasim and Colonel Abd al-Salam Arif. Qasim was a favourite of Abd al-Ilah and Said. He commanded the 19th Brigade in the Third Division, which was stationed in Ba'quba, about forty miles east of Baghdad. Said's order to move the 19th Brigade from Ba'quba to Mafraq gave the conspirators the chance to strike. The most direct route to Mafraq lay through Baghdad. As a precaution against coups, the Iraqi Army's standing orders laid down that any unit passing through the capital should be stripped of its ammunition, but on this occasion the order was not observed. At about three o'clock in the morning on 14 July, Colonel Arif's battalion reached the Faisal Bridge over the Tigris in Baghdad, whence it dispersed to capture the radio station, the railway depot and the principal government buildings. The unit that advanced on the Rihab Palace encountered some resistance from the royal guard. During a pause in the exchange of fire, the king and his uncle went out into the garden to parley with the rebels, but they were killed instantly. The troops and a large crowd then stormed the palace and killed the rest of the royal family, including the women. Abd al-Ilah was beheaded; his body was tied by the feet to a car and dragged through the streets.[22] Nuri as-Said managed to escape from his house disguised as a woman, but he was discovered, mobbed and murdered the following day. His body too was mutilated and dragged through the streets of Baghdad. The British Embassy was burned down. A story was put about that the leaders of the conspiracy had intended to spare the king, but this story is implausible.[23] What is clear is that the entire royal family was mowed down in a terrible exhibition of blood-lust by a group of junior officers.[24] The Free Officers who staged the coup, like the opposition parties, were opposed to the Baghdad Pact and to Iraq's close connection with Britain. There is some evidence to suggest that their decision to kill the three men at the top was made because they feared that they might come back to power with the support of Britain or other Baghdad Pact powers.[25]

News of the bloody revolution in Baghdad reached Hussein at 7:00 a.m. on Monday, 14 July. He was awakened by a telephone call and informed that his cousin had been murdered. This was a bitter personal blow to Hussein because he and Faisal had been so close since their childhood. It was also devastating politically because it signalled the end of the recently formed union with Iraq. Hussein's first impulse was to seize the initiative and to restore Hashemite rule by force. He ordered Sharif Nasser to lead an expeditionary force into Iraq, launch a counter-attack against the rebels and restore the old order. Hussein was no doubt influenced by the precedent of 1941, when the Arab Legion had helped Britain to suppress the pro-Axis revolt of Rashid Ali al-Gaylani and to restore the monarchy. Hussein thought he had a legitimate claim to the throne of Iraq, and he asserted this claim by assuming the presidency of the Arab Union after the death of Faisal. He also hoped that the Iraqi brigade in Mafraq would rally to the royal cause and help to overthrow the newly proclaimed republic. But this was based on nothing more than wishful thinking. The Iraqi brigade, on orders from its headquarters, moved out of Jordan and took up position by the oil-pumping station at H-3. A further setback was the Anglo-American refusal to provide air cover for Sharif Nasser's troops. Last but not least, Samir Rifa'i, who was not known for faint-heartedness, urged caution. All these factors combined to persuade Hussein to recall Sharif Nasser, who was by this time 150 miles inside Iraq.

Hussein had to change his priorities from reversing the revolution in Iraq to safeguarding Jordan and his own regime. Forceful steps were taken to this end. First, Hussein imposed martial law and, with the help of the CIA, purged the army of all potentially subversive elements.[26] Second, he appointed Habis al-Majali as commander-in-chief of the Arab Union forces and Sharif Nasser as military commander of Amman. Third, he repressed the opposition by arrests, curfews, censorship and other draconian measures. But his most significant decision, and one that he knew would not go down well with his people, was to request Britain and America to send troops to Jordan. He felt acutely the need for Western support, not just physical but moral and psychological. The British had been the traditional protectors of Hussein's family and the appeal to them may have saved his throne.

In making the request for military support on 16 July, King Hussein and Samir Rifa'i said they wanted these troops in order to free their own army to deal with a coup that they expected the UAR to launch the following day. It was made clear that the Anglo-American forces would not be used against Jordanians but only to deal with external aggression. Nor would they be used to release Jordanian forces to attack Iraq.[27] The overthrow of the monarchy in Baghdad threatened to alter the entire strategic landscape of the Middle East to Britain's disadvantage. Iraq had not only been a client of Britain but a major oil producer and the keystone of the Baghdad Pact. Prime Minister Harold Macmillan was aware that the future of Jordan was hanging by a thread and that Britain's credibility as an ally was on the line. The risks of military intervention were great, but the dangers of inaction he considered to be even greater. Macmillan convened an emergency cabinet meeting that decided to respond positively to King Hussein's request. In his diary Macmillan wrote, "We all thought the Cabinet were determined to do this rather 'quixotic' act and that we would not forgive ourselves if the King were murdered tomorrow, like the Royal Family of Iraq."[28]

British anxieties were allayed to some extent by the American promise of moral, financial and logistical support for the operation to stabilize Jordan. Britain and America were united in their aim to contain the revolution in Iraq, aid their allies and prevent a chain reaction from unfolding in the region. With the American rebuke over Suez still ringing in their ears, Macmillan and his foreign secretary, Selwyn Lloyd, were extremely nervous about going it alone and took great pains to coordinate all their moves with their senior partner. They continued to argue for an American military escort for the British forces that were about to be dispatched to Jordan. But the Americans preferred to concentrate on Lebanon and to leave it to Britain to rescue Jordan; the day after the coup in Baghdad, 1,500 American marines landed on the beaches of Beirut in response to President Camille Chamoun's appeal for help under the Eisenhower Doctrine. All that Eisenhower could offer Lloyd was a promise that "we would of course not permit the British to get into a jam there." As a token of its commitment and a symbolic show of force, America sent military aircraft to sweep over northern Jordan and the West Bank.[29]

"Operation Fortitude" was launched early in the morning on 17 July from the British base in Cyprus. The task force was commanded by Brigadier Tom Pearson and consisted of two battalions of the Parachute Regiment, one light regiment of Royal Artillery and six Hunter fighters of 28 Squadron RAF. Pearson's mission was to secure the airfield in Amman and to protect King Hussein, the palace, the government and the main government installations. He was also charged with ensuring the protection of British and other friendly nationals. The wider political purpose of the task force was to stabilize the existing regime in Jordan and to deny the country "for a time" to the United Arab Republic.[30]

The task force's problems began before it arrived at its destination. Whitehall had asked Israel for permission to fly over its airspace, but no reply had been received. As time was of the essence, the task force left without clearance. As soon as it reached Israel's airspace, however, it was ordered to land immediately because it had no permission for over-flight. The group, led by Pearson, made a dash for the Jordanian border, but some of the RAF planes returned to Cyprus. Under strong American pressure, Israel relented and allowed Britain as well as America to fly over its territory.

Israel's behaviour in Jordan's hour of need was erratic and unhelpful, partly as a result of internal political divisions.[31] The survival of the Hashemite monarchy in Jordan was regarded by most of the political establishment as essential to Israel's security. In times of crisis, how-ever, Israel always reserved its freedom of action, which in practical terms meant capturing the West Bank if the kingdom disintegrated. On this occasion Israeli intelligence did not rate highly Hussein's chances of survival against the challenge he faced from radical Arab national-ism. On the day of the Iraqi revolution, the chief of staff submitted a proposal for the capture of Hebron and the hills north of Jerusalem.[32] David Ben-Gurion, the prime minister, was torn between the desire to help his eastern neighbour against his opponents and the temptation to exploit his weakness in order to encroach on his territory. Ben-Gurion also hoped to exploit the Western powers' temporary dependence on Israel's goodwill in order to extract far-reaching concessions from them. More specifically, he wanted arms supply, an American security guar-antee and Israeli participation as an equal partner in Western plans for the defence of the Middle East.

This was a ludicrously high price to demand for the privilege of using Israel's airspace. The Americans thought that Ben-Gurion had ideas above his station and politely put him in his place. John Foster Dulles bitterly resented the constant pressure that the Israelis brought to bear on him throughout the long crisis. In his public utterances he was careful not to show his true feelings. But in private Anglo-American exchanges he called Israel "this millstone round our necks."[33] The British were equally resentful and even more resistant to Ben-Gurion's proposal for partnership on a footing of equality. To Evelyn Shuckburgh of the Foreign Office it seemed that if they went along with this pro-posal, "we should simply be adding another heavy link to the chain hanging round our neck which started with the Balfour Declaration and has been steadily drowning us ever since."[34]

If Western support was damaging to Hussein's standing in the Arab world, Israeli support was even more so. But the combination of external and internal challenges that he faced left him little choice. Jordan was under siege, its supply lines were severed by its enemies, and serious food and fuel shortages were beginning to develop. Hussein was grateful for Britain's help and for Israel's part in facilitating it. The situation in Jordan was becoming more ominous by the day, as he recalled many years later: "Suddenly, we found ourselves isolated; our oil tankers were caught up in Iraq and couldn't come through. The Syrian border was closed. Nasser straddled both Syria and Egypt. The Saudis would not permit overflights or the supply of food . . . So we were totally cut off and we needed oil and there was only one way: to fly it across Israel into Jordan. We did not have any direct negotiations over that. The British and Americans did and we certainly appreciated it."[35] In his memoirs Hussein recorded with some bitterness that every gallon of fuel had to be flown over the skies of Israel: "Where an Arab nation refused, an enemy agreed."[36]

Saudi Arabia's refusal to help Jordan was a particularly bitter blow. Jordan's position was precarious because without oil it could not survive. The Americans responded instantly to Hussein's desperate appeal for help with the offer to fly oil in tanker aircraft from the Gulf across Saudi Arabia to Jordan. The first consignment went through, but at this critical juncture the Saudis changed their minds. This about-face reflected an internal shift in the balance of power between King Saud and his brother Faisal, who favoured an accommodation with Nasser. Hussein called King Saud and asked him to explain the hostile stand against Jordan. Saud replied lamely that there was nothing he could do because the government had already met and taken this decision. Turning to his chief of the royal court and others who had been listening, Hussein said bitterly, "This is probably the first time in history that any government has ever taken any decision in Saudi Arabia, or for that matter, even met!"[37]

For the Hashemites in Jordan this was a very trying time. As Hussein's nephew, Talal bin Muhammad, noted, "For us, the Iraqi revolution was the low watermark. We were totally vulnerable. We were completely encircled: Syria and Iraq to the north, Saudi Arabia to the south, and Egypt further afield. Britain had to fly over Israel with our fuel supplies, which was humiliating for us because our so-called Arab brothers would not give us the oil. Our obituary was in the paper every week in anticipation. But through sheer guts a young man was able to pull it off."[38]

The young man was, of course, King Hussein. The grief he felt at the loss of his cousin Faisal seared itself in his mind. Hussein and Faisal had been the best of friends; they were born the same year, and were at Harrow together; their fathers were first cousins and best friends; their grandmothers were sisters; and they became kings on the same day. Prince Talal once asked his uncle what was the most difficult experience that he had gone through in his life. There were so many things Hussein could have said: the assassination of King Abdullah, the June War and the loss of Jerusalem, the death of his wife Alia in a helicopter crash. But Hussein answered that the worst thing was the loss of his cousin Faisal and the manner in which he and his whole family were murdered. This was the thing that grieved him the most in his lifetime. Hussein told Talal that Faisal was too gentle a person for a country like Iraq, and he reserved most of his anger for Abd al-Ilah. Hussein "held Abd al-Ilah entirely responsible for the mishandling of the situation in 1958. He hated him with a passion; he saw him as an oppressor and a bully."[39]

Hussein did not speak much about this period because it was too painful. Nor did he allow himself to wallow in self-pity. The British ambassador, at his first interview with the king and his prime minister on the morning of 18 July, found them in a mood of dour resolution. "After all," said the king, "one can only die once."[40] The death of his cousin was a shattering blow for Hussein but outwardly he struggled to remain calm and composed. In his predicament he convened a press conference on 19 July to tell his countrymen and the world at large where he stood. James Morris, who was at the press conference, gave the following description of Hussein:

He walked into the conference room of his palace closely surrounded by officers, officials, policemen, security guards, walking quickly and tensely to the head of the table. His face was lined and tired, and moisture glistened in the corners of his eyes. The ministers and officers grouped themselves behind his chair (and who could tell, looking at their dark-eyed meditative faces, which of them was loyal, and which had a subversive pay-packet in his office drawer?). The old Prime Minister, hatchet-faced, sat beside him. The King cleared his throat huskily. "I have now had confirmation," he said slowly, "of the murder of my cousin, brother and childhood playmate, King Feisal of Iraq, and all his royal family." He paused, his eyes filling, his lip trembling, a muscle working rhythmically in the side of his jaw, and then he said it again, in identical words, but with a voice that was awkwardly thickening. "I have now received confirmation of the murder of my cousin, brother and childhood playmate, King Feisal of Iraq, and all his royal family." And raising his head from his notes, Hussein added in his strange formal English: "They are only the last in a caravan of martyrs."[41]

"A caravan of martyrs" was how the embattled king, looking back over five decades of struggle and violence, saw the progress of his family. "On one level of analysis they were the mere satellites of an alien empire, waxing and waning with its fortunes. On another they represented a last stand of authority—religious, social, moral, political—against the advancing forces of disorder. On yet a third they were the mercenaries of a retreating civilization, posted on the walls to do or die. Their tragedy was their aloneness . . . They were kings in an age of republicanism; Arabs in a century of Arab impotence; Anglophiles in the last days of British supremacy; Moslems among agnostics; traditionalists amid constant change."[42]

Four days after this sad press conference, further details reached the palace of the horrors that had been committed in Baghdad against the supporters of the royal family during the revolution. Two Jordanian ministers, Ibrahim Hashem and Suleiman Toukan, had also been butchered by the blood-thirsty Baghdad mob. Hussein and Rifa'i were badly shaken by the reports of these atrocities. Outside the British Embassy, the virtually unanimous view of foreign observers in Amman was that the monarchy had no chance of surviving. Most Jordanians too thought that their monarchy was doomed. "This was the period," wrote Charles Johnston, "when the airlift droned gloomily overhead; when, for lack of anything more encouraging, the Hashemite radio went on broadcasting pipe music all day long; when the anterooms of the Palace (normally the best club in Amman, full of cheerful coffee-drinking place-seekers) were deserted except for a few lugubrious tribal sheikhs." One day Johnston found Samir Rifa'i grey-faced in his office, looking at a photograph of an obscenely mutilated body dangling from a balcony. "Abd al-Ilah," he said.[43]

Johnston was one of the very few foreign observers who believed that with a bit of luck and support from the West, Hussein would be able to carry on. Johnston's estimate of the importance of Jordan's survival went further than the thinking in London. But the basic difference was that the British Embassy in Amman believed that Jordan would survive the emergency, whereas the Americans were sure that it would not. In spite of these different estimates, Anglo-American cooperation in Jordan remained excellent. President Eisenhower's advisers were all for supporting Hussein, even though they doubted his chances. On two occasions during the crisis the Americans made plans for the evacuation of Hussein and his family from Jordan. On 17 July the Sixth Fleet was ordered to prepare two passenger planes with appropriate air cover to pick up Hussein and fly him to safety. In mid August, when the situation seemed perilous again, Hussein made arrangements with American and British officials to fly him, his family and his retainers to Europe.[44]

Israel's leaders tried to keep as close as possible to the Americans during the crisis. Towards the end of August, Ben-Gurion sent two very senior officials to a secret meeting with John Foster Dulles at the residence of the American ambassador in London. One was Abba Eban, Israel's ambassador to the United States, and the other was Reuven Shiloah, a former head of the Mossad. They told Dulles that if it was not possible to maintain the status quo in Jordan, Ben-Gurion's thinking was that the West Bank belonged to the land mass of Palestine. The tentative idea he advanced was a union between the eastern part of Jordan and Iraq, and between the western part of Jordan and Israel with the West Bank turned into some kind of an autonomous unit. Dulles pointed out that most of the population of the West Bank were Palestinians who were highly emotional on the question of Israel. Eban and Shiloah did not press this idea but urged America to do everything possible to maintain the status quo in the area and to encourage wider cooperation among the anti-Nasser governments towards this end.[45]

Hussein had good cause to fear both for the independence of his country and for his own life. The general sense that his days were numbered was bound to affect his self-confidence and his morale. Of all the many crises of his career, this one, according to one sympathetic Israeli observer, brought him to the brink of giving up.

Hussein descended into his personal crisis only after the first threat was over. About a week after the "Rihab slaughter" at Baghdad, he virtually locked himself up in his palace, tightly surrounded by his bodyguards and inaccessible to the visitors who normally paid their respects. It was the low point, to this day, of his image as a ruler, of his morale, and of his resilience. There are reports of Hussein's fear of assassination bordering on panic during those days. And it is said that he spoke of going into exile abroad: no such stories are credibly connected with any other emergency through which he has passed.[46]

British moral and material support helped Hussein, more than any other factor, to recover his confidence in himself and his customary resilience. One man in particular made a huge difference: Wing Commander Jock Dalgleish, who had turned up at the airport on the outskirts of Jerusalem after the murder of King Abdullah. When the crisis in the Middle East broke out, Dalgleish was serving in the RAF headquarters in High Wycombe. He was sent to Jordan with the first group of paratroopers to report again to duty. The presence of the British Parachute Brigade in the capital sent a powerful signal to all Hussein's enemies and enabled him to stay on his throne until the shockwaves from the Iraqi capital had subsided. It gave him the breathing space he needed to rebuild his authority and to recapture the initiative. After a period of listlessness, he regained his energy and the courage to leave his fortified hill. He "began a round of successful visits to Army units, showing characteristic courage in moving without an escort through crowded gatherings of troops drawn from units of doubtful allegiance. This programme of visits did more than anything else to restore King Hussein's prestige and personal ascendancy in the Army and throughout the country."[47]

The security situation continued to improve. A further regiment of loyal Bedouins was brought to reinforce the garrison of Amman. The British opened a sea route from Aqaba and a line of communication from Aqaba to Amman. But the crisis was by no means over. On 1 August, Harold Macmillan wrote in his diary, "The position in Jordan is precarious and may blow up at any moment. God grant that we can avoid a disaster. But, of course, our force is too small for any real conflict—if, for instance, the Jordanian Army deserts the King. Its only use is to strengthen the hand of the Government and provide an element of stability. The danger is that it might be overwhelmed. I do not think a mob could do this. But if the Jordanian armoured division went over to Nasser, we should have difficulty in extricating our troops. So it is—

and will be—a continual worry, until we can get a UN force in their place."[48]

On 21 August a Special Session of the UN General Assembly met to consider the situation in the Middle East. Hussein recognized the need for a UN role in resolving the crisis, but he had serious worries that the session would result in an unworkable formula and a premature departure of the British troops. It therefore came as a great relief when the session unanimously adopted an Arab League–sponsored resolution calling on all Arab states to respect the territorial integrity of other states and to observe "strict non-interference in each other's internal affairs." The resolution also called on the secretary-general to make practical arrangements for the evacuation of foreign forces from Lebanon and Jordan. The "Arab resolution" reduced the tension between Nasser's camp and the pro-Western camp and paved the way to the withdrawal of the American marines from Lebanon and of the British paratroops from Jordan. Dag Hammarskjold, the UN secretary-general, arrived in Jordan at the end of the month, expecting, on the basis of press reports, to find it in its last gasp. He was therefore surprised by the calm and stability of the internal situation and impressed with the personalities of Hussein and Rifa'i. They had no difficulty in persuading him that British troops should not be withdrawn except on conditions to be agreed between themselves and the British government.[49] Intervention by the UN also served to enhance Jordan's international legitimacy. Hussein's critics claimed that foreign troops were stationed in Jordan to protect him from his own people. UN involvement was used by him to show that the threat to his regime was external, not internal.

As the UN stepped in, Jordan's Western friends stepped up their financial assistance. The American government pledged a total of $40 million in the current fiscal year, and another $10 million was earmarked for development. The British government promised a million pounds in aid, an interest-free loan and other forms of economic assistance. Despite the offers of aid, some Western policy-makers remained pessimistic about Jordan's prospects of survival. In a letter home on 31 August, Charles Johnston revealed that

There is a school of thought in London and Washington which believes that Jordan is a dead loss and that the best thing is to . . . let Nasser have it, but in a decent-looking way, using Hammarskjold and the UN to do the deed, rather as the Runciman mission was used to scupper Czechoslovakia in 1938. I think this would be not only ignoble but also very foolish of us, and I have been screaming my head off by telegraph against any such thing. Whether my screams were listened to or not, London and Washington have now agreed to keep this place afloat for the time being. An odd twist to the story is that Nasser doesn't really want Jordan anyway. So what with one thing and another the prospects of this Kingdom staggering on for some time are better than could have been expected—barring accidents and bullets of course.[50]

The withdrawal of British troops was carefully managed so as not to disturb the calm and weaken the king's position. It began on 20 October and was completed by 29 October. In his memoirs he noted with gratitude that "The British force was small, but its very presence had given us a chance to breathe. The famous red berets in the streets made people realize we were not alone, that this was no time for despair."[51] Dag Hammarskjold secured from Nasser assurances of "good neighbourliness" and an agreement to lift the blockade of Jordan. On 29 October the UAR announced the resumption of normal land and air communications with Jordan. On the surface at least the crisis seemed to be over.

After the strains and stresses of the last three months Hussein felt in need of a rest. He decided to fly to Lausanne in Switzerland for a three-week holiday with his mother, Queen Zain, his daughter Alia and the rest of his family. He also planned to celebrate his twenty-third birthday with them. On the morning of 10 November, Hussein took off from Amman Airport in his twin-engine De Haviland Dove, which had belonged to his grandfather. His co-pilot was Wing Commander Jock Dalgleish, who stayed behind after the crisis as an air adviser within the Joint Services Mission. The other members of the party were Sharif Nasser and two Jordanian pilots who were to fly the plane back home. The flight path went through Damascus, Beirut and Athens, and all the necessary overflight permits had been obtained. The first sign of trouble was a message from Syrian air flight control that said: "You are not cleared to overfly. You must land at Damascus." The aircraft replied that they were cleared to overfly though not to land at Damascus, but the order to land was repeated more insistently. At this point Hussein and his co-pilot turned the plane around, dropped to a low altitude and made a dash for the nearest point of the Jordanian border. To their dismay, two Syrian MiGs appeared overhead and started to make attacking passes at the Dove. Hussein handed over the controls to Dalgleish, who took repeatedly evasive action and after several near misses landed safely at Amman Airport. The Syrian authorities gave no explanation for this wanton attack on an unarmed aircraft on a lawful flight. Hussein concluded that the motive was to kill him and put an end to the Hashemite Kingdom of Jordan.[52]

A hero's welcome awaited Hussein on his return to Amman. A crowd quickly gathered in the streets and greeted their monarch with scenes of tumultuous enthusiasm and great rejoicing. Hussein's supporters made the most of the incident to boost his image as the brave king who was fighting the evil forces of communism. A few hours after his return, Hussein made a broadcast in which he thanked his people for their enthusiastic welcome and announced that he would not go abroad after all, as "the best holiday and the best place is here with you."[53] The next day was declared a public holiday. Tribal chiefs and other dignitaries went to the palace to congratulate the king on his escape. Crowds danced in the streets and shouted, "Long live the king!" The king's popularity shot up overnight, and there were signs of the new mood even on the normally hostile West Bank. Rumours spread that the king's uncle had been with him in the airplane. Sharif Nasser was respected by the Bedouins for his bravery and generosity but regarded by the Palestinians as the man with the iron fist; it was said that he was going to murder Ali Abu Nuwar and that he was stopped from doing so only by the king. The monarchy in general had been unpopular, but at this point it suited Hussein to have all the complaints and criticism directed at his wicked uncle.[54] The whole episode had a powerful effect in building up the Hussein legend of a brave and resourceful king surrounded on all sides by treacherous enemies. One British diplomat was quoted after the Syrian MiG episode as saying, "This is not a country but a geographical monument to the courage of one young man—Hussein."[55] In the eyes of the population at large the young man fully lived up to his title as "the Lion of Jordan."

9. Arab Foes and Jewish Friends

In the years between the 1958 revolution in Iraq and the June War of 1967, King Hussein continued to consolidate his position as Jordan's principal policy-maker. He also became better known internationally as a result of his frequent visits abroad. As in previous years, Hussein took only a superficial and intermittent interest in economic affairs, delegating them to the government, while he himself was much more directly involved with the army and with foreign relations. The army was the key to the survival of the monarchy and, after the turmoil of the two previous years, it called for careful monitoring. Foreign relations moved in three main spheres: the West, the Arabs and Israel. In all of these Hussein's conduct was governed by dynastic interests. None was predictable or stable. Inter-Arab politics revolved round the rivalry between the conservative and the revolutionary states in what was aptly dubbed "the Arab cold war." These years also saw the emergence, with Nasser's encouragement, of a Palestinian competitor to Hussein's regime, and the transformation, partly as a result of Arab and Palestinian antagonism, of Hussein's perception of Israel from deadly foe to secret friend and ally.

The king's advisers were divided into two rival factions who stood for different foreign policies. One faction was headed by Sharif Nasser. It included two members of the prominent tribal family from Kerak in the south: Hazza' al-Majali, the chief of the royal court, and his cousin Habis al-Majali, the army chief of staff. This faction had a pro-British orientation. It advocated an uncompromising stand in confronting the UAR and a proactive policy of expanding Jordan's role in regional politics. The second faction included Sadiq al-Shar'a, the deputy chief of staff, and Akif al-Fayez, the son of the shaikh of the powerful Bani Sakhr tribal confederation in northern Jordan. This group was allied to prime minister Samir Rifa'i and generally considered pro-American. It favoured a less confrontational policy towards the UAR and believed that Jordan should make an effort to reach accommodation with the radical Arab states. At stake were not just rival foreign and security policies but competition for political and economic power.[1]

As 1958 turned into 1959, Hussein felt secure enough to embark on extended travels abroad. Between February and May he went on a world tour that helped to put Jordan on the map and greatly increased his own range of contacts and stature as a leader. Ahmad al-Lozi, who, as chief of royal protocol, accompanied Hussein on this world tour, has suggested that Hussein valued it as a vehicle to forging friendships between people, a bridge to international cooperation and a means of enabling leaders to discharge their joint responsibilities. One royal tour included Iran, Turkey, Spain, Morocco and some African countries that had yet to gain their independence, such as Ghana, Guinea and Kenya. The visit to Ethiopia produced an unusual gift. Emperor Haile Selasse gave Hussein two lion cubs and a guardian to look after them. The royal party took the cubs on the plane back to Amman, where they were kept in the garden of the palace. When they grew up, they were put in cages. The king used to visit them every day, until they died a few years later.[2] Emperor Haile Selasse had as one of his many titles "the Lion of Judah," and Hussein of course came to be called by his admirers "the Lion of Jordan."

By far the most important country on Hussein's itinerary was the United States, where he went with a large party of aides and advisers in March 1959. The main purpose of the trip was to persuade the Eisenhower administration to increase its economic aid and arms supplies to Jordan; another aim was to present Jordan as a bastion of regional stability in the Middle East and as a strategic asset for the United States in the cold war. The Jordanian line in the talks with American officials was essentially "You don't count dollars and cents when your security is at stake." At the meeting with President Eisenhower at the White House, Hussein outlined his vision for a stable and peaceful Middle East and followed it with a powerful pitch for expanding American aid for his country. He criticized Nasser for helping to bring the Soviet Union into the Middle East and restated Jordan's determination to stand up to Nasser and to preserve its independence. Hussein also rejected the notion that the Arab world could remain neutral in the cold war: he felt that they had to choose between the United States and the USSR. Eisenhower was profoundly impressed with "the brave young king," and made complimentary remarks about his courage and leadership; he also noted that, while Hussein was concerned with Israel, he realized the real danger to the Middle East was communist imperialism. On the public relations front Hussein also scored notable successes. He visited half a dozen American cities and made strong anti-communist speeches that went down well with his listeners, made him the darling of the conservative media and won him many friends in Congress. The concrete outcome of the trip was an aid package of $47.8 million. Beyond that, as Lawrence Tal has noted, the trip was important for Jordan's future security because it established a personal basis for the relationship between the top decision-makers and their American opposite numbers.[3]

Hussein's five-week visit to the United States coincided with a military plot against his regime. Shortly before his departure, Hussein's intelligence service uncovered a plan by some army officers, with outside help, to stage a coup while he was abroad. Major-General Sadiq al-Shar'a was implicated, but there was no hard evidence against him. Hussein decided to take Shar'a with him as part of his entourage in order to keep him under surveillance. While they were in America, news came that thirteen Jordanian officers were arrested at home on a charge of plotting to overthrow the monarchy and to merge Jordan with the UAR. Shar'a showed increasing signs of anxiety and nervousness. During a stop in London on the return journey, he asked Hussein for permission to stay to undergo an operation on his leg. Permission was denied. Once back in Jordan, Shar'a was arrested, court martialled and sentenced to death. Hussein commuted the death sentence to life imprisonment. Four years later Shar'a was released from prison and appointed director of the Jordanian passport office.

Like most plots in Jordanian history, this one was rather tangled, with almost as many different accounts of it as there were participants. The evidence produced in court to incriminate Shar'a was flimsy and certainly not solid enough to substantiate Hussein's claim in his autobiography that the culprits planned to fire with heavy guns on the Zahran Palace where his family was living.[4] Jamal Sha'er, a medical doctor and a Ba'thist who was working in Beirut at the time, claimed that Shar'a sent him a messenger to say that he was about to make an attempt to overthrow the throne and to ask for his support. Sha'er also suggested that Shar'a and Rifa'i had very close links with the Americans and that they collaborated secretly against the regime. Shar'a himself admitted that he planned a coup, but he claimed it was directed against the army high command and not against the king. He told Peter Snow that he wanted to make some changes in the army in the interests of efficiency and that this must have led his opponents to denounce him, falsely, to the king.[5]

The whole affair was part of a wider power struggle that pitted Shar'a and Rifa'i against Sharif Nasser, his sister Queen Zain and the close-knit Majali clan. Queen Zain still wielded considerable power and influence; she was determined to force Rifa'i out of office and to replace him with Hazza' Majali. Majali, for his part, began to flex his muscles even before the king's departure for the United States. Shortly after his return, Hussein accepted Rifa'i's resignation and called upon Hazza' Majali to form a new government. Majali was less independent than his predecessor, and his rise to the top had involved a shift in the balance of power between the government and the palace. Majali's entire cabinet consisted of loyalists. Its main goals were to carry out political and social reforms, to reduce corruption in public affairs and to keep the army from intervention in politics. His broader aim was to work towards some sort of a balance within the kingdom between north and south and between the East Bank and the West Bank. In foreign affairs, on the other hand, there was a shift towards a more aggressive policy of confrontation with the UAR.

The policy was part of a broader concept of Jordan as a "Third Force" in Arab politics. This was not a realistic aim, given Jordan's size, poverty and fragility. The concept was never formalized in any doctrine or document but it was vigorously promoted by the Sharif Nasser faction, which argued that the split between republican Iraq and the UAR provided an opportunity for Jordan to establish itself as an independent centre of power in the region. In one sense this was simply the latest reincarnation of the old Hashemite ambition to unify the Fertile Crescent under their leadership, an ambition that King Abdullah had bequeathed to his grandson. Sharif Nasser and his colleagues, however, were not content to wait upon events but urged Hussein to seize the initiative and implement the Third Force idea by military means. They enjoyed Hussein's trust, having stood by him in the crises of the previous two years, and they skilfully exploited his impulse to avenge the murder of his Iraqi cousins and his desire to strengthen his regional

position. They persuaded him that the regime in Baghdad could be toppled easily because it faced considerable tribal opposition and that
regime change there could have a knock-on effect in Syria and lead to
the breakaway of Syria from the UAR. What they proposed was a Jordanian military assault on Iraq, spearheaded by an armoured division.
Once Hussein was won over to the idea, the military men began to prepare more detailed operational plans.[6]

The plan for a Jordanian military assault on Iraq encountered firm
British opposition. Anyone who knew anything about military affairs
realized that to invade a large country like Iraq without air cover (the
Jordanian air force was tiny) was an act of insanity. But the British considered that action against Iraq risked not just a military disaster but the
end of the regime in Jordan. Britain's ambassador in Amman, Sir
Charles Johnston, warned that the most probable beneficiary of such
military action would be Nasser, and, not for the first time, he found an
ally in Queen Zain. Zain also regarded Nasser and his Syrian stooges as
inherently more dangerous to Jordan than Abd al-Karim Qasim, the
prime minister of Iraq. She told Johnston: "The snake's head is nearer
than its tail," meaning that Damascus was nearer than Baghdad. The
issue was eventually settled not by argument but by Britain's refusal to
allow its advisers to the Royal Jordanian Air Force (RJAF) to participate
in the operation. In mid October, Hussein felt he had little choice but to
call off the invasion. As a result of this decision, the Jordanian trigger-
finger was brought under control, but there was a risk that it might not
be the next time a crisis blew up in Iraq. The obvious course was for
Hussein to sit back and watch the tug-of-war between Nasser and
Qasim. But, as Johnston noted, there were other forces at play: "The
King, who has inherited his Mother's flair for *Realpolitik*, sees this
clearly, but in time of crisis a combination of Iraqi émigré optimism,
Bedouin pugnacity, Hashemite *revanchisme* and his own boyish exu-
berance could easily obscure his better judgement and send him down
the road to Baghdad. How to stop him may well be one of our major preoccupations in 1960."[7]

As it turned out, one of Britain's major preoccupations in 1960 was
to stop Hussein from attacking Syria rather than Iraq. On 29 August
1960 Hazza' Majali and twelve other Jordanians were killed by a bomb
planted in Majali's desk by UAR agents. Twenty minutes later there was
a second explosion that Hussein surmised was intended for him. Hus-

sein was, not surprisingly, enraged by the assassination of his prime minister and friend, and his first impulse was to avenge his death. He also came under strong pressure from Sharif Nasser, Habis Majali and their supporters in the army to retaliate. On Hussein's orders, three brigades were assembled in the north for a lightning strike against Syria. One problem with the plan to march on Damascus, as with the earlier plan to march on Baghdad, had been that the ground forces could not be given air cover; another was that it exposed Jordan's western flank to hostile action from Israel. Hussein needed an understanding with Israel, and he therefore initiated his first direct contact across the battle lines. On 14 September, Lieutenant-Colonel Emil Jamian, a confidant of the king, met secretly in Jerusalem with General Chaim Herzog, Israel's director of military intelligence. Jamian told Herzog, "We shall have to thin out our forces on the border with Israel, and we are asking that you not take advantage of the situation by moving against us." Herzog promised to give an answer as soon as possible. After consulting prime minister David Ben-Gurion, Herzog gave Jordan a positive reply. The message from West Jerusalem to Amman said, "You may rest assured. You have our pledge."[8]

It took the combined pressure of the Western powers to prevail on Hussein to abort the operation. Queen Zain, who was on a visit to London, was asked by British officials to call her son and urge him to reconsider his decision. Charles Johnston, who was on the spot in Amman, gave avuncular advice to the king. In a private letter home, dated 25 September, Johnston wrote: "We have had some uphill work here over the last three weeks. The locals concentrated about a division in the desert facing the Syrian frontier, and everything seemed ready for a dash to Damascus to avenge the PM's murder. I have had to see our neighbour [the king was also Johnston's neighbour] at all hours of the day and night and tell him . . . that you can't win in that sort of thing, that we tried at Suez and look where it got us, etc., that Jordan has a good case before the UN and it would be a pity to spoil it by committing suicide."[9] The Americans had their own reasons for discouraging Hussein. Their policy in the Middle East in the late 1950s and early 1960s consisted primarily of accommodating the populist pan-Arabism of President Nasser. The cornerstone of this policy was to maintain the regional status quo by opposing the pan-Arab ambitions of the Hashemites in Amman.[10] In line with this, the American ambassador urged Hussein to weigh carefully the consequences of his action. Hussein realized he could not defy both Western powers, and he gave the order to cancel the plan for the march on Damascus. The episode served to underline to him the limits of Jordan's power, and it led him to abandon the concept of a Third Force.

Hussein's conflict with the UAR continued, however, in terms of both ideology and propaganda. Radio Cairo denounced him as the "Judas of the Arabs" and as nothing but a cog in the machinery of Western imperialism; he denounced his critics as the servants of Moscow. More unsettling were the repeated attempts by his enemies to have him assassinated. So numerous, cunning and varied were the plots against his person that he sometimes felt like the central character in a detective novel. In his own mind he divided the plots into two categories. The first consisted of major coups aimed at overthrowing the monarchy and the downfall of Jordan. The second consisted of plots aimed at killing him. One such plot involved replacing the medicated nose drops that Hussein used for his sinus trouble with acid strong enough to dissolve the chromium in a bathroom washbasin. Another weird plot resulted in a large number of dead cats being found in the palace grounds. An investigation revealed that an assistant cook had been recruited by the Syrian Deuxième Bureau to poison the king. As the cook was not an expert in poisons, he experimented on the local cat population. This led to the arrest and imprisonment of the cook, until Hussein responded to a plea from the cook's daughter by releasing him to celebrate a Muslim feast with his family.[11] Plots and conspiracies were to dog Hussein for the rest of his life. He was always aware of the danger but he did not allow it to intimidate him. Like his grandfather, he had a rather fatalistic, typically Muslim attitude to death. But the risk and uncertainty were always there, reflected in the title of his autobiography, *Uneasy Lies the Head*.

Most of the plots against Hussein and his regime were hatched by the UAR. The collapse of the union between Syria and Egypt therefore came as a great gift to him. On 28 September 1961 a group of officers overthrew the regime in Damascus and declared their country's independence from Egypt. The rebellion took Hussein by complete surprise, but he welcomed it with enthusiasm and reacted with great speed. He immediately extended official recognition to the new government, and urged Britain and America to follow suit. At the same time he mobilized troops on the border with Syria and got ready to intervene to prevent a counter-coup by Nasser. To the American ambassador, William Macomber, Hussein made it clear that if Nasser did make a move against the new regime, Jordan would intervene militarily to assist it. Macomber was an enthusiastic supporter of the "Brave Young King," but on this occasion he was instructed by his superiors to warn Hussein that military intervention could engulf the whole area in conflict and that it might jeopardize America's political and economic support for Jordan. Macomber reported back that, while Hussein was deferential to American views, he could be stubborn and defiant if he thought that his own long-term survival was at stake. Hussein, added Macomber, had long been convinced that his regime could not survive indefinitely in Jordan unless there was a break in the chain of hostility that surrounded him. He clearly viewed the Syrian rebellion as such a break and was determined to help the insurgents if Nasser moved against them.[12] Nasser broke off diplomatic relations with Jordan, but he did not resort to force to reassert his authority in the northern province. Consequently, the crisis subsided to a point that permitted Hussein to withdraw the troops from his northern frontier.

The British pursued a clear and consistent policy of supporting Hussein in the early 1960s. They had invested a great deal in him, and did all they could to help him overcome the internal and external threats to his regime.[13] They sided with Hussein against Nasser following the break-up of the UAR. The effects of the crisis were aptly summarized in the annual review of the new British ambassador to Jordan, John Henniker-Major. First, the standing threat of invasion from the north had been removed. "Less tangibly, the Syrian defection has given a big psychological boost to King Hussein and his supporters. It was Nasser who chose by his attacks on 'the dwarf King' to personalize his quarrel with Jordan. Goliath is still on his feet; but he is distinctly groggy, and David is correspondingly confident. Jordanians are able to breathe more freely and to look more closely at their internal problems."[14]

The fading away of the threat from the north also provided Hussein with a respite to enjoy his recent marriage to an English girl: Toni Gardiner. After the collapse of his marriage to Dina in 1957, Hussein enhanced his reputation as a playboy with a zest for life, a passionate nature and a penchant for dangerous sports such as aerial acrobatics, car-racing and water-skiing. He was frequently pictured in the press in the company of glamorous women, including models and actresses, both in the Middle East and on holiday in Europe. In his memoirs, however, Hussein painted a much less glamorous picture of life in the fast lane during those years:

Before my marriage, my personal life, if not empty, was made up of endless devices to distract myself. My duties and responsibilities occupied me for the greater part of each day, but once the day's work was ended I knew as much as any man alive the dullness, even the misery, of loneliness. Mine has not, after all, been the life of an ordinary young man. The crises that have threatened my life and country, the constant attacks of my enemies, our lone stand in the Arab Middle East against Communism, the frequent betrayals by people I had great hopes for—all these conspired to turn me into what I did not want to be: a man apart. I was becoming nervous, irritable and bad tempered . . . I was far too young at twenty-five to become a recluse . . . I needed friends more than acquaintances, but it is difficult for a reigning monarch in the Middle East to have close friends. It is even more difficult if one has come to power as early in life as I did. I did have a few personal friends, but I had to be chary about seeing them too frequently. I could not attach myself to any group of people, for fear of causing complications, suspicion and intrigue. In the end I reached the stage where I did not wish to mix with anybody, and even avoided offers of genuine friendship. I was the friend of every Jordanian, but the true, personal friend of scarcely anyone.[15]

All this was changed by the encounter with Toni Gardiner. She was a nineteen-year-old English girl, five feet four inches tall, and not strikingly beautiful. Her father was Lieutenant-Colonel Walker Gardiner, the number three in the British military mission to Jordan. She was a delightful, good-natured and straightforward young woman with no airs and graces, no social ambitions and no intellectual pretensions. She was very much an outdoor girl who enjoyed swimming, water-skiing, horse-riding and go-karting. She also enjoyed dancing, especially Scottish dancing, which was all the craze at that time. Hussein met Toni at a fancy-dress party that he gave at his palace at Shuneh in the Jordan Valley. Hussein was dressed as a pirate and when he was introduced to her, she said, "You look pretty scruffy, Your Majesty!" Hussein was smitten.

It was not love at first sight, but it was the beginning of a very happy, relaxed and uncomplicated relationship. In the months that followed, Toni became a regular member of Hussein's Friday evening Scottish dancing group, and a frequent visitor to the Amman Go-Kart Club, of which he was the president. They also spent a great deal of time together on outdoor sports, and in the palace, listening to pop music and watching films. While respectful of Hussein's rank, Toni obviously liked Hussein as a person and treated him as an ordinary man. Companionship was what he had been yearning for and in Toni he found for the first time in his life someone who took an interest in him as a human being rather than as a king. At impromptu teas with her parents they made no fuss over him, and he felt relaxed and happy. He liked the simplicity of the family and the unaffected way they lived. It was a great relief when Hussein's mother, by whose wisdom he set great store, gave her blessing to the union. When Hussein asked Toni to marry him, she quietly accepted and agreed to convert to Islam. Her Arabic name was to be Muna al-Hussein, which means "Hussein's Delight," and she modestly settled for the title of "princess" in preference to that of "queen."[16] The wedding was announced and the date set for 25 May 1961.

The announcement of Hussein's intention to marry an English girl gave cause for concern among both his own advisers and the British. Although his relations with the British improved dramatically following their intervention to save his throne, they were afraid that the marriage would expose Hussein to attack from his Arab opponents and that it might be tantamount to political suicide. The new British ambassador, Henniker-Major, went to see Hussein to advise him that marrying an English girl was not a good idea. Hussein politely pointed out that he knew the woman he wanted to marry and that he had been on the throne for eight years, whereas the ambassador had just arrived. Thrown on the defensive, Henniker-Major said that he merely wanted to ensure that His Majesty had considered all the possible repercussions. Hussein assured him that he had considered the matter quite thoroughly. Back at the embassy there was a minor insurrection. The novice was told that the marriage could not be allowed to take place and that it would not have happened in the days of Glubb Pasha. Henniker-Major then went to see the prime minister, Bahjat Talhouni, who had with him the chief of staff, Habis Majali. They both looked depressed and sat stroking their beards. Talhouni said, "We can't stand for this. We can't stand for the King's marriage to a Westerner. You must do something about it, Ambassador." Henniker-Major told them he had already tried but promised to see whether he could do anything worthwhile.

Henniker-Major thought that Hussein's action was caused by his desire to show who was in charge in Jordan. So he went back to see the king and, taking a deep breath, said, "Your Majesty, I speak with the utmost reluctance, and feel it is really awful of me to raise this matter again, but I feel I must, as your intended wife is a British subject . . . Our one aim is to ensure your majesty's happiness on the throne, and that there is no trouble of any kind. We all know the type of man Nasser is." The king looked up and said, "Well, I've listened to what you've said, and if you had said it in any other way I'd have asked you to leave. But I won't. I take what you have said in good part. You have been expressing your opinion, and I have to tell you that I am going to disregard it. I've told you already that I need this girl. She's the only one who can make me happy. We shall be married. It is difficult for me and awfully difficult for her, but I feel we must go ahead." Henniker-Major said that he fully accepted his majesty's view, thanked him for being so forbearing and kind, and withdrew.[17]

This conversation is equally revealing of Hussein's firmness in keeping his private life private and of the lingering tendency of the British ruling class to continue to treat Jordan as a colony. If Hussein took the unsolicited advice in good part, the imperial proconsul continued to harbour ill feelings. In his annual review on Jordan for 1961, Henniker-Major gave an exceedingly sour gloss on the whole episode of the royal wedding. Hussein, he wrote,

could hardly, in Arab and Moslem eyes, have made a more unsuitable marriage. He appeared to have placed his personal interests above any consideration of his people's wishes, of his own standing in the Arab world, and of the future of his dynasty. He had revealed a self-indulgent and irresponsible side to his character which his people had hoped did not exist . . . He had been impervious to the advice of his family, his most loyal advisers, and his Western friends. At least he managed, by his adroit handling of the affair, and by agreeing that Muna should not be Queen, to palliate his people's bitterness, and to avoid any disturbances internally or any external attacks. His marriage passed off without incident, and indeed amid some popular rejoicing, on the 25th of May. Arab emotions are short-lived, and by the end of the year his marriage seemed to have passed quietly into history. But the King's choice of wife had impaired his public image and was at hand for his enemies to use when a suitable occasion arose. No one will, I think, have quite the same confidence in him again.[18]

These grim predictions were not borne out. The marriage went ahead without ill effects. Hussein's popularity at home did not suffer as a result of his marriage to the woman he loved. The fact that she was foreign was grist to the propaganda mill of Radio Cairo, but the damage was minimal. In fact, as one Israeli historian has suggested, the marriage strengthened rather than weakened Hussein's position in the long run because it vindicated his own instincts against those of his would-be guardians.[19] Princess Muna endeared herself to the public by her kindness, humility and pleasant manners. Learning Arabic also counted in her favour. Unlike Queen Dina, she was not a great intellectual, and she did not try to involve herself in the affairs of state. What she did do was to provide her husband with a domestic anchor that helped him cope with the strains and stresses of his stormy political life.

The royal couple settled down comfortably and happily in Hussein's little farmhouse at Al-Hummar, about ten miles from Amman. It was a low, two storeyed building of white stone with four bedrooms and two reception rooms. The house was in line with Hussein's simple tastes, and provided a real home and a retreat from the pressures of public life. The house stood on the crest of a hill in open countryside where Hussein and Muna could ride on horseback. In the garden there was a helicopter pad that enabled Hussein to commute in five minutes to his office in the Basman Palace in Amman and occasionally to go home for lunch. Hussein also had a house at Shuneh in the Jordan Valley and a villa on the Red Sea at Aqaba, and he travelled around at great speed by car or helicopter. Muna established close and friendly relations with her formidable mother-in-law. Queen Zain particularly valued Muna for her loyalty and for the effort she made to preserve family bonds and to sustain family life.[20] On 30 January 1962 Muna gave birth to their first son; he was named Abdullah, after his great-grandfather. Hussein already had a daughter from his first marriage, Alia; Muna brought her into the family and arranged for her mother, Dina, to visit her whenever she wanted. Now Hussein had a son and an heir to the Hashemite throne. Abdullah was followed by Faisal, named after his assassinated relative, and twin girls, Zain, named after her grandmother, and Aisha.

Abdullah was appointed crown prince, but it took Hussein another three years to arrange the succession to the Hashemite throne to his satisfaction. Ever since Hussein had ascended the throne, the crown prince, in accordance with the constitution, had been Prince Muhammad. Muhammad was born in 1940, went to boarding school in England and attended the military academy in Baghdad. On his return in 1958, he joined the Jordan Arab Army and became ADC to his elder brother. There were always doubts, however, about Muhammad's suitability for high office. He was said to be mentally unstable, and his behaviour could be erratic and unpredictable. The appointment of Abdullah as crown prince did not solve the problem of the succession because he was an infant, not to mention half English. Hussein may have wanted to protect his son from the dangers involved in being crown prince. He decided to prepare someone else to hold together the house of Hashem if anything happened to him, and the choice fell on his younger brother Hassan. On 1 April 1965, as soon as Hassan came of age, he was appointed crown prince, after the constitution had been changed to make this possible. The amendment to the constitution laid down that the king's eldest son or any of the king's brothers could become crown prince, a change that was to become highly significant during the crisis of the succession in 1999.

The collapse of the UAR gave Jordan a chance to turn its attention to internal affairs—to the problems of insolvency, poverty and unemployment, and the pressing needs of economic development. Hussein seized his chance and came up with his first slogan: *Fal nabni hatha al-balad li nakhdem hathihi al-umma* ("Let us build this country to serve this nation"). This was the theme of a series of speeches and radio broadcasts he made. But lip service was one thing and leadership was another. Rhetoric was not matched by a sustained effort to come to grips with the dismal domestic situation. Hussein had no interest in economic affairs, in contrast to his intense interest in the army and foreign policy. He was temperamentally unsuited to the task of planning because of his deep dislike of any kind of paperwork. Hussein's chief contribution to the cause of economic and political reform lay in his moving round of political elites—and, more specifically, in replacing Bahjat Talhouni with Wasfi al-Tall as prime minister in January 1962.

Talhouni was a time-server and a notoriously corrupt politician who used his high office to enrich himself and his friends. Tall represented a new generation of politicians: young, well educated, efficient and dedicated to the public good.

Wasfi Tall was an outstanding statesman and a towering figure in Jordanian politics in the 1960s. He represented not only a new generation but also a new attempt to find a third way between Arab socialism and old-fashioned Arab reaction. His first government has been labelled by one scholar as "another milestone in the history of modern Jordan; indeed, in some respects it was the birth of modern Jordan."[21] Wasfi Tall came from a well-established family in nothern Jordan, the son of a famous poet; he was educated at the American University of Beirut; he served with distinction as a battalion commander in the First Arab–Israeli War; and he had an impressive record as an administrator and diplomat. Yet Tall remains a controversial figure among his own countrymen, partly because of his authoritarian personality, partly because of the complexity of his political views. In the words of one historian of Jordan: "A volcanic and seemingly contradictory amalgam, Tall was an Arab nationalist and Jordanian nationalist, a fighter for Palestinian rights and a suppressor of Palestinian activists, a patriot but someone who acquired a reputation as a British agent, a former journalist and reformer but a man whose first political appointment was as a government censor, a man who served three times as prime minister but was never a team player."[22]

Tall, aged forty-one, began as he intended to continue: with a frontal attack on vested interests and on Jordan's corrupt political culture. He was committed to radical internal reform and gathered about him a cabinet of youngish intellectuals and well-educated technocrats, none of whom had served as a minister before and none of whom was tainted by corruption. This was the best cabinet that Jordan ever had. It represented the rise of the meritocracy. There was much talk of "a new frontier." Under this slogan the government launched an ambitious Seven-year Plan to raise the gross national product by 70 percent in ten years through a system of "welfare capitalism." The purpose of the plan was to expand domestic sources of revenue, to reduce expenditure on the army and to make the state economically viable. An energetic drive was launched to reorganize and streamline the bureaucracy, and to root out corruption. Seven hundred civil servants were removed from their posts, and nepotism was replaced by a system of competitive examinations. An attempt was made to bring the army under civilian control, though this met with serious resistance. Elections were held in November 1962, and they had the distinction of being the freest in Jordan's history. Fairer elections produced a more representative, reformist parliament, which was treated as a partner of the government rather than as a talking shop. Political prisoners were released, and the press was allowed a much greater measure of freedom. Taken together, these measures represented the beginning of a peaceful revolution in Jordanian public affairs.

Tall was one of a tiny group of Jordanian prime ministers who were capable of standing up to the king, in matters of foreign relations as well as domestic policy. He believed, and tried to persuade the king, that foreign policy should be based on the Jordanian national interest and not on purely dynastic interests. Relations with Iraq were a case in point. Hussein's attitude towards republican Iraq continued to be influenced by the bitterness he felt at the murder of his cousin in 1958. Tall, who became the first Jordanian ambassador to Baghdad after the murder of Faisal II, was more influenced by cold calculations of *realpolitik*. He saw Iraq as a rich and powerful state, and wanted to ally with it in building a broader regional coalition to balance the power of the radical group headed by Nasser.[23]

Tall had especially strong and distinctive views on the Palestine question. Although he ended his career as the scourge of the Palestinians, he began it as one of the foremost supporters of their cause in Jordan. To his way of thinking Jordan and the Palestinians were not rivals but partners in the long-term struggle against Israel to which everything else should be subordinated. His starting point was that Israel was a usurper state and as such had no legitimacy. He described Israel as a cancer in the Arab body politic and argued that they had two options: to eradicate it or to be destroyed by it. Tall emphasized that the failure of the Arab states to coordinate their diplomatic and military strategies in 1948 was a major factor in the loss of Palestine. He therefore wanted the Arabs to build up their military forces and to prepare themselves carefully and rationally for the final showdown with the usurper state. He never spoke of throwing the Jews into the sea, as some Arab leaders did. The Jews as individuals were welcome to stay under Muslim rule. But Palestine was an Arab land, and there was no room and no legitimacy for a Jewish state on it. Finally, and this was crucial, Tall wanted to make Jordan the spearhead of the Arab fight against Israel.[24]

Tall's vision of Jordan as the key to the liberation of Palestine was outlined in the White Paper on Palestine that he issued in July 1962, in which he argued that Jordan's long border with Israel, large refugee population and close historic ties to the West Bank gave the country the right to direct the Arab effort to liberate Palestine.[25] In the meantime, he suggested that Jordan should be regarded as the guardian of the rights of the Palestinians and that its economic, political and military strength should be built up to enable it to perform this role. Predictably, this suggestion was rejected by the radical Arab states because they were never willing to accord to Jordan a central role in the Palestine question. The idea foundered on the cross-currents of inter-Arab suspicions, jealousy and recriminations.[26]

While allowing his radical prime minister to take the lead in internal affairs and in the Palestine question—which straddled internal affairs and foreign policy—Hussein retained his pre-eminent position in the conduct of foreign policy, especially in relation to the more traditional Arab states. As one of Hussein's aides remarked, "Arab loyalties are very personal. In the Arab world of the 1960s, foreign policy was still conducted on a ruler-to-ruler basis, not by foreign ministers. It was a tribal tradition that the chief of the tribe spoke directly to the chief of the other tribe and it was even considered disrespectful to send a subordinate. This is how business was done in the Middle East from time immemorial."[27] At first sight Hussein may not seem a natural candidate for this traditional role because of his Western education and Western orientation. But he was, in fact, a versatile person, equally fluent in English and Arabic, and capable of switching in a second from a Western to an Eastern mode of doing business.

Hussein's dealings with Saudi Arabia at this time are a good example of the king in his Eastern mode. In July 1962 he met a sick and frightened King Saud in Rome. The Saudi king was demoralized by Nasser's relentless propaganda attacks and angry with America for the economic aid it gave him. The foundation was laid for a revival of the old trade union of monarchs. At a subsequent meeting of the two monarchs in Taif in late August, a joint communiqué was issued, announcing a military union between the two countries, the formation of a joint military command, and the coordination of their foreign and inter-Arab policies. Hussein came back with an impressive sounding series of agreements providing for close economic and cultural cooperation, but resistance on the part of Crown Prince Faisal ensured that there was no follow-up. Hussein had been hoping for economic assistance and help in modernizing his army, but by the end of the year nothing had materialized. On the other hand, the public reception of the Taif agreements in Jordan was decidedly unfavourable. The liberals who welcomed the reforms of the Tall government were taken aback at this close association with the feudal Saudi monarchy.[28]

The outbreak of a war in the Yemen in September 1962 preoccupied both countries and had the effect of further deepening the division between the pro- and anti-Nasser camps. A military coup by the pro-Egyptian commander of the Yemeni Army, Abdullah al-Sallal, resulted in the flight of Imam Muhammad al-Badr from Sanaa and the proclamation of the Yemen as a republic with Sallal as its president. Nasser immediately announced his recognition of the republic and began to send troops in ever-growing numbers to fight on the republican side. This brought Nasser into conflict with King Saud and his brother Faisal, who replaced him on the throne in 1964. The Saudis backed the exiled imam as part of a broader policy of keeping the Arabian peninsula under their influence and denying Nasser a foothold in the area.[29] As a result of this external intervention, the conflict between the republican and the royalist sides in the Yemen became one of the dominant issues in inter-Arab politics until 1967.

Hussein reacted rather emotionally to the revolution in the Yemen. He saw it as a fresh victory for Nasser with grave implications for Jordan, Saudi Arabia, Aden and the whole British position in the Persian Gulf. Tall, an outspoken opponent of Nasser, thought that intervention in the Yemen would serve the Jordanian national interest. He therefore encouraged Hussein's penchant for foreign adventure, instead of reining it in. The two thus made an impulsive decision to join the Saudis in supporting the Yemeni royalists against the republicans. They dispatched 62 military advisers and 12,000 rifles to the Saudi–Yemen border, and mounted a vitriolic propaganda campaign against Nasser and his allies. Tall, who had been director of broadcasting and knew something about psychological warfare, was as emotional and vehement as the king about this issue. Jordan's role made little difference in the combat zone, but it provoked criticism at home. "If there was little public enthusiasm in Jordan for the association with Saudi Arabia, there was absolutely none for the restoration of the Imamate in the Yemen." To the British ambassador it seemed that the situation "brought out the obstinate, foolhardy worst in Wasfi's character."[30]

When Egypt poured more troops into the Yemen, the temptation to commit the tiny Jordanian air force proved irresistible. Half a squadron of Hunter fighter planes was dispatched to Taif to help the royalists. This decision backfired disastrously. The recently appointed commander of the air force and two pilots defected with their planes to Cairo. Hussein was shaken and full of remorse, but Tall was unrepentant. "It was a good thing," he said, "that the mice have been flushed out." The defection was only one symptom of growing opposition at home to the anti-Nasser crusade in the Yemen. Another sign of this trend was Dr. Kamal Sha'er's resignation from his post as director of the Development Board. Sha'er resigned in protest against the government's policy towards the revolution in the Yemen. He was one of the most promising technocrats of the new generation, and his departure left the Development Board rudderless. Involvement in the Yemen thus threatened to wreck the liberal, reformist agenda of the Tall government. In the end, however, the king and his prime minister managed to weather the domestic storm. Relations with America also suffered. When America recognized the republican regime, Tall reacted angrily. It was clear, he said, that the Western powers were only concerned with the nuisance value of countries, taking their friends for granted. And these gloomy sentiments were echoed to the British ambassador by Hussein.[31]

In the spring of 1963 Hussein's fortunes took another turn for the worse. On 8 February a Ba'th coup in Baghdad deposed the Qasim regime, and exactly a month later, on 8 March, a military coup in Damascus brought the Ba'th Party to power. Both new leaderships were much more favourably disposed towards Nasser than their predecessors had been, and both were expected to bring their countries into the circle of Arab unity. Tripartite talks were held in Cairo, and, on 17 April, the three heads of government signed a document proclaiming the new United Arab Republic. Once again Jordan was dangerously isolated and vulnerable; it looked as if an ominous ring of anti-monarchist, revolutionary-minded regimes was closing in. Hussein began to pay more attention to the conservative elements, including Bahjat Talhouni, Habis Majali, Queen Zain and other members of the

royal family. Hussein always had a problem reconciling the requirements of security with those of progress. Under the influence of the
conservatives, he placed a disproportionate weight on security. The
conservatives regarded Tall as unstable and unreliable, and they
strongly and persistently opposed the Tall "experiment" on the
grounds that it endangered Jordan's stability. On 27 March, Tall tendered his resignation, and on the same day Hussein invited the diehard
but experienced Samir Rifa'i to form a new government. Some fifty officers of doubtful loyalty were retired on security grounds, although
there were no signs of a plan for a coup. Bahjat Talhouni, "venal but
dependable," went back to his old post as chief of the royal court, and
"Jordan returned to square one in an unedifying and largely unnecessary posture of closed conservative ranks."[32]

Rifa'i was Jordan's traditional leader in times of crisis. This was his
sixth government, and it was to be his last. It was also very short-lived.
The announcement of the tripartite union between Egypt, Syria and
Iraq had a profound effect on Jordan's internal politics. It was followed
by stormy mass rallies in the main towns of the West Bank, Amman and
the northern city of Irbid. The theme of Arab unity captured the popular imagination. Demonstrators chanted anti-monarchy and pro-Nasser
slogans. Pictures of Nasser and banners with four stars expressed their
fervent wish that Jordan should join the tripartite union. Mass rallies
spread to the East Bank and quickly turned from calls for unity into
riots and violent demonstrations against the regime. These were spontaneous, grass-root demonstrations, fuelled by the widespread Palestinian resentment of the regime. Royalists, however, denounced the
demonstrations as interference by Nasser in internal Jordanian politics.
The government decided to use the army to suppress the riots. A strict
curfew was imposed on the West Bank cities. Special, hand-picked
units were assigned to the task and succeeded in re-establishing order
but at a price: 13 dead and 97 wounded. In the lower house of parliament, Rifa'i was openly attacked for his corruption and nepotism, and
for using sledge-hammer tactics in excess to requirements to quell the
riots. A vote of no confidence on 20 April persuaded him to resign. It
was the first time in Jordan's history that a government had fallen as a
result of a vote of no confidence in parliament.

The king retaliated by dissolving parliament and brought in his
great-uncle, Sharif Hussein bin Nasser, as a stopgap premier pending

the holding of fresh elections. Dismissing a freely elected parliament was an astonishingly heavy-handed and arbitrary act on the part of the king. He added insult to injury by telling the new government in a letter, "We are firmly confident that the manner in which members of the House withheld confidence in the Rifa'i government was due to personal motives and attempts to gain private advantage." Members who had voted against Rifa'i, the letter said, were voting against the "national interests of the country."[33] The king's behaviour brings to mind Bertolt Brecht's heavily comical suggestion that, if the people forfeit the confidence of the government, the government should dissolve the people and elect another.

In the first half of the year Hussein had two men of personality and character to advise him: Wasfi Tall and Samir Rifa'i. In the second half he ruled virtually by himself through the well meaning but nominal medium of his great-uncle. Sharif Hussein bin Nasser was depicted as "amiable but ineffectual" and standing at the head of a "Government of nonentities unable or unwilling to say boo to the Royal goose," according to the British ambassador, Roderick Parkes. Hussein promised to find honest ministers of vigour and calibre to support his great-uncle, but was himself a bad judge of character, and most of the men he selected turned out to be colourless or corrupt or both. Sharif Hussein remained in office but was unable to stand up to his nephew, and was often ignored or bypassed. In August, for example, the important decision to establish diplomatic relations with the Soviet Union—in order to gain leverage with the United States—was taken without his knowledge. With no strong prime minister to guide or restrain him, and having already survived so many crises, the king became overconfident and, Parkes feared, in danger of regarding himself as infallible.[34]

Another worry reported by Parkes to Whitehall was the steadily worsening condition of Jordan's public finances. While its leaders tediously repeated their intention to achieve economic viability by 1970, the country was in a state of near-bankruptcy. Poverty apart, the root cause of Jordan's budget deficit was disproportionate expenditure on the armed forces. Parkes recognized that the preservation of Jordan's integrity was an Anglo-American interest and that this was postulated on the survival of the Hashemite dynasty, which in turn depended on the loyalty and morale of its armed forces. But he deplored the air of complete financial unreality in the palace, for which the king and his immediate entourage were responsible. Some of the court officials were venal and thus easy prey for unscrupulous businessmen. The king himself was unable or unwilling to do his financial homework and constantly gave his consent to new extravagances. Jordan was completely dependant on Anglo-American budgetary support, but if the ambassadors dug in their heels, they could be accused of adopting a "colonialist" attitude. The answer, of course, was that Jordan would never be fully sovereign until it was financially self-sufficient. But Parkes suspected that Hussein calculated that in the last resort Britain and America would have no option but to bail him out, since Jordan's survival was an integral part of their Middle East policies.[35]

One of the manifestations of Hussein's growing confidence and independence was his involvement in a direct dialogue with Israeli officials in the aftermath of the April 1963 crisis. On the face of it, this was a curious thing to do. The two countries had been officially at war since 1948. Hatred of Israel was the one sentiment that united nearly all Arabs, regardless of their country, class or political affiliation. The creation of the State of Israel in 1948 involved an egregious injustice to the Palestinians. The bulk of the three quarters of a million dispossessed Palestinian refugees lived in Jordan and harboured a deep sense of grievance against the Jewish state and hopes of liberating their homeland. In Arab eyes Israel was a usurper state with no legitimacy and no right to exist. Contact with Israel was considered a taboo, perhaps the greatest taboo in Arab political culture. King Abdullah of Jordan had paid with his life for breaking this taboo: he was assassinated by a Palestinian nationalist. Now Hussein was poised to follow in his grandfather's footsteps despite all the dangers involved. Why, then, did King Hussein engage in direct talks with Israeli officials?

Hussein's reply to this question was that his purpose throughout the 1960s was to see if there was any way to resolve the dispute with Israel peacefully. He felt that if he was to be in a position of responsibility, next door to Israel, he had to know what he was dealing with. He had to explore, to find out what the thinking was on the other side. There was no future in war and there was no future in further suffering for the people on either side. So he had to break that barrier and begin a dialogue, whether it led anywhere immediately or not. He believed it was important to have it direct and first-hand and not to let other players manipulate the conflict. "And by chance I had a very, very good friend who looked after my health in London, Dr. Herbert, and gradually through conversations we came to this subject. He was a man who really believed in peace in our region and wished to see it happen. So I think he raised the possibility of some contact and I said 'fine.' That is how it started. Trying to explore, trying to find out what the other side of this issue was like. What was the face of it?"[36]

On the Israeli side the desire to establish direct contact with the ruler of Jordan went back a long way. They had the same friend in London. Hussein's doctor and personal friend, Emanuel Herbert, was a Jew from Russia and an ardent Zionist. He had a private clinic in 21 Devonshire Place, near Harley Street. Dr. Herbert was an eminent physician who specialized in heart conditions and counted many foreign dignitaries, including the king of Sweden, among his patients. The British came to trust the Jewish doctor, and, after consultation with the counter-intelligence agency MI5, the Foreign Office recommended him to Hussein as the best man to be his London physician. The king raised no objection, even when he was informed that Dr. Herbert was not just a Jew but a supporter of Israel. The British assured the king that Dr. Herbert's other speciality was discretion.[37] Dr. Herbert was also engaged as the doctor of the Jordanian Embassy in London. At the embassy his Jewish provenance was no bar to the development of very close and warm relationships. As well as attending to the staff of the embassy, Dr. Herbert looked after the Jordanian royal family. His royal patients included King Talal, Sharif Nasser, Queen Zain, her middle son, Muhammad, who had inherited his father's mental instability, and her youngest son, Hassan, who was attending school at Harrow.

Officials at the Israeli Embassy in London began to cultivate Dr. Herbert assiduously as a channel of communications with the Jordanian royal family from 1960 onwards. The files of the Foreign Ministry in Jerusalem bulge with detailed reports on every contact and conversation with Dr. Herbert and records of extensive internal discussions on how to make the most of the opening he offered. From these documents it can be seen that the Israelis regarded Dr. Herbert as a loyal, highly intelligent and subtle man and that they had complete confidence in him. They accordingly treated him as a valued go-between and were careful to avoid the impression that they wanted to use him to spy on his Jordanian patients. Dr. Herbert felt loyalty to both parties and was only too happy to do anything he could to facilitate a dialogue between them.

Eliahu Elath, the Israeli ambassador to London, asked Dr. Herbert to convey a message to King Hussein. It said that Israel viewed with admiration Hussein's firm stand against Nasser in the struggle to defend the independence of his country and that as long as he persisted in this stand he had nothing to fear from the Israeli side. Dr. Herbert did not get a chance to convey the message directly, but did so through the queen's younger brother. He had struck up a friendship with Sharif Nasser, who was by now a brigadier in the Jordanian Army, and one of the subjects they discussed, after the medical examination, was the relationship between Jordan and Israel. Sharif Nasser said that as a member of a Hijazi family he harboured no hostility towards Israel and that this was in fact the position of the entire royal family. Had it not been for the two dictators, Nasser and Qasim, it would have been possible to reach a settlement with Israel. Given the current situation and Palestinian opinion within Jordan, no one dared say this in public. But Sharif Nasser was optimistic about the future. Dr. Herbert told Sharif Nasser that he had been asked to convey a message to King Hussein, but that he had not yet had the chance to see him. Sharif Nasser heard the message from Israel and promised that Herbert would meet Hussein on the king's next visit to London.[38]

The Israelis encouraged Dr. Herbert to make contact with Queen Zain during her visit to London in September 1960. He understood what they were after and promised to try to arrange a private meeting with her when she came to see him in his clinic. But after her visit he told the Israelis that he had nothing of interest to report. As usual, the queen was accompanied by her personal physician, Dr. Shawkat Aziz as-Sati, with whom she conversed in Turkish, and Herbert did not find a convenient opportunity for a proper conversation with her. In her entourage he found considerable anxiety about Nasser's intrigues, but he did not detect any willingness to move closer to Israel as a result. The queen herself was troubled by the rumours of plots to assassinate her. Although the meeting bore no fruit, the Israelis were once again impressed by Herbert's shrewdness and unqualified willingness to help.[39]

A month later Hussein visited London; he stayed at Claridges, and Dr. Herbert received an invitation to have tea with him there. It was a social call with no particular medical purpose. Hussein was extremely friendly and invited his Jewish doctor to visit him in Jordan. Herbert asked the king whether he received the message he had sent him through his uncle. The king replied that indeed he had and added, "I very much appreciate the message and am grateful for it. It was very important for us that during difficult times we had nothing to fear from this side. Over the years a growing confidence has been established which has quietened the border. One day it will be possible through the UN to reach an honourable agreement. Now that contact has been established, we can look forward with increasing confidence to the future." Dr. Herbert recalled that the king mentioned the United Nations twice as a party in reaching a peace settlement. Although the king did not mention Israel by name, he clearly had it in mind and, what is more, he treated his doctor as the representative of the other side.[40] The Israelis were therefore justified in concluding from this private conversation that the king regarded Herbert not just as a doctor and a friend but as a trusted emissary. They went further in thinking that, given the sensitivity of contact with Israel, the king was more likely to put his trust in Dr. Herbert than even in any of his closest advisers. In any case, they felt that at long last they had succeeded in establishing a permanent channel of communication with the king.[41]

Hussein visited London again in December 1961 and saw Dr. Herbert five or six times for various medical check-ups. Hussein was said to be as healthy as an ox but tired and rather tense. Dr. Sati, the family doctor, accompanied Hussein on all of these visits, so there was no opportunity for confidential conversations.[42] Not that the elderly Jordanian physician would have been surprised by the admixture of medicine with covert contacts with the Jews. He himself had been King Abdullah's doctor as well as his most trusted emissary in the secret diplomacy that he conducted with his neighbours across the Jordan River in the crucial phase of the struggle for Palestine. Unlike some of King Abdullah's other aides, who had a personal axe to grind, Dr. Sati had enjoyed Abdullah's absolute confidence and was entrusted by him to carry out the most sensitive of missions. It was Dr. Sati who was usually sent to Jerusalem to convey the king's letters or verbal messages to the officials of the Jewish Agency, who knew that the doctor would not try to inject his personal views and preferences in the process of liaising between the two sides and that any money they handed to him would be faithfully delivered to the right destination.[43]

The patient efforts of the Israelis to make direct contact with Hussein through his Jewish doctor eventually paid off. Following an incident on the border with Jordan, the Israelis asked Dr. Herbert to arrange a meeting for them with Queen Zain, who was staying in London at the time, so they could give her a message for her son. Zain replied, "Why do you want to meet with me? His Majesty is in London and he is ready to meet an authorized representative sent to him by the prime minister of Israel."[44] Levi Eshkol was the prime minister at that time, having recently replaced David Ben-Gurion. Eshkol was a more reasonable and down-to-earth person than his predecessor, and more moderate in his approach to the Arab–Israeli conflict. Whereas Ben-Gurion was a proponent of retaliation, Eshkol was a proponent of negotiation, of practical solutions to practical problems, of dialogue and accommodation. Eshkol's foreign minister was Golda Meir, a participant in the secret contacts with King Abdullah and a not so secret admirer of Abdullah's grandson. During the 1958 crisis in Jordan, Meir told the British foreign secretary, Selwyn Lloyd, "We all pray three times a day for King Hussein's safety and success."[45] She and Eshkol favoured the continuation of the status quo in Jordan and regarded the survival of the Hashemite monarchy in Amman as essential to Israel's security.[46] For the delicate mission of meeting with Hussein, they chose the best qualified person in the Israeli diplomatic service.

Yaacov Herzog (1921–72) was a highly sophisticated, cultured and sensitive man with a profound faith in Israel's destiny. He was the son of the Chief Rabbi of Ireland and the brother of Chaim Herzog, the director of military intelligence and later president of the State of Israel. Yaacov, who was born in Dublin, settled in Palestine in 1939. He graduated in law from the Hebrew University of Jerusalem and obtained a doctorate in international relations from the University of Ottawa. Following in his father's footsteps, he was also ordained as a rabbi and became a considerable Talmudic scholar. As ambassador to Canada he achieved fame by challenging Professor Arnold Toynbee, the eminent historian, to a public debate at McGill University. From 1963 to 1965 he was deputy director general of the Foreign Ministry. Herzog was a practising Jew, very cautious by nature, but with a taste for secret diplomacy and sensitive missions. It was he who established the secret channel to Hussein, and it was he who maintained it almost without a break until 1970. Herzog and Hussein had very little in common except for their admiration for the British way of life, yet they established a relationship based on trust and mutual respect. Apart from all his intellectual talents, Herzog was a meticulous, even fastidious, civil servant who compiled an extraordinarily detailed record of all his contacts and conversations with Hussein and his advisers.[47]

On 24 September 1963 Herzog went straight from the airport to the secret meeting at Dr. Herbert's elegant house in Langford Place, St. John's Wood. When he entered the room, Hussein rose from his chair and stretched out his hand. Herzog bowed to him, shook his hand, and expressed his appreciation that he had agreed to see him. Dr. Herbert stayed with his guests until the end of the meeting after Hussein indicated that he had no objection. Herzog opened the conversation by saying that he was privileged to be the special emissary of the prime minister and foreign minister of the State of Israel and that he brought with him a message of esteem and goodwill. They and indeed the entire people of Israel viewed with sympathy and admiration King Hussein's statesmanship, leadership, and personal courage. While the public posture of their relationship might be touched by the wounds of history, deep down Israelis were aware of the common destiny that bound the two peoples together in their struggle for survival. They were convinced that cooperation between them enshrined a key for stability and progress for the Middle East as a whole. As Herzog spoke in this grandiloquent manner, Hussein alternated between smiles and signs of nervousness. He offered Herzog a cigarette and insisted on lighting it with his lighter.

Herzog proceeded to give a survey of the situation in the Middle East, touching on many of the different conflicts in the area. Hussein broke in with a broad smile and gave his response. With clear signs of nervousness and weighing his words very carefully, he said that he was pleased that Herzog had come to see him. For years he had been endeavouring to build up his country and it was not an easy task because his people had suffered much; there were diverse elements, and he was constantly under pressure from his enemies. He did not want war, as he realized that war would solve nothing. All he sought was to develop a better life for his people. He understood that his people had to recognize and accept Israel as a fact. He admitted that in the past he had been very extremist, but he wanted the Israelis to understand that his family had suffered tragedy. He hoped that a solution would come about, and he was prepared to work towards this goal.

Hussein agreed with Herzog's analysis of the Middle East situation.

His trouble, he said, was with his friends more than with enemies. The Americans supported Nasser to the highest degree and without reservation. They were now also supporting the Ba'th, an unstable and destructive force that would bring communism into the area. Hussein spoke with some bitterness about the Americans and returned to them at several points in the conversation. America took Jordan for granted. He had therefore decided to establish diplomatic relations with the Soviet Union, and he had just completed a successful visit to France. Hussein said that he had nothing personal against Nasser, but that Nasser was incapable of agreeing to a union of equals. He was now careful in his relations with Nasser so as not to provoke him. The Ba'th seemed to be moving on a dangerous course. They were considering a union of Syria and Iraq, and he felt that it was their plan to try to swallow up Jordan.

The more tangible part of the conversation dealt with cooperation in the security, political and economic spheres. Hussein said that he favoured cooperation and asked Herzog to make suggestions. Herzog offered to transmit regularly their assessments of the internal situation in Jordan and of military developments in other Arab countries of the Middle East. He referred in this context to the information they transmitted in 1958 on Mahmud Roussan's plot and to the contact of their head of military intelligence (his brother, Chaim Herzog) with Emil Jamian. Hussein expressed his deep gratitude for their support and for the information they had transmitted to him in the past. Herzog replied that it was vital to establish a means for regular communication about security.

Herzog proceeded to outline a plan for coordinated political action in the Middle East. He argued that America's support for Nasser was due in no small part to the absence of a coordinated initiative on the part of his opponents. If clear lines of policy were worked out between Iran, Turkey, Jordan and Israel, a new concept for the Middle East might evolve and an effective counter-balance to Nasser be created. Hussein seemed particularly impressed with this idea and proceeded to reiterate his criticism of American policy. Herzog replied that Israel could be of assistance in an effort to project a positive image of Hussein and Jordan in the US press and in Congress. Hussein remarked that the situation was growing more difficult and that he would appreciate any help that Israel could proffer. The discussion then moved on to economic issues like water, tourism and the resettlement of the Palestinian refugees. Here the discussion helped to clarify the issues in dispute without leading to any concrete conclusions. But in the course of the conversation both sides had ample opportunity to state their basic position. Herzog emphasized Israel's commitment to the independence and integrity of the Hashemite Kingdom of Jordan. Hussein expressed his deepest admiration for Israel's achievements.

The last part of the meeting was devoted to the technicalities of establishing and maintaining regular communication. Herzog submitted that this was absolutely vital and asked Hussein to appoint two high-level representatives, one for security and military questions, and the other for political and economic questions. Hussein promised to give the matter some thought after his return home and stressed the importance of keeping their contact secret. When Herzog reached the door, he turned towards Hussein and bowed. Hussein acknowledged with a warm smile and with a wave of the hand. To Dr. Herbert, who escorted him out of the residence, Hussein said that he was highly pleased with the meeting.[48]

On the following day Hussein paid another visit to Dr. Herbert and handed him a secret code for contacting him in Amman without any risk of the message being seen or intercepted by any unauthorized persons. Hussein said that he was very pleased with the meeting and that he had been highly impressed by the presentation that had been made to him. Yaacov Herzog needed no reminding about the importance of secrecy because he was by nature an exceedingly careful, discreet and secretive man. Even in his private diary he resorted to codes, but in his official reports he took this habit to ludicrous lengths. He registered in his hotel under the pseudonym "Dr. Davis" and referred to the other participants in the drama by elaborate code names that are not very difficult to decipher from the context. Thus Dr. Herbert was "the lawyer"; Queen Zain was "the cousin"; Jordan was "Menashe"—a reference to one of the twelve biblical tribes of Israel; and Hussein, for some strange reason, was "Charles." At the end of his thirteen-page report on the first meeting, Herzog penned the following impression:

Charles is short and stocky, effusing simultaneously warmth and nervous energy. I was struck by the apparent contradictions in his posture—maturity with leadership, levity with dignity, escapism with responsibility. The almost crushing burden of perilous leadership seemed to have caught his youth unaware. As I watched him at close quarters I recalled the description of Bernard Shaw attributed to Chesterton: "I see in him two personalities and at times they come so close to each other that I had to hold my breath." As I took my leave I said from the depth of my heart that I felt that the meeting was providential and I prayed that the Almighty would guide the unfolding contact and cooperation towards fruition. Charles seemed moved and nodded assent.[49]

The most extraordinary thing about this meeting between the Arab ruler and the Jewish emissary is that it took place at all. One factor that helps to explain it is Hussein's perception that the Americans were wavering in their commitment to the survival of his regime as a result of their desire to accommodate Nasser. Fear that the Americans might abandon him made Hussein more willing to open a strategic dialogue with Israel in September 1963.[50] Meir Amit, the head of military intelligence from 1961 to 1963 and director of the Mossad from 1963 to 1968, stressed the American dimension in Israel's relationship with Jordan. America was important to both Israel and Jordan. Hussein had a feeling that Israel's influence in America was decisive and that affected his attitude towards Israel. Another factor that helped Israel get closer to Hussein was that there were fewer problems and fewer conflicts in Israel's relations with Jordan than in its relations with the other neighbouring Arab states. Amit was not sure whether the word "liberal" was appropriate for Hussein, but he was always more open to contacts with Israel than other Arab rulers. Amit used to say that the sea was stormy and if Israel wanted to continue to swim, it had to swim under the waves. Following this precept turned the Mossad into the secret foreign ministry of the State of Israel and led to the establishment of secret links with a number of Arab states. All these links were grounded in common interests. In the case of Jordan, however, Israel was able to get right up to the top of the pyramid.[51]

The basic premise of Hussein's policy was that Israel was there to stay. The issue for him was how to reach accommodation and how to cooperate in the post-peace period. For him the existence of Israel was never in question and neighbourly relations with her were desirable, if not inevitable. He never harboured any illusions of fighting Israel for the sake of eliminating it. There was thus an obvious tension between his public commitment to Arab unity and to the liberation of Palestine on the one hand, and his private commitment to a peaceful resolution of the conflict over Palestine on the other. This tension did not trouble Hussein, according to one of his close advisers. Hussein knew that Arab leaders always had two languages on Palestine: one was solely for the benefit of the public, while the other reflected their pragmatism and directed their policy. He had no difficulty making use of the same dual discourse.[52]

10. The Palestinian Challenge

Hussein's first face-to-face encounter with an Israeli official was followed by a successful effort to re-establish himself as an Arab and an accepted leader among the Arabs. For the British ambassador this was the most significant feature of 1964: "After all these years in the Arab wilderness, the prophetic lineage tainted by too close links with the West, of suspect zeal in the struggle against Zion, the Old Harrovian tie like a halter round his neck, he has made a remarkable comeback."[1] This comeback was made possible by Hussein's rapprochement with Nasser. The much vaunted and much feared UAR was consigned to the scrap heap as old rivalries and old jealousies reasserted themselves between Nasser and the Ba'th parties of Syria and Iraq.[2] A major realignment was taking place in the Arab world that brought Hussein and Nasser much closer together. Hussein gained unprecedented popularity in Jordan and was able to sleep more soundly in his bed at night. But in the longer term there was bound to be a political price to pay for this association. Some politicians, notably Wasfi Tall, cautioned against what they saw as the appeasement of Nasser, but their warning was disregarded by the increasingly self-confident king.

Nasser invited all the heads of Arab states to a summit meeting in Cairo on 13–17 January 1964. This was a new departure in Arab politics, with "unity of objectives" being replaced by the less ambitious and more inclusive slogan of "unity of ranks." The new approach enabled Jordan to return to the Arab fold, and Hussein was treated by Nasser as a long-lost friend on his arrival in Cairo. One positive outcome of the summit was an agreement to put an end to inter-Arab slanging on the radio and in the press. Below the surface, however, two conflicting forces continued to turn the wheels of Arab politics: the unifying force of the conflict with Israel, and the dividing force of separate and distinctive national interests.[3] Called in part to discuss Arab countermeasures to Israel's plan to divert the headwaters of the Jordan River from their natural storage basin at the Sea of Galilee to the Negev, the summit's hidden agenda was to bolster Nasser's leadership in the Arab world following his fracture with his revolutionary allies.

The summit reached three decisions: the first was to divert water from the tributaries of the Jordan River before it entered the territory of Israel; the second was to set up a United Arab Command to deal with possible military action by Israel; and the third was to form a Palestinian entity. These decisions had far-reaching consequences for Jordan, and Hussein had misgivings about all of them, especially the last two; but, for the sake of his new friendship with Nasser, which enhanced his popularity at home and his legitimacy in the Arab world, he went along with them. The decision on water was the least threatening. It was the result of Nasser's efforts to isolate Syria and to prevent it from undertaking independent military action that risked embroiling the Arab states in a war with Israel for which he knew they were not ready. In 1955 the American envoy, Eric Johnston, presented a plan for distributing the water of the Jordan River and its tributaries. Israel was allocated 40 percent of the water and the remaining 60 percent was to go to Lebanon, Syria and Jordan, with Jordan getting the largest share. The Arab states adhered to their respective quotas but refrained from adopting the plan officially because it implied recognition of the State of Israel. Hussein could live with the summit decision because it did not entail military action and because only the upper tributaries in Lebanon and Syria were to be diverted, not the ones in Jordan. The decision also dovetailed with Jordan's development plan and opened up the prospect of Arab funding for the Jordanian irrigation scheme. The second decision, to set up a United Arab Command, was not welcome because it involved subordination to an overall Egyptian commander, dependence on unreliable external powers and the presence of foreign troops on Jordanian soil. Taken together, these two decisions increased the risk of an armed confrontation between the Arab states and Israel.

But the summit decision with the most profound significance for Jordan was the one that led to the establishment of the Palestine Liberation Organization (PLO). The announcement spoke vaguely of "organizing the Palestinian Arab people to enable it to play its role in liberating its country and determining its future," but the challenge to Jordan was unmistakable. Whereas the United Arab Command threatened to impair Jordan's independence in the making of foreign policy, the PLO threatened to undermine the very foundations of the Hashemite Kingdom of Jordan by claiming to represent its Palestinian population. The magnitude of the challenge can be gauged from the fact that, as stated earlier, two thirds of Jordan's population at this time were Palestinians. Ever since the merger of the West Bank with the kingdom in 1950, the Hashemite regime strove to integrate the Palestinians into Jordanian society and insisted that the population on both banks constituted one indivisible people. The guiding principle of the regime was to oppose the emergence of a separate Palestinian identity and to resist the formation of a separate Palestinian power base. This was reflected in the slogan of the regime: "Jordan is Palestine and Palestine is Jordan."

In line with this policy, Hussein resisted earlier proposals made by Iraq, Syria and Egypt in the Arab League for the creation of a Palestinian entity.[4] These took various forms but they were all intended to encourage Palestinian separatism by allowing them to have their own representatives to international forums. The government of Jordan, by contrast, had always insisted that it alone spoke officially for the Palestinians within its borders. At the Cairo conference, however, Hussein modified this long-held position by going along with the collective decision to create a new Palestinian entity. A compromise was reached whereby the UAR and other Arab governments agreed that a revived Palestinian entity, though it would be institutionalized, would not challenge Jordan's sovereignty over West Jordan.

Going along with this compromise was a serious mistake. It could be argued that the PLO was created not to take the West Bank from Jordan but to liberate Palestine from Israel; the real target was Israel, not Jordan. On the other hand, the West Bank was part of Palestine; the PLO was bound to want to include it in its sphere of operations and make a bid for the loyalty of its inhabitants. So in the long term the PLO posed more of a threat to Jordan than to Israel. As Asher Susser has noted, "There was a fundamental incompatibility between the PLO's ambition to exercise authority and patronage over the Palestinian population, the majority of whom were in Jordan, and the demand of the regime for complete sovereign authority over the territory of the Kingdom and its citizens."[5] At Cairo, Hussein took his first steps on the slippery path that was to lead to war with Israel in 1967, to the loss of the West Bank, and to the civil war on the East Bank in September 1970.

In the short term, however, Hussein could bask in the glory reflected in his rapprochment with Nasser and his progressive posture towards the nascent Palestinian entity. His performance at the summit raised his stature and popularity with the Jordanian public. On his tour of the major West Bank towns he was accorded a hero's welcome. Hussein thought he could control the Palestinian movement in Jordan, but it began to gather its own momentum. The real sponsor of the Palestinian entity was Nasser, and he conceived of it not as an independent force for the liberation of Palestine but as an instrument of Egyptian foreign policy. A constituent assembly had to be convened to give an institutional expression to the summit decision on the Palestinian entity. The choice was between holding it in Jordan and imposing Jordanian conditions or outside Jordan, in which case there would be no restraints. Hussein chose the former as the lesser of two evils. A Palestinian National Congress was held in Jerusalem at the end of May, with King Hussein acting as a reluctant and suspicious host. The congress chose Ahmad Shuquairi, a Palestinian lawyer and demagogue who was close to Syria, as the first chairman of the PLO. It also undertook to refrain from interfering in the internal affairs of the Arab states, and it recognized Jordanian sovereignty on both sides of the Jordan River. This was a conciliatory gesture towards Jordan, promising coexistence. But the congress also resolved that the PLO should have its own flag and anthem, and that it should set up offices at the UN, in the countries of the Soviet bloc and in the Arab states. From the outset it was thus obvious that the attempt to achieve independence for the Palestinians and coexistence with Jordan was an attempt to square a circle.

At Cairo, Hussein came under subtle pressure from Nasser to accept Soviet weapons for his army. Hussein regarded the United States with a mixture of respect and resentment. For some time he had been questioning the wisdom of having "all his eggs in the Western basket," and this had led him to establish diplomatic relations with the Soviet Union. Relations with the Soviet bloc provided him with some sort of a counterweight to dependence on the Western powers. After the Cairo summit he started to play the Russian card in his quest for Western weapons. He let it be known that if Jordan's needs were not met by its friends, he might follow Nasser's lead and start shopping in Moscow for military hardware. The veiled threat secured for Hussein an invitation to an official visit to the United States in April. In his public statements Hussein sought to put his visit in the context of the Arab summit con-

ference decisions. He made it clear that he regarded the Palestine problem as "a question of life and death" and that he intended to convey the
Arab point of view to all whom he met in the course of his trip. But
there was no single Arab point of view, and Hussein faced the complicated problem of trying to do what he knew was in Jordan's interest and
at the same time not getting out of step with his Arab colleagues.

The most important meeting of Hussein's American trip was with
President Lyndon Baines Johnson in the White House on 14 April 1964.
The briefing papers for this meeting described the twenty-eight-year-
old monarch as "capable, courageous, and proud." Despite almost universal doubts that he could survive, he had weathered eleven turbulent
years on the throne. Hussein was also described as "a frank and open
friend of the West" and consequently the target of vitriolic propaganda
by fellow Arabs, who portrayed him as a stooge of America. On his trip
to America, Hussein was buoyed by his improved relations with the
other Arab countries, particularly the UAR, and deeply conscious of his
role as spokesman for all Arab states.[6] Johnson was advised to make it
clear to Hussein that "Jordan can count on us if it plays the game," to
both reassure him of American support and to make him realize that
this was a two-way street. Most interestingly, Johnson was assured that
relations with Israel would not suffer as a result of support for Hussein:
"There will be no Israeli kickback if you're friendly to Hussein, because
they're even more anxious to keep him on the throne than we are. The
last thing they want is another activist Syrian or Nasserite regime sitting right next to them."[7]

Johnson welcomed Hussein in public "both as soldier and wise and
resolute man of peace." But the main item on the working agenda was
the Arab–Israeli conflict, and Johnson had a reputation for being a great
admirer and friend of Israel. Johnson tried to strike an even-handed
posture, but his bias towards Israel was evident throughout. In his characteristically blunt Texan style he reminded Hussein of the large
amount of aid that his country had already given Jordan. He was prepared to consider the supply of arms, but he warned Hussein that flirt-
ing with Moscow was unlikely to go down well in Congress. The final
congressional aid level of support, he said, would be influenced more
by Jordan than by the White House and accepting Soviet equipment
might seriously jeopardize the whole American aid programme. He
also pointed out that the supply of arms to Jordan would prompt Israeli

demands for compensation and could end up fuelling the arms race in the Middle East.

Hussein expressed gratitude for the economic aid that his country received and welcomed the opportunity to tell the Arab side of the story. There was Arab annoyance, he said, that so many sorely needed resources had to be diverted to counter the major threat of Israel, a hostile state that split the Arab worlds of Asia and Africa and complicated the problems of development. Jordan bore the brunt of the problem because of its large numbers of Palestinian refugees. Hussein said that Arab policy at that time was the containment of Israel. Stability in the area depended on the establishment of a balance between Israel and the Arab states. Israel had to be brought to realize that it could not continue to maintain a position in the area based on force. At present, there was no balance between the Arabs and Israel, and this has led the Arabs to look to the Soviets for military equipment. Johnson and his advisers tried to explain and justify their support for Israel. They thought that Arab fears of Israeli expansionism were unfounded. Hussein replied that their differing estimates of Israel's expansionism and capabilities should not prevent them from exploring areas of possible cooperation.[8] None the less he left Washington empty-handed and came under renewed pressure from Nasser to turn to Moscow for arms.

Marching on the path to Arab unity had implications for Hussein's relations with Israel as well as with America. Hussein's public statements and actions gave the Israelis cause for concern, and they sought clarification through the secret channel. Yaacov Herzog requested a meeting with the king, and on 2 May 1964, the meeting took place at the home of Dr. Emanuel Herbert in St. John's Wood, London. Herzog was immediately struck with the change that seemed to have come over Hussein since their meeting the previous September: he looked firm, tranquil and dignified, and had about him an air of calm statesmanship. The meeting lasted an hour and three quarters, and covered a broad range of topics connected with bilateral relations, and regional and international politics. Herzog restated Israel's commitment to the independence and integrity of Jordan, and reported on their lobbying in Washington against cuts in the aid budget to Jordan and attempts to get some private companies to invest money there. Hussein explained that his policy in the Middle East was directed at controlling the extremists. At the conference of the heads of state in Cairo he had tried to keep all the Arab leaders together and in this way to prevent the extremists from acting on their own. The main thing now was to get the Arab leaders to concentrate on economic development.

The dispute over the water of the Jordan River was the principal and the most contentious issue in the discussion. Earlier that month Israel had inaugurated the programme in which the National Water Carrier conveyed water for irrigation from the Sea of Galilee to the Negev. Herzog said that Israel would abide by the American envoy Eric Johnston's allocations if the Arabs did the same. He disputed Hussein's charge that this was causing increased salinity in the lower flow of the Jordan River. Hussein said that he was working to ensure that the Arab plan for diverting the headwaters of the river did not depart from the Johnston Plan. Herzog seized the opportunity to warn that any action contrary to the Johnston Plan would lead to tension. A diversion of the Banias tributary to the Jordan River in Syria or of the Hasbani tributary in Lebanon beyond their immediate vicinity, for example, would be considered by Israel as a flagrant departure from the plan. Whatever the quantities of water involved, Israel would consider itself free from the Johnston framework, which would then fall apart, and serious trouble would ensue. On this issue, there was no meeting of minds.

As in the previous meeting Herzog gave a detailed intelligence survey of the various conflicts in the region and analysed closely Nasser's recent moves. On this occasion, however, Hussein leaped to Nasser's defence. He conceded that Nasser could be impulsive but added that, in their recent conversations, the Egyptian leader admitted that he had made mistakes in the past and asked that these be forgotten. Nasser was now ready to work together with other Arab countries in equality and in mutual respect for the good of the Arab world. He agreed with Hussein that the quarrels between the Arab countries had weakened the Arabs, diverting their attention and economic resources from the more important objective of development. Over the years Hussein had argued for cooperation and the abandonment of any attempt at control by one Arab country of another. Nasser now agreed with him. This was the basis of their relationship.

Having covered all the ground on his agenda, Herzog suggested that he sum up the talk. Hussein nodded assent. Herzog said (1) they had reaffirmed that their common objective was to work towards an ultimate settlement. War could bring only endless tragedy. Peace would open up a great future for the Arab people and Israel. Hussein interpolated to say that war could solve nothing. (2) It was agreed that each side should proceed with water development within the Johnston allocations and without departing from the Johnston framework. (3) Integrity and independence of all countries in the area was their common interest. (4) Israel, for its part, would study ways of assisting Jordanian economic development. (5) Hussein, for his part, would study ways and means of alleviating tension—propaganda, arms race and so on. Somewhat embarrassed at being pinned down, Hussein blushed and nodded simultaneously.

At the end of the meeting they discussed the method of communication. Herzog wanted Hussein to appoint a representative to meet regularly with them, to advance cooperation and exchange impressions. At their last meeting he had felt that this could be arranged. Were there no people he could trust to maintain the contact? Hussein replied that there were those whom he could trust. "At this stage, however, I do not want to take further people into this matter." How then, Herzog asked, could cooperation be developed? Hussein replied that Herzog could come to meet him whenever he went abroad. Moreover, Herzog could communicate with him through their common friend. Hussein then asked whether Herzog ever went to Eilat. When he replied that he did, Hussein said with a broad smile that he was often in Aqaba and thus they were close to each other. Herzog asked him if he had a residence in Jerusalem. Hussein said that he was building a house there. Herzog asked if he could go to visit him there. Smiling broadly Hussein replied, "Not yet."[9] As they rose to leave, Herzog remarked that Allah had preserved the king from his enemies and that he had become a living legend of courage and survival. It was surely the will of merciful Providence that he should be an emissary of peace in the Middle East. Hussein blushed and smiled, they shook hands and he left the room. Herzog went away with the impression that Hussein accepted the permanence of Israel and at any rate considered that war was no solution to the Arab–Israel problem. If Hussein believed otherwise, reasoned Herzog, the risk of continuing the contact would surely have seemed to him greater than the risk of snapping it.[10]

Hussein was unlikely to cut his newly established contact with Israel because his entire foreign policy was based on balancing between rival forces in order to avoid becoming isolated or too dependent. The principle of balancing applied at all levels: the inter-Arab, the regional and the global. In practical terms this meant balancing between Arab conservatives and Arab radicals, between the Arab world on the one hand and Israel on the other, and, at the global level, between the West and the Soviet bloc. At all these different levels, Hussein's dynastic interests were paramount. The survival of the Hashemite dynasty was the guiding principle behind his foreign policy, the key to the constant shifts and manoeuvres, to all the alliances and realignments. Hussein made sure he always had at least one major Arab power on his side to provide protection. Thus, when the UAR threatened him, he forged an alliance with Saudi Arabia. Now that the Syrian militants were pushing the Arab states to a showdown with Israel, he could use his new friendship with Nasser in order to restrain them. The covert contact with Israel afforded him a measure of protection and he also tried to turn it to his advantage in his relationship with America. But Israel was not just one more element to be balanced but a country that was unique in the Middle East by virtue of its history, religion, democracy, military power and special relationship with the United States. In short, Israel was a very complex country to handle, and Hussein's contact with it greatly complicated the rest of his foreign policy.

The most burning issue for Hussein was military hardware. The first Arab summit in January had called for an Arab military build-up as part of the scheme to counter the Israeli diversion of water from Lake Galilee. The richer Arab states agreed to finance the arms purchases of the poorer ones such as Jordan. Nasser exerted subtle but constant pressure on Hussein to accept cheap Soviet arms (and UAR technicians) to equip half a dozen new brigades and a squadron of MiG-21 supersonic jets. Not wishing to become dependent on Soviet arms or UAR technicians, Hussein replied that he could get what he needed from his Western friends. He then turned to the Americans with a big shopping list, including twenty F-104 supersonic starfighters, promising that the other Arabs would pay for it. He freely admitted that, while related to Jordanian defence along the border with Israel, the arms were urgently needed to help Jordan stand up to pressures from the United Arab Command.

This request presented a dilemma for the Americans. They understood that Hussein was in a box: that unless he acted as a good Arab, he might endanger his own throne; but also that if he let UAR technicians into Jordan, he would risk growing UAR influence and a possible coup.

On the other hand, the pressure applied through the United Arab Command for an arms build-up in Jordan was part of a larger Arab effort to attain military parity with Israel, and it threatened important American interests. The first question was how to meet Hussein's arms requests without abandoning their traditional policy of restraint on arms sales in the Middle East. The second question was how to obtain Israel's acquiescence in the sale of US arms to Jordan. Israel shared with America a strong interest in a free Jordan under Hussein as an insurance against another Arab–Israeli flare-up. But the sale of advanced US arms to Jordan was bound to provoke loud protests from Israel and even louder protests from its friends in Washington. The Johnson administration dealt with this dilemma by offering to provide gradually most of the equipment for ground forces that Jordan asked for on a part-credit, part-cash basis and to postpone a decision on supersonic aircraft.[11] The gambit was to buy time rather than to confront Hussein head-on regarding the advanced aircraft.

This offer was sufficient to enable Hussein to resist the pressures on him to go for Soviet MiG-21s during the lead up to the second summit of Arab heads of state that Nasser convened in Alexandria from 5 to 11 September 1964. At the Cairo summit the Arab states had pledged $42 million a year for a number of years to help enlarge and equip the armed forces of Jordan, Syria and Lebanon. At Alexandria the pledge was increased to $56 million a year. The more important decision was to proceed immediately with the construction of a storage dam at Mukheiba on the Yarmouk River and to divert water into it from the Banias and Hasbani rivers. Jordan was promised a contribution from the Arab states towards the cost of constructing the dam, which was estimated at $28.7 million. This was the Arab answer to Israel's extension of the National Water Carrier from the Jordan River Basin to the Negev. But in general the summit took a step back from the brink of actions that might have provoked an immediate Israeli military response. The Mukheiba project was assigned the first priority at the Alexandria summit and this was not particularly provocative. The Lebanese originally maintained that no counter-diversion construction should begin until complete military preparedness had been achieved. In the end, however, they accepted Nasser's "compromise" proposal that construction should begin without delay but that actual diversion be deferred until the military build-up had been completed.[12]

Nasser in fact emerges as the leading conciliator at the summit from a verbal report of the proceedings that Hussein gave to his CIA contact. Nasser was reasonable and moderate throughout the conference, and he succeeded in avoiding open splits and breakdowns. He had apparently concluded that summitry was the best possible vehicle for pursuing his interests. Hussein was expected to be a major antagonist to a number of proposals, such as increasing the authority of the United Arab Command and of the Palestinian entity. Fortuitously, he was relieved of this role by Lebanon, Syria and Saudi Arabia, which took the lead in opposing them. Some of their attacks were so extreme that Hussein ended up defending rather than opposing Shuqairi, who had proposed the stationing of several brigades of Palestinian Arabs in the countries bordering Israel. Another proposal related to the composition and authority of the United Arab Command. Hussein felt that the compromise solutions reached on these issues did not jeopardize Jordan's interests, and indeed that they enabled him to appear more Arab than many of his colleagues. He was therefore confident that summitry would continue and that it enabled the Arabs to follow a moderate and an increasingly realistic course.[13] This was at least partly based on wishful thinking. It glossed over the commitment of the members of the Arab League to assist the PLO and to endorse the decision of the organization to set up the Palestine Liberation Army (PLA). For Jordan this decision was to have far-reaching consequences.

Some of the implications of the conference were reviewed together by King Hussein and Dr. Herzog at their third meeting in London. The meeting again took place at the home of Dr. Emanuel Herbert, on Saturday, 19 December 1964 between 12:10 and 1:20 p.m. Dr. Herbert was present throughout the meeting. Of the three meetings this was the shortest and the most businesslike, but it still covered a lot of ground. At the beginning, Hussein asked a question about the internal political crisis in Israel, and he received a full answer. Herzog, who as usual had been well briefed by intelligence chiefs, gave his assessment of recent developments in the Middle East. Hussein listened intently throughout the presentation and at its conclusion said that he thought the analysis "was correct."

The discussion then turned to bilateral issues, starting with the Unified Arab Command. Herzog said that the unified command opened up possibilities for gradual subversion on the part of the Egyptians. The Egyptians were making efforts to impress Jordanian officers with the strength and efficiency of the Egyptian war-machine, and this process could ultimately be dangerous. Israel had intelligence that the Egyptians had also contemplated using more direct methods to influence a Jordanian Air Force officer by the name of Ibrahim Atmah. On hearing this, Hussein's body stiffened and his face turned serious. Herzog added immediately that they had no information as to whether Atmah had actually been approached and there was certainly no indication that he had agreed to cooperate, at which point Hussein relaxed.

Herzog pointed out that within the framework of the unified command Jordan had moved a further brigade to the West Bank, bringing up the total to three. While he was sure that no aggressive purpose was behind this, a large concentration of troops on the border inevitably created tension. Smiling broadly, Hussein said, "What have you to fear? You know how strong you are." Herzog replied that he was not referring to the overall military balance but to the danger that, with heavy concentrations of troops on both sides of the frontier, things might happen unintentionally. He asked Hussein to withdraw at least a token force to the East Bank. Hussein promised to consider the request. Then, assuming a serious mien and looking straight at Herzog, he said, "I wish to assure you that only defensive plans have been brought before the Unified Command. No plans for offensive action have even been considered. The troops in the Jordanian plain are stationed within the Jordanian defence plan." Thanking him for this assurance, Herzog said that they had heard that the Iraqis had entered Jordan to establish a radar station and ammunition dumps, and that they considered this development to be dangerous to Jordanian security. Hussein reacted with slight emotion to say that "no foreign forces will come into Jordan" and repeated for emphasis "none." He then went on to say, "We are fully aware of the danger of foreign troops in our country. We are carefully watching the dangers."

On President Nasser the two men did not see eye to eye. Herzog regarded the Unified Arab Command as a framework through which Nasser could lay foundations for a later attempt to undermine Jordan. Hussein replied that he had engaged over the past year in a policy of "collective action" that seemed to be working. He spoke frankly of the reasons behind this policy. First, he wished to develop his country in peace and to keep it free from subversion. Second, when the Arab leaders were together there was more responsibility and thus more moderation. Third, when the Arab leaders acted separately, Nasser's influence was far greater than when they acted collectively. Herzog gave his own opinion that Nasser's aim was to destroy Israel. Hussein, on the basis of his private talks with Nasser, felt that Nasser understood the position and that ultimately he would want a settlement.

From Nasser the conversation moved to Ahmad Shuqairi. Herzog noted that the PLO had opened offices in Jerusalem, Nablus, Tulkarem, Irbid and elsewhere, and that they were planning to recruit Palestinians for the Liberation Army. In Israel's assessment, he said, Shuqairi and his movement presented a real danger to Hussein and to the integrity of his country. Hussein replied that there would be no recruiting in his country and that he would not permit any units of Shuqairi's new force to be stationed there. Contemptuously, he said that a few units might be stationed in Gaza. Nevertheless, Hussein had not thought it wise to try to block Shuqairi entirely. The Palestinians had complained for years that they were denied self-expression. Hussein was sure that they would eventually see that the new course would take them nowhere. "I withdraw and let them go their way. They will return," he said confidently. Herzog thought the dangers should not be underestimated. Smiling broadly, Hussein commented that Shuqairi talked of having a government and a people, but that they were watching him.

Another question raised by Herzog was the use of Soviet and Egyptian arms for the expansion of the Jordanian Army. With some emotion Hussein said, "They tried in Cairo to push Soviet arms on me but I refused. I will receive arms from the West and prove that one does not have to rely on the Soviets in order to develop an army." To Herzog it appeared that there were considerable prospects of increasing economic aid to Jordan and that through economic progress the validity of Hussein's view, as compared to that of Egypt, would be effectively proved. Herzog reported that, after their previous meetings, Israel had discreetly encouraged US senators and officials to increase economic aid to Jordan. He considered it important that Hussein too should meet US senators for this purpose. On the water question there was the briefest of exchanges. Herzog thanked Hussein for renewing the flow from the Yarmouk. Hussein noted that the water plans were being developed in accordance with the Johnston Plan. Towards the end of the meeting Herzog reminded Hussein that he had promised to appoint a person on his side to maintain regular contact. Hussein replied that at that stage he could not take anyone else into the secret.

Despite this and other disagreements, Herzog sensed that they were making good progress. At their first meeting in September 1963, Hussein appeared "a hunted man in fear of his safety and seeking the assurance of our continued interest in his survival." At the second meeting "he had sat with majestic airs, clearly himself impressed by the new status he had achieved in the meanwhile in the Arab world through the rapproachement with Nasser." At that meeting Hussein had sought to defend Nasser, at least pro forma. The atmosphere had been strained at times, and on the water problem Herzog felt obliged to speak with some vigour. At the third meeting the atmosphere was more cordial and balanced. On the personal level, at least, Herzog had the feeling of close communication. Hussein was relaxed and frank. He did not seek to defend Nasser but to explain frankly the nature of their relationship. The third conversation not only indicated that the contact for Hussein was of a substantive nature; it also developed the relationship to a point where Herzog could intuitively sense its character, possibilities and limitations.[14]

Israel continued to use its influence in Washington to make the case for American economic and political support for Jordan, although it strongly opposed arms supplies. The White House agreed that support for Hussein was a way of helping Israel. Robert Komer, a senior member of the National Security Council staff, made this point very forcefully in a memo to President Johnson: keeping Soviet arms and UAR trainers out of Jordan served Israel's security interests more than it served America's. "In fact, we have no other major security interest in Jordan than to keep Israel from being surrounded. Our whole half billion dollar subsidy during 1957–65 has been primarily for this purpose; it has actually been indirect aid to Israel."[15] The key issue, wrote Komer in another memo, was "How far to go now in order to keep Hussein on the reservation?"[16]

Philip Talbot, the assistant secretary of state for Near Eastern and South Asian affairs, was sent to Amman to find out. At his meeting with King Hussein, Talbot explained America's dilemma in relation to Jordan's arms request. He emphasized that America would not tolerate the introduction of Soviet supersonic aircraft into Jordan; that such action would only undermine the king's position by enhancing Soviet and Egyptian influence in the Jordanian Air Force; and that it would strengthen Israel's drive for more sophisticated military equipment, because Jordan's request would trigger an immediate and much larger request from Israel. Hussein expressed warm appreciation for the trouble that the American government was taking over Jordan's problems and emphasized the defensive nature of Arab plans. The Palestine problem, he said, had been a serious strain on all of them. His objective was to build a better future for his country and to protect its existence, and in this spirit he had taken part in creating the United Arab Command. Arab leaders had met and reached certain decisions. They decided to build up their air strength and to put a cordon round Israel to prevent it from further expansion. Once Jordan and the Arabs became strong, there would be no threat to his country. Anything short of that would not be good for Jordan. In any case, he could testify that the Arabs had no intention of solving the problem of Israel by force. The Arab military build-up would be wholly defensive. Speaking quietly and slowly, Hussein said that Jordan requested M48A3 Medium Patton tanks with 105-millimetre guns in order to have tanks with the same capacity and gun calibre as those Israel was getting. Talbot made no response.

Talbot alluded to the power of the Jewish lobby when he said that the domestic pressures in America would become unmanageable if Jordan accepted arms from the Soviet Union. Hussein said it frightened him to hear statements of this kind, to hear that pressures from minority groups could influence the powerful United States to act against its own best interests. In Jordan he had never been fortunate enough to enjoy broad backing, yet he had not hesitated to fight alone against communist influence. If Jordan's policy had changed, it was not because his views had altered but because of his disappointment with the policies of Jordan's friends.[17] After lunch with the king on the following day, Talbot sent another report that was quite alarming. During lunch the king expressed his foreboding that the end for the Hashemite kingdom was near and his conviction that the West was letting him down. Talbot did not think that threats to cut off aid would make Hussein turn away from the UAR and that the only solution to the crisis lay in persuading the Israelis that limited American sales to Jordan would best serve Israel's interests as well as those of America. The Israelis had to be made to understand that the consequences to Israel of Hussein buckling under to the United Arab Command would be vastly worse than the arms deal under discussion.[18]

In order to keep Jordan "on the reservation" and to calm down

Israel's friends in Congress, Lyndon Johnson decided to link the sale of arms to Jordan with a particularly attractive arms package to Israel. The package reversed long-standing American policy by including offensive as well as defensive weapons. Robert Komer and Averell Harriman, the under-secretary of state for political affairs, were sent to Israel in late February 1965 to sell the proposed linkage to the Israelis. As expected, the Israelis drove a hard bargain. In return for their agreement not to oppose the Jordanian arms deal they were promised Skyhawks and 200–250 advanced tanks with 105-millimetre guns. This was quite a sweetener for swallowing the bitter pill of the arming of Jordan, but there was more to come. The talks concluded with a written protocol in which Harriman proclaimed that the United States had an understanding with King Hussein that the tanks that the Americans would supply would not cross the Jordan River.[19]

The eventual American arms package to Jordan included 250 M-48 tanks with 90-millimetre guns, help with modernizing the Jordanian Air Force and permission to buy suitable aircraft in Western Europe. In return Hussein had to agree not to move the tanks into the West Bank and also pledge not to seek jet fighters from the Kremlin. Hussein's pledge not to deploy the American-made tanks in the West Bank of his kingdom was both secret and highly significant. It accorded with Hussein's repeated assurances to America that his posture vis-à-vis Israel was purely defensive. But it could not be so easily reconciled with the intentions of the other members of the United Arab Command to build up military strength on all of Israel's frontiers in order to hem it in, which was why it was kept strictly secret and shared only with the Israelis. What the pledge amounted to was a partial agreement to demilitarize the West Bank. The thinner the forces deployed by Jordan on the West Bank, the better it was for Israel. Hussein was left in no doubt on this score after his last meeting with Dr. Yaacov Herzog. The written pledge that Hussein gave to the Johnson administration thus represents another milestone in the evolution of his tacit strategic cooperation with Israel. It complemented Hussein's firm assurance to Herzog that he would not allow any foreign troops to be stationed on his territory. If the other leaders of the United Arab Command had any offensive action against Israel at the back of their minds, Hussein most definitely did not.

In February 1965 Hussein appointed Wasfi Tall as prime minister for the second time. Hussein's back was giving him trouble, and he was beginning to feel the strain of the previous year. Having a strong and competent prime minister left Hussein with some time on his hands, and he used it to take a month-long vacation in Europe and to attend to his health. Tall's main complaint on resuming office was that his original Seven-year Development Plan was now dead, and there had been virtually no economic progress in the intervening two years. For the first few months, he drove himself and his ministers like a man possessed in a frantic effort to get results. But "having huffed and puffed to the limit of his lungs, Wasfi at last began to relax, to everyone's relief."[20] Containing the PLO replaced economic development as the dominant issue for the rest of Tall's second term. From the beginning he had been opposed to the creation of the PLO, predicting that it would be too weak to mount a serious challenge to Israel and that it would end up by making peace. He also suspected that Nasser had originally sponsored the PLO not in order to fight for the liberation of Palestine but in order to saddle it with the responsibility for settling the dispute with Israel. In his more paranoid moods, Tall even spoke of Israel and America as being the evil spirits behind the invention of the PLO. He was certainly in no doubt that the new organization and its leader posed a serious threat to the survival of the Hashemite Kingdom of Jordan.[21]

The foreign minister at that time was Dr. Hazem Nusseibeh, a Princeton-educated member of a prominent Palestinian family from Jerusalem. Nusseibeh put forward a proposal for giving the West Bank a limited degree of autonomy and changing the name of the country from "The Hashemite Kingdom of Jordan" to "The United Kingdom of Palestine and Jordan." He wrote a White Paper on relations between Jordan and the nascent Palestinian organization, and included this idea in it. Nusseibeh believed that the alternative name he suggested could remove the dichotomy and allow the Palestinians to feel included. By allowing the Palestinians to choose their own representatives, he wanted to forestall more radical demands. The king was quite agreeable to the idea after listening attentively to the reasoning behind it. Wasfi Tall, on the other hand, spoke forcefully against it. He feared that it would create friction and lead to divided loyalties among Jordanians and Palestinians. Tall won the argument, as usual. In retrospect, Nusseibeh regretted that his proposal was not adopted because he believed it would have made unnecessary the role that the PLO later assumed, that of being the sole legitimate representative of the Palestinian people. Under Nusseibeh's scheme, the PLO would have been able to call itself a representative of the Palestinian people, but by no means the sole representative of the Palestinian people.[22] But it was a compromise proposal, and Tall did not like compromises.

Within a relatively short time, the tensions between the PLO and the regime came to the surface. The clash became inevitable following the second Arab summit's endorsement of the proposal to create the Palestine Liberation Army. Hussein realized this, but he did not wish to stage a showdown with Shuqairi for fear of jeopardizing his relationship with Nasser. It was Shuqairi who issued the first challenge on arrival in Amman, on 24 February 1965, for talks with the Jordanian government. To allay Jordanian fears, Shuqairi declared that Jordan and the PLO were "two wings of the same bird." His actual proposals, however, revealed an unbridgeable chasm between them. They included the setting-up of Palestinian regiments; the arming and fortification of West Bank villages along the border with Israel; military training for the Palestinians in Jordan; and the raising of "popular resistance" units among the Palestinians there. The purpose of the plan was to transform the Palestinians along the border with Israel into "soldiers in the army of return." In addition, Shuqairi demanded the opening of a PLO office in Amman and the collection of 5 percent of the salaries of Palestinian officials in Jordan for the PLO. What Shuqairi proposed, in effect, was a division of labour between the PLO and the Jordanian government whereby the latter would operate on the official state level while the former would operate on the popular level. Tall rejected all of these requests. Jordan and the PLO were now on a collision course.[23]

The breakdown of the negotiations encouraged militant Palestinians to take direct action against Israel in defiance of the authority of the Jordanian government. Al-Fatah, a militant clandestine group formed by Yasser Arafat and others, advocated a guerrilla war to liberate Palestine. Its general strategy was to drag the Arab states into war with Israel by stoking up the fire along the borders. From Jordanian territory al-Fatah mounted a series of rather ineffectual sabotage operations inside Israel. Israel retaliated against these hit-and-run raids with severe military reprisals against Jordanian targets along the border, which prompted the Jordanian government to step up its efforts to prevent the incursions. Its security services carried out arrests of activists, confiscated small arms and explosives, and rounded up Fatah cells on the West Bank. Al-Fatah acted independently of the PLO, but its operations had the effect of making Shuqairi adopt a more combative posture in relation to Israel, and this in turn widened the rift between him and the Jordanian regime. Various measures were taken by Hussein and Tall to fight Shuqairi's irridenta and to prevent him from consolidating his power base on the West Bank. For example, the National Guard, which was based on the West Bank and provided a focus for a possible Palestinian rebellion against the regime, was disbanded and its units integrated with the regular army.

At the third Arab summit, held in Casablanca from 13 to 17 September 1965, the conflict between Jordan and the PLO came out into the open. The "unity of ranks" forged at the first summit in Cairo collapsed in a welter of disputes and mutual recriminations. Shuqairi's demand that the Palestine Liberation Army be allowed to recruit Palestinians from Jordan met with a firm rebuff from Hussein. Lieutenant General Ali Amir, the Egyptian head of the United Arab Command, pressed for permission to send Iraqi and Saudi troops into Jordan before the actual outbreak of hostilities; Hussein made it clear that Jordan would agree to accommodate Arab forces only following the outbreak of hostilities. There was thus no change in the Jordanian position. Collectively, the Arab leaders endorsed gradualism rather than extremism on the Palestine issue. The other major issue was the diversion of the headwaters of the Jordan River. The secretary-general of the Arab League reported that the diversion work had to be stopped because of Israeli aggression. The Syrian representative vowed to keep up the fight against the Zionist enemy, but Nasser injected a characteristic note of caution by warning against resuming the diversion work before the Arabs had improved their land and air defence capabilities. He hinted that if Syria acted unilaterally it would not be able to count on his assistance. In effect he conceded that Israel had won the water war.

From Casablanca, Hussein went to Paris, where he had a secret meeting with Israel's foreign minister, Golda Meir. The transition from an Arab summit conference at which Israel featured as the greatest enemy to a face-to-face meeting with the representative of this enemy was rather dramatic, but then Hussein's relations with the official enemy were full of paradoxes. At Casablanca the discussions revolved round the conflict with Israel; in Paris the leaders explored avenues of cooperation.[24] This was Hussein's first meeting at the ministerial level with the Israeli side. It was arranged by Israel's ambassador to Paris, Walter Eytan, in a private flat in 19 Rue Reynard in the Sixteenth Arrondissement.

"I have wanted to meet you for a long time, and I am pleased about this meeting," said the king to Mrs. Meir when they were introduced. He referred to her meetings with King Abdullah, and expressed his pleasure at being able to follow in the tradition of his beloved grandfather.[25] Thirty years later Hussein was hazy about the details but he recalled clearly the atmosphere that formed the backdrop to the talk:

It was a good meeting. It was really a meeting of breaking the ice, of getting to know one another. And we talked about our dreams for our children and grandchildren to live in an era of peace in the region and I think she suggested that maybe a day would come when we could put aside all the arms on both sides and create a monument in Jerusalem that would signify peace between us and where our young people could see what a futile struggle it had been and what a heavy burden on both sides. Essentially, it didn't go beyond that. There wasn't very much indeed that happened, just an agreement to keep in touch whenever possible.[26]

There was slightly more substance to the meeting than Hussein remembered. Both sides reaffirmed their agreement to abide by the water quotas allocated to them by Eric Johnston in 1955. Jordan departed from the pan-Arab position in agreeing to Israel's diversion of water to the Negev, while Israel approved Jordan's various water conservation projects. Then there was the question of the balance, security and trust. Hussein was expecting to take delivery of the 250 M48 tanks, and he knew that a bad report on his behaviour from Israel could cause delays and complications. Nor was he oblivious to the power of Israel's friends on Capitol Hill. He was therefore anxious to reassure Meir that Israel had nothing to worry about, that no foreign troops would be allowed on Jordan's soil, and that he would honour his commitment not to deploy the new American tanks on the West Bank. Another topic that came up in the talk concerned keeping the border between their two countries quiet. Meir knew that at the Casablanca summit Hussein had fought against Shuqairi's proposal to extend his sphere of operations in Jordan, but she was not content with declarations. She urged the king to take more energetic steps against the groups who were fomenting trouble along the border and especially against the Fatah men, who were crossing into Israel from Syria via Jordan.[27] From Meir's vantage point too this was a good talk both because of the friendly atmosphere in which it was conducted and because of the specific agreements that were reached. The meeting was only one link in a chain of contacts and communications, but it contributed to the de facto peace that prevailed between Israel and Jordan in the mid 1960s, despite the activities of irregular Palestinian forces operating from Jordan's territory and a limited number of retaliatory raids by Israel.[28]

Hussein placed the meeting in the context of a long-term effort to find a peaceful solution to the Arab–Israeli conflict and the proximity of the parties who lived cheek-by-jowl: "with the passage of years one realized we were not talking about a country hundreds of miles away. We were talking about a people and a country with a destiny, both of us. We were in a very small region and we had to figure out how we could resolve our problems. If we looked at water, it was a problem that both of us suffered from. If we looked at even a flu epidemic, it affected both of us. Every aspect of life was interrelated and interlinked in some way or another. And to simply ignore that was something I could not understand. Maybe others could, others who were distant, who were not equally aware or involved. By now there were Palestinians and Jordanians, and their rights, their future was at stake. One had to do something; one had to explore what was possible and what was not."[29]

11. The Road to War

On 13 November 1966 the IDF launched a devastating attack on the village of Samu', south of Hebron on the West Bank, about four miles from the border with Israel. It was staged in broad daylight by a large force with infantry, an armoured brigade, heavy artillery, mortars, engineers and two Mirage squadrons. A Jordanian Army unit was rushed to the scene, but it careered into an ambush and suffered heavy casualties. As a result, 15 Jordanian soldiers and 5 civilians died, 36 soldiers and 4 civilians were wounded, and 93 houses were destroyed, including the police station, the local school, a medical clinic and a mosque. One Jordanian Hunter aircraft was shot down in an air battle and its pilot was killed. The attack was a reprisal for a landmine that had exploded the previous day on the Israeli side of the border, killing three soldiers.

Israel, as was its wont, exacted an overwhelming revenge, but this time it was exacted from the wrong Arab party. Israel's leaders knew full well that Hussein was doing everything in his power to prevent Fatah from staging sabotage operations from his territory because they heard it directly from him and from his representatives on the Mixed Armistice Commission. The Israelis knew equally well that the militant Syrian regime that had come to power in February was training Fatah saboteurs and supporting Fatah operations against Israel from Jordan. For some time Israel's leaders had been pointing an accusing finger at Syria and threatening dire consequences if these attacks did not cease. So the attack on the Jordanian civilians came as a complete surprise both at home and abroad. The reason given by the IDF spokesman was that the saboteurs who had planted the mines on the Israeli side of the border had come from the Hebron area, but no satisfactory explanation was ever given for the scale or ferocity of the attack. This was no routine reprisal raid but the biggest operation of the IDF since the Suez War.

Inside Jordan, the effects of the raid were highly destabilizing, opening old wounds, exposing dramatically the country's military weakness and fragility, and touching off large-scale unrest and violent protest against the regime. Hussein felt personally betrayed by the Israelis because their action contradicted their previously expressed commitment to the safety and stability of Jordan. Furthermore, the raid occurred on his thirty-first birthday and the pilot who was killed was one of his friends. Speaking about this incident thirty years later, Hussein chose to stress the unbalanced and unreasonable nature of the Israeli action:

It really created a devastating effect in Jordan itself, because the action, if it had been an action from Jordan, was not something that Jordan had condoned or sponsored or supported in any way or form. And to my way of thinking at that time, what I couldn't figure out was why react in this way, if a small irrigation ditch or pipe was blown up (assuming it was, which I didn't necessarily know for sure)? Was there any balance between the two? Why did the Israelis attack instead of trying to figure out a way of dealing with the threats in a different way, in a joint way? So it was a shock and it was not a very pleasant birthday present.[1]

At the time Hussein took a much graver view of the raid on Samu', seeing it as a signal of a change in Israel's attitude towards his regime and possibly even as part of a larger design to provoke a war that would enable the IDF to capture the West Bank. No evidence, however, has come to light to support this suspicion, at least not on the part of the Labour-led government. Itzhak Rabin, the IDF chief of staff at that time, claimed that some of the more serious consequences of the raid were unintended. He had repeatedly emphasized that whereas in Syria the problem was the regime, in Jordan the problem was not the regime but the civilians who assisted Israel's Palestinian enemies. The plan of action he had proposed to the cabinet was not intended to inflict casualties on the Jordanian Army but to serve as a warning to the civilian population not to cooperate with the Palestinian saboteurs. The damage greatly exceeded the estimate he had given the cabinet and he later admitted that Levi Eshkol had good reason to be displeased with him. "We had neither political nor military reasons," said Rabin "to arrive at a confrontation with Jordan or to humiliate Hussein."[2]

Eshkol was in fact furious with Rabin for the bloodshed and destruction. He felt that the IDF top brass had given the cabinet bad advice and that the target should have been Syria, not Jordan. The result, in Eshkol's earthy language, was that Israel hit the wife instead of the wicked mother-in-law. There was also an issue of principle. David Ben-Gurion, as prime minister and minister of defence, rarely called on the IDF to account for its actions. Eshkol also combined the premiership with the defence portfolio but he was determined to assert civilian control over the army. Miriam Eshkol, the prime minister's wife, kept a diary. She recalled her husband's bitterness towards the IDF leaders at that time. After the Samu' raid, her husband said to her, "Write down in your diary that, unlike my predecessor, I am not the representative of the army in the government!"[3] The main reason for Eshkol's anger over the Samu' raid, however, was that it ran counter to his policy of supporting Hussein and helping him in his struggle against the Palestinian guerrilla organizations.

Hussein perceived the attack on Samu' as an act of war rather than as a routine retaliatory raid. He interpreted it as an indication that the Israelis were no longer committed to the survival of his regime and were casting their beady eye on the West Bank of his kingdom. For him Samu' was not an isolated incident but part of a wider Israeli design to escalate the border clashes into a full-scale, expansionist war. Ze'ev Bar-Lavie, who served on the Jordanian desk in Israeli Military Intelligence and used to celebrate the king's birthday, gave the following assessment of the consequences of the operation: "The Samu' affair disturbed Hussein deeply. He saw in it an Israeli intention to prepare the ground for the conquest of the West Bank and an aggressive patrol directed at outflanking the Jordanian defence line-up from the south. All the attempts by the Western powers to calm him down were in vain. Hussein refused to relax and remained fixed in his fear that the Jews would exact from Jordan the price for the Syrian attacks and for the operations of the saboteurs. Why should the Jews content themselves with the destruction of a few inferior Syrian brigades? No, they, the Jews, would go for something more concrete like the conquest of the West Bank, the moment they find an excuse."[4] Wasfi Tall was equally convinced that Israel was looking for an excuse to capture the West Bank. He believed that Israel wanted to provoke Jordanian retaliation, which would provide the opportunity to go to war.[5] In short, both Tall and Hussein suspected that Israel was setting a trap for Jordan, and they took care not to fall into it. Instead of retaliating, they referred the matter to the UN security council.

The attack on Samu' and Hussein's failure to respond with force stirred greater Palestinian antipathy towards him and played into the hands of his enemies. Samu' thus widened the existing rift between the regime and its Palestinian subjects. The regime was accused at home and in the Arab world of neglecting the defences of the country and of failing to protect the inhabitants of Samu' against the enemy. The PLO, Syria and Egypt fanned the flames of popular hatred against the regime by launching a fierce propaganda offensive, much of it directed against the king personally. All the pent-up frustrations suddenly came to the surface and fuelled angry and often violent protest. Mass demonstrations erupted in the refugee camps and in the cities of the West Bank. Serious riots convulsed Hebron, Jericho, Jerusalem, Ramallah, Nablus, Jenin, Tulkarem and Qalqilyah. Demonstrators marched through the streets carrying nationalist placards, shouting pro-Nasser slogans and calling on Hussein to follow the path of Nuri as-Said—the Iraqi premier who was killed by the Baghdad mob in 1958. The main targets of the demonstrators were government offices and police vehicles. The army was called in and instructed to use harsh measures to suppress the riots: curfews, mass arrests, tear gas and firing live ammunition into the crowd. Even with these aggressive methods, it took the army the best part of two weeks to restore order. One new feature of this crisis was the active involvement of West Bank leaders and mayors in the anti-Hashemite protests. Some of these notables styled themselves as the "National Leadership"; they demanded the convocation of "a people's convention to discuss the core issues regarding the Homeland"; and they formulated a "national manifesto" that called for the presence of the Arab armies on Jordan's soil and supported the PLO as the only representative of the Palestinian people's will. The manifesto stopped short of asserting a unilateral Palestinian declaration of independence on the West Bank, but it posed a challenge that the Hashemite regime could not afford to ignore.[6]

By provoking such a fierce domestic backlash, the Samu' raid constituted a turning point in the relations between the Hashemite monarchy and the Palestinians of the West Bank, and, in the words of Israeli expert Moshe Shemesh, a turning point "in Jordan's attitude toward Israel, from a state of guarded coexistence to one of disappointment and

pessimism." "At the heart of Jordan's military and civilian estimate,"
Shemesh has written,

stood the unequivocal conclusion that Israel's main design was conquest of the
West Bank, and that Israel was striving to drag all of the Arab countries into a
general war, in the course of which it would make a grab for the West Bank.
According to this appraisal, in light of Jordan's military weakness and the Arab
world's dithering, Israel believed it would have little trouble in seizing the West
Bank. After Samu', these apprehensions so obsessed the Jordanians that they
should be regarded as the deciding factor in King Hussein's decision to participate in the Six-Day War. He was convinced that Israel would occupy the West
Bank whether Jordan joined the fray or not.[7]

For Israel's leaders the immediate worry after Samu' was that Hussein's regime would collapse and that forces from the neighbouring
Arab states would move into Jordan. Dr. Yaacov Herzog was rushed to
London to undo at least some of the damage that the Samu' raid had
inflicted on bilateral relations with Jordan. A meeting with Hussein
was out of the question, so Herzog drafted a letter for Dr. Emanuel Herbert to send to his friend the king. Although Dr. Herbert was extremely
angry with his Israeli friends, he was prevailed upon to send the letter
in order to save what Herzog described as a central project in Israel's
foreign policy. The letter expressed the deepest regret for the loss of life
and assured the recipient on the basis of "the most reliable information
from the highest authority" that there was no change whatsoever in
basic policy. The letter referred to the action as "a blunder of the gravest
character," but it also mentioned the provocation to which Israel was
subjected by the terrorist gangs and ended with a plea for both sides to
make an effort to alleviate the tension, as they had done in the past.[8] Dr.
Herbert received no reply to this letter, and he reported that the friends
of the king, who came to see him after the raid, spoke about Israel in a
very different and extremely hostile manner.[9]

In mid December 1966 a series of discussions took place in Jerusalem on policy towards Jordan with representatives from the Foreign
Ministry, Military Intelligence and the Mossad. There was a general
consensus that the Hashemite regime had demonstrated its determination to survive during the previous eighteen years but also that it had
virtually no chance of survival in the long term. The question was

whether the survival of Hussein's regime was vital for the State of Israel. Here there were two positions. Those who embraced the first said that Hussein was a problem because the existence of the West Bank in its present form was a catastrophe for Israel and he was an obstacle to change. The second position was the polar opposite of the first. Its adherents believed in the status quo; they wanted Hussein to consolidate it; and they looked forward to coexistence with him. The IDF position was described as being halfway between the two approaches. It was reconciled to the existing situation, but it would be glad for an opportunity to establish a new and more convenient status quo.[10] With such opposing views and tendencies within the political–military establishment, it is not surprising that Hussein was getting mixed messages from the Israeli side.

Mistrust of Israel made Hussein turn to America for reassurance. The Johnson administration sharply rebuked Israel for its raid on Samu' and voted in the Security Council for a resolution condemning the attack. Hussein had strong backing from Findley Burns, Jr., the American ambassador to Amman, and from Jack O'Connell, the CIA station chief in Amman from 1967 to 1971. Burns suspected that Egypt, Syria and Israel were not too worried about the consequences of a short Arab–Israeli war that might end with the collapse of Jordan. He did not imply that the Israeli attack on Samu' was part of a dark plot to set in train an Arab–Israeli war or cause the liquidation of the Hashemites. Nor did he discount the advantages for Jordan's neighbours in retaining the country's present regime. He merely suggested that there could none the less be strong policy considerations in all three countries working against their instincts for caution. For these countries the continuation of a moderate Jordan was "the stopper that keeps the dirty water from running out of the bathtub." For Burns, by contrast, the status quo in Jordan was vital for the maintenance of balance and stability in the Middle East.[11]

Jack O'Connell had a closer relationship with King Hussein than any other American official before or after, one that was based on mutual respect and absolute trust. O'Connell was a well-educated man. As a Fulbright Scholar he did an M.A. in Islamic Law in the University of the Punjab, after which he returned to Georgetown University to do a Ph.D. in international law. During the 1958 crisis he was sent to reinforce the CIA team in Jordan and that was when he and the king bonded. O'Connell was a man of complete integrity and Hussein always found him to be entirely reliable. Hussein reciprocated O'Connell's honesty by being honest with him in turn. Hussein could be vague and give indirect answers, but he did not tell outright lies. As a result of this honesty, the working relationship between the two men was both harmonious and effective. O'Connell gave tremendous assistance to the king and his kingdom. The relationship continued after O'Connell retired from the CIA in 1971 and joined a law firm in Washington. He became the family lawyer of the Hashemites and an adviser and advocate of the Jordanian government.[12]

President Johnson was persuaded by his advisers of the need to support Jordan. On 23 November he sent a secret private letter to Hussein that opened by saying: "Words of sympathy are small comfort when lives have been needlessly destroyed." Johnson went on to make two points. First, he assured Hussein that his administration maintained its interest in the peace and security of Jordan and in the well-being of its people. Second, having heard from Burns about Hussein's concern, Johnson wanted to assure him that Israel's policies had not changed and that Israel did not intend to occupy the West Bank of the Jordan River. America's opposition to the use of force to alter borders in the Near East had been made unmistakably clear to Israel both in private representations and in public statements, and Johnson was certain that it was fully understood and appreciated by the Israelis.[13]

Johnson's letter was significant for the promise it provided to oppose any attempt by Israel to change the border at Jordan's expense, but it did not dispel Hussein's fears. Hussein invited Burns and O'Connell to see him on the evening of 10 December at his private residence at Al-Hummar. Burns had never seen the king so grim or so obviously under pressure. It was apparent that he had to use the utmost self-restraint to keep his emotions from erupting openly. At several points in the conversation Hussein had tears in his eyes. He said that although the demonstrations had abated, pressures under the surface were in fact building up. The discontent on the West Bank was deeper than he had imagined. "The growing split between the East Bank and the West Bank has ruined my dreams." The only thing that bound the army to him, Hussein said, was traditional loyalty, but this was daily growing weaker: "There is near despair in the army and the army no longer has confidence in me."

Hussein said that he was beset on all sides by enemies, outside Jordan and within. Syria was openly calling for his overthrow, publicly offering arms and covertly infiltrating arms and terrorists into Jordan to help achieve this purpose. Hussein concluded by saying that he simply must have Washington's decision on his request for assistance. For a decade he and America had been partners and at that critical hour they were the only friend to whom he could turn. The right answer from the United States would enable him to justify his past policy to his army, to his people, to the PLO and to everyone else. If this was not forthcoming, even he would be forced to conclude that his past policy had been a failure. Repeated delays by America left Hussein no choice, he said, but to agree to the decision of the Arab Defence Council in Cairo to station Saudi and Iraqi troops in Jordan.

If the United States turned down Hussein's request for assistance, three courses were open to him, he said: to turn East; to batten down the hatches and take on all his enemies together; or to declare the West Bank a "military directorate" and call on the Arab states and the PLO to station forces there to protect it. Of these three courses only the third appealed to him because it would enable him to make a redoubt of the East Bank and thus offer him one last chance to serve his cause. There were many indications in the course of the conversation that Hussein had become suspicious of America's intentions with regard to Jordan. America was too closely tied to Israel and this could inhibit its ability to respond to his request for assistance. Hussein also felt that America did not appreciate the seriousness of the situation in Jordan or the depth of the desire of its enemies to liquidate it. Hussein hoped that his views could be brought to the personal attention of the president.[14]

Having finished the business part of the meeting, Hussein asked Burns and O'Connell to stay on. In the privacy of his home at Al-Hummar, free from the formal constraints of the royal court, the king proceeded to reveal to his astonished American guests that he had been in secret contact with Israeli leaders for the past three years through clandestine meetings. The purpose of these exchanges, Hussein explained, was to reach understandings that would ensure peace between their two countries and eventually, he hoped, achieve a negotiated settlement of the Palestine problem. Hussein said he wondered what more he could have done to avert what happened. He then added quietly that no one in his country, except himself, knew about these discussions with the Israelis. Hussein repeated that he did not believe in war as a solution to the Palestine problem. He had consistently followed a course of moderation on the whole question of Palestine in the hope that reasonable men would one day negotiate a just settlement. He had done his utmost to eliminate terrorism against Israel from across Jordan's border. The United States knew all these things and so did the Israelis. The Israelis knew it, he said, because "I told them so personally."

Hussein had warned the Israeli leaders, among other things, that he could not absorb or tolerate a serious retaliatory raid. They accepted the logic of this and promised there would never be one. In addition to these secret meetings, Hussein had maintained a personal and confidential correspondence with the Israeli leaders. These messages served to "underscore and reinforce our understandings." The last message he received from the Israelis was to reassure him that they had no intention of attacking Jordan. That message arrived on 13 November, the very day the Israeli troops attacked Samu'. Hussein added that the message was unsolicited and that it was presumably dispatched twenty-four to forty-eight hours before he received it. "As far as I am concerned," Hussein told his American guests, "this attack was a complete betrayal by them [the Israelis] of everything I had tried to do for the past three years in the interests of peace, stability and moderation at high personal political risk. Strangely, despite our secret discussions and correspondence, despite secret agreements, understandings, and assurances, I never fully trusted their intentions towards me or towards Jordan. In assessing Israeli intentions I ask you to put my experiences with them into your equation." Hussein ended the soliloquy on a bitter note: "This is what one gets for trying to be moderate, or perhaps for being stupid." He asked that this information be held in strictest confidence by as few people as possible. Burns, when writing later of this conversation, underscored Hussein's request by recalling that King Abdullah had been assassinated by a Palestinian when it became known that he had contact with the Israelis.[15]

Reports of the semi-official, semi-private conversation in Al-Hummar fed into a reassessment of American policy towards Jordan that was under way in Washington. The CIA's contribution to this process was an eleven-page memorandum, "The Jordanian Regime: Its Prospects and the Consequences of its Demise," prepared by the Office of National Estimates and coordinated with the Office of Current Intelligence and the Clandestine Services. The name of the author was omitted but the content reflects the private knowledge and the views of Jack O'Connell. Whoever the author, the memorandum sheds much light on what was undoubtedly one of the most critical crises of Hussein's reign. It was noted that "King Hussain has stayed on his throne in Jordan despite slender domestic political support, military weakness relative to his enemies, and the hostility of radical Arabs who regard him as a Western puppet." His survival was attributed in part to his own courage and resourcefulness and in part to US support. Another reason was that the Arab radicals generally tolerated Hussein's rule as an alternative to conflict with Israel for which they knew they were unprepared. "As a consequence Jordan served as a kind of political buffer between irreconcilable opponents and to an important degree kept the unstable elements in the area in equilibrium."

Recent events, however, put the future of Jordan in question and threatened the precarious status quo. The PLO had become more violent in its criticism of Hussein for his refusal to admit Arab military forces to Jordan and to station them on the border with Israel. Al-Fatah stepped up its sabotage raids into Israel, mostly from Jordan, which did its best to prevent them. The Israeli raid on Samu' badly shook Hussein and his government and humiliated the army. In the aftermath of the raid Hussein appeared to his subjects, to his neighbours and perhaps even to himself to have been badly let down by the United States. The Palestinians agitated and demonstrated against him and his government for over three weeks. They were enthusiastically egged on by the Syrian government and by Egyptian and PLO propaganda campaigns. Disaffection in the Jordanian armed forces—the mainstay of the king's position—had grown greatly. "Hussain is aware of his weakened position at home. He probably believes that the threat from Israel is greater than he had calculated, and has probably lost faith in the *modus vivendi*. He is also deeply concerned lest the US fail to give him firm support. Hence, his first priority is to demonstrate to the Jordanian army and citizenry that he continues to enjoy the full backing of the US. He has asked the US for a large additional supply of arms to help him allay dissatisfaction in the armed forces."

The US response to Hussein's request was said to be an important factor in the situation: "A military aid package, if it included prompt delivery of some showy items, would help the king greatly. A US refusal to extend aid, or to give only token amounts of it, would weaken his position and discourage him." The clinching argument was that "Hussain himself already entertains some suspicions that the United States and Israel are collaborating against him, and he would feel that these suspicions were confirmed." While the memorandum conceded that no amount of US aid could guarantee Hussein's tenure, it pointed out that prompt and substantial assistance could help him to maintain political control. "In sum, Hussain's chances of surviving this crisis depend on a number of variables, nearly all of them outside his control. It is clear that he is in deep trouble, and that there are significant dangers to him and to the *modus vivendi* which has helped maintain an uneasy peace in the area."[16]

The review resulted, towards the end of December, in a decision to supply military hardware to Jordan, though not on the scale that Hussein had requested. It was generally understood that the collapse of his regime could precipitate open warfare between the Arabs and Israel and that this would not be to America's advantage. As tangible evidence of his administration's continuing support, President Johnson agreed to airlift to Amman military equipment worth $4.7 million in order to improve the mobility, firepower and effectiveness of the Jordanian Army. American officials hoped that Hussein would use this hardware "to prevent guerrillas from using Jordan as a base for operations against Israel," and not to prepare for war with the Jewish state.[17] Thus, from the beginning to the end of the crisis that finished with the modest package of arms for Jordan, the chief preoccupation of the policy-makers in Washington seemed to be the security of Israel.

Hussein sent a gracious letter to Johnson to thank him for his sympathy, concern and prompt action in helping Jordan to overcome the current crisis. He made no mention of the disappointment of the army chiefs with some aspects of the military aid package. In the negotiations with William Macomber, President Johnson's special envoy, Hussein made it clear that he did not agree with their belief that there had been no basic change in Israeli policy towards Jordan. Hussein understood, however, that the American response was primarily meant to be a way of easing the current situation rather than a way of dealing with a longer-term threat. He could not give a guarantee to keep Arab troops out of his country, but he promised to do all he could, not least because they were not in Jordan's interest either. Finally, Hussein informed Macomber that he intended to continue his moderate policies and measures to enhance regional stability. The only specific measure mentioned in this connection was to persist in the efforts to prevent terrorist infiltration into Israel.[18]

Inside the Jordanian national security establishment there were two very different responses to the Samu' affair. One group argued that Jordan needed the other Arab states as the only possible defence against future Israeli aggression and that meant drawing closer to Nasser. The other group, led by Wasfi Tall, argued that Samu' showed that the United Arab Command was a broken reed and that Jordan should therefore concentrate on building up its own defences. Tall pursued a confrontational policy towards the PLO, Syria and Nasser. Hussein recognized Tall's ability, dynamism and devotion, but he wanted a less abrasive prime minister in order to improve relations with the Arab world. In April 1967 Hussein appointed Saad Juma'a as prime minister but kept Tall by his side as chief of the royal court. Juma'a had served as ambassador to the United States and was generally regarded as pro-Western and anti-Nasser. But he was a malleable character and, once he reached the top, faithfully carried out his master's policy of patching up the old quarrels with Cairo and Damascus and calling for a new round of Arab summitry.

Within six weeks of Hussein's change of course, Jordan was involved in a full-scale war with Israel that culminated in the loss of the West Bank. The loyalist version maintains that Jordan had no choice but to fight alongside its Arab brethren. But there was nothing inevitable about the chain of events that plunged the region into war. The June War was an unnecessary one with disastrous consequences for all the Arab participants, but especially for Jordan. The notion of "no alternative" was invented by the Jordanian policy-makers to cover up their mistakes and their personal responsibility for the catastrophe that they brought upon their country. Hussein was admittedly faced with an extremely difficult situation, but he also had a range of options from which to choose, and he made the wrong choice. Wasfi Tall kept warning him that jumping on the Egyptian bandwagon would lead to war and to the loss of the West Bank and this is precisely what happened: because of his decision, Hussein lost control over the course of events and ended up losing half of his kingdom.

The decisive factor in triggering the crisis that led to the June War was inter-Arab rivalries. It may sound perverse to suggest that the war owed more to the rivalries between the Arab states than to the dispute between them and Israel, but such a view is supported by the facts. The Arab world was in a state of considerable turmoil arising out of the conflict and suspicions between its radical and conservative regimes. The militant Ba'th regime that had captured power in Syria in February 1966 posed as the standard-bearer of Arab unity and continued to agitate for a popular war for the liberation of Palestine. It not only unleashed Fatah units to attack Israel from Jordan's territory but engaged in direct clashes with the Israeli Army along the common border. A major landmark in the spiral of violence was an air battle on 7 April 1967 in which six Soviet-made Syrian MiGs were shot down by the Israeli Air Force (IAF). This was the first time that the IAF penetrated all the way to the Syrian capital. Two of them were in fact shot down in the outskirts of Damascus, turning Syria's military defeat into a public humiliation. All the Israeli planes returned safely to base. The shooting down of the six Syrian MiGs started the countdown to the June War. Syria's conflict with Israel did nothing to improve its relations with Jordan. Relations between the two Arab countries reached their nadir when a Syrian truck loaded with dynamite exploded in the Jordanian customs station at Ramtha on 21 May, causing fourteen deaths and a wave of popular indignation throughout the country. Hussein was convinced that the radicals in Syria saw Jordan, and not Israel, as the real enemy. He described terrorism as an instrument designed by his Syrian enemies to bring about Israeli retaliation in order to destroy Jordan. An immediate rupture of diplomatic relations with Syria was ordered by Hussein on his return from the scene of the explosion.

For President Nasser, Syrian militancy posed a different kind of problem: it threatened to drag the confrontation states prematurely into a war with Israel. Nasser kept repeating that two conditions had to be met before war with Israel could be contemplated: Arab unity and Arab military parity with Israel. Nasser's dilemma was how to restrain the Syrian hotheads while working to achieve these conditions. As a first step Egypt and Syria signed a mutual defence treaty on 7 November 1966. But this merely papered over the cracks. Nasser suspected his Syrian allies of wanting to drag him into a conflict with Israel while they suspected that, if war actually came, he would leave them to face

Israel on their own. Nasser's failure to come to Syria's aid during the air battle of 7 April exposed the hollowness of the treaty and undermined his credibility as an ally. Jordan seized the opportunity to launch a scathing attack on Nasser, contrasting his anti-Israeli rhetoric with the absence of any concrete action. There were two main thrusts to the Jordanian propaganda offensive: the failure to close the Straits of Tiran in the Red Sea to Israeli shipping; and hiding behind the skirts of the United Nations Emergency Force (UNEF) that was stationed in Sinai in the aftermath of the Suez War as a buffer between Egypt and Israel. Jordan's propaganda offensive escalated the Arab cold war and contributed to the crisis slide that culminated in a hot war between the Arabs and Israel.

Thrown on the defensive, Nasser took a series of steps designed to shore up his prestige at home and in the Arab world. He appeared to challenge Israel to a duel, but most observers agree that he neither planned nor wished a war to take place. What he did do was to embark on an exercise in brinkmanship that went well over the brink. On 13 May 1967 Nasser received a Soviet intelligence report that falsely claimed that Israel was massing troops on Syria's border. Nasser responded by taking three successive steps that made war virtually inevitable: he deployed his troops in Sinai near Israel's border on 16 May; he expelled the United Nations Emergency Force from the Gaza Strip and Sinai on 19 May; and he closed the Straits of Tiran to Israeli shipping on 22 May. Nasser's first move, the deployment of the Egyptian Army in Sinai, was not intended as a prelude to an attack on Israel but as a political manoeuvre designed to deter the Israelis from attacking Syria and to rebuild his authority in the Arab camp. But it unleashed a popular current for war that Nasser was not able to contain. Each step that he took impelled him to take the next one and thus drove him closer and closer to the brink.

Hussein became increasingly apprehensive. On the one hand, he realized that Nasser's actions increased the risk of war when the Arab side was not ready, and when there was no Arab cooperation, coordination or joint plan. On the other hand, Nasser's challenge to Israel dramatically increased his popularity inside Jordan and raised expectations that the battle of destiny was at hand and that the liberation of Palestine was imminent. Not only Palestinians but the majority of Jordanians were swept along by the rising tide of Arab nationalism. This

posed a threat to the regime, which reacted by emphasizing its nationalist credentials, by making overtures to the radical Arab states and by
ostentatiously moving armoured units from the East Bank to the Jordan
Valley. Egypt, Syria and Iraq did not reciprocate Jordan's gestures of
conciliation, leaving it completely isolated. To break out of his isolation Hussein made the fateful decision to go to Cairo for a grand reconciliation with Nasser.

Early in the morning of 30 May Hussein, wearing a khaki combat
uniform with field marshal's insignia, took a small group of advisers
and piloted his Caravelle plane to Al-Maza military air base near Cairo.
Nasser, who came in person to the air base to receive his visitor, was
surprised to find him in uniform. "Since your visit is secret, what
would happen if we arrested you?" asked Nasser. "The possibility
never crossed my mind," Hussein replied with a smile. This was an
inauspicious beginning for the talks in the Kubbah Palace, in the course
of which Hussein made one concession after another. Hussein began by
stating that it was absolutely essential for the United Arab Command to
rise out of the ashes. Nasser proposed another solution: to draw up a
pact between their two countries there and then. At Hussein's suggestion, Nasser sent someone to fetch the text of the Egyptian–Syrian
mutual defence treaty. By his own account, Hussein was so anxious to
come to some kind of agreement that he merely skimmed the text and
said to Nasser: "Give me another copy. Put in Jordan instead of Syria
and the matter is settled."[19] The manner in which Hussein negotiated
this important international treaty was strange but in character. It
reflected his impatient, impulsive and irresponsible side as well as his
propensity for taking gambles.

The treaty was one of mutual defence, with each party undertaking
to go to the defence of the other in the event of an armed attack. The
detailed provisions gave Nasser everything he asked for. First, the Jordanian armed forces were placed under the command of Egyptian General Abdel Munim Riad. Second, Hussein agreed to the entry into
Jordan of troops from Egypt, Syria, Iraq and Saudi Arabia. Third, Hussein had to agree to reopen the PLO offices in Amman and to reconciliation with Ahmad Shuqairi, who was summoned to Cairo from Gaza
City for the occasion. Hussein also reluctantly agreed to take Shuqairi
back to Amman with him on his plane. Jordan's role in the event of war
was to tie down a substantial portion of Israel's army and to prevent it

from attacking the other confrontation states one by one. In return, Nasser agreed to augment Jordan's tiny air force with air support from Egypt and Iraq. This promise went some way towards allaying Hussein's anxiety about conducting ground operations with little or no air cover. Hussein warned his hosts of the danger of a surprise Israeli air attack. He pointed out that Israel's first objective would be the Arab air forces, starting with Egypt. Nasser replied that that was obvious and that they were expecting it. He exuded self-confidence and assured Hussein that his army and air force were ready to confront Israel. The signing ceremony of the treaty was broadcast live on Radio Cairo and was followed by a press conference attended by the two heads of state and Ahmad Shuqairi. On his return home later in the day, Hussein basked in the glory of his friendship with Nasser. Jubilant crowds lined the streets as the royal procession drove to the hilltop palace. The king was left in no doubt that his people approved his latest move. The following day the Chamber of Deputies voted overwhelmingly in favour of the pact and dispatched cables of congratulations to the king and the Egyptian president.[20]

Hussein's pact with Nasser was not the brilliant diplomatic coup that it was almost universally perceived to be at the time. Within a week Jordan was at war with Israel alongside its new and feckless Arab allies. After the defeat that overwhelmed his country in this war, Hussein frequently repeated that he had had no real choice in the matter, that events took their own course regardless of his wishes. To the present author he said:

In 1967 I had the impression that various events happened without one having anything to do with them and that this was going to be a problem. We came under pressure to hand over the control of our army and our destiny to a unified Arab command as part of the Arab League. And when Nasser moved his forces across the Suez Canal into Sinai, I knew that war was inevitable. I knew that we were going to lose. I knew that we in Jordan were threatened, threatened by two things: we either followed the course we did or alternately the country would tear itself apart if we stayed out and Israel would march into the West Bank and maybe even beyond. So these were the choices before us. It wasn't a question of our thinking there was any chance of winning. We knew where we were. We knew what the results would be. But it was the only way and we did our best and the results were the disaster we have lived with ever since.[21]

Hussein's retrospective account of the sequence of events that led to war is excessively deterministic. He was not compelled to throw in his lot with Egypt. Egypt had lost two wars to Israel, in 1948 and 1956, and there was no reason to think that it could win a third. Even if one concedes that Hussein had no choice but to sign a mutual defence pact with Egypt, he was responsible for the hasty manner in which it was concluded and for the terms it embodied. Two mistakes stand out above all others. The first and most disastrous was to place the Jordanian armed forces under the command of an Egyptian general. This meant that the most crucial decisions affecting Jordanian security, including the decision to go to war, would be taken in Cairo, not in Amman. It also meant that in the event of war, the Egyptian high command would determine how the Jordanian Army would be deployed and how it would fight. Syria had a defence pact with Egypt but it would never have agreed to place its army under the operational command of a non-Syrian officer. Hussein's second mistake was to agree unconditionally to the entry of Iraqi troops into Jordan. In every previous crisis involving the entry of Iraqi troops into Jordan, Israel reserved its freedom of action. The closure of the Straits of Tiran to Israeli shipping constituted one *casus belli*. The opening of Jordan to Iraqi and other Arab troops raised the perception of threat by Israel and made it more likely that it would take pre-emptive action. Far from providing political and military insurance, the pact with Egypt increased the external perils and dangers facing Jordan.

Having replaced Wasfi Tall with a pliant prime minister, Hussein was left with no persons of stature to advise and support him in the lead up to the war that he now considered inevitable. Field Marshal Habis Majali, the commander-in-chief of the armed forces, was a rather staid and conventional army officer. His deputy, Brigadier Nasser, the king's uncle, was better known for his corrupt practices than for his skills as a staff officer. A British diplomat reported from Amman that the king was "thoroughly fed up with Sharif Nasser's arms and drugs smuggling activities and is determined to put a stop to them once and for all. The king has said that if Sharif Nasser fails to toe the line, he will have to go."[22] The chief of staff was General Amer Khammash, a well-educated professional soldier and planner who led the reorganization of Jordan's armed forces in the mid 1960s. He was the brightest and ablest individual in the king's inner circle. But he was a strong supporter of cooperation with Nasser and the integration of Jordan into the United Arab Command. Khammash was thus not a constraining influence but a contributing factor in the policy that led Jordan down the road to disaster. Other generals also pressed for coordinating Jordan's defence plans with the rest of the confrontation states. Failure to stand together, they argued, would result in losing more soldiers and more territory. The CIA reported that "the army's mood was determined, their argument was irrefutable and the King faced serious morale and loyalty problems if he did not respond to it."[23]

Arab overconfidence and Arab overbidding were among the main causes of the 1967 June War, which thus provides a striking illustration of the perennial predicament of the Arab states: they cannot act separately and they cannot act collectively; they have separate national agendas and they keep getting in each other's way. On this occasion, the level of incompetence displayed by the Arab leaders was quite staggering. After ten years of preparation for what was often referred to as the battle of destiny, and after raising popular passions to a fever pitch with their bombastic rhetoric, the leaders of the confrontation states were caught by complete surprise when Israel took their threats at face value and landed the first blow.

On 1 June, General Abdel Munim Riad arrived in Amman and assumed command of the Jordanian armed forces, under the terms of Hussein's pact with Nasser. From this point on it was the Egyptian who made the key decisions on orders from Cairo. Israel opened hostilities at dawn on Monday 5 June, with a brilliantly planned and executed air strike that annihilated most of Egypt's air force on the ground. Despite three separate warnings from Hussein, the Egyptians were totally unprepared and as a result virtually lost the war on the first day. Elementary decency required the Egyptian high command to inform its allies of the setback and to warn them to take precautionary measures. But there was no decency and no honesty in the relations between the Arab allies.

At about 9:00 a.m. Hussein rushed to his army headquarters after being informed that the Israeli offensive against Egypt had begun. Shortly before his arrival, General Riad had received a cable from Cairo; it was from Field Marshal Abdel Hakim Amer, the first vice-president and deputy supreme commander of the Egyptian armed forces. Amer was a fool who largely owed his rapid promotion to his friendship with Nasser. A major and a Free Officer during the revolution of 1952, Amer became minister of war two years later and was promoted to field marshal in 1958. He was inexperienced in military affairs, corrupt, often drunk and prone to wishful thinking. He was responsible for the lack of preparedness of the Egyptian air force on the eve of battle.

Amer's cable to Riad was a pack of lies. It said that the enemy's planes had started to bomb Egypt's air bases, that the attack had failed, and that 75 percent of the enemy's aircraft had been destroyed or put out of action. It also said that Egypt's forces had engaged the enemy in Sinai and taken the offensive on the ground. On the basis of these alleged successes, Amer ordered Riad to open a new front against the enemy and to launch offensive operations. By the time Hussein arrived at the headquarters, Riad had already given the orders for the artillery to move to the front lines and bombard Israeli air bases and other targets; for an infantry brigade to occupy the Israeli enclave on Mount Scopus in Jerusalem; for the two Egyptian commando battalions to infiltrate enemy territory from the West Bank at dusk; and for the air force to be put on combat alert and commence air strikes immediately. Although these decisions were made in his absence, Hussein made no attempt to cancel them or to delay the opening of fire until the information from Cairo could be checked. Jordan was thus committed to war by the decision of an Egyptian general who was acting on the orders of an idiot in Cairo.

Shortly after his arrival at army headquarters, Hussein was given the first of three Israeli messages urging him not to get involved in the war that had broken out very early that morning. Israel's main enemy was Egypt and the government most emphatically did not want war with Jordan, hence the message that was transmitted through three different channels. The first channel was the Norwegian general with the implausible name of Odd Bull, chief of staff of the United Nations Truce Supervisory Organization (UNTSO). Bull was asked to transmit a message to Hussein expressing the hope of the Israeli government that he would not join in the war. If he stayed out, Israel would not attack him, but if, on the other hand, he chose to come in, Israel would use against him all the means at its disposal. At first Bull hesitated: "This was a threat, pure and simple, and it is not the normal practice of the UN to pass on threats from one government to another." But this message seemed so important that he quickly sent it to Hussein the same morning.[24]

"I did receive the message," Hussein confirmed,

but it was too late in any event. I had already handed over the command of the army to the unified Arab command. There was a unified Arab command with an Egyptian general in army headquarters in charge of the Jordanian armed forces as a part of the defensive effort. The Syrians were not ready, the Iraqis were far away, eventually they moved even before the Syrians and already the first wave had gone in from Jordan into Israel when the UN general called to say that there is a message to keep out of it. I said: "Tell him it's too late." I don't know that the message made any difference because at that time I had these options: either join the Arabs, or Jordan would have torn itself apart. A clash between Palestinians and Jordanians might have led to Jordan's destruction and left the very clear possibility of an Israeli takeover of at least the West Bank and Jerusalem. We did the best we could in the hope that somebody would stop this madness before it developed any further and help us out.[25]

Israel conveyed the same message to Hussein through Colonel Daoud, his representative to the Mixed Armistice Commission, and through the American ambassador to Tel Aviv. Dean Rusk, the American secretary of state at the time, wrote in his memoirs that they tried hard to persuade Hussein not to become embroiled in the fighting, but he said, "I am an Arab and I have to take part." As an Arab, wrote Rusk, Hussein felt honour-bound to assist Egypt, especially since Israel had struck first. Rusk thought that they could have got the Israelis to stay their hand, but Hussein insisted on getting in: "It was one of the sadder moments of this crisis because it certainly was not in Jordan's interest to attack Israel, then lose the West Bank and the old city of Jerusalem."[26]

Jordan did not declare war on Israel but opened hostilities very gently at 9:45 a.m. with isolated shots across the armistice lines in Jerusalem. From Jerusalem the shooting spread to other fronts and involved artillery and tanks. The ministers who had a positive image of the Hashemite dynasty found it difficult to reconcile these acts of belligerence with their experience of coexistence. They hoped that Hussein was making a token gesture of solidarity with Egypt. Abba Eban, the foreign minister, wrote in his autobiography about the Hashemite dynasty: "There was nothing here of the inhuman virulence which marked the attitude of other Arab nationalists toward Israel's existence. Even in wars, an unspoken assumption of ultimate accord hovered over the relations between Israel and Jordan. General Uzi Narkiss, commander of our central front, described the first artillery bombardment of Monday morning in his diary as a 'salvo to uphold Jordanian honour.' But the Jordanian capture of Government House, together with the encirclement of Israeli positions on Mount Scopus, had a far more serious effect. Unlike the dispatch of shells, these measures changed the strategic position to Israel's peril."[27]

Jordan also launched an air attack on Israel on Monday morning. This was utterly pathetic compared to that of the IAF on the Egyptian air bases. The Jordanian Air Force was so tiny—a fleet of twenty-two Hawker Hunters—that it could not carry out any large-scale operations on its own. General Riad realized this and issued an order at 9:00 a.m. for a joint Jordanian–Syrian–Iraqi attack on Israel's air bases. Persistent Iraqi and Syrian delays, however, meant that the attack could not be launched until 11:50 a.m. The Jordanian Hawker Hunters took part in the bombing of air bases and other military targets but, because the Israeli planes were in action, the damage they inflicted was minimal. The Syrian Air Force made one ineffectual sortie and the Iraqi Air Force did not fare much better. By this time the IAF had completed the destruction of the Egyptian Air Force and could turn its full might against the three smaller ones. Amman's airport was bombed while all the Hawker Hunters were refuelling and rearming; they were destroyed on the ground before they could take off. Fifteen minutes later much of Syria's Air Force and the two Iraqi squadrons at H3 suffered the same fate. Israel was now effectively the only air power in the region. By knocking out the Arab air forces so swiftly on the first day, Israel achieved complete mastery in the air and proceeded to use it to very good effect in the land battles that followed. In all, 400 enemy planes were destroyed on the first day and that basically sealed the fate of the Arab armies. Never in the history of modern warfare did air power play so decisive a role in determining the outcome of a conflict.

Israeli pilots appear to have targeted Hussein personally. Zaid Rifa'i, chief of protocol at the royal palace, was an eyewitness. He saw two Israeli Mystères approaching the palace: one was hit by anti-aircraft fire and crashed; the other swept down and fired two missiles that penetrated the conference hall. It came full circle and headed back to the palace at full speed: "This time, it machine-gunned the King's office at point-blank range with a precision and knowledge of its target that was stupefying. Then, finally it disappeared." Rifa'i called Hussein at army headquarters to report the incident. Hussein only asked if anyone had been wounded. The answer was no. "In that case, it's all right," Hussein said calmly, and hung up.[28] Jack O'Connell, the CIA station chief, took the incident more seriously. He reported it to his superiors and asked them to tell the Israelis to knock it off. A message was slipped to the Israelis, and there were no further air attacks threatening King Hussein.[29]

The generals were less indulgent than the ministers towards Hussein and saw no reason to accord him immunity after he had ignored Israel's repeated warnings and initiated hostilities. Once war had broken out, it developed a momentum of its own and offered hope to those with thoughts of territorial expansion. Ezer Weizman, the head of the General Staff Division of the IDF, was a military hawk and an ardent nationalist who was rearing to go once he had the scent of battle in his nostrils. In his memoirs he described his feelings at the time with remarkable frankness:

The "little king," the darling of Israeli politics, Hussein of Jordan, was making vulture-like sounds. Nasser at least had guts: he put a noose around Israel's sensitive neck, threw down the gauntlet—and got his due deserts. Hussein waited. Israel sent him reassuring messages. "Sit still and don't worry. We're not going for you." But Nasser filled Hussein's head full of fanciful tales, telling him Tel Aviv was in flames and Israel was on the verge of collapse, and it would soon be time to divide up the spoils. As soon as he heard "loot," Hussein lost his head and bounded to the carcass for his hunk of meat. Thus Hussein altered the course of the contest, giving it an additional national and historical dimension: as a result of the war, we returned to our ancestral home, to Jerusalem and the Land of the Bible.

At the first reports that the Jordanians had opened fire, there was an inclination in the General Staff to make light of it: "Hussein's just pretending, to keep in with Nasser; but he doesn't mean it in earnest." I must admit that I very much hoped he was in earnest. As long as we had been forced to go to war, I wanted it to give me the chance to write a wish on a slip of paper to be stuffed into one of the cracks in the Western Wall. It soon became clear that Hussein was in earnest—and we were in even greater earnest. The conflagration spread, and the Israeli forces set about restoring Jerusalem, Judaea and Samaria to the Jewish people.[30]

Following the destruction of the Jordanian Air Force, Israel launched a limited counter-offensive with the aim of repelling the Jordanians from Government House, defending Mount Scopus and capturing key strategic positions around Jerusalem. The next forty-eight hours of fighting on the Jordanian front consisted of a catalogue of errors committed by General Riad, each one worse than the last. The Jordanians had a carefully laid plan for the defence of the West Bank. "Operation Tariq" called for concentrating Jordan's forces around Jerusalem, encircling the Jewish side of the city, capturing Mount Scopus, holding on to it until the UN imposed a ceasefire and then using it as a bargaining counter. The Jordanian officers knew the topography of the West Bank well, and this plan was tailored to make the most of their limited military capability. But they were compelled to carry out the orders of an Egyptian general who was a complete newcomer to this front and who acted on the basis of orders from Cairo. Jordan's armoured corps was divided into two brigades of M48 tanks, the 40th and the 60th. Riad's worst blunder was to order the 60th armoured brigade to move from Jericho to Hebron and the 40th brigade to move from the Damia Bridge to Jericho. The intention was that the Jordanian brigades would join up with an Egyptian force that was supposed to be advancing towards Beersheba. But this victorious Egyptian march was simply a myth that subjected the Jordanian Army to muddled and self-defeating manoeuvres and exposed it to unrelenting attacks from the IAF. The Israelis found Riad's juggling of armoured brigades in broad daylight and without air cover to be extremely strange, to say the least.[31]

At dawn on Tuesday, the second day of the war, the full extent of Jordan's reverses became apparent. At a meeting at 5:30 that morning, General Riad offered Hussein the following options: try for a ceasefire through diplomatic channels or order an immediate retreat so as to fall back at dusk to the East Bank of the Jordan. Riad added, "If we don't decide within the next twenty-four hours, you can kiss your army and all of Jordan goodbye! We are on the verge of losing the West Bank; all our forces will be isolated and destroyed." Hussein thought for a moment and then asked the Egyptian general to contact Nasser to find out what he thought. Half an hour later, they got through to Nasser over the regular public telephone system. Egypt had at its disposal an ultra-modern system but the equipment sat idle in Cairo. This was the famous conversation that the Israelis intercepted and publicized round the world. The two leaders agreed to accuse America and Britain of giving Israel air support. "The Big Lie" badly backfired on its inventors by alienating the two governments and public opinion. Hussein maintained, however, that when he charged America and Britain with participation on the side of Israel, he actually believed it.[32]

In the same conversation Hussein and Nasser also discussed the situation on the Jordanian front. At Nasser's suggestion, Riad sent a written report. Riad's coded cable read as follows:

The situation on the West Bank is becoming desperate. The Israelis are attacking on all fronts. We are bombed day and night by the Israeli air force and can offer no resistance because the major part of our combined air power has been put out of commission.

Therefore, we now have three possible solutions:

1. We can call for a political solution in the hope of bringing hostilities to an immediate end. This solution must come from a foreign source—the United States, Soviet Russia, or the UN Security Council.

2. We can evacuate the West Bank tonight.

3. Or, obviously, we can try to stay on the West Bank another 24 hours. But if we do, the total destruction of the Jordanian army is inevitable.

King Hussein has asked me to inform you of the above in order to learn your opinion and your decision at the earliest possible time.

At 12:30 Hussein sent a personal telegram to Nasser in which he reported: "The situation is deteriorating rapidly. In Jerusalem it is critical. In addition to our very heavy losses in men and equipment, for lack of air protection, our tanks are being disabled at the rate of one every ten minutes. And the bulk of the enemy forces are concentrated against the Jordanian army." Hussein requested Nasser's views as soon as possible. At almost the same moment Riad received an answer from Field Marshal Amer that said, "We agree to the retreat from the west bank, and the arming of the civilian population." Hussein answered Amer with another message: "We are still holding on. We are trying to put off the retreat as long as possible. The civilian population has been armed for a long time."

Hussein did not hear from Nasser in response to his telegram until eleven hours later. From a telephone conversation and a cable Hussein learned for the first time that Nasser's air force was out of commission, that his army was in retreat in the Sinai and that the situation on the ground was desperate. "We have been purely and simply crushed by the enemy," Nasser summed up. His advice to Hussein was to evacuate the West Bank and hope that the Security Council would order a cease-fire but not break off diplomatic relations with London and Washington.[33] The UN had called for a ceasefire two hours after the outbreak of hostilities and Israel responded positively, but the fighting continued none the less. On the second day it became clear that unless Israel could be stopped by political means the Jordanian front would collapse. Jordan desperately needed a ceasefire, but it could not say so openly nor could it act on its own without consulting its Arab allies. Hussein got round this problem by asking the Americans to arrange a ceasefire directly with Israel without going through the UN. On the morning of the second day the Americans informed the Israelis of Jordan's readiness to cease hostilities immediately but emphasized the need for secrecy so as not to compromise Hussein's position. This American request prompted the Israeli government to order the army to take the Old City of Jerusalem before the Security Council had a chance to order a ceasefire.[34]

At 11:00 p.m. on 6 June an immediate and unconditional ceasefire was ordered by the Security Council. An hour earlier, with Hussein's agreement, General Riad had issued an order for all the Jordanian forces to retreat from the West Bank to the East Bank. The Security Council resolution gave hope of holding on to the West Bank until the ceasefire came into effect. With this prospect in mind, Riad issued a new order countermanding his earlier order and directing the troops to stay in their positions. A few units had already moved back and had to fight to regain the positions they had just relinquished. The counter-order also led to general confusion because of problems of communication between army headquarters and the units in the field. The IDF did not respect the ceasefire. On the contrary, it intensified its offensive in order to gain as much territory as possible. The Israeli offensive destroyed any lingering Jordanian hope of holding on to the West Bank.

At 2:30 a.m. on the night of 6–7 June, Riad, once again with Hussein's approval, ordered a complete withdrawal from the West Bank. Both men feared that failure to do so would result in the annihilation of the remnants of the Jordanian Army.[35] The retreat of units from the West Bank continued all night.

Wednesday, 7 June, was the third and to all intents and purposes the last day of the war on the Jordanian front. Military and diplomatic events, closely interrelated, unfolded at a bewildering speed: the rapid deterioration in Jordan's military situation led it to intensify its diplomatic efforts to bring about an end to hostilities. The reverse was also true: the unstoppable momentum of the IDF offensive tipped the balance against a ceasefire until the capture of the West Bank had been completed. At noon, Jerusalem, including the Old City, fell after a desperate battle. Following this, a general order was issued for the withdrawal of all the bruised and battered units from the West Bank to the East Bank. The main cities of the West Bank fell in rapid succession. By nightfall the entire West Bank was in Israeli hands. Last to leave were three units that secured the bridges across the Jordan River. The Israelis blew up the bridges in order to sever the link between the two banks and consolidate its control of the territory all the way up to the river.

All day long Hussein persisted in his frantic efforts to secure a ceasefire and stayed in close contact with the ambassadors of the Western powers, who were bringing pressure to bear on Israel. Walworth Barbour, the American ambassador to Israel, forwarded to the Foreign Ministry four telegrams that came directly from Amman, starting at 5:25 in the morning. If the fighting continued, Hussein stated, his regime would be destroyed. In a second telegram that followed half an hour later, Hussein tried to clarify that he was not asking for a formal ceasefire but urging Israel to halt what he described as its punitive actions against his army. Shortly before seven, he warned again that he was in danger of losing control over the situation. These four messages gave Israel a chance to stop before hundreds of thousands of Palestinians came under its rule.[36] Dean Rusk instructed Barbour to convey at the highest level their insistent demand that Israel agree to a ceasefire. The ambassador was to stress that the flood of refugees to the East Bank and the disintegration of the Jordanian security forces created a real danger for the regime and for the large foreign community in the country.[37] Barbour conveyed the message to Levi Eshkol but gained the impression that it was too late, that Israel was no longer interested in keeping the king on his throne, not after he had bombarded Jerusalem, Kfar Saba Netanya and other civilian settlements.[38]

The British ambassador, Michael Hadow, made similar representations. For the rest of the day the press agencies reported that Hussein was ready to start negotiations with Israel for a ceasefire. Moshe Dayan, Israel's minister of defence, rejected this request with some vehemence: "We have been offering the King an opportunity to cut his losses ever since Monday morning. Now we have 500 dead and wounded in Jerusalem. So, tell him that from now on, I'll talk to him only with the gunsights of our tanks!"[39]

London put pressure on Israel to stop shooting and to start talking to Hussein across the conference table. Prime Minister Harold Wilson told the Israeli ambassador that Israel's refusal to respond to Hussein's offer of a ceasefire cast doubt on its claims that its war aims were defensive and not territorial. Julian Amery, a prominent Conservative politician who was both a supporter of Israel and a close personal friend of Hussein, tried hard to reconcile the warring sides. Amery met Prince Hassan, Hussein's younger brother, who was studying Oriental Languages at Christ Church, Oxford, when the war broke out. Hassan told Amery that he spoke to his brother on the telephone and that there was a reasonable prospect for signing a peace agreement. A ceasefire could be made conditional on the immediate start of negotiations for a peace treaty and a comprehensive settlement between the two countries. Amery relayed this report to his Israeli friends and pressed them to act on it.[40]

Another meeting in London involved Amery; Air Vice-Marshal Erik Bennett, who had been an air adviser to Hussein in the early 1960s; the Israeli ambassador, Aharon Remez; and the Mossad representative, Nahum Admoni. The British stated, on the basis of their discussion with Prince Hassan, that there was a reasonable prospect of persuading Hussein to agree to a separate peace treaty with Israel. It was likely that Bennett, who was also a friend of Hussein, would go to Amman the following day with the approval of the British government. Bennett planned to recommend to Hussein the option of a separate peace on a fair basis. He therefore asked the Israelis to indicate to Hussein the kind of terms on which this could be concluded. Bennett realized that the Israelis would need to hold detailed and direct negotiations before entering into a final commitment, but he suggested that it might be decisive to let the king know as soon as possible the kind of terms he might expect to obtain.[41] Bennett's suggestion was not taken up.

Hussein also used a direct British intelligence channel to try to arrest the Israeli assault on his army. Jock Smith, the MI6 representative in Tel Aviv, met his opposite number, Naftali Kenan, at 5:30 p.m. on 7 June at Kenan's house. Smith reported that Hussein saw a very bleak situation: he could either withdraw his army from the West Bank and the result would be his fall from power, or he could throw his army into battle with the IDF, in which case his army would be defeated and the result for himself would be the same—the collapse of his regime. Either course would create a situation that would permit the entry of Syrian troops into Jordan. Hussein estimated that the Syrians had eleven brigades that so far had not been committed to the battlefield. Smith asked his colleague to believe that the long-term interests of both their countries could best be served by "reducing fighting immediately to the level of skirmishes; this would enable the Jordanians to hold their positions until the Egyptians are seen to be defeated and a ceasefire arranged by somebody. The internal situation could then be controlled. If this is not done the King believes his regime will fall and you will be faced with a Syrian-type regime in Jordan." Kenan wanted to know whether this was a service-to-service or a government-to-government approach. Smith replied that it was a service-to-service approach that had the support of the British government. He added that they took into account Hussein's provocative actions during the crisis and after the outbreak of hostilities and his stupid statement about the participation of British airplanes in the fighting alongside Israel, but they still wanted to help him. Kenan asked whether the initiative for this appeal came from Hussein or from the British side. Smith replied that Hussein turned to their representative in Amman and that the assessment and the conclusions that he presented came from Hussein himself. The British government shared Hussein's assessment of the situation and his conclusions, and they supported the course of action that he proposed. Indeed, the British government considered this to be the only way to save Hussein's regime.[42]

These behind-the-scenes manoeuvres did not have any visible effect on Israel's conduct of the war, but they are very revealing of Hussein's state of mind and of his feeling that he and his dynasty might have reached their end. They also reveal the depth of his disenchantment with his Arab allies, and especially with the Syrians. Let down by the Arabs and threatened by the Israelis, he was fighting for political survival. For him the Six-Day War lasted less than three days. In the early hours of Thursday, 8 June, Jordan accepted unconditionally the Security Council call for a ceasefire. Exhausted, his voice cracking with emotion, Hussein addressed his people in a radio broadcast. First, he paid tribute to the heroism with which Jordan's soldiers had fought against overwhelming odds. He went on to express his deep grief over the loss of all their fallen soldiers. "My brothers," he intoned, "I seem to belong to a family which, according to the will of Allah, must suffer and make sacrifices for its country without end. Our calamity is greater than any one could have imagined. But, whatever its size, we must not let it weaken our resolve to regain what we have lost."[43]

The reference to Hussein's family may seem odd in this context but it was not accidental. He was the proud heir to a Hashemite heritage that went back to Hussein, the sharif of Mecca, and the Great Arab Revolt. Throughout his own career, Hussein had to walk a tightrope between Arab nationalism on the one hand and coexistence with Israel on the other. In the mid 1960s he began to lean towards accommodation with Israel. The tacit alliance with Israel was grounded in a common interest in keeping a quiet border, in a common enemy in the shape of radical Arab and Palestinian nationalism and in a common allegiance with the West in the global cold war. Israel's attack on Samu' suddenly destroyed the trust on which this evolving alliance was based. It pushed Hussein into the arms of the radical Arab nationalists. This process culminated in his dramatic reconciliation with Nasser and in the signature of a mutual defence pact with Egypt. From this point on Hussein was locked into the inter-Arab dynamic of escalation that ended in a full-scale war with Israel. Hussein went to war not because he was threatened by Israel but because he feared that he would be denounced as a traitor to the Arab cause if he did not. By this time, in any case, he had relinquished control over his armed forces to an Egyptian general. It was the Egyptians who committed his country to war against the enemy, and it was they who made all the strategic decisions that led to the crushing defeat of his army and to the loss of the Old City of Jerusalem and the West Bank of his kingdom. Hussein was the only Arab ruler who faithfully discharged all his duties to Arab unity during the first few days of the much vaunted battle of destiny. But Arab unity was a snare and a delusion. Hussein made his choice and he paid the price. Within sixty hours of launching his forces in support of Egypt, Hussein lost much of his army, the whole of his air force and half of his territory. Under his leadership, Jordan's part in the June War was brief, ineffective and inglorious.

12. Picking Up the Pieces

The June War opened a new chapter in the life of Hussein. It faced him with the most serious test to date of his ability to survive. His main preoccupation in the weeks that followed the war was with picking up the pieces. In Arabic the defeat of June 1967 was referred to as Al-Naqsah, meaning "The Setback," or temporary reversal. This was in contrast to the Al-Nakbah, or "The Catastrophe," of 1948. For Jordan, however, 1948 was less than a catastrophe, while 1967 was more than a setback. For the Hashemite dynasty the defeat suffered in 1967 was much worse than that suffered in 1948. In 1948 King Abdullah managed to salvage East Jerusalem and the West Bank from the dismal wreckage of Arab Palestine. In June 1967 King Hussein lost what his grandfather had gained on the battlefield and later incorporated into the Hashemite Kingdom of Jordan. A heavy, almost crushing sense of personal responsibility for the loss lay on Hussein's shoulders. The result was an emotionally disturbed state and mood swings that alternated between bouts of resignation and fatalism and sober realism in dealing with the bitter consequences of defeat. Hussein was bitter towards Israel, the West, the Soviet Union, Nasser and the other Arab leaders but above all he was bitter towards himself.

The losses sustained by Jordan in the course of the June War were extremely heavy, and the regime's prospects of survival were correspondingly poor. The government was bewildered and impotent. The army was defeated and dispirited. Seven hundred Jordanian soldiers had died in the war and over 6,000 were wounded or missing. Jordan lost its entire air force, 80 percent of its armour and a great deal of other equipment. At the end of the war only four out of the army's eleven brigades remained operational.[1] The Iraqi troops in Jordan were a destabilizing force. Having arrived too late to take much of a part in battle, they now struck a heroic posture, defying the call for a ceasefire and spoiling for a fight. Hussein wrote to President Arif politely to say that

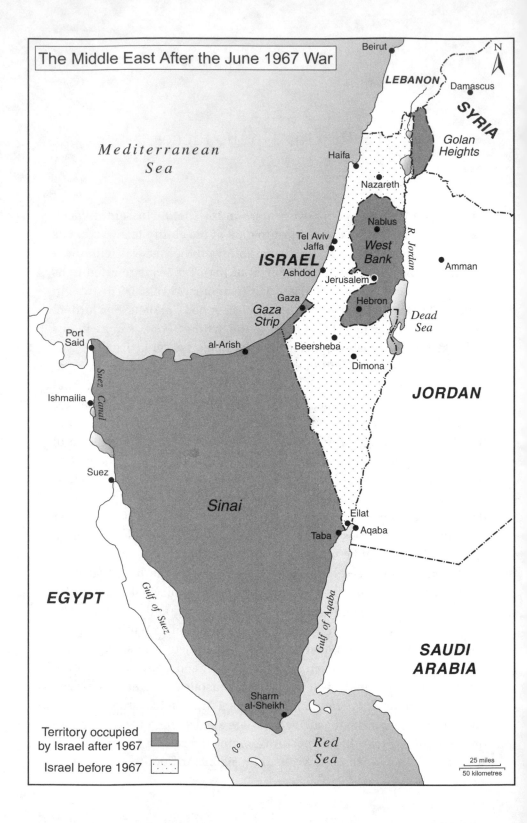

The Middle East After the June 1967 War

Beirut

LEBANON   Damascus

SYRIA

Mediterranean Sea

Haifa

Golan Heights

Nazareth

Nablus

Tel Aviv
Jaffa   *West Bank*

ISRAEL   R. Jordan   Amman

Ashdod

Jerusalem

Gaza   Hebron   *Dead Sea*

Gaza Strip

Port Said   al-Arish   Beersheba   JORDAN

Suez Canal   Dimona

Ishmailia

Suez

Sinai

Eilat
Taba   Aqaba

EGYPT   *Gulf of Suez*   *Gulf of Aqaba*

SAUDI ARABIA

Sharm al-Sheikh

Red Sea

Territory occupied
by Israel after 1967

Israel before 1967

25 miles
50 kilometres

since a military solution to Jordan's difficulties with Israel was not practicable, the Iraqi troops could be withdrawn from Jordan. Syria posed a much more serious threat. The Syrian Army emerged relatively unscathed from the war compared with the Jordanian Army. Jordan was defenceless against Syria, particularly without an air force. Hussein also heard indirectly that the Syrians were well aware that he alone held Jordan together and that they had plans prepared that they would not hesitate to put into effect should Jordan step out of line. He interpreted this to mean that if he embarked on any action that the Syrians considered improper, they would attempt to assassinate him and take over parts of his country.[2]

The economic consequences of the war were also crippling. The Old City of Jerusalem was not just a prize possession but a major source of revenue from tourism, as were some of the West Bank towns like Bethlehem. The West Bank comprised roughly half of the kingdom's inhabited territory, half of its industrial capacity, a quarter of its arable land. It contained valuable water resources and it contributed nearly 40 percent of Jordan's Gross Domestic Product.[3] Israel's occupation of the West Bank resulted in the creation of a new wave of refugees. The influx from the West Bank to the East Bank was estimated at 175,000 by Israel, 250,000 by Jordan and around 200,000 by independent agencies. Many of these were second-time refugees, having first been displaced from their homes in 1948. Israel made it easy for them to cross to the East Bank of the Jordan River but refused to allow them to go back to their homes after the dust had settled. The total number of refugees in Jordan's care increased as a result from about half a million to nearly three quarters of a million. Quite apart from the human suffering involved and the burning sense of injustice, it was a heavy material burden for the truncated and impoverished kingdom to bear.

Hussein's primary aim in the aftermath of the war was to recover the West Bank and East Jerusalem. He knew that this could not be achieved by military means and that diplomacy offered the only hope. His strategy for recovering the West Bank rested on two pillars: Nasser and the United States. The war transformed Nasser from Hussein's worst enemy to his closest ally in the Arab world. Mahmoud Riad, Egypt's foreign minister at the time, has described how impressed Nasser was that Hussein stood shoulder to shoulder with him during the war. On 22 June, Nasser wrote to Hussein, paying tribute to his heroic struggle and offering "to put all we have in the service of the common destiny of our two peoples." He later received Hussein in Cairo and told him that Egypt was ready to share everything it had with Jordan, even if it meant sharing the last loaf of bread between them. "We have entered this war together, lost it together and we must win it together," said Nasser. Nasser also felt that the United States might be more inclined to accommodate Hussein because he was an old friend of theirs, and so he urged him to negotiate with the Americans in any way he wanted to and for as long as he wanted to for a peaceful settlement in the West Bank as long as he refrained from signing a separate peace treaty with Israel.[4]

The importance for Hussein of the new alliance with Nasser cannot be overestimated. Together the two leaders built up an axis of moderation in the Arab world that others were encouraged to join. After their defeat the Arabs faced a fork in the road: one way led to another appeal to arms; the other involved a fundamental change in the Arab policy towards Israel, an official end to the state of belligerency and an attempt to recover the occupied territories by peaceful means. By himself Hussein had no chance of persuading his fellow Arab rulers to follow him down the moderate path; with Nasser's support there was at least a chance. Nasser's support provided Hussein with political cover for working with the Americans, for negotiating with the Israelis, for standing up to the Syrians and for countering the PLO's call for renewing the armed struggle against Israel. It was also crucial for maintaining the legitimacy of the Hashemite regime inside Jordan following the defeat on the battlefield.

The second pillar of Hussein's post-war foreign policy was the alliance with the United States. Hussein's relations with the United States were characterized by many ups and downs. After the 1967 war, however, Hussein believed that Jordan could remain a viable state, and the Hashemites could remain at the head of Jordan, only in the context of a close relationship with the Americans. Moreover, the United States was the only country with the capacity to lean on Israel to relinquish the West Bank. These two considerations led Hussein to put all his eggs in the American basket. The Americans for their part had a clear if not vital interest in preserving Jordan as a viable state with the Hashemite dynasty at its head. America's credibility was tied to the continuation of the moderate and stable regime that it had helped to sustain in Jordan over the previous decade. America was just as committed to the territorial integrity of Jordan as it was to that of Israel. After the war America supported a peace settlement between Jordan and Israel based on a return to the previous borders with only minor modifications. But it gradually drifted away from this principled position, leaving Hussein in the lurch. Hussein's two-pronged strategy ultimately proved unequal to the task of recovering the West Bank. Nasser gave Hussein solid and unswerving support until his death in 1970. By contrast, the Americans turned out to be the most inconstant and unreliable of allies.

Israel's resounding military victory in the war transformed the national mood from deep anxiety to unrestrained triumphalism. It also unleashed a powerful current of opinion in favour of retaining the West Bank, the core of the biblical homeland of the Jewish people. This convergence of religious and secular nationalism constrained the government's room for manoeuvre. The national unity government headed by Levi Eshkol consisted of seven parties and a wide range of ideological positions. It included the right-wing Gahal Party, headed by Menahem Begin, which regarded the West Bank as an integral part of the Land of Israel. The ruling Labour Party was split down the middle. At the dovish end was Abba Eban, the eloquent but politically impotent foreign minister, who wanted to negotiate peace agreements with all of Israel's neighbours based on the pre-war borders with only modest territorial modifications. At the other end was Moshe Dayan, the hardline defence minister, who wanted to keep most of the occupied territories for either security or ideological reasons or a mixture of the two. Levi Eshkol did not like to make irrevocable choices. He was a man of consensus and compromise. His preference for compromise is illustrated by the anecdote of the waiter who asked Eshkol whether he wanted coffee or tea. "Half and half," was the reply. At interminable internal party discussions on the future of the West Bank, Eshkol often taunted his colleagues by pointing out that they liked the dowry but not the bride, meaning that they coveted the land but were less keen on the Arabs who lived there.

Control of the West Bank gave the Israeli government two main alternatives: one was to reach an agreement with Hussein; the other was to give the inhabitants of the West Bank political autonomy under overall Israeli control. The former was called the Jordanian option; the latter the Palestinian option. The conventional view of Israel's post-war policy is that it was based on the Jordanian option, on solving the Palestinian problem by restoring to Hussein most of the territory of the West Bank. According to this view, Israel's leaders were so wedded to the Jordanian option that they failed to consider the alternative. Reuven Pedatzur has challenged this view, arguing that the Palestinian option was the first choice of the Israeli policy-makers and that they only adopted the Jordanian option after attempts to realize the Palestinian option had failed.[5] The truth of the matter is that divisions within the government made it impossible to pursue any clear or consistent policy. It was like a see-saw, veering back and forth between the king and the West Bank notables.[6]

The Israelis no longer regarded Hussein as a reliably moderate figure after he joined the Arab radicals in the run-up to the June War. In the mid 1960s Israel had settled on a policy of cooperating with the king to contain the challenge posed to both of them by the Palestinian national movement. After the war the Israeli policy-makers were indifferent to Hussein and willing to discuss plans for Palestinian self-rule on the West Bank, provided Israel controlled both the western and the eastern borders of the Palestinian entity. This meant that Israel's security border, and possibly also its *de jure* border, would lie along the Jordan River. It also meant that Hussein was no longer necessarily the preferred ruler of the West Bank. For some ministers he was, while for others he was not, and this became evident immediately after the war. On 15 June, Eban reported to a ministerial committee that the British prime minister Harold Wilson had sent a suggestion through an intermediary for direct contact between Israel and Hussein. Eban and Eshkol were in favour but Dayan was against. Dayan argued that since they wanted the Jordan River to be their eastern border, there was no point in entering into negotiations with the king, because he could not possibly accede to their demands. Eshkol's characteristically opaque summing up was that they would agree to negotiate but on condition that the river would be the border.[7] Like his choice of a hot drink, it was half and half.

The deliberations of the cabinet culminated in the decision on 19 June in favour of peace agreements with Egypt and Syria based on the international border and the security needs of Israel. This formula allowed Israel to retain some of the territories it occupied, especially the Gaza Strip and the eastern shore of the Sea of Galilee, and it demanded the demilitarization of the rest. It was a reasonable offer, but unfortunately it was never conveyed to the governments of Egypt and

Syria. As there was no consensus over the West Bank, the cabinet decided to defer decision on the position to be taken up with regard to Jordan. Thus, from the very start, the Israeli cabinet had nothing to offer Jordan.[8] Its initially flexible position on the other fronts gradually hardened with the passage of time. As early as mid July the politicians approved plans for building Jewish settlements on the Golan Heights. In doing so, they reversed their own policy and embarked on the road towards creeping annexation. The decision of 19 June became null even before its formal cancellation in October.[9]

In the Israeli–Jordanian context the most sensitive and intractable issue was the future of Jerusalem. For both sides this was a highly emotive issue. Jerusalem is the third holiest site of Islam after Mecca and Medina, and so was of paramount importance not just to Jordan but to Arabs and Muslims everywhere. It was also the jewel in the Hashemite crown, and a vital symbol of Hussein's legitimacy as an Arab ruler. Hussein was a descendant of the prophet Muhammad, who, according to Muslim tradition, ascended to heaven from the Dome of the Rock in the Old City of Jerusalem. For Jews, Jerusalem has equally powerful symbolic and religious resonance. It was the city of David and the site of the "Wailing Wall," the Western Wall of the Second Temple that was destroyed by the Romans in A.D. 70. The capture of Jerusalem stirred passionate feelings about the historic rights of the Jewish people and of continuity with the past. At noon on 7 June, Moshe Dayan went to the Western Wall and declared that Jerusalem had been "liberated": "We have united Jerusalem, the divided capital of Israel. We have returned to the holiest of our Holy Places, never to part from it again." The Zionist movement's moderate position on Jerusalem disappeared overnight. Suddenly life in the Jewish state without Zion, one of the biblical names for Jerusalem, became difficult to imagine. The Israelis considered that they were sovereign in the unified city and proceeded to act accordingly. On 27 June, in a remarkable display of national unity, the Knesset enacted legislation to extend Israeli law, jurisdiction and administration to Greater Jerusalem, which included the whole of the Old City. This amounted to annexation in all but name, an irreversible step that virtually doomed to failure all the post-war attempts at accommodation between Israel and Jordan.

After recovering his composure Hussein concentrated his efforts on repairing his relationship with friendly states and mobilizing international opinion in the struggle to recover the occupied territories. On 26 June he presented the Arab position to the UN General Assembly, offering peace with Israel in return for territory. Two days later he met with President Johnson and his advisers in the White House. Johnson was always partial to Israel and so were most of his advisers, notably Walt Rostow, the special assistant to the president, his brother Eugene Rostow, the under-secretary of state for political affairs, and Nicholas Katzenbach, the under-secretary of state. Johnson was advised to tell Hussein not to rely on any outside force to settle the dispute and to encourage him to enter into bilateral negotiations with Israel.[10]

The tone of Hussein's meeting with Johnson was marked by seriousness and sympathetic frankness, but there was no real meeting of minds. The king stressed that the Arabs faced very critical decisions. They could opt for either what amounted to a settlement with Israel to be followed by concentration on economic development, or for rearmament, with a view to another round. The king said that he favoured the first course and that he intended to try to sell this position to the other Arabs, since there could be no real stability in the Middle East unless all the Arabs chose a settlement with Israel. Hussein added that he had some reason for hope for success in this regard. He pointed out that, as the Arab leader who had nothing to do with bringing about the confrontation, who had fought the hardest and who had lost the most, he was in a unique position to speak for a moderate course. The Americans agreed that the Arabs had reached a fork in the road and they believed that a peaceful solution was the only solution. But they also told Hussein that they could not impose a settlement, nor could they deliver the Israelis. They steered him, in effect, towards a separate settlement with Israel. His reply was along the following lines: "The first thing I must do is to try to convince all the Arab leaders to adopt a moderate solution. Only if this fails could I consider whether it would be feasible to pursue a solution on my own."[11]

On his way home Hussein stopped in London for a few days. On Sunday, 2 July, he met Dr. Yaacov Herzog at the home of Dr. Emanuel Herbert. This was their fourth meeting and the recent war cast a long shadow over it. It lasted an hour and a half, and Herzog's account of it fills fifteen pages. But there was not much of substance to report. It was essentially an exploratory meeting in which each side tried to figure out the position of the other without committing itself to a particular out-

come. This was especially true of Dr. Herzog. Vagueness was the hallmark of his position at this and all subsequent meetings. He could not
convey the cabinet's terms for a settlement because the cabinet had
reached no decision with regard to the future of the West Bank. Herzog
himself became a proponent of Greater Israel under the impact of the
resounding victory. He was deeply affected by the national mood of
religious and spiritual elation that accompanied the encounter with the
sacred biblical sites of Judea and Samaria, and he set his face against
withdrawing from them. Although he took the initiative in requesting
the meeting with the king, he approached it with some trepidation. His
main worry was that the king would demand a clarification of Israel's
position regarding the West Bank, and, as he recorded in his diary, he
resolved to remain evasive.[12]

As he entered the room, Herzog bowed and said that he was grateful
that the king could receive him despite his heavy preoccupations. He
opened by saying that their contact had been valuable and that he
always felt privileged by the confidence the king had reposed in him.
At their first meeting four years previously he had given the king a "biblical undertaking" that it would remain secret come what may, and he
now wished to renew the promise of secrecy. The prime minister and
the foreign minister asked Herzog to convey personally to the king their
good wishes. They realized the stress under which he had been labouring and regretted deeply the loss of life and suffering on his side. The
object of the visit was to inquire whether he wished to convey anything
to the Israelis on the situation that had developed since the end of the
war. They welcomed clarification of his thoughts. Herzog emphasized
that he was talking to the king on an unofficial basis and invited him to
speak his thoughts in an unfettered fashion.

The king replied that he too valued the contact over the years and
thanked his guest for coming to see him. He spoke without bitterness or
recrimination and even admitted that in the Israelis' place he would
have acted as they had. For some years he had understood that war was
inevitable. He had reached this conclusion from an appraisal of the difficult political and strategic circumstances of Israel. It had seemed to
him inevitable that one day they would try to settle their problem by
force. During the past months he had felt the crisis was approaching.
The Arabs had made great mistakes. He had warned them time and
again. He also bore responsibility for what had happened because he

had not taken sufficient action to drive home his warnings. The Middle East was now at the crossroads. It could move towards a better future or it could become embroiled in further war, which would surely spread beyond the frontiers of the area. After the war, he had suggested an Arab summit conference with the view of achieving a common Arab purpose and a joint line. Other Arab leaders had refused. Now, however, he felt the summit would probably take place shortly. If the summit did not reach agreement, each country would be free to act individually as it wished.

Herzog replied that the king had been labouring under a basic misunderstanding. They had never planned war and they had no need for it. Their preparations over the years had been to meet an attack. Herzog then described the events that led to war in minute and often unnecessary detail in order to underline that Israel's position had been purely defensive. There were two central points that Arab leaders never understood, he said. First, for a people that had been subjected to persecution down the ages culminating in the Nazi Holocaust, an assault on any individual Jew was an assault on the entire Jewish people. They could not live in Jerusalem or Tel Aviv with farmers being shot down in frontier settlements. The general Jewish reaction to the murder of individual Jews flowed from the transcendental unity of the Jewish people, a unity forged in faith and fortified in the struggle for survival throughout history.

Second, the Arab leaders had never understood the nature of Israel's link with the land, which was unique in that it sprang from the distinctive spiritual sources of the Jewish people. Instead of trying to understand this phenomenon, the Arab leaders had sought rational explanations for the Jewish renaissance in the land of their fathers. They assumed that the Jews had returned to the land only as refugees, that the Jewish national movement was an artificial creation without basic roots, and that it drew its strength largely from political and financial machinations in Western capitals. Nazi persecution had indeed lent a great momentum to the Zionist movement. Influence by Jews throughout the world had been a vital contribution. But the basis had been, and remained, the undying attachment of the Jews to the Land of Israel. The acceptance of this central fact by the Arabs was an essential prelude to peace.

To this grandiloquent lecture on the roots of Jewish nationalism Hussein responded with a down-to-earth account of the origins of the recent war. For him the attack on Samu' was a great shock. It convinced him that, for Israel, Jordan and Syria were in the same class despite all of his actions against Fatah. When he visited Cairo, Nasser was convinced that Israel was about to attack Syria. As an Arab leader, Hussein had no choice but to get ready. He was absolutely sure that there had been no intention of mounting an all-out attack on Israel. There had been no cooperation and no joint planning for such an attack. Verbal threats meant nothing.

From the prelude to the war Hussein moved to the war itself, slipping into the mode of a detached military analyst. In his assessment, there were three major factors behind Israel's victory: its aircraft, its intelligence and its communications systems. Israel had shown remarkable organization and a capacity to move troops from point to point with great rapidity. Its striking power in the air and on the ground had been overwhelming. "Such is war," he said wistfully.

What was past was past, said Herzog; what of the future? Hussein returned to the subject of the proposed Arab summit. Herzog asked whether he sought unity to prepare new aggression or to make peace. The question was crucial to Israel's calculations. He therefore had to insist on an answer. Hussein replied very slowly and hesitantly:

The extremists (sarcasm touched his voice) have one course, I have another. I must say frankly to you, if it is peace, it will have to be peace with dignity and honour (the last words were uttered firmly and in a deep tone). What you said earlier about the historic link with the land I have understood for some time now; others have not. This is the most difficult point for the Arabs to accept. Our basic problem is how to maintain Arab identity in the area. Not only you have rights. We also have rights. Do not push us into a corner. If you do this, even if there be no hope, we will have no alternative but to follow the extremist line. So much depends in the coming weeks on how you behave and how we behave. Be careful of our emotions. Treat them with respect and understanding. The area is now at a crossroads. I hope we will take a positive course. So much depends on you.

Herzog remarked that the time had come for the moderate Arab group to speak out frankly for peace. The king had spoken of peace with dignity and honour but had yet to tell him officially that he was ready to enter into peace negotiations; and, until he did so, Herzog could not discuss the details of a peace settlement. He repeated that he had been sent on an unofficial basis to take away a clear idea of the king's thoughts. All he could offer was his personal vision of peace, namely, an economic union between Jordan and Israel, with a joint effort to settle the refugee problem. He painted a dark picture of the future of the region without peace. Would the pattern of tension and aggression continue to be the pattern, or would they link hands to build a new Middle East? Hussein replied, "Give me a short time. I shall not hesitate to insist on my views and to state them publicly." Herzog summed up: Hussein was trying to get a summit meeting in order to achieve a united line on peace. If he did not succeed, he would feel free to act unilaterally in relation to Israel. Hussein nodded agreement. They parted with a warm handshake.

At the end of his report Herzog recorded his general impressions. At their various meetings over four years, Hussein's mood and presence had reflected the pendulum of his relations within the Arab world and particularly with Cairo and Damascus. "This time his expression bore the marks of what had recently passed over him, yet the mood seemed more of sadness and fatalism rather than of anger and bitterness. The furtive look at some of the previous meetings had left him. He seemed downcast and liberated at the same time. Throughout the talk it occurred to me that while he had lost a war and with it a large part of his kingdom, he had for the first time achieved real status in Arab leadership, his patriotism no longer challenged, his motives no longer suspect. The shock of events did not seem to have affected the inner core of his personality. At once he was sad and carefree, contemplative but easy of communication, broken and yet apparently filled with hope."[13]

Herzog assumed Hussein refrained from raising the question of the West Bank and Jerusalem in order to avoid putting Israel's position on the record. But it was he who wanted to leave the question open. Hussein knew that time was not on his side, whereas Herzog was convinced that it was on Israel's: that with the passage of time the chances of withdrawal from the West Bank would diminish. His ploy was to spin out the talks with Hussein in order to avert an internal cabinet crisis and to fend off external pressures on Israel to withdraw. To Yigal Allon, Herzog confessed that he and Abba Eban were divided: Eban believed that there was a chance of reaching agreement with Hussein, while Herzog did not. For him the importance of the talks was purely tactical. To Menachem Begin, Herzog said that he favoured the continuation of the contact with Hussein, although he was certain that nothing would come out of it.[14] In this respect Herzog was the perfect representative for a divided government that preferred land to peace with Jordan. Meir Amit, the director of the Mossad, was even more cynical. He wanted to use the contact with Hussein in order to bring about division in the Arab camp on the issue of peace.[15]

The day after the meeting with the evasive envoy, Hussein went to 10 Downing Street for a working lunch with Prime Minister Harold Wilson and Foreign Secretary George Brown. Wilson's brief for the meeting told him that "The Americans (or at least Mr. Eugene Rostow) seem to have been persuaded by the Israelis into acceptance of the Israeli thesis that the way to a settlement is to press King Hussein into separate negotiations and the conclusion of an agreement within the next few weeks, using the threat that he will otherwise lose his West Bank territories." The Foreign Office view, on the other hand, was that it would be virtual suicide for Hussein to engage in separate negotiations at that time. There was no Palestinian tolerance even for heavily conditional engagement in negotiations. Consequently there was no scope for Hussein to challenge Israel publicly with the offer of peace for full withdrawal. The Foreign Office experts also assumed that separate negotiations would not recover the occupied territories. Moreover, the separation of the West Bank from Jordan was not seen as an attractive prospect for a stable settlement of the Arab–Israel dispute or for the future of the two halves of Jordan. Besides, Britain's interests elsewhere in the Arab world required that they should continue to be seen to support Jordan, and should not under any circumstances get involved in the promotion of a settlement based on its dismemberment.[16]

At the meeting Wilson and Brown expressed regret at the disaster that had befallen Jordan and inquired whether he was thinking of negotiating a separate peace with Israel. Hussein said that there were naturally grave tensions and difficulties in Jordan, an influx of refugees and the general shock to Arab morale resulting from their military defeat. There was also the danger of Soviet exploitation of the situation in an East–West context. But he was confident that he could hold the situation in Jordan satisfactorily, provided the Arab cause was not rebuffed at the United Nations and provided Israel were obliged to withdraw from the territories it had occupied. With regard to a separate peace, his first objective was, as he had said to Herzog the previous day, an Arab summit to try to concert a common stand. If this failed, then he might indeed have to "go it alone," including some kind of separate settlement with Israel. Wilson commented that it would be a very rough summit meeting if it took place, and Hussein agreed. Brown thought the king had shown himself by his recent behaviour to be one of the bravest men alive; but he believed that the king could not afford, without serious risk to himself, to take any position in relation to Israel that put him too far ahead of his Arab colleagues in other countries.[17]

Wilson had a back channel to the Israeli Embassy in London that did not go through the Foreign Office. Before leaving London, Dr. Herzog asked Wilson's contact man whether the prime minister would agree to convey to them his impressions from his talks with Hussein. Late on Monday night, the contact man relayed the following message: first, Wilson was impressed by Hussein as a man; second, Israel should not press for bilateral contact with him, as such contact would endanger his life, or, as Wilson phrased it, "put an end to the Hashemite kingdom." This was Wilson's direct impression, which had been supported by a British Embassy report from Amman. The Israelis also received a report on the meeting through official channels. On the instructions of George Brown, a senior official at the Foreign Office gave details of Hussein's talks to the Israeli ambassador.[18]

On 10 July, Hussein flew to Cairo to report to Nasser on his talks in the West and to coordinate their diplomatic strategy. The Algerian president, Houari Boumedienne, was also there. Boumedienne supported the hard-line Syrian position of continuing the struggle against Israel with the help of the USSR. Nasser told Hussein that he now regretted cutting his links so completely with the West. In the interests of the Arabs as a whole, he agreed that Jordan should maintain its relations with the West. He himself was completely dependent on the USSR. His advice to Hussein was to get in touch with the Americans and to ask for their help in arranging negotiations between Jordan and Israel, advice that he later repeated, at Hussein's request, in front of the Egyptian, Algerian and Jordanian delegations.[19]

On his return from Cairo, Hussein informed both the UK and the US ambassadors that, as no overall settlement of the Arab–Israeli conflict was in sight, he might very discreetly seek a separate settlement with

Israel. Before doing so, however, he wished to elicit the views of the two governments and the extent of their support in facilitating such a settlement. Anglo-American discussions of Hussein's options revealed significant differences. Britain's prime interest in the Middle East was to get the Suez Canal reopened. The British were unwilling to encourage Hussein to enter separate negotiations with Israel. They wanted Hussein to continue to rule Jordan, but they were not prepared to invest much in supporting him. They were unwilling to intervene, as they had done in 1958, to save the Hashemite regime. Their advice to Hussein was to wait a while. America's view, on the other hand, was that, despite the risks involved, it was essential to encourage a settlement between Jordan and Israel. The Americans accordingly advised Hussein to enter into direct negotiations but they declined to lean on Israel to offer him terms that would enable him to survive.[20] Hussein's reaction was one of deep disappointment at what he saw as inadequate American support for the course of action he had hoped to take. He felt unable to move forward in the direction of a bilateral settlement with Israel.[21] Instead he took the lead in steering Arab policy towards a political solution to the crisis and in preparing the ground for an Arab summit.

The fourth Arab summit conference was held in Khartoum, the Sudanese capital, between 28 August and 1 September. It was the first meeting of the Arab leaders since their defeat in the June War. The conference ended with the adoption of the famous three "noes" of Khartoum: no negotiation, no recognition and no peace with Israel. These were a propaganda gift for Israel, and were often cited by critics as proof of the intransigence of the Arabs and of the inability of pan-Arabism to formulate a realistic policy. In fact, surprising as it may sound, the conference was a victory for the Arab moderates. The debates of the heads of state revealed profound disunity within the Arab fold. Algeria, Syria and the PLO wanted to continue the fight against Israel and the West with the support of the Soviet Union. The PLO, in particular, wanted the all-Arab aim to be the liberation of Palestine rather than merely the recovery of the territories captured by Israel in the recent war. The moderates, led by Nasser and Hussein, had a more limited aim and argued in favour of trying to obtain Israel's withdrawal by political rather than military means and in cooperation with the West. Nasser stated bluntly that the Arabs at that time had no military option and that the only hope of recovering the land lay in political action. He also pointed out that the recovery of the West Bank was a more urgent Arab need than the recovery of the Sinai, that America alone could compel Israel to withdraw, and that Hussein should therefore approach the Americans. Hussein stressed that time was of the essence because the longer the West Bank remained in Jewish hands, the more difficult it would be to regain it.[22] The Khartoum summit thus marked a real turning point in Nasser's attitude to Israel: a departure from the previous approach of military confrontation and the beginning of the quest not simply for dialogue but for a peaceful settlement. His moderate line earned him the support of King Faisal of Saudi Arabia and the hostility of his erstwhile allies.[23] Hussein gave the following account of the realignment of Arab forces at Khartoum:

At Khartoum I fought very much against the three noes. But the atmosphere there developed into one where all the people who used to support Nasser . . . turned on him and turned on him in such a vicious way that I found myself morally unable to continue to take any stand but to come closer to him and defend him and accuse them of responsibility for the things that had happened. That was the first collision I had with many of my friends in the Arab world.

But then we talked about the need for a resolution and the need for a peaceful solution to the problem. And Nasser's approach was that "I feel responsible. We lost the West Bank and Gaza and they come first. I am not going to ask for any withdrawal from the Suez Canal. It can stay closed until such time as the issue of the West Bank and of Gaza is resolved and the issue of the Palestinian people is resolved. So go and speak of that and speak of a comprehensive solution to the problem and a comprehensive peace and go and do anything you can short of signing a separate peace." And I said that in any event I was not considering signing a separate peace because we wanted to resolve this problem in a comprehensive fashion.[24]

At the close of the summit the following communiqué was issued: "The Arab Monarchs and Heads of State agreed on unifying their efforts in political action on the international and diplomatic level to remove the traces of aggression, and to ensure the withdrawal of Israeli forces from the Arab territories that have been occupied since 5 June. This is within the framework of the basic principles by which the Arab states abide, namely: no peace with Israel, or recognition of her, no negotiation with her, and the upholding of the right of the Palestinian people in their homeland."[25] The first sentence opened the door to diplomatic activity. The last sentence was inserted to reassure the Palestinians that their interests would not be abandoned in the climate of accommodation that followed defeat in the June War. Arab spokesmen interpreted the Khartoum declarations to mean no formal peace *treaty* but not a rejection of a state of peace; no *direct* negotiations but not a refusal to talk through third parties; and no *de jure* recognition of Israel but acceptance of its existence as a fait accompli.[26] Israeli propaganda, however, seized on the last sentence to discredit the summit and to portray the Arab position as incorrigibly rejectionist, absolutely uncompromising and threatening.

Hussein returned from Khartoum well satisfied with the success of the moderates in imposing their views on the extremists and with the support that Jordan obtained, both moral and financial, from the other Arab states. The oil-producing states pledged economic aid to the confrontation states until "the traces of aggression" had been removed, with the sum of £40 million allocated to Jordan. King Faisal had never seen Nasser "so frank, humble, sincere or courageous." Syria was isolated and saddled with most of the responsibility for having provoked hostilities. President Arif agreed to withdraw Iraqi troops from Jordan. President Nasser agreed to withdraw Egyptian troops from Yemen, where they had been since 1962. Hussein was asked to mediate in the Algerian–Moroccan dispute.[27] And all the participants agreed to revive the Arab solidarity pact and conduct no hostile propaganda against one another.

The Khartoum summit effectively allowed Hussein to explore the possibility of arriving at an accommodation with Israel. The problem was one of timing, of choosing the optimal moment and the most promising avenue for negotiations. His instinct was that it was too soon to take the initiative on his own. Arab leaders were ahead of their people in appreciating the implications of their recent defeat by Israel. He and his advisers decided to wait for the next meeting of the Security Council in the hope that, with the support of the Great Powers, it would take a step towards imposing a solution. When the Americans suggested to Hussein direct negotiations with Israel, his reaction was that the time was not right. Hussein reminded the American ambassador that he never hesitated in the past to have direct contact whenever he felt it to be useful and assured him that he would not hesitate in the future.[28]

During a visit to Cairo on 30 September, Hussein secured Nasser's agreement to a draft resolution that he hoped the United States and the USSR would submit to the Security Council. In the early days of the following month Hussein made his first official visit to Moscow. According to an Israeli intelligence report, the king was amazed by the honour and special treatment that he was accorded there. He discovered that the Russians were not quite the monsters he had assumed them to be. They made strenuous efforts to sell him arms, but he agreed only to economic aid and cultural relations. The primary reason for the visit was thought to be to form a personal impression of the Russians and to assess their ability to help break the Arab–Israeli impasse.[29] According to Hussein's own report, he had found the Russians very understanding and ready to support an early Security Council resolution along the lines of the draft formulated by Arthur Goldberg, the American permanent representative at the UN, and Andrei Gromyko, the Soviet foreign minister. Hussein submitted to the Russians a revised version of this draft, which they said they were ready to accept. They warned him, however, that the Americans were becoming increasingly intransigent and that he might have difficulty in securing their acceptance.[30]

Hussein wrote a long letter to President Johnson, giving his view of the Middle East situation following the Khartoum Conference and his subsequent trips to Cairo and Moscow. It was a strongly worded but dignified letter. Hussein expressed his deep hurt at America's pro-Israeli position and lamented the double standard it applied to Arabs and Israelis. This kind of discrimination, he said humbly, was not worthy of a great leader or a great nation. He pointed out that at Khartoum the Arabs reached a reasonable and responsible position. Now it was up to the great powers to act, since they were the ones who had created Israel in the first place. In conclusion, Hussein strongly urged the US government to cooperate with others in convening the Security Council and adopting without delay a resolution along the lines of the draft he had discussed in Moscow.[31]

Hussein intensified his efforts to influence American policy during a visit to Washington in the early part of November. In a series of meetings with US officials he succeeded in obtaining a promise that America would exert its influence to preserve the territorial integrity of Jordan. At a meeting in New York on 3 November, Ambassador Goldberg gave Hussein the following summary of US policy: "The United States as a matter of policy does not envisage a Jordan which consists only of the East Bank. The United States is prepared to support a return of the West Bank to Jordan with minor boundary rectifications. However, the United States would use its influence to obtain compensation to Jordan for any territory it is required to give up . . . In short, we are prepared to make a maximum effort to obtain for Jordan the best possible deal in terms of settlement with Israel." Secretary of State Dean Rusk formally confirmed these assurances to Hussein and President Johnson was also informed. When Hussein went to the White House on 8 November, Johnson pressed him hard to support the resolution that America was about to submit to the Security Council, despite its lack of precision on the withdrawal of Israeli forces.[32] Hussein left Washington with the clear impression that he had reached an understanding with the administration that if he supported the American resolution, they would see to its implementation and that the Israeli forces would be withdrawn from the West Bank within six months.[33]

On his way back from the United States, Hussein stopped in London and there he renewed his contact with the Israelis after an interval of four months. In the intervening period Israel had received offers to arrange a secret meeting with Hussein from several quarters but it deflected all of them. The most persistent efforts to get the two sides together were made by Julian Amery, now minister of aviation, but the Israelis kept stalling. Amery was valuable to them because of his senior position in the Conservative Party and his close contacts with the intelligence community, but they did not need him as a link man to Hussein and so they kept fobbing him off with various excuses. They also kept him in the dark about Dr. Emanuel Herbert, whom they preferred as their link man because he was not a politician and because he did not have his own agenda. Herzog's account of all the conversations he had with and about Amery fills up twenty pages. The one mildly interesting point to emerge is that Hussein expressed a wish to meet Moshe Dayan and to talk to him as one soldier to another, and that Abba Eban and Levi Eshkol opposed the idea because of their political rivalry with Dayan. But the basic reason for Herzog's reluctance to meet with Hussein was quite simple—he had nothing to say to him. He believed that it was in Israel's interest to delay the contact with Hussein for as long as possible.[34]

Despite these reservations Herzog had not one but two meetings with

Hussein in London. The meeting on 19 November took place in the home of Julian Amery and the one on the following day took place in the home of Dr. Emanuel Herbert. Also present at Amery's home was Erik Bennett, Hussein's friend and former air adviser. Hussein and Herzog pretended that this was their first meeting, but Hussein gave the game away by asking Herzog whether he had stopped smoking. Herzog opened the meeting with a long review of the Middle East scene designed to destroy any hope that Hussein might have had of help from the Russians or from Nasser. After the survey Herzog said that the prime minister had instructed him to meet the king in order to ask whether he had reached a decision on direct negotiations with Israel that might lead to a peace treaty. Hussein replied that he had always felt that the resources of the countries of the Middle East should be concentrated on constructive efforts, and he still held to this view. In close coordination with Nasser, he had succeeded at Khartoum in getting a decision to seek a political settlement of the problem. After Khartoum he and Nasser remained in regular contact. They both agreed to a settlement comprising the end of belligerency; recognition of Israel in return for its evacuation of the territories it had occupied; freedom of passage for Israeli shipping in the Suez Canal and in the Gulf of Aqaba; and a settlement of the refugee problem that was part of the state of war.

Hussein said that the Middle East was at a turning point. Without a settlement, extremist policies would prevail. "I do not think of today but of the distant future," he said. "After all that has passed over me I do not care what happens today. I hope that history will judge that I was true to my principles. I hope you will understand that we have gone to the utmost limit." He and Nasser were in agreement about their approach, and the other Arab States had promised not to interfere. He hoped that Israel would not prove too obstinate and now make the same mistake the Arabs had over many years. If a settlement were not found, the Middle East would be thrown into turmoil and become an arena of conflict between East and West.

Herzog belittled the significance of Hussein's achievements and argued that his proposals amounted to no more than the armistice agreements that had not been fulfilled for twenty years. He gave another version of the lecture that Hussein had heard before about the Jewish link with the Land of Israel. At the root of the Arab–Israeli problem, he said, lay the refusal of the Arabs to acknowledge the nature of this link.

Israel insisted on direct negotiations as a symbol of recognition. Hussein agreed that direct negotiations should be official and public but he repeated his advice to Israel not to be obstinate. Herzog asked whether Hussein would enter into negotiations with Israel on his own in the event of his failing to carry his colleagues with him. Hussein replied that he would if the people of the West Bank approached him. But he could not go into negotiations without knowing in advance where he stood. What were the limits to Israel's claims to the land? This was the question that Herzog had dreaded and to which he could give no answer. He had to confess that he had been sent to listen and not to pronounce. All he could do by way of background was to tell the king that there were differing views in Israel. Some thought that the present position should continue unchanged. Others felt that Hussein had no rights whatsoever on the West Bank and that Israel should seek a settlement with the Palestinians. Yet others considered that in order to achieve peace with Jordan, they should negotiate with him on the West Bank. Even the last school of thought, the minimalists, emphasized security considerations as well as historical associations with the land. In Herzog's view this was not expansionism, though one is left to wonder what would have constituted expansionism in his view. The meeting, in any case, ended inconclusively. Hussein remarked that the question of Jerusalem was crucial. Herzog did not react because he wished to leave him with the impression that this was not even a matter for discussion.[35]

In the evening Hussein went to Dr. Herbert's home on his own initiative and asked to see Herzog again. By the time that Herbert found Herzog it was too late so they met the following morning. It was not clear why Hussein wanted the meeting because he said very little at the beginning, as was his custom. Herzog explained that he had met him at Amery's home only because Amery claimed that he had requested the meeting. Hussein looked embarrassed and said he hoped that Amery did not know about their secret channel through Dr. Herbert. Herzog then referred to the Fatah incursions across the Jordan River in the Beisan area and warned that these guerrilla operations could have serious consequences. Hussein replied that he gave the army orders to put an end to these operations and that they had already arrested 150 Palestinian fighters. Herzog summed up what he thought they had agreed the previous day: the UN mediator would move between the capitals with a view to bringing the two sides to direct negotiations. Hussein confirmed this understanding. They also agreed to avoid Julian Amery and to continue to use Dr. Herbert as their link.[36]

With the approach of the Security Council debate, both sides stepped up their lobbying: Jordan for a strong resolution and Israel for as weak a resolution as possible. Hussein remained actively involved in the discussions and the drafting behind the scenes with American, British and Arab diplomats. In the end a British resolution was unanimously adopted by the Security Council on 22 November 1967. In Jordan this came to be called "the Jordanian resolution." It was considered a great triumph for Hussein and became the cornerstone of Jordanian foreign policy. Resolution 242 was the most significant international pronouncement on the Arab–Israeli dispute after the June War. The preamble to the resolution emphasized the inadmissibility of the acquisition of territory by force and the need to work for a just and lasting peace. Article 1 stated that a just and lasting peace should include two principles: (i) "withdrawal of Israeli armed forces from territories occupied in the recent conflict" and (ii) respect for the right of every state in the area "to live in peace within secure and recognized boundaries free from threats or acts of force." The resolution went on to affirm the necessity for guaranteeing freedom of navigation and for achieving a just settlement of the refugee problem. The resolution supported the Arabs on the issue of territory and Israel on the issue of peace. Basically, the resolution proposed a package deal in which Israel would get peace in exchange for returning to the Arab states their territories.

The resolution was a masterpiece of British ambiguity, and it was this ambiguity that won for it the support of the United States, the Soviet Union, Jordan and Egypt, though not of Syria. Israel had many successes on the long road that led to the adoption of this resolution. It defeated a series of Arab and Soviet proposals that called for withdrawal without peace. Another success was to avoid the requirement of withdrawing from "the territories" or "all the territories" occupied in the recent war. The final wording in the English text was "withdrawal from territories," and this gave Israel some room for manoeuvre. The French text of Resolution 242 spoke explicitly of withdrawal from *les territoires*—from *the* territories. This made it absolutely clear that the drafters of the resolution had in mind Israel's withdrawal from *all* the territories it had occupied in the war. Everyone except Israel understood the resolution in this sense. Israel, however, exploited the ambiguity in the English text to defy international pressure for complete withdrawal. Israel's interpretation of Resolution 242 also differed from the Arab interpretation in other respects. Egypt and Jordan agreed to peace but insisted that the first step must be complete Israeli withdrawal. Israel insisted that before it would withdraw from any part of the territories, there must be direct negotiations leading to a contractual peace agreement that incorporated secure and recognized boundaries. In sum, 242 invited Israel to trade land for peace, but Israel was more interested in keeping the land than in achieving peace.

Dr. Gunnar Jarring, the Swedish ambassador to Moscow, was appointed by the UN secretary-general to promote an Arab–Israeli settlement on the basis of Resolution 242. Having rejected 242, Syria declined to participate in his mission. The other Arab states had high expectations of Jarring, whereas Israel had no expectations at all, perceiving him as personally unimaginative and ineffectual. But the real problem was that Israel had no trust in the impartiality of the UN or in its capacity to mediate. The Israeli tactic was to keep feeding Jarring with proposals and documents to which he was to obtain Arab reactions. The aim was to keep his mission alive and prevent the matter from going back to the UN, where Israel would be blamed for the failure. Abba Eban's colleagues were happy to leave it to him to conduct the elaborate exchange of notes with Jarring as long as he did not make any substantive concessions. Eban understood better than any of them both the limits and the possibilities of Jarring's mission. "Some of my colleagues," noted Eban, "did not understand that even a tactical exercise fills a vacuum. Even diplomatic activity that is not leading anywhere is better than no diplomatic activity at all. Activity itself gives Arab moderates an alibi for avoiding the military option."[37] A diplomatic vacuum there certainly was but a vacuum of Israel's making. The urbane and witty Eban liked to say that the Arabs never missed an opportunity to miss an opportunity for peace, but after 1967 this description fitted Israel much better than it did the other side. Hussein's hope of using the Jarring mission to pave the way to direct negotiations between the moderate Arab states and Israel bore no fruit because Israel had no interest in any kind of purposeful diplomacy.

Fearful that Hussein was about to sell them out at the conference table, Fatah and the more extremist groups resumed guerrilla raids

against Israel in the autumn of 1967. First they tried to instigate a popular liberation war on the West Bank, but when this failed they moved
their operational bases to the East Bank of the Jordan and to Lebanon
and started mounting hit-and-run raids against the Israelis from there.
They enjoyed a great deal of popular support, and attracted floods of
volunteers from Palestinian and non-Palestinian communities throughout the Arab world.[38] After the defeat of the regular Arab armies, they
became the standard-bearers of Arab nationalism. The Palestinian
cause as a whole began to attract more international sympathy and support. In the past the conflict was perceived as one between the large
Arab states and little Israel. After 1967 it was increasingly perceived as
a conflict between an oppressed people and an oppressive, colonialist
state. The biblical image of David and Goliath was reversed, with Israel
assuming the unaccustomed role of Goliath.

The Palestinian guerrilla organizations also commanded support at
all levels of Jordanian society. Ex-prime minister Wasfi Tall was a member of a royal consultative committee created to advise the king on strategy and policy in the wake of the June War. Tall believed that Israel had
no intention of withdrawing from the lands it occupied and no real
interest in a political settlement with the Arabs, since this would entail
withdrawal. He therefore concluded that the Arabs had no alternative
but to resort to prolonged guerrilla warfare in order to drive Israel out.
Active resistance, argued Tall, was necessary to provide the Arabs with
the "psychological umbrella" to proceed to a political settlement in the
unlikely event that Israel changed course. Above all, the "psychological
umbrella" was essential to re-establish the king's authority over his
people and to provide the nation with some hope and purpose. Tall's
argument was that a peace based on humiliation would not endure and
that any Arab leader who accepted it would be repudiated.[39] Within the
army the urge to expiate the defeat and to purge the humiliation was
particularly acute. Although there was no direct challenge to the king's
authority, his orders were not invariably obeyed. The official policy
was to stop Palestinian guerrilla organizations from using Jordan as a
springboard for attacks on Israel. Army commanders stationed in the
border areas, however, often gave passive and sometimes even active
support to the guerrilla fighters.

Trapped between Israeli hardliners and Palestinian radicals, Hussein
complained that "Jordan had given everything and got nothing" from

the United States. With the United States stalling on his request to resume arms supplies, he again hinted that it might be necessary to move towards the Soviets. It was unusual for him to play hardball, but his credibility with the army was at stake. He was also beginning to give up hope that the United States would use its muscle to prevent the Israelis from presenting him with a massive fait accompli on the West Bank. His confidence in the Johnson administration began to crumble. Walt Rostow informed Lyndon Johnson that "Hussein is wondering whether a Soviet ring around Israel wouldn't better bring Israel to terms. This is, of course, the thinking of an increasingly desperate man who sees his choices diminishing."[40] In his despair Hussein began to relax the policy of reining in the fedayeen. Sometimes he would be very tough on them, at other times very lenient. The Israelis noted this change in policy. In the past the Jordanian authorities regarded the fedayeen as an element that endangered the regime. They used to monitor them and to carry out arrests. But they came to see fedayeen harassment of the Israeli forces and settlers on the West Bank as something that helped Jordan domestically and in the inter-Arab arena.[41]

Regardless of whether Hussein was unwilling or unable to prevent the attacks from his territory, the Israeli conclusion was the same: to strike at the Fatah bases. Having chased the fedayeen from the West Bank, the Israelis pressed the offensive with raids against their positions on the East Bank inside Jordan proper. The process of escalation reached its climax with a massive attack on Karameh, a village about four miles east of the Jordan River where Fatah's headquarters were located. Jordanian intelligence alerted Fatah to an imminent Israeli attack on the village and suggested that they make themselves scarce. Fatah's reply was that it was their duty to set an example and to prove that Arabs are capable of courage and dignity. At dawn on 21 March 1968 a massive Israeli armoured force, supported by helicopters and infantry, attacked Karameh. There were only about 300 Fatah men, but they were well prepared and ably supported by Jordanian artillery, which was stationed near by.[42] The casualties were heavy on all sides: 28 Israelis, 61 Jordanians and 92 fedayeen were killed. But all the glory went to Fatah. *Karameh* is the Arabic word for "honour," and by their brave stand the fedayeen were seen to have redeemed that of the Arabs. The Arab media presented the battle as a turning point and as the first defeat inflicted on the IDF by the Arabs. In the forty-eight hours after the battle, 5,000 new recruits applied to join Fatah. Hussein could not afford to go against the tide and was driven to express his sympathy with the fedayeen in public. "It is difficult to distinguish between fedayeen and others," he said. "We may reach the stage when we shall all become fedayeen."

However, the aims of Hussein and the fedayeen remained incompatible. He wanted to recover his land, whereas they challenged Israel's very existence. After Karameh they acted more independently in mounting operations against Israel, and these provoked Israeli reprisals. Hussein was thus caught between the Palestinian militants, who were encouraged by Syria, and Israel's insistence that he had to bear the responsibility for their hostile acts. Israel bombarded Fatah positions in the Jordan Valley and Jordanian Army bases, as well as the towns of Salt and Irbid, inflicting heavy civilian casualties. These punitive raids, especially the ones involving aircraft (against which Jordan had no defence), undermined Hussein's position. On the one hand he recognized the right of the Palestinians to resist occupation. But on the other, as he recalled,

we had a very turbulent internal situation; we had continuous reprisals and fire-fights on the long front, essentially from the Dead Sea or just south of the Dead Sea to the northernmost part. And we were hit by both sides. We had an internal problem, we had an external problem, our army was being hit, and one was trying one's best to ameliorate this situation or save the situation from deteriorating . . . The Israelis considered that they had to retaliate against actions from Jordan. I kept saying that these actions were by people resisting occupation but it didn't necessarily mean that Jordan was fighting. Jordan was deployed on the longest border and its army was trying its best to see what could be done. But we had our own problems . . . I was very worried at the increase of what was almost perpetual fighting until the Egyptians started the so-called War of Attrition.[43]

This endless chain of fedayeen raids and Israeli counter-raids greatly complicated the search for a peaceful solution to the Arab–Israeli conflict.

13. Dialogue Across the Battle Lines

Remarkably, although in the aftermath of the June War it held very few cards, Jordan became a major player in Arab diplomacy. How did such a small, impoverished and insignificant country come to occupy such a prominent part in regional and international politics? The answer largely lies in the personality and policies of King Hussein. He was a strong, energetic and charismatic leader who commanded the attention of the great powers by sheer persistence and force of personality. Hussein's unique brand of personal diplomacy enabled Jordan to exert an influence in foreign affairs that was out of all proportion to its real power. Hussein was the only Arab ruler who had intimate relations with America and relations of any kind at all with Israel, the greatest taboo in Arab politics. And he positioned himself very carefully between the Arab world, the United States and Israel. It was a difficult balancing act but one that Hussein succeeded in sustaining. Other Arab rulers, including Nasser, knew about Hussein's contacts with their problematic neighbour only what he himself chose to tell them. Nasser needed Hussein as a channel both to Washington and to Jerusalem, and Hussein carried on his contacts with Israel in a way that did not exclude him from the Arab fold. He did not overstep the mark by going public, as Anwar Sadat had in the 1970s, and he did not pay the price that Sadat had for making a separate peace with Israel: the expulsion of Egypt from the Arab League. Hussein developed a network of bilateral relations, and he alone knew where he stood with each of his partners.

Whereas before 1967 the Israelis needed Hussein more than he needed them, after the war it was he who desperately needed something from them: his land. Despite all the obstacles along the road, he never despaired of reaching a peaceful settlement. He requested direct contact with Israel at the highest possible level. Prime Minister Levi Eshkol was reluctant to go in person, but the cabinet eventually agreed to send the foreign minister to a meeting with Hussein in London. Abba

Eban was instructed to stress that he could put forward only private proposals without the approval of the cabinet. The meeting took place at the home of Dr. Herbert in St. John's Wood on 3 May 1968. Eban was accompanied by Dr. Herzog and Hussein by Zaid Rifa'i, his private secretary. Zaid was the eldest son of the former prime minister Samir Rifa'i. He had been educated at the Bishop's School and Victoria College, where he formed a close friendship with the future king, and at Harvard, where he took a degree in political science and international law. Zaid Rifa'i was to play a key role alongside his friend the king in the conduct of the secret talks with Israeli officials over the next two decades. He was the adviser, the organizer, the note-taker and the negotiator. His thoughts on these talks, which were related to the present author, therefore merit serious attention.

To understand the course of the next thirty years, Rifa'i believed, one first of all had to understand Hussein's personality. Hussein was truly a man of peace who hated war. He was intelligent, shrewd and pragmatic enough to know that the Arab–Israeli conflict could not be settled by violence. Only through negotiations and agreement would it be possible for their two peoples to live together in peace. This was Hussein's frame of mind before and after the June War. The loss of Jerusalem hurt him more than anything else: it had been under Arab sovereignty and was lost on his watch. Regaining it, therefore, was of paramount importance to him. Here again he realized that this could not be done through war, feeling very strongly that only through negotiations and agreement would it be possible for him to get Israel to withdraw from the West Bank and East Jerusalem.

Rifa'i believed that, from the outset, Hussein doubted that Israel's intentions in going to war in 1967 were as claimed: to defend itself from an imminent Arab attack or to gain recognition from the Arab countries. Rather, Hussein started to suspect that the Israelis had wanted to expand all along. What disturbed him most was the Israeli response to an offer he made at their early post-war meetings and kept repeating: to sign a formal peace treaty in return for Israel's complete withdrawal from the West Bank and East Jerusalem. Hussein realized he was taking a big risk, but he was willing to chance it and to accept the judgement of his people, the Arab nation and history. He also thought that his offer was a very major sacrifice because it would have meant the breaking of an Arab taboo. And he was shocked when the Israeli response was that they were willing to sign a peace treaty with Jordan but only if Jordan agreed to cede parts of the West Bank and all of Arab East Jerusalem to them.

At Rifa'i's first meeting with the Israelis the question was how the recent war could be used as a window for making peace. It was clear to him from the beginning that it was going to be exceptionally difficult: "Both sides were interested in making peace: one party wanted to annex Jerusalem and some areas in the West Bank, and the other was not willing even to consider making any territorial concessions. That was the deadlock right from the beginning. The intent for peace was there, but His Majesty was adamant that Israel must return *all* the territories captured in the war. And the Israelis were unwilling to accept it."[1] Rifa'i's allegation of Israeli territorial expansionism and diplomatic intransigence after the war is fully supported by the Israeli documentary record.

According to the Israeli record of this first meeting, Abba Eban said that he had come not to negotiate or to make commitments but to clarify two questions. First, could Jordan negotiate and sign a peace treaty with Israel on a separate basis without being dependent on another neighbour? And second, what could the king do to ensure an end to terrorist activities? Hussein's answer to the first question was that "It is not impossible." But before taking such a difficult step, he needed to know what kind of a settlement Israel was prepared for. Eban's answer was evasive: his government saw no reason to come to a binding decision until and unless it was convinced that it had a serious Arab partner for peacemaking. There were three schools of thought, Eban elaborated: those who wanted to keep all the territory west of the Jordan River; those who favoured a settlement with the Palestine Arabs; and those who favoured peace with Jordan on the basis of a new, agreed and secure frontier. Even the last school of thought insisted on four conditions: no return to the borders of 4 June 1967; the changes would take account of security needs and historic association; the area west of the Jordan River would have to be demilitarized; and Jerusalem would remain united as the capital of Israel.

Hussein ignored the specific terms and merely suggested that they meet under the auspices of Gunnar Jarring, the UN mediator, as well as privately. He also wanted to consult with Cairo before proceeding with separate negotiations. Rifa'i was more militant and seemed worried that Hussein had not reacted to the substance of Eban's presentation. "All your ideas, including the third," Rifa'i told Eban, "are for Arab surrender, not for agreement." Jordan's starting point would be the 4 June territorial situation with minor changes and on a reciprocal basis. There had to be Arab, and not merely Muslim, status in parts of Jerusalem. Israel's security would lie in a full peace settlement, not in topography. Hussein's final words were that a further effort should be made to get enough Egyptian consent to enable open negotiations to take place.[2]

Two days later Herzog took the initiative in arranging a follow-up meeting with Rifa'i. Herzog was evidently very impressed with Rifa'i, describing him in his report to the cabinet as a shrewd and even brilliant man who knew his subject inside out. At the second meeting Rifa'i stressed that Cairo's approval was vital for them because their hands were tied by the Khartoum decisions—no recognition, no negotiation and no peace with Israel. They could not go to New York for talks with Israeli representatives under Jarring's auspices unless the Egyptians went along with them. When the king visited Nasser in Cairo on 6–7 April, the Egyptian president had expressed scepticism about meeting with the Jews but agreed to reconsider if the Jordanians insisted. Nasser wanted Egypt to be present at the first meeting with Dr. Jarring but he did not rule out independent Jordanian negotiations subsequently. Rifa'i talked at length about Nasser. During the king's last visit to Cairo, Nasser told him that he did not want young Egyptians to continue to sacrifice their lives. He was willing to end the state of war if Israel withdrew from all the occupied territories. But he would never agree to meet with the Israelis face to face. Israel and the West had defeated him militarily and economically; if he met with them, he would be defeated politically too. Should Israel continue to refuse to withdraw, he estimated that he would be ready to take military action at the end of 1969 or the beginning of 1970.[3]

On the following day, 6 May, the two men met again. Rifa'i reported that he had received a message from Cairo in which Nasser said the following: "Don't trust the Jews. First, they will not carry out the Security Council resolution. Second, they will not give up Jerusalem. Third, they will not give up Gaza. Fourth, they will not withdraw to the borders of 4 June 1967. This whole business is an illusion and a danger. But, if you insist, I, Nasser, will order my permanent representative at the UN to meet with Jarring, not with the Israelis, and we'll see. I'll give you this chance." Rifa'i emphasized Nasser's moral debt to Jordan: he had involved them in the war and thus he could not stop them from proceeding to peace talks. In practical terms this meant two stages. In the first the Jordanian and Egyptian representatives would meet with Jarring. In the second the Egyptians would withdraw and the Jordanians would move forward to substantive talks. On his return home Herzog gave a detailed report to the cabinet on the three meetings and on the procedure proposed by Jordan for moving to a settlement. In the subsequent discussion a multitude of opinions were expressed. The most telling remark came from the mouth of the prime minister. Levi Eshkol repeated what he had told his colleagues many times before: "I fear the day when we have to sit face to face and conduct negotiations."[4]

Herzog was allocated the task, which he executed with considerable skill and ingenuity, of maintaining the contact with the king and his adviser but without making any concrete proposals and without entering into negotiations. At his meeting in London with Rifa'i on 19 and 20 June, arrangements were made for a trip by Hussein to the Gulf of Aqaba on 8 August.[5] The meeting was to take place on a ship 500 metres south of Coral Island.[6] But on 4 August the Israeli Air Force twice bombed the Fatah camps near Salt, on the East Bank, inflicting heavy civilian casualties and hitting four ambulances. Two days later a cable arrived from Dr. Herbert, who was on holiday in Crete, to say that the consultation was cancelled owing to the hostilities. During a visit to London two weeks later, Hussein saw his doctor and discussed having another meeting there. At first Hussein said that he would see Herzog only if Herzog had something new to say, but he later changed his mind. Rifa'i told Herzog at a meeting on 22 August that the king wanted to see him on the 24th at 6 p.m. at the doctor's home. That evening, close to midnight, Herzog and Rifa'i met again for a summing-up talk. Herzog read his notes on the position stated by the king and received Rifa'i's comments. The doctor was present throughout all these meetings.

Altogether the three meetings took up four to five hours, with Herzog's report taking up twenty-four pages of precise, polished, Mandarin-like prose. Hussein said that Israeli attacks, like the ones on Karameh and Salt, solved nothing and only made Fatah stronger. Did

the Israelis think that through the use of force they could gain acceptance by the Arabs? It was his impression that there were three voices
in the government: those who sought a separate settlement with the
Palestinians; those who were working for peace with the kingdom of
Jordan; and the extremists who would try to ensure that the road to
peace was always blocked at decisive moments. On the Arab side there
was growing despair because of the lack of progress, and time was running out. Hinting that he himself might be overthrown, Hussein exclaimed, "Make up your minds. Will it be easier for you to yield to the
extremists when they are in power than to yield now?" Rifa'i talked
about Nasser's predicament. On the one hand he faced a danger from
within because of inaction, and on the other the danger of further defeat
if he acted against Israel. If he was forced to do so, Nasser would choose
to act and to go under as an Arab patriot in the eyes of history. He feared
above all else his removal from within, which would destroy his image
for ever. After Karameh, with tears in his eyes, Nasser had expressed
his gratitude to Hussein for the success of the Arab Legion in preventing Israeli forces from taking the hills. Nasser said that had the Israelis
succeeded, he would have had no alternative but to intervene and that
would have meant suicide.

The only practical outcome of the wide-ranging discussions in June
and August was a decision to hold a further high-level meeting in London towards the end of September.[7] Despite the lack of concrete results
these meetings with Hussein were hugely significant for Israel. In his
self-congratulatory second volume of memoirs, Abba Eban noted both
the significance of the meetings and the unique qualities of the man
with whom they met:

The very existence of those talks gave Israelis a feeling that Arab–Israeli conflicts are not inherently irreconcilable. Here was an Arab statesman, descended
from the prophet Muhammad, who held a record for longevity in leadership of
an Arab country, expressing his belief, however reluctant, that Israel was an
immutable part of the Middle East. Hussein never failed to enunciate a passionately Arab national pride, but he respected the allegiances of his Israeli interlocutors. Meetings with him, and a study of his Arabic rhetoric, which was
classically perfect in diction and in range of expression, were for me an antidote to Dayan's bleak theory that struggle had been eternally "decreed" as the
law of Arab–Israeli relations . . .

The impression that I deduced from contacts with King Hussein was that he would give Israeli interlocutors maximum courtesy and minimal commitment. Our encounters took place in the home of a British friend of the king, not far from the Israeli embassy residence in North West London, or in a motor launch swaying from side to side in Red Sea waters off the Jordanian–Israeli coast, or on a coral island near Eilat. It was conventional for us to believe that our London encounters, at least, were concealed from the British authorities by skillful maneuvring, but one day Prime Minister Wilson said to me: "There are rumors that you saw King Hussein today. Absurd, isn't it?" Wilson then winked at me with prodigious emphasis in a gesture of conspiratorial reassurance . . .

Hussein was consistently rigorous in the formulation of his role. He believes that Israel and the Arabs have no option except eventual coexistence. He has sometimes envisaged the possibility of an individual peace initiative by Jordan, but only if he can succeed in a total restoration of Arab rule in all the occupied territories. He has never been ready to be a pioneer both in the ideology of peace and in the explosive principle of territorial bargaining. His slogan has always been that Israel can have either peace or territory, but not both. This is not far from being a universal international consensus, and King Hussein was the first Arab leader to make it so.[8]

Herzog, the real initiator of the link with the descendant of the prophet, was no longer certain of its value. One of the first things that Herzog said to Hussein on 22 August was that, in his opinion, their meetings had not been a waste of time. But nor were they going anywhere. One therefore has to ask the question: why did Hussein continue with the contact, even when it became abundantly clear that the Israelis were simply stringing him along? The answer is twofold: fear and hope. The fear was that the extremists in Israel would gain the upper hand and try to topple him or that they might try to capture more land on the East Bank of his kingdom, such as the hills round Karameh. He knew that the Arabs had no military option; he sensed that the Israelis had no desire for peace and speculated that their posture on terrorism owed something to this underlying attitude. He concluded that Israel wished to hold on to the land it occupied for religious and cultural reasons, and needed certain additional territories to consolidate its position. Combating terrorism provided the excuse for further expansion.[9] Hussein was worried by rumours of an imminent Israeli attempt to seize territory on the East Bank in northern Jordan from which some fedayeen operated. He therefore asked Ambassador Harrison Symmes for a statement from the highest authority in the US government of its attitude to the independence and territorial integrity of Jordan.[10] The Americans discounted the rumours and reaffirmed their commitment to Jordan's integrity, but they did not succeed in dispelling Hussein's fears. By continuing his contact with the Israelis he tried to forestall further Israeli encroachment on his land. Hussein also kept alive the hope that America would eventually fulfil its promise to him and start putting pressure on Israel to withdraw from the West Bank. Despite the frequent frustrations caused by America's partiality towards Israel, he kept trying. He was virtually the only member of the Jordanian political elite who had not completely given up on America by this time. Similarly, with Israel, Hussein had no cards to play and nothing concrete to offer except peace; yet he was always hopeful that he would eventually succeed in persuading the Israelis to make peace with Jordan on the basis of the 1967 borders.[11] In the meantime, as Winston Churchill liked to say, jaw-jaw was better than war-war.

The Americans were kept informed of the state of play in the bilateral talks by Itzhak Rabin, the former chief of staff who was now ambassador to Washington. Rabin had undergone a remarkable conversion from the Palestinian option to the so-called Jordanian option. After the June War, Rabin advised Eshkol that, from the security point of view, the only possible solution on the West Bank was the creation of a mini Palestinian state. Towards the end of the year, however, the scales tilted in favour of an agreement with Jordan. Rabin was converted to the Jordanian option and tried to advance it as ambassador to Washington. In his second term as prime minister in the early 1990s he made it into the cornerstone of his foreign policy.[12] Rabin was treated in Washington with the utmost respect because he was a renowned soldier who had scored a decisive victory over the Arabs, in sharp contrast to the poor performance of America's generals in Vietnam. During a discussion of other matters on 4 June 1968 with senior American officials, Rabin alluded to the question of Jordan–Israel peace talks. He said that Nasser had given Hussein the green light to go further than Egypt. Nasser had also said, however, that Hussein could make no agreement affecting Jerusalem without the approval of the Arab world, since Jerusalem belonged not only to Jordan but to all Arabs. Israel had good information about the thinking of Hussein and his entourage, but it was committed to not discussing this matter in detail and Rabin was therefore limited in what he could say. He could tell the Americans, however, that Hussein was ready for a peace treaty through secret, direct negotiations under the cover of the Jarring Mission. There was an argument in Israel as to whether Hussein could be relied upon. Government policy, however, was to maintain the Jarring Mission while trying to make progress secretly with Hussein. The Jarring cover was necessary in view of the basic differences between Hussein and Nasser. Israel knew what kind of settlement Hussein wanted and there was hope for a settlement with Jordan. There was no more talk of overthrowing Hussein. All key members of the Israeli cabinet apparently agreed that "everything will be adjusted to this policy."[13]

A further glimpse into Hussein's thinking was gained by McGeorge Bundy, special consultant to the president, during a visit to the Middle East. Bundy thought that Hussein had regained some of the confidence he lacked during the summer of 1967 when he seemed "very shaky." Hussein stressed the importance of progress towards a just solution by the end of the year and the necessity of having something tangible before he could directly confront the fedayeen. Bundy, who had just come from Israel, urged Hussein not to wait for others to solve his problem for him but to tackle it directly with someone like Moshe Dayan, the minister of defence. Bundy also conveyed Dayan's warning that if fedayeen forays into Israel continued, Israel might be forced to strike at Jordan again, causing further population displacement. Hussein frequently used the word "just" in much the same manner as the Israelis used the word "peace." A settlement in which all the parties had confidence was the only solution, said Hussein. He obviously considered that what Israel had offered the Arabs so far was "thin soup." Hussein repeated to Bundy his frequently used description of Israel as possessing three faces: the extremist one, which sought the downfall of Jordan and Israeli occupation of the West Bank; the seemingly reasonable one, which wanted a Palestinian entity; and the moderate one. Hussein said that it was the face of moderation that he was trying to find.[14]

Hussein's own moderation helped to win him friends and admirers in Israel. One of them was Golda Meir, who had had a face-to-face meeting with Hussein in Paris in 1965 when she served as foreign minister under Levi Eshkol. In August 1968 Theodor Sorensen, a former senior aide to President Kennedy, visited the Middle East. Through Sorensen,

Meir sent a message to Hussein that said, "I hope that Your Majesty knows that Israel is your best friend in the Middle East." When the king received the message, he smiled and said, "Some people think that I am Israel's best friend in the Middle East."[15] The little exchange revealed a degree of goodwill at both the political and personal levels that was without parallel in Arab–Israeli relations. Israel and Jordan were not the best of friends, but they could be described as the best of enemies.

The Americans encouraged Israel to develop this special relationship into a separate peace settlement with Hussein. Pleasing President Johnson was one of the reasons that Eshkol cited in cabinet to overcome resistance to talks with Hussein. Eshkol himself was still adamant that he would not himself meet Hussein but he was happy for Eban to represent the government in the talks. Eshkol valued Eban more as a spokesman than as a policy-maker. He called Eban "the clever fool" because he had the gift of the gab but not much common sense. Eban belonged to the school of thought that favoured a settlement with Hussein. But since few, if any, of his cabinet colleagues were prepared to go as far as he was, he began to emphasize the tactical value of the talks: the back channel to Hussein could be used to deflect American and UN pressures on Israel to implement Resolution 242. Eban stressed that continuing the contact was important because "so long as the great powers believe that we have independent contacts—it would constrain Jarring and America."[16]

To counterbalance the moderate Eban, Herzog suggested to Eshkol that Yigal Allon, the deputy-prime minister and minister for labour, should represent the government alongside the foreign minister. Allon was a former general, a hawk and an arch-expansionist. During the year he had spent at St. Antony's College, Oxford, in 1957, he improved his English and acquired some surface polish, but underneath he remained a ruthless land-grabber. Sending Allon to the meeting with Hussein was a terrible mistake if the aim was to reach a settlement; but if, on the other hand, the preferred destination of the talks was deadlock he was the ideal candidate. Allon was personally and politically hostile to Hussein. When the cabinet discussed Jordan on 7 April, following an approach from President Johnson, Allon said, "After all, we don't owe Hussein anything. He violated his commitment to the United States on the eve of the Six-Day War by moving tanks to the West Bank. I would not take the initiative to topple Hussein, but nor would I recoil from

active defence measures which are necessary for Israel." To the aston-
ishment of his colleagues Allon added, "I would not rule out the possibility that if a Palestinian government emerged in Jordan, it would dare
to negotiate with us more than Hussein's government."[17]

Two weeks after the end of the June War, Allon had submitted to the
cabinet the famous plan that would bear his name. It called for incorporating into Israel the following areas: a strip of land 10–15 kilometres
wide along the Jordan River; most of the Judaean Desert round the Dead
Sea; and a substantial area round Greater Jerusalem, including the
Latrun salient (see map on p. 294). The plan was designed to include as
few Arabs as possible in the area claimed for Israel, and it envisaged
building permanent settlements and army bases in these areas. Finally,
it called for opening negotiations with local leaders on turning the
remaining parts of the West Bank into an autonomous region that
would be linked to Israel. In no sense could it be described as a peace
plan: it was a unilateral Israeli device to annex large chunks of the West
Bank in total disregard for Arab rights. The Palestinian state would
have been surrounded by Israel on all sides. There was never a chance
that any Arab leader would accept it. When nationalistic Jewish settlers
heard about the plan, they were surprised and hurt. Allon justified it by
saying, "Jews have to be smart. No Arab will ever accept this plan."[18]
Having given up hope of reaching agreement with the West Bank leaders, Allon proposed to hand over the parts of the West Bank that Israel
did not need to Jordan. Allon did not change the map of July 1967 but
instead of offering to share the West Bank with the Palestinians, he
offered to share it with King Hussein.[19] No decision was taken on the
Allon Plan, but its author was authorized to discuss it in general terms
with Hussein at their meeting.

This was held in London on 27 September 1968. Hussein was
accompanied by his tough and trusted adviser Zaid Rifa'i. Abba Eban
was accompanied by Allon and Herzog. Eban opened the meeting by
describing it as a historic occasion. He said they had been instructed to
discuss the possibility of a permanent peace but hinted that if the king
rejected the principles presented to him, they would have to find tracks
to a settlement with the Palestinians without reference to Jordan. Allon
described the meeting with Hussein as the happiest moment of his life.
He spoke of the dangers of Soviet–Arab cooperation for the Jordanian
regime and suggested that an agreement with Israel would serve to

guarantee the regime against external intervention and domestic instability. Eban explained that the aim was to move from a state of war to a
contractual peace embodied in a treaty, and then posed a series of questions. Was the king capable of controlling Fatah? Could he sign a peace
agreement without Nasser's consent? Eban and Allon indicated that the
cabinet had not yet reached a decision on the future of the West Bank,
but, if the king was interested in their ideas, they would go back and
seek its authority to negotiate.

The king responded by saying, "My feelings are genuine. I hope we
will not lose the chance for peace. In order for it to be a lasting peace, it
must be an honourable peace. If not honourable, it will not last. We
want permanent and lasting peace. We recognize you are strong and
could use your forces for a period of time. If this were to happen, some
will lose, some will win. But, to be frank, if force is to be the only solution for the problem, the peace of the region and, indeed, world peace
will be in danger. You may win many victories, but you cannot afford to
lose one single battle. If a just permanent lasting peace will come about,
we will all win. I wish in what is left of my life to contribute towards
this. At long last, I have been pleased to hear the position of the Israel
Government."[20]

Eban then outlined six principles that underlay the Israeli approach
to a settlement with Jordan. Allon said he could not support any agreement that did not involve significant territorial changes and defensible
borders. Israel was not after fertile land or additional population but
security, and without security there could be no concessions. Hussein
replied that in the Arab world too there were different currents of opinion. His problem was how to explain the solution to his people. He
thought that the Security Council could be the framework for a comprehensive settlement in the region. To his way of thinking, security was
not a territorial question but a function of the feelings of the people. It
was a question of trust between nations. Allon disagreed and argued
that in modern warfare territory was still vital. Topography was more
important than goodwill. To promote mutual security, he also suggested a meeting between their respective chiefs of staff.

As far as the Security Council resolution was concerned, Eban said
that there was no disagreement and that Israel's principles were in line
with it. At this point Rifa'i intervened to point out that the Security
Council resolution proscribed the acquisition of territory by force. Eban

replied that the resolution spoke of withdrawal from "territories," not from "the territories." Rifa'i retorted that Eban's ideas added nothing to what he had said at their meeting in May.[21] In his autobiography Eban wrote, "The first reaction of Jordan was one of interest. But when the conception behind our policy found expression in a map attributed to Minster of Labour Yigal Allon, the Jordanian attitude became adamant. It was clear that King Hussein would rather leave Israel under international criticism in possession of all the West Bank than take on himself the responsibility of ceding 33 percent of it to us."[22] This was a rather odd way of summing up the meeting. The position taken by the king was a principled one. He agreed to a contractual peace treaty with minor border modifications. He was utterly opposed to Israel's retention of a third of the West Bank. Eban could hardly have been surprised by the king's stand. It was he, not the king, who was posturing and playing games. In a handwritten note on Claridges writing paper, Eban wrote to Eshkol, "For the time being we should focus on the tactical objective of ensuring the continuation of the talks." Eban added that he was going to make sure that the Americans knew that Israel had substantive contact with Hussein's government; that he was offered an honourable way out of his predicament; and that pressure should be put on him to display a more realistic attitude and not to miss his chance.[23] The Israeli proposal was derogatory and incompatible with the king's concept of a just and honourable peace. Sixteen months had elapsed since the guns fell silent, and this was the first concrete proposal to come from the Israeli side for a settlement. It was unsatisfactory and problematic. But, worst of all, even if the king accepted it, there was no way of telling whether Israel's land-hungry cabinet would give their sanction.

Although the king rejected the Allon Plan without any hesitation, the Israeli ministers proposed another meeting within the next fortnight to give him a chance to reconsider his position. The king did not need a fortnight. A day later Rifa'i called Herzog and arranged to meet with him on the following day. Rifa'i gave Herzog a document listing his master's six principles, in reply to Eban's six principles. The fifth paragraph dealt with secure borders. It gave the king's unambiguous answer to the Allon Plan: "The plan itself is wholly unacceptable since it infringes Jordanian sovereignty. The only way is to exchange territory on the basis of reciprocity." The document served to demonstrate just

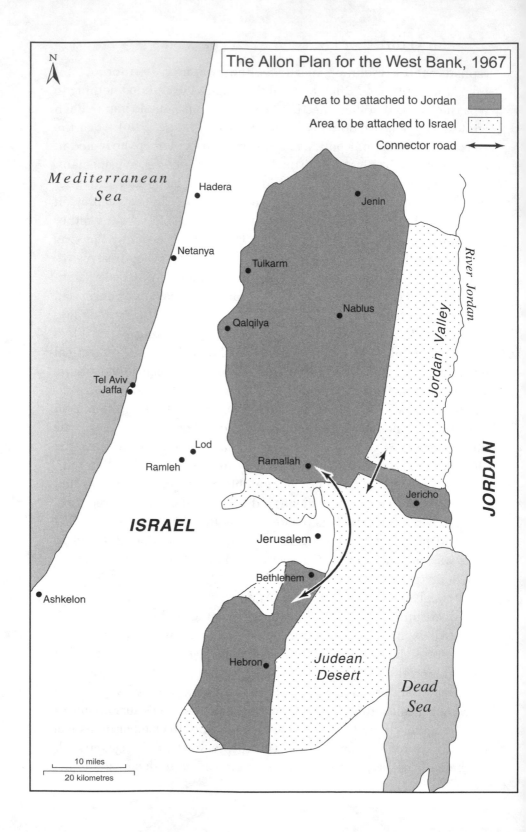

The Allon Plan for the West Bank, 1967

Area to be attached to Jordan
Area to be attached to Israel
Connector road

Mediterranean Sea

Hadera

Jenin

Netanya

Tulkarm

Nablus

Qalqilya

River Jordan

Tel Aviv
Jaffa

Jordan Valley

Lod

Ramleh

Ramallah

Jericho

ISRAEL

JORDAN

Jerusalem

Bethlehem

Ashkelon

Hebron

Judean Desert

Dead Sea

10 miles
20 kilometres

how wide the gulf between the Israeli and Jordanian positions was. The meeting thus dealt a blow to the idea of a separate Israeli–Jordanian settlement ahead of any of the other Arab countries.

Although the king had rejected the Israeli terms for a settlement, the secret meetings with him continued until the conclusion of the peace treaty between Israel and Jordan in October 1994. It was only after this had been signed that the king agreed to speak on the record about his covert meetings with Israeli leaders over the previous three decades. When discussing the Allon Plan he did not mince his words:

This was totally rejected. And in point of fact in the subsequent period of negotiations and discussions and so on, I was offered the return of something like 90 plus percent of the territory, 98 percent even, excluding Jerusalem, but I couldn't accept. As far as I am concerned it was either every single inch that I was responsible for, or nothing. This was against the background of what happened in 1948 when the whole West Bank was saved, including the Old City of Jerusalem. Yet my grandfather eventually paid with his life for his attempts to make peace. If it were to be my responsibility, I had to return everything, not personally to me, but to be placed under international auspices for the people to determine what their future ought to be. We were perfectly happy with that. But I could not compromise. And so this repeated itself time and time and time again throughout the many years until 1990.[24]

The Israelis saw every advantage in continuing the secret contacts despite the uncharacteristically categorical royal rejection of their proposal for a territorial settlement. One purpose that the secret channel served was to deal with current security and, more specifically, to put pressure on the king to do more to curb fedayeen attacks from Jordan's territory against Israel. Chief of Staff Chaim Bar-Lev was sent to London for a meeting with his opposite number, Amer Khammash. Bar-Lev was given strict instructions by the cabinet to confine himself to current security and not to stray into political issues. He travelled in disguise, wearing a black wig and spectacles that completely changed his appearance and startled Dr. Herbert. (Mrs. Herbert, on the other hand, liked the wig so much that Herzog promised to bring her one on his next visit to London.) The meeting took place on 16 October in the Herberts' home, with Herzog and Rifa'i in attendance. For two hours the generals discussed the situation along the border and ways and means of limiting fedayeen raids and Israeli retaliation against Jordanian targets. They compared notes about their favourite Cuban cigars and the meeting was conducted in a haze of smoke.

Two days later a second meeting took place, with the king, on his own initiative, joining the four original participants. At this meeting too General Bar-Lev stuck to his brief and outlined again his views on border security. The king, like his chief of staff before him, said that they were doing their best to prevent incidents but that they could not stop them altogether in the absence of a settlement. A settlement would enable them to take additional measures against the fedayeen. Bar-Lev stated that in his opinion the West Bank was a vital area for Israel's security and that the natural border, from the security point of view, was the Jordan River. Even if a settlement was reached with Jordan, there would still be danger from Iraq, Syria and Egypt. That was an additional reason for basing Israel's security on the West Bank and the Jordan River.

Herzog discussed with the king the most recent developments in the Jarring Mission. He complained that, despite the king's promise to give them more time, they had come under renewed pressure from Dr. Jarring to declare that they accepted UN Resolution 242 and to state their terms for a settlement with Jordan. The king expressed surprise that Israel was still not ready to turn to the implementation of 242. He was prepared to delay the talks in New York under the auspices of Dr. Jarring until another secret bilateral meeting had taken place. But if they failed to reach agreement, both sides should convey their substantive positions to Dr. Jarring and the UN would judge. Resolution 242, he emphasized, was the only framework for moving forward. Herzog remarked that 242 was open to different interpretations. Israel was prepared to make peace but the Allon Plan was the minimum it aspired to. The Jordanians retorted angrily that they thought it was the maximum. Herzog replied that the cabinet had not approved the Allon Plan, and that even Eban and Allon saw it as the minimum and hoped for more. Bar-Lev remarked that the presence of the army along the entire Jordan Valley was vital to Israel's security. The king said he understood the Israeli point of view, but that he had to sell any agreement that was reached to the Arab world and he could do so only if the agreement was a just one. Nevertheless, the door was not closed. The king added that some of the great powers supported his position and that he was coordinating his moves with Nasser.

ABOVE LEFT: Hussein ibn Ali, King of the Hijaz, 1924

ABOVE RIGHT: King Abdullah of Trans-Jordan in the Royal Compound, Amman, 1948

BELOW LEFT: Sir John Glubb, 1951

BELOW RIGHT: Hussein with his father, Prince Talal, and his mother, Princess Zain Al-Sharaf, 1939

ABOVE: Members of the royal family standing behind the flag-draped coffin of assassinated King Abdullah in the royal cemetery at Amman. *From right to left behind coffin:* Hussein, Prince Naif, Prince Abd al-Ilah, the Iraqi Regent, and Prince Fahd of Saudi Arabia, July 1951

RIGHT: Hussein entering the Parliament building for the Accession to the Throne Ceremony, 2 May 1953. Sharif Nasser bin Jamil, his uncle and ADC, is seen behind him

ABOVE: Hussein as a cadet with his detail on
the shooting range, Sandhurst, 1953

BELOW: Eighteen-year-old Hussein and twenty-four-year-old
Dina Abdul Hamid dancing in London, 1953

ABOVE: Hussein with his cousin Faisal II
of Iraq during a visit to Baghdad, 1955

BELOW: Hussein and his British wife, Princess Muna,
on their wedding day, 25 May 1961

ABOVE LEFT: Hussein at the wheel of his Mercedes Gull Wing, Lebanon, c. 1960

ABOVE RIGHT: Crown Prince Abdullah, wearing the dagger that originally belonged to his great-grandfather, 1963

BELOW: Hussein with the royal family *(back row, left to right):* Prince Mohammad and Princess Ferial, Crown Prince Hassan, Princess Basma, Princess Muna, the King, Alia *(front row):* Queen Zain with Faisal and Abdullah (on her lap), c. 1965

ABOVE: Hussein walks through frontline trenches during his visit to the Jordan-Israel frontier, 29 May 1967, accompanied by his officers

BELOW: Hussein with his cousin, Sharif Zaid bin Shaker *(left),* his uncle, Sharif Nasser bin Jamil, and Prince Ali bin Naif of the 60th Armoured Brigade in the Jordan Valley on the eve of the June 1967 war

ABOVE LEFT: Hussein announcing the loss of the
West Bank at a press conference, Amman, 8 June 1967

ABOVE RIGHT: Hussein meets Wasfi al-Tall during Black September 1970

BELOW: Arab heads of state meet at the Nile Hilton in Cairo *(left to right):*
Libyan leader Muammar Gaddafi, PLO chief Yasser Arafat,
Egyptian President Gamal Abdel Nasser, and
Hussein, 27 September 1970

ABOVE: Outgoing Foreign Minister Yigal Allon (*left*) with his successor
Moshe Dayan. On the far right, Shlomo Avineri. Jerusalem, 1977

BELOW LEFT: Hussein in a secret meeting with Dr. Yaacov Herzog, c. 1968-69

BELOW RIGHT: Golda Meir, 1970

ABOVE: Hussein confers with President Nixon and Secretary of State Henry Kissinger in the Oval Office of the White House, March 1974

BELOW LEFT: Zaid al-Rifa'i, as Jordanian ambassador to Great Britain, 1970

BELOW RIGHT: Hussein with his third wife, Queen Alia—pictured a few months before the helicopter crash that killed her—with their children Ali and Haya and their adopted child, Abir *(left),* 1976

ABOVE: Hussein announces his engagement to Lisa Halaby, May 1978

BELOW: President Carter *(left)*, Hussein and Mohammad Reza Pahlavi, the Shah of Iran, at the Niavaran Palace, Tehran, 1978

ABOVE: Hussein with Saddam Hussein, 1980

BELOW: Hussein with President Hafiz Al-Asad of Syria, 1985

ABOVE: Celebrating Jordanian Independence Day, 1992

BELOW: Israeli Prime Minister Itzhak Rabin and Hussein shake hands
as President Clinton watches, Washington, 26 July 1994

ABOVE: Hussein addressing the audience during the Israel-Jordan
Peace Treaty signing ceremony, Wadi Araba, 26 October 1994

BELOW: The heads of state adjust their neckwear in preparation for the "Oslo II" signing ceremony at
the White House, 28 September 1995 *(left to right):* Rabin, Mubarak, Hussein, Clinton and Arafat

ABOVE: King Hussein and Queen Noor's twentieth wedding anniversary, 1998 *(front row, from left):* Prince Hamzah, Prince Ali, Prince Hashim; *(back row):* Princess Iman, Princess Haya, Queen Noor, King Hussein, Princess Raiyah and Abir

BELOW. Hussein praying with Prince Abdullah *(right)* and Prince Hamzah *(left)* at the Prophet's Tomb in Medina, Saudi Arabia, 1998

ABOVE: Hussein returns home to Jordan after six months'
medical treatment in the United States, 19 January 1999

BELOW: Hussein appointing Abdullah Crown Prince
over Hassan, 25 January 1999

ABOVE: Mourners at Hussein's funeral, 8 February 1999, including Crown Prince Mohammed of Morocco, Arafat, Clinton, Sultan Qaboos of Oman, Carter and Ford

LEFT: King Abdullah salutes a portrait of his father before taking the oath of office, February 1999

Herzog thought that the secret talks would allow Israel to stave off a crisis at the UN for about two months, but he sensed that the tactic of playing for time was about to be exhausted. He surmised that Nasser had agreed Hussein should engage in direct talks in New York, provided Israel agreed to proceed to the implementation of Resolution 242. Herzog guessed that Hussein's plan was to use the secret talks to influence Israel to display more flexibility and at the same time mobilize the support of the Great Powers for his position.[25] This was indeed Hussein's intention. He gave the American ambassador in Amman, in the strictest confidence, information about his bilateral negotiations with the Israelis without revealing the channel being used. He appealed to America to make one more effort to convince the Israelis to say something sufficiently constructive to enable negotiations through Jarring to go forward. Hussein explained that the Jarring channel was the basic one and the other channel would be used mainly to clear up differences that might arise in it. But before anything could happen it was essential for the Israelis to come out clearly on the point of the implementation of the UN resolution. Hussein's dilemma was an acute one: he desperately needed a satisfactory Israeli statement to be able to sell the idea of negotiations to his own people and the rest of the Arab world. But if he could not go forward with negotiations through Jarring, the bankruptcy of his previous policy of seeking a negotiated peace would be exposed and the pressures on him to adopt a more extreme course would mount. He also badly needed the negotiations to justify the measures he was taking against fedayeen groups operating from Jordan. Everything now depended on the Israelis.[26]

The Israelis, however, continued to stall, not least because of internal divisions within the cabinet. The next high-level meeting took place on 19 November 1968 aboard an Israeli ship in the Bay of Aqaba near Eilat. The Jordanian side was represented by Hussein, Rifa'i and Sharif Nasser bin Jamil; the Israeli side by Eban, Allon and Herzog. The Jordanian team came to the meeting by boat from Hussein's villa in Aqaba, conveniently located right on the border. This was the first meeting to be held in the region, and the Israelis took advantage of their position as hosts to secretly record the discussions: a copy of the transcript, which was preserved in Herzog's papers, runs to fifty-two pages. From this it is clear that, although Eban and Allon spoke at great length, they had absolutely nothing new to say. They went on and on about the Allon Plan, which the Jordanians had already dismissed as "totally unacceptable" and which in any case the Israeli cabinet had still not ratified. Allon elaborated again on the strategic reasons that impelled Israel to insist on a military presence along the Jordan River, while Eban dwelt on Israel's magnanimity in offering to place most of the West Bank territory and nearly all its population under Jordanian sovereignty. But these arguments convinced no one on the other side. They completely ignored Jordan's security needs and the civilian Jewish settlements on the West Bank that served no security purpose. The Israeli officials used security to justify what was in essence a Zionist colonial project beyond the 1967 line.

Hussein felt that the Israelis were going round and round in circles, while his objective was a permanent, durable and just peace. Everything, he said, hinged on acceptance of the UN resolution. The one new idea that he introduced into the discussion was the possibility of yielding territory on the West Bank in return for Jordanian control over the Gaza Strip and access to the sea. This, he said, had the merit of placing all the Palestinians under one umbrella. The Israeli representatives had no authority to take his suggestion any further. They admitted frankly that a common border between Jordan and Egypt would not be in their interests. They also knew that the cabinet intended to annex the Gaza Strip and that it had a secret plan to "encourage" the emigration of the Palestinian refugees from this crowded area.[27] Hussein's idea did not fit in with these expansionist plans.

Rifa'i was outspoken and even vehement in his rebuttal of the Israeli arguments. The Israeli government, he said, was starting with the wrong premise. If it was interested in property and territory, it could not be interested in peace as far as Jordan was concerned. As the king had explained, no agreement could be reached if it entailed the annexation of Jordanian territory. With the terms on offer, it was impossible for the king to make peace, simply impossible. The only basis for peace was adjustment of the existing armistice lines on a reciprocal basis. Jordan had accepted Resolution 242 and Israel's right to live in peace and security within recognized boundaries. But in return, Israel had to accept unconditionally the principle of withdrawal. The Israelis thought that security would breed peace. Rifa'i assured them that it was the other way round, that peace would breed security. Allon retorted that for him security came first. Nothing was achieved at this meeting except for a decision to hold another meeting in Europe the following month.[28]

It is difficult to judge whether king Hussein was more disappointed with Israel or with America. He certainly felt that America owed it to itself, to its Arab friends and to the Israeli moderates to use its influence to bring about a peaceful settlement. America's failure to play an active role in Middle Eastern peacemaking, he pointed out, only encouraged the extremists in Israel.[29] Hussein missed no opportunity to impress these points upon any American official who visited his country. To Governor William Scranton, President-elect Richard Nixon's special envoy to the Middle East, he handed a paper in December 1968 that summarized his conclusions: that Jordanian contacts with Israel, both direct and indirect, had failed to produce progress towards a peaceful settlement. For whatever reasons, Israel was not truly serious about negotiating a settlement with Jordan; it was determined to annex significant portions of the West Bank to improve its security; and it was also unable or unwilling to leave East Jerusalem. Neither he nor any other Arab leader could accept the terms proposed by Israel. There was nothing more he could do to achieve a settlement. Only massive outside pressure might induce Israel to agree to reasonable terms that the Arabs could accept. And the only country capable of exerting that degree of pressure was the United States.[30] Hussein realized, however, that such a dramatic change in the American approach was unlikely in the dying days of the Johnson administration. He could only hope that the incoming Republican administration headed by Richard Nixon would be more even-handed between Israel and the Arabs, and play a more assertive role in Middle Eastern peacemaking.

Ambassador Harrison Symmes's reading of the situation was that the Jordanians, with strong support from Egypt and the other Arabs, would put a challenge to the new administration and that this, coupled with the political impasse, called for a policy review. The Israeli government's inability to develop a consensus not only made it unlikely that Jarring could succeed but was also a major stumbling block in the path of a breakthrough in the purely Jordanian–Israeli context. More and more, Israeli spokesmen were defining security in terms of the acquisition of territory. The Israelis "seemed unable to grasp that the Allon Plan and its variations are not only unacceptable to Jordan but that it also represents the kind of arrangement that would perpetuate hostility." What Symmes called the Israeli "clarification process" with Jordan had up to that point been *singularly unrealistic, unspecific, and unproductive.*" Symmes had been baffled all along by what the Israelis were telling the Americans. But Hussein's comments to Governor Scranton forced him to conclude that, in addition to pulling the wool over their eyes, the Israelis had definitely moved too slowly and failed to come to grips with reality as far as Jordan was concerned. Symmes reminded his superiors that the explicit assurances they had given Hussein—to support the return of the West Bank with minor border rectifications and a meaningful role in the future of Jerusalem—could not be squared with the Israeli demands to surrender substantial parts of his kingdom, including East Jerusalem. Hussein saw these assurances as his final fallback position. Symmes recommended that they continue to make this clear to the Israelis. Finally, Symmes pointed out that in stressing that "the parties to the conflict must be the parties to the peace," America was in danger of forgetting that it was itself a very interested party, with high stakes of its own. The past year had demonstrated that if America left peacemaking to the Israelis and the Arabs, there would be no forward movement.[31]

Whether the new administration would rise to the challenge was yet to be seen. In the meantime, Hussein could not afford to break off the contact with the Israelis. He knew that they were making much of their meetings with him and believed that their motive was to give the Western powers the misleading impression that the two sides were actually getting somewhere. He also felt that Israel's obduracy stood in the way of progress. Nevertheless, he did not threaten to sever the contact. Whenever the Israelis asked for a meeting, he readily agreed. Dates and detailed arrangements for meetings were made by Herzog and Rifa'i with the help of Dr. Herbert. On 19 December the two met in London to set up a high-level meeting. Rifa'i wanted to know whether the prime minister and the defence minister would take part, but he received no clear answer. He also said that His Majesty saw no point in holding a meeting unless the Israelis had something new to say. Herzog replied that he was not authorized to say what Eban and Allon would propose, but that both attached importance to continuing the contact.[32]

Levi Eshkol was still not prepared to meet Hussein face to face. His refusal is noteworthy against the often repeated official claim that Israel's leaders were indefatigable in their search for peace but there was no one to talk to on the other side. This time Eshkol asked Defence Minister Moshe Dayan to meet with Hussein. Dayan favoured direct talks with the West Bank leaders without the involvement of the Jordanian monarch. Were he to meet Hussein, he warned, it would take him ten minutes to state his views and their side would be the loser, because the game of playing for time would be over.[33] Dayan, unsuited to these tactics, stayed at home so the game could go on.

Herzog and Rifa'i met again at the home of Dr. Herbert on 26 January 1969. Herzog said that the prime minister would be happy to go any-where at any time for a meeting with Hussein, but that he could not take part in political talks so long as there was no cabinet decision, and that there could not be such a decision until the two sides were close enough to require it. This was a convoluted way of saying that Eshkol did not want to meet Hussein. Rifa'i replied that he understood the prime minister's position and that the king would not complain. In his report to Jerusalem about the meeting, the Israeli ambassador to Lon-don wrote, "The infant most definitely does not want to sever the con-tact with us."[34]

The following day Herzog called Dr. Herbert and expressed a wish to meet Hussein, who was staying in London. By coincidence, Dr. Herbert had a similar request from Hussein and a meeting was arranged for the evening of the 28th. Herzog opened the meeting by saying that Eshkol greatly appreciated the king's courage and his dedication to peace. He repeated the official line: Eshkol could not participate personally in political discussions so long as there was no cabinet decision, but in the meantime it was hoped that the clarification process would con-tinue with his two ministers. Herzog implied that direct contact was also in Hussein's interests because the special relationship that had developed between them had led Israel to exercise restraint in respond-ing to fedayeen provocations from Jordanian territory. Hussein nodded to indicate he understood. A long debate ensued between the two advisers about Nasser's latest speech, in which he seemed to justify the continuation of Fatah operations against Israel. Rifa'i argued that the Israelis misunderstood Nasser's meaning because of their complex about him, while Herzog argued that Nasser's aggression and subver-sion were nothing new and that in the past they had not been confined to Israel. At this point Hussein turned to Rifa'i and said, "Let us face facts. The man sometimes says crazy things and does crazy things." Hussein spoke at length about his vision of peace and of the need to convince his people and the people of the region that its terms were just. He described the Middle East as a mess but was encouraged by the signs that the Great Powers wanted to help resolve their problems. Herzog warned him against pinning his hopes on an externally imposed solution. The atmosphere remained friendly throughout the meeting.[35]

The next meeting took place on Hussein's boat in the Bay of Aqaba, on the evening of 20 February. After eating and drinking the serious conversation began. They dealt first with the security situation, and Allon did most of the talking. He warned Hussein against Fatah attacks on Israeli targets from his side of the border. Hussein replied that he was doing all he could and that he had divided up the brigade stationed in the border area into smaller units to achieve better control. Allon said that if Hussein could not control Fatah activities, Israel would be prepared to help him by sending its own forces into his territory, meaning the East Bank. The implication that the West Bank was no longer his territory could not have been lost on Hussein. With a bitter smile he thanked Allon for the offer but turned it down.

Eban talked at inordinate length about all the issues involved in holding talks under the auspices of Jarring. His main point was that the proposals they had made at the previous meetings were only a starting point for negotiations and that the Jordanians were free to criticize them and to modify them. This went down well with the Jordanians, and Hussein said that for the first time he was greatly encouraged. Herzog steered the conversation towards Nasser, and Allon asked Hussein to try to arrange a meeting for him with Nasser. Herzog argued that progress on the Egyptian front would facilitate progress on the Jordanian front. On this occasion Hussein spoke with some hesitation about Nasser, but he did say that he had sent Bahjat Talhouni to ask Nasser whether he still supported a settlement based on the Security Council resolution, and that Nasser had sent him a letter with a positive reply. Nasser also agreed to Hussein's continuing his contacts with the Israelis.

Why was Hussein, in his own words, greatly encouraged by this meeting, although the Israeli officials had brought nothing new to the table? One possible explanation is that Eban presented the Allon Plan in a much more flexible manner than before, and Allon himself did not repeat his usual mantra that security came before peace. At any rate, the possibility of breaking off contact was never mentioned. Nor did the Jordanians press for a meeting with Eshkol, who died six days later after a long illness.

Allon and Eban were not as strict as Herzog in protecting the secrecy of the dialogue that took place across the battle lines. At the beginning of their conversation Eban had looked for a pen to make notes, and when he could not find one, Hussein handed him his own gold pen with the Hashemite crown at the top. The pen remained on the table, and at the end of the meeting Hussein gave it to Eban as a present. Later Eban waved the pen with the royal crown under the noses of Israeli newspaper editors.[36] Allon committed a more serious indiscretion by telling a Vienna-based US correspondent that, public denials notwithstanding, he and Eban had had a meeting with Hussein that had come to naught, with Hussein declaring that he would not go down in history as the first Arab ruler to surrender Jerusalem to Israel.[37] The new American secretary of state, William Rogers, found Allon's indiscretion extremely disturbing. "Nothing," he wrote to the ambassador in Tel Aviv, "could be better designed to undermine Hussein's support for a peaceful settlement and, indeed, to jeopardize his regime if not his life than to give credence to reports that he has met with Israelis."[38]

The international context for Jordanian diplomacy changed in two respects in the early months of 1969. In Washington the Nixon administration replaced the Johnson administration. The key foreign policy-maker alongside Nixon was his national security adviser, Henry Kissinger, rather than Secretary of State William Rogers. Nixon and Kissinger were cold-war warriors who looked at the Middle East through the prism of America's global contest with the Soviet Union. For them Jordan was not a player in the cold war, whereas Egypt was, and therefore concerned them more. Hussein established good personal relations with members of the new administration, but he could not persuade them to lean more heavily on Israel for the sake of a settlement.

In Israel, Golda Meir replaced Eshkol as Labour Party leader and prime minister. Meir was a much more rigid and inflexible person than her predecessor. She had a black-and-white view of the world in which the Arabs featured as an untrustworthy, sinister and implacable adversary. In anything that touched Israel's security she was completely intransigent. As she noted in her autobiography, "intransigent" was to become her middle name.[39] But in their thinking about the future of the West Bank she and Eshkol were not all that far apart. Both wanted to preserve the Jewish and democratic character of the State of Israel, and both were therefore opposed to the annexation of the West Bank. Both came round to the view that the most promising solution to the Palestinian problem lay in a territorial compromise with Jordan that would keep the bulk of the Palestinian population outside Israel's borders. The difference was largely one of presentation: Eshkol put the emphasis on what Israel was prepared to concede for the sake of a settlement with the Arabs, whereas Meir put the emphasis on Israel's security-related conditions.[40] Apart from her preference for the Jordanian over the Palestinian option, Meir had a personal liking for Hussein that went back to their meeting in Paris in 1965 when she served as foreign minister. As far as Israel's terms for a settlement were concerned, however, there was no improvement whatsoever as a result of the change at the top.

At home Hussein had to contend with the rising power of the Palestinian resistance movement. Popular support for the movement's objective for "liberating" the whole of Palestine, combined with the lack of any tangible progress on the diplomatic front, had the effect of undermining the idea of a "peaceful solution." The component parts of the resistance movement were in some disarray, but the trend was towards greater cohesion. Although the resistance movement had not established itself as a credible military force, it none the less brought about an upsurge in Palestinian self-confidence that made it more and more difficult to sell the alternative of a diplomatic solution. Most Jordanians and most Arabs had come round to the view that sooner or later they would have to fight Israel again. The election in February 1969 of Fatah leader Yasser Arafat as chairman of the PLO enhanced his standing and that of his organization in the Arab world. In April the Palestine Armed Struggle Command was set up with the purpose of coordinating paramilitary operations and overall strategy. Its progress was slow, but it included all the groups except the Popular Front for the Liberation of Palestine and its extremist offshoots. These extremist groups succeeded in embarrassing the fedayeen "establishment" by mounting operations that alienated international public opinion.[41] The activities of both the establishment and the fringe groups became a burning issue in the dialogue across the battle lines.

Herzog met Rifa'i at the home of Dr. Herbert in London on 23 April and recited a long list of recent cross-border raids in some of which, he alleged, the Jordanian Army was complicit. He then conveyed Meir's request for a meeting between her chief of staff and the king. Rifa'i, who looked very tense, asked Herzog whether this was the only message he had brought. Herzog replied that he understood from a cable Hussein had sent from Paris that he wanted the two of them to set up another high-level meeting. Rifa'i reacted angrily by reading a prepared statement, the gist of which was that there had been numerous meetings since the previous May and that His Majesty was shocked that nothing had been achieved and that the Israelis had exploited the contacts to dissuade Jarring and the Americans from taking steps of their own. Rifa'i also warned that, if there was no progress on the political front, the security situation might deteriorate beyond their ability to control it. His Majesty had assumed a personal risk in formulating a six-point Arab peace plan and in getting Nasser to support it publicly. Israel had a first and last chance for true peace. If it responded, a new chapter would be opened, and Israel would be accepted as a sister state in the Middle East. On the other hand, if it chose to keep Arab territories, it would remain under siege until the Arabs decided to launch another round. Israel's military power enabled it to reject peace proposals but not to impose a settlement. Rifa'i concluded by reading a statement from Hussein that said he saw no point in continuing the high-level talks with Israeli leaders unless they declared that they were ready to implement the Security Council Resolution 242. Herzog, however, asked for another meeting with Hussein before the talks were suspended.[42]

Hussein visited Washington in April to launch his six-point peace plan. At a meeting with President Nixon he presented the plan as a joint Jordanian–Egyptian initiative. In a speech to the National Press Club the king emphasized that the joint plan was based on UN Resolution 242. He proposed an end to belligerency, and the acknowledgement of Israel's sovereignty, territorial integrity and right to live within secure and recognized borders. He also offered to guarantee Israel's freedom of navigation through the Red Sea and the Suez Canal. In return he expected Israel to withdraw from the territories it occupied in June 1967 in accordance with the Arab interpretation of Resolution 242. Both he and the Egyptian president, he said, were prepared to sign an agreement with the Israeli government that fell short of a formal peace treaty, if the resolution was implemented. Israeli spokespersons immediately rejected the six-point plan. They insisted on the signing of a contractual peace treaty incorporating secure and recognized borders before withdrawal could begin. They pointed out that 242 did not demand complete withdrawal. And they insisted on direct negotiations between themselves and the neighbouring Arab states, although 242 did not require direct negotiations.[43]

Hussein's patience with the Israelis was being stretched to breaking point. He met with Herzog on 25 April in Rifa'i's room in the Dorchester Hotel in London. It was a tense meeting. Hussein said that if no political progress was achieved in the coming months, the clashes would escalate to the point where war would become inescapable. In response to a question, he said that the previous statement he had sent through Rifa'i referred to the suspension of the talks and not to breaking off contact. Since their last meeting the internal pressures on him had increased, and the situation along the border had deteriorated. In the Arab world he was under attack for striving for peace, while at the UN he heard that Israel was using the bilateral talks in order to prevent international action to deal with the dispute. Hussein wanted Israel to clarify its position regarding 242 before he would agree to another meeting. Herzog replied that he could not accept conditions for holding talks that were in their mutual interest but noted Hussein's desire to have a detailed clarification of Israel's stand at the next meeting. Hussein hoped to be presented with a clear and realistic stand rather than with a bargaining position. In his report on the meeting, Herzog commented that it was the first time that he had seen the king so deeply stressed.[44] He paid a brief visit to Rifa'i two days later, and they set up another high-level meeting, in Aqaba Bay for 25 May.

This time the meeting took place neither on an Israeli ship nor on Hussein's but on Coral Island. It started at eight in the evening, to enable the Israelis to leave Eilat under the cover of darkness. The conversation concluded with a decision that Eban would prepare a memorandum of principles for a peace settlement and that the advisers would meet again in June or July to take matters forward. Whereas in London Hussein had been very tense, on the island he seemed more relaxed and confident.[45]

Royal confidence was gradually eroded over the summer as a result of the escalation of the border war between the fedayeen and Israel. Paradoxically but unsurprisingly, the effort of the Jordanian government to assert control over the various fedayeen groups only drove them closer together. The border war took the form of guerrilla hit-and-run raids; Israeli shelling of fedayeen bases and Jordanian Army positions that gave them cover; heavy artillery battles in the Jordan Valley;

and guerrilla incursions in the area of the Dead Sea and Eilat. On one occasion there was an exchange of fire near the king's house in Aqaba. Under the leadership of defence minister Moshe Dayan, the IDF pursued an aggressive policy of retaliation that did not spare civilians, cities like Irbid and Salt, or regular army units suspected of extending active or passive support to the fedayeen. In Jordan the fedayeen were widely seen as brave freedom-fighters. In Israel they were seen as terrorists pure and simple, and dealt with as such.

A particularly vulnerable civilian target was the East Ghor Canal, which carried water from the Yarmouk River in the north of Jordan. It was literally the lifeline of that part of the Jordan Valley that was still cultivated and populated despite the border war. On 23 May an Israeli patrol destroyed a section of the canal. Repeated Jordanian efforts to repair the damage were frustrated until the Israelis received private assurances that serious new measures would be taken to prevent fedayeen attacks on the kibbutzim across the river. The publicity given by the Israelis to these private assurances made effective enforcement politically impossible. A period of calm lasted long enough to enable essential repairs to be made. But the canal was breached by the IDF a second time in August and a third time in December.[46] Dayan was the chief advocate of holding the East Ghor Canal hostage to effective Jordanian policing of the irregular forces on their territory. If the policy failed to achieve its declared objective, Dayan advocated raising the threshold of pain. He was reluctant to accept any political constraints on military action, his policy being to meet force with much greater force. It was simply the latest version of the policy he had followed as chief of staff in the 1950s. Within the cabinet this met with only mild opposition and he could usually rely on the support of the hawkish prime minister. At a cabinet meeting on 11 August a proposal to put the East Ghor Canal out of action again was agreed to, with no votes against and only one abstention. The only real debate was whether to use the army or the air force to do so.[47]

The harder Israel struck at the fedayeen, the more popular the latter became in Jordan, and the greater was the threat they posed to the Hashemite regime. Hussein understood that the Palestinian resistance movement was eroding his power base. There was increasingly loud criticism of the royal family for their extravagances and for surrounding themselves with sycophants who kept them in ignorance of the true state of the nation.[48] Hussein reacted to the challenge by moving further away from the Palestinians rather than towards them. He seemed tempted to abandon the policy of associating Palestinians with his regime and to fall back on xenophobic East Bankers. He embarked on a major reorganization of the army structure and command, appointing a group of officers with unsavoury past histories, described by one British defence attaché as "the Mafia," to senior posts. "As he looked wistfully around at the possibilities of withdrawal into his Transjordanian shell he began the formation of a private army outside the normal chain of military command, responsible for his own protection as well as for use in case of need in an internal security role; and an atmosphere of 'good old Transjordan' prevailed at a series of light-hearted cricket matches between the Court and the British community."[49]

The most notable change was the appointment in June of Sharif Nasser bin Jamil as commander-in-chief of the armed forces. Sharif Nasser was controversial because of his forceful personality and ostentatious lifestyle. He liked hunting, riding and fast cars, women, drinking and gambling. Hussein's uncle appeared to outsiders to be one of his closest advisers, friends and supporters. But his notorious illegal traffic in arms and drugs placed a strain on his relationship with Hussein. An ultraconservative monarchist who was entirely dependent on the king's favour, he was also one of the regime's strongest bulwarks and was known to maintain an extensive intelligence network within the army. Even those officers who hated him and all he represented acknowledged respect for him as a soldier and leader of men. Nevertheless, his image was poor; he was feared and hated by Palestinians throughout the kingdom and especially on the West Bank. In foreign policy Sharif Nasser was pro-Western, anti-Communist and anti his Egyptian namesake. He had not forgiven the Iraqis for overthrowing the Hashemite monarchy in Iraq in 1958, and he remained an implacable opponent of any republican regime in Baghdad.[50]

What is less well known is that beneath the surface Hussein had serious misgivings about his Iraqi-born maternal uncle. One member of the family described Sharif Nasser as a very destructive influence and as Hussein's *bête noire*. According to this source, Sharif Nasser was a good tactical field commander at battalion or brigade level but a disaster at HQ or as commander-in-chief. He interfered in everything. One problem was that Sharif Nasser had a warehouse full of weapons in his house in the Ghor. He always tried to have his own feudal enclave, as if the laws of Jordan did not apply to him. He also had his own entourage of royal guards. Many times Hussein had to surround his uncle's house with armoured cars from a loyal regiment to bring him to heel. On one occasion the problem nearly got out of hand. The army was going to seize the arms warehouse, and Sharif Nasser's guards resisted. But before it turned into a shoot-out, Hussein intervened personally to defuse the crisis. Sharif Nasser was a member of Hussein's family, so the king could not throw him out; he could only try to contain him.[51] The two qualities that probably recommended Sharif Nasser to Hussein as commander-in-chief of the armed forces in 1969 were his unswerving loyalty to the regime and his rabidly anti-Palestinian sentiments. His brief was to bring the Palestinian guerrilla groups under control and to prevent their attacks on Israel.

Hussein's mood changed perceptibly during the summer. In the past he had frequently referred to the need for visible progress within a matter of a few months at the outside if the chance of peaceful settlement was not to be lost and extremists were not to gain control of the situation. Now he seemed to adjust his mind to the thought that quick progress was simply not possible and that Jordan would have to face a long period of stalemate.[52] The secret meetings between Rifa'i and Herzog continued but led nowhere. One meeting took place in London on 26 July and another on 17 September. Herzog used these meetings to give the Jordanians a pat on the back for the renewed efforts they had made to rein in the fedayeen and to urge them to intensify these efforts and to coordinate them more closely with Israel's military commanders. Yet a written paper with Israel's principles for a peace treaty that had been promised did not materialize, and the excuse given, rather illogically, was the persistence of fedayeen attacks. Rifa'i said that they had been waiting in vain for this paper since May. Israel's position on Jerusalem was particularly perplexing. On the one hand it said that the Jerusalem question was open to negotiations and on the other it persisted in presenting the world with faits accomplis. Its record was such that everyone in Jordan had become a pessimist regarding Israel's interest in a peace settlement.[53]

Although Israel evinced no interest in peace talks, Hussein did not give up; he turned to the Americans. His basic objective since June 1967 remained unchanged: to recover the West Bank. He still needed

Nasser to protect his back from his Arab opponents. Initially, he had visualized America as the trump card in forcing the Israelis into a conciliatory mood, but he was repeatedly let down by them. Despite all his disappointments, he did not despair; he tried one tack after another. The reason for this persistence was that, even though his close relationship with America did not gain him his land, it did give him security. It deterred the Israelis from toying with the idea of overthrowing him. It afforded him a measure of protection against hardline Israelis, such as Moshe Dayan, who saw him as an obstacle to a direct deal with the local Palestinian leaders on the West Bank. Moreover, time was not on Hussein's side; the clock kept ticking on the hopes for a settlement. His own popularity in Jordan had long since peaked, and political, economic and administrative paralysis was spreading in his country. Israel exploited this weakness to consolidate its control over the West Bank and East Jerusalem.

With the talks with the Israelis failing to progress in the summer of 1969, Hussein made another approach to the Nixon administration. Rifa'i told Joseph Sisco, the assistant secretary of state for Near Eastern Affairs, that, on the authority of Hussein, he was prepared to commence direct, secret negotiations with the Israelis, with Sisco present, on condition that advance assurances were supplied by either the United States or Israel that the Jerusalem issue would really be negotiable. Rifa'i indicated that US assurances in this respect mattered more than Israeli ones. The assurances sought by Rifa'i were that the United States would live up to the spirit as well as the letter of its November 1967 commitments regarding the Jordanian role in Jerusalem.[54] The State Department noted that Hussein had concluded that Jordan's national survival required a settlement with Israel. It pointed out that the outcome of the negotiations might be decisive for Hussein's life and for the life of his country. But it also noted that, despite some ambiguity on some elements of a settlement, Israel's position seemed firm in respect of a unified Jerusalem under its control. Nor did Israel wish to deal with Jordan through any intermediary. Hussein's approach produced no results. The only help the administration was willing to give him was in finding a competent and discreet American law firm.[55] This was not what Hussein had had in mind.

American indifference and Palestinian militancy drove Hussein back into the arms of the Israelis. Ultimately, Israel was the only party that could bring about a change in the status quo. One of the most interesting meetings in the dialogue across the battle lines occurred in London on 28 September. The Jordanian side was represented by Rifa'i and Sharif Nasser; the Israeli side by Herzog and Chief of Staff Chaim Bar-Lev. Sharif Nasser said he intended to deal sternly with Fatah and requested Israel's help in expelling the organization to Syria. This was music to Herzog's ears. Well versed in the history of the Hashemites and the bitterness they felt at the setbacks they had suffered in their ancestral home in the Hijaz and in Iraq, Herzog steered the conversation towards other possibilities of regional cooperation and away from the West Bank. He spoke with enthusiasm about the possibilities that awaited the Hashemite kingdom to the south in Saudi Arabia and to the north in Iraq. In his notes Herzog described the Jordanian commander-in-chief as "macho" and as much more energetic than his predecessor, Amer Khammash. Unlike Khammash, Sharif Nasser regarded Fatah as a threat to the Hashemite Kingdom of Jordan and appeared to stand altogether outside the circle of Arab political thought. The only point he made that did not please Herzog was that he could not prevent Fatah operations in the occupied part of Jordan. Rifa'i reported that Hussein agreed to another meeting after the Israeli elections and that he hoped the prime minister would participate.[56]

The cabinet defence committee received a full report on the London meeting. Herzog was proud of the fact that they had skirted round political issues and concentrated mainly on military cooperation. Dayan was not impressed. He said that the Jordanians were playing games, and that while the chief of staff was receiving promises in London, there was heavy shelling at the front. He gave notice that he intended to submit proposals for military action against Jordan to the cabinet.

The news from and about Jordan in general was not encouraging. There was secret information that the British were preparing a contingency plan to evacuate the king and his entourage in the event of his regime collapsing. In Amman it was announced that the security forces had aborted a plot by an extremist religious group to assassinate the king. There were other pieces of information about the disruption of public order by terrorists in Amman and in the rest of the country. A meeting was therefore convened by Meir on 9 October, to which the security chiefs were invited, to discuss possible courses of action in the event that the regime in Amman collapsed.

At that meeting Zvi Zamir, the head of the Mossad, revealed that back in April Hussein had discussed with Harold Wilson the formation of a personal British bodyguard for him under the command of Colonel David Stirling, the founder of the SAS regiment, and that this plan did not materialize partly due to Israeli objections. Eli Zeira gave the assessment of the Military Intelligence branch that there was no imminent threat to the Jordanian regime because the Egyptians had no interest in bringing it down. He said that potential revolutionaries were trying to make contact with the Iraqis, who had a large military force stationed not far from Amman. He assumed that if a coup did take place, Suleiman Nabulsi might assume control and that Arafat might be invited to share power. Dayan said that in the event of a coup he would have to implement a particular plan. He was not specific, but it was probably for the capture of certain areas that were considered essential for Israel's security. He also raised the question of preventing the pro-Soviet extremists from taking over Jordan and of talking to the Americans about action to stop the entry of Syrian and Iraqi forces into the country. He assumed that the conquest of Jordan was always in the minds of the Iraqi leaders. In the event of an actual regime change in Amman, he was of the opinion that Israel should strive towards peace with the Palestinians and enter into talks with certain of their leaders on the West Bank. In addition, he suggested making contact with Hussein's brother Muhammad, who was reputed to be anti-Palestinian, to coordinate action against Fatah. Herzog pointed out that Hussein was opposed to such contact, but Dayan did not see this as a sufficient reason not to go ahead. He seemed to think that Muhammad might be able to reveal to them the location of Fatah bases.[57]

America's approach towards the Arab–Israeli conflict was, as so often in the past, a tug of war between the even-handed position of the State Department and the Israel-first position of the White House. Towards the end of 1969 Secretary of State William Rogers became convinced that a new American initiative was called for to break the deadlock in the Jarring Mission. Abba Eban tried to dissuade him, claiming that Israel was engaged in delicate bilateral negotiations with Jordan on the basis of the Allon Plan, though Eban failed to mention that Jordan had categorically rejected it. On 9 December, Rogers presented his peace plan for the Middle East at a conference in Washington, D.C. It was based on UN Resolution 242 and envisaged Israel's return to the international border with its neighbours, with only minor modifications and a solution to the Palestinian refugee problem. Egypt rejected it. On 18 December, Charles Yost, the US permanent representative to the UN, proposed guidelines for a settlement between Israel and Jordan based on the Rogers Plan. Yost advocated Israeli withdrawal from most of the West Bank, Jordanian administration for East Jerusalem and a settlement of the Palestinian refugee problem. Meir termed the Rogers Plan "a disaster for Israel" and rejected with vehemence all the American proposals—which robbed the plan of any practical significance. The Jordanian government accepted the plan but was unable to pursue it after Egypt and Israel had rejected it.

Despite the differences over the Rogers Plan, it was vital for Hussein to keep in step with Nasser in order to retain the material support of the Arab world. He therefore worked closely with Nasser to prepare the way for the fifth Arab League summit, which convened in Rabat on 21 December. He hoped for a reaffirmation of the commitment to a peaceful settlement of the dispute with Israel and for the continuation of aid from the oil-producing states. He argued that the Jordanian Army, not the fedayeen, was bearing the brunt of the confrontation with Israel and pleaded for increased financial aid to purchase arms. But the summit quickly degenerated into a squabble between Colonel Muamar Gaddafy, the revolutionary ruler of Libya, and King Faisal of Saudi Arabia. Nasser walked out in a huff, and the summit disbanded without adopting any resolutions.[58] Its collapse left Hussein isolated and Nasser totally dependent on the Soviet Union economically and militarily.

While the Rabat summit was still in session, Israel escalated the fighting on both the Egyptian and the Jordanian fronts. Back in March, Nasser had launched the "War of Attrition" to give substance to his slogan "That which was taken by force can only be recovered by force." The War of Attrition took the form of heavy artillery bombardment of Israel's positions on the Suez Canal, occasional air attacks and hit-and-run commando raids. Israel intensified the shelling in the Canal Zone and later resorted to deep-penetration bombing inside Egypt with the aim of toppling the regime. The result was to rally domestic support behind Nasser and to bring about deeper Soviet military involvement on his side. At the same time Israel stepped up the pressure on Jordan. On 19 December the IDF began intermittent shelling of Irbid from the Golan Heights, which lasted to the end of the year. Two days later there was a heavy Israeli air raid on Kufr Asad in which seven soldiers were killed. On 28 December the radar station in Ajlun was bombed, and on the last day of the year Israel launched severe artillery and air attacks in the north and in the south. The year thus ended with the Arab League in complete disarray, diplomatic deadlock, a sour stand-off in the secret Jordanian–Israeli dialogue, and dangerous military escalation on both the Egyptian and the Jordanian fronts.

14. Civil War

Everything else that happened in Jordan in 1970 was overshadowed by the conflict between the army and the fedayeen. One clash after another, punctuated by untenable compromises, led inexorably to a full-blown civil war in September of that year. The British ambassador to Amman began his annual review for 1969 with the terse prescription "the mixture as before." His successor, John Phillips, recorded that in the following year "the mixture became so volatile that the container exploded."[1]

The showdown between the regime and the fedayeen in September 1970 was short and sharp, but the process that led to it was protracted and complex. Fedayeen in Arabic means "self-sacrificers." The power and prestige of the fedayeen throughout the region, and especially in Jordan, grew rapidly in the aftermath of the battle of Karameh. They received material help from various Arab governments and enjoyed widespread popular support. Fedayeen raids into Israel and the Israeli-occupied West Bank continued to provoke savage Israeli reprisals against cities and civilians on the East Bank, but these attacks intensified rather than undermined the fedayeen's support. Nor did the failure of the armed struggle to liberate any part of Palestine or the occupied territories constrain the growth of the Palestinian resistance movement. On the contrary, the conduct of the armed struggle against the Zionist enemy gave Palestinian nationalism a symbol in the shape of the fighting Palestinian; it enhanced the legitimacy of the PLO; and it enabled the PLO to build up its political, economic and social institutions. Armed struggle and state-building went hand in hand: one reinforced the other.[2] Inside their own camps, the fedayeen groups enjoyed considerable administrative autonomy, had their own finance departments and ran their own welfare services. Outside the camps, they enjoyed freedom of movement and special rights, while exercising growing influence over the Jordanian part of the population. By the beginning of

1970 the Palestinian resistance movement had to all intents and purposes established a state within a state in Jordan.

The resistance movement was not a monolithic body, however, but a
collection of different and divided guerrilla organizations loosely gathered under the umbrella of the PLO. And the PLO itself was not an
independent actor but a microcosm of Arab politics, representing the
different ideological trends as well as the interests of the states who
supported the different factions within it. Fatah was the largest group,
and its leader, Yasser Arafat, was also the chairman of the PLO. As
well as being the largest, Fatah was also the most moderate and mainstream of all the guerrilla groups. Its core ideology was one of non-
intervention in the internal affairs of the Arab states. Its leadership was
accordingly reluctant to take a public stand against the regime in Jordan. The precept of non-intervention, however, was not observed by
the more radical guerrilla organizations such as the Popular Front for
the Liberation of Palestine (PFLP), led by Dr. George Habash, or by the
Popular Democratic Front for the Liberation of Palestine (PDFLP), led
by Nayef Hawatmeh. Nor was it observed by the more marginal but no
less radical Al-Saiqa ("the storm"), which was a wing of the Syrian
Ba'th Party, or the Arab Liberation Front, which was a wing of the Iraqi
Ba'th Party. Hussein was seen by all these groups as "a reactionary," "a
puppet of Western imperialism" and "a Zionist tool"; a confrontation
with him was therefore regarded not only as desirable but as ideologically necessary.[3] By the beginning of 1970 Habash and Hawatmeh were
openly calling for the overthrow of the Jordanian monarchy and its
replacement by a revolutionary regime. They wanted to transform
Amman into an Arab Hanoi and proclaimed that the road to Tel Aviv
passed through it.

Growing power and prestige were accompanied by growing arrogance, insolence and heavy-handedness. The fedayeen, regardless of
what group they belonged to, were overbearing: "They drove noisily
around Amman in jeeps with loaded weapons, like an army of occupation; they extorted financial contributions from individuals, sometimes
foreigners, in their homes and in public places; they disregarded routine traffic regulations, failed to register and license their vehicles, and
refused to stop at army checkpoints; they boasted about their role of
destiny against Israel and belittled the worth of the army. Their very
presence in Amman, far from the battlefield, seemed like a challenge to
the regime."[4]

The arrogance and the indiscipline of the fedayeen placed Hussein in an acute dilemma. If he used force to crush them, he would alienate his Palestinian subjects and the Arab world. Yet if he failed to act against them, he would forfeit the respect of his Jordanian subjects and, even more seriously, that of the army, the mainstay of his regime. The dilemma was not eased by pressure from the army to confront the fedayeen challenge to the regime head-on. In February 1970 Hussein went to Cairo to see Nasser and won his support, or at least his acquiescence, in a tougher policy in dealing with the fedayeen. Nasser was prepared to use his influence with the fedayeen to get them to reduce their pressure on the regime, provided Hussein restrained his army from openly clashing with them.[5] Immediately after Hussein's return from Cairo, the Jordanian government issued new regulations that required the fedayeen to carry identity cards and to license their cars like everybody else. The new regulations also prohibited the carrying of arms in public, the storing of ammunition in towns, and the holding of unlawful meetings and demonstrations. The fedayeen reacted sharply and violently to this, and forced Hussein to climb down and "freeze" the new regulations. He also yielded to fedayeen pressure by dismissing the hardline minister of the interior, Major-General Muhammad Rasul al-Kilani.

Western newspapers now started to carry stories saying that Hussein might abdicate soon, as he was gradually losing control over his kingdom. These reports, however, were based more on rumour than on fact. Far from thinking about abdication, Hussein was preparing for the next round, which he regarded as inescapable. His concessions to the fedayeen were a tactical move designed to gain time, rather than an admission of defeat. It was *reculer pour mieux sauter*. Moreover, in line with his perennial policy of balancing, he began to mobilize external support to help him in his battle against his internal opponents. The two countries he turned to were the United States and Israel. Both had their drawbacks as allies. News that the ruler of Jordan was turning to America and Israel for help against fellow Arabs would have provided powerful ammunition to his enemies and enabled them to drive home the charges that he was "a puppet of Western imperialism" and a "Zionist tool." But he had no other options. On 17 February the US deputy chief of mission in Tel Aviv, Owen Zurhellen, conveyed an urgent message from Hussein to Foreign Minister Abba Eban. In this message the king put three questions:

1. Does Israel agree to avoid taking advantage of the opportunity of Hussein having to thin down his forces on the border to deal with subversive elements at home?

2. Can Israel agree to avoid responding to provocations by the terrorists, who will try to carry out attacks while Jordanian forces are being thinned down, with the purpose of drawing Israel into retaliatory actions?

3. Can Hussein count on Israeli forces to assist him should the forces of neighbouring countries come to the aid of the Palestinian terrorists while he tries to knock them out?

Eban was not surprised that Hussein chose to convey these questions via Washington, even though he had the means of asking the questions and receiving the answers directly. Eban realized that Hussein sought not only an Israeli promise but also an American guarantee. In the cabinet debate regarding the reply, Defence Minister Moshe Dayan had the greatest reservations about helping their embattled neighbour. He did not want to help, and he did not believe that Hussein would be able to hold out. But there was a majority in the cabinet in favour of a positive response. Accordingly, the message that the Americans were asked to convey to the king went as follows:

1. Israel will not take advantage of the thinning down of forces on the Jordanian border to attack Jordan.

2. In case of terrorist provocations on the Jordanian border, Israel will respond vigorously.

3. Israel is willing to discuss the question of assisting Jordan, should the need arise.[6]

The February incident set the pattern for the next seven months, during which "the mainstream of events, diverted only briefly now and then by side currents, eddies and minor obstructions, moved inexorably towards September and civil war."[7] One of the eddies resulted from fedayeen attacks on Israel and Israeli retaliation against Jordan. A rocket attack on Beit Shean was followed, on 3 June, by Israeli air and artillery attacks on Irbid, in which seven civilians and one soldier were killed and twenty-six civilians wounded. On the same day the Jordanian Army shelled Tiberias for the first time since 1948. Having ordered the shelling, Hussein recognized that this was a dangerous new cycle of violence that had to be stopped somewhere. He therefore approached the Israelis through the US Embassy in Amman to suggest that if they would give him a period without retaliation, he would take strong measures against the fedayeen. The message said: "Jordanian Government was doing everything it could to prevent fedayeen rocket attacks on Israel. King deeply regretted rocket attacks. Jordan Army under orders to shoot to kill any fedayeen attempting to fire rockets and fedayeen leaders had been told again evening of June 3 that violators would be shot on sight." The Americans believed that the Jordanians had no wish to escalate further, but they wanted to see this chapter closed. Irbid, however, was the key point, and if it were shelled again, or if Israel renewed her assaults on civilians, the Jordanians might feel they had to retaliate again. In view of these indications, the Americans urged the Israeli government to give a breathing space to permit further discussions in an attempt to call a halt to rising violence and to restore the ceasefire.[8] The Israelis decided to give the king what he wanted. It was true that Hussein had made similar protestations in the past about controlling the fedayeen, but the strength of his language on this occasion impressed them. Nor did they place any time limit on the truce. The important thing was to see if he could make his intentions effective.[9]

Difficulties assailed Hussein from all directions. While straining to prevent the fedayeen from provoking Israel, he also had to restrain the army from settling scores with them. After the IDF had driven the fedayeen out of the Jordan Valley, they moved into the cities and instituted what can only be described as a reign of terror. Army bases were located outside the cities, but many of the serving soldiers had their families in urban areas. Their patience was strained beyond endurance by the lawlessness of the fedayeen, by the liberties they took in a country that was not theirs and by their mistreatment of civilians. Increasingly, army commanders began to take the law into their own hands. By the early summer it became apparent that, if Hussein did not act, the military would rebel against him because they could not take any more humiliation from the fedayeen. After one incident, a tank battalion moved from the valley to Amman with no orders to do so and it took Sharif Zaid bin Shaker, the commander of the Third Armoured Division, and the king to stop its onslaught on the perpetrators. Hussein and Shaker drove out and intercepted the tanks. Shaker stood on the road in front of them and ordered the commander to return back to base. When the commander refused, Shaker said he was ordering him in the name of the king. The commander said to Shaker, "If you don't get out of the way, I'll run you over." Hussein then came out of the car and repeated the order. The commander obeyed reluctantly. The incident showed that the army was desperate to confront the fedayeen and put them in their place. It could no longer tolerate the abuse and humiliation heaped on Jordan by its Palestinian guests.[10]

Hussein thus had his work cut out for him. As he recalled,

We had thousands of incidents of breaking the law, of attacking people. It was a very unruly state of affairs in the country and I continued to try. I went to Egypt. I called in the Arabs to help in any way they could—particularly as some of them were sponsoring some of these movements in one form or another—but without much success, and towards the end I felt I was losing control. In the last six months leading up to the crisis the army began to rebel. I had to spend most of my time running to those units that had left their positions and were going to the capital, or to some other part of Jordan, to sort out people who were attacking their families or attacking their soldiers on leave. I think that the gamble was probably the army would fracture along Palestinian–Jordanian lines. That never happened, thank God.[11]

On 7 June fighting broke out between the army and the fedayeen in Zarqa. Hussein himself was the target of two assassination attempts. On 9 June some fedayeen opened fire on the government's intelligence headquarters in Amman, and Hussein insisted on rushing to the scene. His motorcade came under heavy machine-gun fire, and one of his guards was killed. News of the ambush of the king was hardly out when the crack Bedouin units of the army took matters into their own hands. Al-Wahdat and Al-Husseini, the large refugee camps on the outskirts of Amman, were shelled, and heavy fighting between the army and the fedayeen continued for three days.[12] Rifa'i went to the US Embassy and reported that an attempt had been made on the life of his "boss," but that he escaped unharmed. Rifa'i said that the situation was getting very serious, and that the king would have to pull back some of his troops from the border areas. Hussein requested that the Americans relay this information to the Israelis and urge them to exercise maximum forbearance in the event of incidents on the border.[13] The Israelis replied that if Hussein wanted to withdraw his forces, particularly tanks, from the front, he could do so with impunity as far as they were concerned.[14]

The Israelis followed closely the events unfolding on the other side of the border. Major-General Aharon Yariv, the director of Military Intelligence, gave the IDF General Staff a full report on the fighting. According to this, Hussein had brought in reinforcements for the battle in Amman. In Amman there were 1,500 to 2,000 Fatah fighters armed with Katyusha rockets and some mortars. Although the army had superior forces and firepower, Yariv thought it moved too slowly and that the king recoiled, as on previous occasions, from using the capacity available to him because he did not want a massacre on his hands, especially one of civilians. Hussein's advisers were said to be divided. Some urged him to go forward and finish the job, while others warned him that it could be accomplished only at the cost of several thousand casualties, which was unacceptable. Hussein drew back, and the outcome was inconclusive. The toll of the fighting was 250 to 300 dead and about 700 wounded, some of them non-combatants.[15]

After three days of fighting Hussein and Arafat announced the terms of a ceasefire and urged their followers to return to their normal lives. The main features of the ceasefire were an agreement by both sides to return to their bases and a commitment to release the prisoners they held. The PFLP, however, refused to abide by the ceasefire. It held sixty-eight foreign hostages in two hotels in Amman and threatened to blow up the buildings unless prominent army officers, including Sharif Nasser bin Jamil and Sharif Zaid bin Shaker, were dismissed and the Special Forces unit of paratroopers was disbanded. Fear of losing ground in public opinion to the PFLP led Arafat to associate himself with these demands. Hussein yielded to the combined pressure and dismissed his uncle and his cousin. The British ambassador remarked that the departure of Sharif Nasser bin Jamil was "a purgation which brought relief to many other than the fedayeen."[16] Only after its demands had been met did the PFLP release the hostages. Not long after the departure of the commander-in-chief came the resignation of the equally corrupt prime minister nicknamed "10 percent Talhouni" and his government. Talhouni was replaced by Abdul Mun'im Rifa'i, an honest man acceptable to both sides but a rather weak politician. He was the brother of Samir and the uncle of Zaid Rifa'i. Six of the ministers in the new government were ardent Palestinian nationalists. On the military side too the new chief of staff, Manshur Hadithah, came from a moderate wing of the army that leaned towards compromise. Hadithah had good relations with Yasser Arafat. He was in favour of opening a second front in the War of Attrition against Israel and of cooperation with the fedayeen. According to Israeli intelligence, his influence within the army was considerable, as two out of the three divisional commanders were his close friends.[17]

There can be little doubt that Hussein emerged from the crisis with his power and authority gravely weakened. He had opted for compromise and coexistence with the Palestinian resistance movement, but this involved a change of policy as well as personnel on his part. The sacrifice of his uncle and his cousin was particularly painful because, like himself, they were pillars of the establishment and symbols of Hashemite rule in Jordan. Dr. Henry Kissinger, President Nixon's national security adviser, had privately encouraged Hussein to crack down on the fedayeen.[18] In his memoirs Kissinger wrote that "By the summer of 1970 the young, able, and courageous King was in grave peril. The guerrillas, resentful of his efforts to promote a political settlement with Israel, increasingly challenged his army." For his favouritism towards the young king, Kissinger gave the following reasons: "Hussein had always advocated moderation, resisted the radical tide, and avoided fashionable anti-Western slogans. He was in difficulty because of his reluctance to permit the guerrillas free rein. His collapse would radicalize the entire Middle East. Israel would not acquiesce in the establishment of guerrilla bases all along its Jordanian frontier. Another Middle East war would be extremely likely. Thus, Jordan, in my view, was a test of our capacity to control events in the region. Nixon shared this perception."[19] During the crisis Kissinger began to make plans both for the evacuation of American civilians from Jordan and for other unspecified contingencies. The signs were not hopeful. A report to the president drafted by Harold Saunders, one of Kissinger's staff, in early July abounded with ominous phrases: "The authority and prestige of the Hashemite regime will continue to decline. The international credibility of Jordan will be further compromised . . . Greater fedayeen freedom of action will inevitably result in more serious breaches of the ceasefire in the Jordan Valley . . . Hussein faces an uncertain political future."[20]

June 1970 was one of the low points of Hashemite rule in Jordan. Most foreign observers, including American diplomats based in Amman, thought that events had favoured the Palestinian guerrilla organizations and that it was only a matter of time before Hashemite rule was swept away. Some members of the royal family were also beginning to wonder how much longer they could hold out against the advancing tide. One of them was Sharif Nasser, who came to the conclusion that there was no future for the Hashemite family in Jordan. So he went to his nephew and told him that they should consider leaving.[21] Those who knew Sharif Nasser would hardly have believed that he could advise quitting without a fight. In the army he was renowned for courage rather than cowardice.[22]

Sharif Nasser was a very forceful man, but Hussein rejected his advice on this occasion, just as he had during the crisis of April 1957. For Sharif Nasser abdication and exile were an option, but for his nephew they were not. Not only was Sharif Nasser ten years older than Hussein but the formative experiences in his life were very different. He came from the branch of the Hashemite family that had been driven out of Baghdad in 1958. For them living in exile was almost a normal state of affairs.[23] Hussein, on the other hand, was born in Jordan, grew up there and never suffered from any sense of being an outsider. His passionate identification with the country and its people was further reinforced by a strong sense that, as a Hashemite, it was his duty to rule and to lead from the front. He was absolutely determined to stand his ground and defend his dynasty. Abdication to him looked like an easy option, tantamount to cowardice and treason.[24]

In the eyes of Prince Zaid bin Hussein, the ruler of Jordan passed the test of Hashemite kingship with flying colours. Zaid was the youngest son of Hussein, the sharif of Mecca, and the only one who did not become a king in the aftermath of the Arab Revolt against the Ottoman Empire in the First World War. In early June 1970 Prince Zaid, who was seventy-two years old and lived in London, paid a visit to his royal relative in Amman. Hussein greeted Zaid at the airport and hosted him in the Nadwa Palace. The following day fighting broke out between the army and the fedayeen, and the house guest had to stay indoors for about ten days. During this period Zaid had ample opportunity to watch the king in action, dealing with the government and the army, and trying to arrange a ceasefire with the PLO. The elderly and taciturn guest was greatly impressed with the way in which the young king coped with all the problems, pressures and challenges that the country faced at a time when the odds were stacked up against the monarchy. Before leaving Amman, Zaid told his son Raad that he considered Hussein to be the most genuine, able and courageous Hashemite he had ever met, as well as the greatest leader among all the Hashemite kings. This was high praise from a man who had known all the Hashemite kings of his time and had nothing but admiration for his brother Faisal I of Iraq.[25]

Neither Hussein nor Arafat wanted to fight a pitched battle to settle the question of who ruled Jordan. Both were moderates who sought ground rules for coexistence, but neither was entirely master in his own house. Both men strove to avoid polarization, but the extremists on the Palestinian side bolstered up the extremists on the Jordanian, eroding the middle ground in the process. On 10 July, Hussein and Arafat signed another ceasefire agreement. This one recognized the central committee of the Palestinian resistance and legalized the presence of the fedayeen in Jordan. The government undertook to repeal the emergency measures it had adopted during the crisis, and the PLO entered into commitments restraining the behaviour of its members. A joint committee was set up to implement the agreement.

But the dispute between the two sides was rekindled by the announcement of a new American diplomatic initiative to bring about peace between the Arab states and Israel. The second Rogers Plan called for a ceasefire, a standstill along the Suez Canal and a renewed effort by Dr. Gunnar Jarring to bring the parties to a settlement on the basis of Security Council Resolution 242. Hussein was in favour of the Rogers Plan, but he needed to keep in step with Nasser, whose support was crucial in the fight that was brewing up at home with the fedayeen. On 24 July the Egyptian government accepted the new American initiative and two days later Jordan's government followed suit. "What you accept, we accept, and what you reject, we reject" ran the cable Hussein sent to Nasser on the 26th.[26] Arafat rejected the American proposals but refrained from personal attacks on Nasser and Hussein. The central committee of the PLO condemned the proposals as a plot to liquidate the Palestinian resistance. The PFLP and the PDFLP attacked Nasser and Hussein directly in the strongest language and organized peaceful demonstrations against the plan. The Israeli government accepted the second Rogers Plan but only after Menachem Begin and his colleagues in the right-wing Gahal Party walked out in protest at what they saw as a plot to force Israel out of the West Bank. The ceasefire on the Egyptian front went into effect on 7 August, ending the War of Attrition. On the same day Egypt violated the terms of the standstill by moving missiles to the edge of the Suez Canal. Israel protested about the Egyptian violations and suspended its participation in the Jarring talks. The second Rogers Plan thus ended the War of Attrition but failed to move the parties forward towards a peaceful settlement.

Feeling betrayed by Nasser but unable to do anything about it, the fedayeen turned their wrath against his friend in Jordan. On 15 August, Arafat was reported as saying, "We have decided to convert Jordan into a cemetery for all conspirators—Amman shall be the Hanoi of the revolution."[27] This was mild stuff by comparison with the Maoist revolutionary rhetoric of Dr. Habash and Mr. Hawatmeh. The PFLP was a Marxist organization that was receiving limited quantities of arms and advisers from China. It spawned an even more extreme offshoot that called itself PFLP–General Command and was headed by a former Syrian Army officer named Ahmad Jibril. The challenge posed by these groups to the regime in Jordan became increasingly blatant. Their leaders began to call more and more openly for the overthrow of the reactionary Hashemite monarchy as a prelude to the launching of a popular war for the liberation of Palestine. Fighting flared up again between the army and the fedayeen towards the end of August. The stage was set for a civil war.

Like all civil wars, the one in Jordan was a complex, multi-layered and murky affair. The Jordanian Army enjoyed a clear superiority in numbers and armament over its opponents. It had 65,000 well-trained and well-equipped troops facing around 15,000 hastily trained and very lightly armed militiamen.[28] But since the army included a large number of Palestinians, there was the ever-present danger that it would fracture along Jordanian–Palestinian lines and that some Palestinian commanders might desert if ordered to shoot fellow Palestinians. On the other side was a collection of separate and divided guerrilla groups, supported by rival Arab countries. Nor was it a straightforward contest between the army and the fedayeen. It was more like an inter-Arab civil war in which Syria, Iraq, Algeria and Libya supported the fedayeen against the monarchy, with Egypt occupying an uncertain middle ground. Hussein knew that he had the military power at his disposal to crush the fedayeen. The outcome of a contest in which they received external support was more difficult to predict. With the odds against him rising, there was the risk that he would lose unless he too received external support. In his case such support could come from only two sources: America or Israel.

In the event, it was the radical fedayeen that precipitated the show-down. On 1 September, Hussein's motor cavalcade came under heavy fire on its way to the airport. This was the second attempt on his life in three months, and it immediately triggered fighting between loyalist troops and the fedayeen in various parts of Amman. The Iraqi govern-ment sent a note to Jordan to say that if the Jordanian shelling did not stop, "it would not be able to stop individuals from the Iraqi forces from intervening in favour of the fedayeen." As there were 17,000 Iraqi troops stationed in eastern Jordan, this was no idle threat. These troops had been in Jordan since the June War of 1967, and they had long out-stayed their welcome. (At the Khartoum summit in late August 1967, President Arif had agreed to withdraw the Iraqi troops from Jordan. But, for reasons connected with internal politics, the Iraqi government preferred to have them stay in Jordan rather than return home.) Later in the day Zaid Rifa'i, the chief of the royal court, informed the US Embassy of the Iraqi ultimatum and expressed the hope that they could count on American support. He also asked whether the Americans knew what Israel would do if Iraq moved. Rifa'i had been a student of Dr. Henry Kissinger at Harvard, and he shared his view that interna-tional relations are about power and state interests rather than about sentiments or morality. Both men were extremely clever, deeply con-servative and well versed in the theory as well as the practice of Machi-avellian power-politics.

The Americans had difficulty in answering Rifa'i's questions be-cause of serious differences of opinion between the State Department on the one hand and the CIA and the White House on the other. The State Department view was that the monarchy was doomed, that the fedayeen were likely to emerge on top, that the best policy was to hedge one's bets and that in the meantime it was prudent to open lines of communications with the opposition. At any rate, this was the view of the ambassador Harry Symmes, whose sympathy lay with the Palestini-ans. By bugging his phone the security services discovered that he was in contact with some of the fedayeen leaders; he was declared a *per-*

sona non grata; and he was recalled home. It took several months to replace him, and during the interval reporting from the embassy was limited and uninformed. The key person during that period was Jack O'Connell, the experienced and staunchly pro-royalist CIA station chief in Amman. O'Connell knew a lot of people in the army, and from the beginning he predicted that the army would win because it was strong, tough and determined to restore order. His reports said that the king could control the situation and that with a little bit of help from his friends he would unquestionably come out on top. Kissinger and Nixon rejected the State Department's recommendations and adopted O'Connell's.[29]

Kissinger assumed that Israel was unlikely to remain inactive if the Iraqi forces moved closer to its borders or if the Palestinian guerrillas occupied the Jordan Valley. But he also realized that for Hussein to be joined by Israeli forces in his conflict was no trivial matter: "In defending his political independence he had no incentive to destroy his moral position in the Arab world." According to Kissinger, the State Department adopted its not uncommon practice of procrastination. The American chargé in Amman responded to renewed Jordanian queries about Israeli intentions by saying that he could not imagine Jordan's accepting help from its enemy Israel against a fellow Arab country. "The king," noted Kissinger, "was, of course, much too subtle to put the issue this way and much too intelligent to require lectures by American officials about the implications of his own query."[30]

While waiting for an answer from his allies, Hussein's authority at home came under serious challenge. On 6 September the PFLP hijacked four Western-owned airliners with several hundred passengers and forced them to land in Dawson's Field, an abandoned airfield near Zarqa, which was renamed "Revolution Airstrip." The hijackers offered to release the hostages, except for those holding Israeli or dual Israeli–American citizenship, in return for the freeing of Palestinian prisoners held in Swiss, German or British jails. A spokesman for the Popular Front said in Beirut that the airliners were hijacked in order to "teach the Americans a lesson for their support for Israel over the years." Arafat was opposed to hijacking but felt compelled to associate himself with the demands of the hijackers to avoid becoming marginalized. On 12 September the hijackers blew up the airliners in front of the world media and released all but fifty-four of the passengers. Two days

later a Fatah newspaper called for a general strike and the establishment of a national authority in Jordan that would remove "malevolent
elements and agents from the State, army and public security
machines." The PLO central committee resolved to make "a decisive
stand" in defence of the Palestinian revolution. Revolutionary rhetoric
was matched by revolutionary deeds. On 15 September the fedayeen
took over Irbid and declared it a liberated area under a people's government. The international community began to doubt Hussein's ability to
govern his own kingdom. So did a growing number of his loyal
Bedouin troops. Armoured units started flying brassieres from their
tank antennas. The message they conveyed was: "If we are forced to act
like women, we might as well dress like women!"

   For Hussein, the hijacking of the airliners was the last straw. Since
the beginning of the hijack crisis he had been subjected to mounting
pressure from the army, his close advisers, and his brothers Muhammad and Hassan to reassert his authority. The army, where the hardliners were taking over, was on the point of mutiny and could not be
restrained for much longer. In the midst of the crisis, on 9 September,
Manshur Hadithah al-Jazi, the conciliatory and pro-Palestinian army
chief of staff, resigned. He was replaced by the loyalist Field Marshal
Habis Majali, who was recalled from retirement. Natheer Rasheed, who
had been appointed the director of Military Intelligence the previous
month, claimed that Arafat paid al-Jazi 200,000 dinars to get him to
defect. Rasheed also claimed that al-Jazi's letter of resignation had been
written by the PLO. Rasheed had first-class intelligence on the fedayeen
through phone tapping and knew without a shadow of a doubt that
their aim was to overthrow the royalist regime. At the height of the
hijack crisis he told the king in the presence of Sharif Zaid bin Shaker
that he could not stay in his post if the king did not fight back. He added
that if the king wanted him to stay, he knew exactly what to do. The
king asked him to stay and continued, "Enough is enough. It is time to
put things straight."[31] Shaker, who had been reinstated in the army the
previous month and promoted to deputy chief of staff for operations,
also believed that the showdown with the fedayeen could not be put off
any longer.

   Some observers thought that Hussein lost his nerve during the crisis.
A more likely explanation was that, realizing a showdown was
inescapable, he was simply biding his time and giving the fedayeen

enough rope to hang themselves. He refrained from drastic action because he did not wish to compromise his position as king of the whole Jordanian nation. Three stages can be discerned in his policy towards the PLO in 1970: conciliation, containment and confrontation. Hussein was extremely patient by nature and knew the importance of timing. He wanted to leave his people in no doubt that he had done everything in his power to avoid the shedding of blood. The hijacking of planes and the holding of hostages finally tipped public opinion at home and abroad against the fedayeen. The time for action had come. On the evening of 15 September, Hussein summoned his closest advisers to an emergency meeting at his house in Al-Hummar on the outskirts of Amman. Among those present were Wasfi Tall, Zaid Rifa'i, Sharif Zaid bin Shaker and Habis Majali. All of these men had been urging him to crack down on the fedayeen for some time. The military men estimated that it would take the army two to three days to clear the fedayeen out of the major cities.

Before ordering the army to move, Hussein decided to dismiss the civilian government and appoint a military government headed by Brigadier Muhammad Daoud. Daoud was in fact a Palestinian, but he was loyal to the king and favoured firm action in defence of the regime. Hussein preferred to see the coming conflict not as a war between Jordanians and Palestinians but as a contest between the forces of law and order and the forces of anarchy. Most of the members of this government were military men though not all of them were high ranking. Adnan Abu-Odeh, an obscure major in the General Intelligence Department (Mukhabarat), was appointed minister of information. Earlier that year he had been sent to the UK to attend a psychological warfare course. Abu-Odeh came from humble Palestinian origins and had been a schoolteacher and member of the Jordanian Communist Party before joining the Mukhabarat. Hussein knew all this, but he greatly respected the sharpness of his analysis and his eloquence. Abu-Odeh's task was to explain the government's policy and to conduct psychological warfare in the middle of the military operation. His selection for the post reflected Hussein's desire to have Palestinians among his ministers and his keen awareness of the importance of public relations. He was later to become one of Hussein's closest political advisers. One day Abu-Odeh asked the king what was the most difficult decision he ever made. The king replied, "The decision to recapture my capital."[32]

Early in the morning of 17 September the civil war began. The 60th Armoured Brigade entered Amman from different directions and started bombarding the Wahadat and Al-Hussein refugee camps, where the fedayeen had their headquarters. The fedayeen were well prepared and offered very stiff resistance. The army pounded with tanks, artillery and mortars not only the fedayeen strongholds but also the Palestinian population centres in and around Amman. Heavy fighting continued without a break for the next ten days. At the same time the army surrounded and bombarded other cities controlled by the fedayeen—Irbid, Jerash, Salt and Zarqa—but refrained from entering them. Here there was no house-to-house and street-to-street fighting, as in the capital, but many buildings and blocks of apartments were reduced to rubble, and there were heavy casualties. According to PLO figures, the death toll in the first ten days of fighting was as high as 3,400. The initial estimate that it would take two to three days to dislodge the fedayeen from the cities turned out to be wide of the mark. As the days went by, Arab leaders stepped up the pressure on Hussein to put an end to the fighting and to reach a compromise with the fedayeen.

Jordanian fears of external intervention in the conflict were soon realized. On the morning of 18 September a small Syrian armoured force crossed the border near Rathma and headed for Irbid, which was under the control of the fedayeen. The 40th Armoured Brigade engaged the invading force in fierce combat, knocked out some of its tanks and managed to block its advance. Later in the day there was a second incursion across the border but on a larger scale. This time two armoured brigades with nearly 300 tanks and a mechanized infantry brigade were dispatched towards Irbid. The Syrian tanks had PLA markings, but the PLA had no tanks and it was obvious that the invaders were regular army units. The motives behind the Syrian invasion remained obscure, and no statement was issued to clarify them. It is the received wisdom that the Syrian leadership's aim was to help the guerrillas overthrow Hussein. But, if this was indeed the aim, it is not clear why the Syrian intervention was so cautious and circumscribed. A more likely explanation is that the Syrian leaders wanted to protect the Palestinians from a massacre by helping them to create a safe haven in northern Jordan from which they could negotiate terms with the king.[33]

That evening Hussein convened an emergency meeting of his three-

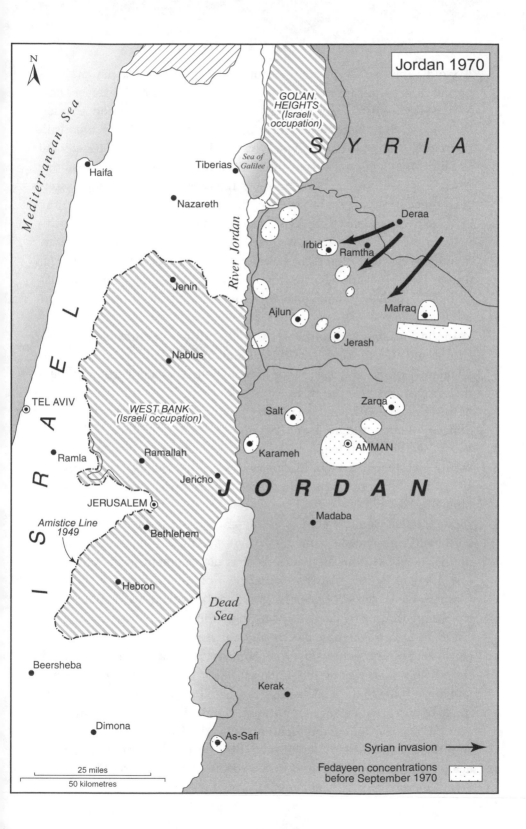

Jordan 1970

N

Mediterranean Sea

GOLAN HEIGHTS
(Israeli occupation)

S Y R I A

Haifa

Tiberias
Sea of Galilee

Nazareth

River Jordan

Deraa

Irbid
Ramtha

Jenin

Mafraq

Ajlun

Jerash

Nablus

TEL AVIV

WEST BANK
(Israeli occupation)

Zarqa

Salt

Ramla

Ramallah

Karameh

AMMAN

Jericho

J O R D A N

JERUSALEM

Madaba

Amistice Line
1949

Bethlehem

I S R A E L

Hebron

Dead Sea

Beersheba

Kerak

Dimona

As-Safi

Syrian invasion

Fedayeen concentrations
before September 1970

25 miles

50 kilometres

day-old cabinet. The purpose of the meeting was to get the cabinet's permission to call for outside help if it became absolutely necessary. Most of the ministers were soldiers and the king was their commander-in-chief, so they were rather surprised that the king chose to consult them rather than to issue orders. What the king said to the cabinet went as follows: "The Syrians have entered the country and are approaching Irbid. Our troops are fighting back but the Syrians are still progressing. As a precaution we might need the help of friends, and I want you to give me the mandate to ask for such help if I have to do so." Some ministers did not like what they heard, but only vague comments were made in response. Their faces revealed their displeasure. Noticing their unease Hussein said, "Gentlemen, I leave you alone to discuss the idea among yourselves. When you reach a decision, please call me." And he left the room.

In the subsequent discussion two rather different attitudes emerged. One group of ministers saw this as an internal Arab affair and was adamantly opposed to asking for outside help. A second group thought that Jordan was engaged in an existential struggle for survival and saw nothing wrong with asking a friend to help, provided it was the United States or Britain and not Israel. No one suspected that the friend could be Israel; they all thought that, because of the precedent of 1958, it would be either or both of the Western allies. At the end of the discussion, the second group prevailed, and the king was given the mandate he had asked for.[34]

Sunday, 20 September, was a long and stressful day. Events on the battlefield influenced the manner in which Hussein used the mandate he had received from his ministers. His management of the crisis was also affected by the recurrent breakdown of communications between the palace and the US Embassy. Walkie-talkies were used some of the time, and the fedayeen who controlled the area round the embassy could eavesdrop on the conversations. Another constraint was the absence of direct "across the river" contact with the Israelis. Zaid Rifa'i, the trusted aide, was by his monarch's side throughout the crisis and conveyed most of the sensitive messages to his Western allies. Hussein made his first request for help through the British Embassy because his normal channels of communications with the US Embassy were interrupted. He called for "Israeli or other air intervention or threat thereof" against the Syrian troops and he asked the British government to consider this request and to convey it to Israel.

In Britain there was virtually unanimous opposition to military intervention. The experts in the Foreign and Commonwealth Office believed that the Palestinians would eventually win the struggle against the king and that it would be damaging to British interests in the Arab world to take action to save his throne. Peter Tripp, who served on the Jordanian desk in the FCO, explained the British predicament: "You cannot just nail your colours to the mast and say well, we'll go down with the ship. I mean, there's a certain amount of self-interest in all this."[35] The Conservative government headed by Edward Heath shared the view of the experts. Sir Alec Douglas-Home, the foreign secretary, advised the prime minister that Western intervention would be deeply resented by the Arab countries: "The Palestinian revolt strikes a very deep chord in Arab hearts. Any Western country therefore which intervenes to try to save Jordan will be involving itself in a deep quarrel in Arabia as a whole, the consequences and end of which none could foretell." The other argument against intervention was stated even more bluntly: "Jordan as it is is not a viable country."[36] After discussion the cabinet rejected any idea of military intervention and feebly decided to transmit the king's message only to the Americans and to leave it to their discretion whether to convey the message to Israel.[37] The truth was that Britain had an each-way bet on the king and on Arafat.

Shortly after his conversation with the British ambassador, Hussein managed to contact the new American ambassador, Dean Brown, who arrived at the height of the hijack crisis and was taken to the palace to present his credentials in an armoured personnel carrier. Hussein made an urgent appeal for air strikes and air cover "from any quarter." Hussein did not explicitly mention Israel this time but the substance of his appeal was passed on to the Israeli representative in Washington.[38] Kissinger and Nixon saw the Syrian invasion as a Soviet challenge that had to be met. Kissinger told Nixon that the Soviets were pushing the Syrians and the Syrians were pushing the Palestinians. Nixon shared the conviction that the Kremlin orchestrated the Jordanian crisis in order to challenge US credibility throughout the Third World. In his memoirs Nixon wrote, "We could not allow Hussein to be overthrown by a Soviet-inspired insurrection. If it succeeded, the entire Middle East might erupt in war . . . It was like a ghastly game of dominoes, with a nuclear war waiting at the end."[39] Kissinger and Nixon tended to see every regional conflict through the lens of their global rivalry with the

Soviet Union; in their view, a Russian soldier lurked behind every olive tree in the Middle East. And both men vastly exaggerated the superpower dimension of the Jordanian crisis. There was no concrete evidence at that time to support the theory that the Soviet Union had instigated the Syrian invasion; the little evidence that came to light later on, in fact, pointed the other way. The Egyptian foreign minister, for example, noted in his memoirs that the Soviets made efforts to defuse the crisis and that they also asked Nasser to put pressure on the Syrians to end their military involvement in Jordan.[40]

The perception of high stakes drove Kissinger and Nixon to respond robustly to Hussein's plea for help. Nixon enthusiastically approved all the military deployments recommended by his hawkish adviser. Apparently, they appealed to his macho streak. "The main thing," Nixon said, "is there's nothing better than a little confrontation now and then, a little excitement."[41] Nixon ordered the 82nd Airborne Division on full alert; the Sixth Fleet to move demonstratively towards the area of tension in the eastern Mediterranean; a reconnaissance plane to fly from an aircraft carrier to Tel Aviv to pick up targeting information and signal that American military action might be approaching; and a warning to be delivered to the Soviets to restrain their Syrian clients. Kissinger preferred Israeli military intervention against Syria with America holding the ring against Soviet interference with Israeli operations; Nixon was reluctant to rely on Israel and wanted only American forces to be used if a confrontation could not be avoided. In the evening, however, Nixon received a more desperate message from Hussein, which led him to reverse his position on the use of Israeli forces. The message from Hussein said that the situation had deteriorated seriously, that Syrian forces occupied Irbid, and that the troops in the capital were disquieted. Hussein also said that air strikes against the invading forces were imperative to save his country and that he might soon have to request ground troops as well. Reversing his earlier procedure, Hussein asked the Americans to inform Britain of his plight.

Kissinger called Itzhak Rabin, the Israeli ambassador to Washington, and told him that the president and the secretary of state would look favourably on an Israeli air attack, that they would make up any material losses, and that they would do their utmost to prevent Soviet interference. Rabin said he would consult with Prime Minister Golda Meir, who happened to be in New York. Late that night Rabin called back with her answer. Israel would fly reconnaissance at first light. The situation around Irbid was described as "quite unpleasant." Israel's military leaders assessed that air action alone might not be sufficient. But they promised to consult again before taking any action.[42]

Monday, 21 September, was another momentous day. In Jerusalem, the cabinet, chaired by Yigal Allon, met in the morning to consider Hussein's extraordinary request. One group favoured the preservation and the strengthening of Hussein's regime. It argued that among all the Arab countries the Hashemite dynasty had the best relations with Israel. According to this group, the June War was a tactical mistake on the part of the king that should not be allowed to damage the basically positive relationship between the two sides. This group also considered Hussein to be the most promising Arab candidate for a peace settlement. Another group was in favour of turning the Hashemite Kingdom of Jordan into a Palestinian state. The more extreme members of this group advocated active Israeli support for the PLO in bringing this about. Yasser Arafat's declaration of independence in Irbid helped members of this group to press their case. They recommended allowing the PLO to achieve its goals and to gain control of the whole country. For them this was the ideal solution to the problem of Palestinian independence.[43]

The pro-Hussein lobby included Meir, Allon, Eban and Rabin. The second group included right-wing politicians, notably Ezer Weizmann and right-wing generals such as Rehavam Ze'evi and Ariel Sharon. Moshe Dayan and Shimon Peres, who were also ministers in the Labour-led government, told the media that they would not shed tears if the Palestinians replaced Hussein. Some of the participants in the cabinet debate were worried that, if Israel intervened to save Hussein at America's behest, it would look like a gun for hire. Yaacov Herzog kept all the little notes he received during that debate. Shimon Peres referred to Hussein as "the amateur king" and gave his opinion that "it is not possible to save him but it is possible to stain our reputation." Gideon Rafael of the Foreign Ministry warned against getting caught up in all the excitement generated by "Dr. Strangelove Kissinger and Rabin."

The cabinet's reply to the Americans, on 21 September, said that air operations alone were considered inadequate to the situation unfolding in Jordan and that ground troops would be necessary; the air force alone could not remove 300 tanks from the battlefield. In view of the risk of war involved, the cabinet sought reassurance and submitted a list of eight questions about American policy in the event of escalation. Could the king make his approach to Israel directly and make arrangements to coordinate their moves? What guarantees could America give Israel against Soviet military intervention? It took the State Department the best part of the day to prepare written answers to these and the other questions. Israel's caution and insatiable quest for reassurance took Kissinger by surprise. His advice to Rabin was: "Don't try to extract too many conditions before moving. Conditions don't mean much any more. If you lick the Syrians that will count."[44] Acting on this advice, the Israelis prepared for an air strike, laid plans for a pincer movement against the Syrian forces in Jordan from north and east, and ostentatiously mobilized their ground forces along the borders with Syria and Jordan. The IDF General Staff also prepared a contingency plan in case Jordan disintegrated and there was a general land-grab involving its Syrian, Iraqi and Saudi neighbours. The military commanders thought that, with or without America's permission, the IDF should move swiftly to secure the Gilead Heights, Kerak and Aqaba.[45]

Allon, the acting prime minister, was the most fervent proponent of prompt action to save Hussein. Through the American ambassador in Tel Aviv, Allon sent a friendly message to the king at 9:13 p.m.: "Following developments with deep sympathy and goodwill. In view clarify situation suggest immediate meeting with you or with your authorized competent representative. Place time your convenience."[46] Through this message Allon sought to reassure his neighbour not only that Israel would not take advantage of his domestic difficulties but that it was ready to help him against any and all of his Arab enemies.[47] An hour later came the reply: "Extremely grateful to old friend for concern. Situation very grave up north. Trying to reorganize and given a chance we may be able to contain threat. However, serious threat of a breakthrough does exist. And this will require immediate action. I would have loved to have this chance to meet, but physically impossible at this time. Will arrange meeting as soon as possible. Meantime please keep in touch through this channel. Best regards and wishes."[48] This extraordinary message reveals, first, Hussein's relief at re-establishing the direct "across the river" contact and, second, that he wanted to keep all his options open.

Part of the problem was that Hussein kept changing his mind during the day about the kind of help his army needed. In the morning he asked for an immediate air strike to check the advance of the Syrian armour. His second message was more desperate and gave notice that he might soon be requesting support from ground forces as well. But in the evening he qualified his request by saying that Israeli ground operations would be fine as long as they operated only in Syria and did not enter Jordan. Two considerations probably prompted Hussein to rule out Israeli ground operations in Jordan: they would have damaged his already tarnished reputation in the Arab world, and there was no guarantee that the Israeli troops would leave the country when they were no longer needed. The Iraqi precedent was not at all encouraging in this respect. Nevertheless, Hussein was evidently very happy to receive the Israeli offer of help.

Tuesday, 22 September, saw the turn of the tide. Emboldened by American and Israeli backing, Hussein ordered his small air force to move against the Syrian forces in the north of the country. Both the air force and the army went into action, and, in a well-coordinated air–ground offensive, inflicted heavy losses on the Syrians. Early signs could be detected that the Syrian forces were preparing to withdraw from Irbid and from the area around it. The great worry of the Jordanian military commanders was that Syria would deploy its air force, which was substantially larger than theirs. Hussein, however, believed all along that the Syrians would not use their air force. He interpreted the PLA markings on the tanks as an attempt to dissociate Syria from the invasion, and considered Hafiz al-Asad, the former minister of defence and commander of the air force, to be a rational and pragmatic man who would not risk an all-out war and super-power involvement.[49] It later transpired that Asad had held back the air force for reasons connected with his internal power struggle with Salah Jadid, the deputy secretary-general of the Ba'th Party, who had ordered the invasion. By refusing to commit the air force to the battle, Asad doomed the venture to failure. Shortly after the débâcle in Jordan, Asad ousted Jadid and seized power in Damascus.

Meanwhile, success on the battlefield led Hussein once again to reassess his earlier request for Israeli support against Syria. In the course of the afternoon the Americans received two messages, one from Jordan, the other from Israel. Hussein was becoming ambivalent about

Israeli air strikes and negative about Israeli ground support. The Israelis were prepared to undertake ground operations but only in Jordan, not in Syria.[50] Israel's help was evidently no longer required either in the air or on the ground; nonetheless, the Israeli Air Force played a part in deterring the Syrians from further escalation of the conflict with Jordan. Phantom jets of the IAF flew low over the Syrian units and created sonic booms to suggest that worse might come if they did not turn round and go back where they came from.[51]

If Israeli support was one factor that helped the Jordanians to gain the upper hand in the conflict with the Syrians, Iraqi neutrality was another. Iraq had two divisions, with about 17,000 troops and 200 tanks, stationed in Jordan. When the fighting erupted the government in Baghdad pledged to use these forces to protect the Palestinian resistance against the royalist army. In an ominous move the Iraqis surrounded the Jordanian Air Force base in Mafraq. Syria's invasion raised the fear that the Iraqis and the Syrians had joined up to help the resistance overthrow the regime. Both countries had extremist Ba'th regimes, but they were bitter enemies with old scores to settle and they suspected each other of plotting to gain control over Jordan. There were also bitter rivalries inside the Iraqi Ba'th Party that made the behaviour of the Iraqi Army in Jordan all the more unpredictable. The one encouraging factor was that the Iraqi Ba'thists hated the Syrian Ba'thists even more than they hated Hussein. The Iraqi leadership's main concern was to stop Jordan from falling into the hands of the Syrians, possibly because they wanted Jordan for themselves. In any case, the worst-case scenario did not materialize: there was no coordinated PLO–Syrian–Iraqi effort to overthrow the regime in Amman; each party had its own objectives.[52] Upon the outbreak of the civil war, General Hardan al-Takriti, the Iraqi vice-president, took personal charge of the forces in Jordan. Takriti turned out to be much better disposed towards Jordan than his colleagues.[53] Fatah's intelligence chief later claimed that he listened to a taped telephone conversation in which Takriti assured Hussein that his country would not intervene militarily. Takriti was as good as his word. The Iraqis allowed large Jordanian Army units to pass through their lines to attack guerrilla strongholds in and around Zarqa on 17–18 September.[54] When the Syrians invaded, the Iraqis remained inactive. When the Syrians withdrew, the guerrillas were left to fend for themselves. Takriti was dismissed for his role in these events and assassinated in Kuwait a year later.[55]

With the Iraqis remaining on the sidelines, the Jordanians launched continuous attacks on the Syrians. At nightfall, 22 September, the Syrians began to withdraw across the border, having lost some 120 tanks and armoured personnel carriers and suffered around 600 casualties. The withdrawal of the Syrians enabled the Jordanian Army to mount an all-out offensive against the fedayeen and to drive them out of the cities and their major strongholds. The Palestinians sustained further heavy losses, and some of their leaders were captured, but there were around 300 defections from the Jordanian Army, including an infantry brigade commander. Political pressures from the Arab world forced Hussein to call a halt to the fighting. Accusations that a massacre of the Palestinians was taking place in Jordan circulated in the Arab media. Nasser convened an emergency summit in Cairo at which Jordan was represented by Prime Minister Muhammad Daoud. But soon after his arrival there Daoud—under heavy pressure from Colonel Muamar Gaddafy, who posed as the champion of the Palestinians—resigned his post and went to live in Libya. In the palace there were conflicting opinions as to whether the king should leave the country in the middle of the crisis to attend the Cairo summit in person. A telephone call from Nasser tipped the balance in favour of going. It took some courage on the part of Hussein to agree to face his accusers directly at a time when Arab sympathy was turning rapidly away from him.

Hussein flew to Cairo on 26 September to a hostile reception from the Arab heads of state and a chilly meeting with Arafat. But the next day an agreement was signed by Hussein and Arafat in the presence of Nasser, who had served as its broker. This was to be the Egyptian leader's last service to the cause of Arab unity: he died of a heart attack the following day. After ten days of fighting the guns fell silent, and the two leaders shook hands over "a sea of blood." The Cairo Agreement provided for an immediate ceasefire all over Jordan, the withdrawal of the Jordanian Army and the Palestinian resistance from all cities before sunset the same day, the release of all prisoners and the formation of an Arab commission to supervise the implementation of the agreement. In victory Hussein displayed magnanimity. He invited Ahmad Toukan, a loyalist Palestinian, to form a government. In his letter of appointment Hussein urged the new prime minister to "bandage the wounds" and combat "regionalism" and Palestinian–Jordanian animosity.[56]

After his victory, Hussein took the initiative and arranged to meet with his old friend Yigal Allon. On 3 October, with Rifa'i and Herzog in attendance, the King of Jordan and the deputy prime minister of Israel carried on an uninterrupted conversation for ninety minutes in an air-conditioned car parked in the Araba Desert north of Eilat.[57]

The king opened the conversation by expressing his heartfelt thanks for the willingness that Israel had shown to help him in the recent crisis. He then proceeded to shed some new light on what had happened in Jordan. There was a serious plan for a revolution to coincide with the general strike, and he had pre-empted it by only three days. In the Amman area alone he discovered 360 subterranean bases, modelled on those of the Vietcong. He held about 20,000 detainees—among them some Chinese "advisers"—and planned to screen the rest thoroughly before releasing them. In the Fatah bases a lot of documents were captured that would be very valuable in tracking down the terrorists. The king thought he had succeeded in breaking the backbone of the terror organizations. Paradoxically, he said, Nasser's last deed was to prevent the complete ostracizing of Jordan in Cairo. Hussein's impression was that Nasser had not been opposed to the action against the fedayeen but was troubled by the length of time it took. Nasser thought that, had the Syrians got into trouble in Jordan, the Iraqis would have invaded Syria. Saudi Arabia and Kuwait had not stopped their financial support for Jordan because of its actions; only Libya had done so. Arafat was a liar, and chiefly responsible for the crisis; but it was necessary to continue to deal with him because, in addition to being the leader of Fatah, he was the chairman of the umbrella Palestinian organization. Hussein said he was determined to build a new Jordanian society. There was no longer a place for the old politicians. He could not repeat the operation he had just carried out and only by building new foundations could a similar crisis be averted in future.

The more concrete part of the conversation concerned joint action against the fedayeen and against Iraq. Hussein reported that the fedayeen were concentrated mainly in the Ajlun area. He kept forces between them and the border with Israel and also behind them. He promised to do his utmost to prevent fedayeen attacks against Israel and agreed to examine Allon's suggestion of forming mobile units to patrol the border area. According to Hussein, the area south of Amman, including the area from the Dead Sea to Eilat, had been cleared of terrorists. He indicated that the forces he had stationed along the border were very slight because the bulk of them were engaged in completing the task of restoring order. Hussein also reported that he had started work on getting the Iraqi forces out of Jordan. He said he wanted to have a swift means of communication with the Israelis because he might again need to ask them at short notice for an air strike—this time against the Iraqis.

There was some discussion about resuming the peace talks under the auspices of Dr. Jarring, which had been suspended by Israel following the Egyptian violation of the terms of the Rogers Plan ceasefire. Hussein claimed that by accepting the plan, Nasser had in effect agreed to enter into peace talks with Israel. Nasser had told him that before agreeing, he had placed his deputy, Anwar Sadat, under house arrest to silence his opposition to the American initiative. Hussein himself wanted to resume the talks but could not do so until the talks with Egypt had begun. Allon suggested secret trilateral talks between Israel, Jordan and Egypt, but Hussein did not see this as a real possibility. He pointed out that the second stage of the Jarring talks involved direct negotiations between Israel and the Arabs.

Finally, Allon put forward the idea of forming a Palestinian entity on the West Bank that would serve as an alternative to the guerrilla leaders and eventually link up with the Palestinians on the East Bank. In its original version, the Allon Plan envisaged a link between the West Bank and Israel. Hussein said that he accepted the idea in principle but could not make any commitments until he was presented with the details. Allon explained that this was a private idea of his for an interim settlement and that it had not been approved by the cabinet.[58] Allon added that he had had this idea since 1967 and that he was prepared to raise it in cabinet since Hussein's reaction was positive. Allon was encouraged by the fact that, having rejected the Allon Plan as a permanent settlement, Hussein was now willing to consider it as an interim one.

After securing Hussein's agreement, Allon presented his idea to the prime minister. He argued that a pro-Hashemite autonomy on the West Bank would provide the best available interim solution, with Israel remaining in the Jordan Valley and Hussein in charge of law and order in the heavily populated Palestinian areas. Allon also pointed out that an interim settlement could go on indefinitely. Meir convened an informal group of ministers who discussed the idea and rejected it unanimously, with Moshe Dayan leading the opposition. So Allon could not go back to Hussein with an official proposal, and the plan fell by the wayside. Allon considered Hussein's agreement in principle to the plan of Palestinian autonomy as highly significant and the cabinet's rejection of it as a cardinal error.[59]

The more pressing issue for Hussein was how to regulate the presence of the Palestinian organizations on the East Bank of his kingdom. On 13 October he signed another agreement with Arafat. The Amman Agreement required the fedayeen to respect the laws of Jordan, to disband their bases and not to be in uniform or bear arms in public. But the fedayeen won one major victory: recognition by the Jordanian government of the PLO as the representative of the Palestinian people. This clause enabled the fedayeen spokesmen to claim that, although they lost the battle militarily, they won it politically. Since the Palestinians constituted well over half the population of Jordan, the agreement implied recognition of Arafat as co-sovereign of the country. This was the first formal recognition of the PLO's independent role by an Arab state, and it set in motion a process that culminated in the Rabat summit decision of 1974, which designated the PLO as the sole legitimate representative of the Palestinian people. Wasfi Tall strongly objected to this clause, but Hussein disregarded his warning, saying they would find a way round it.[60] On the Palestinian side Habash and Hawatmeh rejected the Amman Agreement and resumed their attacks on the monarchy. They openly called for the liberation of Jordan as a necessary prelude to the liberation of Palestine. Faced with a renewed challenge to his authority from radical Palestinian factions, Hussein invited Tall to form a new government.

At the end of October, Tall thus became prime minister for the third time. The fedayeen regarded him as their arch-enemy and suspected that he was appointed to continue the war against them. This public image was not entirely justified. From the beginning of his political career Tall identified with the plight of the Palestinians and advocated turning Jordan into a springboard for the liberation of Palestine. His main criticism of the PLO was that, instead of pursuing the struggle against Israel, it became involved in subversion against the Jordanian regime. Tall also had a low opinion of Arafat and questioned his motives. On one occasion Tall lost his temper with Arafat and shouted at him: "You are a liar; you don't want to fight!"[61] On becoming prime minister, Tall insisted on strict observance of all previous agreements with the government by all the fedayeen organizations. His first priority was law and order for the sake of internal security and stability.

Within a week of Tall's installation, clashes occurred between the army and the PFLP and the PDFLP. Tall was much tougher and more uncompromising than Hussein, and very popular in the army. His name was a byword for loyalty to the crown, courage, honesty and, above all, integrity. Under Tall's vigorous leadership the army continued to consolidate its control of the cities and of the roads leading to them, and in January 1971 launched an offensive against the fedayeen bases along the road from Amman to Jerash. In March it drove the fedayeen out of Irbid, their principal stronghold in the north. In April, Tall ordered the PLO to remove all the fedayeen from the capital and to relocate them in the wooded hills between Jerash and Ajlun. The fedayeen put up some resistance, but they were hopelessly outnumbered and outgunned. In the middle of July the army launched the final assault in the Jerash–Ajlun area and after four days of fighting overpowered the last pockets of resistance. About 2,000 fedayeen surrendered and were later allowed to move to Syria, and about 200 crossed the river, preferring to surrender to the Israeli rather than to the Jordanian Army. The rupture between Jordan and the PLO was complete. The PLO state within a state was snuffed out and exclusive Jordanian sovereignty was re-established over the country. At a press conference on 17 July, Hussein stated that Jordan was "completely quiet" and that there was "no problem" now.[62]

Jordan had erupted into civil war not because of the relationship between the regime and its Palestinian population but because of the challenge to the regime mounted by the fedayeen as an armed movement. By driving out the fedayeen, the regime solved the immediate problem. But it also left behind a bitter legacy of mistrust and resentment, and an overwhelming desire to exact revenge. The civil war was one of the darkest chapters in the history of the Palestinians, and it came to be known as Eylul al-Aswad, or "Black September." Fatah felt betrayed and humiliated by what it called the CIA-backed regime, and it formed a commando group that went by the name of Black September. Its first operation was an act of revenge against the regime that had driven all resistance out of Jordan. On 28 November 1971 four members of Black September assassinated Wasfi Tall outside the Sheraton Hotel in Cairo. His last words were: "They killed me. Murderers . . . they believe only in fire and destruction." Egyptian security was very lax, and the murderers were released a few months later, giving rise to Jordanian suspicions that the Egyptians and the Palestinians had plotted the murder together.[63] The following day Tall was buried with full military honours in the Royal Cemetery adjoining Hussein's palace in Amman. Hussein, who was said to be "desolated" by the death of his prime minister, could not hold back his tears as he headed the thousands of mourners who accompanied Tall on his last journey.[64]

The civil war of 1970–71 was a major landmark in the career of Hussein both internally and externally. Internally, it marked the emergence of a distinct Jordanian identity. Until the civil war Hussein had made a sustained effort to blur the distinction between Jordanians and Palestinians, and cultivated the myth that all his subjects were one big happy family. After the civil war Hussein embarked on a process of Jordanization of the civil service and of the armed forces of the kingdom. The rift between Hussein and his Palestinian subjects also weakened his will to reimpose his sovereignty over the West Bank. Hussein began a very slow and uncertain process of political disengagement from the West Bank of his kingdom, a process that reached its climax in 1988.

In foreign relations too the crisis of September 1970 was rich in lessons and consequences for the king. On the one hand, it underlined Jordan's isolation in the Arab world and its dependence on Western and Israeli support. The oil-producing states cut their subsidies to Jordan after the repression of the fedayeen. On the other, the courage and decisiveness with which Hussein eventually acted to defend his rule against the combined Palestinian–Syrian challenge greatly impressed the Western powers and Israel. Before the showdown the prevalent view among Anglo-American diplomats in Amman was that the monarchy was doomed and that the Palestinians were well on the way to taking over the country. Right-wing Israelis not only expected but wanted actively to support the PLO in its drive to transform the Hashemite Kingdom of Jordan into the Republic of Palestine. By crushing the fedayeen, Hussein confounded the prophets of doom and demonstrated to his enemies the staying power of his dynasty. Nixon commended him on his performance, authorized $10 million in aid to Jordan and requested another $30 million from Congress to reinforce the regime against its enemies. Hussein's victory also persuaded some, though by no means all, right-wing Israelis that they could not solve the Palestinian problem at Jordan's expense. From Hussein's point of view the covert relationship with the Israeli political establishment gained even greater significance as a result of the role it played during the crisis. Israel became a crucial factor in the complex formula that governed Hussein's foreign policy—one in which everything was variable except the interests of Jordan and the survival of the monarchy.

15. The United Arab Kingdom Plan

Hussein's victory over the fedayeen in 1970–71 restored his control over the East Bank of his kingdom but left unresolved many issues about the future of the West Bank. First among them was Israel's consolidation of its presence through the steady expansion of civilian settlements. Hussein was also troubled by growing separatist tendencies: one on the East Bank, which had the support of an influential faction in Amman, including his mother; and another on the West Bank, which favoured drifting away from Jordan and towards coexistence with Israel. There was growing Arab and international support for the idea of a separate Palestinian entity. On top of all these concerns was the suspicion that Egypt and its closest allies were plotting a deal whereby the PLO would tacitly accept UN Resolution 242 in return for a Palestinian state comprising the Gaza Strip, the West Bank and north-western Jordan. For Hussein this was too high a price to pay for ridding himself of the Palestinians and their aspirations—and even if he had been willing to pay it, his army would not have let him.[1]

In fact, Hussein's thinking was moving not towards cutting his losses on the West Bank but towards a more creative solution based on recognizing the emergence of a Palestinian identity and granting his Palestinian subjects the right to self-determination. Having defeated the fedayeen, he wanted to offer the Palestinians at least limited political independence. In the aftermath of the civil war, Hussein saw three possible solutions: for the West Bank to be reunited with Jordan in a unitary state as it had been from 1950 to 1967; a federation between the two banks of the Jordan; or an independent Palestinian state on the West Bank. Hussein favoured the second, federal, solution. All of these, however, were predicated on Israeli withdrawal from the West Bank and Palestinian agreement. Hussein was convinced that the party that had the best chance of regaining the West Bank was Jordan. He also felt a personal duty to regain Jerusalem. He claimed that he wanted Israel to withdraw not so that Jordan could re-establish its rule over the West Bank but so that the Palestinians would be able to choose their own future. He was even prepared to give the Arab League a mandate over the West Bank in the event of an Israeli withdrawal. But it was very difficult to persuade either the PLO or the Arab states that this was his true motive.[2]

Suspicion was fuelled by what the British ambassador described as "a measure of schizophrenia" in Hussein's attitude to the West Bank. Once, in the dark days of September 1970, Hussein remarked that in order to get the Palestinians off his back he would gladly wash his hands of the West Bank and content himself with old Transjordan. Later, he started talking of self-determination for the West Bank after a settlement. Then "Jordanian Jerusalem" became a sticking point. And finally he started speaking of giving the West Bankers a chance after a settlement to opt for self-government within a federation.[3] If royal inconsistency was one problem, Palestinian disunity was another. Hussein thought that the Palestinians were so hopelessly split that they could never agree on anything among themselves. In the occupied territories alone there were at least three identifiable factions, not to mention the proliferation of ideologically opposed Palestinian organizations in Jordan and elsewhere. He concluded that they would be able to sort themselves out only after the imposition of a settlement.[4]

On 15 March 1972, in an address to parliament, Hussein launched his plan for the radical reorganization of his kingdom. The plan was the product of a committee that had conducted its work in secret under the chairmanship of Crown Prince Hassan. The Hashemite Kingdom of Jordan was to be renamed the United Arab Kingdom (UAK) and to consist of two autonomous regions, Jordan and Palestine, united under a central government, with a National Assembly in Amman. Amman was to be the capital of the Jordanian region while Arab Jerusalem was to be the capital of the Palestinian region. Each region was to have its own governor-general, a government and a directly elected "People's Council." The central government was to be responsible for foreign affairs and defence, and there was to be one army with the king as its "Supreme Commander." A supreme court was to serve as the central authority for both regions. In essence, Hussein's speech was an affirmation of his belief in the unity of the kingdom but also the acknowledgement of some sort of separate Palestinian entity—a major development.[5]

Hussein issued his manifesto for a United Arab Kingdom for several reasons. It offered a rallying point for the Palestinians, and especially the West Bankers: maintaining a Palestinian identity with a fellow Arab state would, he thought, always be preferable to maintaining it with Israel, which would inevitably dominate any Palestinian "independence." Also, the plan staked a claim for the Jordanian monarch, and not the multi-vocal fedayeen leaders, to represent the Palestinians and to find a solution for the West Bank that could bring long-term security to his kingdom. Finally, by asserting himself as the champion of the Palestinians, Hussein hoped to regain respectability in the eyes of moderate Arab opinion and to create the conditions for the resumption of the subsidies from the oil-producing Arab states that were cut off following the repression of the fedayeen in Jordan.

Hussein's plan was an unmitigated failure that fell between every conceivable stool. It was greeted with a unanimous chorus of condemnation in the Arab world. Hussein was personally attacked in unusually strong language and his plan rejected out of hand. It was as if he were trying to steal something that did not belong to him: the land of the Palestinians. The general Arab view seemed to be that the whole thing was a plot between the Americans, the Israelis and the king. Hussein had succeeded in uniting all the Palestinian guerrilla organizations but, ironically, in total opposition to his proposals. Rejection, especially by the radical factions, was immediate, vehement, vitriolic and even violent. On the day after Hussein spoke, the PLO's Executive Committee issued a statement that said the people of Palestine alone had the right to decide their own future and the future of their cause. The Jordanian regime was denounced for its cooperation with world imperialism and for "offering itself as an accomplice to the Zionist enemy." The conflict was said to be not between Jordanian and Palestinian but "between a subservient and collusive regime and a people who have adopted armed struggle as a way to achieve their wishes and to recover their rights." Hussein was charged with going against the Arab consensus "by breaking the isolation of the Israeli wild beast and unleashing it on the Arab nation" through the United Arab Kingdom plan. The plan itself was said to be Arab only in name, "while its mind and will would be Israeli." The statement ended with a rousing call on all patriotic Arabs to frustrate the plot by the "feudalist" Hashemite regime to liquidate the Palestinian resistance.[6]

Fatah, the largest commando organization, went further in its reply and called for the overthrow of Hussein. Fatah's statement said that "the centre of the dispute is the king, the Hashemite dynasty and the regime." The dynasty was denounced for its history of conspiracy against the Palestinian people and for its role in serving imperialist objectives in the region. Hussein's plan was described as an "artificial and fake structure with reactionary contents designed to consecrate subjugation to imperialism and Zionism." Accordingly, the statement called for "getting rid of the dynasty and overthrowing the monarchy in Jordan."[7] The Arab press generally sided with the Palestinians against the regime. Its comments were either negative or lukewarm about the plan, and there was the familiar preoccupation with restating Palestinian "rights" rather than with any realistic discussion of how these might be realized.[8] Reactions of the mayors on the West Bank were largely unenthusiastic or negative, although a few welcomed the plan. The mayor of Hebron captured the prevalent mood of scepticism when he remarked, using an old Arab saying, that the king was selling fish in the sea.[9]

The Arab leaders, with very few exceptions, none of them heroic, joined in the chorus of condemnation. The PLO claimed to be the only party with the right to represent the Palestinians, and most Arab leaders found it convenient to placate the PLO by endorsing this claim. Some may have been motivated by genuine commitment to the Palestinian cause, while others played the Palestinian card for cynical reasons of their own. Foremost among the latter was Anwar Sadat, Nasser's successor. For Hussein the death of Nasser removed his most weighty supporter in the Arab world and caused the collapse of the Amman–Cairo alliance. Sadat would reverse Nasser's foreign policy by moving from pan-Arabism to an Egypt-first attitude, by changing from a pro-Soviet to a pro-American orientation and by abandoning the commitment to a comprehensive settlement in favour of a separate deal with Israel. The change and the camouflage are illustrated by a popular story about Sadat and his driver. As they were approaching a crossroads, the driver asked Sadat which way to turn. Sadat asked which way Nasser used to go and the driver replied that Nasser used to turn left. Sadat's instruction was "In that case, indicate left and turn right!"

Sadat's attitude towards Hussein was hostile from the beginning. Soon after Sadat became president, Hussein suggested a visit to Cairo in the hope of establishing a good working relationship. Against the background of rumours that Hussein had met with Yigal Allon, Sadat thought that a meeting with the Jordanian king would look like giving a blessing to his clandestine contacts with the Israelis. So, on 23 November, Sadat sent his chief of staff, General Muhammad Sadiq, to Amman to ask Hussein bluntly whether he had seen any Israeli leader recently. Although Hussein was evasive, Sadiq got the firm impression that Hussein had seen Allon, and the proposed visit was delayed.[10] Another unfriendly act by Sadat was the release from prison of the assassins of Wasfi Tall. Sadat suspected Hussein of planning to make a separate deal with Israel over the West Bank, while Hussein suspected Sadat of planning to make a separate deal with Israel over Sinai. Sadat came under attack from the PLO for his own overtures towards Israel, and specifically for the offer of 4 February 1971 of an interim settlement based on the reopening of the Suez Canal and the withdrawal of the Israeli forces to the Sinai Passes. By posing as the champion of the Palestinians, Sadat sought to deflect their anger from himself to the Jordanian monarch. Sadat's response to the launching of the United Arab Kingdom scheme was a dramatic announcement, at the Palestine Peoples Conference in Cairo, of his decision to sever diplomatic relations with Jordan. Objection to a hypothetical plan that had next to nothing to do with Egypt was a bizarre reason for breaking off diplomatic relations, but the decision was well received by the conference and the radical Arab states.

Syria, Algeria and Libya had already broken off diplomatic relations with Jordan in September 1970. The Algerian press saw Hussein's plan as proof of a Zionist–imperialist plot aimed at putting a double seal on the fate of the whole of Palestine, with one part administered from Amman and the other from Tel Aviv. A leading article in the government-controlled daily *El Moudjahid* labelled the Jordanian initiative as the Allon Plan under a different guise and found in it further evidence of the permanent collusion between Jordan and Israel.[11] The Algerian article was typical of the entire Arab reaction to the UAK plan. Arab politicians and the Arab media worked themselves into a state of frenzy—over a plan that had no chance of being realized for the obvious reason that the area in question was under Israeli occupation. The sensible response would have been to let the whole thing drift into oblivion. The greatest irony of all was that on this occasion there was no consultation, let alone collusion, between Hussein and Israel prior to his speech.

The initial Israeli reaction to Hussein's announcement was overtly hostile. Israel rejected the king's federal plan on the grounds that the king was presuming to regulate the future of Israeli-controlled territory before negotiating its return. If he wanted to recover the West Bank, he first had to negotiate with them and find out their conditions.[12] But although Golda Meir's rejection of the plan was swift, it was not absolute. She did not reject the federal idea, only the territorial conception behind the plan. In a speech to the Knesset on 16 March, she said that Israel never interfered in the internal structure or form of an Arab regime. If the King of Jordan had seen fit to change the name of his kingdom to "Palestine" and modify its internal structure, she would have raised no objections. But she had strong objections to the king's initiative because it affected Israel's borders and security. She criticized Hussein's speech for ignoring Israel's presence on the West Bank; for making no mention of willingness to negotiate with Israel or to make peace with it before making changes to the status quo; and for treating the State of Israel as nothing but "a Zionist plot to gain control over Palestine." The plan itself, according to Meir, was "a pretentious and one-sided statement which not only does not serve the interest of peace, but is liable to spur on all the extremist elements whose aim is war against Israel." Meir's strident rejection of Hussein's federal plan was music to the ears of Yasser Arafat, the leader of Fatah and chairman of the PLO. Arafat and his colleagues regarded the king's move as "an attempt to put the PLO out of business." Arafat told his biographer that if Israel had agreed to withdraw from the West Bank, Hussein would have made peace with it immediately "and the PLO would have been finished. Absolutely finished. Sometimes I think we are lucky to have the Israelis as our enemies. They have saved us many times!"[13]

Nothing could have been further removed from Meir's intention than helping the PLO. Her rejection of it was absolute and unconditional. She had never shown any interest in the Palestinian option because she regarded the Palestinians as the irreconcilable enemy of Israel. Her views about the Palestinians had been formed in the pre-independence period and had hardly changed. In November 1947 she and King Abdullah had reached an agreement to partition Palestine at the expense of the Palestinians, and that policy held until early June 1967. After June

1967 she remained unremittingly hostile towards Palestinian nationalism; in fact, she refused to acknowledge that the Palestinians were a
nation or that they had any right to national self-determination. As
prime minister she was well known for her anachronistic and hardline
views about the Palestinian problem, and she achieved notoriety for her
statement that there was no such thing as a Palestinian people. "It is not
as though there was a Palestinian people in Palestine considering itself
as a Palestinian people and we came and threw them out and took their
country away from them," she told journalists in June 1969. "They did
not exist."[14]

Simha Dinitz, who served as director-general of the prime minister's
office from 1969 to 1973, explained: "For Golda the only realistic solution to the Palestinian problem, from the demographic and the geographic point of view, was to place them under Jordan's jurisdiction.
An attempt to deal with the Palestinian question without linking it to
Jordan, in other words, an attempt to create an additional state between
Israel and Jordan, would not succeed because such a state would not
have an adequate geographic or demographic base. This was the foundation of her thinking. Consequently, in order to arrive at a solution to
the Palestinian problem, a link with Jordan had to be forged. Hence all
the meetings and discussions with Hussein." Dinitz also argued that,
although a peace agreement was not achieved, Israel's dealings with
Jordan were successful in a number of different ways:

First, the dialogue with Jordan prevented the rise of the PLO as a central force
in the Palestinian arena. As long as the dialogue continued, the PLO was prevented from becoming the main spokesman of the Palestinians or the most
important spokesman.

Second, the contact yielded all sorts of agreements, ranging from the fight
against terrorists to the fight against mosquitoes. These practical and security
agreements between Israel and Hussein created a situation of de facto peace,
though not de jure peace. On the one hand, there was the policy of open bridges
across the Jordan River; on the other hand, there was a coordinated effort to
suppress the terrorists who threatened both Jordan and us. There was also
cooperation in practical matters such as the division of land, farming, pest control and irrigation.

Third, the contacts with Hussein created a precedent for a direct dialogue
with an Arab leader. They made Sadat's trip to Jerusalem seem less revolutionary and less incredible than it would have otherwise.[15]

Unlike Meir, Allon changed his position on the preferred partner for a settlement after 1967, largely as a result of the personal relationship he had formed with Hussein. Whereas the meetings with Hussein merely reinforced Meir's basic pro-Hashemite views, in Allon's case they brought about a change of orientation. Having been a proponent of the Palestinian option after the June War, Allon became the most fervent proponent of the Jordanian option. In an interview with the daily newspaper *Ma'ariv*, Allon tried to soften the impression created by Meir's speech in the Knesset. He said that there was no absolute conflict between the Allon Plan and Hussein's plan as far as the political structure of the Jordanian–Palestinian entity was concerned; the difference related to the borders with Israel. Hussein's premise of a return to the pre-1967 borders was totally unacceptable to the Israeli deputy prime minister.[16] Allon's favourable comments about Hussein's plan fed the rumours of collusion across the Jordan. But there had been no collusion and no prior agreement.

Discussion between Hussein and the Israeli prime minister about the United Arab Kingdom plan took place after, not before, its public announcement. The meeting took place in an air-conditioned caravan in the Araba Desert, south of the Dead Sea, on 21 March 1972. By that time defence minister Moshe Dayan had established his ascendancy in the cabinet over his rival Allon. The exclusion of Allon from the meeting with his "old friend" heralded a hardening of the Israeli position. Allon advocated peace with Jordan based on territorial compromise over the West Bank. Dayan wanted to maintain Israeli control over the whole of the West Bank even if it meant no peace treaty with Jordan. He advocated a functional solution, the essence of which was that the Palestinians would run their own affairs on the West Bank with open bridges to the East Bank, while Israel remained in charge of security and continued to build Jewish settlements there. This, too, was unacceptable to the king.[17] Dayan's position was dictated by internal politics and made no sense in terms of foreign policy. In her speech in the Knesset, Meir was prepared to go along with it and rebuked the king for ignoring the need to negotiate with Israel. But she offered no realistic alternative basis for negotiations.

The Israeli plan was of course completely unacceptable to Hussein, but his interest in continuing to meet with the Israeli leaders was unaffected by their intransigence. He continued to believe that secret contact with the Israelis was important: first, it was essential to limit the extent of clashes that took place along the ceasefire line; second, he needed to check regularly for any sign of a less inflexible attitude on Israel's part towards a settlement.[18] At the start of the meeting on 21 March, Meir complained that Hussein had not given her advance warning of the United Arab Kingdom plan. Hussein apologized and said that his intention was to implement the plan after reaching a peace agreement with Israel. Meir was not mollified and complained further that in his speech Hussein spoke of liberating all the occupied territories—"Maybe you mean Tel Aviv as well?" she inquired sarcastically. Since Hussein was not ready for significant territorial changes, she suggested seeking temporary arrangements. Hussein asked her to allow him access to the people of the West Bank in order to build up support for the federal plan. Meir replied that this was a complex matter that carried the risk of raising false hopes of a territorial settlement among the Palestinians.

She then posed two questions of her own: could His Majesty sign a separate peace agreement with Israel; and could the peace agreement be based on substantial border modifications? To the first question Hussein gave an affirmative reply, provided the peace agreement could be fitted into an appropriate framework. He spoke of a peace that would put an end to all the wars. Regarding the second question, Hussein saw no possibility of significant border changes. The whole of the West Bank, including East Jerusalem, had to be part of the federation under his crown. He realized that since 1967 Israel had built Jewish neighbourhoods in Jerusalem and dispossessed many Arabs, but the eastern part of the city had to remain under Arab rule. To reinforce his words, and to address the Israeli concern with security, Hussein presented a working paper in which Jordan agreed to the demilitarization of the entire West Bank after its transfer, along with the Gaza Strip, to Jordanian rule. Jerusalem would serve as the capital of the two nations and did not have to be redivided.

Hussein argued that Jordan and Israel had a common interest in preventing the Syrians and the Iraqis from gaining political dominance over the Palestinians. Meir suggested that Jordan should not be part of an eastern front against Israel in the event of war; that Syrian and Iraqi forces should not be stationed on Jordanian territory; and that Jordan and Israel should prepare joint contingency plans to meet changes in the regional status quo. Hussein did not respond to these specific suggestions but asked again to be allowed to develop his links with the inhabitants of the West Bank. Meir made no promises but offered to send an authorized representative to discuss the matter. This would be Moshe Dayan, who as minister of defence was responsible for security in all the occupied territories.[19]

On 29 June 1972 Dayan accompanied Meir to a meeting in Wadi Araba with Hussein and Zaid Rifa'i. Dayan urged Hussein to seek a settlement with Meir because of her strong position at home and her flexibility, but he warned that even she could not settle without significant border changes. In the absence of a settlement, the danger of war increased. The question was whether Jordan would join Egypt if Egypt went to war against Israel. Hussein rejected this approach and repeated his earlier request for access to the Palestinians of the West Bank. "I hoped you would come up with new ideas, as the prime minister promised," he said. Dayan, however, continued to make his pitch for an agreement with Meir: "Leave aside the Palestinian issue for twenty years. It is in your interest to reach an arrangement with Golda. Her line would be more convenient for you than my line." The most that Hussein was prepared to consider was changes to the 1949 armistice agreement that separated villages from their land. Dayan's next move was to offer Hussein a defence pact. The idea was to formalize Israel's policy of preserving the territorial integrity of Jordan in return for a Jordanian commitment not to join any Arab war coalition against Israel, as it did in 1967. "Israel," said Dayan, "is prepared to rush to Jordan's aid, possibly in cooperation with the United States, if pressure on Jordan increases as a result of its refusal to join in the war. We are even prepared for a defence pact."

Hussein and Rifa'i did not wish to pursue the suggestion of a secret agreement. They preferred to concentrate on practical matters such as the building of a security fence along the border in the south to prevent infiltration and terrorist attacks. Although Hussein did not take up Dayan's specific offer, he sought to preserve the option of Israeli aid in a crisis without a written pledge on either side. He also knew that the extremists in Israel had wanted to topple the monarchy in September 1970, and he was anxious to persuade Israel's leaders that one day he might be able to overcome Arab constraints and make a peace settlement with them. But both he and Rifa'i made it clear to Dayan that neither IDF bases nor civilian settlements could remain on the West Bank once a peace agreement was reached. In response to Dayan's question about their ideas for a permanent settlement, Rifa'i replied that it must be based on the 4 June 1967 border. The only concession that Rifa'i would consider was not to station Jordan's army on the West Bank following the Israeli withdrawal.[20]

A third meeting between the two sides occurred at the same place on 19 November 1972. The suggestion of a defence pact was not raised again. Hussein and Rifa'i made a specific request for a corridor between the West Bank and the Gaza Strip. Meir suggested leaving the territorial question for negotiations at a later stage and pressed for a clear commitment that the Jordanian Army would not cross the Jordan River. The terms she proposed for a settlement were that the unpopulated part of the West Bank would remain in Israeli hands and the Jewish settlements would stay. "I believe that I have a majority in the Knesset and in the government in favour of this principle," she said. "Gahal [the right-wing opposition party] and the religious parties will be opposed but I have a majority." Hussein rejected the proposal out of hand. "I understand that you are offering me the Allon Plan," he said, "maybe more limited in scope, but it is out of the question." Meir stressed that she just wanted to keep unpopulated areas and estimated that there were only about 25,000 Arab inhabitants on the western side of the Jordan Valley. Hussein held to his position and explained to Meir that significant border changes would arouse the opposition of the Arab world. He reminded her that after he announced his federal plan Sadat severed diplomatic relations with Jordan.[21]

The picture that emerged from the three meetings between Hussein and the Israeli leaders was bleak. Hussein had tried every approach in an effort to stimulate motion, but he reached a dead end. The positions of the two sides as presented at the talks were simply irreconcilable. Hussein's position was clear and consistent, whereas the Israeli position was vague and evasive. One of the problems was that there was no official Israeli position at all: Meir's offer, paltry as it was, had not been endorsed by her government. Even if Hussein had been foolhardy enough to accept it, there was no guarantee that the divided government would sanction it. The fact that Meir made this offer at all reflected her preference for land over peace as well as her indifference to Arab sensitivities. Israeli supremacy reinforced her natural intransigence. The truth of the matter was that Israel was in a position of unassailable power and did not therefore have to yield ground; and, because of this power, the only opinions the Israelis had to consider were internal ones. Time and again since the beginning of the secret meetings, Hussein told his Israeli interlocutors that he was ready for a peaceful settlement with them provided he could defend it in front of the Arab world. In Arab eyes land was sacred and inseparable from national honour. If Hussein had agreed to Meir's terms he would have been instantly denounced by the entire Arab world as a traitor and as a collaborator with the enemy. Her offer was therefore a complete non-starter, just as all previous versions of the Allon Plan had been. Dayan, to his credit, at least recognized the futility of making an offer for a peace settlement that had no chance of being accepted. He therefore offered Hussein a defence pact in return for a pledge not to join an Arab war coalition against Israel. But this approach was no more successful because Hussein could not run the risk of becoming a pariah by relying on Israel for protection against his Arab neighbours. So in his relations with Israel, Hussein reached a stalemate.

Jordan's isolation in the Arab world increased its dependence on Anglo-American aid. British aid was small compared to that of America, and this contributed to the spreading of a sense of disillusion in Jordan with its "oldest friend." There was a belief that the British were losing interest in the Hashemite struggle for survival and that they were content to allow American influence to supplant British influence in the region. The question for the hard-headed policy-makers in Whitehall was whether the stability and survival of Hashemite Jordan mattered to Britain, given that Jordan had no oil or major potential as an export market, and that the Americans were already pouring a lot of money into the country. Glen Balfour-Paul, the new British ambassador, effectively answered these doubts. He argued to the Foreign Office that the Middle East would be a worse place without Hussein's Jordan and that the Jordanians looked to Britain, indeed their "oldest friend," to help with the development of their state and the stability of their regime. If Britain allowed Hussein to become too dependent on the Americans, his standing could suffer. It was in the interest of regional stability to strengthen the Hashemite regime and to diminish the risk of its replacement by a radical Arab demagogue. Balfour-Paul therefore suggested increasing British economic aid and arms sales to Jordan. Even if the Americans wished Jordan to be regarded as *chasse guardée*, he did not see why Britain should relinquish all hunting rights. He reminded his superiors that this was a military regime at least to the extent that military considerations played as much a part as any other in policy-making. Consequently, Britain's standing in Jordan depended very considerably on its readiness to help over the problems of the armed forces.[22] These arguments carried the day and resulted in a more supportive British policy towards the regime in Jordan.

At about this time Prince Hassan, Hussein's heir designate, was becoming increasingly involved in the affairs of state and taking over the supervision of more and more government business, particularly in the fields of economics and development. Hassan was unusual among the younger generation of Hashemite princes in not going to a military academy. He was the intellectual in the family. At Harrow, Hassan had a notably more distinguished academic career than his elder brother; and he went on to Christ Church, Oxford, where he took a degree in Oriental Languages, including Hebrew. Very soon after his return home, Hassan went into the family business. Jordan's constitution does not assign any specific responsibilities to the crown prince; it was entirely at Hussein's discretion to decide what duties to assign to his younger brother. From the beginning, the two developed a very good working relationship. In personality and style they were very different, yet they worked harmoniously. Hussein was intuitive, unsystematic and somewhat superficial; Hassan was serious, painstaking and methodical. Hussein relied on the personal touch to solve problems; he was impatient with paperwork, and he was pretty useless at keeping records. Hassan had an infinitely better understanding of the importance of research and record-keeping in the conduct of government business. Hussein was only too happy to delegate to his brother responsibility for overseeing complex projects that required sustained attention, such as the Five-Year plans. Within a short time, Hassan became Hussein's main adviser. Because the crown prince was without specific powers, tensions sometimes arose between Hassan and the government. But Hussein had full trust in Hassan's judgement, and he could discuss issues with him in complete confidence. For this reason Hussein could also entrust Hassan with sensitive briefs like preparing the plan for the United Arab Kingdom and holding a secret meeting with the Israeli minister of agriculture, Chaim Givati.

In his valedictory dispatch from Amman, John Phillips noted that his period of service had seen the Hashemite regime emerge from the shadows into the sunlight. He found the dynastic rulers of Jordan rather more admirable in triumph than his predecessor had found them in the defeat of 1967. "King Hussein has some considerable qualifications for his job including physical courage, resilience, a disarming readiness to admit that he had made a nonsense of something . . . a good deal of personal charm and the capacity to inspire loyalty; also a large slice of luck. Prince Hassan is intelligent and very hard-working but his abrasiveness combined with his suspicious nature has made and may continue to make enemies of some who wish his country well." Hassan's untrusting nature, on the other hand, also enabled him to see through and expose the motives of some of those who used their membership of the king's inner circle for their own disreputable ends. Phillips therefore hoped that in future they would see less of "the slick exploiting the thick."[23]

Glen Balfour-Paul gave an eloquent account of his first impressions of the king and his brother. Their three-fold policy objectives were said to be a modus vivendi with the Israelis, reconciliation with the Palestinians and the development of the economy. Despite the façade of parliament and a ministerial system, he observed, it was in the person of the king, and increasingly in that of the crown prince, that authority was concentrated: "Hussein and Hassan, vicar and curate of this truncated Arab parish who have been ex-communicated by the Bishops of Confrontation but who continue to serve the Mass (or the masses) after their own dissident doctrine." The first thing that struck the new ambassador was how harmoniously the two brothers complemented each other, the division of labour between the pair suiting their respective turns of mind. The king concerned himself with external affairs and public relations, the crown prince with internal affairs, planning and the economy. "The middle brother Mohammed, having inherited from his hapless father not only his gentle charm but also his less marketable qualities, has been put out to grass, though his functions as the Head of the Tribal Council are not purely honorary." As a man to talk to, Balfour-Paul thought that the crown prince outclassed the king: "At twenty-six his powers of intellectual concentration . . . are formidable, his jokes sophisticated, his English distinctly more fluent than mine."[24]

In the personal life of Hussein 1972 was noteworthy for the breakdown of his marriage to his second wife, Princess Muna. Hussein had embarked on this marriage a decade earlier despite opposition from the British ambassador and his own advisers. It was a source of much happiness in its early years and had produced two sons and two daughters. How and why it broke down is not known because both sides maintained a dignified silence. Recurrent rumours of Hussein's marital infidelity were at least one likely source of strain. In any case, Hussein fell in love with another woman, and it was he who decided to dissolve the marriage.

The woman who swept Hussein off his feet was Alia Toukan, who came from a prominent Palestinian family from Nablus. Alia was born in Cairo in 1948 to Baha Uddin Toukan, the Jordanian ambassador to Egypt. Young Hussein was a frequent visitor who stayed with the Toukans during school holidays and on his way to and from Victoria College in Alexandria. Alia was one year old when they first met, and he used to play with her. Baha Uddin Toukan subsequently served as Jordan's ambassador to Ankara, London and the United Nations in New York, where Alia did an M.A. in Business and Public Relations at Hunter College. She was a beautiful and sophisticated young woman with an appreciation of the arts and a social conscience, very interested in human rights and the welfare of the poor. She was also lively and outgoing, and communicated easily with people from all walks of life. Her ambition was to become an ambassador for her country. When Hussein met her again she was working for Royal Jordanian Airlines, and he was very taken with her. It was he who asked her to oversee the International Water Ski Festival in Aqaba. Their romance flourished, and they got married in Amman on 24 December 1972, when he was thirty-seven and she was twenty-four. The title she assumed was Queen Alia Al-Hussein. Alia was a popular queen not least on account of her Palestinian background. She seemed to embody her husband's vision of one united Jordanian–Palestinian family.

16. The October War

All diplomatic activity to resolve the Arab–Israeli conflict was suspended in the second half of 1972. Israel had no real interest in negotiating with any of its Arab neighbours; the principal aim of its policy was to preserve the territorial status quo on all fronts and make no concessions for the sake of peace. Underlying this was the assumption that the present state of affairs could be perpetuated indefinitely because Israel's military power would deter the Arabs from going to war. Egypt, as the largest and most powerful of the Arab states, was the main target of the Israeli strategy of attrition. The essence of this strategy was to let President Sadat "sweat it out," with his range of alternatives narrowing all the time, eventually, it was supposed, driving him to settle the conflict on Israel's terms. Richard Nixon and Henry Kissinger, who replaced William Rogers as secretary of state, abandoned the effort to mediate between the Arab states and Israel. They adopted the Israeli belief that the stalemate in the Middle East served American as well as Israeli interests and that it worked against the Soviet Union and her Arab allies. With tacit American backing, Israel was free to pursue the policy that could fairly be described as "destination deadlock."

In relation to Jordan too Israel's leaders displayed no diplomatic flexibility and no interest in a peace agreement. Under the influence of Moshe Dayan, the Labour-led government continued to consolidate its military control over the West Bank and to build more and more settlements in the Jordan Valley. Practical cooperation with the Jordanian authorities continued over a wide range of practical issues, including agriculture, the management of water resources, trade, taxation, banking, electricity, the provision of medical services and the repatriation of refugees. Paradoxically, what Simha Dinitz described as the state of de facto peace enjoyed by Israel reduced the incentive to strive for a formal, or *de jure*, peace: functional cooperation between Jordan and

Israel contributed to the diplomatic stalemate in the Middle East.[1] Hussein was convinced that if this was not broken, the result would be instability, turbulence and, eventually, war. In early February 1973 he arrived in Washington to share his forebodings with President Nixon and other senior American policy-makers. Kissinger describes the king's predicament with insight and sympathy:

Hussein repeated his willingness to make peace with Israel. But despite secret contacts he faced an impasse. Hussein symbolized the fate of Arab moderates. He was caught between his inability to sustain a war with Israel and his unwillingness to make a common cause with the radicals. He was prepared for a diplomatic solution, even a generous one, but Israel saw no incentive for negotiations as long as Hussein stood alone. Any return of conquered territories seemed to it less secure than the status quo. And the West Bank with its historic legacy would unleash violent domestic controversy in Israel—the National Religious Party, without which the governing coalition could not rule, was adamantly opposed to the return of any part of the West Bank.

When Hussein returned to Washington on 27 February, Kissinger briefed him on the latest Egyptian proposals for resolving the conflict. Hussein's reaction revealed the depth of his distrust for Sadat. Kissinger thus had indications of two separate approaches from two Arab leaders whose mutual suspicions kept them from combining. Sadat was using the Palestinians to gain a veto over Jordanian actions, while Hussein invoked American fears of Soviet intransigence to slow down a separate peace between Egypt and Israel.[2]

Alone among Arab leaders at that time, Hussein was prepared to be specific about peace terms. At his second meeting with Kissinger he handed him a paper that spelled out the elements he had described at the first: "Jordan would negotiate directly with Israel over the West Bank. There would be some border changes provided the Gaza Strip was given in return. If Jordanian sovereignty was restored, there could be Israeli outposts along the Jordan River or even Israeli settlements, provided they were isolated enclaves on Jordanian territory; he could not agree to the annexation of the Jordan Valley by Israel. Wryly the King said that all these proposals had already been made directly to Israel and been rejected. What was needed was an American proposal, not another Jordanian one." The paper in fact represented an improvement on Hussein's previous offer to the Israelis. At the secret meeting with Moshe Dayan on 29 June 1972, Hussein had ruled out Israeli bases and settlements on Jordanian territory, whereas the paper to Kissinger allowed for enclaves. The next visitor to Washington was Golda Meir. At a meeting with Nixon on 1 March 1973, she proclaimed that "we have never had it so good" and insisted that the stalemate was safe because the Arabs had no military option. The Americans accepted her argument and stepped up their economic and military aid to Israel.[3] No American proposal followed Hussein's visit, and his conversations with Kissinger led nowhere.

The complacency and conceit that Meir displayed in Washington also coloured her attitude to Jordan. She and Hussein met secretly on Israeli territory on 9 May 1973, at a time when there were clashes between the Lebanese Army and the PLO forces in southern Lebanon; there were also early signs that Egypt and Syria were preparing for military action against Israel. Hussein sent warnings to Washington that the Egyptian and Syrian military preparations were too realistic to be considered manoeuvres.[4] At the meeting the king asked the prime minister to stop Israeli planes flying over Jordan on their return from surveillance missions in Syria. Meir flatly rejected the request. Syrian threats to attack Israel, she said, made it impossible to accede to the king's request. Another meeting took place on 6 August, which dealt mainly with economic issues such as Israeli encouragement for foreign investment in Jordan, Jordanian–Israeli cooperation in exploiting the mineral resources of the Dead Sea, measures to relieve the housing shortage in Amman and agricultural development in the Jordan Valley. A peace settlement was no longer on the agenda for the top-level bilateral meetings.[5]

Israel's diplomatic intransigence and Arab threats of war placed Hussein in an awkward position. He did not want to repeat the mistake he had made in 1967 of allowing other Arab leaders to drag Jordan into a war with Israel for which Jordan had been completely unprepared. To do so it was necessary to communicate with the leaders of the other confrontation states, but both Egypt and Syria had broken off diplomatic relations with Jordan: Egypt over the United Arab Kingdom plan and Syria over Black September. So in early December 1972 Hussein sent Zaid Rifa'i on a secret mission to Cairo to meet with Sadat. The meeting lasted six hours, and Sadat was very frank. He told Rifa'i, "I know I am not Tarzan. I realize my limitations. I am not good at blitzkrieg. The Israelis are good at blitzkrieg. I will fight a war of political reactivation and not of military liberation. I will wage a limited war: cross the canal, secure a bridgehead and stop. Then I will ask the Security Council to call for a ceasefire. This strategy will ensure my victory in the battle, cut my losses and reactivate the peace process." Rifa'i pointed out to his host the risks involved in this strategy, but Sadat was not convinced. On the other hand, Sadat welcomed Rifa'i's suggestion that the king visit him in Cairo. At first Sadat stipulated conditions for the meeting but later dropped them and invited Hussein to join him and President Asad of Syria for a three-day summit in Cairo, beginning 10 September 1973.[6]

The main items on the agenda of the Cairo summit were to settle the differences between the three countries, to coordinate their military–political strategy and to re-establish diplomatic relations. Hussein conceded that if Israel refused to withdraw from the occupied territories, the Arabs would only be left with the option of liberating them by military means. But he stressed that war required careful preparation and the support of the oil-producing states. Sadat's comment was that the confrontation states alone had the responsibility for liberating their own territories. He then dropped the subject of war and raised the subject of the PLO, hinting that Jordan would have to take back the Palestinian guerrillas as the price for restoring diplomatic relations. Hussein refused point blank and threatened to leave Cairo. Sadat backed down and agreed to re-establish diplomatic relations with Jordan immediately; Asad pretended he needed to consult his colleagues and a few days later Syria announced the re-establishment of formal relations with Jordan. The summit thus looked like a triumph for the king: "War was discussed as a possible option but only after proper preparation. For the time being Jordan would be expected to play a purely defensive role and deter an Israeli attack on the rear of Syrian forces through Jordan. Relations were re-established with Jordan and the king did not give in to Sadat's conditions."[7]

What Hussein did not know at the time was that during his stay in Cairo, Sadat and Asad held a secret meeting to put the final touches on a joint war plan. What Asad did not know was that Sadat had his own separate war plan. After the war, Asad told Zaid Rifa'i that Sadat had double-crossed him. The two leaders agreed to wage war to liberate their occupied territories, but Sadat planned only a limited war to reactivate the political process. In accordance with the joint plan, the Syrian Army would go into battle to liberate the whole of the Golan Heights. Sadat's war aim, however, was much more limited. Instead of keeping up his attack against the Israeli Army in Sinai and advancing to the Giddi and Mitla Passes, he crossed the canal and stopped. This, Asad complained, enabled Israel to concentrate all its might against Syria.[8] What is reasonably clear about this generally murky summit is that Sadat and Asad did not divulge to Hussein their war plan. Support for Hussein's assertion that he was not told at the summit of the plan to go to war comes from an unexpected source: Abu Iyad (Salah Khalaf), the PLO leader. Abu Iyad wrote in his memoirs that he, Yasser Arafat and Faruk Qaddumi heard from Sadat about the imminent war on 9 September, whereas Hussein, who arrived in Cairo the following day, was told nothing: Sadat informed the PLO leaders that he had no intention of breathing a word to Hussein. The main purpose of the summit, said Sadat, was to restore normal relations with Jordan in order to create suitable conditions on the "Eastern Front" during the coming hostilities.[9]

Hussein's next secret meeting was with Meir in Tel Aviv on 25 September 1973. Less than two weeks later, on 6 October, Egypt and Syria launched their carefully coordinated attack against the Israeli Army in Sinai and in the Golan Heights. In Israel this war became known as the Yom Kippur War because it started on the Day of Atonement, the holiest day in the Jewish calendar; in the Arab world it is usually referred to as Operation Bader or the Ramadan War; and the most commonly used name is the October War. The proximity between the three dates gave rise to suspicions in Arab quarters that Hussein went to meet with the Israeli leader to give her advance warning of the imminent Egyptian–Syrian attack. These allegations make the meeting of 25 September more controversial than any of Hussein's numerous other meetings with Israeli leaders. Hussein routinely denied the rumours about these meetings, but, if pressed, he could have argued that direct contact was necessary for the defence of his country and that he never conceded a single inch of Arab territory to Israel. On the other hand, if Hussein disclosed to the Israelis secret Arab war plans, he would have been a traitor to the Arab cause. Hence Hussein's anger at the tendentious Israeli leaks from this particular meeting and the lengths to which he went to rebut the specific Arab allegations of duplicity and betrayal.[10] Special care is therefore called for in analysing the meeting that preceded the October War.

The meeting was arranged at short notice in response to a request made by the king on 23 September. The principal participants were Hussein; Zaid Rifa'i, who had become prime minister in May 1973; General Fathi Abu Taleb, the director of military intelligence; and, for the Israelis, Meir and Mordechai Gazit, the director-general of the prime minister's office. Hussein flew his helicopter from his house in Shuneh and landed on the Israeli side of the Dead Sea near the Caves of Komran.[11] An IAF helicopter then flew the Jordanians to the outskirts of Tel Aviv, and the rest of the journey was completed in cars provided by the General Security Service (Shabak). The meeting took place in the Midrasha, the Mossad headquarters in Herzelia, just north of Tel Aviv, and lasted about three hours, from nine in the evening until close to midnight. The meeting of Hussein, Rifa'i, Meir and Gazit was secretly filmed and transmitted by CCTV to another room in the building where Meir's military secretary and three senior intelligence officers were sitting. At the same time, General Fathi Abu Taleb met in another room with Colonel Aharon Lavran from Israeli military intelligence and with Zvi Zamir, the director of the Mossad.[12]

Hussein opened the meeting with a description of the Cairo summit of 10–12 September. He commented favourably on Sadat's courtesy and kindness but was much more reserved about Asad. He stressed that neither Sadat nor Asad was prepared to tolerate a continuing state of neither peace nor war; he added that he too shared their view but hoped that before Arab patience was exhausted something would happen to prevent war from breaking out. In this connection he reported that the two other leaders sounded him out for his opinion about the renewal of the eastern front and that his reply was: "Leave me alone." Meir questioned Hussein about his intentions to allow the fedayeen to return to his kingdom. He replied that he intended to allow the PLO and other fedayeen organizations to open offices in Jordan but that he would prevent them from undertaking any military or terrorist operations from his territory. After reassuring Meir on this score, the two leaders moved on to discuss the Soviet arms that had started flowing to Egypt and Syria.[13] At this point Hussein became more specific and said the following:

HUSSEIN: From a very, very sensitive source in Syria, [from whom] we have had information in the past and passed it on, [we have learned that] all the units that were meant to be in training and were prepared to take part in this Syrian action are now, as of the last two days or so, in position of pre-attack. That were meant to be part of the plan, except for one minor modification— the Third Division is meant also to cater for any possible Israeli movement through Jordan on their flank. That includes their aircraft, their missiles and everything else that is out on the front at this stage. Now this has all come under the guise of training but in accordance with the information we had previously, these are the pre-jump positions and all the units are now in these positions. Whether it means anything or not, nobody knows. But I have my doubts. However, one cannot be sure. One must take those as facts.

MEIR: Is it conceivable that the Syrians would start something without full cooperation with the Egyptians?

HUSSEIN: I don't think so. I think they would cooperate.[14]

Whether this passage amounted to a warning of war is a subject of some contention in Israel. Hussein did not speak of an Arab war plan but about the situation on the Syrian front, referring to Egypt only in response to a question. He did not say that Syria was planning to attack but that it was ready to attack without further preparations. Meir's critics claimed that she should have questioned him much more closely and probed for further information, but the king was not a prisoner of war under interrogation, he was a friendly head of state who had come on his own initiative because he was worried and wanted to share his concern with one of the parties involved. Alerting Israel to the danger of war was, perhaps, a service to the enemy but it was also an attempt to protect the security of his own country. The charge that Meir did not heed her visitor's warning is baseless. As soon as the meeting ended, close to midnight, she called Dayan at his home and repeated to him what she had just heard. Dayan convened two meetings the following day to evaluate the conversation as well as all the other data at their disposal. The consensus among the Israeli experts, with one or two exceptions, was that there was nothing new in what the king had to say: his information about Syrian military deployments simply confirmed what the IDF already knew. This was also the opinion of Zvi Zamir, the director of the Mossad. Zamir noted that throughout the meeting the king argued that the status quo would lead to military confrontation but he gave no date and did not speak of cooperation between the Syrians and the Egyptians.[15] Furthermore, Zamir was distressed by the publicity given to the meeting and took a dim view of those Israelis who created the impression that Hussein was an agent of the Mossad.[16]

The present author interviewed three of the participants at that meeting: Hussein, Rifa'i and Gazit. All denied that specific Arab war plans were revealed or discussed at the meeting. Hussein replied as follows:

I can only say that, as far as I was concerned, I was caught completely off guard. I was riding a motorbike with my late wife [Alia] behind me in the suburbs of Amman when a security car behind started flashing us to stop and then I was told that a war had started. I had no idea that anything of that nature would happen and certainly not at that time. I had met with Anwar Sadat and Hafiz al-Asad in Cairo shortly before the outbreak of war. We didn't have relations with either of them at the time. Egypt restored relations and Asad didn't until the day before the war, if I am not mistaken. Sadat wanted the fedayeen to be permitted back into Jordan and I refused that. At the same time we were told that they were afraid of an Israeli attack through Jordan and I said that if that ever happened, we will fight it. We were not going to leave our territory open for anyone. So they seemed satisfied with that and I returned to Jordan and a few days later we had the October War. We were totally excluded from any knowledge of what the plan was.

After this emphatic denial, Hussein was asked for his reaction to Ezer Weizmann's assessment that he made two big mistakes in his relations with Israel: one in joining in the June War and the other in not joining in the October War. After reviewing at length the road to war in 1967, Hussein continued: "In 1973 I wasn't a part of it and, in any event, I had embarked on a course of trying to achieve peace and I could not be double-faced about it even if they [Sadat and Asad] had told me about the plan to go to war. Thank God I wasn't told anyway."[17]

Zaid Rifa'i insisted that Hussein could not have given advance warning of the October War for at least three reasons. First, he would never have betrayed the Arab cause for the sake of the Israelis or anyone else. Second, Hussein was invited to the Cairo summit to restore diplomatic relations, not to participate in planning a war. Third, Rifa'i dismissed the notion that Jordan could have information that no other intelligence service had. How could anyone in their right mind, he asked, think that Jordanian military intelligence was more capable than the Mossad, the CIA, MI6 or the KGB? And even if Jordan had information that no one else did, was it conceivable that it would share it only with Israel? Hussein did not prepare for a war, Rifa'i concluded, because he did not know there was going to be one.[18]

The background to Mordechai Gazit's testimony is the claim by Major-General Eli Zeira that at the meeting of 25 September Hussein passed on to Meir a warning about the approaching war and that she failed to appreciate the significance of what he said or to act on his warning.[19] Zeira was the director of military intelligence in 1973. The Agranat Commission of Inquiry held him and Chief of Staff David Elazar responsible for the intelligence failure that preceded the October War, and both were forced to resign. Meir and Dayan, who were responsible for the policy failure that made the war inevitable, were allowed to stay in their posts. Zeira, not unreasonably, felt that it was unfair to blame only the military echelon and to exonerate their political counterparts. But his account of Hussein's visit is coloured by the desire to shift responsibility for the intelligence failure from himself to the prime minister. Writing and talking to the press about this meeting was in itself an indiscreet act that damaged both Zeira's credibility and, more importantly, Israel's relations with a friendly Arab king. Mordechai Gazit is an honest civil servant with no axe to grind. He regards the allegations made by Zeira as groundless.

According to Gazit, Hussein did not come to warn Meir of an impending war but to review the situation and to underline the dangers of the continuing stalemate. Gazit also had the impression that Hussein wanted to share with Meir his thoughts following the Cairo summit. Sadat had become president in 1970 and this was Hussein's first meeting with him. What Sadat told him had implications for Israel as well as for Jordan. Gazit did detect a note of urgency in what the king had to say. Hussein's message was that the Arabs could not go on waiting for ever; that the situation of no war and no peace was inherently unstable; and that the danger of war was increasing all the time. In this connection Hussein also pointed out that the Syrian Army was fully mobilized on the border and that it was ready for war. When Meir asked him whether Syria would dare attack Israel without Egypt, he replied that this was unlikely. Hussein did not come to talk about something that was about to happen immediately but to warn that the situation was intolerable and that it could not go on like that indefinitely. Switching suddenly from Hebrew to English, Gazit exclaimed, "This is the whole story. You have to believe me. I was there!"[20]

The attack on 6 October 1973 caught the Israelis by surprise, and this helped the Arabs to score impressive military victories in the first few days of the fighting. The Egyptian Army crossed the Suez Canal in force, captured the Bar-Lev line of strongholds along the canal, advanced twenty kilometres into Sinai, and inflicted heavy losses on Israel in troops, tanks and aircraft. The Syrian Army launched a highly effective armoured thrust on the Golan Heights, and for a short period it seemed unstoppable. Hussein's main preoccupation following the outbreak of war was the protection of his country. But the poor state of IDF preparedness, with only seventy tanks deployed along the entire eastern front, constituted a temptation to engage in the battle. The king's advisers were divided. Rifa'i was opposed to Jordanian involvement, as was Amer Khammash, the former chief of staff. Mreiwad Tall, the king's private secretary, and a number of army commanders, on the other hand, believed that Jordan should fight. Some members of the cabinet also thought that the regime could not sit out a war in which its fellow Arab states were fighting with the avowed aim of liberating the occupied territories.[21] Arab leaders with whom Hussein was in almost daily contact were also giving him conflicting advice. Sadat encouraged Hussein to maintain his defensive posture because a third front could get in the way of his strictly limited political ends. Asad, on the other hand, kept urging Hussein to open a third front and to commit his 70,000-strong army to the battle for the liberation of the West Bank and Jerusalem. Hussein was always a good listener, and during the war he listened to a wide range of opinions, but the Hussein of 1973 was very different to the one who jumped on Nasser's bandwagon in 1967. Then Hussein had been impatient, impulsive and imprudent. He paid the price and learned his lesson. Now he was much more calm, cautious and calculating. At the outset he settled on a defensive strategy and adhered to it, despite all the conflicting pressures and the vicissitudes of war. He found a formula that enabled him to participate in the war while avoiding a military confrontation along the Jordanian–Israeli front.

While walking a tightrope between Israel and the Arabs, Hussein also had to deal with the rival superpowers. The Soviet Union was encouraging other Arab states, particularly Algeria and Jordan, to enter the fray. On 9 October the Soviet chargé in Amman told Hussein that the Soviet Union fully supported the Arabs in the conflict with Israel and thought that all the Arab states should enter the battle. Sadat also reversed his position and started putting pressure on Hussein to join the battle. Hussein had the idea of sending an armoured brigade to Syria in order to avoid the more dangerous course of opening a third front by attacking Israel along the Jordan River. Henry Kissinger appealed to Hussein to delay any decision for at least 48 hours. Kissinger said that he was making a major effort through diplomatic channels to end the fighting and that he needed Hussein's help. "Hussein did not reply, which was prudent, but he accepted the recommendation, which was statesmanlike."[22] On the same day Hussein received a stern message from Israel warning him of the consequences of opening a front along the Jordan River. The warning was required because of the enormous risk that the IDF took in moving its only strategic reserve division from the central front to the northern front. Some Israeli generals wanted to move this division to the southern front. One of the arguments for moving it north was that dealing a serious blow to Syria might deter Hussein from entering the war.[23]

Popular support was building up in the Arab world for participation in what was being described as a battle of destiny. King Faisal appealed to Hussein to allow a Saudi brigade stationed in Jordan to move to Syria. At first Hussein refused to give permission but later relented. The Saudi brigade lost its way in Jordan, and Hussein had to send a desert patrol to find it and to lead it to Syria. The PLO did not wish to be left out and started to put pressure on Hussein to allow 1,000 fedayeen to cross from Jordan into southern Israel to carry out sabotage operations. Hussein refused permission because this would have amounted to the opening of a third front against Israel from his territory. Abu Iyad, Yasser Arafat's deputy, called Sadat and asked him to intercede on the PLO's behalf. Sadat doubted that there was much he could do. He suspected that Hussein would enter the battle only after the Israelis had been so severely weakened that they were in no position to give him much trouble. But Sadat passed on the PLO request anyway. Hussein sent Amer Khammash to Cairo to tell Sadat that he was against opening up a Jordanian front because his country lacked air defences and that he preferred to send units of his army to give support on the Syrian front.[24]

Hussein wanted to refurbish his credentials as an Arab nationalist by extending support to a neighbouring Arab state but also to ensure that this did not entail an Israeli attack on his country. In other words, he wanted to have his cake and eat it. In the first instance Hussein approached the British prime minister Edward Heath for help. Late on 11 October, Heath called Kissinger about the ever-mounting pressure on Hussein to do something on behalf of his Arab brethren. Hussein was thinking of moving an armoured brigade into Syria, as much out of harm's way as he could manage. He wanted Israel's acquiescence or at least an assurance that Israel would not use it as a pretext for an attack on Jordan. In his memoirs Kissinger remarked, "Only in the Middle East is it conceivable that a belligerent would ask an adversary's approval for engaging in an act of war against it." Israel predictably refused to agree formally to the reinforcement of its enemies but made no threat of retaliation or of expanding the war. Israel's mild message crossed with one from Hussein telling Kissinger that the 48-hour delay was up and that Jordan had to take the least provocative move, which was to send a brigade to Syria. Jordan's purpose was to counterbalance "Iraqi–Soviet designs" and to contain the conflict within the smallest possible area. Kissinger replied urging Hussein to continue his efforts to circumscribe the area and scale of the fighting.[25]

On 13 October, Jordan's 40th Armoured Brigade was ordered to move to the Golan front. By a curious historical irony, it was the same brigade that in September 1970 had been sent to resist the Syrian invasion. Now it was sent to help the Syrians, but the reception it received was less than cordial. Prince Talal bin Muhammad, Hussein's nephew, described the encounter between the Arab comrades-in-arms: "There was no coordination between the Syrians, the Iraqis and us. The different armies were not talking to each other. We were not met at the border, there was no liaison officer, and nobody showed us where the frontline was. We had to make our own way up to the frontline. We groped our way blind to the Golan Heights. It was complete chaos. The Saudis sent a brigade. They went up a hill one night and they decided to go to sleep, only to wake up the next morning surrounded by Israeli soldiers. They did not know what they were doing. As in 1967, they showed up after the fighting was over. Their artillery did not even have ammunition. It was a typical Arab shambles."[26]

While the 40th Armoured Brigade moved to the Golan front, the bridges across the Jordan remained open to traffic in both directions, indicating that there was no war between Jordan and Israel. In his memoirs Dayan noted that "The Jordanians never threatened to open war and when they sent a unit of theirs to help the Syrian Army in the Yom Kippur War—this did not come to us as a surprise."[27] Dayan knew that Hussein sent a brigade to the Golan in order to avoid a direct confrontation with Israel. Dayan was worried, however, that if Syria looked like gaining the upper hand, Jordan might be tempted to open a third front. He therefore ordered the Israeli chief of staff to intensify the attacks on Syria with a view to deterring Jordan. Army headquarters received intelligence that the Jordanian brigade was ready to go on the offensive. On 16 October the Israeli cabinet authorized the army to hit any Jordanian unit that got involved directly in fighting but without extending operations into Jordanian territory. That day a short and sharp encounter took place on the Golan Heights in which the Jordanian unit lost twenty-two tanks to Israeli fire and six to Iraqi fire: the Iraqis mistook the Jordanian Centurions for Israeli tanks. The fighting did not spread, but the Jordanians continued to reinforce their expeditionary force with armour, artillery and infantry. By the time the ceasefire came into force on 22 October, Jordan had almost a division on the northern front.[28]

It was obvious from the start that something had gone wrong on the Arab side on the northern front. The Syrian, Iraqi and Jordanian attacks were uncoordinated, with Israel only too well prepared to take advantage of the confusion. Major-General Chaim Herzog, later the president of Israel, observed: "Inter-Arab coordination proved to be very faulty on the battlefield. Every morning between 10:00 and 11:00 hours, a counter-attack was mounted against the southern flank of the Israeli enclave by the Iraqis and Jordanians, supported by the Syrian and Iraqi air forces. Rarely did they succeed in coordinating and establishing a common language: on two occasions the Jordanians attacked while the Iraqis failed to join in; frequently Iraqi artillery support fell on the advancing or withdrawing Jordanians; and, on a number of occasions, Syrian aircraft attacked and shot down Iraqi aircraft. In general, the Iraqi forces moved slowly and cautiously, and were led without any imagination or flair."[29]

An episode that is particularly revealing of the intricate nature of Jordanian–Israeli relations during the October War involved the Israelis' unwillingness to kill Hussein. One day the IAF received orders to bomb a Jordanian unit because it blocked the path of advance of the Israeli Army towards Damascus. By coincidence, one of the officers at the front was Ze'ev Bar-Lavie, the head of the "Jordan desk" in the IDF Military Intelligence branch. Looking across the enemy lines through binoculars, he picked up a few clues of unusual activity that suggested to him that the king was visiting his troops at the front. Bar-Lavie, who had a particular fondness for the king, hurriedly consulted with the intelligence chief and with the chief of staff, and they decided not to bomb the gathering. It was a decision that may well have spared Hussein's life. At a much later meeting with Zvi Zamir, Hussein confirmed that he had been at the front and thanked him for sparing his life.[30]

So in the October War, as in the First Arab–Israeli War of 1948, Israel and Jordan were "the best of enemies." Whereas the relations between the Israelis and Hussein were characterized by respect and mutual restraint, inter-Arab relations were marked by profound mistrust and bitter rivalry. One of the little known aspects of the October War is the secret channel that Sadat had with Kissinger. It was through this channel that Sadat requested, on 20 October, a ceasefire without consulting or informing Asad, thereby beginning the break-up of the Egyptian–Syrian alliance. Nor did Sadat bother to inform Hussein of his unilateral decision to terminate hostilities. On the contrary, just as he was preparing to bring the war to an end, Sadat made an effort to get Jordan involved. He did this by renewing the request to Hussein to allow the fedayeen to cross from Jordan to carry out sabotage operations in southern Israel. Hussein stalled, sensing that the project made no military sense, and suspecting that Sadat's real motive was to drag Jordan into the war.[31] The plan for a Security Council ceasefire to be followed by negotiations between the parties on a fundamental settlement was revealed to Hussein by the American secretary of state. On 18 October, Kissinger wrote, "In such a settlement, Your Majesty, it is inconceivable that the interests of Jordan . . . would not be fully protected . . . Your views will, I can assure you, be given the full weight they deserve."[32] These assurances were transparently insincere and worthless.

After the guns fell silent on the Sinai and Golan fronts, the turn of the diplomats came on 26 October 1973. The most important figure in the international diplomacy surrounding the Arab–Israeli conflict in the aftermath of war was Henry Kissinger, and the key to understanding this diplomacy is the collusion between Kissinger and Sadat. Sadat knew that Asad would not agree to make peace with Israel unless Israel withdrew from all the occupied Arab territories. Sadat also knew that the West Bank was the core of the Arab–Israeli conflict and that Israel would never agree to complete withdrawal from it. This left the possibility of a separate Israeli–Egyptian deal over Sinai. Kissinger was more than happy to proceed along these lines. He was the chief proponent on the American side of the strategic partnership with Israel. Now Egypt, the largest and most powerful of the Arab states, was offering itself as a second major ally alongside Israel. One did not have to be a Harvard professor of international relations to grasp the potential for excluding the Soviet Union from the Middle East and for building up *pax Americana* on the twin pillars of the two strongest countries in the region. This is what Kissinger proceeded to try to achieve. In the pipe-smoking Egyptian leader, Kissinger found a congenial companion for playing the game of nations. Sentiments, morality and justice did not count, only state interests. Jordan, a friendly but feeble Arab state, was assigned a very minor role in this grand design. Its role was to enable Kissinger and Sadat to dress up what was essentially a bilateral Egyptian–Israeli deal as a first step towards comprehensive peace in the Middle East.

17. The Road to Rabat

On 22 October 1973 the UN Security Council passed Resolution 338, calling on the parties to cease hostilities and to begin direct negotiations for a settlement of the conflict on the basis of Resolution 242. Israel, Egypt and Jordan promptly accepted but Syria did so only after a short delay to register its resentment at not being consulted. Hussein was not only willing but anxious to engage in direct negotiations with Israel to restore Jordan's sovereignty over the West Bank, but he was let down by both Israel and the United States.[1] With the ceasefire in place, Kissinger embarked on his first trip to the Middle East to prepare the ground for an international conference. He arrived in Amman on 8 November at the end of his tour of the capitals of the region. Hussein received him with his customary courtesy, and stated his position clearly: Jordan was the Arab country most involved in the conflict in terms of both territory and population; it was its duty to recover the West Bank with minor changes on a reciprocal basis; and it could not give up its responsibility for the Muslim and Christian parts of Jerusalem. In his memoirs Kissinger wrote, "It was one of our sorrows that our best Arab friend was at the periphery of this phase of the peace process."[2] But Kissinger's actions suggest that he was in fact two-faced, colluding with Egypt and Israel to keep Jordan marginalized.

Hussein was clearly concerned that his interests in the Palestinian question would be neglected in the American-dominated peace process. Kissinger told him that the best way for these to be protected would be for Jordan to become a founding member of the Geneva Peace Conference: this would make it a spokesman for the Palestinians. Hussein agreed to attend the conference, hoping that it would lead to a comprehensive settlement of the conflict on the basis of UN resolutions 242 and 338—now the cornerstones of Jordanian foreign policy. Kissinger's purpose, however, was limited to preserving the ceasefire, separating the combatants, and enabling Israel and Egypt to proceed to a bilateral settlement. He knew that Jordanian participation would necessitate negotiations over the West Bank and, sooner or later, Jerusalem—subjects he wished to avoid.

The conference opened in Geneva on 21 December formally under the auspices of the UN and with the United States and the Soviet Union as co-sponsors. Kurt Waldheim, the UN secretary-general, chaired the opening session but the choreography was arranged by the hyperactive American secretary of state to suit his own agenda. Israel, Egypt and Jordan accepted the invitation but President Asad of Syria declined because the conference did not have the clear objective of bringing about Israeli withdrawal from all the occupied Arab territories, and Israel vetoed PLO participation. Jordan was represented by Prime Minister Zaid Rifa'i. This was the most peculiar conference Rifa'i had ever attended, with no terms of reference, no rules of procedure and no agenda.

In his opening speech Rifa'i insisted on the complete withdrawal of Israeli forces from all the occupied territories, including East Jerusalem. Stressing that Syria's absence from the conference did not prejudice its right to demand Israel's withdrawal from the Golan Heights, Rifa'i declared, "The question of withdrawal, boundaries, Palestinian rights, refugees, obligations of peace and the status of Jerusalem are all common concerns and collective responsibilities. My delegation therefore is not prepared to conclude any partial settlement with Israel on matters that are of joint interest with our Arab brothers." Egypt's foreign minister, Ismail Fahmy, refused to coordinate with Rifa'i before the conference started and failed to exchange even a word with him while it took place. In his opening speech Fahmy referred to the West Bank as Palestinian territory, thus implicitly denying Jordan's right to represent the Palestinians. Abba Eban stressed in his speech that Israel would not return to the 1967 lines and that Jerusalem was its eternal, united capital. Kissinger proposed the formation of a joint Egyptian–Israeli military working group to discuss the disengagement of forces. Rifa'i objected and said that the purpose of the conference was to implement Security Council resolutions and to arrive at a comprehensive settlement. Kissinger replied that comprehensive peace could not be attained immediately but only result from a series of steps. This gave Rifa'i the opportunity to propose the formation of a Jordanian–Israeli working group to discuss disengagement on their two fronts. Eban objected to this, arguing that their forces were not actually engaged and that the withdrawal of Israeli forces from any part of the West Bank could be discussed only within the framework of an overall settlement and a peace treaty. Rifa'i's protests that Jordan was being penalized for not participating in the war were in vain.

Rifa'i began to suspect that the real purpose of the conference was to provide diplomatic cover for a separate Egyptian–Israeli accord. This suspicion was confirmed in 1988 by Peter Rodman, an American official who had accompanied Kissinger to the conference. Rodman said that Geneva had a limited end: a disengagement agreement between Israel and Egypt. He also intimated that a secret agreement had been made between America, Israel and Egypt before the conference convened. Even before this admission of Kissinger's and Sadat's duplicity, Hussein had concluded, on the basis of the actual outcome of the conference, that it was no more than an elaborate charade to provide legitimacy and to pave the way for a separate deal between Egypt and Israel.[3] Geneva was not a proper international conference but a con. The inaugural session of this peculiar gathering turned out to be its last. Jordan was left holding an empty bag.

Following the adjournment of the Geneva conference, Kissinger embarked on what became known as his "shuttle diplomacy." The first fruit of this was the military disengagement agreement between Israel and Egypt, which was signed on 18 January 1974. Kissinger's next target was a military disengagement between Israel and Syria but in the meantime he needed to stop in Jordan "to demonstrate that King Hussein, that moderate ruler and old friend, would not suffer for his refusal to pressure us." Hussein invited Kissinger to visit him in Aqaba, Jordan's holiday resort on the Red Sea. Still a passionate pilot, Hussein would occasionally fly out to greet visitors to whom he wished to pay special respect. "On this occasion," wrote Kissinger, "it pleased His Majesty to come out in a helicopter and perform aerobatics in the narrow space between the right wing of *SAM 86970* [Boeing plane] and the Saudi mountains. Had there been a Jordanian official aboard our plane, he could have easily got us to sign any document as the price of getting his monarch to return to earth." On Saturday afternoon, 19 January, they met in Hussein's bungalow by the sea, 800 meters from the barbed-wire fence that denoted the frontier with Israel. Hussein, his brother

Crown Prince Hassan, Prime Minister Zaid Rifa'i and Chief of Staff General Zaid bin Shaker received the Americans as friends. The Jordanians were warm in their praise of the disengagement agreement. Hussein described it as a tremendous achievement.

Kissinger sensed that this achievement also filled his Jordanian hosts with foreboding. They recognized that Syria had to be next, but they wanted to be sure that their turn would come soon after. In the meantime, they wanted some working-level discussions on an initial Israeli withdrawal from the West Bank, emulating the procedures in the Egyptian case. "Jordan's nightmare was that its Arab brethren would deprive it of the right to recover the territory it had lost to Israel in 1967. Jordan, in fact, had two nightmares about the West Bank: either indefinite Israeli occupation or a PLO state whose first target would be the Hashemite Kingdom." Kissinger claims that he was sympathetic and that he shared Hussein's strategic assessment. "Either it [Israel] can deal with Arafat or it can deal with Your Majesty. If I were an Israeli Prime Minister . . . I would rush into negotiations with Your Majesty because that is the best guarantee against Arafat." But stating the alternatives did not advance matters, because Israel wanted neither.

So the discussions in Aqaba were a replay of what had occurred on Kissinger's previous visit in November. On that occasion he had presented to Israeli leaders Rifa'i's suggestion of a very modest "disengagement," involving principally withdrawal from the city of Jericho with its exclusively Arab population and its location close to the Jordan River. Jericho would have symbolized Hussein's claim to the West Bank and established him as Israel's interlocutor in West Bank negotiations. The suggestion had been rejected as inconsistent with the Allon Plan, which claimed the Jordan Valley as Israel's security border. Kissinger suggested that since Yigal Allon was in the room, there was nothing to keep the author from modifying his plan. This was treated as a joke. But when Kissinger asked whether some disengagement scheme based on the Allon Plan could be put forward, he hit an obstacle: the Allon Plan could not be the basis of disengagement on the Jordanian front because the Labour Party's coalition partner, the National Religious Party, was absolutely opposed to giving up any territory on the West Bank. "Thus Israel would reject a proposal inconsistent with the Allon plan but would refuse to negotiate the Allon Plan because it could not get the full cabinet behind."[4] Kissinger's analysis of the Israeli position is accurate enough. What he does not say is that he himself, for his own reasons, wanted to avoid negotiations on the West Bank. In countless private conversations Kissinger in fact encouraged Israeli intransigence by telling Allon: "If I were you, I wouldn't settle for less than the Allon Plan."[5]

At the meeting in Aqaba, Hussein put forward another disengagement plan in which Jordan and Israel would each pull back their military forces eight kilometres from the river to the foothills of the mountain ranges that marked the Jordan Valley. Jordanian civil administration would be established in the area vacated by Israel, especially in the town of Jericho. A working group would be formed as rapidly as possible to establish Jordan's claim to represent the Palestinians. Kissinger was non-committal. He told the king that he would discuss his ideas with the Israelis in the coming weeks. Kissinger describes Hussein's approach as moderate and statesmanlike but futile while a new Israeli coalition was being formed, including a party that opposed any territorial change on the West Bank. That state of affairs, according to Kissinger, precluded even the formation of a working group.[6]

None the less, Hussein persevered in his efforts to engage in the diplomatic process. Kissinger's obvious reluctance to involve Jordan in his step-by-step diplomacy impelled Hussein to renew his direct contacts across the river. In the early part of 1974 he had two meetings with Meir, who was facing a storm of domestic protest for the failure to anticipate the Arab attack. With great difficulty she managed to assemble a coalition government following the election of 31 December 1973 but this government had the shortest lifespan in Israel's history. Even at the height of her power Meir was not noted for her flexibility but now she had less room for manoeuvre than ever before. Hussein had little enough himself. Rifa'i accompanied him to both meetings with Meir and her ministers. By this time Rifa'i had gained a great deal of experience in regional and international diplomacy, and had grown considerably in stature and authority. There was a division of labour between the Jordanian monarch and his prime minister in accordance with the model prescribed in the constitution: the monarch determined the broad lines of policy, while the prime minister was in charge of carrying it out. The monarch set the tone; the prime minister's role was to deal with the details, to clarify the issues and to dispel ambiguity. He also took notes during the discussion and produced records after the meetings.[7] Hussein was courteous, soft-spoken and skilful at creating a congenial atmosphere for negotiations; Rifa'i was a shrewd and hard-headed politician and a tough negotiator who robustly defended Jordanian interests. They were an impressive duo, but they had a very weak hand to play.

On 26 January 1974 Hussein and Rifa'i crossed into Israeli territory to meet with Meir, Dayan and Gazit. The meeting took place in the Araba Desert on the border between the two countries in an air-conditioned caravan. Both sides wanted to move forward towards a disengagement agreement, but they had conflicting ideas about the nature and scale of Israeli withdrawal from the West Bank. Essentially, the Israelis thought in terms of very limited disengagement, whereas the Jordanians demanded vertical disengagement along the entire front. Meir favoured a gradual approach and offered to restore to Jordanian rule the city of Jericho and the heavily populated Arab areas at the centre of the West Bank. Although this was a modest offer, Meir emphasized that it was only a beginning and not the end of the process.[8] Hussein, on the other hand, demanded that Israel vacate a strip of land along the entire length of the Jordan River, which would have entailed the dismantling of some Israeli settlements. He regarded her offer as a rehashed version of the Allon Plan, which he had repeatedly rejected as "totally unacceptable." The rationale behind his demand was that even a modest Israeli retreat along the entire ceasefire line would give the Palestinians hope for the future and restore their faith in Jordan.[9] The following dialogue took place:

HUSSEIN: If you agree in principle to my proposal for an Israeli withdrawal from the Jordan River to a depth of fifteen kilometres, enabling me to establish a Jordanian civil administration in this strip, we can move on in stages to its implementation. It will help us distance the Palestinians from the PLO.

MEIR: It's possible to find other ways of separating [our forces] through a corridor connecting you to the Palestinian population.

HUSSEIN: We refuse to be confined to a narrow corridor to the West Bank; and there will be no progress without your withdrawal from the Jordan Valley.

DAYAN: This means that the IDF must pull back from the entire valley?

RIFA'I: Yes, definitely. But we shall not introduce a Jordanian army there.

DAYAN: And what about Jewish settlements in the Jordan Valley?

RIFA'I: They must be totally removed.

DAYAN: If so, what will your final border be?
RIFA'I: Identical with the 1967 lines. We are ready to achieve this in stages.

The dialogue continued but the deadlock could not be broken. Dayan was adamant that in any accommodation, the Jewish settlements and military bases in the Jordan Valley had to stay in place. Meir added that to get agreement even to a corridor from the Knesset would be a tough struggle. Rifa'i was no less adamant that withdrawal could not begin with a corridor. "We need 'frontage' along the entire Jordan River," he said to the Israeli premier. "If the Allon Plan is Israel's goal, there's no prospect of a settlement." So as not to end on a sour note and to keep the lines of communication open, Hussein concluded by saying, "Even if there's no agreement, we could continue with our good relations."[10]

A second meeting with the same cast of characters took place in the same caravan on 7 March. Once again Hussein raised the demand for an Israeli withdrawal along the entire front. Meir pointed out that the disengagement with Egypt was not from the whole Suez line but only from part of it. Hussein's response betrayed his frustration: "Would I have had to fight you in the October War to bring you to a disengagement agreement along the whole border?" The discussion did not go anywhere:

HUSSEIN: If there is peace, we'll prevent terrorism, but as long as you reject our proposals they [the Palestinians] get stronger . . .
MEIR: What if the Palestinians on the West Bank want to establish an independent Palestinian state?
HUSSEIN: It will be all right. Such a state would be like a sandwich between you and us and there is nothing to fear.
DAYAN: Can strongholds and settlements remain under Israeli sovereignty?
HUSSEIN: It is difficult for us to accept that.

Dayan continued to press for an Israeli presence in the Jordan Valley but Rifa'i rejected this idea much more categorically than the king. Dayan threatened to ask the Palestinian leaders on the West Bank whether they would agree to Israel's presence there in return for suitable payment. Rifa'i dismissed the threat by stating confidently that they would not agree. Dayan said, "We'll either strive for an agreement with the Palestinians or you agree to significant border changes." Rifa'i retorted, "At the moment we are discussing the separation of forces." Meir became agitated. The question, she said, was: did the Jordanians accept Israel's right to be on the West Bank? She pleaded with Hussein to move forward step by step without a commitment to total Israeli retreat at the end of the road. She pointed out that the separation of forces with Egypt did not require Israel to pull out of Sharm el-Sheikh. "Why is what I am proposing," she asked, "so unacceptable to you?" "The reasons," replied Hussein, "are psychological. You created a psychological problem with the Allon Plan." Another point made by Hussein was that the Palestinians could be more generous in making concessions with their own territory and their own rights than he could. "I most certainly have no such right nor the will to exercise it on their behalf," he added with uncharacteristic bluntness.[11] The meeting ended without any agreement. As Hussein had remarked at the beginning, they were back to square one.

Mordechai Gazit was a largely silent but highly perceptive participant in these meetings. What struck him most was the complete consistency with which Hussein adhered to his basic position, namely, that the price of peace was Israel's withdrawal from all the territory it had captured in 1967, including East Jerusalem. Hussein was prepared to settle for phased withdrawal from the West Bank, provided Israel accepted at the outset the principle that it should eventually be total. At the last meeting Hussein made it crystal clear that he could make no compromises over this territory because it belonged to the Palestinians. This was not a new departure but a more forceful statement of Hussein's consistent position ever since the end of the June War. This principled position stood in marked contrast to the popular Arab view of Hussein as a traitor who was prepared to trade with the Jews on Palestinian rights. Gazit was therefore moved to tell his Palestinian interlocutors that they had no idea how loyal Hussein was to them in all his dealings with Israel or how staunch he was in defence of their interests. Meir was difficult to deal with because she tended to view Arabs as a monolithic and implacable enemy. "Do you know one Arab who is prepared to make peace with us?" she would ask, glowering at her advisers. "King Hussein!" they would reply in unison. She would concede the point about King Hussein but not about any other Arab.[12] It is testimony to Hussein's skills as a diplomat that he managed to remain on good terms until the end with a leader who was unusually truculent and self-righteous, even by Israeli standards. On 10 April, Meir tendered her resignation following the publication of the Agranat Commission's report. The Labour Party chose Itzhak Rabin to succeed her, and a long chapter in Jordanian-Israeli relations came to an end.

One trend was clear: "The longer the delay of negotiations to relieve Israeli occupation of the West Bank, the more inexorable the growth of the political status and weight of the PLO. Stalemate on the West Bank spelled humiliation for King Hussein; it undercut his claim that his moderate course would return Palestinian lands to Arab control."[13] Not surprisingly, Hussein was in a sombre mood when he arrived in Washington. He confided to Kissinger that the Israelis had flatly rejected his proposal for disengagement and countered with their old scheme of inviting him to take over civil administration in the West Bank while their military occupation continued. Kissinger wrote that it was "an amazing reflection of how little the Israelis understood Arab psychology that the proposal was continually put forward; not even the most moderate Arab head of government could accept administering the West Bank under Israeli occupation." Hussein was depressed and seriously considered withdrawing from the negotiations altogether. This, however, would have made the PLO Israel's only valid negotiating partner, and Hussein continued to be convinced that its hostility towards him and his dynasty was implacable. Kissinger shared Hussein's frustration, and during the king's call on Nixon, on 12 March, he said, "Israel hasn't faced what their real alternatives are. They have to deal either with King Hussein or with Arafat. They can't deal with neither."[14] But Kissinger also had his own priorities and these did not include negotiation over the West Bank. His main aim was to exclude the Soviet Union from playing a part in Middle East diplomacy. He embarked again on his solo shuttle diplomacy, and on 31 May delivered a military disengagement agreement between Israel and Syria on the Golan front. Hussein hoped it would be his turn next. But Sadat pressed for a second agreement with Israel that would give him another slice of Sinai, and the political situation in Israel was not conducive to negotiations on the West Bank.

The government that Rabin presented to the Knesset on 3 June was weak and divided. Allon became minister of defence and Peres foreign minister. The trio had different priorities: Rabin favoured negotiations with Egypt; Allon had a pro-Hashemite orientation; and Peres preferred an agreement with the Palestinian leaders on the West Bank. Peres acknowledged that Hussein was willing to conduct negotiations with Israel for a permanent peace settlement, "But he is a weak candidate for peace—because of the weakness of his position . . . His first problem is that of status and authority. A king is not a president or a prime minister. His authority does not spring from popular elections or from an appointment, backed by force, but from a title inherited from his father. Monarchs today are few and rare, and they are fast disappearing from the world's landscape. Even a courageous king is not a representative leader, as is the rule in most modern countries, but is born to the title, as in olden times, and most of his thoughts and energies are inevitably concerned with how to preserve it."[15] Allon was not interested in political legitimacy but in an arrangement that would enable Israel to keep substantial portions of the West Bank without responsibility for its Palestinian population. He knew that Hussein was unwilling to compromise on Arab land, but he believed that sooner or later he would be compelled to accept Israel's terms because he had no alternative if he wished to survive. Allon was also an ardent supporter of the settlement movement in the occupied territories. For him, as for the Zionist leaders in the pre-independence period, settlement established a claim to the land and put paid to the option of negotiations and compromise. In line with this old Zionist logic, the Rabin government continued to expand the settlement project of its predecessors. This project was illegal and, in political terms, a disastrous mistake. Yet, like its predecessors, the Rabin government proceeded on the premise that peace was dispensable while territory was essential.

Rabin and Peres could hardly cooperate in seeking peace with the Arabs because they were at war with one another. As prime minister Rabin suffered from the additional handicap of presiding over a coalition that had the narrowest of parliamentary majorities: 61 supporters in the 120-member Knesset. The National Religious Party (NRP), which had ten seats in the Knesset, declined to join the coalition. In the hope of attracting the NRP, Rabin had at the outset committed his government to hold an election before concluding a peace agreement that involved the surrender of any territory on the West Bank. In September 1974 the NRP joined the coalition, which broadened the parliamentary base of the government but at the same time it seriously curtailed

Rabin's freedom of action in relation to Jordan and the Palestinians. His party was committed to territorial compromise over the West Bank; the NRP was committed to keeping the whole of the West Bank within Greater Israel.

The PLO was gaining international legitimacy but Rabin's position remained firm and inflexible: Israel would never recognize or enter into any negotiations with the PLO and it would not agree to the establishment of a Palestinian state. If personal conviction precluded Rabin from offering anything to the PLO, domestic political constraints precluded him from offering anything of substance to Hussein. Rabin's American friends urged him to talk to the pro-Western monarch. Two weeks after Rabin was sworn in, Richard Nixon (who was soon to lose the presidency because of the Watergate scandal) came to Israel on a state visit. Nixon urged that the military disengagement agreements with Egypt and Syria be followed up with a similar agreement with Jordan.[16] Rabin, however, had tied his own hands by pledging to submit any withdrawal on the West Bank to the verdict of the Israeli electorate, and he was unwilling to risk another election. Consequently, he had nothing to offer Hussein, and the negotiations between them came to nothing. Some of Rabin's advisers favoured "Egypt first," while others favoured "Syria first," but none favoured "Jordan first."[17] Hussein could not make any headway because there was no Israeli partner for peace. The gulf between the two sides could not be bridged and the stalemate persisted.

Although Rabin was not ready for a deal on the West Bank, he valued the contact with Hussein. During the three years of his premiership Rabin, accompanied by Allon and Peres, had half a dozen meetings with the king, who was always accompanied by Zaid Rifa'i. All the meetings took place on Israeli soil, one in Tel Aviv, the rest in Wadi Araba, in the air-conditioned caravan that kept changing its location for security reasons. They would begin with a survey of the regional and global situations, and, since both Rabin and Hussein spoke slowly, this would take a relatively long time. On the Israeli side each meeting was carefully prepared in advance by officials who also produced a detailed record of the discussions. Israel had four main aims in these discussions: to explore the possibilities of a deal with Jordan; to solve minor problems that affected both countries; to promote economic cooperation; and to coordinate policy towards the West Bank and the Palestinian guerrilla organizations. Jordan put forward two proposals in these discussions: an interim agreement involving partial Israeli withdrawal along the Jordan River; and a full peace agreement in return for complete Israeli withdrawal.[18]

The first meeting took place on 28 August 1974. Allon introduced Rabin and Peres to Hussein. The king repeated the proposal he had already made to Meir for a military disengagement involving a withdrawal of about eight kilometres on both sides of the Jordan River. Rabin rejected the proposal out of hand and added that he could not even consider it as an option for the future. Peres then put forward a proposal of his own—another instance of an individual minister floating a proposal to relieve the cabinet of collective responsibility. Peres sought to solve the Palestinian problem by means of an Israeli–Jordanian condominium. He proposed the creation of three political entities: Israel, Jordan and a Palestinian entity that would be administered by them jointly. The Palestinian entity, comprising the West Bank and the Gaza Strip, would be wholly demilitarized and fall under no single sovereignty. The three entities would form a single economic unit, open to the free movement of goods, of persons and of ideas. Peres conceded that his plan might seem fantastic but argued that "fantasy is the only way to solve this situation." The king remarked impatiently that he wanted to talk about the present and that meant a military disengagement agreement. Allon stepped in to save the meeting from failure. He suggested that the town of Jericho and the area surrounding it be turned over to Jordan to set up a civil administration and to serve as a bridgehead to the West Bank. This was simply a new version of the Allon Plan. The king rejected the proposal and restated his demand for an Israeli withdrawal along the entire front, as in the case of Sinai and the Golan Heights. The meeting ended, unsurprisingly, without any agreement being reached.[19]

The second meeting was held on 19 October. An Arab summit conference was scheduled to take place in Rabat at the end of the month and in the Arab world support was rapidly growing for replacing Jordan with the PLO as the representative of the Palestinians. Hussein was now more anxious than ever for a disengagement agreement to shore up his position and to extend his influence on the West Bank. Without an agreement he was in danger of being supplanted by the PLO at the upcoming Arab summit. But Rabin, having just brought the NRP into the government, was unwilling to cede the Jericho enclave, let alone vertical disengagement, because he feared the collapse of his fragile coalition. He was terrified of going forward with Hussein because any territorial concession entailed either the departure of the NRP or new elections. Rabin could have soldiered on without the NRP but he was too passive and pusillanimous to take any risks. It was a classic example of the impact of domestic politics on foreign policy. What it meant in practical terms was that Rabin once again had nothing concrete to offer. Rabin sought to reassure Hussein that his government would have no truck with the PLO. "As far as the Palestinian problem in the West Bank is concerned," said Rabin, "Israel has one and only one partner: Jordan." Peres's ideas of a condominium over the West Bank and Gaza were also predicated on Jordan as Israel's partner in dealing with the Palestinian problem.[20] But secret assurances of Israel's fidelity to the traditional alliance with the Hashemite rulers of Jordan were no substitute for a public disengagement agreement along the lines of the Egyptian and Syrian models. Hussein left the meeting with nothing.

Itzhak Rabin estimated that the chances of a second agreement with Egypt were better than the chances of an agreement with Hussein on the West Bank. Rabin also made it clear to the Americans that Egypt was his first priority. He urged them to leave the Palestinian problem to one side and to focus on Sadat's Egypt. Kissinger's conduct was rather more convoluted and his statements were contradicted by his actions. He too was fixated on a second disengagement agreement between Israel and Egypt, and, in the slightly longer term, on removing Egypt altogether from the circle of the confrontation states surrounding Israel. Kissinger wanted Jordan to attend the Rabat summit. During his last visit to Amman before the summit, his former student, Zaid Rifa'i, told him that there was a serious risk that a resolution would be passed at Rabat to deprive Jordan of the right to negotiate over the West Bank and to appoint the PLO to that role. Kissinger assured Rifa'i that the United States was using its influence in Arab capitals, and that Egypt, Morocco and Saudi Arabia would all reject the pressure from the radical Arab states to promote the PLO at the expense of Jordan. Jordan's position was secure, Kissinger concluded, and there was nothing to worry about. Mreiwad Tall, the private secretary, strongly advised Hussein not to go to Rabat so as not to be bound by any anti-Jordanian decisions that might be taken there. Kissinger's assurances played a part in persuading Hussein to reject this advice and to go. Shortly before the summit, the Moroccan authorities uncovered a Fatah plot to assassinate Hussein on arrival at Rabat. But this did not deter Hussein from attending the Arab League summit.[21]

The Arab heads of state and Yasser Arafat, the chairman of the PLO, convened in Rabat on 26 October. The dispute between Jordan and the PLO dominated the discussions. Hussein opened the discussions with a long speech that emphasized his country's historic responsibility for the fate of the West Bank. He identified two distinct phases in the struggle that lay ahead: liberating the occupied territory and settlement of the Palestinian problem. He urged his colleagues to support Jordan in its efforts to recover the West Bank and promised to give its inhabitants an opportunity to determine their own future once Israel withdrew. Towards the end of the speech came the warning: if the Arab states allocated to the PLO sole responsibility for both phases of the Palestinian problem, they would have to bear the consequences, including withdrawal of the civil administration from the West Bank and ending the payment of salaries of civil servants, judges and teachers by the central government. Yasser Arafat argued in his speech for an exclusive role for the PLO both in the negotiations to recover the West Bank and in determining its future. The vote went in favour of the PLO. Egypt, Morocco and Saudi Arabia all joined the radical states in voting against Jordan. The final resolutions of the summit designated the PLO as "the sole legitimate representative of the Palestinian people" and affirmed the right of the Palestinian people to set up an independent national authority, led by the PLO, on any part of Palestine that was liberated. In the meantime, Jordan was asked not to sever its links with the West Bank. Hussein had always felt very strongly about Jordan's responsibilities towards its citizens under occupation, and he decided, despite his threats, not to desert them. He had no choice but to go along with the summit resolution on Palestinian representation but he did not want the Palestinians under occupation to pay the price. He therefore announced that Jordan would continue its administration of the West Bank and would continue to assist and support its inhabitants until liberation. The Arab leaders gave him a standing ovation.[22]

Despite the round of applause at the end, Hussein regarded the Rabat summit as a major political and diplomatic defeat. He felt let down by Israel, abandoned by the Arab moderates and double-crossed by the

American secretary of state. A month after Rabat, Kissinger stopped in Amman on his tour of the Middle East. Rifa'i reminded him of his assurances that America's Arab allies would back Jordan at the summit. Kissinger's only reply was: "We overestimated our manipulative capabilities." Rifa'i, however, concluded that the Rabat decision was the direct result of Kissinger's machinations. It was clear all along that Israel would refuse to negotiate with the PLO. Kissinger secretly wanted the PLO to replace Jordan as the spokesman for the Palestinian people to ensure that there would be no negotiations over the West Bank. Kissinger undermined Jordan's position not to help the PLO but to help Israel and Egypt move forward towards another bilateral deal over Sinai.[23] Rifa'i assessed the Rabat summit succinctly: "The only way for Kissinger to rid himself of Jordanian demands was to knock us out, once and for all. Kissinger plotted against the Arab nation. And Sadat took part in the plot. The rest of the Arabs fell into the trap."[24] Hussein shared his prime minister's suspicions about the collusion between Kissinger and Sadat on the road to Rabat. But the additional point he chose to stress was that the Arab rulers had their own reason for voting for the Rabat decision: they were tired of the Palestinian problem and by crowning the PLO as the sole representative of the Palestinian people they hoped to divest themselves of further responsibility for it. "The Palestinians wanted their way and their say. The Arabs wanted it, the Muslims wanted it, and the whole world wanted it."[25]

Hussein did not feel he could go alone against the current, and in the end he actually voted for the Rabat resolutions. But formal adoption of the resolutions was not the same as genuine acceptance. The claim to represent the Palestinians was a vital part of Hussein's Hashemite heritage. At Rabat this role was taken away from him and given to the PLO, his deadly rival. The message that the Rabat summit sent to Hussein was that he no longer had any say in the affairs of the occupied territories and that he could no longer speak on behalf of the Palestinians in international fora. To an ambitious monarch this was a depressing message. He saw it as "a betrayal of the Hashemite custody of the Palestinian cause."[26] As Foreign Minister Dr. Kamel Abu Jaber confessed, "Hussein did not like it and never accepted the Rabat summit resolution. He thought of the PLO as a tool to reach a political settlement, not as a substitute to Jordan. This was obvious from his movements between 1974 and 1988. We continued to try to get around the Rabat formula and to persuade the Palestinians, the Arab world and the international community that Jordan is the place to talk about the Palestinians—that it is the door to be knocked on. Eventually, Hussein reluctantly accepted the necessity to disengage."[27]

Rabat was thus a watershed in Hussein's troubled relationship with the Palestinians: he could no longer claim that they were under his crown. But Rabat represented an opportunity as well as a setback. It opened the door to a "Jordan-first" policy, to concentrating on the political and economic development of the East Bank. Some of his advisers from the East Bank elite, led by Mreiwad Tall, urged him to adopt such a policy, to cut his losses on the West Bank and to leave the representation of the Palestinians to the PLO in accordance with the Arab consensus. Crown Prince Hassan sided with this group of advisers, arguing that Jordan should cut its ties with the West Bank and that for all practical purposes the "unity of the two banks" idea should be revoked.[28] At this stage, however, Hussein was not ready for an official break with the West Bank. Following the Rabat summit, parliament was dissolved and a new government, headed once again by Rifa'i, was appointed by royal decree. West Bank representation in the Senate and the Chamber of Deputies was reduced, and national elections were postponed until March 1975. The citizenship rights of Palestinians on the East Bank were curtailed, giving rise to tensions. Eventually the king defused the crisis by assuring the Palestinians that they would have the right to choose their citizenship at the appropriate time.

Hussein eventually heeded the advice he was given after Rabat—but only in July 1988, when he severed Jordan's legal and administrative links with the West Bank. He could have opted for constitutional separation in 1974. One reason for not doing so has already been noted—his sense of moral obligation as a Hashemite towards the people of the West Bank. But there was a second and related reason, namely, his dynastic interests and, more specifically, his belief that the Hashemites were destined to play a major role in the affairs of the Middle East. He was obsessed with projecting Jordan as a key player in regional and international politics. This sense of mission impelled him to continue to invest most of his time and energy not on internal development and consolidation but on diplomatic efforts to recover the West Bank of the kingdom that his grandfather had bequeathed to him.

The Rabat decision weakened further Hussein's already very weak hand in dealing with the Israelis. After Rabat the secret meetings resumed because both sides saw some value in staying in contact, but the regional context had changed and the sense of urgency had gone. Nevertheless, Hussein always liked to avoid complete isolation. In addition, contact with the Israelis enabled him to bypass the Rabat resolutions and to maintain his links with his supporters on the West Bank. In Israel the morale of military intelligence was at its nadir because of the débâcle of the October War. Mossad, on the other hand, emerged largely unscathed. Rabin rewarded Mossad by assigning to it responsibility for coordinating his clandestine contacts with Hussein— the most sensitive aspect in Israel's foreign relations. One of the results was a top-secret intelligence exchange between the Mossad and the Mukhabarat.[29] The Mossad had passed messages to Hussein in the past and alerted him to plots against his life, but the relationship was now institutionalized for the first time.

Hussein's next meeting with the Israelis did not take place until 28 May 1975. Hussein spoke more in sorrow than in anger about their attitude on the eve of the Rabat summit. He believed that, had they reached a disengagement agreement with him, the Rabat defeat could have been avoided. The Israelis tried to shift the conversation from the past to the future by raising the possibility of territorial compromise. "We are out of the picture," Hussein replied angrily. "Please talk to the PLO and then we'll see." By this time Israel had started negotiating a second disengagement agreement with Egypt. Hussein feared that such an agreement would further weaken Jordan's position in the Middle East, but there was little he could do except to cast doubt on Sadat's reliability. Like the previous two meetings, this one ended without any agreement being reached. Yet during the meeting Hussein indicated that there was some point in continuing the dialogue.[30]

Jordan had been relegated to the margins of the diplomacy surrounding the Arab–Israeli conflict. Kissinger resumed his shuttle between Cairo and Tel Aviv, and, on 1 September 1975, the two countries signed an interim agreement, popularly known as Sinai II. It was a freestanding agreement that did not include any commitment by Israel to enter into negotiations over the Golan Heights or the West Bank. Sinai II was well received in Israel but not in Jordan. Adnan Abu-Odeh explained: "We were very unhappy because we were not included in the disengagement agreements that were reached between Egypt and

Israel. Jordan's exclusion was also received with fear and worry in Amman. It was taken as a first indicator that Jordan would gradually be excluded from a solution to the Palestine question. Exclusion meant a great deal to us at the time: above all, it meant that Jordan would become gradually irrelevant. Irrelevance to Jordan means that getting rid of the Hashemites would become more possible. In other words, that the Palestinian question could be solved at Jordan's expense."[31]

Sinai II had the unintended effect of improving the relations between Jordan and Syria. Asad shared Hussein's mistrust of Sadat, of Kissinger and of Kissinger's step-by-step diplomacy, which seemed to be directed at dividing the Arab world, avoiding the core issues of the Arab–Israeli conflict and frustrating the search for a comprehensive settlement. The Syrians tried to compensate for Sadat's "defection" by forming a banana-shaped front round Israel and by consolidating their influence in Lebanon.

After its expulsion from Jordan in 1970–71 the PLO began to build a state within a state in Lebanon. A civil war broke out in April 1975 between the leftist–PLO coalition on the one hand and the various Christian militias on the other. Syria and Israel were the main external actors in the Lebanese conflict, and there was a danger that they would be dragged in by their respective allies. Hussein played a part in arranging the tacit understanding between Asad and the Israelis. The king advised the Maronite Christians that if they wanted to survive in the Middle East, they should turn to Israel for protection. He also offered to serve as a messenger for Asad, who knew about his channels to the Israeli leaders. Asad wanted Israeli acquiescence in the presence of Syrian troops up to a certain point in Lebanon. One night in April 1976 Gideon Rafael, Israel's ambassador in London, was asked to meet Hussein urgently at the house of a mutual friend. The king was deeply concerned about the mounting tension in the Levant. It was in their mutual interest, he argued, to contain the present fighting in Lebanon. The message he conveyed from Asad to Rabin was that Syria's intervention in Lebanon was designed to protect the Christians and that there was no intention of harming Israel's interests there. Asad promised to keep his forces away from the Israeli border and asked the Israelis not to intervene. A few hours later Rafael was on his way to Israel. Rabin appreciated the message. A special meeting of the cabinet was convened: it was decided to accept the Syrian explanation and to refrain from direct intervention in Lebanon. Rafael flew back to London to convey the reassuring message to the king, who promptly dispatched it to Damascus.[32]

Thus the dialogue among the principals across the battle lines continued, but the emphasis shifted from the discussion of a political settlement to dealing with day-to-day problems. Among the subjects that came up were the combating of terrorist activities by the radical Palestinian factions, ecology, water, aviation, shipping in the Gulf of Aqaba and border demarcation.[33] There were minor complaints by the king about Israeli planes flying over his palace and Israeli boats booming around his house in Aqaba, and appropriate action followed. Crown Prince Hassan, who was in charge of the Jordanian development plan, had two long meetings with Allon. They discussed projects for building hydroelectric stations, for more effective management of water resources, for free passage between Eilat and Aqaba, and even for giving Jordan access to the Mediterranean through Gaza. Allon was most impressed by Hassan's expertise in economics and development. He also seized the opportunity to find out whether there was any basis to the rumours that Hassan was opposed to Jordan's return to the West Bank. Hassan burst out laughing and said that rumour had already reached his ears. The truth of the matter was that he did not wish to give up the West Bank not because he was in love with its inhabitants but because he did not want his political rivals to have it.[34]

Politically, the deadlock continued. The PLO was unable to represent the Palestinians in negotiations over the future of the West Bank because Israel and the United States refused to deal with it. As a result of the Rabat resolution the Palestinians were thus left in limbo. The advent of a Democratic administration in January 1976 under Jimmy Carter carried hopes of a change in the American position. Carter put the emphasis on human rights in foreign policy and came out publicly in support of a homeland for the Palestinians. He was thus the first US president to champion the right of the Palestinians to national self-determination, and he used the terms PLO and Palestinians interchangeably. Jordan and Israel feared that this formula might lead to the emergence of a Palestinian state as a wedge between them. So there were grounds for exploring again various views about territorial or functional compromises, such as Peres's scheme of a condominium over the West Bank and the Gaza Strip.

A meeting was arranged between Hussein and the triumvirate led by Rabin towards the end of March 1977. This time Hussein and Rifa'i were driven to the Mossad-operated guest-house just north of Tel Aviv. The talks, however, proved futile as neither side was ready to yield, especially on the question of Jerusalem.[35] On the issues that really mattered, according to Hussein, "Rabin was very rigid, very polite, very cordial but rigid and impossible to alter." During Rabin's second term as prime minister, in 1992–95, he recalled their last meeting to Hussein, saying, "You were very stubborn." Hussein replied, "Yes, I was because I could not give an inch of Palestinian territory or an iota of Palestinian rights." Hussein remembered that Rabin had said: "Well, there is nothing that can be done. Wait for ten years, maybe things will change on the ground." Hussein had replied, "Well, too bad."[36]

18. The Camp David Accords

The year 1977 was the silver jubilee of Hussein's accession, but it was one of tragedy in his private life and of frustration in his political career. On 9 February 1977 Queen Alia, his third wife, died in an air accident. She had visited a hospital in Tafila in the south of Jordan when the royal helicopter in which she was travelling crashed in a rainstorm. The other casualties were the minister of health who accompanied her and Lieutenant-Colonel Bader Zaza, her husband's pilot and friend. Hussein was completely devastated by the death of his young wife, his grief deepened by a sense of guilt at having allowed Alia to travel to a remote part of the country in such atrocious weather conditions. Alia left behind three little children—Haya, Ali and Abir. Hussein was plunged into dark depression and for a while withdrew into a kind of monastic seclusion.

Hussein's performance of his public duties was not surprisingly affected by his private grief. His attention span shortened, his level of energy seriously declined, and he looked dour and distracted. The first foreign trip after the tragic event was to the United States. On 24 April, Hussein had a meeting in the White House with President Jimmy Carter and his advisers. They all liked him, enjoyed his visit and believed he would be a staunch ally in the conference on the Middle East they were planning to hold later in the year. Hussein said that for the first time in many years he was hopeful that they could reach some agreements. Late that night Carter, his wife, Rosalynn, and their royal guest sat on the Truman Balcony, watching the planes land and take off from Washington National Airport, and talked about both diplomatic affairs and personal matters. Hussein was still emotionally drained. When he told Rosalynn Carter how much he had appreciated the handwritten letter that the president had sent him, he began to weep, and their hearts went out to him. Carter asked him if he would like to visit the Georgia coast for a few days of rest, and Hussein gratefully accepted the invitation.[1]

Jimmy Carter was the sixth American president that Hussein had worked with. Despite their promising start, relations between the two men were strained when it became evident that Jordan was assigned only a minor role in the Middle East plans of the Carter administration. Another source of strain on Jordanian–American relations was the rise to power in Israel, after the May 1977 elections, of a right-wing Likud government under the leadership of Menachem Begin. Rabin resigned on 7 April because of a minor foreign currency violation, and the Labour Party elected Peres to succeed him. But the Likud victory brought to an end three decades of Labour hegemony. It also brought about a major change in Israel's foreign policy. Labour is a pragmatic party preoccupied with security, whereas Likud is an ideological party dedicated to Greater Israel. According to Likud's nationalist ideology, Judea and Samaria, the biblical terms for the West Bank, are an integral part of *Eretz Israel*, the "Land of Israel." The Likud categorically denied that Jordan had any claim to sovereignty over this area. Equally vehement was the Likud's denial that the Palestinians had a right to self-determination in this area. *Shlemut hamoledet*, the integrity of the homeland, was an article of faith in the Likud's political creed. This was clearly stated in the party's manifesto for the 1977 election: "The right of the Jewish people to the Land of Israel is eternal, and is an integral part of its right to security and peace. Judea and Samaria shall therefore not be relinquished to foreign rule; between the sea and the Jordan, there will be Jewish sovereignty alone." This programme abruptly brought to an end the special relationship that had developed over the previous seven decades between the Labour Zionist leaders and the Hashemite rulers of Jordan. Unlike Labour, the Likud was not committed to the survival of the monarchy in Amman.

Jordan's leaders were virtually panic-stricken. They feared that the new Israeli government would not only annex the West Bank but that it would carry out large-scale expulsions of Palestinians from the West Bank to the East Bank. The personal record of the new prime minister— as the leader of a right-wing terrorist group in the pre-independence period and as a member of Levi Eshkol's national unity government— was also a major cause for concern. Hussein viewed Begin with deep distaste on account of his terrorist past and his extremist approach to politics.[2] His misgivings were shared by other members of the royal family. Prince Zaid bin Shaker recalled: "The Likud people said that

Palestine is on the East of the River and the only thing that needs to change is the monarchy because the great majority of the people here are Palestinians, which is untrue. We had contingency plans for the possibility of expulsion. His Majesty had contacts with all our allies. It was a period of anxiety in Jordan."[3]

The Jordanian leadership felt threatened by both the programme and the composition of the new government. Ezer Weizman, the hawkish former commander of the Israeli Air Force and a loud-mouthed enemy of the Hashemites, became minister of defence. Ariel Sharon, another hawkish former general, became minister of agriculture. Sharon was one of the most aggressive proponents of the right-wing thesis that "Jordan is Palestine." According to this thesis, there was already in existence a Palestinian state on the East Bank of the Jordan River and the West Bank should be incorporated into Greater Israel by accelerating the pace of Jewish settlement there. During the September 1970 crisis in Jordan, Sharon was one of the very few members of the IDF General Staff who were opposed to helping Hussein beat the challenge to his regime from the PLO. Sharon wanted to help the PLO topple the regime in Jordan and turn the country into a Palestinian state. One of the most surprising decisions made by Begin was to invite the Labour Party's Moshe Dayan to serve as foreign minister. One of the reasons for offering Dayan this key post was to stress the continuity in Israel's foreign policy. Begin was well aware that outside Israel he was widely perceived as an extremist, a fanatic and a warmonger. He knew of the widespread fears that his rise to power would cause tension between Israel and its neighbours. To allay these fears, he tried to give the impression of being reasonable and responsible.

With the Likud and Dayan in power, the Jordanian orientation in Israel's foreign policy was replaced by one in favour of Egypt. But, before issuing any peace feelers to Egypt, Dayan arranged a secret meeting with Hussein in London on 22 August at the home of Dr. Emmanuel Herbert. Dr. Herbert was now seventy-nine years old and in poor health, and this was to be the last secret meeting he hosted at his home between his Jordanian and Israeli friends. It was also the last meeting between the king and the Likud leadership for a decade. Dayan's account of the meeting is as follows:

King Hussein was late, and he apologized as he greeted me with a handshake and a broad smile. He had had guests, he explained, and could not get away till they had left. I found him greatly changed, not in appearance but in spirit. He was not the same man I had last seen. He was now withdrawn, subdued, without sparkle, and the political topics I raised did not seem to touch him deeply. His language was clipped, his answers to my questions often monosyllabic, rarely more than yes and no and without clear explanation. His depression may have been caused by the tragic death of his wife, who had been killed shortly before in a helicopter crash. Or it may have sprung from one of the decisions of the 1974 Rabat Conference of Arab States, of which he was bitterly critical. This was the decision to recognize the PLO as the sole authorized representative of the Palestinians and withdraw Hussein from that role. Now, he said, he was concerning himself exclusively with administering the East Bank of the river—his kingdom of Jordan. He was neither able nor anxious to clash with the Arab countries and the PLO on this matter. If they did not want him, they could run the affairs of the Palestinians without him.

Dayan then asked the king whether he would agree to a peace treaty with Israel based on the partition of the West Bank between Jordan and Israel. By his own account, Dayan received not only an unequivocal answer but an instructive lesson. The king rejected the idea out of hand, saying that he, as an Arab monarch, could not propose to the people of even a single village that they cut themselves off from their brother Arabs and become Israelis. Agreement to such a plan would be regarded as treachery. He would be charged with "selling" Arab land to the Jews so that he could enlarge his own kingdom. "Was Hussein," Dayan wondered, "still the King of Jordan or only the shadow of a ruler? Was he really looking after his country or was he spending most of his time gallivanting abroad? In any event, his attitude toward the subject of our discussion—the attempt to find a suitable and agreed-upon arrangement for the problem of the West Bank and the Gaza Strip—seemed to be one of indifference."[4] The disenchantment was mutual. Hussein's account of the meeting may be plain, but it has the merit of clarity: "I saw my friend Moshe Dayan who had become the Foreign Minister of the Likud here in London. His attitude was even harder than it had been earlier and that was the end of that. We never had any contact for a long period."[5]

The meeting contained no surprises. Hussein's position had not changed since he had met Dayan in his earlier incarnation as the minister of defence and member of the Labour Party. Dayan received the answers he expected, which simply confirmed Begin's view that the king would not agree to relinquish any territory to Israel on the West Bank and that he also rejected any possibility of power-sharing. On many subsequent occasions, Begin would quote the king's words to Dayan that the division of the land was "totally unacceptable."[6] Territorial compromise between Israel and Jordan was now ruled out by both sides. The "Jordanian option" was buried. This left Begin and Dayan free to explore the "Egyptian option," and they stepped up their diplomatic efforts to persuade Sadat that Israel wanted to begin bilateral negotiations.

Jimmy Carter and Menachem Begin were at cross purposes from the beginning. Carter replaced Henry Kissinger's step-by-step approach, which had suited Israel very well, with an attempt at a comprehensive approach, which did not suit Israel at all. Carter saw the Palestinian problem as the core of the Middle East conflict and considered it to be in American interests to promote a solution to it. The solution he favoured was a Palestinian homeland on the West Bank and the Gaza Strip linked to Jordan. He worked for the reconvening of the Geneva conference with the participation of the Soviet Union and all the parties to the conflict, including the Palestinians. Begin denied that the Palestinians had any national rights; he was opposed to an international conference and to the Soviet participation that it would entail; and he did not consider that UN Resolution 242 applied to the West Bank or Gaza. What he wanted was direct bilateral negotiations between Israel and Egypt without the involvement of any other Arab party, least of all the PLO, which he regarded simply as a terrorist organization. By raising endless procedural problems, Begin succeeded in sabotaging Carter's plans for an international conference.

There were also problems on the Arab side. Asad and Hussein favoured a unified Arab delegation to the reconstituted Geneva conference, while Sadat preferred separate national delegations. Hussein welcomed the American initiative for a conference because it was based on UN resolutions, because it promised a comprehensive settlement, and because it assigned a major role to Jordan. His approach at the preparatory stage was both constructive and creative. The Israelis had vetoed PLO participation in the conference, but Hussein proposed to include non-PLO Palestinian leaders as members of the Jordanian delegation to ensure Palestinian representation. He also made a tour of Arab capitals in an effort to forge a unified front. In Cairo, Sadat was in no mood to consult or take advice on anything. From the beginning there was no trust and no chemistry between the two leaders. Hussein offered Sadat the benefit of his experience in dealing with the Israelis. He wanted to give him an idea of what the difficulties might be, but no reaction was forthcoming. So Hussein said pointedly that he had been in touch with "their neighbours" and invited Sadat to ask questions about these contacts; Sadat replied that he would assume his own responsibilities in this respect. His attitude was all the more disappointing against the background of Nasser's commitment after the June War to give priority to the recovery of the West Bank in any peace negotiations. Hussein's efforts to find common ground between Sadat and Asad also came to nothing.[7] Sadat had decided to act alone and failed to inform any of the other players of the dramatic political initiative on which he had set his mind. On 9 November, in an address to the Egyptian parliament, he dropped his bombshell. "I am prepared to go to the ends of the earth for peace even to the Knesset itself," he announced. Ten days later he embarked on his historic journey to Jerusalem. Sadat finally scuttled the Geneva conference and the comprehensive approach to which it was closely linked.

Sadat's visit to Jerusalem caused disarray and disunity in the Arab world. Some Arab leaders supported his initiative; some opposed it furiously; and some adopted a wait-and-see attitude. Hussein held the last view. Although Sadat's move took him by complete surprise at a time when he was working for a unified Arab stand, his reaction was surprisingly mild. He refused to condemn the move despite the pressure to do so from the radical Arab states, from the PLO and from domestic opinion. In a televised broadcast to the nation, Hussein criticized both Sadat's unilateral initiative and the emotional reaction it elicited from other Arabs. He praised Sadat for his courage in bypassing the customs, traditions and psychological barriers that constrained the Arab approach towards Israel, but expressed reservations about the form and substance of the Egyptian initiative. The speech was essentially a call on Arab leaders to close ranks. The Arabs could not hope to regain their rights, warned Hussein, "if the effort to liberate our territories and secure a just peace is unilateral or partial or not committed to the bond of common action."[8] In effect, Hussein was acting as an elder statesman and putting himself as a mediator and peacemaker between the rival camps.

The moderate tone of Hussein's response to the Sadat initiative was to some extent a reflection of the growing influence of Sharif Abdul Hamid Sharaf, the chief of the royal court, on foreign policy. Sharaf was born in Baghdad in 1939 to an Iraqi branch of the Hashemite family. He was a distant cousin of Hussein, but relations between them had been strained because he was an Arab nationalist; he had joined the Arab Nationalist Movement during his studies at the American University of Beirut. He married Laila Najjar, a Lebanese Druze, a fellow student at AUB who was also an ardent Arab nationalist. Sharif Zaid bin Shaker played an important role in reconciling the king to his other cousin and in enabling Sharaf to return to Jordan and to join the Ministry of Foreign Affairs. Following the June War, Hussein appointed Sharaf as ambassador to Washington, where he stayed for five years; he then moved to the UN in New York. The king trusted Sharaf and was happy with his work in the United States. The old tension was diluted. In 1976 Sharaf and his wife returned to Jordan, and he accepted the post of chief of the royal court. From that point onwards, his relationship with the king became extremely intimate. Sharaf was a proactive chief, and the king relied on him for advice and trusted his judgement. Sharaf believed in a balanced relationship between Jordan and the other Arab countries.[9] Mudar Badran, the prime minister at that time, was dogmatically opposed to the Egyptian initiative. Sharaf counselled that outright Jordanian rejection would leave Sadat isolated and vulnerable to Israeli pressure and that Egypt's isolation would accelerate the process of fragmentation among the remaining Arab states.[10] His advice prevailed because it was more in tune both with the king's style and with his strategy.

By visiting Jerusalem, Sadat succeeded in breaking the psychological barrier that, according to him, constituted 90 percent of the Arab–Israeli conflict. He persuaded the majority of Israelis that peace with the Arabs was a real possibility but that it could be achieved only at a price: withdrawal from the occupied territories. Yet Sadat made no dent in the political barrier to peace, namely, the Likud's refusal to withdraw from the West Bank. In this respect his visit was a failure but one that he refused to admit. Negotiations continued after the visit, and in December Begin presented Sadat with a plan for Palestinian autonomy in the West Bank and the Gaza Strip. This plan was unacceptable to any Arab, including Sadat, because it amounted to an attempt to legalize Israel's occupation of these areas, including East Jerusalem. Negotiations dragged on, but it became clear to all concerned that the Sadat initiative had reached a dead end. In the summer of 1978 President Carter intervened with an initiative of his own: an invitation to Egypt and Israel to a peace conference under American auspices at Camp David, the presidential retreat in Maryland. Hussein received no invitation, only a letter from President Carter outlining his plans.[11]

Carter's initiative represented his abandonment of a comprehensive approach in favour of a bilateral Israeli–Egyptian one, and it relegated Jordan to the periphery of Middle East peacemaking. Hussein replied to Carter with a long letter wishing him success but also pointing out the pitfalls along his path. He began by noting that Israel's negative response to President Sadat's brave initiative increased the belief in Arab minds that it was opposed to withdrawal from the territories it occupied by force in 1967 under any circumstances and that it did not intend to allow any reasonable solution to the Palestinian question. The Israeli government, wrote Hussein, added to the obstacles to peace by refusing to admit that the West Bank was occupied Jordanian territory. Jordan was ready to participate positively in the efforts to construct peace, but before entering into negotiations it needed a clear and unambiguous indication that the result would be total Israeli withdrawal from all the occupied territories. Implicit in the letter was a warning that a separate settlement would not be acceptable to Jordan or its Arab allies.[12]

Some reports in the American press suggested that Jordan was invited to the Camp David summit but that it declined to participate. These reports were untrue but they may have stemmed from Hussein's ambivalent position on the eve of the summit, when he seemed to be angling for an invitation but insisting on conditions that made it difficult to include him. The summit meeting at Camp David lasted thirteen days, starting on 5 September 1978 and ending on 17 September. Throughout this period Hussein remained in London, feeling excluded and following developments nervously. Ashraf Marwan, a wealthy Egyptian businessman, the son-in-law of Nasser and a confidant of Sadat, happened to be in London at the time, and Hussein asked to see him. He told Marwan in strict confidence of his interest in joining the summit and asked him to sound out Sadat. Marwan flew to Washington, spoke to one of Sadat's senior aides and returned to London to convey a negative response to the king. Sadat did not want Hussein at Camp David partly because he neither liked nor trusted him, but more importantly, because he feared that Hussein's presence at Camp David would complicate the process and block the path to progress. Sadat understood that Hussein was bound to raise the question of Palestinian self-determination and to insist on a comprehensive settlement to the dispute. When Begin's press secretary asked Sadat why he had declined Hussein's request, Sadat replied simply, "Because if Hussein had arrived at Camp David, we would not have reached any agreement."[13]

Yet Sadat did not want to fall out with Hussein: his support could be valuable in countering the inevitable Arab opposition to a partial agreement with Israel, and Sadat needed a façade of legitimacy. The role assigned to Hussein in Sadat's grand design was not that of an equal partner but that of the *sabi as-sutra*. When a woman leaves her house with a less than honourable purpose in mind, she might take a boy with her to make it appear like an innocent family outing. Literally, *sabi as-sutra* means the youth who protects the honour of women. Hussein's role, according to this analogy, was not to play an independent part in peace negotiations but to lend legitimacy to what in Arab eyes was bound to look like a shady deal. Sadat reckoned that with combined Egyptian–American pressure, Hussein would have no choice but to fall in line. Sadat had a low opinion of his fellow Arab rulers and often referred to them as dwarfs and clowns. In his meetings with American officials, he often bad-mouthed and belittled Hussein. This contributed to the American tendency to take Hussein for granted and to ignore his repeated warnings against a separate agreement. On this, as on other occasions, particularly during the Johnson administration, the White House officials treated Hussein as a "cheap date."

The most contentious issues at Camp David were Jerusalem, Palestinian rights and the future of the Jewish settlements on the West Bank. The media reported that deadlock was reached on all of these issues. On 14 September, the tenth day of the conference, Hussein, with the encouragement of Ashraf Marwan, called Sadat at the presidential retreat in Maryland. Sadat told Hussein that the negotiations were foundering on the Palestinian issue, that he was very depressed, and that he was preparing to pack his bags to go back home. Hussein saluted Sadat for having tried and encouraged him to hold his ground and to put the responsibility for failure where it belonged. He also arranged to meet Sadat in Morocco on his way back from the United States and to accompany him on a tour of Arab capitals to explain what had gone wrong and to work out a joint strategy. Hussein in effect offered to help Sadat to break the fall and restore his position in the Arab world. Three days later, Hussein heard on the BBC that agreement had been reached at Camp David. Hussein was very angry because he thought that Sadat had deliberately deceived him, so instead of going to Morocco he went back to Jordan.[14]

The Camp David Accords were in two parts. The first accord was entitled "A Framework for the Conclusion of a Peace Treaty between Israel and Egypt." The treaty was to rest on four principles: complete Israeli withdrawal from Sinai and recognition of Egyptian sovereignty over this territory; demilitarization of most of Sinai; the stationing of UN forces to supervise demilitarization and to ensure freedom of navigation in the Gulf of Suez and the Suez Canal; and full normalization in the relations between Egypt and Israel. The second, entitled "A Framework for Peace in the Middle East," dealt with the Palestinian problem. This called for the election of Palestinian representatives to negotiate the establishment of limited local autonomy on the West Bank and Gaza with Israel. Although this accord was also based on Resolution 242, it fudged the question of Israeli withdrawal, leaving it for "final status" negotiations after a transitional period of autonomy during which Israel would maintain military control. There was no mention of the PLO or of Palestinian self-determination, and no commitment to Israeli withdrawal except from Sinai. As a result, the Camp David Accords were immediately rejected by the PLO, Syria and the other radical Arab states.

Hussein was in a state of shock when he read the text of the accords, especially in the light of the assurances he had received from Sadat only three days earlier. His nightmare scenario became a reality: Egypt had opted for a separate deal; Jordan and the Palestinians had been sidelined; and the Arab world was in complete disarray. Hussein feared that endorsement of Sadat's deal would strain relations with the Palestinians and the rest of the Arab world. He felt insulted by the crude manner in which the Americans had tried to involve him. He refused to legitimize Israel's occupation or to play the part of Israel's policeman on the West Bank; and he particularly resented the assumption that Jordan could be forced to play the role assigned to it in the Camp David script. The "Framework for Peace in the Middle East" mentions Jordan no less than fourteen times, although Jordan was not consulted about the role assigned to it by the writers. Hussein and his government repeatedly emphasized that Jordan was not legally or morally bound by accords that it took no part in formulating. Jordan, they said, would continue to insist on Israeli withdrawal from all the occupied territories and on the right to self-determination of the Palestinian people.

Hussein believed that Sadat simply deceived him, but the sequence of events towards the end of the summit suggests that it was Begin who deceived all the other participants. On Friday morning, 15 September, Sadat told Cyrus Vance, the secretary of state, that he had decided to go home, as he saw no hope of an agreement. At the end of an hour-long conversation, Carter persuaded Sadat to stay. On Saturday evening Carter and Vance met with Begin and his senior advisers for six hours, and it was felt that a major breakthrough had been reached on the question of settlements. Begin agreed to write a letter to Carter to be made public, saying that no new settlements would be built during the five-year transitional period to Palestinian autonomy. Begin's commitment was a major argument in persuading Sadat to sign the Camp David Accords in Washington on Sunday, the seventeenth. On Monday, Begin's letter arrived. It limited the moratorium on the building of new settlements to the three-month period of negotiations on the peace treaty between Israel and Egypt. Carter's notes were quite clear—that the settlements freeze would continue until all negotiations were completed—and Vance confirmed his interpretation.[15] Begin said that there must have been a misunderstanding, but there was no misunderstanding: he behaved dishonestly and dishonourably. Carter was so appalled by Begin's duplicity that he ended up by describing him as a "psycho."[16] An Israeli settlement freeze on the West Bank was the one concession that might have persuaded the Arabs that America was committed to peace with justice. By withdrawing this concession, Begin brought about an ignominious collapse of the American position in the Arab world. Even the most moderate and pro-Western Arab leaders were now reluctant to endorse the defective and deficient accords signed by Egypt.

Yet America lobbied vigorously for Jordanian and Saudi support. In his memoirs Carter writes that he called Hussein in Amman and discovered that he was under pressure from some of the other Arabs to reject any role in the forthcoming negotiations to implement the Camp David accords. Carter explained the advantages of the accords to Jordan and the Palestinians, and Hussein promised, somewhat reluctantly, not to make any decision or public comment until he had been informed thoroughly about the documents.[17] There is no mention in Carter's memoirs of the letter that Hussein had written to him on 27 August warning him precisely against the outcome that was eventually reached at the summit.

As soon as it was concluded, Carter sent Cyrus Vance to Jordan and Saudi Arabia to drum up support for the settlement. Vance was the victim of the political geography of Washington. The State Department building is a mile away from the White House while the national security adviser's office adjoins the Oval Office. Zbigniew Brzezinski, Carter's national security adviser, intervened destructively after the conclusion of the Accords. He adopted a tough line, saying, in effect, that beggars cannot be choosers. Brzezinski ignored the State Department warning that the Jordanians and the Saudis would take a long time to accept the new situation. He enraged both states by ill-disguised briefings to the American press in which he claimed that they were simply putting up token opposition before joining enlarged talks.[18]

The triumphalist tone of the American media worked against Vance during his visit to the Middle East. Hussein and Crown Prince Fahd were angry with Sadat. They believed that he had given them an explicit commitment before the summit to negotiate a comprehensive settlement in which the rest of the Arabs, including the Palestinians, could join, or that they could at least support, without unacceptable political risk. Instead, Hussein and Fahd told Vance, most of the Arab world was attacking Sadat and no recognized Palestinian leader was prepared to participate in the autonomy negotiations. Sadat had let them down by making a separate peace with Israel in exchange for the return of Sinai. Vance argued that the autonomy arrangements could lead eventually to Palestinian self-determination. His hosts doubted that Israel would abide by the terms and the spirit of the accords. At the conclusion of a lengthy discussion, Hussein said he had additional questions to which he needed answers before he could give his considered response, and promised to send them shortly.[19]

Most of Hussein's advisers were ambivalent about joining the Camp David negotiations. They did not want to damage relations with America, but they also felt that involvement entailed unacceptable personal and political risks for the king, the greatest of which was being compromised by joining Sadat and emerging empty-handed. Hussein and his advisers understood that this was a process, but they wanted to be certain about the intended outcome before embarking on the journey. In particular, they needed to be assured that the result would be a comprehensive settlement and Israeli withdrawal from all the occupied territories. Hussein appointed a committee of five officials under the chairmanship of Sharaf to draft the questions. The committee prepared a list of fourteen searching questions mostly about the American interpretation of the Camp David Accords and the American role in implementing them. President Carter personally signed the answers and sent Harold Saunders, the assistant secretary of state, to deliver them to the king on 16 October. The answers stated that America's interpretation of 242 had not changed since 1967, and they elaborated on America's view of specific issues in the Camp David Accords, but they did not contain the assurances that Jordan had sought. There was no indication that the Carter administration was prepared to apply to Israel the kind of pressure it was applying to the Arabs. All the contentious issues, the American document said, had to be resolved by direct negotiations between the parties themselves. The imbalance of power between the parties was not addressed. The consensus among the king's advisers was that the answers were opaque, non-committal and unsatisfactory.[20]

Harold Saunders spent hours with the king's advisers and had two meetings with the king himself. Hussein was still anxious to be constructive, but he was not prepared to take the plunge on his own. He told Saunders that Jordan could not participate in the negotiations to implement the Camp David Accords without the support of the Palestinians or the Saudis. Saunders met with West Bank leaders but could elicit no support for Jordanian participation. He also went to Saudi Arabia but fared no better than Cyrus Vance. Saunders put the question directly to Crown Prince Fahd: would Saudi Arabia back Hussein if he came out in support of the Camp David Accords? Fahd's reply was anything but direct. He gave an oblique and undecipherable answer and then changed the subject. Saunders went back to Amman to a meeting with the king at which he candidly admitted the failure of his mission.[21] Despite all his disappointments, the king did not want to exclude all future possibilities of discussion. In his memoirs Carter writes: "I received a typically equivocal message from Hussein, leaving open the possibility that either the Jordanians or the Palestinians might negotiate as agreed at Camp David, but making no commitment."[22] In private conversations Carter used less diplomatic language, describing Hussein as the weak king of a weak country.[23]

Jordan depended heavily on subsidies from the Gulf states, so there would be an economic price to pay for a break with the Arab consensus. The military threat from Iraq and Syria to Hashemite rule in Jordan would also be exacerbated by a break, and there was a danger to domestic stability from any move that defied the Rabat resolution and displeased the Palestinian population of the kingdom. Under these circumstances, Hussein's usual balancing act became practically untenable; Jordan was indeed a weak country. He moved closer to the Arab rejectionists by accepting an invitation to attend a summit in Baghdad from which Egypt was excluded. Baghdad was not the most congenial of Arab capitals for Hussein to visit because it was the city in which the Hashemite royal family had been murderously ejected twenty years previously. This was to be his first visit to Baghdad since 1958. Great care was taken to make him feel welcome. Ba'th officials were sent to the overgrown royal cemetery to scythe down the long grass around the graves of the Hashemites in case Hussein wanted to visit them.[24]

The other twenty members of the Arab League attended the meeting in Baghdad from 2–5 November. At the summit Hussein positioned Jordan at the heart of the new Arab consensus. In his speech to the delegates he outlined a framework for joint action to protect the Arab world against Israeli expansionism and to secure the peaceful recovery of the occupied territories. All their resources had to be mobilized, he argued, to meet the common danger. The meeting resolved to suspend Egypt's membership of the Arab League and to transfer the headquarters of the Arab League from Cairo to Tunis. It declared Camp David to be in contradiction to the resolutions of the Arab summit in Rabat and confirmed Arab support for the PLO as the sole legitimate representative of the Palestinian people. It also voted to extend financial support over a period of ten years to Syria, Jordan and the PLO. Jordan was allocated a third of the total—$1,250 million over ten years. This financial support by the Arab oil-producing countries for the Eastern Front was intended to correct the imbalance of power caused by Egypt's defection.[25]

The Baghdad summit marked the beginning of a close personal

friendship and political partnership between the Hashemite king and Saddam Hussein, the young vice-president of Iraq. Saddam was the strongman of the Ba'th regime who within a few months was to take over the presidency from the ailing Ahmad Bakr. At the summit Saddam played a major part in persuading the wealthy Arab states to extend financial aid to the remaining confrontation states with a common border with Israel. Hussein was most impressed with the energetic Iraqi leader, who spoke eloquently about the need for unity among the Arab states and their collective responsibility to make sure that no Arab went hungry. Saddam treated Hussein with great courtesy and showed real understanding and sympathy for his predicament. Later on Saddam would reveal himself as a dissembling psychopath, but on this occasion all the members of the Jordanian delegation found him to be a perfect host and a man of considerable charm. Like other members of the Hashemite royal family, Hussein viewed Iraq with a mixture of admiration and loathing: admiration for its power and wealth and loathing for the savage massacre of their relatives in the revolution of 1958.[26] Hussein's fledgling friendship with the Iraqi leader tilted the balance in favour of admiration and helped him to overcome the bitter memories of the past. But the personal friendship was to assume growing political significance. Hussein always looked for an Arab regional order that would be conducive to the survival of the Hashemite dynasty. Iraq was to become the anchor of this political order during the following decade.

America reacted aggressively to Jordan's rejection of the Camp David Accords. The Carter administration intensified the pressure to compel Jordan to change course and to join in the Camp David negotiations. It cut economic aid and advised its allies in the Gulf not to help Jordan. Jordan experienced difficulty in obtaining grants for development projects from the World Bank, and there were times when it was unable to pay the wages of the army. In March 1979 Zbigniew Brzezinski visited Amman and threatened to restrict arms supplies if Jordan did not change its attitude towards the American-sponsored peace process. Jordanian officials thought that he also implied that unless there was a change of attitude, America might not protect Jordan against a future Israeli attack. The explicit threat met with a cool response from Hussein, who said that Jordan would have to look around for alternative sources of military equipment. Hussein also accused America of double standards in encouraging Islamic resistance to the Soviet invasion of Afghanistan while portraying the Palestinians as criminals for resisting the occupation of their land by Israel. Relations between Jordan and America sank to an all-time low. Jimmy Carter cut aid to Jordan from $40 million in 1978 to $20 million in 1980. Jordan's request to buy F-16 aircraft was ignored. The House of Representatives approved a military aid bill denying Jordan any funds until it played the role assigned to it in the Camp David Accords. In Jordan this bill was regarded as black-mail. The Americans attached so many conditions to their offer to sell 300 M60A3 Main Battle tanks that Hussein ended up buying 274 British Chieftain tanks with the help of Saudi Arabia. Hussein's personal relations with Carter also suffered. Carter described Hussein as "a slender reed" on which to rest the prospects of peace.[27] On 17 June 1980 Hussein visited Washington for talks with Carter. Hussein explained the importance of the arms denied by Congress in view of Jordan's vulnerability. But he also repeated his objections to the Camp David Accords, and stressed the need to convene an international conference under UN auspices, to provide for Palestinian representation and to address the question of Palestinian self-determination.[28]

The entire saga of the peace process revolved round the tension between a comprehensive settlement and a separate settlement. The accords that were eventually concluded at Camp David were incompatible with the basic principles of Jordanian foreign policy. Hussein understood that Israel and Egypt ranked much higher than Jordan on the list of America's allies in the Middle East. But he felt that, in his desperate search for a foreign policy success, Carter made the Arabs pay the price for Israel's intransigence. There was no way that Jordan could negotiate on the basis that the West Bank was Israeli-liberated territory. Nor could Jordan afford to play the dangerous and humiliating role spelled out for it in its absence: to act as Israel's policeman in the occupied territories and to safeguard Israel's security while it pursued its expansionist project. After a long period of sitting on the fence, Hussein therefore finally decided to come down on the side of the Arab rejectionists. Hussein's Arab opponents habitually portrayed him as an American stooge. In 1978, however, he defied strong American pressure to make peace on Israel's terms. Paradoxically, from his point of view, the one good thing that came out of Camp David was the breaking of the taboo on direct peace negotiations with Israel.

19. Lebanon and the Reagan Plan

The most momentous event in the private life of Hussein in 1978 was his marriage to Lisa Halaby in a simple ceremony in Amman on 15 June. She was a highly intelligent, cosmopolitan and strikingly beautiful blonde: slim, athletic and tall. She was considerably taller than the man she married and younger by sixteen years. She was born into a prominent Arab–American family, raised in privilege and sent to exclusive private schools. Her father, Najeeb Halaby, was a successful businessman and an aviation executive. Lisa Halaby joined the first class at Princeton to accept women, graduating in 1974 with a degree in architecture and urban planning. After graduating, she worked in the urban planning field in Australia and Iran before joining Royal Jordanian Airlines as director of planning and design projects.

In 2003 Lisa Halaby published a revealing and engaging autobiographical book. *Leap of Faith: Memoirs of an Unexpected Life* is the story of her remarkable journey into Hussein's heart and of the twenty-one years of their marriage, ending with the king's death in 1999. For the king it was evidently love at first sight. Following her move to Jordan, Lisa had several fleeting encounters with Hussein, usually in Amman airport. For the young and independent-minded American woman, the courtship involved some doubts and hesitations. The king was a widower with eight children from three previous marriages and a reputation as a playboy. "I will not deny that the idea of being his fourth wife, or anybody's fourth wife, was troubling to me," she writes.[1] But the king was an assiduous suitor; he would even sing to her.

Having accepted the royal proposal of marriage, Lisa Halaby changed her name to Noor Al Hussein, the "Light of Hussein." She also converted to Islam and began to learn Arabic in earnest. She became a stepmother to Hussein's eight children, including his very young children with Alia. In the early years of their marriage, Noor gave birth to

four more children: Hamzah, Hashim, Iman and Raiyah. Her love affair
with Hussein developed into a love affair with his desert kingdom. As
well as being an intimate portrait of a marriage and motherhood, *Leap
of Faith* conveys a deep commitment to the people, culture and natural
beauty of Jordan. "I had found myself spellbound," writes Noor, "by the
serene expanse of desert landscape washed golden by the retreating sun
at dusk. I was overwhelmed by an extraordinary sensation of belonging,
an almost mystical sense of peace."[2]

There was precious little peace, however, inside the royal palace.
Noor realized that she had to make adjustments to her new environment, but she found the lack of privacy irksome and unsettling. Court
officials were ubiquitous and constantly intruded into what she
regarded as her private space. Noor also had to fight to carve out a
meaningful role for herself. Many in Jordan thought a queen should be
a glamorous figure on a pedestal, perhaps engaged from a distance in
charity work. Noor had no intention of being a mere figurehead and
spending her time simply opening bazaars and exhibitions. On the contrary, she wanted to be involved in tackling real problems.

Through the United Nations and other organizations Noor became
involved in issues that were important to her, such as global peacekeep-
ing, refugee assistance and the Land Mine Ban Treaty. Most of her time
and energy, however, were taken up with work in the areas of women's
and children's welfare, human rights, health, education and the environment. She became acutely aware that all of these problems, which
were tackled in isolation by individual ministries and charities, were
fundamentally interrelated. Her role, as she saw it, was to serve as a cat-
alyst for consensus-building and action. In 1985 the Noor Al Hussein
Foundation was established. Its aim was to provide strategies for sustainable development in Jordan and to integrate efforts to tackle these
various problems in a concerted manner.

While Hussein supported his wife's domestic initiatives, he himself
remained mainly preoccupied with foreign affairs and with his quest
for peace in the Middle East. International politics thus became a constant companion to Queen Noor throughout the years of her marriage.
One theme that crops up again and again in the narrative of *Leap of
Faith* is the frustration and anger she feels in the face of American double standards towards the Middle East. From Jordan she began to see
the land of her birth through new eyes—and the image that she saw of

America was not a positive one. Noor had grown up believing in America's commitment to freedom, justice and human rights, but she gives many examples of Washington's failure to uphold these principles in its treatment of Jordan. She complains, with justice, that America's support for Israel has too often been at the expense of Arab human rights and in violation of international law and United Nations resolutions. During the 1980s Noor undertook several intensive speaking tours in America, gruelling two-week marathons of speeches and interviews. She was uniquely placed to educate her fellow Americans about the problems of the region and did her best to do so, but Israel had a magical hold on the American media and the American political psyche generally. A Jordan Information Office was established in Washington, but it was no match for the Israel lobby.

Whereas in foreign affairs Noor was a valuable source of advice and support to her husband, in domestic politics being a foreigner often counted against her. On at least one issue Noor was at odds with her husband and the leaders of her adopted country: press freedom. From the first years of their marriage, she started lobbying her husband and his key officials to reconsider their restrictive attitude towards personal and institutional freedoms. The press in Jordan, though privately owned, was effectively government controlled. Truly independent reporting did not exist. A combination of conservatism and insecurity made the government apprehensive about allowing the people to read dissenting opinions and about the destabilizing impact of free political reporting. By her own account, Noor's pleas fell on largely deaf ears.[3]

The early years of Hussein's marriage to Noor coincided with considerable turbulence in the region, beginning with the Islamic Revolution in Iran and ending with the Lebanon War. The shah of Iran was an old personal friend and ally, and his fall from power on 1 February 1979 was to Hussein a deeply worrying event. The designation of the shah as "the policeman of the Gulf" reflected his country's importance in American eyes for maintaining regional stability. Now the policeman was gone and his place was taken by Ayatollah Khomeini, a Shi'ite cleric and the leader of the Islamic Revolution. Hussein's friendship with the shah did not stand him in good stead with the new rulers of Iran, who referred to him as "Shah Hussein." The new rulers also threatened Jordan by their support for the PLO and the Palestinian revolutionary groups. Hussein feared that an alliance between the two revolutionary movements would have a radicalizing effect on the Palestinian refugees. But beyond his immediate concerns, Hussein could see the danger that this new regime posed to the security and stability of the entire Gulf. Khomeini openly declared his ambition to export his version of the Islamic Revolution beyond Iran's borders and to topple the corrupt Sunni monarchies of the Gulf. So, following the inauguration of the reign of the ayatollahs in Iran, Hussein and Crown Prince Hassan redoubled their efforts to present Jordan to the West as a bastion of stability in a turbulent region. They emphasized Jordan's reasonableness and moderation and its rejection of all extremist doctrines, be they of the Islamic or the communist variety. But while Jordan could serve as an example, it could not match the Islamic Republic of Iran either in power or in popular appeal. An effective counterweight to balance Iran was needed, and the Arab country best qualified to play that part was Iraq.

The Gulf states also looked to Iraq for protection against Iran because they were weak and vulnerable, even virtually defenceless, and certainly no match for Iranian military power either individually or collectively. Oman was still preoccupied with domestic affairs after suppressing an insurgency in Dhofar. Qatar had a population of 150,000. The United Arab Emirates were tiny. So was Kuwait. Saudi Arabia was an economic giant but a military dwarf. Gulf stability rested essentially on the balance of power between Iran and Iraq. Khomeini was deeply hostile to Iraq and openly incited Iraq's Shi'ite population to rise up and overthrow their secular Ba'thi oppressors. On 17 September 1980 Saddam, who was by now president, launched a full-scale attack on Iran. Hussein went to Baghdad to find out from Saddam the reasons for this attack. Saddam replied that Crown Prince Fahd had encouraged him to do so. Prince Fahd had allegedly told Saddam Hussein that if he attacked Iran, the Saudis would support him financially. Saddam also thought that the internal upheaval in Iran provided Iraq with a unique chance to regain the strategically vital Shatt al-Arab Waterway, which was his declared war aim. Iran was in disarray following the revolution, and there was fear that the revolution would indeed begin to spread. This, said Saddam, was the golden opportunity to neutralize Iran.[4]

Islamic Iran turned out to be a much tougher military opponent than Saddam had expected. The Iran–Iraq War lasted eight gruelling years, from 1980 until 1988. From the outset Jordan backed Iraq against Iran. The war transformed the personal friendship between the two rulers into an enduring strategic alliance between their countries. Jordan began to support Iraq so as to contain the spread of the Islamic Revolution, defend the Arab homeland and protect the Gulf monarchies. A special logistics and supply unit, the Yarmouk Brigade, was formed from ex-service volunteers and sent to assist the Iraqi war effort. The Yarmouk Brigade did not take part in actual fighting, but it freed Iraqi personnel for front-line duty. Hussein used his extensive connections abroad to support Iraq in terms of public relations and to explain that Iraq was also defending vital Western interests in keeping the oil flowing and its price down. The Western powers encouraged Hussein to persist in his efforts to mobilize international and Arab support behind Iraq. America in particular looked with favour on the emerging front against Iran because Iran became its main enemy in the region after the fall of the shah. Hussein played a minor part in bringing Saddam and the CIA together to collaborate against the common enemy, but Saddam had his own independent link with the CIA through his half-brother Barzan Takriti, the director of military intelligence who later became ambassador to Geneva. CIA officers warned Saddam twice about plans for coups against him, once in 1979 and once in the early 1980s, and they informed the Jordanians of what they had done. Every time Hussein asked the CIA to support Saddam, the reply was that they had always supported him. And when the Iranians looked as if they were gaining the upper hand, Hussein pleaded with the Americans to give Saddam more tangible support. The general view in Hussein's inner circle was that, had it not been for American support, the Iranians would have crushed Saddam's forces.[5]

There were economic as well as geostrategic reasons for Jordan's support for Iraq during the Iran–Iraq War. The oil-producing oligarchies of the Gulf, and especially Saudi Arabia, were now virtually Jordan's only source of foreign financial help. Had these regimes been toppled, foreign aid to Jordan would have dried up. Jordan also depended on oil from Iraq: Jordan's only refinery was geared to take Iraq's "heavy" type of crude oil. This gave Saddam great leverage over Jordan. Jordan benefited directly from the war between Iraq and Iran. Many factories were built in Jordan to export goods to Iraq, and there was a particularly significant expansion in the transport sector. Because Iraq is practically landlocked and Basra was blocked by the war, the Jordanian port of Aqaba on the Red Sea became the principal transit point in the supply of goods and services to Iraq. Finally, Jordan derived significant benefits from its military missions to friendly Gulf states during the 1970s and 1980s. Jordan had the most impressive army in the Arab world, the best trained and the most professional if not the best equipped, and it was very willing to extend advice and assistance to the conservative monarchies of the Arabian peninsula. If Jordan had the military expertise, they had the wealth. Personal relations between Hussein and the ruler of the individual Gulf State concerned invariably determined the scope and nature of military cooperation.

Jordan's oldest and most extensive military assistance programme was to Oman. Sultan Qaboos ibn Said, the ruler of Oman, deposed his father in a bloodless coup in 1970. His aim was to develop and modernize his country but before he could do so he had to bring under control the leftist insurgency in the south-western region of Dhofar. Jordan offered him not only advice and training but its own troops to fight the insurgents. Hussein and Qaboos were kindred spirits: both had been to Sandhurst; both were friendly to the West; and both shared a pragmatic attitude towards Israel. By the mid 1970s the situation was stable enough for Qaboos to start building a modern military, with Hussein as his guide. Air Marshal Sir Erik Bennett went to Oman in 1975 on Hussein's recommendation to create an air force out of a ragtag collection of aircraft. Qaboos wanted a comprehensive assessment of the threats facing his realm and advice on strategies to deal with them. Twenty people in foreign uniform arrived in an aircraft, spent several weeks in Oman, produced a report and left. An American ambassador to Oman a decade later was told that the foreign advisers were from Israel and that the broker had been Hussein. Qaboos showed his appreciation by giving Hussein very generous financial support.[6] The number of Jordanian military advisers in the Gulf increased rapidly following Khomeini's rise to power. Jordanian officers were seconded to the United Arab Emirates, Bahrain and other states which felt the need to retrain and reequip their armies. Bahrain, for example, engaged General Ihsan Shurdom, the retired chief of the Jordanian Air Force, to advise them on the training of pilots and the purchase of aircraft. Income was generated for the Jordanian Army and for the royal purse from the provision of these services.

The one Arab country with which Jordan's relations became strained after the outbreak of the Iran–Iraq War, apart from Egypt, was Syria. A rapprochement had taken place as a result of Jordan's rejection of the Camp David Accords. But the war with Iran rekindled tensions between Syria and Jordan, Iraq's new ally. Both Iraq and Syria were ruled by Ba'th parties, but they were bitter rivals and Syria supported Iran in the war against Iraq. American support for Saddam was one of the considerations that led Asad to take the unusual step of backing a non-Arab state against fellow Arabs. Saddam was getting support from most of the Arab world, and Asad's worry was that the Iraqi Ba'th would overthrow his regime and take power in Syria. Asad suspected that Hussein was plotting against him with Saddam and that he was trying to foment domestic strife in Syria by inciting the Islamic opposition against the regime. In November 1980 Syria mobilized its army on Jordan's northern border, giving Jordanian support for the Muslim Brotherhood, a small ultra-conservative group opposed to the Ba'th regime, as the reason for its action. The immediate crisis was defused, but the underlying tension remained.

The alliance with Iraq helped Hussein to pursue his traditional policy of maintaining a regional equilibrium and to fend off threats from whatever source: Iran, Syria or Israel. The Likud government became more hardline and more aggressive in its attitude to the Arab world following the conclusion of the peace treaty with Egypt in March 1979. Sadat was assassinated in October 1981 by a fundamentalist officer from his own army, but his successor, Hosni Mubarak, persevered in his policy of peace and normalization with Israel. The Likud used the treaty with Egypt not to go forward with the peace process but to consolidate its control of the West Bank and to act with impunity towards the rest of the Arab world. In July 1980 it passed the Jerusalem Law, which stated that "Jerusalem, complete and united, is the capital of Israel." The motive behind this was to foreclose any negotiations over the status of the city; the *New York Times* called it "capital folly." In June 1981 the Israeli Air Force bombed the Iraqi nuclear reactor near Baghdad, and in December the Knesset extended Israeli law, jurisdiction and civil administration to the Golan Heights, which had been under military occupation since 1967. The composition of Menachem Begin's government also changed in a more hawkish direction following the resignations of Moshe Dayan and Ezer Weizman. Itzhak Shamir, a former leader of the terrorist Stern Gang and an opponent of withdrawal from any of the occupied territories, became foreign minister. Ariel Sharon, the most aggressive general in the history of the IDF, became minister of defence. Sharon continued to hold the view that the Hashemite regime in Jordan was the chief obstacle to the incorporation of the West Bank into Greater Israel.

Hussein, for his part, increasingly looked to Iraq to offset the threat of an expansionist Israel. The alliance with Iraq compensated to some extent for Egypt's disengagement from the Arab–Israeli conflict. It gave Jordan strategic depth and acted as a deterrent to an Israeli attack. King Abdullah II has commented: "Iraq, as a counterbalance to Israel, would be a lot stronger than Syria or Saudi Arabia. It was a dividend of the relationship that was built in fighting Iran. The dividend of having a strong neighbour like Iraq allowed my father to have a much firmer position in dealing with the Israeli governments at the time."[7] Alignment with Baghdad was also relevant for diplomatic bargaining with Israel. As Prince Talal bin Muhammad has observed: "His Majesty saw Iraq as providing the Arabs with strategic parity with the Israelis to enable us to resume negotiations from a position of strength. He believed that the only thing that would break the deadlock would be Arab strategic parity with Israel. Israel would then be forced to come to the negotiating table. We would be able to negotiate from a position of equality rather than inferiority."[8]

The prospects for breaking the diplomatic deadlock were not enhanced by the election of a Republican administration headed by Ronald Reagan in November 1980. Reagan was one of the most passionately pro-Israeli presidents in American history. In his memoirs Reagan wrote: "I've believed many things in my life, but no conviction I've ever held has been stronger than my belief that the United States must ensure the survival of Israel."[9] Like Nixon and Kissinger before him, Reagan also emphatically perceived world politics through the prism of his country's global rivalry with the Soviet Union. Israel for him was not only a beacon of freedom but a strategic asset in countering Soviet advances in the area. Initially, he was reluctant to get involved in the diplomacy of the Arab–Israeli conflict, although he did wish to cultivate good relations with moderate Arab rulers. With Hussein, Reagan quickly developed a warm personal relationship. He and his wife Nancy enjoyed the glamour that went with entertaining royalty, and

Hussein was the first foreign leader to be invited to Washington on a state visit after Reagan was elected. Reagan said to Richard Viets, the American ambassador to Amman, "That man is a straight shooter and I believe we can do business together." The king subsequently began to realize that Reagan was not always on top of his brief, to put it mildly. Conversation between them often wandered off course.[10]

One major issue in American–Jordanian relations during Reagan's first term of office was the conflict in Lebanon. The traditional rivalry there between Muslims and Maronite Christians was accentuated by the arrival of the Palestinian guerrilla organizations after their expulsion from Jordan. Palestinian attacks on Israel from Lebanese territory further fuelled the cycle of violence by provoking Israeli reprisals. Jordan was not directly involved but Hussein felt all along that Lebanon should be stabilized and that it should not be used as a battlefield. Jordan's interest lay in containing the violence and in calming things down. Accordingly, Hussein used what influence he had to promote reconciliation among the various parties to the civil war but of course he had no influence over the PLO. On 14 March 1978, following a serious terrorist attack, Israel invaded Lebanon and occupied the south of the country between the border and the Litani River. The aim of "Operation Litani" was to destroy the PLO bases and to widen the buffer zone under the renegade Lebanese Army officer Major Saad Haddad, Israel's surrogate in southern Lebanon. The price the Lebanese paid for the incursion was 700 dead, scores of villages devastated, and the flight from the war zone of 225,000 civilians. There was no Arab military resistance to this incursion, and Hussein, in a nationwide speech, deplored what he called the atmosphere of lethargy and indifference that prevailed in the Arab world. He called on the Arab leaders to rise to their national responsibility and so stop the Arab nation from having to "see itself being eroded bit by bit, its limbs chopped off and its honour humiliated."[11] Hussein feared that Jordan could be just as vulnerable to Israeli aggression as southern Lebanon in the absence of united Arab action. On more than one occasion he referred to this first Israeli invasion as one of the most troubling moments in his career because if Israel did to Jordan what it had done to Lebanon, the Arab reaction would be the same: silence and impotence.[12]

Silence and impotence were the hallmarks of the Arab response to Israel's second invasion of Lebanon on 6 June 1982. The invasion was called "Operation Peace for Galilee" in an attempt to portray it as a defensive measure to stop PLO attacks. But it was an offensive war that violated a year-long ceasefire brokered by the US. Menachem Begin was nominally in charge, but the real driving force behind the war was Ariel Sharon. From his first day at the defence ministry, Sharon started planning the invasion of Lebanon. He developed what came to be known as the "Big Plan" for using Israel's military power to establish political hegemony in the Middle East. The first aim of Sharon's plan was to destroy the PLO's military infrastructure in Lebanon and to undermine it as a political organization. The second was to establish a new political order in Lebanon by helping Israel's Maronite friends to form a government that would proceed to sign a peace treaty with Israel. The third was to expel the Syrian forces from Lebanon or at least to weaken seriously the Syrian presence there. In Sharon's big plan, the war in Lebanon was intended to transform the situation not only in Lebanon but in the whole Middle East.[13] The destruction of the PLO would break the backbone of Palestinian nationalism and facilitate the absorption of the West Bank into Greater Israel. The resulting influx of Palestinians from Lebanon and the West Bank into Jordan would eventually sweep away the Hashemite monarchy and transform the East Bank into a Palestinian state. Sharon reasoned that Jordan's conversion into a Palestinian state would ease international pressure on Israel and give it a freer hand to determine the fate of the West Bank and the Gaza Strip. To his close friends Sharon disclosed that had he been prime minister he would have actively helped the Palestinians depose Hussein and establish a Palestinian state in Jordan. He said he would give Hussein twenty-four hours to get out of Amman, but he did not say what would happen if Hussein declined.[14] Begin was not privy to all aspects of Sharon's ambitious geopolitical scenario, but they were united by their desire to act against the PLO in Lebanon.

Israel's war in Lebanon affected Hussein both psychologically and politically. He was in uniform most of the time and looked tense and troubled. His army was not involved, but its morale was adversely affected by seeing another Arab country being humiliated by the Israelis. As their supreme commander Hussein was duty-bound to raise the morale of his soldiers by staying in close touch with them. Most of all he was upset by the loss of Lebanese life and by the suffering inflicted on innocent civilians. In pursuit of the PLO the IDF soon reached the outskirts of Beirut and laid siege to the city. Seeing an Arab capital being occupied by the Israeli Army was a bitter blow to Hussein both as an Arab and as a Hashemite.[15] More ominous was the political fallout from the war. As Zaid bin Shaker, the commander of the Jordanian armed forces at the time, recalled, "There was a very severe reaction in Jordan to the Israeli invasion of Lebanon, especially as the war leader was Sharon and the prime minister was Begin. This was extremely worrying. We had an alert in the armed forces. The situation was unpredictable because the Likud government was an aggressive, expansionist organization."[16] Anxiety about Israel's intentions led Hussein to send his cousin on a secret trip to Washington at the end of July to meet with George Shultz, the new secretary of state. Shaker sought reaffirmation of America's military and political support for Jordan. Hussein, he said, feared that Israel intended to carry out Sharon's threat to create a Palestinian state in Jordan by overthrowing the king. Hussein's fears had been heightened by the lengths to which Israel had gone in Lebanon. Shultz reassured Shaker that they could continue to count on American support for Jordan's independence and territorial integrity.[17]

One of George Shultz's first acts as secretary of state was to send Philip Habib to negotiate an end to the fighting round Beirut. Arafat let it be known that he was prepared to withdraw his men from the city, if appropriate terms and guarantees could be worked out. The withdrawal of the PLO was then only a matter of time: the difficulty was that they had nowhere to go. Sharon came up with a suggestion. He asked an Egyptian intermediary to persuade Arafat to lead the PLO back to Jordan and said that, if Arafat accepted, Israel would force Hussein to make way for the organization. "One speech by me," boasted Sharon, "will make King Hussein realize that the time has come to pack his bags." The message was conveyed to Arafat, who asked the intermediary to give Sharon an immediate reply: "1. Jordan is not the home of the Palestinians. 2. You are trying to exploit the agony of the Palestinian people by turning a Palestinian–Lebanese dispute into a Palestinian–Jordanian contradiction." Arafat also suggested that Sharon wanted to provoke a Palestinian–Jordanian conflict to give Israel an excuse for occupying the East Bank of the Jordan. When Sharon heard Arafat's reply, he responded with an obscene curse in Arabic.[18]

Habib eventually succeeded in arranging for the withdrawal of the

PLO to Tunisia. A first contingent of fighters left Lebanon by sea on 21 August. Arafat left on 30 August aboard a Greek merchant ship, with the US Sixth Fleet providing cover. After seventy-five days of heavy fighting, the remnants of the PLO were banished from its stronghold in Lebanon to the periphery of the Arab world. But in Lebanon itself the strife and violence continued. One consequence of the Lebanon War was the Reagan administration's disenchantment with the Likud. Another was its recognition that one of the root causes of disorder and instability in the Middle East was the plight of the Palestinians.[19] This led to the launching of the Reagan peace plan on 1 September 1982. In the speech unveiling the plan, Reagan said that the departure of the Palestinians from Beirut dramatized more than ever the homelessness of the Palestinian people. His plan was for self-government by the Palestinians of the West Bank and Gaza in association with Jordan. He ruled out both an independent Palestinian state and annexation by Israel. Additional Israeli settlements in the territories would be an obstacle to peace, said Reagan, and the status of Jerusalem had still to be decided. The message was clear: the United States rejected the Israeli claim for permanent control over the West Bank and Gaza. Equally clear was another message: the United States did not think that Israel was entitled to exploit the recent carnage in Lebanon to implement her grand design for Greater Israel. Reagan, however, did not recognize the PLO, and he was unwilling to talk to its leaders. He wanted Hussein, not Arafat, to represent the Palestinians in negotiations on a settlement with Israel. The Reagan Plan sought to bypass the PLO and to bring Hussein and Jordan back into the centre of the scene.

So, shortly before the public unveiling of the Reagan Plan, Nicholas Veliotis, the assistant secretary of state for the Near East and a former ambassador to Jordan, was sent on a secret mission to Amman to present the plan to Hussein and to try to enlist his support. The plan was favourable to Jordan and in its basic conception it was not all that different from Hussein's own United Arab Kingdom project of a decade earlier. Veliotis reiterated the American position that there should be Israeli withdrawal from the West Bank, but he did not say how much. On the other hand, he promised American support for a real settlement freeze. Hussein thought that something really might come out of this initiative and cautiously agreed to join the negotiations on the plan, provided the United States stood by its provisions.[20] He also proceeded to relaunch his earlier project for a Jordanian–Palestinian federation. Menachem Begin rejected the Reagan Plan with all the vehemence he could muster. He had always opposed Palestinian or Jordanian sovereignty over the West Bank and he stuck to his position. He also announced the building of new settlements on the West Bank and used Israel's continuing occupation of Lebanon to derail the Reagan Plan.

Despite Israel's categorical rejection, Hussein remained optimistic and continued to shuttle round the capitals of the region in an attempt to build up an Arab consensus in the plan's favour. But the consensus that emerged at the Arab League summit in Fez, Morocco, the week after Reagan had spoken, was not entirely to Hussein's satisfaction. The summit indirectly recognized Israel and opted for a two-state solution. This represented a fresh pragmatism in the Arab position on Israel—but it went no further. Instead of endorsing a Jordanian–Palestinian delegation to negotiate with Israel, the summit reaffirmed the PLO as the sole legitimate representative of the Palestinian people. The plain fact was that Hussein was acceptable both to the United States and to Israel as a negotiating partner, whereas the PLO was not.[21] Moreover, the Fez summit called for the establishment of an independent Palestinian state in the West Bank and Gaza, whereas the Reagan Plan envisaged Palestinian autonomy in association with Jordan. Despite his best efforts, Hussein failed to secure an unambiguous Arab mandate to proceed with the American initiative.

Following the departure of the PLO fighters, the situation in Lebanon went from bad to worse. On 14 September, Bashir Gemayel, the recently elected Maronite president and Sharon's ally in the war against the PLO, was assassinated by pro-Syrian elements. Two days later Gemayel's followers, with their Israeli allies standing by, entered the refugee camps of Sabra and Shatila, and systematically massacred as many as 800 Palestinian civilians. Once again, the Palestinian issue was entangled with murky Lebanese politics. Hussein watched with mounting dismay America's inability to restrain Israel. Lebanon for him became a test case of American resolve. He, like many Arabs, considered that unless America could get the Israelis out of Lebanon, there was little chance of dislodging them from the West Bank.[22]

In December, Hussein visited Washington for talks with Reagan and his advisers. The Americans tried to persuade the king to continue to support their initiative. At the end of the talks Reagan gave Hussein a letter in which he committed himself to trying to halt the Israeli settlements and to arrange military and financial assistance to Jordan if Jordan entered negotiations. As always, Reagan and Hussein got on well and the meeting seemed to be a success but nothing happened. Although Hussein declared himself to be optimistic as a result of the visit, the differences on the nature of Palestinian autonomy and the question of Palestinian participation in the talks had not been resolved. Hussein's greatest concern was that in the likely event that the negotiations failed, the Begin government would be free to retain the territories. He had doubts about engaging in a process that failed to guarantee the principal objective of his foreign policy: Israeli withdrawal from the occupied territories. On occasion Hussein may have given the impression that he would be willing to proceed without Arafat if the PLO chairman turned out to be intransigent. American wishful thinking probably contributed to this impression.[23]

The risks of proceeding without the PLO were too great because the organization was supported by an all-Arab consensus. If Hussein proceeded on his own and failed, the blame would have been laid fairly and squarely on his shoulders. Hussein therefore needed Arafat's support, and he made a sustained effort to get it. Arafat had his own reasons for wanting to cooperate with his old rival. Weakened by the expulsion of his organization from Lebanon and anxious to recover, Arafat arrived in Amman on 1 April 1983. Hussein impressed on his guest the merits of the Reagan Plan and the advantages of a Jordanian–Palestinian federation. He proposed a coordinated Jordanian–PLO effort to recover the occupied territories and the subsequent establishment of a federation along the lines of the UAK plan. Hussein's aim was to marry the American and the Arab plans: to utilize the Reagan Plan as a vehicle for realizing the principles of the Fez summit. After three days of intensive discussions, Hussein and Arafat drew up an agreement for joint action on the basis of the Fez plan. Before signing the final text, Arafat asked for a delay to make a quick trip to Kuwait to get the approval of the PLO Executive Committee. He promised to come back within forty-eight hours with the signed document. Hussein had no choice but to agree, though he feared that the committee would be divided between moderates and hardliners. This is what indeed happened: the hardliners argued that coordination with Jordan infringed the independence of the PLO and that the reference to Resolution 242 would make Jordan a key player in the negotiations over the West Bank. Arafat did not return to Jordan for more than a year. The Jordan–PLO document was a dead letter.

On 10 April, Hussein called Reagan to inform him that his talks with Arafat had failed and that he was not prepared to go forward on his own. The same day the Jordanian government officially declined to take up Reagan's initiative. Its statement read: "We in Jordan, having refused from the beginning to negotiate on behalf of the Palestinians, will neither act separately nor in lieu of anybody in Middle East peace negotiations."[24] The announcement strained relations between the Reagan administration and Hussein. To Reagan and his advisers it appeared Hussein had never fully accepted their plan; that he did not fight for it; and that he walked away from it after Arafat had double-crossed him.[25] In his memoirs Reagan wrote that his plan was part of a long American effort to persuade Hussein to take part in negotiations with Israel, but "we were never able to get him completely on board."[26]

American comments on Hussein's caution are not unfair, but they serve to obscure other, more fundamental reasons for the failure of the Reagan Plan: the consistent tendency of the PLO to shoot itself in the foot and to put doctrinal purity above practical progress; and the impossibility, for any Arab leader, of ignoring the Arab consensus, as defined by the Rabat and Fez summits, which prevented entry into negotiations with Israel while its troops were occupying another Arab country. The lion's share of the responsibility for the failure of the Reagan Plan, however, goes to Israel, not only because it angrily and absolutely rejected it but because it deliberately sabotaged it by dragging its feet in Lebanon. The Arab response to the Reagan Plan was divided, incoherent and incompetent. But no Arab response could have overcome Israel's opposition. Last but not least were the errors and mistakes committed by the Americans themselves. Jordanians saw no evidence that the Reagan administration was prepared to apply to Israel the degree of pressure required to secure its withdrawal from the occupied territories. The administration was not noted for its courage. Its failure to back its own initiative weighed more heavily with the Arabs than Begin's objections. The Reagan Plan was a sensible, fair-minded and timely initiative to tackle the Arab–Israeli dispute that collapsed for want of American political will and staying power. In the final analysis it was not Hussein who let down Reagan but Reagan who let down Jordan and the Palestinians.

20. Peace Partnership with the PLO

Eighteen months after the collapse of the Reagan Plan, Hussein reckoned that the time was ripe for another attempt at a peaceful resolution of the Arab–Israeli dispute. In the past Jordan had usually responded to the plans of others. This time Hussein adopted a more proactive policy and launched an initiative of his own. One scholar has described it as "the only real example of a Jordanian peace initiative in modern times."[1] Its key element was the invitation to the PLO to forge a common strategy in the quest for a peaceful settlement. Competition with the PLO did not come to an end, but a serious effort got under way to moderate its policies and to turn it into a junior partner in the peace process. Hussein's strategic objective remained the same: the recovery of the occupied territories through negotiations on the basis of UN resolutions 242 and 338. What changed was the part he assigned to the PLO within this framework.

What was behind this shift from competition to co-option of the PLO? First and foremost was the Arab consensus as defined by Arab League summit resolutions. The Rabat summit in 1974 had endorsed the PLO as the sole legitimate representative of the Palestinian people. Hussein therefore could not enter into official negotiations with Israel without their approval. The Fez summit in 1982 had endorsed the idea of negotiations with Israel but only within the framework of an international conference. Hussein therefore could not embark on separate negotiations with Israel without the Arab world turning against him, perhaps fatally. To overcome these problems he proposed an international conference with the participation of the five permanent members of the UN Security Council and of all the parties to the conflict, including the PLO. An international conference, he hoped, would enable him to remain within the limits of the inter-Arab consensus while providing a cover for direct talks with the Israelis.

Another factor in Hussein's calculations was the internal situation in

Israel. The Likud government pursued its expansionist agenda on the West Bank without any inhibitions. It also applied pressure on the indigenous population to move from the West Bank to the East Bank, and its more extreme members talked openly about turning Jordan into an alternative homeland for the Palestinians. The inconclusive outcome of the July 1984 elections resulted in a national unity government with Labour and Likud, and a curious rotation agreement: for the first two years in the life of the government, Shimon Peres was to serve as prime minister and Itzhak Shamir as foreign minister; after two years they were to change places. Itzhak Rabin was to remain minister of defence throughout the life of the government. Labour dominance in the first two years provided a window of opportunity for Jordan. Peres, by his own account, had preferred Jordan over the Palestinians as the partner in negotiations over the West Bank—the Jordanian option—more consistently than any other figure within the Israeli political establishment.[2] Virtually from his first day in office, he began to work through private channels to renew the dialogue with Jordan.

The response from Amman was guarded but encouraging. Hussein seemed willing to explore ways of starting negotiations without assurances regarding the final outcome, something that he had always demanded in the past. Now he was prepared to consider commencing negotiations without preconditions. The reason for the change was that in the new scenario the PLO would negotiate on behalf of the Palestinians, so the risks involved in making concessions would be shared between the king and the PLO. Arafat was prepared to take some risks because he needed Hussein's help to break out of his isolation in Tunis and re-establish his organization as a player in regional politics.

Hussein came to Arafat's rescue when other Arab countries, including Algeria and South Yemen, declined to host the meeting of the Palestine National Council (PNC). Because the Palestinians had no homeland, their parliament-in-exile could meet only in the capitals of friendly Arab states. On 27 September 1984 Hussein received Arafat, accompanied by other members of the PLO leadership, in the Nadwa Palace. Hussein readily agreed to the request of his guests to convene the PNC in Amman despite pressure from Syria and other Arab countries. Syria massed troops on Jordan's border and threatened to invade. Hussein's courage in resisting pressure from Syria was greatly appreciated by Arafat and helped to open a new page in Jordanian–Palestinian relations. Some of Arafat's colleagues, however, could not put behind them the bitter memories of the past or trust the Jordanian monarch to act in the interest of the Palestinians. They were being asked to recognize Israel as the price of admission into an international conference without any certainty that Israel would agree to negotiate with them or, ultimately, to withdraw from the occupied territories. Though there were always some extremists in the PLO who rejected whatever was on the table, many others also now feared that they might play their best card—which they could do only once—and end up with nothing to show for it.

The seventeenth PNC convened in Amman on 22 November 1984. Hussein's opening speech was transmitted by Jordanian television and radio to the inhabitants of the West Bank and the Gaza Strip. It was intended to strengthen the moderate elements within the PLO and to generate grassroots support for the diplomatic option. Hussein called for an international conference at which all the parties to the conflict would be represented, including the PLO. On the other hand, he insisted that UN Resolution 242 had to be the "non-negotiable" framework for a peace conference. Hussein knew that 242 had been rejected by the PLO because it spoke of the Palestinian problem simply in terms of refugees, not in terms of national self-determination. So he presented the Palestinian people with a choice:

If you find this option convincing . . . we are prepared to go with you along this path and present the world with a joint initiative for which we will marshal support. If, on the other hand, you believe that the PLO is capable of going it alone, then we say to you "Godspeed: You have our support." In the final analysis, the decision is yours. Whatever it is, we will respect it because it emanates from your esteemed Council, which is the representative of the Palestinian people.[3]

In January 1985 Hussein received the reply that the Executive Council of the PLO had chosen to work with him on his proposal for joint political action. A series of meetings followed and were concluded by the signing, on 11 February 1986, of a Jordanian–Palestinian accord. By signing the Amman Accord, the Hashemite Kingdom of Jordan and the PLO agreed to move together towards a peaceful settlement of the Middle East conflict. The settlement was to be based on the following principles: total Israeli withdrawal from the occupied territories; the right of self-determination of the Palestinian people within the framework of a confederation with Jordan; and resolution of the problem of the Palestinian refugees in accordance with UN resolutions. Neither Israel nor 242 were explicitly mentioned in the text. Nevertheless, the accord represented a real triumph for Jordanian diplomacy. It was the first time in the history of the conflict that the PLO leaders agreed to a peaceful resolution of the dispute with the State of Israel.

Jordan's foreign minister at the time was Taher al-Masri, a member of a prominent Palestinian family from the city of Nablus on the West Bank. The thinking behind the Jordan–PLO agreement, according to Masri, was as follows: "Jordan and the Palestinians are the two major parties concerned with the Palestinian question. If we could build together a solid understanding, then we could go to the outer circle—certain Arab states that support our view—and develop with them a similar understanding based on our bilateral accord. Basically, we would be able to go to an Arab summit and get the approval of other Arab states. In other words, Jordan and the PLO should be the nucleus of an agreement on the Palestinian question and wider Arab support could be built around this nucleus. This was King Hussein's philosophy."[4]

The Amman Accord breathed new life into the moribund peace process. It became a focal point of discussions both regionally and internationally. It also provided grounds for hope to the Palestinians living under Israeli occupation. But Arab support for the accord fell a long way short of what its signatories had expected. King Fahd of Saudi Arabia was on a visit to Washington at that time. On the day that the accord was signed, Hussein called him to convey the good news. They agreed that King Fahd would talk to President Reagan about the accord and urge the Americans to support it. The Jordanians learned later that Fahd did not even mention the accord during his meeting with Reagan. President Hosni Mubarak of Egypt was in favour of the accord. Although diplomatic relations between Jordan and Egypt had been broken when Egypt signed a separate peace treaty with Israel in 1979 and was expelled from the Arab League, they were restored in September 1984. Given Egypt's continuing isolation, however, Mubarak's support was of limited value. Syria's reaction was predictably hostile. The Syrian claim that the Palestine cause was too important to be left to the Palestinians implied that the PLO had no right to act independently. In reality the Syrians wanted to keep the Palestinian card in their own hands.

So did the Soviets. They saw the accord in cold-war terms, as serving American interests by trying to remove the PLO from the Soviet sphere of influence. They were particularly annoyed because Jordan proposed a joint delegation with the PLO to the international conference. Jordan, they felt, had delivered the PLO to the Americans. Masri flew to Moscow to explain and defend Jordan's position. His request for a meeting with Foreign Minister Andrey Gromyko was first turned down and then granted grudgingly. At their meeting Gromyko was very harsh and accusing. He said that Jordan had taken away their best card, the Palestinian card, by agreeing to a joint delegation. Masri denied the charge. He stressed that Jordan envisaged an international conference under the auspices of the UN with the United States and the Soviet Union as joint sponsors and that PLO participation would serve Soviet, not US, interests. Gromyko was not convinced, and the official Soviet position did not change.[5]

The Reagan administration's attitude towards the Jordan–PLO accord was lukewarm. It was reluctant to get involved in Middle East diplomacy so soon after the failure of its own initiative, which had also called for a Palestinian homeland in association with Jordan. A cold-war mindset instinctively inclined it to seek to exclude the Soviet Union from Middle East diplomacy. Secretary of State George Shultz was close to the Israeli position. He had no confidence in Arab leaders and considered that an international conference would achieve nothing beyond providing a platform for vilifying the American and Israeli governments. He saw direct negotiations between the Arabs and Israel as the only path to peace and regarded the idea of an international gathering as an attempt to circumvent such a path. He needed to be convinced that the PLO would remain in the shadows. Shultz did not place high value on Jordan as an ally or on its ruler as a friend. After one fruitless meeting at the White House, Shultz remarked to Reagan, "Sometimes the king acts like a spoiled child." "George, he's a king," the president sighed.[6]

In his memoirs George Shultz describes King Hussein as "a tightrope walker." "His decision to walk was itself courageous," Shultz concedes, "but he took each step with the utmost caution—and at times, when the wire swayed, he would dart back to the platform for safety and survival."[7] But Hussein was cautious for good reason, and Shultz was out of his depth in the complex world of Middle East diplomacy. He wanted Hussein to ditch the PLO and cut a deal with Israel, so he was not particularly supportive of the king's efforts to bring the PLO on board. On 11 May, Shultz visited Hussein in the holiday resort of Aqaba on the Red Sea and evidently liked what he saw: "King Hussein's palace on the Gulf of Aqaba is a collection of beautifully appointed low-lying structures linked by flower-lined walks, lawns, and gardens. Every detail is exquisite."[8] But there was no real basis for Shultz's impression that they were on the verge of a breakthrough. Later in the month Hussein paid a visit to Washington, and once again the results were disappointing. Hussein went armed with the text of a press statement that Arafat had approved in advance. The statement said that Jordan and the PLO were ready to negotiate "a peaceful settlement on the basis of the pertinent UN resolutions, including 242, and 338." Hussein read out this statement in the Rose Garden of the White House after his meeting with Reagan.[9]

The significance of this statement seems to have been lost on Shultz, who kept pressing Hussein to issue a statement of non-belligerency that would please the Israelis. He was disappointed that the best Hussein could do, in a question and answer session, was to express "a genuine desire for negotiations, proceeding in a non-belligerent manner." "This," writes Shultz, "was not enough for Congress, not enough for Peres, not enough for me."[10] Congress punished Jordan by linking American arms sales to Jordan, which was a bilateral issue, to the peace effort, which was a multilateral issue. Against Shultz's advice, the administration informed Congress of its intention to sell Jordan $1.5 billion to $1.9 billion in arms. Congress vetoed any arms transfers until Jordan and Israel began "direct and meaningful peace negotiations."[11] This was a slap in the face to Hussein, who, as he told Shultz, wanted to engage in direct negotiations with Israel. The ban served no American interest, unless appeasing the Israel lobby is defined as an American interest. Congress is sometimes described as "Israeli-occupied territory," and in this instance the jibe was not unmerited.

To prepare the ground for direct public negotiations, Hussein resumed his covert contacts with Israeli leaders. He met Shimon Peres in London on 19 July 1985, their first face-to-face meeting in nearly ten years. The meeting took place in the king's house in Palace Green,

Kensington, which was conveniently located in the diplomatic enclave a few doors away from the Israeli Embassy. It was a large, three-storey house, surrounded by private lawns and a high wall. The meeting was very friendly and fruitful. The discussion revolved round various possibilities for the future. Peres told Hussein that the preferred option for him was the Jordanian one and that he was ready to help him mobilize support among the inhabitants of the West Bank.[12] The king and the prime minister agreed to move forward in stages. In the first stage a joint Jordanian–Palestinian delegation would meet with Richard Murphy, the US assistant secretary of state for Near East and East Asia affairs; in the second stage the PLO would meet the American conditions for a dialogue; and in the third stage the peace negotiations would begin. There was one point, however, on which they were unable to agree. The king wanted the joint delegation to include some supporters of the PLO. This was unacceptable to the prime minister.[13]

However, Peres later decided he was sufficiently interested in the king's scenario to ask the Americans to give it a try. As Shultz reveals in his memoirs, on 5 August, Simha Dinitz, a former Israeli ambassador to Washington, came to his home with some startling news. He had been sent by Peres, without the knowledge of the cabinet, to report on his meeting with Hussein. But in addition to reporting on the progress made at that meeting, Dinitz informed Shultz of something that Peres had apparently not told the king: if some PLO supporters were included in the delegation to the preliminary talks with Richard Murphy, Israel would have to live with it—after stating its objections publicly. Shultz received a rather different message from Itzhak Shamir, the hawkish foreign minister, through Washington attorney Len Garment. Garment said that Shamir did not want Richard Murphy to meet *any* Palestinians and questioned their judgement in even considering such a meeting, which he felt would break both the letter and spirit of their 1975 commitment not to meet with PLO members, tear apart the Israeli government and jeopardize US–Israeli relations. It was only one more example of the government of national unity speaking with two voices. Shultz consulted Reagan, who ruled that there should be no ambiguity about their refusal to deal with anyone even vaguely connected with the PLO.[14]

Israel's position regarding the PLO was much closer to that of the United States than to that of Jordan. Jordan argued the PLO was relatively weak and could therefore be pressed to make concessions. Israel replied, much like America, that if the PLO was weak it should be excluded altogether from the diplomatic process. This divergence was a major reason for the failure to get peace talks off the ground. As one student of Israeli–Jordanian relations has observed: "For Peres and the Labour Party, the higher the profile of the PLO in any negotiations, the harder to create a political majority for the process in Israel. For Hussein and the Hashemites, the higher the profile of the PLO the fewer the risks in any negotiations, both in the regional and in the Jordanian domestic framework. Hussein felt he could not proceed without the PLO; Peres could not proceed with it."[15]

Arafat helped Hussein by providing a list of names of seven moderate Palestinians for inclusion in the unified Jordanian–Palestinian delegation. None of the seven were prominent members of the PLO. Hussein passed on the list in confidence to the Americans and asked them to select four out of the seven. The Americans went back on their promise and leaked the names to the Israelis, whereupon the secret list became public knowledge. This enabled right-wing Israelis and their even more right-wing supporters in Washington to wage a vigorous campaign on Capitol Hill and in the media against the holding of talks with anyone connected with the PLO. Shultz had authorized Murphy to go to Amman to hold talks with the Jordanian-Palestinian delegation. For a short while it looked as if the Reagan administration was about to break with the tradition of allowing the Israel lobby to dictate American policy in the Middle East. Murphy impressed on his boss that no peace process worthy of the name could be started unless they honoured their commitment to Hussein. But Shultz buckled under the pressure of the lobby and ordered Murphy to cancel his trip to Amman. To the Arabs it seemed that American policy was to erect a series of obstacles to peace and that as soon as one obstacle was removed by Arab effort, another was put in its place. Hussein and Arafat were not alone in their despair. Shimon Peres was said to be very angry in private. He told his close friends that Shultz was "a very stupid man" who had "blown it." What Shultz should have done, in Peres's view, was to ignore the protests, to go ahead with the meeting and to present Israel with a fait accompli.[16]

The aborting of the Murphy mission gave the hardliners on both sides their chance and was consequently followed by a cycle of terrorism and counter-terrorism. Palestinian terrorists murdered three Israelis thought to be Mossad agents in the port of Larnaca, Cyprus. Sharon, the minister of trade and industry, publicly demanded that Israel retaliate against "the terrorist headquarters in Amman." Sharon wanted to destroy any chance of renewing the dialogue with Jordan and to destabilize the country. He had always opposed the Jordanian option, and pointed to the pact between Hussein and Arafat as evidence that Hussein was not a suitable partner for peace talks. Peres and Rabin resisted Sharon's demand to undertake an operation inside Jordan, but they could not afford to appear "soft" compared with the Likud half of the administration.[17] They therefore proposed to the inner cabinet a strike by the IAF on the PLO headquarters in Tunis. On 1 October eight Israeli F-16s carried out the raid against Hamam el-Shaat, the military compound in the PLO headquarters, killing 56 Palestinians and 15 Tunisians and wounding about a hundred others. Arafat himself narrowly escaped. The Security Council and many countries condemned the raid, but the United States condoned it as a legitimate response to terrorism. Reagan sent Peres a message expressing his satisfaction with the operation.

On 5 October, only four days after the raid on Tunis, Hussein had another meeting with Peres. Hussein was accompanied by his prime minister, Zaid Rifa'i, and Peres was accompanied by the young and very dovish director-general of the Foreign Ministry, Yossi Beilin. The meeting took place in the country cottage of Lord Mishcon, a British Jew, a distinguished lawyer, a member of the British Labour Party and a close friend of the king. Hussein's younger sister, Princess Basma, went to school and university with the daughter of Lord Mishcon. He liaised between Hussein and Peres, and his flat in Hyde Park Gardens in central London was used on several occasions for private meetings between them.[18] The relationship between Victor Mishcon and Hussein was one of mutual respect and admiration; Mishcon thought Hussein was a great and very brave man. Mishcon's role in the 1980s was rather similar to that played by Dr. Emanuel Herbert, Hussein's Jewish physician, in the 1960s.[19]

The king summarized his contacts with the PLO and his efforts to set up a joint Jordanian-Palestinian delegation for peace talks with Israel. He stressed that the negotiations would have to be part of an international conference. Peres summarized his country's complicated domestic political scene in order to underscore the importance of speed. He would have to change places with Shamir in a year's time, he said, and then it would be harder to move towards peace. The king expressed concern that the government of Israel, as a result of its unusual structure, was paralysed and incapable of making difficult decisions. The prime minister responded by saying that if and when the moment of decision arrived, and the Likud ministers were the final obstacle to peace negotiations with Jordan, he would not hesitate to dismantle the coalition. The two leaders exchanged views about the speeches they were due to give later that month at the annual session of the UN General Assembly. The meeting ended with polite smiles, handshakes and an agreement to meet again "to advance the peace process."[20]

Within the PLO the hardliners began to pose a challenge to Arafat's leadership and to devise ways of arresting his drift towards accommodation with the enemy. They worked behind his back to mount terrorist attacks on Israeli targets with the intention of scuppering the diplomatic option. The most spectacular of these acts of terror was the hijacking of the Italian cruise ship *Achille Lauro* by four gunmen off the coast of Egypt on 7 October. Before the end of the incident, an elderly American Jew confined to a wheelchair was murdered and thrown overboard. Although the operation was carried out by a minor faction of the PLO, the Palestine Liberation Front (PLF), it seriously damaged the credibility of the entire organization. For Hussein this episode was almost the last straw. "At the end of the day Arafat didn't deliver, and that," according to Taher al-Masri, "was the beginning of the severing of relations between them."[21] In the aftermath of this episode Hussein came under growing pressure, especially from America, to dump Arafat as a negotiating partner and go forward with Israel on his own.

Gradual estrangement from Arafat paved the way for Hussein's reconciliation with his old enemy, President Asad of Syria. Asad had opposed the Jordan–PLO accord from the outset and warned that the effort to arrange direct talks with Israel could lead to another Camp David. Hussein was forced to conclude that Syrian claims could not be ignored if the peace process was to move forward. Zaid Rifa'i activated his back channel to Asad to prepare the ground for a reconciliation. The price of reconciliation with Damascus was a confession of past misdeeds in aiding and abetting the domestic opponents of the Ba'th regime. Hussein was obliged to acknowledge in a letter to his prime minister that underground Syrian Muslim groups had been allowed to

operate from Jordan's territory in their violent struggle to overthrow the
Asad regime. At the end of the year Hussein and Asad met in Damascus
for the first time in six years. The meeting secured Jordan's flank with
Syria and further isolated the PLO, setting the stage for the final break
between the king and the PLO leader.

In January 1986 Hussein made a private medical visit to London.
During the visit he also had two rounds of talks with Richard Murphy.
These dealt with two main issues: defining the mandate of the international conference, at which he was still aiming, and Palestinian representation. Murphy displayed considerable flexibility, and Hussein
asked him for a clear statement of the American position to convey to
the PLO. Their joint efforts seemed to bear fruit. On 25 January, after his
return to Amman, Hussein received a final reply from the Reagan
administration concerning PLO participation in the proposed conference. The reply came in the form of a written commitment that said:
"When it is clearly on the public record that the PLO has accepted Resolutions 242 and 338, is prepared to negotiate peace with Israel, and
has renounced terrorism, the United States accepts the fact that an invitation will be issued to the PLO to attend an International Conference."

Hussein felt that his persistence had at long last paid off and that the
ball was now in the PLO's court. He proudly presented the American
text to the PLO delegation headed by Arafat that came from Tunis to
Amman on 21 January. The talks went on for four days. The upshot was
that the PLO would not accept 242 unless America recognized the
Palestinian right to self-determination. Hussein argued that the important thing was to achieve Israeli withdrawal first and then to proceed to
a confederation along the lines of the 11 February accord. But since
Arafat insisted, Hussein referred the matter back to the State Department and received an amended text. The new text contained a reference to "the legitimate rights of the Palestinian people." Arafat
informed Rifa'i that, despite the positive development of the American
position, recognition of the legitimate rights of the Palestinian people
did not encompass the right to self-determination. There was nothing
more that Hussein could do, and both he and the Americans finally
gave up on Arafat. Hussein concluded that Arafat would never be able
to show the vision and leadership necessary to accept the conditions
that would make a peace conference possible. One American described
Arafat as a "mud puppy"—a bottom-feeding salamander in the canals

of the South, which flaps about to muddy the water whenever anything approaches.[22]

Angry and downcast, Hussein asked Adnan Abu-Odeh, his political adviser, to draft a lengthy speech detailing why his efforts to forge a peace partnership with the PLO had ended in failure. On 19 February 1986, in a speech from the throne that lasted three and a half hours, Hussein gave his side of the story. He characterized Arafat as untrustworthy and said that the problem lay in Arafat's unwillingness to accept unconditionally resolutions 242 and 338 as the price for participation in an international conference. "After two long attempts," Hussein said, "I and the Government of the Hashemite Kingdom of Jordan hereby announce that we are unable to continue to coordinate politically with the PLO leadership until such time as their word becomes their bond, characterized by commitment, credibility and constancy."[23] The long speech marked not just the end of a phase but the end of an era in which Jordan was the leading actor in the search for a peaceful solution to the Middle East conflict.

The rift between Hussein and Arafat revived hopes in the Peres camp that the Jordanian option might be realized after all. The Israeli government supported Hussein in his efforts to rebuild his political influence on the West Bank. As a means to this end, Jordan launched an ambitious five-year plan for improving economic conditions on the West Bank. However, the PLO's assassination of Zafir al-Masri, the pro-Jordanian mayor of Nablus, on 2 March 1986 sent a strong signal that it intended to fight for its position as the sole representative of the Palestinian people. Political rivalry thus undermined joint action between the Jordanian government and the PLO to promote the economic well-being of the West Bank population. The Joint Commission to Support the Steadfastness of the Palestinian People was established, with Taher Kanaan, the Jordanian minister of occupied territories affairs, as head of its Jordanian side and Khalil al-Wazir (Abu Jihad) as head of its Palestinian side.

The Palestinians had complete confidence in Kanaan, who was himself of Palestinian origins. When Jordan launched the West Bank Development Plan, Kanaan approached it as an economist. He advocated a whole menu of measures to improve the everyday life of the people of the West Bank in education, health and welfare. But Prime Minister Zaid Rifa'i had a *political* agenda that affected economic and technical cooperation with the PLO. Rifa'i was trying to prove that a large section of the West Bank population was still loyal to Jordan. He also wanted to demonstrate that the PLO was inadequate and that Jordan was indispensable. Kanaan, by his own account, performed poorly because he did not understand the political game. He was therefore moved to the Ministry of Planning and replaced by Marwan Doudin, who knew much less about economics but much more about politics.[24]

High-level contacts with Israel were resumed when discord grew between Jordan and the PLO. Hussein had a secret meeting with Itzhak Rabin near Strasbourg in France in March 1986. The last time they had met was in 1977 when Rabin was prime minister. Now he was minister of defence with responsibility for the occupied territories. Rabin expressed his concern about the increase in PLO guerrilla activity and asked Hussein to curb the PLO leaders who lived in Jordan. Hussein said he had no intention of allowing the PLO to step up their attacks on Israel, and asked for Israel's help in strengthening the economic and institutional links between the Palestinian population of the West Bank and the Jordanian government. Soon after his return home Hussein ordered the closing down of the PLO offices in Amman and the expulsion of Khalil al-Wazir, the PLO chief of operations and Arafat's deputy. These measures raised tension between Jordan and the PLO to new heights, and they did nothing to enhance Hussein's popular appeal. A poll conducted by the East Jerusalem paper *Al-Fajr* indicated that Hussein had lost favour among the West Bank Palestinians: 93.5 percent regarded the PLO as the "sole legitimate representative of the Palestinian people"; 77.9 percent supported the establishment of an independent Palestinian state; 1 percent supported a link with Jordan; and 60 percent called for continuation of the "armed struggle" against Israel.[25]

The erosion of Hussein's constituency on the West Bank made him more dependent on Israel. Coordination with the Israeli officials became more frequent and more detailed. Rabin and Peres paid a clandestine visit to Hussein at his holiday house in Aqaba in July. This was the house that George Shultz had liked so much. It was a short distance by speedboat from Eilat to Hussein's private wharf in the Gulf of Aqaba. Rabin and Peres were accompanied by Chief of Staff Moshe Levy and Hussein by Zaid Rifa'i. The talks went on for more than four hours, and it was well past midnight when the Israelis set off on their journey back home. The question of an international peace conference inevitably came up for discussion. Peres said that he would continue to work on this after he stepped down to become foreign minister and that Rabin would also represent an element of continuity in the Israeli team.

Hussein agreed with the Israelis that there was no sense in waiting for the PLO to adopt a single unified and realistic stance. He said that he would continue to cultivate moderate leaders from the occupied territories as an alternative to the PLO. The discussion then turned to Jordan's West Bank Development Plan. The Israelis promised to use their influences in Washington, but the American response was disappointing. Jordan was looking for $1.5 billion over the five years of the plan but Congress had allocated only $90 million. The Israelis reaffirmed their policy of providing economic incentives and encouragement to the pro-Jordanian elements on the West Bank. This policy was publicly stated by Rabin in an interview to a newspaper in September: "The policy of Israel is to strengthen the position of Jordan in Judea and Samaria and to strike at the PLO."[26] The use of the Hebrew terminology was rather revealing. It suggested that Israel, like the PLO, was not about to surrender its own claim to the West Bank.

Another aspect of Israeli policy, which deeply troubled Hussein when he found out about it, was the supply of arms to Iran. Hussein saw Iran as a threat not only to Iraq but to the entire Arab world. He was therefore totally committed to Iraq, and assiduously cultivated Arab and Western support for it in its war against Iran. Israel, on the other hand, had a stake in prolonging the Iran–Iraq War: the Khomeini regime in Tehran and the Ba'th regime in Baghdad were both supporters of the PLO, and it suited Israel that they were at war with one another. Israel's interest was believed to be best served by a long and inconclusive war that weakened the two sides. Henry Kissinger once said that America wanted both sides to lose the Iran–Iraq War, and the same was true of Israel. In the spring of 1985 Israel secretly began to sell American-made weapons to Iran. It subsequently involved the Reagan administration itself in the sordid swap of arms to the Khomeini regime for the release of American hostages held by Islamic militants in Lebanon. The Israelis also suggested the spurious strategic guise in which this idea was dressed up, namely, that by supplying modest amounts of arms, America would help the moderates prevail against the radicals in the Khomeini regime and then win back Iran for the West. Soon the scandal was given a name by the American media: Irangate.

The damage from Irangate was serious. As George Shultz noted:

We have assaulted our own Middle East policy. The Arabs counted on us to play a strong and responsible role to contain and eventually bring the Gulf War to an end. Now we are seen to be aiding the most radical forces in the region. We have acted directly counter to our own major effort to dry up the war by denying the weapons needed to continue it. The Jordanians—and other moderate Arabs—are appalled at what we have done.[27]

The revelation that America was actually arming Iran against Iraq outraged Hussein. The additional news that Colonel Oliver North of the National Security Council was supplying Iran with US intelligence in the ongoing war against Iraq was equally disturbing, as Iran had just scored a major victory in the Fao Peninsula in February 1986. Against this backdrop came the news that the Reagan administration was postponing indefinitely the sale of weapons to Jordan. Small wonder that Hussein's mood grew more and more sombre.[28] In a letter to the Reagan administration towards the end of the year, Hussein said that he failed to see how its arms shipments to Iran constituted neutrality. He was convinced that these weapons prolonged the war, strengthened the pro-war faction in the Iranian government and encouraged more hostage-taking. He warned that American actions offered the Soviets an opening to expand their regional influence.[29]

Unlike the Americans, Hussein was completely consistent and unswerving in his support for Iraq. At the personal level the close working relationship between the king and Saddam Hussein developed into a genuine friendship. This was obvious from the way they talked to one another in the company of others. Saddam treated Hussein with great respect and evident affection, calling him "Abu Abdullah," or "father of Abdullah." The two leaders also trusted one another. This helped them to reach a level of mutual understanding and strategic cooperation beyond what was normal in inter-Arab relations.[30] So close was the relationship that the years 1980–90 might be described as the Iraqi decade in Jordanian foreign relations. During this time Hussein visited Baghdad sixty-one times. Important issues did not arise on every occasion, but the king chose to go to Baghdad to sustain the friendship with Saddam and to show solidarity with the Iraqi people.

During the first eight years of the decade, when the Iran–Iraq War was going on, the pattern of these meetings did not change much. Hussein would go to Baghdad with a retinue of aides and advisers. The two delegations would meet in a conference room. Iraqi officers would give a briefing on the war with Iran, including a report from the battlefield. Saddam would add a few comments of his own, saying that he remained confident they were doing the right thing and that they had a solution to all the problems. His subordinates never contradicted him. Hussein would follow up with his own evaluation of regional and international developments. The two leaders would then go into a room on their own for a private conversation without any aides or note-takers. Hussein rarely told his people what transpired at these face-to-face meetings, but some of the issues they discussed were clearly highly sensitive. Saddam, for example, used the king to pass information and messages to many countries, including America and Britain.[31]

Throughout the 1980s America and Britain used Hussein and his generals to arm Saddam Hussein covertly. The Jordanian monarch not only provided facilities for transferring arms for Iraq; he also acted as a lobbyist for Saddam's unsavoury regime in the West. In March 1982 Hussein seized on intelligence reports to Washington, suggesting that the Iraqi Army was in serious trouble militarily, to urge swift action to forestall the possibility of its defeat at the hands of Iran. Jordan was the perfect front for covert American operations, whether they involved intelligence sharing or the supply of arms: Jordan had a long and open border with Iraq, and arms shipments could arrive by way of the Red Sea to the port of Aqaba and from there travel overland to Baghdad. Jordan's pro-Iraqi generals, supine bureaucracy and corrupt army of middlemen also made it the ideal staging ground for arms trafficking. The CIA station in Amman played a part in promoting these clandestine arms shipments to Baghdad. In June 1982, when an Iranian victory seemed imminent, the White House was persuaded to share some of America's most sensitive photographic intelligence with Saddam. The person chosen to hand-carry the satellite photographs to Baghdad was no spy, no courier and no special agent, but the Jordanian monarch himself. Later, as intelligence sharing became more frequent, arrangements were made for trusted Iraqi agents to pick up the sensitive data in Amman.[32]

The financial rewards of the alliance with Iraq were very considerable for Jordan's business community, as well as for the king personally.

The Iran–Iraq War ushered in a new era of close economic cooperation. Iraqi purchases of Jordanian products grew steadily throughout the 1980s. Jordanian exports to Iraq increased from $168 million in 1985 to $212.3 million in 1989. By the end of the decade the Iraqi market accounted for nearly a quarter of all Jordanian exports.[33] Iraq was a very wealthy oil-producing country, and Saddam was a very big spender. No figures are available on the financial support that Saddam extended to the king because this was treated as a private matter between them, but the sums involved were probably very large.[34] Iraqi largesse helped to liberate the king from his financial dependence on the Gulf states. Hussein always felt uneasy about his relationship with some of the Gulf shaikhdoms, especially Saudi Arabia and Kuwait. He felt that the rulers of these countries did not always treat him with the respect he deserved. For a proud man it could be a humiliating experience to have to go to these rulers again and again to beg for money for his country. The aid he received helped to keep Jordan afloat but was not sufficient to fund major development projects. Saddam, by contrast, always treated Hussein as an equal partner and as a valued friend, and the help he gave was on a much more generous scale.[35]

Throughout his reign Hussein prided himself on his Pan-Arabism and on his services to the cause of Arab unity. In the mid 1980s he made a dramatic but little-known attempt to heal the rift between his giant neighbours to the north, Iraq and Syria. The main purpose of this attempt was to bring to an end Syrian support for Iran and to rally the entire Arab world behind Iraq. In April 1986, after reaching his own rapprochement with President Asad, Hussein shuttled between Baghdad and Damascus in an effort to bring about a similar reconciliation between the rival Ba'th regimes. His efforts bore fruit, and he succeeded in persuading first Saddam and then Asad to meet secretly under his auspices in Jordan.

The meeting took place at the Jafar Air Base in the eastern desert near Ma'an. One of the little houses on the base was prepared for the occasion. The king went into the house with his guests and stayed with them for an hour and then withdrew to let them talk privately. Saddam Hussein and Asad worked continuously for eighteen hours with some breaks: Saddam would go for a walk round the base with his bodyguards; Asad would go to his chalet to sit down and talk with Abdel Halim Khaddam, his vice-president. The king was slightly worried that his guests were taking so long. Saddam told him afterwards that he had spoken for half an hour and that Asad had spoken for the other seventeen and a half hours. Asad was extremely shrewd and decisive but notoriously long-winded. When Saddam and Asad said they had finished, Hussein rejoined them in the little house. They told him that the talks had failed to close the gap between them. Asad wanted the announcement of a union between Iraq and Syria before anything else could happen, and Saddam rejected this condition. Asad was uncompromising throughout and unrepentant about his support for Iran; Saddam struck the posture of an Arab nationalist. An Arab country like Syria, he said, should not help a non-Arab country against a fellow Arab country. The fact that Asad and Saddam were Ba'thists who subscribed to the same ideology made no real difference. Each was entrenched in his own worldview and each was single-minded in the pursuit of his own interests. The irony of this abortive exercise in peacemaking was that a Hashemite king had tried to mediate between two Ba'thists in the interests of Arab unity.[36]

21. The London Agreement

After his break with the PLO, Hussein pursued a very assertive policy of building up support for his leadership of the Palestinian cause on the West Bank. In a speech at the opening of parliament on 1 November 1986, he stated that the Palestine question remained Jordan's central concern, and that the Jordanian and the Palestinian people would continue to swim together in the same historical current.[1] Hussein also placed renewed emphasis on the now ageing idea of an international conference as a vehicle for solving the Palestine problem. A separate peace with Israel on the Camp David model was out of the question. A conference was needed in order to give negotiations with Israel international legitimacy and to base them on UN resolutions. As always, Hussein also needed some Arab cover for dealing directly with Israel, and the break with the PLO made it all the more necessary to coordinate his moves with Syria. The Syrians had had a phobia about bilateral deals ever since Sadat signed the Camp David Accords. They wanted an international conference in order to balance the weight of Israel and its superpower sponsor. The traditional Syrian position was that peace talks would be meaningful only when the Arabs achieved some sort of strategic parity with Israel, but that was at best a very distant prospect. For the time being an international conference provided them with an incentive to go along with Hussein's diplomatic efforts. The problem was not Syria but Israel, or rather the deep division within the national unity government between Likud and the Labour Party. In October 1986, as pre-arranged, Shamir and Peres swapped places: Shamir became prime minister and Peres stepped down to become foreign minister. Abba Eban aptly described the change as "ushering in the tunnel at the end of the light."

Once Shamir had rotated into the top job, he was as indefatigable in resisting diplomatic initiatives to change the status quo as Peres had been in promoting them. But demotion in no way weakened Peres's urgent sense that the Jordanian opening had to be pursued with vigour and determination. The Jordanians would proceed to bilateral negotiations with Israel only under the cover of an international conference but Shamir flatly rejected the idea. "As long as I am prime minister," Shamir declared in the Knesset, "there will be no international conference." The Americans too remained cool towards the idea of convening an international conference because they wanted to keep the Soviet Union out of Middle Eastern diplomacy. As the official diplomatic channels produced no movement, Peres tried to reach a breakthrough by means of a secret summit. He accepted with alacrity the offer of his old friend Lord Mishcon to set up a meeting. As we have seen, Mishcon had often liaised between Peres and Hussein, and he enjoyed the complete trust of both. He carried messages back and forth across the bridge on the River Jordan and succeeded in arranging a meeting. The time and place were fixed for Saturday, 11 April 1987, at Mishcon's flat in central London. Peres told Shamir about the meeting and received his grudging consent. To Peres's aide Shamir remarked that he was pleased about this channel to Jordan: it would not bring peace but talking helped to prevent war. On Friday, Peres took off for London aboard a small executive jet, accompanied by Dr. Yossi Beilin, the political director-general of the Foreign Ministry, and Efraim Halevy, the deputy-director of the Mossad. During the flight Peres and Beilin jotted down some notes that later helped with the drafting of what became known as the London Agreement.[2]

Hussein came to the meeting in Hyde Park Gardens with Zaid Rifa'i, still his prime minister and confidant. The domestic staff had been given the day off, and Lady Mishcon cooked and served a delicious meal herself. The king was in sparkling form, weaving amusing anecdotes into his pithy political assessments. He made people laugh by recounting that Ronald Reagan once asked him about fishing in the Dead Sea. Rifa'i told an amusing anecdote of his own about a sleepy guard at a government guest house in Cairo who only let him in one night when he pretended to be Shimon Peres. After lunch the politicians settled down to serious business. Their discussion was to continue for seven hours. It began with a survey of the events of the previous year. The conversation flowed smoothly and pleasantly, and gradually turned to the real issues.

Hussein thought that the Reagan administration was thoroughly confused as to what it was trying to achieve in their region, but he reserved his sharpest comments for the PLO. They were ambiguous in their basic political positions, he said, and this ambiguity, far from being constructive, simply reflected their vague and indeterminate political thinking. The PLO continued to engage in terror and effectively rejected all openings for productive negotiations. The king stressed that his vision of an international conference did not embrace the PLO as long as it continued to reject resolutions 242 and 338. But the Palestinians would not want to be left out altogether, so they were likely to agree to a joint delegation with Jordan and to put forward representatives who would be acceptable to Israel. Hussein also predicted that in the long term the PLO would lose the support of the main players in the Arab world. Peres agreed that neither Israel nor Jordan could regard the PLO, committed by its charter to seek the destruction of Israel, as a partner for peace. Israel certainly did not want to see Arafat ruling Amman, he added in what amounted to a reaffirmation of the Labour Party's traditional policy of support for the House of Hashem. Peres reported that a Soviet envoy turned up at a Socialist International meeting in Rome specifically to see him and that his message was that Moscow accepted the concept of a "non-coercive" international conference. The king observed that Soviet policy-making was undergoing very real and positive changes, even though many of the officials remained the same.

The two leaders found themselves in agreement on many, though not all, of the key issues. They agreed that the time was ripe to move towards a resolution of the conflict. They also agreed that an international conference should be convened to launch the process, but that it should not have the power to impose solutions. Their idea was that the conference should assemble once and that every subsequent session would require the prior consent of all the parties. They agreed too that there should be a joint Jordanian–Palestinian delegation that would not include avowed members of the PLO. Finally, they agreed that after the opening session, negotiations would be carried out face to face in bilateral committees consisting of Israelis and their Arab opponents. According to Peres, "The King spoke enthusiastically of this agenda. He stressed the urgency of reaching a comprehensive settlement. His commitment to the peace process was clear and unequivocal, he said. 'This is a holy challenge for me,' he declared, 'a religious duty.' He explained that he understood Israel's reservations about an international conference, 'But the goal is peace, not a conference.' " Zaid Rifa'i said that he too agreed with the key points that Peres had articulated. "Well, then," said Peres, "why don't we try to write down our agreement?" The king said he could not do this, as he had another engagement that would take him one hour. He suggested that in the meantime the Israelis draft two documents: one detailing the principles and procedures of the proposed international conference, and the other setting out the agreements and understandings between Israel and Jordan. The king and Rifa'i left, and the Israelis quickly got down to work. Lord Mishcon, a distinguished lawyer and a skilled draftsman, helped them to write the text. By the time the king and Rifa'i returned, the two papers were ready. They read them carefully, and Rifa'i started to suggest changes, but Hussein stopped him, saying the two drafts accurately reflected the agreements they had reached. They decided, finally, to transmit the paper to the Americans and to ask them to present it as an American paper. The meeting ended on a note of high hope. Both leaders were deeply gratified with the results of the day's work.[3] For Peres the document represented a major achievement. There had been countless clandestine meetings with the king of Jordan, but this was the first meeting that produced an agreement in writing. Hussein's achievement consisted of getting an Israeli agreement in principle to an international conference and thus meeting the basic Arab condition, laid down at the Fez summit of 1982, for negotiations with Israel.

Unsigned but with the date and venue at the bottom, the London Agreement was typed in English on a single sheet of paper. It was divided into three parts. The first proposed that the UN secretary-general should invite the five permanent members of the Security Council and the parties to the Arab–Israeli conflict to negotiate a peaceful settlement based on resolutions 242 and 338 "with the object of bringing a comprehensive peace to the area, security to its states, and to respond to the legitimate rights of the Palestinian people." The second proposed that the conference should invite the parties to form bilateral committees to negotiate on issues of mutual interest. It was the third, however, that was the key, for it summarized all the points on which Jordan and Israel had agreed:

1. The international conference will not impose any solution or veto any agreement arrived at between the parties.

2. The negotiations will be conducted in bilateral committees directly.
3. The Palestinian issue will be dealt with in the committee of the Jordanian–Palestinian and Israeli delegations.
4. The Palestinians' representatives will be included in the Jordanian–Palestinian delegation.
5. Participation in the conference will be based on the parties' acceptance of resolutions 242 and 338 and the renunciation of violence and terrorism.
6. Each committee will negotiate independently.
7. Other issues will be decided by mutual agreement between Jordan and Israel.

Finally, it was stated that the document was subject to approval by the respective governments of Jordan and Israel and that it would be shown and recommended to the United States.[4]

The PLO was not mentioned anywhere, and this was bound to upset its supporters. On the other hand, an international conference, however impotent, was bound to upset right-wing Israelis. Both Hussein and Peres needed US help in order to overcome opposition to their agreement from within their own camps. Not long after his return home, Hussein contacted George Shultz and explained what had been agreed, urging the secretary of state to give his blessing. Peres acted with greater dispatch by sending Yossi Beilin to Helsinki to intercept Shultz, who was on his way to Moscow to arrange a summit meeting between Ronald Reagan and Mikhail Gorbachev, the new president of the Soviet Union.

Peres himself called on Shamir as soon as he got home, early on Sunday morning. They arranged to meet alone, after the weekly cabinet session. Peres gave Shamir a full account of his talks with Hussein and read to him the text of the document. Shamir asked Peres to read it again, and he did so. But when Shamir asked for a copy of the document, Peres refused. He told Shamir frankly that he was afraid of leaks not by the prime minister but by his staff. Peres added, a bit disingenuously, that as the arrangement was for the Americans to put forward the plan as their idea, it would be better if Shamir received it directly from them. Shamir said nothing.[5] Shamir and his colleagues did not trust Peres, and, although the London Agreement dealt only with procedures, they suspected that Peres had made secret concessions on substance. The fact that Hussein, who in the past had always insisted on knowing the outcome before official negotiations could start, now agreed to negotiations without any preconditions seemed to them to support these suspicions. Besides, even though the London Agreement did not formally commit Israel to anything of substance in advance, Shamir feared that it might open the door to the territorial compromise favoured by the Labour Party.

In Helsinki, Beilin gave Shultz a full account of the London meeting, describing it as an historic breakthrough, and urging him to adopt it as an American plan. "Don't let it evaporate," Beilin said. "It's in your hands now." Shultz had no difficulty with the idea of a carefully controlled international conference that would meet to propel the parties into direct, bilateral negotiations. Yet he thought it was extraordinary for the foreign minister of Israel's government of national unity to ask him to sell to Israel's prime minister, the head of a rival party, an agreement made with a foreign head of state. The problem was compounded by the fact that Shamir, in his Passover message to Reagan on 1 April, had stated that it was "inconceivable that there may be in the US support of the idea of an international conference, which will inevitably reintroduce the Soviets into our region in a major role."[6]

On 22 April, Shultz telephoned Shamir to tell him that he had been informed of the London Agreement by his foreign minister and by the king of Jordan, and to say that he was ready to go to the Middle East to move forward with him in the peace process. Shamir replied that he wanted to think the idea over for a day or two, but Shultz could sense that he was dead against it. Two hours later Elyakim Rubinstein, Shamir's aide, called from Jerusalem to give Shamir's answer. Shamir did not want to say this directly, but the London document had no appeal for him and he would not welcome a visit by the American secretary of state. An international conference would amass pressure on behalf of the Arabs on Israel. If the United Nations was involved, it was inevitable that the PLO would be as well. The next day, 23 April, word came from Peres: he was pleased with the way Shultz had handled the issue with Shamir; he recognized that he would have to risk breaking the government over this; but he would not be party to Israel missing this opportunity. "In London, Israel and Jordan had been in direct negotiations and had achieved agreement. Would the Israeli prime minister now turn away from this opportunity?" Peres asked.

A tug of war was taking place between the Israeli foreign minister and prime minister for the attention of the US secretary of state. It was as if the two men were pulling the stocky American by the arms in opposite directions. On 24 April, Moshe Arens, the hawkish minister of defence, turned up at Shultz's office, sent by Shamir without the knowledge of his foreign minister. Arens said bluntly that the prime minister and their party were opposed to the holding of an international conference on the Middle East and that if Shultz visited Israel to present the Peres–Hussein agreement, he would find himself embroiled in an internal Israeli political debate. Shultz described to Arens in great detail exactly how a conference could work and be kept under control, but Arens refused to budge. Nothing could go forward, Arens concluded, until Shamir and King Hussein met face to face. The conversation ended on this sour note but with what amounted to a request for help in arranging such an encounter.[7]

All the Likud ministers shared Shamir's hostility to the London Agreement. Ariel Sharon did not want any peace negotiations with the House of Hashem, with or without an international conference. His solution to the Palestinian problem was still to topple the monarchy in Amman and to replace it with a Palestinian regime that would be dependent on Israel. On 6 May, Peres presented to the inner cabinet a detailed proposal based on the London Agreement and met with unanimous opposition from the Likud ministers. He could have put the matter to a vote, but decided not to do so, as the outcome was certain to be a five–five split.[8] After the meeting Peres continued to lobby for an international conference at home and abroad, arguing that there was no cabinet decision against it. Shamir said that his coalition partner was exceeding his powers, since there was no cabinet decision in favour of it either. He went further and described his foreign minister's plan as a "perverse and criminal idea" that must be "wiped off" the cabinet table.[9] Peres considered resigning, but this would have entailed stating his reasons in public and thus violating the pledge of secrecy he had given Hussein at their meeting in London.[10]

So the progress promised by the London Agreement ground to a halt. Hussein was bitterly disappointed and tended to think, in retrospect, that Peres had underestimated the strength of the domestic opposition he would face and overestimated his capacity to mobilize American support for the plan:

The London Agreement foundered on two levels. Shimon Peres came as foreign minister and we reached an agreement in London and initialled it. He said he would go back and he would send it immediately to George Shultz and within forty-eight hours it would come as an American addendum to the Reagan Plan. Peres also said that the agreement would be accepted by Israel and I promised it would be accepted by Jordan. So he left. Two weeks later nothing had happened. And then a letter was sent by Shultz to the Israeli prime minister at the time, Itzhak Shamir, telling him that this was the agreement that Peres and I had reached and asking him for his views. And of course Shamir took a negative stand against it and the whole thing fell apart. I cannot say what happened in Israel but Peres, as far as I was concerned, was the Israeli interlocutor. I talked with him. I agreed with him on something and he couldn't deliver.[11]

The London Agreement was another missed opportunity of great importance. Ali Shukri, the director of Hussein's private office, emphasized that this time it was not the Arabs but the Israelis who blocked the path to progress:

Why did Shamir reject the plan? Our belief is that Peres did not have a complete mandate from Shamir to go and make an agreement. Even when Peres was discussing this agreement in London, he did not consult with Shamir. So Shamir was faced with an agreement that he did not approve about to be announced to the world as an American plan. The Americans did not force the issue on the Israeli government. So the plan was not taken any further. It died. The Americans did not even announce it. It was a beautifully crafted plan but Shamir buried it. Hussein believed that it was the inner fighting within the Israel government that shut it down. Whether it was the rivalry between Likud and Labour, or Shamir and Peres, it was shut down. It was also a clear message for the Americans that the Israelis were not ready to discuss peace. We were ready but the Israelis shut it down. The collapse of the London Agreement left Hussein completely in the cold. He said about Peres: "The man agreed but couldn't deliver. This is really serious!" Hussein always asked himself: "What was Peres doing in London?" This agreement could have been a real milestone in the Middle East. The question kept turning in Hussein's mind: what is happening in Israel? Do they really want peace or not? Hussein just couldn't answer this question until Itzhak Rabin became prime minister five years later.[12]

Peres, the leading proponent of the Jordanian option, consequently lost credibility in Jordan. Hussein took a dim view of his failure to bring down the government following Shamir's rejection of their agreement. He had no confidence in Peres, and he did not meet with him again until after the Oslo Accord was concluded with the PLO in 1993.[13]

Shamir was nothing if not consistent. His foreign policy was dictated by the ideology of Greater Israel and he rigidly adhered to it. After scuttling the London Agreement, he sought to arrange a meeting with Hussein. It was far from clear what the purpose of such a meeting would be, since the king's overriding aim was to recover the territory he had lost in June 1967, whereas Shamir was adamant that this territory belonged to Israel and he was determined to hang on to it in perpetuity. The last sentence in Shamir's autobiography is highly revealing in this respect. "If history remembers me at all, in any way," he writes, "I hope it will be as a man who loved the Land of Israel and watched over it in every way he could, all his life."[14] In any case, Shamir did succeed, with discreet American help, in arranging a meeting with Hussein. It took place at Castlewood House, Hussein's home bordering on Windsor Great Park in Surrey. (This was the smaller of Hussein's two country homes in England, the larger being Buckhurst Park in Ascot.) The meeting took place on 18 July 1987. Shamir was accompanied by Elyakim Rubinstein, a senior aide; Brigadier Azriel Nevo, the prime minister's military secretary; and Efraim Halevy, the deputy-director of the Mossad. Shamir's aim was to persuade Hussein to abandon the idea of an international conference, the centrepiece of the London Agreement. Halevy thought that Shamir and Hussein had similar interests: neither wanted a quick solution to the Palestinian problem, and neither trusted Arafat. The king, according to Halevy, never forgot that Arafat had tried to overthrow the Hashemite regime in the summer of 1970 and to assassinate him. Consequently, neither was in a hurry to change the status quo.[15] Halevy's view however, is a more accurate guide to Shamir's thinking than to Hussein's.

Shamir knew that the Jordanians were worried that the extremists within the Likud wanted to expel Palestinians from the West Bank to the East Bank in line with the slogan "Jordan is Palestine." He therefore tried to reassure Hussein that this was not the policy of his party or of the government he headed. Shamir opened the meeting by telling Hussein that the survival and stability of Jordan was a high priority for himself and his colleagues, and that they would not do anything to disturb his country.[16] The London Agreement was not even mentioned. What Shamir did do was to present to Hussein the reasons for his rejection of the conference idea: "I opposed the convening of an international conference first and foremost because of the participation of the Soviet Union, which was very hostile to Israel and supported the PLO and the establishment of a Palestinian state . . . The Soviet Union also opposes Jordan ideologically and, therefore, the best chance for peace is through direct negotiations between us and Jordan, without mediators."[17] Shamir also presented a series of proposals for cooperation between Israel and Jordan in matters of common concern such as water, ecology, tourism and the development of the Eilat–Aqaba region.

Hussein went into the meeting to see if he could make any headway with the right-wing Israeli prime minister. He found that he could not. Queen Noor was told by her husband that the meeting was inconclusive and that the atmosphere at Castlewood House had been very tense: "Shamir's staff were so suspicious that they wanted to search Hussein's secretary's bags and to examine the food. The Israelis would not even use the house phone. They went into the nearby village to make their phone calls from a public phone booth."[18] To his aides Hussein said after the meeting with the diminutive Israeli prime minister: "From this midget nothing came out." The remark was serious and humorous at the same time because Hussein was not much taller than Shamir.[19] At an interview many years later Hussein elaborated: "I found that he [Itzhak Shamir] was very blunt, there was not very much room for putting any of the ideas, or hopes, or aspirations, that I had in mind into reality. He had the philosophy that the whole of Palestine was a part of Israel. At best the Palestinians could have some possibility of ruling themselves, and looking after their own affairs. So there wasn't much that we could really talk about or agree about. However, it was the first contact to see . . . where we stood, and I explained where we stood, and that was the end of that."[20] Hussein's son Abdullah was in charge of security for the meeting. He was standing by a car outside when Shamir came out of the house, and he shook hands with him. Abdullah too recalled his father's remark that nothing came out of the midget.[21]

The Israeli prime minister and the Jordanian monarch each gave George Shultz a rather different assessment of the meeting. Shamir's report was conveyed by a senior Israeli aide, Dan Meridor. Meridor described the event to Shultz as a turning point because it was the first time in history that a Likud prime minister had met with the king of Jordan.[22] The meeting went on for five hours, beginning formally, ending warmly. According to Meridor, Shamir put forward a long list of cooperative steps that could be taken jointly by Israel and Jordan, and went over the interim arrangements for Palestinian self-rule that had been launched at Camp David. This was the way to proceed, said Shamir, not by way of international conference. Shultz tentatively raised the possibility of a cosmetic international conference that would set the stage for direct negotiations and then disperse. "We are against an international conference," Meridor said. It was obvious that Shamir wanted to focus on his own private contacts with the king. The two had agreed, Meridor said, that Shamir would send an emissary to Amman soon. Was there a chance here, Shultz wondered, that Shamir had caught a mild case of peace fever? Might he want to compete with Peres as peacemaker but do it in his own way—secretly with King Hussein and without the backdrop of an international conference?

The contrasting report from Amman gave no grounds for such optimism. In effect, Hussein was saying that Shamir was hopeless and that he could not work with him. This stood in sharp opposition to Shamir's claim that he could work directly with Hussein and did not need any help from outside. Each insisted that Shultz should not reveal his assessment of the encounter to the other. Shultz specifically asked Hussein for permission to reveal to Shamir that he had received his report of the session. The answer was no. Both parties seemed to Shultz to disparage and discount the importance of the United States in all this.[23]

Since the sides had made no headway on their own, Shultz came up with the idea of linking Middle East peace talks to the Reagan–Gorbachev summit that was due to take place in Washington at the end of the year. His idea was that Reagan and Gorbachev, as an adjunct to their summit, would invite Hussein and Shamir, as well as representatives from Egypt, Syria and Lebanon, to meet in the United States under US–Soviet auspices and with the secretary-general of the United Nations in attendance. The gathering would call on the parties to engage in direct negotiations, and the Jordanian delegation would include Palestinians acceptable to Israel. Reagan, who was growing weary of the Middle East and the incessant manoeuvring of its leaders, gave the go-ahead. "But the first guy who vetoes it kills it," he said. In mid October, Shultz flew to Israel to put the idea to Shamir. Shamir asked dozens of questions, all implying that, on reflection, he could not say yes. "Okay," said Shultz, "I don't want to waste your time. Just say no." Shamir wanted time to think and to consult. Their next session was brief. "Well, Mr. Secretary," Shamir concluded, "you know our dreams and you know our nightmares. We trust you. Go ahead."[24]

From Tel Aviv, Shultz flew to London, and on 19 October in the evening he and Richard Murphy paid a visit to Hussein at his residence on Palace Green. Shultz presented the idea of an adjunct to the superpower summit to Hussein, Taher al-Masri and Marwan Kasim. He went over the proposal in great detail and invited the Jordanians to ask questions and to reflect on it overnight. Hussein was taken aback by the new US proposal, which completely ignored his agreement with Shimon Peres and was consistent, virtually word for word, with the Likud position: "Forget any international conference and negotiate directly with Shamir without the PLO or the permanent members of the UN Security Council." The king said he could not oblige.[25] He was about to host an Arab summit in Amman and would have been laughed out of court if instead of the much coveted international conference he presented the idea of a conversation with Itzhak Shamir at the tail-end of a superpower summit. After Shultz departed, the Jordanians found his briefing folder behind a cushion on the couch. It was a thirty-two-page file marked "Secret/Sensitive." The Jordanians promptly made a photocopy and put the folder back in its place; when an American diplomat came to look for it, they pretended they had not noticed it. The king was upset by the content of the file.[26] It was riddled with ambiguities and evasions on the critical issues, and it was full of double-speak. It smacked of craven appeasement to Shamir and displayed indifference towards Arab sensitivities. Hussein could call the meeting an "international conference," Shamir could deny that it was, and the Americans could simply say that it was "an historic event." The file included an Israeli "non-paper" with a list of conditions for participating in this historic event and another long list of assurances that America was to give Israel with Jordan's knowledge. The section "Tactics for Dealing with Hussein" began with the subheading "His Likely Mood." It said: "Hussein is fearful that renewed peace process diplomacy could complicate his Arab summit. Substantively, he is wary of any effort to push him into a Shamir-designed negotiation, with little international cover, a non-existent or weak link between final status negotiations and transitional arrangements."[27] These were indeed Hussein's concerns. There was nothing he could do if after reaching an interim agreement, Shamir refused to proceed to final status negotiations. By the time Shultz went to Palace Green the next day, 20 October, Hussein had made up his mind: his answer was no. He gave two reasons. His nerves were raw at the very mention of Shamir. "I can't be alone with that man," he said in an aside to Richard Murphy. Hussein did not believe that Shamir would ever permit negotiations to go beyond the issue of "transitional" arrangements for those living in the West Bank and Gaza. And he also did not believe Shamir would ever give up an inch of territory or work on a "final status" agreement for the territories. A third reason was implied but not stated. The king knew that President Asad of Syria would reject the proposal and that the Soviet Union would side with Syria. So no, and that was that, said the king.[28]

Once the American proposal was dismissed Hussein turned his attention to the Arab League summit that he had taken the lead in organizing. The summit opened in Amman on 8 November 1987 and lasted three days. It was a high point of Arab unity and cooperation, and one of the king's finest hours. Hussein was the only Arab leader on good terms with all the rival blocs, and he took great pleasure in playing the part of peacemaker. His two main achievements were in mobilizing general Arab support behind Iraq in the war against Iran and behind Jordan's leadership in the Middle East peace process. His earlier effort to reconcile Asad with Saddam Hussein, though not entirely successful, contributed to harmony at the summit. The two arch enemies did not become allies but nor did they allow their differences to disrupt the display of Arab unity. Another long-term effort that bore fruit at the summit was to bring Egypt back into the Arab fold. Libya, Syria and the PLO were opposed to the readmission of Egypt into the Arab League, but Hussein's proposal to do so was adopted, leaving it to each member state to decide whether to re-establish diplomatic relations with Egypt. The collective Arab boycott of Egypt was lifted. Hussein exploited his dominant position in the councils of the Arab mighty to weaken and marginalize the PLO. He deliberately snubbed Arafat by not going to the airport to meet him, a pronounced omission, as he usually went to meet all heads of state. Instead, he sent Zaid Rifa'i, Arafat's nemesis.[29] In his opening speech Hussein made only a passing reference to the PLO and again called for an international conference on the basis of UN resolutions 242 and 338, which the PLO had not yet accepted.[30] The summit greatly enhanced Hussein's prestige and legitimacy in the Arab world. He himself described it as one of the best and brightest moments in his life.[31]

22. Intifada and Disengagement

The spark that ignited the Palestinian uprising, or *intifada*, was the seemingly intentional killing, on 9 December 1987, of four residents of Jabaliyah, the largest of the eight refugee camps in the Gaza Strip, by an Israeli truck driver. The accident set off disturbances both in the Jabaliyah camp and in the rest of Gaza that rapidly spread to the West Bank. Within days the occupied territories were engulfed in a wave of street demonstrations and commercial strikes on an unprecedented scale. Equally unprecedented was the extent of mass participation in these disturbances: tens of thousands of ordinary civilians, including women and children. Demonstrators burned tyres, threw stones and Molotov cocktails at Israeli cars, brandished iron bars and waved the Palestinian flag. The standard of revolt against Israeli rule had been raised. The security forces used the full panoply of crowd-control measures to quell the disturbances—cudgels, night sticks, tear gas, water cannons, rubber bullets and live ammunition—but they only gathered momentum.

The eruption of the intifada was completely spontaneous. There was no preparation or planning by the local Palestinian elite or the PLO, but the PLO was quick to jump on the bandwagon of popular discontent against Israeli rule and to play a leading role alongside a newly formed body, the Unified National Command (UNC). But, equally, it was not without real underlying causes. In origin it was not a nationalist revolt. It had its roots in poverty, in the miserable living conditions of the refugee camps, in hatred of the occupation and, above all, in the humiliation that the Palestinians had had to endure over the previous twenty years. The aims of the intifada were not stated at the outset; they emerged in the course of the struggle and developed into a statement of major political import. The ultimate aim was self-determination and the establishment of an independent Palestinian state. In this respect the intifada may be seen as the Palestinian war of independence.

Events in the occupied territories received intense media coverage. The world was assailed by disturbing pictures of Israeli troops firing on stone-throwing demonstrators, or beating with cudgels those they caught, among them women and children. Israel's image suffered serious damage as a result of this media coverage. The Israelis complained the reporting was biased and that it focused deliberately on scenes of brutality in what was a normal effort to restore order. But no amount of pleading could obscure the message that constantly came across in pictures in the newspapers and on the television screens: a powerful army was being unleashed against a civilian population that was fighting for basic human rights, especially the right to political self-determination. The biblical image of David and Goliath now seemed to be reversed, with Israel looking like an overbearing Goliath and the Palestinians with the stones as a vulnerable David.

The intifada had far-reaching consequences for Jordan. It had begun as a revolt against Israeli rule, but it turned into a demonstration of support for the PLO and very quickly assumed an anti-Jordanian dimension. Although Jordan's security was not immediately affected, there was a clear danger that the intifada would spread, with the nationalist sparks lit on the West Bank inflaming the Palestinians on the East Bank and threatening internal stability. Jordan's influence in the occupied territories had been steadily declining over the previous two decades, and this sudden upsurge of Palestinian nationalism was a further setback. It tilted the balance in the ongoing power struggle between the monarchy and the PLO in favour of the latter. After the Lebanon War the PLO had lost ground to Hussein; the intifada had the opposite effect. Hussein's claim that the PLO leadership had been imposed by a decision of the Arab League on an unwilling population could no longer be sustained. Indeed, leaflets stated very clearly that the Palestinians saw the PLO as their only representative and that Hussein had no mandate to speak on their behalf. Another consequence of the trouble on the West Bank was to increase support on the Israeli right for the dangerous idea of converting Jordan into an alternative homeland for the Palestinian people. Thus, as a result of the intifada and its ramifications in Israel, Jordan had to reconsider both its position on the West Bank and its role in the Middle East peace process.

The uprising also brought about a re-evaluation of US policy towards the Arab–Israeli conflict, culminating by the end of 1988 in recognition of the PLO as a legitimate party in peace negotiations. There was a marked shift at all levels of American public opinion away from its traditional support for Israel and towards sympathy for the Palestinians. For the first time since the war in Lebanon, it even prompted some of the leaders of American Jewry to raise questions about the wisdom of Israel's policies and the morality of its methods. In government circles there was concern that close American association with Israel could have negative repercussions for American interests throughout the Middle East and the Gulf.[1] The Hussein–Peres plan for an international conference had floundered mainly because of Likud opposition but partly because of American passivity. With the intifada gathering momentum, George Shultz became personally involved again. The result was the first major US effort to solve the Arab–Israeli conflict since the Reagan Plan of 1982.

Shultz put forward publicly, on 4 March 1988, a package that came to be known as the Shultz Initiative. The package followed in the path of the Camp David Accords in calling for Palestinian self-rule but with an accelerated timetable. There was also an important new element: an "interlock," or built-in connection, between the talks on the transitional period of self-rule and the talks on final status. This was intended to give assurances to the Palestinians against Israeli foot-dragging. Events were expected to move forward at a rapid pace. First, the secretary-general of the UN would convene all the parties to the Arab–Israeli conflict and the five permanent members of the Security Council to an international conference. This conference had no power to impose solutions on the participants or to veto any agreements reached by them. Second, negotiations between an Israeli and a Jordanian–Palestinian delegation were to start on 1 May and end by 1 November. Third, the transition period was to start three months later and last three years. Fourth, negotiations on final status were to begin before the start of the transition period and be completed within a year. In other words, negotiations on final status were to start regardless of the outcome of the first phase of negotiations.

Peres supported the Shultz Initiative and said so publicly. So did President Mubarak of Egypt. The Palestinian response added up to a chorus repeating the old refrain that the one and only address for any proposals was the PLO in Tunis. And the PLO leaders in Tunis had no intention of letting the "insiders" steal the show by meeting with the

American secretary of state. But the fiercest opposition to the Shultz Initiative came from Israel's prime minister. Shamir again blasted the idea of an international conference and rejected the interlock concept as contrary to the Camp David Accords. He said he was ready to negotiate peace with Hussein, and with any Palestinians he might bring along with him, but that he was not ready to relinquish any territory for peace.[2] One story has it that when Shamir received a letter outlining the American proposals, he said, "I reject the whole initiative, I only accept two words in it, and the two words are the signature—George Shultz—and nothing else!"[3] The story may be apocryphal, but Shultz and his aides had a feeling that America's policy in the Middle East had fallen hostage to Israel's intransigence or inability to make decisions.[4]

Hussein approached the Shultz Initiative with an open mind. He agreed to the general principle, giving rise to hope in the State Department that he could be persuaded to subscribe to the plan.[5] The response of the other Jordanian decision-makers to the new initiative was also tepid. They saw it as a thinly disguised version of the principles set out in the Camp David Accords. Although the initiative did not meet their requirements, they were unwilling to reject it out of hand. They welcomed the Reagan administration's re-engagement in the diplomatic process but felt that its thinking lagged behind events. The Americans recognized that the situation in the territories had been fundamentally altered by the intifada, but they failed to understand the implications. Consequently, the Shultz Initiative continued to promote the Jordanian role in negotiations and to exclude the PLO. Jordanian thinking, however, had changed by this time in two respects. First, they began to stress that any settlement to the conflict with Israel should fulfil the Palestinian right to self-determination. Second, they emphasized the need for PLO participation in an international conference and made it clear that Jordan could not serve as an alternative interlocutor.[6] When Shultz visited Amman in late February, the senior officials he met told him that they liked his ideas but that this was basically a PLO matter. Shultz met Hussein, on 1 March, at his house on 7 Palace Green in London and went over his initiative in detail. Hussein raised two issues: the PLO had to play a central role; and direct negotiations had to take place within the setting of an international conference that could weigh in on issues of substance. Hussein would not say yes and would not say no, but only "Keep working." Shultz could not take any encouragement from the King's comments.[7] Ultimately, he did not understand the changes on the ground that circumscribed Hussein's freedom of action. Indeed, Shultz's inadequate grasp of the local forces at play was one of the factors that contributed to the failure of his initiative.

From the outset the Unified National Command of the uprising declared its support for the PLO. It also attacked the concept of unity between the two banks and accused the Jordanian regime of collaborating with the Israeli government in perpetuating the occupation. From time to time, the UNC issued communiqués with guidance and instructions to its followers. On 11 March 1988 it issued its tenth communiqué, calling on the people to "intensify the mass pressure against the occupation army and the settlers and against collaborators and personnel of the Jordanian regime." It also called on the West Bank representatives in the Jordanian parliament to resign their seats and "align with the people. Otherwise, there will be no room for them on our land." The king described the communiqué as "a horrible sign of ingratitude" and concluded that his strategy of substituting a partnership with the Palestinians in the occupied territories for one with the PLO had fallen apart. All his efforts to work with the Palestinians towards a peaceful settlement with Israel had come to nothing and only one thing remained—the nightmare of Jordan becoming an alternative homeland for the Palestinians. The Jordanian nationalists had been critical of his attempts. They argued that Jordan would be a safer place without the West Bank and without the Palestinians. Every defeat that Hussein suffered in his quest for a partnership with the Palestinians was a source of satisfaction for them. Now they seemed to have a point. After reading the tenth communiqué, Hussein himself began to consider seriously disengaging from the West Bank.[8]

Late in the afternoon on 11 March, Hussein went into the royal court looking grim-faced and angry, and he let off steam about the communiqué to his political adviser, Adnan Abu-Odeh. Abu-Odeh was a Palestinian from Nablus who first came to the attention of the king as a junior officer in the Intelligence Service. For someone so used to command, the king was an exceptionally good listener, and he always encouraged Abu-Odeh to speak his mind. On this occasion, Abu-Odeh argued that the tenth communiqué should not be viewed simply as an act of ingratitude on the part of the West Bankers but as a sign of political maturity. For the first time since 1967 they had risen up to resist the occupation and to assert their independence and dignity. The king did not reject or challenge this analysis but encouraged his adviser to continue. Earlier on in his career, Abu-Odeh had worked as a schoolteacher in Kuwait, and he proceeded in a Socratic mode, by posing questions. Abu-Odeh recalled the conversation that followed:

I asked the king: "Would you make peace with Israel without the recovery of the whole of the West Bank?" He answered saying no. I then asked him: "Would you make peace with Israel without recovering East Jerusalem?" He said no. I then said to him: "Do you think that the Israelis would make peace with you on the basis of the return of the whole of the West Bank and East Jerusalem?" He thought a little and said no. I said to him: "Then let us be frank, by doing this we cannot make peace with Israel." He did not comment. I continued by saying: "Israel, America and the West believe that you are the one who will make peace with Israel. We have agreed that you cannot make peace with Israel. This situation will only cause more suffering for the Palestinians because those among them who want to make peace cannot do so. This situation will only bring about the continuation of the occupation and more torture for the Palestinians." He kept silent. I then said: "Don't you think it is time to consider a disengagement from the West Bank?" He said: "But to leave it to whom?" I said: "You leave it to nobody; you leave it to the PLO. The whole Arab world at Rabat acknowledged the PLO as the sole representative of the Palestinian people. The PLO has been fighting against us for years to establish that role. By disengaging we would be responding to the Arab world and to the Palestinians. The Palestinians in the West Bank do not challenge the PLO. The only two parties that do not consider the PLO as the Palestinian representative are Israel and the West. By disengaging we would not only be helping the Palestinians, we would also be helping ourselves." The king left the office.[9]

Abu-Odeh understood that the king wanted to reflect on their conversation. He did not claim it was the beginning of the king's decision to disengage from the West Bank, but he did feel that it accelerated the king's thinking and made disengagement a more practical option for him to pursue. Two weeks later there was a meeting of the king's men over lunch at his residence. The lunch was attended by Zaid Rifa'i, the prime minister; Zaid bin Shaker, the commander-in-chief of the armed forces; Marwan Kasim, the chief of the royal court; Tariq Alaiddin, the director of intelligence; and Adnan Abu-Odeh, the political adviser.

The king unexpectedly turned to Abu-Odeh and said, "Abu Said, tell our brothers what you told me the other day." The political adviser presented to the others the argument he had shared with the king. When he finished, the king asked the rest of the company for their thoughts. The first to respond was Rifa'i. He thought that disengagement from the West Bank was a brilliant idea. Everyone else concurred. All of them were Transjordanians except for Abu-Odeh, who was a Palestinian. Most other Palestinians in high office, including Foreign Minister Taher al-Masri, who was not present at this meeting, were opposed to disengagement. Three months later disengagement took place.[10] In as much as any one meeting can be said to have made the strategic decision to disengage, this was it. The group of five continued to meet informally and to prepare for the king ideas, proposals and plans for disengagement. At every stage they waited for the green light from the king before proceeding to the next stage.[11]

The first stage was to clarify Jordan's position in relation to the Shultz Initiative. The Jordanians had gone along with Shultz's plan but stated publicly that they were wary of any move designed to "defuse" or "contain" the intifada. "The Jordanians clearly did not want to appear to be pulling the chestnuts out of the fire for the sake of Israel and the United States by cooperating in what could be seen by the Palestinians as an exercise to frustrate their national aspirations."[12] In early April, Shultz embarked on another tour of Middle East capitals in an effort to push forward his plan. In Jerusalem he saw no inclination on the part of Shamir to give him anything at all to work with. Shultz offered to take a message from Shamir to Hussein, and the prime minister gave him a paragraph that urged direct Israeli–Jordanian negotiations. This was precisely what the king could not possibly agree to at this juncture. Shultz made the same offer to Peres, who drafted a message urging the king to accept the American initiative. Shultz was frustrated by Shamir's inflexibility and by the fact that the divided government meant that no one could be held responsible and accountable. "When I arrived in Jordan," writes Shultz, "I found King Hussein candid and gloomy: he again gave me nothing but wanted me to 'persevere.' "[13]

If Hussein looked gloomy it was because he had a lot to be gloomy about, not least Shultz's subservience towards Shamir. Nevertheless, on 6 April, Hussein handed Shultz a paper outlining "Jordan's constants," or its principles for the settlement of the Arab-Israeli dispute. These principles were broadcast on Radio Amman the same day. Some of them were familiar: the inadmissibility of the acquisition of territory by war; Israeli withdrawal from the occupied territories as the basis for a settlement, one that had to be comprehensive; Security Council Resolution 242 applied to all of the occupied Arab territories; the international conference had to be more than a ceremonial gathering and to "reflect the moral and constant weight of the five permanent members of the Security Council in assisting all the parties to the conflict to arrive at a comprehensive, just and lasting peace." Two additional points, however, were indicative of the shift in Jordanian foreign policy since the outbreak of the intifada. One was the emphasis on the right of the Palestinian people to self-determination. The other point made it clear that Jordan could not represent the Palestinian people at the conference or negotiate the settlement of the Palestinian problem on behalf of the PLO. Jordan was, however, prepared to attend the conference in a joint Jordanian–Palestinian delegation if this arrangement was acceptable to the parties concerned.[14]

At the summit conference of the Arab League in Algiers on 7–9 June, Hussein urged the other members not to reject the Shultz Initiative, but by this time his own influence was rapidly declining. The time and place of the summit were not of his own choosing. It was an emergency summit to consider the intifada and financial support for the uprising was the main item on the agenda. Jordan was thrown on the defensive, as it had been at the Rabat summit fourteen years earlier. The intifada refocused the attention of the Arab world on the Palestinian problem. The courage of the Palestinians in resisting Israeli occupation put the rest of the Arab world to shame. Sympathy translated into material and political support for the Palestinians.

In his speech Hussein tried to dispel the suspicions that Jordan still hoped to recover the West Bank for itself and that it was still competing with the PLO, but his words were greeted with scepticism. His other aim was to defend Jordan's role as a channel for Arab aid for the occupied territories in cooperation with the PLO. He reminded his audience that Jordanian law still applied to the West Bank, that Jordanian currency and passports were still in use there, and that Jordan still paid the salaries of 18,000 civil servants on the West Bank and another 6,000 in the Gaza Strip. He also pointed out that some of the Gulf states had failed to honour the commitment of financial aid that they had made at the Baghdad summit in 1978, causing Jordan to incur large debts. If support was not forthcoming, he warned, Jordan might be forced to terminate its role in the occupied territories.

Hussein's impassioned speech fell on deaf ears. The summit resolutions ignored Jordan and affirmed Arab support for the right of the Palestinians to independent statehood under the leadership of the PLO. The commitments made at the Baghdad summit were not renewed, and Jordan was excluded from the new Arab aid package. Moreover, all Arab aid in support of the intifada was to be channelled exclusively through the PLO and not, as previously, through a joint committee. This disappointing and indeed humiliating outcome reflected the sharp decline in Jordan's stature as a regional power and the corresponding improvement in the position of its rival. For Hussein it was also a personal defeat. Only seven months previously, at the Amman summit, he was a dominant figure on the Arab stage. At Algiers he was isolated, frustrated and impotent. For him the Algiers summit resolutions were the last straw and a major encouragement to disengage from the West Bank.

Practical steps towards disengagement were undertaken in the bitter aftermath of the Algiers summit. On 1 July the Ministry of Occupied Territories Affairs was abolished and its responsibilities transferred to the Palestinian Affairs Department linked to the Foreign Ministry. From his vantage point across the river, Labour Party leader Shimon Peres was troubled by this trend because he realized that it spelled the end of the so-called "Jordanian option." For if Jordan relinquished its claim to the West Bank, and the PLO became the sole representative of the Palestinians in fact as well as in name, Israel would have to deal with an organization that did not recognize its right to exist. Peres knew that Hussein still held him responsible for the failure of their joint plan for an international conference. But, on 26 July, he sent a letter that was designed to make the king stop and think. Peres acknowledged that in the past there had been moments when they misjudged each other's intentions. The purpose of his letter was to reiterate his commitment to "the London document approach." Peres still thought that the London Agreement held the most promising prospect for progress, and he gave his reasons for this view. Towards the end of the letter Peres extended to the king his best wishes for the end of the holiday of Eid al-Adha, which commemorated the sacrifice of Abraham, their common father. But he could hear again the bells of belligerency ringing in their region, and he entreated the king to introduce his voice, "both sober and moving," in favour of peace.[15]

Hussein replied the following day to assure his "dear friend" that his commitment to the peaceful resolution of the Arab–Israeli conflict remained firm. The purpose of any action Jordan might take would be to break the long-standing stalemate in the peace process. "We may disengage from the West Bank," wrote the king, "but we would never disengage from the peace process. We may disengage from managing a people that is under occupation, but we would never be able to disengage from the Palestinian people and the Palestinian problem." Hussein said he shared his friend's vision of peace and agreed that the means to that end was an international conference along the lines they had discussed in London. Moreover, he hoped that Jordan's move would make the Palestinians see the light and do what was required of them for the sake of peace in the region. Hussein thanked Peres for his good wishes for Eid al-Adha, which reminded Hussein of the sacrifices that both of them had made for the sake of peace, and he promised to continue to work, from an improved position, for this noble cause.[16]

The move towards disengagement was by now irreversible. On 28 July the Jordanian government announced the termination of the five-year West Bank Development Plan. The reason given for this move was to allow the PLO to assume more responsibility for this area. Two days later a royal decree dissolved the Chamber of Deputies, thereby terminating West Bank representation in the Jordanian legislature. Finally, on 31 July, in a televised address to the nation, the king formally announced the severing of Jordan's legal and administrative ties with the West Bank. The speech was a major landmark in Jordan's history. Adnan Abu-Odeh, who prepared the draft of the speech for the king, placed it in the context of the Hashemite heritage:

Since its creation, Jordan has been faced with the challenge of survival. This challenge became ingrained in the political psychology of its elite. There was a real fear that without an outside strategic partner, Jordan might evaporate. In order for it to secure such a partner, Jordan needed to develop a regional role. Historically and up until 1956, Jordan had this role imposed upon it by the British. After 1956, the US became Jordan's strategic ally and its main role at the time was to combat Communism and Nasserism in the region. After 1967, Jordan developed two new regional roles. On the one hand it became the advocate of peace in the region. From 1973 onwards it also came to defend Western interests in the Gulf.

From early on, the king realized that his grandfather's project regarding the West Bank was wrong. But he could not disengage himself because that would mean giving up Jordan's regional role, Jordan's credentials for survival. When Gulf oil gained importance and Jordan was granted a second regional role, it became easier for the king to abandon the first role. In the 1980s, after the failure of the Jordanian–PLO partnership, it became apparent that the king felt that his grandfather's enterprise was a source of trouble. It also became apparent that the solution that he was hoping to reach was to separate from the Palestinians on the West Bank. In the 1980s therefore one could detect that the king was on the verge of disengaging himself from Palestine. From a historical perspective, the king's disengagement decision was a move to undo what his grandfather had built.[17]

The decision to disengage was warmly received by the East Bankers but not by the Palestinians who lived on the East Bank. Some East Bank politicians felt they got nothing but ingratitude for their efforts to help the Palestinians and that the time had come to cut their losses. They welcomed the opportunity to make the East Bank their priority and to relinquish all responsibility for the West Bank and its population. The king himself felt that Jordan was fighting a losing battle in defending positions that had already fallen to the PLO. After two decades of trying to blur the distinction between the East Bank and the West Bank, he felt that the time had come to assert that the East Bank was not Palestine and that it was up to the Palestinians to decide what they wanted to do with the West Bank and to deal with the Israelis directly over its future. The old Hashemite slogan had been "Jordan is Palestine and Palestine is Jordan." This was replaced by a new slogan that said "Jordan is Jordan and Palestine is Palestine." Disappointment with his Palestinian subjects was a factor in the king's decision. Using the royal "we," he explained:

It was the intifada that really caused our decision on disengagement from the West Bank. It was again our lack of ability to get any agreement with our Palestinian brethren. I wish to God they had been frank enough about what they wanted and they would have got it a long time before. But we were torn apart trying to get all the pieces of the jigsaw together to help them. However, suspicions and doubts got in the way. But beyond that, we recognized there was a definite trend that had started before the Rabat resolution of 1974 and continued all the way through. They could give, they could take, and they could do whatever they liked. They could probably give more than we could but they decided that they wanted to have their say regarding their future and I simply tried to help them by that decision.[18]

This account exaggerates the element of altruism in the decision. The controlling consideration behind the decision was Hussein's own dynastic interest. Hussein's speech to the nation ignored the second and played up the first. Disengagement was described as "a series of measures to enhance the Palestinian national orientation and highlight the Palestinian identity; our goal is to benefit the Palestinian cause and the Arab Palestinian people." Jordan respected, said Hussein, the wish of the PLO to secede and establish an independent state. The institutional links with Jordan were said to be an obstacle along the Palestinian road to independence, so these links were going to be severed. The new measures, however, would apply only to the occupied territories and not to Jordanian citizens of Palestinian origin. Palestinians outside Jordan's borders were promised that Jordan would continue to support their struggle: "No one outside Palestine has had or will ever have a connection with Palestine or with its cause that is stronger than the connection of Jordan or of my family with it." The Great Arab Revolt was mentioned only in passing, but the message was clear: the Hashemite Kingdom of Jordan would remain the proud bearer of the standard of Arab unity and would continue to play a major regional role.[19]

Hussein's speech spoke only of severing Jordan's legal and administrative links with the West Bank; it did not renounce irrevocably the Hashemite claim to this territory. The 1950 Act of Union between the two banks was not repealed. The constitution was not amended. Parliament passed no legislation affecting Jordanian sovereignty over the West Bank. The move was meaningless under international law. These omissions fed Palestinian suspicions that disengagement was just a tactical move and that the Hashemite claim was only held in abeyance rather than abandoned. About the Hashemite trusteeship of the holy places in Jerusalem there was no ambiguity: it was to continue. As a Hashemite and as a descendant of the Prophet, Hussein was anxious to protect the Islamic religious and cultural legacy in the Old City. Disengagement did not apply to the 3,000 employees of the Ministry of Religious Endowments and Religious Affairs who worked in Jerusalem. Hussein viewed Jerusalem as a personal responsibility and as a political necessity, since there was no guarantee that the Israelis would allow the Palestinians sovereignty over the disputed sites.[20]

Hussein did not consult the PLO before making his dramatic announcement, and he did nothing to smooth the transition to PLO rule. In the words of Taher Kanaan, a Jordanian of Palestinian origin and a former head of the Ministry of Occupied Territories Affairs, "The decision to disengage was not a favour to the PLO; it was a provocation to show that the PLO could not do it. The decision did not mean giving up Jordan's role in the West Bank. It was intended to demonstrate that the PLO was inadequate and Jordan was indispensable."[21] Taher al-Masri, the foreign minister, did not know the content of the king's speech until he heard it on television that evening. He was particularly worried that there might be a backlash against the Palestinian population of the East Bank. That evening he went to dinner at Prince Hassan's house, and he was seething with anger. He said to Prince Hassan, "This is a black day in your record as Hashemites!"[22]

Jordan's disengagement from the West Bank came as a disappointment to George Shultz because his initiative depended crucially on cooperation with Hussein. In a press conference on 7 August the king said that never again would Jordan assume the role of negotiating on behalf of the Palestinians. This statement was probably not meant to be as final as it sounded. But it was taken by the American secretary of state to mark the end of his initiative. A few weeks after the king had announced his decision, he asked the State Department to pass a message to Shimon Peres: the decision to remove Jordan from the peace process was taken in the hope that it would cause the PLO to "see the light and come to terms with reality."[23]

This private message, however, could do no more than soften the blow that the king's latest move was bound to inflict on his partner in the abortive London Agreement. The effect of the public message was to strengthen the position of the PLO and to undermine the Labour Party's so-called Jordanian option. The king himself had never liked the term "the Jordanian option," for it implied an agreement between Israel and Jordan over the heads of the Palestinians. In his speech and his press conference he therefore cleared the air. He said, in effect, that if a Jordanian option for settling the Palestinian problem had ever existed, it was now definitely dead.

From Israel's standpoint, the king's speech marked the collapse of a very popular idea. It meant that Jordan was no longer prepared to negotiate on the Palestinian problem with Israel; the only issue it would discuss was the question of its own borders. The Israelis were stunned by the speech and initially interpreted it as no more than a tactical move by the king to get the Palestinians to say that they still wanted him to represent them. But when the king asked his supporters on the West Bank not to sponsor petitions urging him to relent, the Israelis were forced to recognize that disengagement was a strategic move, not a tactical one. Even Likud leaders had reason to regret this move because they realized that the forecasts of all the prophets of doom had come true: Israel now found herself all alone in the arena with the PLO.[24] What Israeli leaders of both major parties failed to grasp was the contribution that their intransigence had made to Hussein's frustration, from which sprang the decision to leave the field to the PLO.

Another consequence of the intifada was the birth of Hamas. The name is an Arabic word meaning "zeal," and also an acronym for the Islamic Resistance Movement. Hamas was founded in Gaza in 1988 by Shaikh Ahmed Yassin, a paralysed religious teacher, as a wing of the long-established Muslim Brothers in Palestine. To obtain a permit from the Israeli authorities, the movement was obliged to pledge that its fight for Palestinian rights would be conducted within the limits of the law and without the use of arms. Ironically, the Israeli authorities at first encouraged Hamas in the hope of weakening the secular nationalism of the PLO. But the Palestinian uprising had a radicalizing effect on Hamas, and its members began to step outside the bounds of the law. The Israelis repeatedly cracked down on the organization, but the roots it put down sprouted again, giving rise to more violence each time. In 1989 the Israelis arrested Shaikh Ahmed Yassin and kept him in prison until 1997. Hamas, however, continued to shift from the use of stones to the use of firearms. In 1994 it began, through its military wing, to launch suicide bombers inside Israel. The suicide attacks were mounted by individual members of Hamas who carried explosives on their body and detonated them in crowded places such as buses and markets. Israel's tactic of "divide and rule" had backfired disastrously.

While radicalizing Hamas, the intifada had a moderating effect on the secular Palestinians. On the one hand, the intifada raised the morale and boosted the pride and self-confidence of the Palestinian community. On the other, it did not bring an end to Israeli occupation, and living conditions deteriorated in the course of the struggle. Local leaders realized that a Palestinian peace initiative was essential. They were worried that the intifada would come to an end without yielding any concrete political gains. Consequently, they started to put pressure on the PLO chiefs in Tunis to meet the conditions that would enable them to enter into negotiations with Israel. Over the years the PLO mainstream had moved towards more moderate positions, but it avoided saying this in any clear-cut fashion, for fear of alienating the militant factions of the organization. The local leaders now threw all their weight behind the moderate mainstream. They urged the PLO chiefs in Tunis to recognize Israel, to accept a two-state solution, to declare a Palestinian state and to establish a government-in-exile.

Hussein could claim a share of the credit for compelling the PLO to shoulder its responsibilities and to adopt a more moderate position. Under pressure from above and below, the PLO rose to the challenge. Disengagement helped to force it, in the words of Hussein's message to Peres, to "see the light and come to terms with reality." A revolution in Palestinian political thinking took place, and the man who presided over it was none other than Hussein's old sparring partner, Arafat. The success of the intifada challenged Arafat and his followers to moderate their political programme. It gave prominence and credibility to the internal leadership. The external leadership in Tunis risked being left behind. They were forced to move. At the meeting of the Palestine National Congress (PNC) in Algiers in mid November 1988, Arafat won a majority for the historic decision to recognize Israel's legitimacy, to accept all the relevant UN resolutions going back to 29 November 1947 and to adopt the principle of a two-state solution. The claim to the whole of Palestine, enshrined in the Palestinian National Charter, was finally laid to rest and a declaration of independence was issued for a mini-state in the West Bank and Gaza with East Jerusalem as its capital. The resolutions of the PNC were well received in Jordan. The PLO, Hussein noted, was "shouldering its responsibilities" and had demonstrated its willingness to join in an "historic reconciliation between Arabs and Israelis." Jordan immediately recognized the independent Palestinian State, and, in early January 1989, the PLO office in Amman became the embassy of Palestine.[25] A month after the PNC meeting, at a press conference in Geneva, Arafat renounced all forms of terrorism. These changes made possible the initiation of a dialogue between the US government and the PLO, but Israel's rejection of the PLO remained absolute and unconditional.

Following Hussein's voluntary abdication as the key Arab player in the diplomacy surrounding the Arab–Israeli conflict, he pursued more vigorously Jordan's second role as a promoter of Arab unity and a defender of Western interests in the Arab Gulf. Hussein always sought an Arab order that could guarantee the survival of his dynasty. Between 1988 and 1990 the main thrust of his foreign policy shifted towards the Arab world. This was manifested in efforts to improve bilateral relations with all the Arab states, in the promotion of inter-Arab dialogue and in the establishment of the Arab Cooperation Council (ACC)—a regional alliance that brought together Jordan, Iraq, Egypt and North Yemen.[26]

The eight-year-old Iran–Iraq War was ended by a UN-negotiated ceasefire in July 1988. Despite the ceasefire, Iran and Iraq were unable to overcome their antagonism. The difference was that after the guns fell silent Iran turned to domestic reconstruction, whereas Saddam Hussein continued to spend a substantial portion of Iraq's oil revenues on building up his country's military capabilities, both conventional and unconventional. As a consequence, Iraq continued to rely on Jordan for services and logistical support, and the friendship between the two leaders continued to flourish. Saddam became increasingly aggressive and threatening, and occasionally reduced his friend to the role of an apologist. The worst example of Saddam's bluster was his threat, on 2 April 1990, "to burn half of Israel." Hussein did not dissociate himself from this statement, and his own relations with Israel became strained as a result. "If Saddam was an unguided missile in 1989 and 1990," writes Philip Robins, "King Hussein failed to provide him with a guidance system."[27] This is true but it was not for lack of trying. After the Iran–Iraq War ended, the king repeatedly advised Saddam to become a more positive element in the region, to improve his country's image in the West, to make a speech at the UN, to travel, to visit at least the countries of the five permanent members of the Security Council. But the advice was not heeded.[28]

The Arab Cooperation Council was an extension of the Iraqi–Jordanian alliance. The idea behind it was to harness Iraqi resources and Jordanian know-how and to move towards economic integration. The time also seemed right for forming a moderate, pro-Western Arab coalition to take the Middle East into a new phase. On 16 February 1989, the rulers of Iraq, Jordan, Egypt and North Yemen met in Baghdad to launch the new regional grouping. Back in 1981 the six-member Gulf Cooperation Council (GCC) had set an example of collective Arab defence, with Saudi Arabia taking the lead in its formation, following the outbreak of the Iran–Iraq War. (Hussein reportedly made a bid for associate membership but his request was ignored.)[29] North Yemen was brought into the new grouping because it was practically the only Gulf country that was not a member of the GCC. Egypt was included at Saddam's insistence, while Syria was not invited because Saddam preferred not to have it as a founding member. The charter of the ACC left the door open for other Arab states to join, and Hussein hoped that Syria might do so at a later date.

The ACC was not a well-thought-out project and did not live up to the expectations of any of its founding members. The main problems seem to have been Saudi suspicions and Egyptian intrigues. The Saudis were concerned about the ACC from the beginning, believing, mistakenly, that it was directed against the GCC in general and against themselves in particular. President Mubarak had close links with the Saudis, who were the main source of foreign aid for his impoverished country. The Saudis expressed their concern about the ACC to Mubarak, and the inclusion of North Yemen was at the top of their concerns. North Yemen had been problematic for the Saudis, especially regarding the border question, ever since the days of Imam Ahmad. The Saudis were on bad terms with Abdullah al-Sallal, a Free Officer who had overthrown Imam Ahmad in a military coup in 1962 and established a republic. The Saudis thought that Yemen's inclusion in the ACC was intended to encircle their country and this frightened them. The suspicion was unfounded: Yemen was included because it was an important Arab country. Mubarak, however, blamed the inclusion of Yemen on Hussein. Hussein always had good relations with Ali Abdullah Salih, who had become president of North Yemen in 1978, but he had no interest in seeing the Saudis and Yemenis at war or on the brink of war. The Jordanians believed that Mubarak was playing on these Saudi sensitivities for his own ends—so that he would get more aid and Jordan would get nothing. Reports reached Amman that Mubarak insinuated that Hussein and President Salih were plotting against the Saudis.[30] With this degree of mistrust at the heart of the ACC, it is hardly surprising that it was not a success. It was also short-lived. Less than two years after its birth the ACC was wrecked by Egypt's participation in the US-led coalition to eject Iraq from Kuwait.

George H. W. Bush's victory in the American presidential elections of November 1988 gave Hussein some cause for optimism. A friendship between the two men had been formed when Bush was director of the CIA and during the eight years that he served as vice-president under Ronald Reagan. A day after the election Hussein called the president-elect to congratulate him on his victory. On 21 November, Bush wrote an effusive letter to Hussein: "I want to reach out to you and a few other world leaders to whom I feel particularly close. One of the greatest satisfactions I derived from winning this election is the knowledge that I will be able to continue the wonderful working relationship with you that we have developed over the last several years . . . You and your countrymen are on my mind. As I begin to form my foreign policy agenda, Jordan and the Middle East will remain one of my top priorities. I want to work together with you to forge fair and just solutions to the region's problems. I want you to know that I will be involved personally in that search." The typewritten letter ended with "warm personal regards." In his own hand, Bush scrawled at the bottom: "P. S. On the personal side, Barbara sends her love to Queen Noor and all the family. I value our friendship—I really do! George." Hussein's reply, hand-delivered to Bush by the Jordanian ambassador to Washington two days later, was similarly warm and upbeat, beginning with "Dear George." Hussein reviewed his recent efforts to promote a settlement and added: "One hand cannot clap by itself. I think the time has arrived for all of us to encourage our cousins across the river to accept to become our peace partners." The friendly message thus contained a warning that nothing would move unless the United States brought its weight to bear on Israel.[31]

Hussein's first meeting with Bush as president took place in Tokyo in February 1989. The occasion was the funeral of the Emperor Hirohito.

Although Tokyo was swarming with dignitaries, Bush suggested as a special mark of friendship that Hussein leave some time open for an unpublicized get-together. Accordingly, a late dinner was arranged for just the two men and their wives without aides or note-takers. There is no record of what was said at this intimate meeting. But there is a copy of a twelve-page dossier that Hussein handed to Bush at the meeting. The dossier was stamped "Top Secret/Sensitive" and entitled "Personal for the President." It consisted of a long letter and two enclosures: a "Chronology of Jordanian Efforts for Peace 1967–1989" and a list of "United States Commitments and Positions on Peace Settlement." The letter began by noting that Bush was the sixth president to lead his country since 1967 and that instead of the promised era of peace, the Middle East was engulfed in two decades of uninterrupted conflict, death and destruction. A series of myths was said to have surrounded the problem and to have obstructed a solution.

Myth number one was that providing Israel with overwhelming military superiority was an inducement to peace. The record allegedly demonstrated that this policy produced the opposite result by promoting greater Israeli aggrandizement and intransigence. Myth number two was the belief that direct negotiations between Israel, Jordan and the Palestinians could produce withdrawal and peace. But it was patently beyond the capacity of Jordan and Israel, on their own, to reach a comprehensive settlement. The previous twenty-two years had been replete with peace opportunities but every effort had ended in failure. At this point a note of bitterness overlay the analysis: "I speak with special authority because during the past two decades I have personally met in secret, on more than 150 occasions, totalling approximately 1,000 hours of talks, with almost every top Israeli official including, most recently, specifically at US request, with Prime Minister Shamir. To my eternal dismay and frustration, all those efforts have not brought us any closer to the peace I am determined to achieve."

A third myth was that the United States conceived of the Arab–Israeli conflict as a foreign policy issue, when, in fact, it had a major and pervasive domestic political component. The reference here was to the power and influence of the Israel lobby in Washington: "Israel understands this and takes advantage of it. The Arabs have little recourse except to endure the consequences. This dichotomy must be resolved if the United States is to be a truly effective partner in the peace process. If this does not occur, I fear that the US mediation role will be rendered increasingly irrelevant." Hussein's fourth myth involved the morality and legality of the Israeli policy of retaining permanent control of the West Bank and Gaza. A fifth myth was the belief that Israel's leaders sincerely wanted to solve the conflict by exchanging land for peace. The truth, according to Hussein, was that they only paid lip service to a negotiated peace while creating excuses for inaction. A sixth myth was that anyone could negotiate on behalf of the Palestinians except the PLO. The Israeli refusal to deal with the PLO prevented negotiations and perpetuated the stalemate that remained the goal of the Israeli government. The next myth was the contention that the acquisition and retention of territory was essential for military security. This, according to Hussein, was neither an accepted principle nor a practicable proposition. Genuine security, he asserted, could be achieved only through peaceful coexistence: "Land-grabbing is not a guarantee for security, but a prescription for continuing hostilities."

Despite all the myths, lost opportunities, frustrations and failures, Hussein declared himself to be optimistic. The source of this optimism was the existence of an Arab–Palestinian consensus to accept the existence of the State of Israel and to negotiate a comprehensive peace with it in accordance with the provisions of Security Council Resolution 242. The importance of this achievement could not be overestimated. The only remaining obstacle was the refusal of Israel to agree to enter negotiations for the same purpose on the same terms. "Mr. President," Hussein concluded, "please allow me to say, in all candor and friendship, that I feel I have done my best. I have worked hard to create the consensus the Arabs and Palestinians have achieved. Based on assurances I have received from the United States I have met every request, made every concession and honored every commitment which the United States has asked of me, often at risk to my person and my country. The history of the problem and the record of past negotiations make it clear that the only remaining viable vehicle for negotiations is an international conference, the terms for which are already substantially agreed upon and to which all the parties, except Israel, are committed to attend. The convening of a congress, within this year, must be our highest priority and we must leave no stone unturned until that goal is achieved."[32] The dinner and the dossier enabled Hussein to get in on the ground floor of the Bush administration.

Hussein's zest for foreign affairs and foreign travel had its counterpart in a deplorable neglect of internal affairs and especially the welfare of his people. Hopeless at managing his private financial affairs and prone to getting into debt, he was certainly not up to the task of managing the financial affairs of his kingdom. Moreover, his own alleged habit of taking commissions on major government contracts meant that he was not a shining example of probity or transparency. Hassan, his younger brother, was both able and willing to take charge of economic policy, but as crown prince he had no authority under the constitution to do so. The constitution entrusted the prime minister and the Council of Ministers with responsibility for administering the affairs of state. The prime minister at the time was Zaid Rifa'i, in his third term in office. Rifa'i was a clever, experienced and shrewd politician, but, like his master, he was much more interested in foreign affairs than in domestic ones. Rifa'i held office by grace of the king, his classmate and friend, and it was widely believed that he used this public office to amass a personal fortune. Rifa'i was far from unique in this respect. Indeed, he was typical of the nepotism, patronage, lack of accountability and disdain for the common people that were all too common within the ruling class in Jordan.

Rifa'i was unpopular in the country at large, and had many opponents and enemies in the ruling class. The charge of corruption was frequently levelled against him and against his government. It was an era of economic prosperity, business opportunity and unregulated growth. Commissions, backhanders and bribes were the order of the day. Marwan Kasim, the chief of the royal court, regarded Rifa'i as brilliant but unreliable and untrustworthy. He also thought that his extreme free market economic policies were not in the best long-term interests of the country. On one occasion Kasim told Rifa'i in the presence of the king that a very rotten smell was coming out of his government. The king cautioned Kasim not to believe all the rumours he heard. Kasim replied that everything he said was validated. The king dropped the subject, but he then asked Rifa'i to get rid of the thieves in his cabinet.[33] In general the king was far too lenient and too forgiving, and it was he who was ultimately responsible for the rotten smell of corruption that continued to pollute the public sphere.

One of the few senior persons in the regime who resisted corruption and upheld higher standards of honesty and integrity in public life was

Crown Prince Hassan. Hassan understood that taking commissions and cuts compromised one's independence, and he was determined to preserve his own. Without the backing of his brother or the prime minister, however, there was not much that he could do to root out corruption. Hassan recalled a conversation he had with Rifa'i in 1969 when Rifa'i came with an envelope full of money. Hassan said, "What is this?" Rifa'i allegedly replied, "It is an envelope from your brother." Hassan gave it back to him saying that he could not accept anything from his brother through either Rifa'i's hands or anyone else's. Once Hussein came into the room with an envelope stuffed with dollar bills and tumbled the bills on Hassan's head. Hassan was not amused. But, although Hassan took a dim view of this aspect of his brother's reign, he did not confront him directly on the issue.[34]

With indifference and incompetence at the top of the pyramid of power, economic conditions inside Jordan continued to deteriorate, culminating in the outbreak of bread riots in Ma'an on 18 April 1989. The background to the crisis was a sudden drop in Iraqi demand for Jordanian goods following the end of the Iran–Iraq War; an economic recession in the Gulf and a consequent dwindling of foreign aid; a decline in the remittances made by Jordanian nationals working in the Gulf; rising unemployment; declining living standards; profligate government spending that led to the depletion of foreign currency reserves; a 30 percent devaluation of the dinar; and widespread corruption at all levels of the government. The immediate trigger for the riots was the sudden withdrawal of food subsidies and the ham-fisted imposition of austerity measures by the government on the advice of the International Monetary Fund (IMF). The two main charges against the government were authoritarianism and corruption. People did not see why they should have to tighten their belts when the ministers were using their official positions to line their own pockets. The riots broke out in underdeveloped towns and villages of the south, traditionally the most loyal supporters of the regime. They started in Ma'an, Tafila and Kerak, and spread to Salt in the north. The rioters denounced the austerity measures and demanded the resignation of Zaid Rifa'i. A petition from Kerak demanded, in addition, a reform of the existing electoral laws; the holding of parliamentary elections; the lifting of martial law; and the removal of restrictions on freedom of the press and freedom of expression.[35]

The riots in the Hashemite heartland were a serious blow to the regime, shaking it to its core. Prince Hassan went down to the south to try to pacify the people and restore order but his car was stoned by the angry crowd. Hussein cut short his state visit to the United States and returned home immediately to take charge. He was the object of his people's wrath for being out of touch, for his extravagant life style, and for failing to curb the rampant corruption of his ministers. The chief of the royal court at the time considered the Ma'an riots as one of the three most painful episodes of Hussein's reign, the other two being the loss of Jerusalem in June 1967 and the Gulf War of January 1991.[36] In 1989 Hussein went on a series of trips to the south as part of an exercise in damage limitation. These enabled him to talk to the people directly, to listen and to hear their pain. Some of the people he met were militant. An old peasant from Ma'an pointed his finger at the king and said to him, "You know that we gave our loyalty to your grandfather when he came to this country and you know that we give the same loyalty to you. What made us revolt was the move by your ministers to deprive us of eggs, onions, potatoes and tomatoes. These basic foodstuffs are no longer available because the prices shot up and we cannot afford them."[37] The king heaped ashes on his head.

A tribal chief in Wadi Rum loudly reprimanded the king by saying, "Abu Abdullah, where have you been all these days? We have missed you. We need water, we need electricity, and we need clinics. Your prime minister is a thief; your ministers are no good." The king responded to this tongue-lashing by apologizing for not being around to attend to their needs, and he promised to put everything right when he got home with the help of those responsible in the government. When Prince Raad bin Zaid, the lord chamberlain, called the tribal chief to order, Hussein brushed him aside and let his irate subject have his say. Later, when Raad bin Zaid asked the king how he had managed to be so kind, the king replied, "We have to allow our countrymen to vent their feelings, and it is up to us to listen and to take action whenever possible." This episode struck the loyal lord chamberlain as an example of democracy in action Arab style.[38]

Hussein was stunned by the bread riots, but he immediately grasped the depth of the crisis. He realized that the political status quo was not sustainable and that greater freedom had to be conceded, especially as the price rises could not be revoked. One of the first things he did on his return home was to dismiss Rifa'i and to ask his trusted cousin Zaid bin Shaker to form a new government. The government lasted seven months and seven days. Hussein's instructions to his cousin were to lift martial law; to stabilize the country and restore it to its normal routine; and, most importantly, to prepare the ground for a general parliamentary election.[39] On 8 November elections were held after a gap of twenty-two years. They were generally free and fair, and represented the beginning of the process of democratic reform. Women had their first opportunity to cast their vote and to run for office after being enfranchised in 1974. The Muslim Brotherhood, by origin an ultra-conservative religious association, participated in the elections through its political wing. Its conception of Islam was basically fundamentalist, mixed with pan-Arabist and anti-Zionist sentiments. Candidates from the Muslim Brotherhood and their allies were the biggest winners, gaining 34 out of the 80 seats in the Chamber of Deputies.

Relations between the king and the Muslim Brotherhood had been through many ups and downs. It was created during the Second World War as a branch of the Egyptian Muslim Brotherhood. But during the Arab Cold War in the 1950s and 1960s it did not support Gamal Abdel Nasser's attempts to overthrow Hussein and turned increasingly pro-Hussein during the decade that followed the June War. Ideologically it was opposed to the Ba'th Party and the communists. Moreover, after considering the alternatives, it concluded that its own interests were best served by the continuation of Hussein in power at the head of an independent state that aimed to preserve the status quo.[40] Hussein's legitimacy in Islamist eyes was further enhanced by the fact that he was a direct descendant of the Prophet. The success of the Islamists raised the alarm in conservative political circles, but Hussein took comfort from the fact that they were now part of the very government they had been challenging. "They had been living on slogans," he told his wife. "Now they are going to have to deliver results."[41]

A further step on the road to democracy was the appointment, in April 1990, of a royal commission to draft the National Charter (*Al-mithaq al-watani*). The purpose of the exercise was to provide a legal framework for regulating the political life of the kingdom and especially of the political parties. Most of the members of the sixty-strong drafting commission were supporters of the regime, but a fair number of outsiders and even critics of the monarchy were included. The charter, which was ratified by parliament in the late spring of 1991, became part of the organic law of the kingdom. At its heart was a social contract between the king and the people. The king accepted pluralist and participatory politics. In return, the people had to acknowledge Jordan as a legitimate territorial state and the king as the legitimate head of state.[42] The National Charter fell a long way short of true democracy, but it was a significant move in a more liberal direction. Although the democratic experiment was an internal domestic affair, it had important ramifications in the Arab world. As Prince Raad bin Zaid noted: "Many Arab leaders were not pleased about this. They felt that King Hussein was letting the genie out of the bottle. In addition, they accused him of interfering indirectly in their domestic politics. They were especially critical of the notion of citizens' rights. The Saudis and others felt that Islamic law, the Shari'a, included that. They were apprehensive. They did not understand the relevance of democracy to the Saudi people. For them the Shari'a was all that the Saudi people needed."[43] Suspicion of Jordan's cautious move towards democracy and its leading role in the ACC possibly influenced the Saudi attitude towards Hussein during the Gulf crisis that was to come.

23. The Gulf Crisis and War

The Iraqi invasion of Kuwait on 2 August 1990 precipitated a major regional and international crisis. Failure to resolve the dispute by diplomatic means culminated, six months later, in a full-scale war, mandated by the United Nations, to eject Iraq out of Kuwait. Jordan remained neutral during the crisis, and resisted all the pressures and blandishments to join the American-led military coalition against Iraq.

There are two conflicting versions of Jordan's role in the Gulf crisis and war that may be termed the Republican and the royalist. The American version is that Jordan betrayed its allies and cast its lot with the aggressor in a critical challenge to the post–cold war international order. The bill of particulars against Hussein included the following charges: he had foreknowledge of Saddam Hussein's plan to invade Kuwait; he gave him tacit support during the crisis; he helped him to circumvent the UN-decreed sanctions against Iraq; and he conspired with him to follow up the annexation of Kuwait with a Jordanian annexation of choice parts of Saudi Arabia. The Jordanian version maintains that the king had no foreknowledge of Saddam's plan; that the kingdom consistently opposed the invasion and annexation of Kuwait; that it worked to promote an Arab solution to the dispute; that it abided by the UN sanctions at great cost to itself; and that it remained opposed throughout to the use of military force. In support of its version, the Jordanian government took the unusual step of publishing, in August 1991, a seventy-eight-page white paper, which included its account of the crisis, and fifteen official documents. A critical scrutiny of all the available evidence invalidates the American version on a number of counts without fully substantiating the Jordanian one.

Iraq's invasion of Kuwait took Hussein by complete surprise. The four main issues were Iraqi debts from the era of the Iran–Iraq War, Kuwaiti oil-pricing policy, oil-production quotas from the joint Rumeila Oil Field and a border dispute. Although tension between Iraq and Kuwait had been escalating over these and other issues, Saddam assured Hussein that he would not resort to force so long as there were negotiations in progress, and Hussein conveyed these assurances to his old friend who now occupied the White House. At 5:50 a.m. on 2 August, King Fahd of Saudi Arabia called Hussein with the startling news that Iraqi forces had crossed the border into Kuwait. Hussein was at that time the chairman of the Arab Cooperation Council, so the invasion occurred on his watch. The other members of the ACC were Iraq, Egypt and North Yemen. Fahd asked Hussein to urge the Iraqi leader to limit the invasion to the disputed territories and to stop the thrust into Kuwait. Hussein asked how far the Iraqi forces had penetrated and was shocked to learn that they were six kilometres from Kuwait City and still moving towards the capital. Hussein immediately telephoned the Iraqi leader, but Saddam did not return his call until just after midday. By this time the Iraqi Army was in Kuwait City. Hussein urged Saddam to withdraw. Saddam said that if the Arab governments refrained from condemning and threatening Iraq, the army would begin to withdraw within days and complete its withdrawal within weeks.[1] After learning about the Iraqi move from King Fahd, Hussein called General Ihsan Shurdom and ordered him, as a precaution, to put the Jordanian Air Force on a war footing.[2]

From this point on Hussein worked indefatigably to keep the dispute within the Arab family and to promote an Arab solution to the crisis. He was the only leader in the world who could describe himself as a personal friend of Saddam Hussein, and he was anxious to talk to him. Hussein also felt that it was his duty to do whatever he could to contain the crisis. Shortly after his conversation with Saddam, Hussein flew to Alexandria for an emergency meeting with President Mubarak. The two agreed that the matter should be resolved inside the Arab family with no outside intervention, and Mubarak urged Hussein to visit Baghdad as soon as possible. King Fahd, who was consulted by phone, endorsed this plan. Hussein and Mubarak also spoke to President Bush. Hussein told Bush that he was about to go to Saudi Arabia and Iraq. "I really implore you, sir, to keep calm," he said. "We want to deal with this in an Arab context, to find a way that gives us a foundation for a better future." Bush told the king that the world would not accept the new status quo, and that it was unacceptable to the United States. "I'm sure Saddam Hussein knows this, but you can tell him that from me." The king replied that Iraq was "determined to pull out as soon as possible, maybe in days," and promised to push for withdrawal.[3] He said he needed forty-eight hours to travel to Baghdad to get specific commitments from Saddam and finished the call under the impression that Bush concurred with this. Mubarak agreed that the Arab League should defer issuing a condemnation of Iraq until the king had a chance to find out whether the Iraqi government would give a commitment to withdraw as soon as possible and to attend a mini-summit to discuss all aspects of the dispute with Kuwait. The crux of the matter was to find a face-saving formula, that is, to facilitate Saddam's withdrawal by undertaking to address simultaneously his grievances against Kuwait.

On the following day, 3 August, Hussein flew to Baghdad in the morning to a meeting with Saddam. Hussein secured Saddam's agreement to resolve the crisis within an Arab context: Iraq would attend a mini-summit to be held in Jeddah on 5 August and inform Hussein of the details of its withdrawal before he landed back in Amman. Saddam was adamant, however, that he would respond positively to the proposals of the three Arab heads of state only if the Arab League abstained from condemning Iraq. In other words, Saddam was prepared to start withdrawing his troops, but not if he was under duress. He thought he had legitimate reasons for invading Kuwait, and he wanted to withdraw voluntarily and in a manner that would preserve his dignity. Saddam, in Hussein's view, seemed to be genuinely interested in defusing the crisis on this occasion. That very day, the Iraqi government announced its intention to start withdrawing its troops from Kuwait at 7:00 p.m. on 5 August. Hussein was elated: he had asked for 48 hours to work out an Arab solution and appeared to be on the verge of a breakthrough within that time.

On arrival back in Amman, Hussein called Mubarak to report on the success of his mission, only to discover that the Egyptian leader had changed his mind. In fact, while Hussein was on his way to Baghdad, the Egyptian government issued a statement condemning the Iraqi invasion of Kuwait. Hussein called Mubarak to inform him of the agreement he had reached and to express his regret at the Egyptian statement. Mubarak explained that he was under strong internal and external pressure not to make any concessions to Saddam and added that he had spoken to King Fahd, who was very angry about the situation. Mubarak now rejected the terms that Hussein had secured and insisted on Iraq's unconditional withdrawal from Kuwait and the immediate restoration of the Kuwaiti ruling family. At the meeting of the Council of the Arab League in Cairo that evening, the Egyptian foreign minister steamrollered through a resolution condemning Iraq. Jordan's foreign minister, Marwan Kasim, warned that the resolution would cut across Hussein's plan for a mini-summit to contain the crisis. The Council, however, adopted the resolution by a majority of fourteen.[4] This resolution led to the hardening of the Iraqi position and to the internationalization of the crisis.

Mubarak's U-turn calls for an explanation. Egypt was economically dependent on the United States, and Mubarak came under heavy pressure from Bush to demand an immediate and unconditional Iraqi retreat. Bush, by his own account, was wary of an "Arab solution," fearing that it might end up in a compromise with Saddam.[5] He regarded the invasion as a blatant transgression that had to be dealt with quickly and firmly. Mubarak wanted to impress upon Bush that Egypt was the leader of the Arab world; he was therefore reluctant to give Hussein the credit for resolving the crisis. Egyptians in general had a low opinion of the Hashemites, regarding them as vagabonds from the Hijaz and their country as the accidental product of the dissolution of the Ottoman Empire. There was a general perception that Hussein could not be relied on to play a constructive role in the crisis because he was too beholden to Saddam in economic matters and because he was constrained by the size of the Palestinian community in Jordan. Mubarak himself shared this haughty attitude, questioning Jordan's legitimacy and Hussein's right to rule.[6] To the Americans he freely expressed his disdain for Hussein and accused him of engaging in a conspiracy with the Iraqi dictator to take over Kuwait and divide the spoils of occupation.[7]

Distrust was rampant in the Arab world and helped to destroy the possibility of an Arab solution. The view of a benign Jordanian role in the run-up to the invasion was not shared by the countries most directly affected. The Kuwaitis suspected Hussein of being privy to Iraq's military intentions and of having concealed this knowledge. Saudi Arabia, after being informed that Iraqi troops were massing on the kingdom's border, suspected Hussein of plotting to join forces with Iraq in order to regain the Hijaz.[8] At a later stage in the crisis, when Hussein reminded the world of his title of sharif, this was seized upon by the suspicious Saudis as evidence that he had territorial ambitions of his own. What Hussein actually said, in an address to the Jordanian parliament on 12 August, was the following: "I will be for ever honoured to be a soldier serving this nation. This is the history of my family and my circumstances. I plead with you as brothers: who wants to honour me shall call me by my name, and he who wants to honour me more shall call me Sharif Hussein."[9] There was no mention of the Hijaz or of Saudi Arabia. Rather, the purpose of the speech was to invoke the old Hashemite mission of leading and uniting the Arab nation.

On the morning of 4 August, King Fahd called Hussein and informed him of the American claims that Iraqi troops were advancing towards the border with Saudi Arabia. Hussein did not believe these claims but offered to check them with Saddam. Saddam was also surprised and, after conferring with his senior military staff, reported that their nearest forces were 30 to 40 kilometres from the border, adding that he had just given his generals orders to keep a distance of at least 50 kilometres. Hussein relayed these assurances to King Fahd and suggested a bilateral meeting. Fahd clearly did not want a meeting and offered to send his foreign minister, Prince Saud al-Faisal, to Amman instead. Prince Saud arrived in Amman the following day with the news that the Americans had given King Fahd a photograph that allegedly showed Iraqi troops advancing. Hussein repeated the assurances that Saddam had given him and added that Iraq had officially notified the UN of its intention to withdraw from Kuwait. As a mark of his own confidence in Saddam's assurances, Hussein offered to send half his army to patrol the border area between Kuwait and Saudi Arabia so that his men would be the first to face any advancing Iraqi troops. The Saudis did not respond to the offer, not surprisingly given their suspicions, and the offer ran into the sand.[10]

What Hussein did not know was that, in view of the allegedly suspicious Iraqi troop movements towards the Saudi border, an offer to send American troops to defend Saudi Arabia had been communicated to Riyadh as early as 2 August, six days before the official announcement was made. On 5 August, Saddam both announced and made a modest start with the withdrawal of troops from Kuwait. This gesture, however, was dismissed by Mubarak as "only redeployment" and by Bush as "insubstantial." The Bush administration spent the period 2–6 August secretly negotiating with Saudi Arabia on the size and composition of the American forces to be dispatched. Initially, King Fahd was very reluctant to have American troops on his sacred soil, so a good deal of scaremongering and arm-twisting by the president and his aides were required to secure his consent. The first contingent arrived as early as 6 August. Mubarak was informed about these negotiations, and he too committed and dispatched troops to Saudi Arabia. This explains his abrupt change of course, his rejection out of hand of Saddam's proposals and the haste with which he moved to denounce Iraq. There was no way Mubarak and Fahd could attend a mini-summit with Saddam while American and Egyptian troops were arriving in Saudi Arabia to challenge him. Within less than two days, the two Iraqi conditions—no condemnation and no foreign troops—were breached, and the dialogue with Iraq was summarily suspended. Hussein's credibility as a mediator was destroyed and the possibility of an Arab solution was undermined by the very parties who had asked him to mediate in the first place. It is worth noting that UN Security Council Resolution 660 of 2 August was almost identical to the proposal that Saddam accepted, namely, withdrawal and negotiations. This is a critical part of the story that the American version of the Gulf crisis completely overlooks.[11]

Hussein's heart sank when he heard about the arrival of American forces in Saudi Arabia. The foreign intervention in the affairs of the region that he so much dreaded had now come about. Overnight an Arab–Arab dispute was transformed into a major international crisis pitting America and its allies against Iraq. Suddenly, Saddam had to "lose face," and conciliation was replaced by confrontation. Hussein's role as a mediator was over: he was outside the tent. Jordan was no longer a player in the issues that interested America. For the next six months America was absorbed in the logistics of deploying forces in the Gulf and in building up a broad military coalition against Iraq. On 6 August the Security Council imposed an embargo on Iraq. In response Saddam declared that his invasion of Kuwait was irreversible, and two days later Iraq announced the annexation of Kuwait in its entirety.

Until then it was generally assumed in the Arab capitals that Iraq intended to occupy Kuwait only for a short period. Saddam Hussein later explained the thinking behind the annexation to the king: "I realized that the Americans were determined to go to war." He felt that if Kuwait was not part of Iraq, the Iraqi forces there would not be strongly motivated to defend it. It was one thing to expect the Iraqi Army to defend Iraq unto death and another to ask them to die for the defence of Kuwait. If Kuwait was officially part of Iraq, it would make all the difference. "That's why I did it at the time."[12] But from the point of view of the international community, this was the point of no return: the brutal Iraqi dictator had snuffed out a sovereign nation-state and a member of the United Nations, and he could not be allowed to get away with it. Jordan, like the rest of the international community, refused to recognize Saddam's puppet regime in Kuwait.

Hussein felt let down by his Iraqi friend, and there was nothing he could do to retrieve the situation. American aid to Jordan was cut off. The Gulf countries that joined the military coalition cut off their aid as well. The imposition of sanctions against Iraq by Security Council Resolution 661 had disastrous economic consequences for Jordan. Another blow to the crippled Jordanian economy was the flood of destitute refugees from the Gulf. So anguished was Hussein that, on 8 August, he talked to his wife about abdication. Given the degree to which he was being personally targeted and maligned, he wondered whether Jordan might suffer less if he handed over his responsibilities to someone else. But a steady stream of messages and phone calls told him that the entire country was behind him. Queen Noor added her encouragement and support. There was no point in abdicating during the crisis, she told him. His people needed him now more than ever, as did others round the world who counted on his moderation to counterbalance the war fever that was sweeping the region.[13]

Hussein's popularity at home reached a zenith. The overwhelming majority of Jordanians, both in the country and in the army, sympathized with the Iraqi people. There was also a popular perception that, with the exception of Saddam, the rulers of the Gulf states were an indolent, greedy and venal lot who refused to share their fortuitous wealth with the poor and needy of the Arab world. America stood accused of upholding double standards, on the one hand condoning Israel's occupation of Arab lands and on the other hand condemning Iraq's occupation of Kuwait. Hussein's stand in the crisis boosted the legitimacy of the regime. For the first time in Jordanian history, the regime allowed and even encouraged the holding of anti-Western demonstrations in public places. The Muslim Brotherhood was given a fairly free hand to mobilize popular support for the king's policy of opposing Western military intervention in the Gulf.[14] The Gulf crisis was one of the few episodes in Jordan's history with almost complete convergence between the positions of the regime, the army, parliament and public opinion.

Hussein's popularity at home came at considerable cost to his relations with the West. The West was aware that Iraq and Jordan were allies and that this called for a more pragmatic foreign policy. Nevertheless, Western goodwill was severely strained by material Jordanian support for Saddam in evading UN sanctions and by what was seen as Hussein's failure of leadership in the early days of the crisis. It was felt that had the king thought more astutely, he would have realized that Jordan's real interest lay in joining with the rest of the international community against the lawbreaker. Hussein could have told his people that the principle of the inadmissibility of the acquisition of territory by force was vital to Jordan and that Jordan's stand in the current crisis was anchored in this principle. Saddam therefore should not expect any moral or material support from Jordan. Hussein's lack of leadership at home, it was claimed, had the effect of increasing popular support for Iraq and of intensifying the animus against Kuwait and Saudi Arabia. Western experts knew that the position of Jordan's various Bedouin tribes varied according to their connections with Kuwait and Saudi Arabia but that generally they were not in favour of the implicit Jordanian support for Saddam. Hussein's behaviour was regarded by these experts as emotional and impulsive. He was making one mistake after another and inflicting serious damage on Jordan's relations with the Gulf Cooperation Council countries. The term "plucky little king" went out of fashion.[15]

Hussein became somewhat divorced from reality in seeing himself as the victim of cynical Western and Arab politicians who promoted their own selfish interests behind the cloak of international legality. But he was not the only saint in a world of sinners, as the official Jordanian version of the Gulf crisis would have us believe. Although the conspiracy theories that linked him to the invasion of Kuwait were not substantiated, he was strangely naive in what he thought he could achieve. This may have been a case when, once again, his strategic sense let him down. His younger brother certainly thought so. One of the very few flaming rows between the two brothers was on the subject of Saddam. Hassan warned Hussein repeatedly that Saddam was an incorrigible and dangerous despot, but Hussein would not listen. The material benefits of the association with Saddam warped his judgement and blinded him to the dangers. Hussein was always hopeful of restoring Jordanian–Iraqi relations to their pre-1958 glory, hence his sympathy for Saddam. He thought that, through Saddam, Jordan might be able to retrieve the position it lost in Iraq as a result of the July 1958 revolution.[16] In the course of one of their periodic rows on the subject, Hussein said to Hassan, "If you don't take this man seriously, I'm really beginning to question, to have my doubts about you." "Fine," retorted Hassan, "make your choice." During the Gulf War, Hussein was angry and truculent and at times even seemed prepared to throw caution to the wind and to join in the battle alongside the Iraqi dictator. Hassan thought he detected the same suicidal tendency in his elder brother during the Gulf War that he had noticed before, notably in pushing for a second front against Israel in October 1956 and in taking the plunge, without thinking about the consequences, in June 1967.[17]

The truth of the matter is that Hussein was only a minor actor in this particular drama. His efforts to find a peaceful way out, sincere and persistent as they were, could not deflect the slide towards war. President Mubarak took the initiative in convening another emergency meeting of the Arab League in Cairo on 10 August. Attempts to revive mediation efforts were brushed aside. The text of a resolution that was probably a translation from English into Arabic was quickly pushed through. It repeated the previous condemnation of Iraq; it refused to recognize the annexation of Kuwait; and it responded affirmatively to the appeal of Saudi Arabia and other Gulf states for Arab forces to help defend their territory against outside aggression. Jordan, Yemen and Algeria abstained because they saw the resolution as a cover for foreign intervention.[18] Hussein sat with his hands on his cheeks in a cloud of gloom. "I felt right away, from the first instant, that this was going to be the most tragic summit in the history of the Arab nation," he told the secretary-general.[19]

Two days later, on 12 August, Saddam, in what amounted to a rare political master-stroke, suggested that Iraq might withdraw from Kuwait if Israel withdrew from all occupied Arab territory and Syria withdrew from Lebanon. It was this proposal that introduced the concept of linkage into the Middle East diplomatic lexicon. Overnight Saddam became the hero of the Arab masses and the saviour of the Palestinians. The Gulf conflict and the Arab–Israeli conflict became linked in the public mind. An Israeli government spokesman dismissed Saddam's proposal as a cheap propaganda ploy. But the proposal landed the Bush administration on the horns of a dilemma. On the one hand, they did not want to reward Saddam for his aggression; on the other hand, they could hardly deny that the long-festering Arab–Israeli conflict also required a settlement. Bush's way round this dilemma was to deny that there was any parallel between the two occupations but to promise that once Iraq left Kuwait, a settlement of the Arab–Israeli problem would be high on his administration's agenda. In other words, he rejected the simultaneous linkage of the two conflicts in favour of a deferred linkage.

Baghdad's linkage proposal motivated Hussein to embark on a tour of Western capitals in a desperate attempt to scale down the crisis. On 13 August he flew to Baghdad for a meeting with Saddam, giving rise to speculation in the media that he came away carrying a message from Saddam. Hussein said there was no message but once again he put himself forward as an intermediary. He was the only Arab leader who was still talking to Saddam, and he hoped that the Americans would use him as a channel of communications to Baghdad. On his return, he called Bush and requested a meeting. Bush was in Kennebunkport, his summer resort in Maine, and the meeting was arranged for 16 August. A small royal party arrived by helicopter at the summer resort for what turned out to be a rather raw experience. Bush himself was courteous but truculent and dismissed out of hand the king's negotiations with Saddam for a peaceful withdrawal. Bush expected a message from Baghdad, but, if there was one, the king never mentioned it to him. Hussein appeared to be seeking to play a role as an intermediary but Bush saw nothing to negotiate. In his diary Bush recorded:

We talked very frankly about the differences. I kept trying to say that the friendship was intact . . . He [pressed] for some middle ground that could solve the problem, and I kept saying, there isn't any—it's got to be withdrawal and restoration of the Kuwaiti regime. There cannot be any middle ground, because tomorrow, it will be somebody else's aggression . . . Hussein refuses to admit that this is a madman. He talked about the "haves and the have-nots" . . .[20]

Bush emphasized that, for America, oil was a way of life, and he wanted Hussein to understand America's resolve. Hussein may have hoped that, because of the historic ties between Jordan and America and their personal friendship, America would moderate or move a little; but, although Bush valued the friendship, he refused to budge. At one point he exclaimed, "I will not let that little dictator control 25 percent of the civilized world's oil!" Sharif Zaid bin Shaker found the remark doubly disturbing on account of the property rights it assumed over Gulf oil and the implication that the Arabs were not civilized.[21] The remark also inadvertently revealed that in seeking a showdown with Saddam, Bush's primary concern was with Western access to Gulf oil rather than with upholding international legality. After all, the Reagan administration, in which Bush had been vice-president, supported Saddam throughout the eight years of his war against Iran. That war was a textbook case of unprovoked aggression, and yet not once did the United States condemn Iraq. Nor did Saddam's brutal oppression of his own people and his gassing of the Kurds at Halabja make any difference to American foreign policy. Saddam was a monster in human form but he was America's monster. His great mistake was to tread on America's toe by attacking its client and threatening its access to Gulf oil. Hussein's efforts at mediation were now treated as a personal betrayal of his friendship with Bush. You were either with them or against them.

Bush may also have thought that he had Jordan backed into a corner. He knew that the country was economically dependent on Iraq, from which it imported 95 percent of its oil and to which it sold 45 percent of its exports. Bush heard from President Mubarak that Saddam had bought off the Jordanian and Yemeni rulers with the offer of a certain percentage of Kuwait's oil in return for supporting the invasion. The story was completely groundless, but it was a factor in Bush's thinking. To wean Hussein away from Iraq, the Bush administration began considering international financial help as well as emergency Arab oil assistance, provided he implemented the UN sanctions.[22] Bush said he realized Hussein was worried about Jordan's economic situation and suggested that the other Arab countries could help. Hussein reportedly replied, "I didn't come to raise that subject. I came because of something bigger: the subject of peace."[23]

To Jordanian officials this looked like an attempt to persuade their king to join the allied coalition against Iraq by the offer of financial rewards. They took a dim view of this attempt, particularly against the backdrop of American failure to extend financial help at the height of the crisis the previous year. Hussein, for his part, remained dedicated to finding an Arab solution to an Arab problem, and he was not tempted by the carrot dangled under his nose. As Adiba Mango has observed, "had it been a matter of financial payoff, the Jordanian leadership would have been more likely to take up Bush's offer of financial largesse rather than rely on promises from a cash-strapped Iraqi neighbour."[24]

At Kennebunkport the diplomatic shutters were briskly pulled down. The meeting was disappointing for Bush but not half as disappointing as it was for Hussein. It marked the parting of the ways between the two old friends. Bush turned to the task of building up a military coalition against "the little Iraqi dictator" while Hussein continued to seek a peaceful resolution of the conflict. Washington's attitude towards Jordan hardened, and its tone gradually became more hostile and menacing. To Roger Harrison, the new American ambassador to Amman, fell the difficult task of maintaining contact between the two capitals. In the aftermath of the Kennebunkport meeting, Harrison handed to His Majesty the following message:

We recognize that Jordan, because of its geographical location, is vulnerable to Iraqi pressure. But you should have no illusion that Iraqi success in its invasion of Kuwait will satisfy Saddam Hussein's ambitions to dominate the region. No neighbour is safe.

It is vital for Jordan's essential interest that it not be neutral in the struggle between Iraq and the great majority of the Arab states.

The perception of a de facto Iraqi–Jordanian alliance has already damaged the reputation of Jordan in the United States and elsewhere. We sincerely hope that you would take firm steps to reverse this deterioration . . .

Hussein described this message to an American journalist as "nasty" and "very, very rude."[25]

In the last week in August, Hussein visited Yemen, Sudan, Libya, Tunisia, Algeria, Mauritania and Morocco. His purpose was to find some common ground among the Arab states that were opposed to foreign intervention. In the first week in September he visited Spain, Britain, Germany, France and Italy. In all these countries he met with heads of state or government and presented to them the Jordanian version of the origins and causes of the crisis. His main purpose was to persuade them to support a peaceful solution. In all these countries, except Britain, he was encouraged to persevere in his efforts at mediation. Britain's prime minister at that time was Margaret Thatcher, with whom Hussein had always had close and cordial relations in the past. He was a man with authority who knew how to command her sympathy and support, and she clearly liked him.[26] Recent events in the Gulf, however, placed a serious strain on their relationship. Thatcher had successfully led her country into the Falklands War and considered herself an expert on dealing with dictators. She was firmly of the opinion that you do not negotiate with dictators; you throw them out on their ear. On day one of the crisis she dogmatically ruled out diplomacy. She happened to be with Bush in Aspen, Colorado, when news of the invasion arrived, and he talked about referring the matter to the Security Council. Thatcher apparently brushed aside the idea. "This is no time to go wobbly, George!" she said.

At their working lunch in Downing Street, Hussein found Thatcher so inflexible and belligerent that he had doubts about her sanity. She assumed a Churchillian posture, glowered at him and sounded like a megalomaniac. She began by asking the king why he was backing Saddam, whom she described as "an evil man." "I am not backing anybody. I am trying to save peace in our area," the king replied. He told her frankly that gunboat diplomacy belonged to the nineteenth century. Her famous eyes blazed with anger. "You are backing a loser and I want you to know that before it is too late," she said. She dismissed Saddam disdainfully as "a third-class dictator."[27] In an imperious voice she concluded by saying, "Your Majesty, you have no more of a role in the Middle East." Adnan Abu-Odeh was the note-taker, and he wrote at the end of his notes of the meeting: "Oh, God, it was like Queen Victoria speaking to an Indian maharaja." He felt as humiliated as the rest of the party. The friendship between the king and the prime minister ended during that working lunch, and the subsequent correspondence between them was less than civil, at least on her part.[28]

After the lunch with Thatcher, Hussein held a secret meeting with Israeli officials in London. A fascinating glimpse of the evolving relationship is provided in a book written by Efraim Halevy, who was deputy director of the Mossad at that time and probably the king's closest Israeli contact. The Israelis were watching events from the sidelines with mounting anxiety. Israel had intelligence that Jordanian pilots were being trained together with Iraqi pilots in Iraq. When this intelligence was first presented to the king he did not deny it but explained it in terms of cost-savings; it did not signal a change of policy towards Israel. After the Iraqi invasion of Kuwait, the Israelis discovered that Iraqi aircraft bearing the insignia of the Royal Jordanian Air Force were patrolling the border between Jordan and Israel south of the Dead Sea, virtually within striking distance of the atomic reactor in Dimona. It was inconceivable that these flights were taking place without the king's approval. In Jerusalem strident voices were raised, calling for an end to the secret honeymoon between Israel and Jordan. Proponents of a Palestinian state on the East Bank saw the approaching war as a chance to achieve two things simultaneously: retaliate against possible Iraqi missile attacks on Israel and strike at the Jordanian Air Force. They knew that this scenario, if carried to its logical conclusion, would spell the end of the monarchy. A decision was taken to confront the king about the consequences of this latest development. He was presented with a stiff warning that the Iraqi flights had to stop instantly. The warning was delivered to the king on the day of his working lunch at 10 Downing Street. In a later conversation the king remarked that while Thatcher's tone had been bitter and unpleasant, the Israeli message was more threatening in content.[29]

The king seized the opportunity to explain to the Israelis some of the facts of life as he saw them. In the eyes of the Arab masses Saddam was the real hero. He had saved the Sunni Muslims from the onslaught of the Iranian Shi'ites. He commanded not only respect but awe and fear. He personified the dream of glory, sacrifice and success. What in Western eyes looked like ruthlessness and cruelty stood in Arab eyes for courage, strength and pride. One must never forget the importance of pride, the king kept repeating. He was especially bitter about the treatment he was receiving from Bush. He had known every American president since Eisenhower, and he had invested a great deal of effort in cultivating the friendship with Bush when he was director of the CIA and after. But now he simply could not yield to Bush's naked pressure with regard to the Iraqi affair. After years of patient cultivation of relations with the United States, he had reached a dead end. His relationship with his long-standing ally was falling apart. For Jordan and for him personally, this was disastrous, but he was powerless to stop the drift towards war. Every time Efraim Halevy met him during those months, the king repeated to him that he was convinced that he had behaved honourably and that he was prepared to confront his fate, just as he had been many times in the past when faced with threats to his life and to the survival of his kingdom. During the lead up to the Gulf War, Halevy saw a leader in a sombre and fatalistic mood but at peace with himself and ready to accept whatever Allah had ordained for him.[30]

On 5 September, Hussein returned from his tour of Europe's capitals and flew straight to Baghdad to try once again to persuade Saddam to withdraw from Kuwait. This was the second of three trips he made to Baghdad in the quest for a peaceful settlement. On this trip he conveyed to Saddam his firm conviction that the Western leaders and their allies were not going to allow him to stay in Kuwait. "Make a brave decision and withdraw your forces," Hussein advised the Iraqi leader. "If you don't, you will be forced out." Saddam, however, remained unmoved.[31] He was less concerned with the future of Kuwait than with his own future. He probably calculated that if he ordered his army to execute a humiliating retreat, his own leadership would be called into question. The Western logic said that if he did not withdraw voluntarily and unconditionally, he would be compelled to withdraw by force. From his own perspective, however, it was probably less risky to let his army be driven out by force than to lose face with an unconditional surrender. Pride in the Arab world was very important, as Hussein was reminding his Israeli friends.

Hussein's perseverance in the role of peacemaker in the face of so many rebuffs is nothing short of astounding. He felt deeply that the Middle East could not afford another war and that the world should not impose one on it. His next venture was a Maghrebi peace initiative. On 19 September, King Hassan II of Morocco hosted in Rabat a meeting to which President Chadli ben Jedid of Algeria was also invited. The prospects of an Arab solution to the crisis were far from promising, but the assembled heads of state agreed to make another effort. Three days later Hussein addressed a long letter to the Iraqi leader in which he conveyed their collective wisdom. The core of the letter was the advice to Saddam to withdraw from Kuwait and to avoid the approaching war. It was made clear to Saddam that the Arab governments could not accept the acquisition of territory by force not only as a matter of principle but because failure to uphold it would play into Israel's hands. The letter appealed to Saddam's ego by extolling his leadership and Iraq's achievements under his leadership. But it also spoke of the ambitions of the large industrial powers to dominate the region and warned him that a war would spell disaster not only for Iraq but for the entire Arab world. These powers were deliberately laying a trap for Iraq, he was told. Saddam was invited to state his precise demands on the subject of Kuwait to enable the three leaders to work for an Arab solution. Having articulated his fears, Hussein placed himself at Saddam's disposal. "I left Baghdad for Jordan anxious and saddened," he wrote. "I was hoping to continue my activities to prevent the deterioration that has been going on ever since. Will you not respond to my call, and the call of every sincere Arab, before it is too late?"

Saddam's reply was carried to Amman by the Iraqi foreign minister on 29 September. It did not respond to the call. Saddam was prepared to take up the challenge of war because he believed, or at least he said he believed, that war would be a disaster not for Iraq but for the United States and its allies. Saddam was prepared to accept one of two solutions to the crisis: an Arab solution along the lines originally proposed by His Majesty on 3 August or an international solution along the lines he himself had proposed on 12 August, linking the question of Kuwait to the problems of Palestine and Lebanon.[32] The letter contained no new ideas for breaking the deadlock. The Arab solution had effectively been rejected by Kuwait and Saudi Arabia, while the international solution had been rejected by America and Britain. Hussein's letter failed to avert war, but it established his credentials as someone who had been opposed to the invasion and annexation of Kuwait from the beginning. It showed that he was a good deal tougher on Saddam than his American detractors realized.

Bush remained firm in his assessment that only military force would drive the Iraqi forces out of Kuwait. In October the decision was taken to increase the number of American troops in Saudi Arabia to 400,000. The mission of this huge military force changed from defensive to offensive. The original aim of the American deployment was the defence of the kingdom but additional forces were required for the purpose of evicting Iraq from Kuwait. Bush denied it, but the doubling of American ground forces marked the critical transition from Operation Desert Shield to Operation Desert Storm. An intensified diplomatic campaign accompanied the dispatch of land, sea and air forces to Saudi

Arabia. On 29 November the Security Council passed Resolution 678, which authorized the use of "all necessary means" against Iraq unless it complied with all previous resolutions within six weeks. It was promptly dubbed "the mother of all resolutions," echoing Saddam's threat that if Iraq was attacked, it would wage "the mother of all battles." The radical shift in the American position persuaded Hussein that a military confrontation was imminent, yet he persisted in his efforts to contain the crisis, focusing in particular on securing the release of the Western hostages held by Iraq since the outbreak of the crisis.

A mini-summit took place in Baghdad on 4 December. It was Hussein's third and last visit to the Iraqi capital in the course of the crisis. Yasser Arafat, the chairman of the PLO, and Ali Salem Al-Bid, the vice-president of Yemen, were also there, and they all pleaded with Saddam to pull back from the brink but to no avail. They argued that the consequences of a clash of arms would be disastrous for Iraq, Kuwait and the whole region, but Saddam could not be moved. Sharif Zaid bin Shaker intervened in the discussion as a military expert to underline the seriousness of the situation, but his words too were ignored. His impression was that Saddam and his key advisers were nowhere near as worried by the prospect of war as they should have been. Their understanding of the outside world was very limited. They had no idea about America's military capability or of the way its political system worked. They said that the Americans were cowards; they would suffer casualties and withdraw. Hussein intervened to tell Saddam that this assessment was wrong, that they would be hit very severely by the allies, and that he should withdraw before it was too late.[33] The Iraqi military advisers were even more ignorant of the outside world than their political masters and just as confident and boastful. They said that they were ready for the Americans and that if the Americans came, they would crush them under their boots like cockroaches.[34]

A more immediate issue was the fate of the Western hostages, or "guests," held by Iraq. "We argued and argued," recalled the king. "Eventually we managed to get the so-called guests out of Iraq. That is the only positive thing that came out of it."[35] After the summit the Iraqi government announced that all foreign nationals would be allowed to leave the country. As a mark of respect, Saddam personally accompanied Hussein to the airport. At the airport he said to the king, "Abu

Abdullah, don't worry. The whole world is against us but God is with us and we are going to win." Hussein said, "This is beyond my ability to comprehend or to deal with. I leave very saddened and very distressed and I know that the results as they appear to me are going to be disastrous everywhere. But I will be back home. If there is anything I can further do, then you know how to get in touch with me." Saddam never called, and the war broke out the following month.[36]

Having failed to avert a military confrontation between Iraq and the American-led coalition, Hussein turned his attention to limiting the consequences of the conflict for Jordan. His primary concern was to avoid being dragged into a war to which Jordan was not a party. Iraq and Israel were preparing for war, and Hussein was fearful that his kingdom would be crushed between the two. Late in the afternoon on 31 December 1990, Adnan Abu-Odeh flew to Baghdad in a private plane to deliver an oral message from Hussein to Saddam. When Abu-Odeh arrived, he was told that Saddam could not see him because he was outside Baghdad. So he saw Vice-President Taha Yasin Ramadan and Foreign Minister Tariq Aziz, and delivered his message. It was only two sentences: "I carry His Majesty's greetings to the president and His Majesty's wish is to let you know that in case war flares up he does not want to see Jordanian territory or Jordanian skies violated by anyone." In other words, Jordan did not want to be involved in any military action, and it would defend its territory and airspace against any incursion from any side.[37] The verbal warning was followed up by the dispatch of an armoured division to the eastern front. Prince Abdullah was sent to the Iraqi border with a Cobra helicopter squadron. They did not know whether they would be attacked by the Iraqis, the Israelis or the Americans. But the message to Saddam was very clear: "If you try to come to Jordan with your troops, you'll go straight into a military confrontation."[38]

Hussein's role was the subject of much comment in the Western media, mostly hostile. Those who were beating the drums of war portrayed him as the ally of the Iraqi dictator and as an accomplice in the assault on Kuwait. Those who were still seeking a peaceful solution to the crisis saw him as the most sincere and helpful of all the Arab leaders. In his public statements Hussein tried to counter the media campaign that was being directed against him. He reiterated that Jordan was opposed to the acquisition of territory by force, that it continued to rec-

ognize the state and government of Kuwait, and that it was implement-
ing the UN sanctions against Iraq at considerable cost to itself. What
Jordan was opposed to, he explained, was the military build-up in the
Gulf. He warned that a war would have incalculable consequences for
Arabs and Muslims the world over for generations to come. He also
appealed directly to the American public to support his efforts to
achieve a diplomatic settlement based on Security Council resolutions.
But he might as well have been talking to himself, for all the good it did.

Hussein's public utterances failed to impress the Saudis, and his
efforts to distance himself from Iraq failed to scotch their suspicions
that he was secretly in cahoots with Saddam. Here is what Prince
Khaled bin Sultan, a member of the Saudi royal family and the commander of the joint forces in the Gulf War, wrote in his autobiography:
"With Saddam's armies at the door, it was not far-fetched to fear that
King Hussein dreamed of retaking the Hijaz, once ruled by his great-
grandfather; that President Ali Abdallah Salih of Yemen dreamed of
seizing our border province of Asir; that the Palestinians, present in
Kuwait in large numbers, imagined that they might establish there a
temporary homeland under Saddam's aegis, pending the recovery of
Palestine from the Jews."[39] This passage discloses a disturbing inability
to distinguish between fact and fiction. Hussein's indication to his own
people that they could call him either king or sharif further deepened
Saudi suspicions. "Sharif" is an honorific title reserved for those who
can claim descent from the Prophet Muhammad. However, the king's
words angered and alarmed the Saudi leadership because they seemed
to signal his ambition to seize territory in the Hijaz that had once been
ruled by his great-grandfather, Hussein bin Ali, the sharif of Mecca.[40]
But when Hussein grew a sharif-like white beard, which made him look
remarkably like his great-grandfather, the jittery Saudis were terrified:
it seemed to them to be reviving the Hashemite dynasty's claim to the
Hijaz. The truth, however, was much more prosaic: the king suffered
from a stress-induced skin condition that made it painful to shave.

Saudi conspiracy theories were not supported by any concrete evi-
dence, and they were denied by Hussein with some vehemence.
"Somehow it turned out that our position had been undermined in the
Arab world," he said. "There was talk of Jordan conspiring with Iraq.
Totally unfounded! We had never done it and if we had done it, we
would have done something much better than that. It is against our

nature. All we were trying to do is to avert the human disaster, the economic disaster, the breaking of bones . . . in the region . . . And all we
wanted was a chance. If we had been given that chance and Iraq had
proved that we couldn't succeed, we probably would have been
amongst the first troops to enter Iraq . . . But we weren't given the
chance." Hussein went on to describe the mood in Jordan on the eve of
the war:

The pressure built up on us in such a way that we were totally isolated but we
mobilized and that was another one of the best moments I have ever seen in Jordan. Our people came together and we of course received 400,000 refugees
from the bidun, those who had no citizenship rights, from Kuwait and from the
Gulf on top of all the other problems we had to cope with. We were encircled.
We mobilized almost a quarter of a million Jordanians and through that we controlled the situation. We made it very clear to Iraqis, we spoke to the Israelis, we
spoke to everybody else who might attack us, we said: "We may be small, but
we will cause a lot of damage. We are not saying we are invincible, we are not.
But neither our land nor our air space can be used by them." We had our forces
deployed facing Iraq and facing Israel, facing north and facing south.[41]

Israel did not fail to pick up the signs of the state of high alert in Jordan. In Israel too the mood was tense as 1990 turned into 1991 and the
crisis approached its climax. With war looming on the horizon, Jordan
assumed ever greater importance as a buffer or potential battleground
between Iraq and Israel. Likud leaders suddenly discovered the value
of having a stable country under a moderate ruler on their eastern border. The change of tune was unmistakable. Instead of issuing threats,
the government began to send, through third parties, soothing messages
to Amman to assure the king that they had no plans to attack and to
urge him not to allow the entry of Iraqi troops into Jordan.[42] As soon as
the crisis erupted, Shamir wrote to Bush to warn that the entry of Iraqi
forces into Jordan would be a "red line" from Israel's point of view.
Shamir also made it clear that Israel had no hostile intentions towards
Hussein and asked Bush to discourage the king from serving the Iraqi
dictator's aggressive purposes.[43]

At the start of 1991 there were worrying signs that Jordan was concentrating forces east of the Jordan River and that the king was losing
control of the situation. A more direct channel of communication with

Amman was needed. Efraim Halevy, the deputy director of the Mossad, took the initiative in trying to arrange a meeting. The purpose of the summit meeting was to prevent Iraq from using Jordanian facilities to attack Israel in the event of war. Hussein agreed to a meeting but doubted whether Shamir would be interested, given the differences that emerged at their one and only meeting in July 1987. When Halevy asked Hussein whether he would come to a meeting if Shamir came, the immediate reply was "Yes!" On his return to Israel, Halevy sounded out Shamir on a face-to-face meeting with their neighbour. Shamir welcomed the idea but doubted whether Hussein would accept the risk of a leak that would damage his standing with his Palestinian subjects and upset his delicate relationship with Iraq and with Saddam Hussein in particular. Halevy reported that the king had already agreed and that the summit meeting could indeed take place. But he did not underestimate the risks involved. The failure of the meeting could provide the anti-Jordanian lobby in Israel with a powerful boost for its policy. At the previous meeting the basic positions of the two leaders were irreconcilable. If they parted again without agreement, the consequences could be serious.[44]

The meeting took place at Buckhurst Park, Hussein's secluded and well-protected country residence in Ascot. The guests arrived before sundown on Friday, 4 January 1991, and left after the end of the Sabbath on the following day. Shamir was accompanied by Elyakim Rubinstein, the cabinet secretary, Yossi Ben-Aharon, the director-general of the prime minister's office, and Major-General Ehud Barak, the IDF deputy chief of staff. The royal party included Sharif Zaid bin Shaker, the chief of the royal court, Adnan Abu-Odeh, Hussein's political adviser, and Colonel Ali Shukri, the director of Hussein's private office. For Abu-Odeh, a Palestinian originally from Nablus, this was the first encounter with Israeli officials on state business. The king did not brief him about the previous meetings, and he did not wish to appear inquisitive by asking. As far as he was concerned, the principal purpose of the talks was to preserve Jordanian neutrality in the coming conflict. In this respect the meeting with the Israelis was a logical sequel to the king's recent mission to Baghdad.[45]

Ali Shukri was born in 1950 and entered the king's service in 1976, after receiving a degree in Electrical and Electronic Engineering from Cardiff University and serving briefly in the Jordanian Signal Corps.

When Shukri entered the king's service he was a lieutenant and when he left in 1998 he was a major-general. Among the various aides, Shukri was the king's closest confidant: he travelled with him everywhere and attended most of his meetings with foreign leaders, including sixty-one meetings with Saddam in the 1990s. Shukri was entrusted by the king with the sensitive task of arranging the clandestine meetings with the Israelis and of maintaining the contact in between meetings. Another task that usually fell to Ali Shukri, as the junior member of the Jordanian party, was that of note-taker. Although the king had little patience for paperwork, Shukri took copious notes at the meetings with the Israelis and produced typed reports in English that he gave to the king after each meeting. Because of their special sensitivity, these records were not kept in the royal court but taken home by the king and kept with the rest of his private papers.[46]

Shamir was sympathetic to Jordan's predicament. He understood that Jordan's geopolitical situation ruled out participation in the coalition against Iraq because Iraq could hurt Jordan. Hussein's success in keeping his country out of the October War of 1973 was an encouraging precedent in this respect. According to Shamir, Hussein began with a survey of his difficulties: the Americans had abandoned him; the Saudis were hostile to him; and he was isolated in the Arab world. At home the Palestinians were liable to cause riots if he publicly dissociated himself from the actions taken by Saddam. He did not want war: he feared its destabilizing effects, and his sole desire was that Jordan should not be turned into a battleground between Israel and Iraq. He asked for an Israeli promise not to infringe the territorial integrity of Jordan by land or by air, and he hoped that this would help him to procure a similar promise from Iraq.[47]

Hussein's account of the meeting suggests that it was Shamir who sought assurances that Jordan would not attack Israel:

Shamir said, "Look, I have a dilemma. In October 1973 our people were not vigilant enough and the Arab attack took place and caused us a lot of damage. Now you have your troops mobilized and my generals are calling for me to do the same and to have our troops facing yours. There isn't much distance in the Jordan Valley and it would be totally irresponsible, they say, if I did not take the same measures." So I said, "Prime Minister, you are perfectly within your rights to take the same measures if you feel like it, but let me suggest that if that happens then the possibility of an accidental war developing between us is very real." He said, "Well, what is your position?" I said, "My position is purely defensive." He said, "Do I have your word?" I said, "Yes, you have my word." He said, "That is good enough for me and I will prevent our people from moving anywhere." And he did. And that was one of the events I will always remember. He recognized that my word was good enough and this is the way people should deal with each other.[48]

Ehud Barak was still troubled by the concentration of troops on Israel's border. Shaker, who was a man of few words, intervened in the discussion to allay his anxieties. This was Shaker's first meeting with Barak, and he found that he rather liked him. He was the military expert, having spent thirty-five years in the army, and Hussein's right-hand man. He amplified Hussein's position and went into detail. He and Hussein were extremely close. They had discussed and prepared the meeting beforehand, and were always in total agreement. Shaker had no reservations about meeting Israelis. He conducted himself at this meeting in a professional manner and spoke to Barak as one soldier to another. He said to Barak: "Your reconnaissance planes are flying all the time. We are professional soldiers. You know the difference between defensive and offensive postures."[49] Barak kept demanding more assurances until Shamir lost his patience. "King Hussein has given me his word," he said firmly, "and that is enough for me."[50] With a gesture of his hand, the diminutive and taciturn man ordered the most highly decorated soldier in Israel's army to shut up and to take away the maps and the rest of the paraphernalia used to make his presentation.

The issue of the potential threat that Jordan posed to Israel was settled in the end to everybody's satisfaction. The king solemnly undertook to prevent the military use of his country in any shape or form against Israel. A second issue was more difficult to resolve. Jordan could not prevent the use of its air space by Iraqi ballistic missiles bound for Israel. Israel therefore sought Jordan's tacit acquiescence in the limited use of its air space should it be forced to retaliate against an Iraqi missile attack. The request implied that if Jordan's Air Force and its anti-aircraft systems engaged the IAF, Israel would be obliged to destroy Jordan's capabilities, which could lead to an Israeli–Jordanian war. But Hussein resolutely refused to accede to the request of the

Israeli prime minister. He explained at length that he could not afford to be seen to collude with Israel, if the latter felt obliged to attack Iraq. He stated unambiguously that if Israel violated Jordan's airspace, he would give the order to protect his country's sovereignty. The two leaders parted amicably but without reaching agreement on this life-and-death issue.[51]

An issue that was not raised because it did not directly concern Jordan was Iraq's possession of weapons of mass destruction. The Israelis knew, and the Americans confirmed, that Iraq had ballistic missiles that could be fitted with chemical warheads.[52] For a nation haunted by the memories of the Nazi gas chambers, this was a highly sensitive issue. Shamir's mother and sister had been taken away in carts from their village in Poland to Treblinka, where they perished at the hands of the Nazis long after he had settled in Palestine. He rarely talked about the Holocaust but it taught him an unforgettable object lesson and instilled in him, as in so many other survivors, a feeling of "Never Again!" In his public statements Shamir warned that if Iraq attacked Israel, terrible retribution would follow. This was taken by commentators to mean that an Iraqi attack on Israel with chemical weapons could provoke an Israeli nuclear response. Shamir did nothing to contradict this interpretation of his statements. In the course of the weekend the Israelis told their hosts that an Iraqi attack with chemical or biological weapons would set off instant retaliation.

In the intimate atmosphere of an English country house, Barak was the most forthright. "We have been gassed once," he said to Shukri, "and we are not going to be gassed again. If one single chemical warhead falls on Israel, we'll hit them with everything we have got. If unconventional weapons are used against us, look at your watch and 40 minutes later an Iraqi city will be reduced to ashes." "Could it be Baghdad?" asked the stunned Jordanian. "It could be," was the reply. The Jordanians passed on the warning to Baghdad. Several years after the war, Shukri found out that the Israeli warnings indeed had the desired deterrent effect. Hussein Kamel, Saddam's son-in-law who had defected to Jordan, confirmed that during the Gulf War the Iraqi Army had missiles armed with chemical warheads ready to be fired on Israel but the order from the president never came.[53]

The meeting succeeded beyond all expectations. A relationship of mutual trust was established between the two leaders. A strategic understanding was reached that Jordan would remain neutral when the bombs in the Gulf started falling and that Israel would respect its neutrality. This understanding goes a long way towards explaining the uncharacteristic restraint that Israel exercised during the Gulf War but also Jordan's success in avoiding being sucked into this war. "It was odd," Hussein observed, "that two countries at war over so many years should have had that degree of understanding to avoid war."[54] Hussein gave most of the credit for this achievement to his opponent. Looking back, Hussein described this meeting to a Likud minister as a turning point and said how impressed he had been with Shamir on this occasion.[55] To his son Abdullah, Hussein said that it was a very good meeting, that Shamir treated his word as trustworthy, and that they agreed, in soldiers' language, that "We won't go for you, if you don't go for us."[56] Shaker also paid tribute to Shamir, describing him as "the most polite and pleasant of the Israelis" and adding that "On that occasion he was a perfect gentleman."[57]

Although he did not claim it, Hussein too deserved a share of the credit for the amazing success of the meeting. On this occasion, as at every other meeting with the Israelis, Hussein was as tactful as the most polished diplomat. Respect for the Jews, the People of the Book, was a Hashemite family tradition that Hussein had learned from his grandfather and passed on to his son. In addition to good manners, Hussein had deep insight into the sources of the insecurity that many Israelis feel despite their patent military superiority over all the Arab states. His close aides and family were well aware of the importance he attached to sensitive handling of the Israelis. He educated the people around him about the need to show understanding and sympathy to the other side. His key point, in the words of his son Abdullah, was: "If you deal with an opponent, and at that point the Israelis were opponents, you have to put yourself in their shoes . . . You have to see their concerns, their paranoia and their fears."[58]

The understanding reached at the summit remained a closely guarded secret. The possibility of a clash with Jordan excited some reckless talk in Jerusalem. Some politicians on the extreme right did not share in the sudden conversion of their normally hardline leader to the royalist cause. Ariel Sharon was not impressed with the argument that Israel had to do its utmost to stop Jordan getting embroiled in the Gulf conflict. On the contrary, one of his motives for advocating swift and forceful military action against Iraq was his persistent desire to destabilize the regime in Amman. The cabinet continued to receive intelligence briefings on the situation in Jordan, but, following the expiry of the ultimatum for Iraqi withdrawal, it redirected its attention to developments further east.[59]

Operation Desert Storm was launched on 16 January and lasted forty-three days. The air war lasted thirty-nine days and the ground war four days, a hundred hours to be precise. Like the Iraqi invasion of Kuwait, it was achieved with virtually no resistance at all. So great was the disparity in the firepower and competence of the two sides that the encounter between them could hardly be called a war. America, under a UN banner, led a coalition of some thirty countries, including Saudi Arabia, Egypt and Syria. After the outbreak of hostilities, Saddam persisted in his efforts to mobilize Arab public opinion on his side by turning what started as an Arab–Arab dispute into a conflict between the Arab nationalists on the one hand and Western imperialism and Israel on the other. His use of Islamic imagery and his call for a jihad against the infidels appealed to Muslim fundamentalists throughout the region.

On the night of 18 January the first barrage of eight Iraqi Scud missiles landed in Tel Aviv and Haifa. After months of uncertainty and bluster, Saddam carried out his threat to attack the Jewish state, dramatically raising the stakes in the Gulf War. It was the first air attack on an Israeli city since 1948. Altogether thirty-nine missiles landed in Israel during the war, resulting in only one direct casualty. The material damage caused was limited, but the psychological impact of the attack was profound. Uncharacteristically, Israel took punches on the chin without retaliating. Two main considerations accounted for this passivity in the face of provocation. One was the understanding that Shamir had reached with Hussein to respect Jordan's neutrality and to refrain from actions that would destabilize it. The other was the strong pressure applied by the Bush administration on Shamir to keep out of the war so that the fragile coalition against Iraq could remain intact. As well as applying pressure, the administration supplied Israel with positive inducements in the shape of Patriot anti-missile defence systems.

Hussein managed to keep his country out of the Gulf War, despite all the external pressures to join the coalition and the internal pressures to wade in on the side of Iraq. Popular sympathy for the Iraqis was fuelled by scenes of the aerial bombardment of their cities and villages by the coalition forces. Another source of mounting anger was the bombing by coalition planes of vehicles carrying vital oil supplies to Jordan from Iraq and the loss of Jordanian lives. Hussein got out in front of his people in a fiery address to the nation he made on 6 February. It was the most overtly anti-Western speech of his entire political career. He bitterly denounced the US-led assault on Iraq as "ferocious" and "unjust," and claimed that the war was going well beyond its UN mandate to liberate Kuwait. Washington and its allies rejected Jordan's attempts to resolve the problem peacefully. Why?

Because the real purpose behind this destructive war, as proven by its scope, and as attested to by the declarations of the parties, is to destroy Iraq, and rearrange the area in a manner far more dangerous to our nation's present and future than the Sykes–Picot agreement. This arrangement would put the nation, its aspirations and its resources under direct foreign hegemony and would shred all ties between its parts, thus further weakening and fragmenting it.

Hussein reserved his harshest criticism for the Arab participants in the US-led coalition in the war against Iraq:

When Arab and Islamic lands are offered as bases for the allied armies from which to launch attacks to destroy Arab Muslim Iraq, when Arab money is financing this war with unprecedented generosity unknown to us and our Palestinian brothers, while we shoulder our national responsibilities; when this takes place, I say that any Arab or Muslim can realize the magnitude of this crime committed against his religion and his nation.[60]

Hussein's speech was a surprising escalation in the propaganda war against America and its Arab allies but it had no material effect on the course of the shooting war. On 28 February, when the coalition forces had overrun Kuwait and southern Iraq and the Iraqi Army was in full flight, Bush gave the order for a ceasefire. The mother of all battles threatened by Saddam had ended in a military catastrophe. But, while Operation Desert Storm was a triumph of advanced military technology against an army that lacked the will to fight, its political aftermath was much more problematic. The basic objectives of the operation were achieved: the Iraqi forces had been ejected from Kuwait and the government-in-exile was restored to its capital. But Saddam retained his hold on power in Baghdad. He had sown the wind; his army and people were left to reap the whirlwind. During the war Bush repeatedly stated that he would not allow the government of Saddam to survive and openly called on the Iraqi people to rise up against their leader. On 1 March, the day after the ceasefire, the Shi'ites rose up in the south, and a few days later the Kurds rose up in the north. If Bush was serious about toppling Saddam, now was his chance. But when the moment of truth arrived, Bush recoiled from pursuing his policy to its logical conclusion. His advisers told him that a Kurdish victory would lead to the dismemberment of Iraq and that their call for help should therefore go unanswered.

Behind the decision to abandon the rebels to Saddam's mercies lay the pessimistic view that Iraq was unsuitable for democracy and that the formula of Sunni minority rule through military force was the only way to keep the country in one piece. Saddam was free to use whatever equipment he had salvaged from the defeat, including helicopters, to suppress the uprisings. The Shi'ites were crushed and fled to the marshes. The Kurds were crushed and fled to the mountains. The suppression of the uprisings quickly punctured the euphoria of victory. In calling for Saddam's overthrow, Bush evidently had in mind a military coup, reshuffling Sunni gangsters in Baghdad rather than helping the opposition to create a freer and more liberal political order. By holding back, Bush ended up by snatching defeat from the jaws of victory. He himself proudly proclaimed that the victory against the aggressor in the Gulf laid the foundations for a New World Order, but the new order was more rhetoric than reality.

The period between Iraq's invasion of Kuwait and the end of the Gulf War was one of the most stressful and unhappy in Hussein's entire reign. Despite all the defeats and disappointments he suffered, Hussein remained an irrepressible peacemaker. From the first day he volunteered his services as a mediator and persisted in his efforts to find a peaceful solution to the problem until the outbreak of hostilities. He made trips to about twenty countries, including three to Baghdad, in an effort to avert a military confrontation, but all to no avail. The American version claims that an Arab solution to the crisis was not possible because Saddam could not be ejected out of Kuwait without the resort to military force. The Jordanian version claims that Hussein persuaded Saddam to begin to withdraw and attend a mini-summit but that

American–Arab condemnation and intimidation pushed him into a corner. According to this version, Hussein, with the approval of Egypt, Saudi Arabia and America, secured the beginning of an Arab solution, but these countries changed their minds and scuttled his efforts.

What went on in Saddam's dark and devious mind we shall probably never know. What is fairly clear, however, is that Hussein's allies promised him forty-eight hours to work out an Arab solution but that they did not keep their promise. Not only did they renege just as Hussein was on his way to Baghdad, but they vilified him, accused him of secretly supporting the invasion—which he had not—and attributed to him sinister designs against Saudi Arabia, which were not supported by a scintilla of evidence. Consequently, Hussein felt used and abused by the Americans. Although he hesitated to say it publicly, he suspected that Bush double-crossed him and that he deliberately killed off his attempt at mediation because, under the influence of Thatcher, he came to equate negotiations with appeasement. With remarkable rapidity it became clear that Bush would settle for nothing less than Saddam's head. Unfortunately, in the end he did settle for less and at a horrendous cost to the Iraqi people.

With so many enemies on all sides, Hussein's success in preserving his throne and in keeping Jordan out of the Gulf War is all the more remarkable. The general consensus in the American media was that he had irreparably blotted his record and that he was unlikely to survive. In the event, he did survive, albeit with difficulty. It took, however, all his skills as a tightrope walker to do so. On the eve of war he scored his most significant success by persuading Shamir to respect Jordan's neutrality. It is the supreme irony that in a crisis in which the survival of the Hashemite dynasty was at stake, Hussein's only true ally was Israel and his only reliable partner was Shamir, the leader of the party that stood for overthrowing the monarchy and turning Jordan into an alternative homeland for the Palestinians.

24. From Madrid to Oslo

The Gulf crisis was very taxing emotionally and psychologically for the lonely, fifty-five-year-old monarch, and it also affected his health. There was a series of minor incidents of ill-health; one, involving cardiac fibrillation, required a few days in hospital until his heart reverted to its normal rhythm. The following year Hussein had his first brush with cancer. Despite the new and more constructive challenges of the post-war era, his mood did not improve. His wife was worried because "he seemed to be retreating more and more into his own world, as if he were trying to disengage from anything that reminded him of the agonies of the Gulf crisis. Uncharacteristically, he began to avoid dealing with complicated problems. He kept saying he was just too tired, even when it came to resolving parenting issues. He did not shirk his responsibilities, but he became somewhat detached from what was happening at work and at home—a highly unusual development for a man who customarily involved himself 150 per cent in everything he did."[1]

Jordan emerged from the Gulf war internally united but politically isolated and economically devastated. A UN-sponsored report estimated that the overall cost of the crisis to Jordan, including the implementation of UN sanctions, reached $1.5 billion in 1990, climbing to $3.6 billion in 1991. The true magnitude of the loss can be appreciated only by noting that Jordan's total GDP in 1990 stood at $4.2 billion and $4.7 billion in 1991.[2] On top of all its other problems, Jordan had to cope with 300,000 Palestinian–Jordanian refugees and other Arabs without citizenship who had been expelled from Kuwait following the Iraqi invasion. Crown Prince Hassan continued to provide energetic leadership in dealing with the financial and humanitarian consequences of the crisis, but the problem was as much political as it was economic. The challenge was how to get Jordan out of the political mire so that the flow of external aid could be resumed. Hussein went about meeting this challenge by rehabilitating Jordan in the eyes of America, by supporting the US-sponsored Arab–Israeli peace process and by building on the strategic understanding he had reached with Prime Minister Itzhak Shamir on the eve of the Gulf War. Shamir turned out to be surprisingly supportive of the king's efforts to repair his relations with the Americans, but he was none the less a reluctant participant in the peace process.

The first order of business was to overcome the crisis in Jordanian–American relations. The end of the cold war in 1990–91 and victory in the Gulf War gave the Bush administration the impetus to re-engage in the Arab–Israeli peace process. The key figure in this enterprise was Secretary of State James Baker. Baker was a blunt and straightforward Texan lawyer who had the rare merit among American politicians of being as tough with the Israelis as he was with the Arabs. Baker's ambitious aim was to get the parties to the conference table in order to deal with all aspects of the Arab–Israeli conflict. After the guns fell silent he made several trips to the region, and in the first two deliberately avoided Jordan to show his displeasure with its recent conduct. His first meeting with Foreign Minister Taher al-Masri took place in Geneva, not in Amman. But on his third trip, in April 1991, Baker did pay a visit to Hussein in the relaxed surroundings of the summer palace in Aqaba.

George Bush was still so angry with Hussein that he refused several requests for a meeting. Baker was just as upset, but they understood that there would be no peace process without Jordan's active participation. Jordan was crucial in persuading the Palestinians to come to the conference table. Like Jordan, the PLO was in disfavour because of its support for Iraq following the invasion of Kuwait. Baker was determined to exclude the PLO but to allow moderate individuals from the occupied territories to represent the Palestinians at the conference. The endgame he had in mind was a Palestinian entity that possessed more than autonomy but less than statehood. From his point of view the ideal solution was a joint Jordanian–Palestinian delegation, but for this he needed Jordan's cooperation. He also had considerable leverage to exert: "Simply stated, the King was broke and he needed America's help to persuade his longtime benefactors in Riyadh to bail him out. There was every practical reason to believe that the King would be willing to do almost anything to end his political isolation and to reclaim

the good graces of the United States." At their meeting Baker told the
king that they were willing to move step by step to let bygones be
bygones but only if Jordan enlisted actively in the US peace initiative.
He wanted the king to know that it was going to be "a tough row to hoe
to repair Jordan's relationship with the United States." Baker also told
the king that despite their differences, "We'll do what we can to help
you patch things up with the Saudis." During lunch the king gave a
long rationalization of his behaviour during the war, which Baker considered wholly unconvincing.[3]

Nevertheless, Baker found the meeting encouraging because the king
understood a simple dynamic: for America to help him he needed to
play on America's terms. The Jordanian preference was for a UN-
sponsored international conference with an ongoing role, aimed at
tackling the Arab–Israeli conflict and the Palestinian issue simultaneously, and on the basis of resolutions 242 and 338 and the principle of
"land for peace." Baker proposed a superpower-sponsored international conference followed by a twin-track approach in the form of
bilateral negotiations between Israel and the Arab states, and Israel and
the Palestinians. Hussein expressed scepticism, fearing that the Palestinian issue, the core of the conflict, would be lost and that the whole
process would be liable to break down.[4] But in fairly short order Hussein endorsed the American proposal and declared that Jordan would
attend the conference even if Syria did not. He also agreed to Shamir's
idea of a joint Jordanian–Palestinian delegation and settled for Baker's
compromise of UN observer status.[5] Palestinian representation at the
conference was a key issue. Hussein preferred separate Jordanian and
Palestinian delegations each with its own separate agenda. The idea of
a joint delegation had surfaced in his abortive peace partnership with
Arafat in 1985–86 but it was overtaken by Jordan's disengagement from
the West Bank and by the subsequent process of democratization on the
East Bank. At their next meeting, on 14 May, Hussein told Baker he was
willing to put together a joint delegation but only if the Palestinians
asked him to do so. As a sweetener to encourage his continued cooperation, Baker told the king that, despite congressional objections, the
administration would shortly deliver $27 million in food assistance to
Jordan.[6]

Why did Hussein agree to play on America's terms? Quite simply,
because he believed Baker when he said that the peace bus would come

only once and anyone who did not get on would be left standing on the kerb. Hussein had been waiting for the peace bus since 1967, and he was determined not to miss it. He also agreed to provide an "umbrella" for Palestinian participation in the peace conference—not as a favour to the Americans or the Palestinians but because it was in Jordan's interest. "I thought," he recalled, "that a process was about to start that was irreversible, and that we had to go. The Palestinians had to go and speak for themselves, and we had to provide them with the umbrella they needed. And that's what we did."[7] It was Shamir who continued to quibble over the fare, the driver, the rights of other passengers, and the bus's speed, route and destination.

Shamir, thought the American secretary of state, looked as if he had bitten into a sour persimmon. There was one and only one Arab leader who enjoyed Shamir's trust and that was the ruler of Jordan. Shamir carried his support for Hussein to the point of confrontation with the Bush administration. He insisted that the administration should do everything possible to keep the king in power despite his support for Saddam during the war. A stable Jordan, said Shamir, was crucial to the long-term prospects for peace. At one of Baker's frequent visits to Jerusalem, Shamir told him that he had met secretly with Hussein, that Hussein was critical to peace, and that some sort of confederation with Jordan at some distant point in the future was the likeliest solution to the problem of the West Bank.[8] Shamir also used Israel's influence in both houses of Congress to moderate their punitive attitude towards the Jordanian monarch. Some Americans did not want to forget or forgive, but Israel and its friends in Washington gave them little choice. For Shamir this curious stand was a logical continuation of his meeting with Hussein in Ascot on the weekend of 4–5 January 1990. Shamir insisted in his talks with the Americans that Hussein's stand during the war was justified and that this was accepted by Israel.[9] Dan Meridor, a Likud leader and a lawyer by profession, recalled a meeting with Baker and his team of peace processors shortly after the end of the Gulf War. Meridor urged them to visit the king and to rehabilitate him. The Americans reacted sharply by saying, "Who are you, the king's lawyer?"[10]

Inside Jordan, the king needed no advocates because his policy of democratization gained him widespread support from all parts of the political spectrum. But whereas the move towards democracy commanded general support, engagement in the peace process with the enemy did not. To give peace a chance Hussein replaced, in June 1991, the conservative prime minister Mudar Badran with Taher al-Masri, the soft-spoken Jordanian of Palestinian extraction and liberal leanings. Badran and some of his ministers had indicated their unwillingness to negotiate with Israel. The appointment of a Palestinian to the top post was intended to foster a climate of trust and national unity. In his letter of appointment to Masri, the king emphasized Jordan's commitment to a negotiated settlement and support for international efforts to resolve the Arab–Israeli conflict peacefully.[11] But the Muslim Brotherhood persisted in their opposition to the peace policy of the king and tabled a motion of no-confidence in the new government in parliament. It also refused to participate in the National Congress that the king convened in order to rally popular support for his peace policy.

Another obstacle that had to be cleared on the road to the peace conference was Syria. Hussein decided to speak to Asad directly. Relations between the two men were superficially correct. But the president had the power to intimidate and to undermine the king. He had resorted to subversion in the past against what he saw as the archetypal "imperial lackey" and he could do so again if he chose. Baker was dubious about Asad, and he thought there was a chance that Hussein could be persuaded to participate unilaterally. He wanted a commitment from Jordan to attend regardless of whether Syria came. "I'll be the master of my own destiny," Hussein told Baker. "I'm going to Damascus only for reasons of form." Although Baker was still cautious, he saw this as a plausible reason to end Hussein's political and economic isolation.[12] On 19 August, Hussein made the trip to Latakia, accompanied by his liberal prime minister. They informed Asad that Baker insisted on a joint Jordanian–Palestinian delegation and that they agreed to form one. Although Jordan preferred to have separate delegations, they said, this was unacceptable to America and Israel. They asked for Asad's understanding of their position, and he reluctantly gave his consent.[13]

Once Asad had been squared, the arduous task of forming the joint delegation began. For Hussein it was like squaring a circle. He had to preserve the fiction that the PLO was not represented, while assuring the PLO that within the joint delegation the Palestinians would be able to speak with an independent voice. Arafat feared that once the conference began, the fiction would become a reality and that this was the king's intention. But this was not the case. He respected the right of the

Palestinians to represent themselves, and he entreated the members of the Jordanian delegation to treat their Palestinian colleagues honestly and fairly, and to give them all the help and assistance they needed. Hussein understood the sensitivities of the Palestinians and the constraints under which they were operating. His general approach to international relations was one of empathy, and this worked well with the Palestinians.[14]

An agreement between the Jordanian government and the PLO was signed on the modalities of coordination and cooperation. Dr. Kamel Abu Jaber, the foreign minister and former academic, was appointed as head of the joint delegation, which consisted of twenty-eight members, fourteen Jordanians and fourteen Palestinians. Dr. Abdul Salam Majali, who hailed from one of the largest and most influential East Bank families, was appointed as head of the Jordanian delegation. He was a former chief medical officer in the army and a former president of Jordan University; he had extensive ministerial experience; and he was proud of the fact that his name meant "the servant of peace" in Arabic. Half the members of the Palestinian delegation were doctors and university professors. The head of their delegation was Dr. Haidar Abdel Shafi, an elderly physician from Gaza and a much respected public figure. Faisal Husseini headed the Palestinian Guidance Committee and Dr. Hanan Ashrawi was its spokesperson. Husseini and Ashrawi knew only too well the complex legacy of resentments and conflicting claims between the Hashemites and the Palestinian nationalists. But they felt that the king was quite sincere in seeking new relationships with the Palestinians based on candour and trust.[15]

The formal letter of invitation to the Madrid peace conference assured Jordan that negotiations would be based on UN Security Council resolutions 242 and 338 and that the aim was to achieve a comprehensive peace. In an address to the Jordanian National Congress on 12 October, the king declared: "Peace demands no less courage than war. It is the courage to meet the adversary, his attitudes and arguments, the courage to face hardships, the courage to bury senseless illusions, the courage to surmount impeding obstacles, the courage to engage in a dialogue to tear down the walls of fear and suspicion. It is the courage to face reality." He rejected the arguments of the Islamic opposition to peace negotiations. Negotiations, he claimed, represented the only means to induce Israel to accept the principle of land for peace. Apart from seeking a solution to the Palestinian problem, Jordan had a number of specific interests to safeguard through negotiations, namely, security, the environment, water and economic development.

A great deal of preparatory work on all of these issues was carried out in the weeks and months before the conference under the supervision of Prince Hassan. He was very active in chairing meetings, in brain-storming sessions, in devising negotiating tactics, in preparing position papers and in presenting Jordan's views to the media. Hussein himself did not get involved in the details or issue any general policy guidelines. But he had a talent for inspiring loyalty to the cause and fostering a team spirit. Some of the officials were reluctant to meet with the Israelis, but his humble and diffident manner moved them to want to serve king and country. Hussein went to the airport to bid farewell to the team. He spoke very briefly but movingly to say it was a national call, to ask them to do their best and to express his full confidence in them.[16]

In an interview with an American newspaper just before the conference opened, the king remarked that he had "almost forty years on active duty." He conceded that he was tired, had contemplated stepping down and was increasingly conscious of his own mortality. He hoped that the lasting achievement of his nearly forty years on the throne would be "to contribute towards peace and to see it coming." He warned that if the Israelis proved inflexible at the peace conference and continued to build Jewish settlements in the occupied territories, a very dark phase in the life of the entire region would result. He worried that the status quo would only solidify Israel's hold on the occupied territories and said that if the Madrid meeting failed, the flickering hopes of peaceful coexistence would be snuffed out.[17]

The Middle East peace conference opened in the Palacio Real in Madrid on 30 October 1991 with the United States and the Soviet Union as co-sponsors, the UN as an observer and delegations from all the parties to the conflict in attendance. The Soviet Union, bankrupt and in the final phase of disintegration, had virtually no influence over the proceedings. The conference was carefully staged by the Americans, with Baker acting as the master of ceremonies. Jordan's two main objectives at the conference were to begin negotiations for the resolution of its dispute with Israel and to enable the Palestinians to engage in separate negotiations with Israel about the future of the occupied territories. In other words, Jordan wanted the Palestinians and Israel to settle the dispute between them but not at its expense.[18] In his opening speech Kamel Abu Jaber delivered a clear message that Jordan was there to negotiate an enduring peace based on international legality. He focused sharply on UN resolutions embodying the principle that land must not be acquired by force. He was preceded by Shamir and followed by Haidar Abdel Shafi.

Shamir's opening speech confirmed the Jordanians' worst fears. The whole tone of the speech was anachronistic, saturated with the stale rhetoric of the past and wholly inappropriate for the occasion. His version of the Arab–Israeli conflict was singularly narrow and blinkered, portraying Israel simply as the victim of Arab aggression and refusing to acknowledge that any evolution had taken place in the Arab or Palestinian attitude to Israel. All Arabs, according to Shamir, wanted to see Israel destroyed; the only difference between them was over the ways to bring about its destruction. His speech, while long on anti-Arab clichés, was exceedingly short on substance. By insisting that the root cause of the conflict was not territory but the Arab refusal to recognize the legitimacy of the State of Israel, he came dangerously close to rejecting the whole basis of the conference: UN resolutions and the principle of land for peace.

The contrast between Shamir's speech and the speech of Dr. Haidar Abdel Shafi, the head of the Palestinian delegation, could hardly have been more striking in tone, spirit or substance. The principal aim of the speech, an aim endorsed by the PLO leaders in Tunis, was to convince the Israeli public that the Palestinians were genuinely committed to peaceful coexistence. Abdel Shafi reminded the audience that it was time for the Palestinians to narrate their own story. While touching on the past, his speech was forward-looking. His basic message was that Israeli occupation had to end, that the Palestinians had a right to self-determination, and that they would pursue this right relentlessly until they had achieved statehood. But, while staking a claim to Palestinian statehood, Abdel Shafi qualified it in two significant ways. First, he accepted the need for a transitional stage. Second, he envisaged a confederation between an ultimately independent Palestine and Jordan. No PLO official had ever been able to declare so unambiguously that a Palestinian state would be ready for a confederation with Jordan. Abdel Shafi's speech was both the most eloquent and the most moderate presentation of the Palestinian case made by an official Palestinian spokesman since the beginning of the conflict at the end of the nineteenth century. As the head of the Palestinian delegation was delivering his speech, Israel's stone-faced prime minister passed a note to a colleague. One of the 5,000 journalists covering the conference speculated that the note could well have said: "We made a big mistake. We should have insisted that the PLO is the sole legitimate representative of the Palestinian people."

What distinguished Madrid from previous Arab–Israeli conferences was that there the Palestinians were represented for the first time on a footing of equality with Israel. Madrid registered the arrival of the Palestinians, long the missing party, at the Middle East conference table. The mere presence of official Palestinian representatives in Madrid marked a change, if not a reversal, of Israel's long-standing refusal to consider the Palestinians as a partner to negotiations, as an *interlocuteur valable*. The principal outcome of Madrid was, as Baker had intended, to establish a twin-track framework for bilateral negotiations between the parties: an Israeli–Arab track and an Israeli–Palestinian track. Although no progress was made on substantive issues, a framework for ongoing negotiations was established.

Both parts of the joint delegation considered the Madrid conference a success. The Palestinians took charge of their own diplomatic struggle for independence and kept open the option of an eventual confederation with Jordan. The Jordanians, after more than two decades of futile diplomacy, were finally engaged in a serious international effort to achieve a comprehensive peace in the Middle East on the basis of UN resolutions. In addition, Jordan's participation at the conference went some way towards repairing the damage caused by its conduct during the Gulf crisis. Most importantly, at Madrid, Jordan succeeded in making a clear distinction between the Jordanian national identity and the Palestinian national identity and in discrediting the notion of *al-watan al-badeel*, of Jordan as an "alternative homeland" for the Palestinians. From this point, Jordan was free to pursue its own peace diplomacy in conformity with the general Arab consensus rather than in defiance of it, as Sadat had done a decade earlier.[19]

In the Jordanian parliament, Islamic opposition to the peace talks with Israel was stepped up in the aftermath of Madrid. The Muslim Brotherhood merged with independent Islamists to form the Islamic

Action Front (IAF). The new party conducted a campaign against the government of Taher Masri because he was a secular liberal, because some of his ministers were considered leftists and above all because of the government's peace policy. Fifty out of the eighty members of parliament voted for a motion of no confidence in the government. The king urged Masri to soldier on regardless of the opposition. But if he had done so, the opposition would have brought down the whole government, forcing the king to dissolve parliament and hold new elections. Masri considered that an internal upheaval would hurt the democratization process and damage Jordan's relations with the West, so, on 19 November, he tendered his resignation but not that of his government.[20] He was replaced by Zaid bin Shaker, the king's trusted adviser and friend, and a conservative who also had the advantage of being a sharif, a descendant of the Prophet. Shaker's appointment restored the tacit alliance between the palace and the Islamists against radicals and leftists that had its origins in the 1950s.

The clandestine contact between the palace and Israel was resumed several weeks after the end of the public gathering in the Spanish capital. Elyakim Rubinstein and Efraim Halevy were conveyed by boat from Eilat to a meeting point in the Gulf of Aqaba one stormy night in December 1991. They moved to a tiny boat driven by Colonel Ali Shukri and Nasser Judeh, Prince Hassan's son-in-law and a future minister of information. The meeting the next day was positive. It established what Prince Hassan called a "safety net" for the forthcoming bilateral negotiations in Washington. These were to proceed simultaneously on two parallel tracks—one public in Washington and one secret in the region. The safety net was a formula arrived at by the Jordanian and Israeli leadership. Essentially it meant that when deadlock was reached in the official negotiations, another meeting would be held privately to move things along. The Jordanian side of the safety net would consist of Hussein, Prince Hassan and, later, a number of senior advisers. The Israeli side would consist of Itzhak Rabin, sometimes Peres, Rubinstein and Halevy.[21]

The public track of the peace process was held under American auspices and American management. As a follow-up to the Madrid conference, the Bush administration invited all the parties to hold substantive bilateral peace talks in Washington starting on 10 December. Lebanon, Syria, Jordan and the Palestinians accepted the invitation without any conditions. The Israelis were less enthusiastic. The last thing they wanted was the kind of brisk and concrete down-to-business approach urged by the Americans. The issue used by the Israelis to delay the start of the talks was the status of the Palestinians. On the last day of the Madrid talks an understanding was reached that in the bilateral phase the Israelis would negotiate separately with the Palestinians and the Jordanians. Accordingly, the Americans prepared two rooms in the State Department, one for the Israeli and Palestinian teams, and one for the Israeli and Jordanian teams. But on arrival at the State Department, the Israelis insisted on negotiating with a joint Jordanian–Palestinian delegation to underline their opposition to a separate Palestinian entity. For six days the heads of the Israeli and Palestinian delegations haggled in the corridor of the State Department, even unable to agree to enter the conference room. The American hosts thoughtfully placed a sofa in the corridor. Rubinstein, the head of the Israeli delegation, felt personally safe sitting between two medical doctors. But the scene was bizarre, and it added a new term to the rich lexicon of the Arab–Israeli conflict—corridor diplomacy. After another round of talks a compromise was reached on the status of the Palestinians that enabled both sides to claim victory. Israel was to negotiate with two separate subcommittees consisting of nine Palestinians and two Jordanians on Palestinian-related issues, and nine Jordanians and two Palestinians on Jordan-related issues. With a sigh of relief Hanan Ashrawi, the Palestinian spokeswoman, announced that "corridor diplomacy" had ended.

From this point on the Jordanians and Palestinians operated essentially as two independent delegations, but they continued to consult and to coordinate their activities. Even after the substantive negotiations began, their progress was painfully slow, and often they ground to a complete halt. Caution was the hallmark of the Jordanian approach. On the one hand, the Jordanians did not wish to be separated from the Palestinians; on the other, they were careful not to speak in their name. Jordan followed closely developments on the Palestinian track, which was under its umbrella but not under its control. Everyone recognized that the critical track was the Palestinian one. The Jordanian delegation was the first to acknowledge this, but it was dogged by suspicions that its real aim was to restore Jordanian sovereignty over the West Bank. Majali sought to dispel these suspicions both in the conference room and in interviews to the media. Jordan, he kept repeating, was not a plenipotentiary for the Palestinians nor did it wish to rule over the Palestinian territories. The one formula Jordan was prepared to consider was a confederation but only if that was the Palestinians' own choice.

The Jordanian delegation devoted most of its time and effort in Washington to preparing its position on specific bilateral issues and to defending Jordanian interests in the negotiations with the Israelis. The Washington talks went on from December 1991 until September 1993. The most significant achievement of this period was the drafting of a common agenda for negotiations on a peace treaty between Jordan and Israel. The common agenda was completed on 28 October 1992, and its text was published in the Arabic newspapers *Al-Ra'i* and *Al-Dustur* two days later. The overarching aim was to reach a state of peace based on UN resolutions 242 and 338. The more specific issues included mutual security, water, refugees, borders and regional cooperation. The agenda spelled out what needed to be discussed in all these different areas and in what contexts. The problem of refugees, for example, was to be dealt with in the context of international law. Regional cooperation covered natural resources, the environment, human resources, transport and tourism. Once the Jordanians had reached this broad agreement on how to go forward with the Israelis, it was essentially a matter of marking time, of waiting for a breakthrough on the Palestinian track. One basic difference in approach, however, was already evident at this early stage. The Jordanians wanted to safeguard their national rights first and to move towards regional cooperation later. The Israelis resisted this. Their priority was to achieve mutual recognition and normalization within the existing status quo and only then to address specific Jordanian grievances.[22]

At home, illness and fatigue led Hussein to rely increasingly on his younger brother in the conduct of the affairs of state. In his youth, and especially during the civil war, Prince Hassan acquired a reputation for being anti-Palestinian. In fact, he was not anti-Palestinian but anti-fedayeen, as were the rest of the Jordanian political elite. But since then a lot of water had flowed down the Jordan, and his views on relations with the Palestinians and Israel were now scarcely distinguishable from those of his elder brother. There was complete trust between the two brothers and a very close working relationship, despite the wide differences in their ages, educational backgrounds, temperaments and lifestyles. Hassan had an office in the royal compound, and he visited the royal court or spoke to his brother on the phone almost every day. He also provided an element of continuity against the background of frequent changes of foreign ministers and prime ministers. Decision-making in Amman during the bilateral talks was rather informal. Abdul Salam Majali, the head of the delegation in Washington, reported to Foreign Minister Kamel Abu Jaber; he, in turn, reported to Prime Minister Zaid bin Shaker, sometimes to Prince Hassan and sometimes to the king. The four men had frequent meetings, often over lunch in the prime minister's home. Abu Jaber, by his own account, made no important decisions on his own; he acted more like a civil servant than like a minister. Although the king did not involve himself in the details, he remained throughout the leader of the team and the ultimate decision-maker.[23]

Hussein's performance as a policy-maker was increasingly affected by insomnia and ill-health. In August 1992 he displayed symptoms of a urological problem and tests showed some cells that needed further study. His doctors recommended the Mayo Clinic in Rochester, Minnesota. Initial tests confirmed that the doctors needed to operate on a partial obstruction to Hussein's left ureter, the duct by which urine passes from kidney to bladder, and that the obstruction might be malignant. "I am stunned," wrote Queen Noor in her journal. "Sidi is quiet and brave, but I know he must be terrified. He speaks fatalistically of being in the process of putting things in order, having sensed this for some time." During the operation the doctors found a few pre-cancerous cells in the ureter leading to the kidney, but they had not spread. The doctors removed the kidney as a precaution, and it contained no signs of abnormality. No further treatment was considered necessary. The days that followed were, in Queen Noor's view, a turning point in her husband's life: "The cancer scare snapped Hussein out of his depression, and he became once again the eager and engaged person he had been before the Gulf War."[24]

Hussein returned home from the Mayo in late September to a hero's welcome. Nearly a third of the kingdom's population poured into the streets to greet him in a spontaneous demonstration of affection and support. Although officials insisted that the king had completely recovered, there was public concern about the recurrence of the illness and his life expectancy. On 5 November, in a remarkably frank speech to the nation, Hussein summed up his own life and the history of the Hashemite dynasty. He said that the life of an enlightened nation is not measured by the life of one individual. He spoke of his grandfather Abdullah, the founder of the kingdom, who "told me that he perceived his life as a link in a continuous chain of those who served the nation and that he expected me to be a new and strong link in that chain." Hussein recalled the moment when he vowed to follow in Abdullah's footsteps to carry out the Hashemite ambition. The three pillars of the Hashemite project that Hussein listed were pan-Arabism, Islam and democratization. This was the ideological foundation on which Hussein based his claim to leadership both at home and in the Arab world beyond Jordan's borders.

In a speech to the staff college on 23 November, Hussein adopted a more aggressive tone, confronting his opponents at home and abroad. He made it clear that, despite the recent bout of ill-health, he had no intention of stepping down. He attacked the extremist groups in Jordan, on the left and on the right, for their opposition to the peace talks with Israel. He warned them not to interpret the process of democratization as a sign of weakness or his magnanimity as a sign of fear. He also attacked Iran for the support it gave to Islamic groups attempting to subvert his regime. He was surprisingly blunt in his criticism of the Gulf states for their undemocratic nature and of their rulers for their reliance on imperialist support to preserve their thrones. Kuwait was attacked for its expulsion of hundreds of thousands of Palestinians who had served it faithfully. Hussein distanced himself from Saddam by calling for the introduction of democracy in Iraq so that the Iraqi people could lead a normal life without international sanctions—a passage that could be interpreted as a call for the removal of Saddam from power. Turning to the Palestine question, Hussein asserted that Jordan would never agree to become an alternative homeland for the Palestinians. Finally, Hussein stressed Jordan's commitment to continue the peace talks with Israel. The impression created by his earlier speech—that his days on the throne were numbered because there was no cure for his cancer—seemed to be countered in this one.

While the Likud remained in power, very little headway was made on either the Israeli–Palestinian track or on any of the Israeli–Arab tracks. It was only after the Labour Party's victory over the Likud in June 1992 that the Israeli position began to be modified, at least on the

Arab track. On the Palestinian issue the Israeli position displayed more continuity than change following the rise of the Labour government under the leadership of Rabin. Consequently, the official talks in Washington continued to make slow progress. This led both Israel and the PLO to seek a back channel for communicating, a decision that constituted a diplomatic revolution in Israel's foreign policy and paved the way to the Oslo Accord.

The talks between the representatives of the Israeli government and the PLO were held behind a thick veil of secrecy in the Norwegian capital. They proceeded parallel to the bilateral talks in Washington but without the knowledge of the official Israeli and Palestinian negotiators. In fact, Arafat deliberately instructed the official delegation to adopt uncompromising positions in Washington in order to make possible the secret deal in Oslo. The first Oslo Accord was signed in the White House on 13 September 1993 and sealed with a handshake between Arafat and Rabin. It consisted of two parts: the first was mutual recognition between Israel and the PLO; the second was the Declaration of Principles on Interim Self-Government Arrangements in Gaza and the West Bank city of Jericho. Essentially, Israel recognized the PLO as the representative of the Palestinian people, the PLO recognized Israel's right to live in peace and security, and the two sides agreed to resolve all their outstanding differences by peaceful means.

The Oslo Accord took Hussein, his government and the Jordanian delegation to the Washington talks completely by surprise. Arafat's deputy, Mahmoud Abbas, popularly known as Abu Mazen, admits in his memoirs that PLO Tunis was at fault:

A few months after Oslo had got under way we began to feel very embarrassed for not having informed Jordan and in particular His Majesty King Hussein personally of this development. Jordan had been our partner in the formal negotiations, had given us the legal cover to go to Madrid, and had helped us during the "corridor negotiations" in the first Washington sessions to separate the Jordanian from the Palestinian track. Furthermore, we had constantly spoken of a confederation with Jordan because of the special relations binding the Jordanian and Palestinian peoples. For these important reasons we shuddered even to contemplate the consequences of King Hussein's anger if we were to reach an agreement with the Israelis that took him completely by surprise.

Abu Mazen relates that he made three attempts to speak to the king in private, all unsuccessful. So he visited him on 17 October and explained the matter from beginning to end. "I do not know whether he accepted my excuses or not," writes Mahmoud Abbas, "but I do say that he had every right to be reproachful."[25]

The Clinton administration was told of the breakthrough only shortly before it was made public. Norway had upstaged them in brokering the Israel–PLO accord, but they quickly turned the accord to their advantage. The accord was made in Oslo, but it was signed in Washington with Clinton basking in the glory. Although it was not he who brought together the lugubrious old soldier and the grinning guerrilla leader, they handed him one of the very few foreign policy successes of his administration. Moreover, the Americans could not fail to understand the opportunities that the breakthrough presented. As one American diplomat put it: "First you get an Israeli–Palestinian deal cut, and then the other accounts can be settled more rapidly and more successfully."[26]

The other Arab participants in the peace process were more sceptical. The initial reaction of the neighbouring Arab states to the Israel–PLO accord was one of suspicion and resentment. Syria and Lebanon were as surprised as Jordan by Arafat's solo diplomacy, fearing that he was making a separate deal with Israel, and they were suspicious of Israel's intentions. Arafat defended his decision to sign the accord by presenting it as the first step towards comprehensive peace in the Middle East. There was a general feeling, however, that the PLO chairman had broken rank and, like Sadat fifteen years earlier, played into Israel's hands. The country most directly affected by the Israel–PLO accord was, of course, Jordan, for which it posed acute economic, political, constitutional and security problems. As the Jordanian academic Mustafa Hamarneh explained to a foreign journalist: "These are extremely challenging times for Jordan. Yasser Arafat did not pull a rabbit out of his hat but a damned camel."[27]

The Israelis had also kept Hussein in the dark about their secret talks with the PLO representatives in Oslo. Halevy, who held the "Jordan file" in the Mossad and had particularly close relations with Hussein, felt a sense of guilt not unlike that recorded by Mahmoud Abbas. "During the months preceding the surprise announcement of the Palestinian Oslo agreement," writes Halevy,

I was privy to numerous reports of meetings and negotiations between Israeli figures and Palestinian counterparts, all of a secret and clandestine nature. Some of these reports or rumours reached King Hussein. He repeatedly asked me about them since he was concerned that he would be surprised by an Israel–Palestinian agreement that would adversely affect his country, a country whose population was more than half Palestinian in origin. Since he was dialoguing secretly with Israel on the possibility of reaching a peace agreement, he believed it only right that he should be kept abreast of developments that had a direct effect on his vital interests. Needless to say, I relayed these fears back to Mr. Rabin, and he demonstratively dismissed them with his customary wave of the hand, instructing me to reassure King Hussein and to allay his fears and suspicions.[28]

One reason for Rabin's reticence was that, until very near the end, he assumed that the Oslo channel would remain inconclusive and unimportant. Hussein, however, had every reason to be reproachful when presented with a fait accompli.

One day in late August, Arafat requested an urgent meeting with the king and came to Amman to inform him that the PLO had concluded an interim peace agreement with Israel. Hussein was very upset. He never liked or trusted Arafat but now his worst suspicions were confirmed. "Why not coordinate?" he said. "How can we possibly work this way?"[29] Hussein also thought that the Palestinians had given away too much. He himself had been careful ever since 1967 not to bargain away any Palestinian rights to the land, whereas the agreement negotiated by the PLO was vague and imprecise. More troubling to Hussein was the fact that substantive issues like Jerusalem, borders and refugees were not addressed in the accord but deferred for future negotiations.[30] Hussein was all the more angry because he had been holding back on the common agenda for almost a year, waiting for progress on the Palestinian track, and now the Palestinians had gone ahead without him. He felt he had been treated shabbily after all the help he had given the Palestinians, especially by providing an umbrella for Madrid. Yet Hussein had no viable alternative to accepting the agreement. He had accepted the PLO as the sole legitimate representative of the Palestinian people, and he could not object to the agreement it had reached with the Israeli government. All the king's men confirm that his first reaction was one of surprise and anger but also that he quickly came to terms with the new reality. The most revealing account, however, is the one Hussein himself gave in an interview for a TV programme:

I am afraid at that point I decided the best thing was for me to shut myself off for a couple of days to calm down and collect myself and reflect on what to do. And finally I came up with the conclusion that we should close up the umbrella and really get it into the closet of history, and move on our own to deal with our own problems, and as far as our Palestinian brethren were concerned to give them all the support we could. That was their decision, that was what they had sought all along, that was their leadership assuming a position of responsibility. And I implored them all to gather round this leadership, and not to fragment, and I have supported them ever since.[31]

On the positive side the PLO–Israel accord cleared the path to progress on the Jordanian–Israeli track. Arafat had broken the Arab taboo on making peace with the Jewish state: so Hussein was free to proceed along the path charted in the common agenda. The senior Jordanian representatives in Washington were Dr. Fayez Tarawneh, the ambassador, and Marwan Muasher, the director of the Jordan Information Bureau. (Tarawneh had replaced Abdul Salam Majali as the head of the Jordanian delegation to the bilateral talks when Majali was appointed prime minister.) Warren Christopher, the secretary of state, called Tarawneh to say that Arafat was coming and to suggest signing the common agenda in the same White House ceremony that was being organized for the PLO–Israel accord. Tarawneh thought that the common agenda should not detract from the Declaration of Principles, but he promised to consult the king. The king told Tarawneh that this was a Palestinian day of celebration and that the common agenda could wait another day. Accordingly, the following day Tarawneh and Elyakim Rubinstein signed the common agenda in the presence of Christopher and Andrei Possobliuk, a senior Russian representative, in a modest ceremony at the State Department.[32]

This, however, is not the whole story. While Hussein moved very quickly from denunciation to acceptance of Oslo, he continued to harbour dark suspicions about the motives of the two signatories. Jordan and Israel had been tacit allies for decades, but now Israel seemed to have changed tack. Hussein feared that Israel might have abandoned its policy of partnership with Jordan in favour of a new partnership with the PLO. Another worry was that Jordan would be shut out of the economic boom that was expected to result from an Israeli–Palestinian peace. Rabin's abrupt reversal raised doubts about the depth of his commitment to the traditional pro-Hashemite policy of the Labour Party. More than half of Jordan's 3.9 million people were Palestinian, and there was the risk of increased pressure from them to turn the Hashemite Kingdom of Jordan into the Republic of Palestine, as most Palestinians and some Israeli extremists wanted. It is no exaggeration to say that in some respects the accord appeared to endanger Jordan's stability, security and survival as an independent state. In the words of Adnan Abu-Odeh: "King Hussein feared that Israel may have reached with Arafat an agreement that would weaken or threaten Jordan. Regarding the Palestinian question, the king was always afraid of being left out of the picture. This was for good reason because it might entice some to think that 'Jordan is Palestine.' The king had to listen to an Israeli, and not to Arafat, to make sure that nothing was being plotted against him."[33]

The initiative for a meeting came from the Israeli side. Halevy, burdened by a lingering sense of guilt towards the king, saw the need to clarify the Labour government's policy towards Jordan better than most. The Israeli daily newspaper *Ma'ariv* quoted intelligence reports that said the king felt "cheated and neglected" over the accord. "King Hussein's political world has collapsed around him and the most direct means are required to calm him down," the Israeli prime minister was reportedly told. Rabin heeded this advice.[34] The meeting took place at the king's palace in the Red Sea resort of Aqaba on Sunday, 26 September. Rabin was accompanied by Halevy, Rubinstein, and Eitan Haber, the director of the prime minister's office. The king had with him Prince Hassan, Zaid bin Shaker and Ali Shukri. Given the sensitivity of the situation the domestic staff was kept to the minimum. Queen Noor and her house manager attended to all the details of the preparation. Her most distinct memory of that meeting was the sound of Itzhak Rabin's deep, sonorous voice for what seemed hours on end. It was at this meeting, according to Queen Noor, that her husband began to establish the mutual trust and respect with Rabin that would lead a year later to the peace treaty.[35]

Rabin reassured the king about the continuing strategic value placed on his kingdom by the Israelis, more specifically, that Israel remained firmly committed to upholding his regime; that Jordanian interests would be protected in dealing with the Palestinian issue; and that future peace strategy would be closely coordinated with Jordan.[36] Reaffirming the pre-Oslo alliance between Israel and the Hashemite dynasty was one major purpose of the meeting; planning for the future was another. Both sides agreed that the ultimate aim was a peace settlement but differed on the means to achieve it. Rabin wanted to sign a peace treaty first and then attend to the technical details and to the practical problems of implementing it. Hussein firmly rejected this proposal. He took the common-sense view that first you negotiate and reach agreement on all the outstanding issues and only then do you sign the treaty. In support of this approach Hussein invoked the authority of his friend, the lawyer Lord Mishcon. When consulted, Mishcon told Hussein that no one with any sense would sign a treaty first and discuss its technical clauses afterwards.

After a lengthy discussion Rabin deferred to the superior wisdom of the king and his Jewish friend, as well as to some members of the Israeli delegation. Broad agreement was reached on the format of the negotiations but not on a timetable. Detailed discussions were to take place between experts from the two sides on all bilateral issues such as borders, border crossings, security, refugees, trade, water and the environment. Rabin urged the king to hold the Jordanian elections on time because Israel wanted to make peace with the Jordanian people and not just with the regime. A further subject that came up for discussion was the sequence of peace treaties between Israel and the Arabs. Rabin was under the impression that Jordan would not sign a peace treaty with Israel until Syria had done so. This was what Peres had repeatedly told him, though it was not clear on what basis. Hussein made it clear that once agreement had been reached on all the cardinal issues Jordan would be ready to sign a peace treaty, regardless of the situation with Syria. All in all, the meeting was highly significant in restoring trust between the two sides and in laying the foundations for progress towards peace.[37]

In the negotiations that led to the peace treaty the four principal players were Hussein, Hassan, Rabin and Peres. The Americans encouraged and supported progress on the Jordanian track, but they did not play an active mediating role, as they did on the Syrian track, because the leaders enjoyed direct channels of communication. On the

Jordanian side, Hussein was the visionary, the leader and the principal decision-maker. To the talks with the Israelis he brought a rich experience of regional and international affairs, a sense of purpose and renowned social skills, which helped to create a positive, problem-solving atmosphere. Hassan also played a major role in the conduct of peace negotiations. He combined expertise in economic affairs with a wide range of intellectual interests, including medieval Jewish theology. He would surprise and delight the Israeli negotiators by giving them copies of his erudite articles and books with a dedication in Hebrew, a language he had studied at Oxford.[38]

Hussein's attitude towards Peres was ambivalent. He respected his energy, his commitment to the cause of peace and the imaginative ideas he constantly generated. Yet Hussein could not forget that Peres had let him down over the London Agreement of April 1987. Peres, in Hussein's eyes, was both a dreamer and a publicity-seeker who could not be fully trusted. Peres was also the chief architect of the Oslo Accord, which was taken to indicate a preference for partnership with the Palestinians. Keeping Hussein in the dark about the Oslo channel was Israeli state policy, for which Peres could not be held personally responsible. But Hussein believed that Peres had a preference for the emergence of a strong Palestinian entity as a substitute for the traditional alliance with Jordan.[39] Peres denied any such preference. The Oslo Accord, he convincingly argued, was not against Jordan; it was with the Palestinians. Israel's policy had changed towards the West Bank, not towards the Hashemite Kingdom of Jordan. The king, argued Peres, had no valid grounds for complaint, since he himself had disengaged from the West Bank in 1988, making it necessary for Israel to deal directly with the Palestinians. Even after Oslo, Peres stood by his claim that he was the most consistent advocate of the "Jordanian option."[40]

For Rabin, the king had considerable respect, which only grew with the passage of time, because he spoke with the precision of a military man and because he was usually as good as his word. Personal trust between the king and the prime minister was the key to progress on the Jordanian track. "We had a unique relationship," said the king wistfully after Rabin's death. "I felt he had placed himself in my position many times. I placed myself in his position. We did not try to score points off each other. We tried to develop something that was workable, that was acceptable to both our peoples, something that was balanced, something that was reasonable. And that's the approach we had and that's how we managed to get there."[41] Rabin and Hussein took the lead in the political and security-centred negotiations, while Hassan was largely responsible for the economic and technical aspects of the peace process. "The personal relationship between the late king and the late Prime Minister Rabin," remarked Hassan, "was the magic and the salve that resulted in the achievement of the peace treaty."[42] The remark glosses over the crucial part played by Hassan himself in driving and coordinating the work of the negotiating teams. He was the unsung hero of the peace process.

Rabin's mistrust of his foreign minister was a complicating factor. Rabin felt that Peres had received most of the credit for the breakthrough on the Palestinian track, and he wanted to keep for himself all the credit for achieving the breakthrough on the Jordanian track. Rabin therefore confined Peres to the low politics of the peace process and excluded him as far as possible from the high. A couple of weeks after the signature of the Oslo Accord and the common agenda, Peres and Hassan travelled to Washington to attend a donors' conference to support Middle East peace. On 1 October the two stood in front of the press with President Clinton at the White House. This was the first high-level public meeting between Jordan and Israel, and it attracted considerable publicity. Clinton's participation signalled his administration's backing for the two countries in their effort to move forward. On the substantive side, a trilateral Israel–Jordan–US economic committee was established at the meeting. This forum convened first in Washington and then periodically in the region. Subgroups were established to discuss specific issues such as trade, finance, banking, civil aviation and Jordan Valley joint projects. One of the committee's main tasks was to consider how development projects could be put together and funded.

The meeting at the White House persuaded Peres, as he put it to his aides, that it was "time to storm Jordan!" Four weeks later, disguised with a porkpie hat and a moustache, the peripatetic foreign minister crossed the Allenby Bridge and made his way to the royal palace in Amman. He was accompanied by Avi Gil, his chief of staff, and Halevy of the Mossad. In the palace he met Hussein, Hassan and Dr. Abdul Salam Majali, now prime minister. Peres "assaulted" his host with a vision of regional peace and prosperity, and the role of the Hashemite kingdom in realizing it. The discussion resulted in an understanding on the parameters of a future peace treaty and in the initialling of a four-page document. Showing his customary flair for the economics of peace, Peres proposed a daring initiative. "What do you think, Your Majesty," he asked, "of inviting four thousand businessmen to Amman to discuss investing in the New Middle East?" Hussein agreed in principle, and the idea was added to the prospectus.[43]

There were three key points in the document. First, Israel would restore land it had appropriated in Wadi Araba and the Dead Sea to Jordanian sovereignty, but these lands would be leased to Israel for a nominal rent. Second, the two countries would establish normal relations and exchange ambassadors. Third, the two countries would cooperate in the fields of agriculture, transport and tourism, and in the development of energy resources. A large international economic conference was to be held in Amman with senior business figures from Israel and the Arab world. Several informal understandings were also reached. Israel would use its influence with the Clinton administration and with Congress to try to secure the remission of Jordan's heavy external debt. The Jordanian dinar was to remain legal tender in the area of Palestinian self-government. Israel was to provide a military umbrella for Jordan and defend it in the event of attack by a third party. The document was prepared in advance and initialled by Peres and Hassan after nine hours of discussions on the night of 2–3 November. It was a highly significant meeting that foreshadowed much of what came later. The king confided to Peres that he did not feel well, that he may not have many more years to live, and that he wanted to leave the peace treaty as his legacy for future generations.[44]

Peres was overjoyed by the results of the meeting with the man he once referred to as "His Royal Shyness." He returned to Israel in a euphoric mood, dropping hefty hints that a peace treaty with Jordan was imminent. "Put 3 November in your calendars as an historic date," he told journalists. Peres had, of course, gone to Amman with Rabin's permission. Prior to his departure he had told Rabin that if they met the king's demands on land, water and guardianship of the Muslim holy places in Jerusalem, a peace treaty would be possible. Rabin doubted that the king would be ready to move so fast.[45] He also made allowance for the possibility that the king might get cold feet and change his mind, as he had on some past occasions.

Hussein was incensed by Peres's indiscretion. He was not ready yet to commit himself to bilateral peace negotiations in public. The rumours that the Israeli foreign secretary had visited him in Amman were liable to complicate his relations with the Palestinians and to antagonize Syria and Saudi Arabia. Strict secrecy was an explicit condition governing the clandestine contacts, and all Israeli officials going back to Dr. Yaacov Herzog respected that. Peres, however, apparently could not contain his excitement. In self-defence he pointed out that he made no mention of Jordan, its ruler, the meeting or its subject matter. But there was not a single Israeli journalist who did not know what Peres was talking about. Nor was there any doubt that he was seeking publicity for his achievement. This, at any rate, was how Hussein saw the matter. The disclosure caused a crisis in Jordanian–Israeli relations. Hussein complained to Rabin about his colleague's indiscretion and warned him that there would be no more secret meetings if they could not be kept secret.

Rabin did not need much persuasion to relegate his foreign secretary to the sidelines and to keep all contacts with the palace in his own hands. He suggested that he and the king should appoint a number of aides whom they could trust implicitly to keep a secret. The king appointed Hassan, Shaker, Majali and Shukri. Rabin appointed Rubinstein, Halevy, Haber and General Danny Yatom, his military secretary. Rabin ordered his aides in no uncertain terms not to report to Peres and to take every necessary measure to prevent him from knowing what was going on.[46] Rabin was a brutal military man who liked a clear chain of command. He used Peres's indiscretion to gather all the reins of power into his own hands and to set himself up as mover, negotiator and only decision-maker in the peace process with Jordan.

The Oslo Accord had implications not only for Jordan's relations with Israel but also for its progress towards democracy. This process got under way with the election of November 1989, in which the Muslim Brotherhood did well. Another election was scheduled for 8 November 1993. Arafat's deal, however, meant that some Palestinians could end up voting for two legislatures, one in Amman and one in Jericho. Under the initial shock of the Oslo surprise, Hussein gave a clear signal of his intention to postpone the election. The assurances given to him by Rabin at a meeting in Aqaba lay behind the subsequent decision to go ahead as planned. The general election held on 8 November was the first multi-party election since 1956. A change in the electoral law,

replacing the old bloc-voting system with a one-person, one-vote formula, was calculated to limit the strength of the Islamic opposition.[47]
The amendment had the desired effect: a strengthening of the conservative, tribal and independent blocs and a resounding rebuff to the
Islamic Action Front, whose principal platform was opposition to the
peace talks with Israel. IAF representation in the eighty-member lower
house declined from 34 to 21 seats. A large majority in the new house
were moderate-to-conservative independents generally supportive of
the regime and of its pursuit of the peace process. The king subsequently appointed the forty-member Senate from the ranks of his own
supporters on 18 November. This gave him a pliant parliament for proceeding with the task of Arab–Israeli peacemaking, which remained at
the top of his agenda. It also gave rise to speculation that the signing of
a Jordanian–Israeli peace accord was imminent.

25. Peace Treaty

The signature of a peace treaty with Israel represented, in Hussein's own words, the "crowning achievement" of his political career. It was also the culmination of almost half a century of Hashemite efforts to secure their kingdom and to carve for themselves an enduring regional role through the settlement of the Arab–Israeli conflict. In this respect, Hussein was the true heir to his revered grandfather, Abdullah bin Hussein. Abdullah I initialled in 1950 a peace treaty with Israel, but an overall settlement was beyond his reach and the following year he was assassinated by a Palestinian nationalist. Hussein followed in his grandfather's footsteps because he shared his conception of the vital interests of their dynasty and their country. The most important of these was to protect the Hashemite Kingdom of Jordan against external threats. In the aftermath of the Oslo Accord this interest narrowed down to the protection of the East Bank against threats from whatever quarter, whether Israeli, Palestinian or Syrian.

A peace treaty with Israel was needed in order to fend off the challenge of Palestinian militants and Israeli extremists who wanted to convert Jordan into an alternative homeland for the Palestinians. By concluding a peace treaty with Israel Hussein hoped to achieve other aims as well, such as securing the status of the Hashemite dynasty as the guardian of the Muslim holy places in Jerusalem, an economic link with the West Bank, a resolution of the refugee problem and American economic aid. But defence of the realm was the paramount consideration. The treaty was intended to renew and institutionalize the strategic understanding with Israel, so that Jordan would not be hurt when Israel and the Palestinians proceeded to a final settlement.

Like his grandfather, Hussein relied heavily on personal diplomacy in working for an understanding with his neighbour across the river. The trust between him and Itzhak Rabin was crucial to progress on the road to peace. But there was one other Israeli official who played an important role because he fitted in with the king's peculiar brand of personal diplomacy and that was Efraim Halevy, the deputy head of the Mossad. Halevy, who had been born in Britain and had earlier headed the Foreign Liaisons Division of the Mossad, formed an unusually close working relationship with the king, which over time developed into a personal friendship. Hussein trusted Halevy, and he often sought his advice on sensitive internal issues that did not concern Israel directly. Halevy's principal task was to serve as a back channel between the prime minister and the king, and to step in whenever the negotiations reached an impasse. Halevy made countless secret visits to the king and his brother, the pattern of which was remarkably uniform. Halevy would arrive for a meeting with Prince Hassan around eleven in the morning, and they would spend two and a half hours together. At 1:30 Hassan would go to brief his elder brother, and the two would return half an hour later. Lunch would last a couple of hours and the conversation would continue for another couple of hours in the garden. Hussein needed time to think and to explore issues from different angles. He did not like the Israeli habit of getting straight down to specifics, and Halevy easily accommodated to the king's pace and method of doing business.[1]

In the last months of 1993 and the early months of 1994 Israel was preoccupied with the implementation of the Declaration of Principles on Interim Self-government and with negotiations on the Syrian track. Hussein was concerned that Jordan would be left behind. His concern seemed justified by the refusal of the Palestinians to take into account Jordan's interests in their negotiations with Israel. On 4 May 1994 Israel and the PLO reached an agreement on extending self-rule from Gaza and Jericho to the rest of the West Bank. This agreement threatened Jordanian access to the markets of the West Bank and the status of the dinar there. By posing a threat to the Jordanian economy, the agreement provided an impetus to the slow-moving talks between Jordan and Israel. On 19 May, Hussein had a meeting in his house in London with Itzhak Rabin. The other participants were Prince Hassan, Elyakim Rubinstein and Efraim Halevy. Hussein asked Rabin whether he was ready to move forward on the Jordanian track, and he received a positive answer. At this meeting Hussein heard for the first time that Israel would be prepared to grant Jordan a privileged position in looking after the Muslim holy places in Jerusalem in any future peace settlement.

This was the turning point in the talks. Hussein agreed to start drafting a peace treaty; that detailed negotiations would move from Washington to the region; and then, in principle, a public meeting with Rabin could take place in the White House. Rabin, in return, promised to recommend to the American president and Congress the cancellation of Jordan's debt to the United States.[2] Hussein himself presented the decision to go public as a joint decision that arose naturally from the progress in the talks:

The fact that we did not announce peace contacts publicly all through the past was due to a mutual agreement. At first we were so far apart that there would have been no benefit in announcing the meetings. These meetings enabled us to get to know each other. They enabled us to examine our positions every now and then to see if there was any chance of progress. They certainly changed the atmosphere, but it was a mutual agreement from the word go that we keep them quiet until we had something of substance so that when we reached the right moment all this would not be lost.[3]

In June, Hussein went to Washington to coordinate the peace moves with the Clinton administration and to present his case for the renewal of the American economic and military aid that had been cut off during the Gulf crisis. In Congress and in public opinion there was still resentment towards the king and the kingdom from the Gulf War. At Hussein's request Halevy was dispatched to Washington to help behind the scenes. Israel's ambassador to Washington at that time, Professor Itamar Rabinovich, was a friend and a tennis partner of Prime Minister Rabin, and he too was active behind the scenes in lobbying on behalf of the Jordanian cause.[4] If Hussein expected his courageous step in authorizing direct talks with Israel to be rewarded, he was in for a shock. The American officials he met told him that to get any aid he would have to make a more visible move towards peace with Israel. Going back home with an empty bag could have serious consequences, especially in relation to the army, which had been starved of supplies for a number of years. In his distress, Hussein turned to his Israeli friends. Rabin himself authorized Halevy and Rabinovich to go to the rescue. At a meeting with Dennis Ross, the peace process coordinator, Halevy strongly argued the Jordanian case, including the request for a squadron of F-16 fighter aircraft to upgrade their air force. Ross turned to Halevy and said, "Tell me, Efraim, who are you representing here? Israel or Jordan?" Without hesitation Halevy blurted out, "Both!"[5]

Halevy advised Hussein to prepare a letter detailing Jordan's specific requests prior to his meeting with the president. The meeting took place in the White House on 22 June. Clinton conducted the meeting without any notes but having thoroughly studied Jordan's submission. His mastery of his brief persuaded Hussein and his aides that Clinton was certainly looking for ways to respond. After going over what he could and could not do, Clinton turned to Jordan's crippling debt burden. Jordan's debt to America amounted to $700 million. Clinton said he knew that this was the most important of all of Jordan's economic requests. But the political reality was that Congress would reject debt forgiveness unless he had a powerful argument to use on Jordan's behalf: "A public meeting with Rabin would give me that argument." Clinton offered to host such a meeting and asked the king to think about it. In political terms the main outcome of this visit was the president's personal engagement. This was very reassuring for Hussein because he placed so much store by personal relations. The king told his aides that he had not had such a meeting with any president since Dwight Eisenhower. Halevy reported that the king had been "amazed" by the president and was "thrilled" by his visit to Washington. On 4 July, Hussein sent a message suggesting a trilateral meeting at ministerial level by the Dead Sea preceded by a meeting of the Jordanian and Israeli negotiators. The Americans understood that the sequence was the king's way of conditioning his public, and the Israelis accepted it with alacrity.[6] The sequel was described by the king:

I returned home and gathered parliament and told them that we had decided to meet. I also made a statement in the United States that I was not against a public meeting with Rabin. That's the way people do business; there is no other way. And we prepared the document that turned out to be the Washington Declaration. At first I wanted the first meeting to be held in Wadi Araba. But when we told the Americans, President Clinton invited us to the White House, and both of us felt that the Americans had been our partners in trying to get somewhere for so long, particularly President Clinton. So we accepted. And we went with the paper agreed to its last detail and we gave it to the president's office at the last possible moment in the evening so it could not get into the newspapers until it was ratified by us the next morning.[7]

In his speech to parliament on 9 July, Hussein stated that it was time for Jordan to pursue its own peace agenda and that a public meeting with the Israeli leadership would be an important step towards that end. Three days later he sent a letter to Clinton proposing a public meeting with Rabin on the border between Jordan and Israel followed three or four days later by a meeting in Washington. Hussein wanted the first meeting to be in the region, not at the White House, as if it were some media replay of Arafat's meeting with Rabin. "Follow your instincts," Queen Noor told him. "Don't let anyone hijack this critical historic moment for their own short-term political benefit." But the Americans were dangling all sorts of financial incentives, including the forgiveness of Jordan's $700 million debt. In the end, Hussein felt he had no choice. "This is the only time I've ever compromised for profit to the country," he said. The next day he was informed that Clinton was about to break the secrecy of the negotiations and announce the upcoming meeting in Washington. Only after the news announcement did the king and queen learn that the official trip included a banquet, a White House ceremony, and an invitation to both Hussein and Rabin to address a joint session of the United States Congress. This elaborate plan gave Hussein just the opportunity he was looking for to take his vision of peace directly to the American decision-makers.[8]

From this point on events moved at a rapid pace. On 18 July the heads of the Jordanian and Israeli delegations appeared together in Wadi Araba to announce the commencement of peace negotiations between the two countries. The meeting took place in a tent pitched on the border, seventeen miles north of Aqaba. "The tent is temporary, but the peace will be permanent," said Rubinstein in his opening speech. Two days later, Majali, Peres and Christopher held a public meeting at the Dead Sea Spa Hotel in Jordan. They discussed plans for a Red–Dead Sea canal, joining their electricity grids, and turning the barren Wadi Araba Desert into a "Valley of Peace" with thriving farming, industrial and tourist centres. "The flight," said Peres, "took only fifteen minutes but it crossed the gulf of forty-six years of hatred and war." The meeting was of great symbolic significance and helped to prepare the Jordanian public for the much more dramatic meeting between their king and the Israeli prime minister in the White House.

Negotiations and drafting of what became known as the Washington Declaration were conducted directly between Hussein and Rabin through a back channel with the help of their most trusted aides, Ali Shukri and Efraim Halevy. Hussein insisted on absolute secrecy and on excluding the two foreign ministries and the State Department. Negotiations went on literally until the last minute and, as planned, the text of the declaration was not disclosed to the Americans until the evening before the ceremony. The much publicized ceremony took place on the White House lawn on 25 July 1994. Clinton read the text, and his two guests signed it. The Washington Declaration terminated the state of belligerency between Jordan and Israel, and committed the two countries to seek a just, lasting and comprehensive peace based on UN resolutions 242 and 338. Israel formally undertook to respect the special role of the Hashemite Kingdom of Jordan in the Muslim holy shrines in Jerusalem and to give priority to this role in the negotiations with the Palestinians on final status. This was a serious blow to Arafat, who regarded control of the holy places as a Palestinian prerogative and claimed Jerusalem as the capital of a future Palestinian state. Finally, various bilateral measures were announced, such as the establishment of direct telephone links, joint electricity grids, new border crossings, free access to third-country tourists, and cooperation between the two police forces in combating crime and drug smuggling.

All three leaders made eloquent speeches on the White House lawn, but Hussein's speech was the most moving. Without a note in hand he spoke at some length about peace as the realization of a dream. He spoke with particular insight about the mental adjustments that were needed to attain real peace. "I have felt over the recent past that many of us in our part of the world, both in Israel and in Jordan, had to begin the inevitable readjustments, psychologically, after so many years of denial of our right to live normally together, to build and to move ahead. And, as I have said before, unfortunately, the abnormal became normal, which is indeed a tragic state of affairs." Hussein's clear and unqualified statement that the state of war had come to an end was greeted with a spontaneous round of applause and featured prominently in the media reports of the ceremony.

After the ceremony the principals adjourned to the cabinet room. As this was supposed to be only the second meeting between Rabin and Hussein, Clinton was mildly surprised to see how well acquainted they seemed. "Tell me, how long have you known one another?" he asked. "Twenty-one years, Mr. President," Rabin replied. Hussein corrected him with a benign smile: it was "only" twenty years. On a more serious note, Hussein emphasized the need for the Jordanian people to enjoy the material fruits of peace. Clinton explained to Rabin that only Congress had the power to write off Jordan's debt, and he asked for his help in persuading Congress to do so. "Yes, Mr. President," replied Rabin slowly. "We will do our best." To the Jordanians present this brief exchange provided a remarkable demonstration of the political clout wielded by Israel and its friends on Capitol Hill. In the evening a banquet was laid on in honour of the two visiting dignitaries and their delegations. Clinton lavished praise on Hussein for his courage and commitment, comparing him to King Abdullah, his grandfather. No comparison could have been more flattering to Hussein, and Clinton knew this. Rabin added his own words of praise for Hussein but he was more prosaic and more forward-looking. Hussein was visibly moved.[9]

The following day, 26 July, Hussein and Rabin addressed a joint session of Congress. Both speeches were well received. In his speech, Hussein outlined his vision for a bold peace. He spoke of his great-grandfather, who had led the Arab Revolt, and of King Abdullah, who was martyred at the doors of the Al-Aqsa Mosque: "He was a man of peace who gave his life for an ideal. I have pledged my life to fulfilling his dream." Hussein came across as a man who understood the fears of his neighbours and only wished to live in peace with them. Towards the end of his speech Hussein touched on America's role in facilitating and supporting the move of the two countries from a state of war to a state of peace. He was greeted with a standing ovation. None of Jordan's Arab neighbours accepted his claim to leadership, while the Oslo Accord threatened the security of his kingdom. Now, in Itzhak Rabin, he had found a true friend and an ally who understood his anxieties better than any Arab ruler and was willing to help him. According to Taher al-Masri, Hussein felt a deep debt of gratitude to Rabin for pleading his case in Washington and for procuring for him the much coveted invitation to address the two houses of Congress. This personal attachment to the strong Israeli leader, in Masri's opinion, is the key to understanding Hussein's decisions and actions from this point onwards.[10]

Some of Hussein's senior advisers had reservations about the speed with which he was moving towards a formal peace treaty with Israel. Masri, now the speaker of the lower house, warned Hussein that his rush to normalization was counter-productive. For decades the Jordanian people had been conditioned to think of Israel as the enemy, and the abrupt reversal of attitudes that Hussein was proposing was simply not realistic. The transition had to be gradual or it might provoke a backlash. Masri also objected to the Jerusalem clause in the Washington Declaration, the text of which he did not see until only a few hours before it was announced. He felt that it was a mistake to ask Israel to acknowledge Jordan's special status in Jerusalem because Israel was an occupying power with no legal standing in this matter.[11] Adnan Abu-Odeh, now Jordan's permanent representative to the UN, believed that Hussein had to proceed to a peace treaty with Israel, but he too objected to the Jerusalem article in the Washington Declaration because it implied that Israel was the legal owner of Jerusalem. He also believed that it would give rise to problems between Jordanian and Palestinian officials because it gave priority to the former in administering the Muslim holy places in Jerusalem. Hussein was not pleased to hear these criticisms.[12]

The very effective support that Hussein received from Israeli officials during his visit to Washington reinforced his determination to move forward swiftly. Rabinovich played a major role in lobbying for Jordanian debt forgiveness by Congress, and Hussein was very appreciative of his efforts. They had a number of extended meetings both in the Four Seasons Hotel and in Hussein's home on the Potomac outside Washington, D.C. Halevy delayed his return home by five days at Hussein's request in order to assist with the campaign for congressional debt forgiveness. He left Washington aboard the royal aircraft. During the flight Hussein was in high spirits and in a celebratory mood. He was well on the way to having Jordan's debt written off; his armed forces stood to receive sorely needed spare parts and upgraded equipment, including a first squadron of F-16 fighter aircraft; and his relationship with the American superpower had been repaired. Among the friends Hussein called to thank from his airborne satellite telephone in the presence of Halevy were Rabinovich and Rabin.[13]

It was Hussein's nature to act intuitively and sometimes impulsively. Perhaps because of his recent physical ordeals, Queen Noor felt particularly protective of him and worried that he would be let down. They had lived through many failed attempts but they remained cautiously optimistic. Her husband described to her his relationship with Rabin as one between two military men who dealt directly, and often bluntly, with each other. Two weeks after the signing of the Washington Declaration, the royal family went to Aqaba to prepare for the inauguration of the first open crossing point between Jordan and Israel. Christopher flew in for the historic event with several of his officials. Israel sent a large delegation, including Rabin, Peres, army officers and journalists. The telephone lines that the Washington Declaration called for between the two countries had just opened, and Hussein inaugurated them with a conversation with Ezer Weizman, Israel's President.[14]

Teams of experts from the two sides got down to work on the sensitive issues of water allocation, border demarcation and mutual security. Most of the meetings took place in the house of Crown Prince Hassan in Aqaba. The Jordanian team included General Ihsan Shurdom, the former head of the air force; Dr. Munther Haddadin, a tough-minded water expert; Dr. Ahmad Mango, an economist and a senior adviser to Prince Hassan; and Awn Khasawneh, the chief of the royal court and a distinguished jurist who was later appointed to the bench of the International Court of Justice in the Hague. The Jordanians also brought another expert in international law, the Australian-born Professor James Crawford from Cambridge. Crawford had been Khasawneh's tutor at Cambridge, and he was a leading expert on refugees under international law. Refugees were a particularly complex issue because the great bulk of them were Palestinians, not East Bank Jordanians. Initially, the Israelis wanted no reference whatsoever to the question of refugees. Crawford and Khasawneh sat with Rubinstein, and Khasawneh explained to him that it was impossible for Jordan to enter into a treaty of peace without reference to the question of refugees. Khasawneh spoke for eighteen minutes and when he finished, Crawford said to his former student: "Those were the most dramatic eighteen minutes of my whole professional life, including my appearances before the International Court of Justice." A compromise was eventually reached, and, though it was not completely satisfactory to the Jordanians, at least it allowed for a reference to the question of refugees in the treaty.[15] Discussions on all the issues were intense, and, when the differences had been sufficiently narrowed, the negotiators reported to their principals that the time was ripe for a top-level meeting.[16]

This took place in Aqaba on 29 September. The most intractable issues were land and water. In the aftermath of 1967 Israel encroached on Jordanian land south of the Dead Sea and built a string of agricultural settlements that specialized in growing flowers. To supply these farms with water, Israel bored wells deep inside Jordanian territory. In total Israel stole more than 380 square kilometres, roughly the area of the Gaza Strip. Jordan demanded the return of all this land and an end to the exploitation of its water resources. At the meeting Rabin proposed to Hussein that Israel would recognize Jordanian sovereignty over the entire area in return for an agreement to lease it back to the agricultural settlements. Hussein did not reject the proposal out of hand and seemed willing to bargain. But the following day Ali Shukri arrived in Jerusalem by helicopter and handed the prime minister an urgent letter from the king with an absolute rejection of his proposal. Hussein stated that unless he received all 380 square kilometres that he demanded of Israel, he would not be able to sign a peace treaty. At first it looked as if all was lost. But Rubinstein and Halevy were dispatched for an intensive round of talks with the king and his brother, and eventually they came up with a saving formula.

The compromise was endorsed by Hussein and Rabin at their meeting in the Hashimiyya Palace west of Amman on 12 October. Rabin assured his host that he did not intend to keep either one inch of Jordanian territory or a drop of Jordan's water. The two leaders agreed that some minor adjustments could be made to the borders in Wadi Araba by exchanging territory of exactly the same size. Israel would retain Jordanian lands that its farmers had been exploiting in the border zone in return for ceding to Jordan uncultivated land of equal size. The other element of the deal concerned water quotas. Israel offered a package with three components of fifty million cubic metres each. The first fifty would come from what Israel had been using, the second from dams that the two countries were to build jointly, and the third had no specific source.[17]

The following day Prince Hassan returned to Aqaba and reported to his aides the outcome of the summit. Munther Haddadin was dissatisfied with the water quotas and said so bluntly. The Israelis returned to Aqaba that evening to resume negotiations. No agreement could be reached over the water wells in Wadi Araba. The Israelis wanted to annex them, and, Haddadin, who was more pugnacious than any of the Israeli negotiators, refused to cede Jordanian territory. Negotiations broke up without agreement, and Rabin subsequently complained to Prince Hassan that Dr. Haddadin did not appear to want peace.[18]

Rabin and Hussein had to be called in to resolve outstanding problems one last time. They met again in the Hashimiyya Palace with a large number of aides on the evening of 16 October and worked through the night. Rabin and Hussein went through the agreement paragraph by paragraph, solving problems as they went along. When the border issue came up, they got down on their hands and knees to pore over a huge map laid out on the floor. Together, they worked out the whole line from Eilat and Aqaba in the south to the point of convergence with Syria in the north. They settled with military precision all the border demarcation issues and the land exchanges. They agreed to special regimes for Naharyim in the northern Jordan Valley and for Zofar in Wadi Araba. In other areas Hussein agreed, with characteristic magnanimity, to allow Israeli farmers to continue to use the land they had been cultivating after it reverted to Jordanian sovereignty. As for water, Israel agreed to supply Jordan with fifty million cubic metres a year. This was a net gain for Jordan. It was also agreed that Jordan and Israel would cooperate in finding sources for the supply to Jordan of an additional quantity of fifty million cubic metres of water of drinkable standard. The two countries undertook to alleviate the water shortage by developing new water resources, by preventing contamination and by reducing wastage. In the south, Israel was to retain the use of the wells in the areas that reverted to Jordanian sovereignty. The security article of the treaty was unique in that it did not entail the involvement of the UN or any other third party. There was a mutual commitment not to enter hostile coalitions, to combat terrorism and to strive for regional security in the spirit of the Helsinki agreements in Europe. Israel's commitment to respect Jordan's special role in the Muslim holy shrines in Jerusalem was incorporated into the treaty. Finally, the two parties agreed to work together to alleviate the position of the Palestinian refugees who had found refuge in Jordan.[19]

Hussein and Rabin worked until 4:00 a.m., then took a rest while the officials tied up the loose ends and produced the final draft. Khasawneh was the first person the king saw after the initialling of the treaty. He was sitting in the Hashimiyya Palace reading a newspaper, as was his habit in the morning. He invited Khasawneh to come in and sit next to him. Hussein noticed that Khasawneh had been unhappy about the way the meeting went the night before. He said, "Please don't think that I entered into this treaty of peace for my own sake. I am but a transient person. When I came back after the treatment for my illness in America, and I saw how the people of Jordan came out to greet me, I thought it my duty to do everything within my power to bring security to them. This is why I concluded this treaty." The king then started thanking Khasawneh and said, "I will be for ever indebted to you until the day I die for what you did in negotiating this treaty." Khasawneh replied, "Your Majesty, I am a civil servant and I only did my duty."[20] In the days after the marathon session Hussein was in an elated and triumphant mood. Everyone who saw him commented on how happy he looked and on the strong sense of satisfaction he radiated at having overcome all the obstacles and accomplished his mission.[21]

The treaty of peace between the Hashemite Kingdom of Jordan and the State of Israel was signed on 26 October 1994 at a border point in Wadi Araba that had been a minefield just a few days before. The treaty was signed by prime ministers Abdul Salam Majali and Itzhak Rabin with President Clinton as a witness. A large number of foreign dignitaries attended the ceremony, including the foreign ministers of America, Russia and Egypt, and representatives from several other Arab countries. The event was telecast to a vast audience around the world. It was the second treaty concluded between Israel and an Arab state in fifteen years and the first to be signed in the region. Itzhak Rabin, who had displayed by his body language so much discomfort when shaking Arafat's hand in the White House a year earlier, was now in a positively festive mood. He and Hussein seemed to enjoy the carnival-like setting as thousands of balloons were released into the air, and senior Israeli and Jordanian officers exchanged gifts. Rabin said it was time to make the desert bloom, and Hussein promised a warm peace, unlike the cold peace with Egypt. The public ceremony was the culmination of thirty-one years of secret dialogue across the battle lines.

The Jordan–Israel treaty carried the potential for building peace in the full sense of the word. Jordan was the second Arab country to sign a peace treaty with Israel, but in one respect it was the first: no other Arab country preceded it in offering a warm peace. The two countries exchanged ambassadors: Professor Shimon Shamir, an eminent historian of the Middle East from Tel Aviv University, was appointed as Israel's first ambassador to Amman, while Marwan Muasher, an accomplished and forward-looking diplomat, was appointed as Jordan's first ambassador to Tel Aviv. Shamir, who had served as Israel's ambassador to Egypt, emphasized the uniqueness of the Jordanian approach to peace. The peace with Egypt was concluded under the pressure of renewed hostilities, in the teeth of opposition from the other Arab countries and in a world dominated by the cold war. Security arrangements in Sinai were consequently at the centre of this peace treaty, while normalization was merely a bargaining chip for the Egyptians. The peace treaty with Jordan, on the other hand, was concluded after years of quiet dialogue and tacit understandings, with legitimacy provided by Madrid and Oslo, and in a world whose beacons were globalization, interdependence and the free market. Accordingly, the treaty said little about security and a great deal about economic cooperation. The word "cooperation" appeared twenty times in the text. Jordan's leaders preferred the term "peacemaking" to "normalization" because it denoted a joint enterprise for the benefit of both countries.

Hussein saw peace as the crowning achievement of his long reign and hoped to see its fruits in his own lifetime. Whenever it was suggested to him that the pace of progress in peacemaking should be controlled, he replied that, on the contrary, cooperation should be accelerated and expanded in order to consolidate the peace. He realized that the peace treaty took his people by surprise, that many of his Palestinian subjects found it difficult to accept, and that the Islamic and radical opposition would do everything in their power to subvert it. But he also hoped that, in the final analysis, the peace settlement would be judged by its practical results. Hence the importance he attached to turning the peace with Israel into an economic success story whose benefits would reach the ordinary man in the street.[22] The cold peace that characterized the relations between Egypt and Israel was alien to his entire way of thinking:

I can't understand the term cold peace. I don't understand what it means. You either have war, or a state of no war and no peace, or you have peace. And peace is by its very nature a resolution of all problems. It is the tearing down of barriers between people. It is people coming together, coming to know one another. It is the children of martyrs on both sides embracing. It is soldiers who fought each other coming together and exchanging reminiscences about the impossible conditions they had faced in a totally different atmosphere. It is people getting together and doing business. Real peace is not between governments but between individuals who discover that they have the same worries, the same concerns, that they have suffered in the same way, and that there is something they can both put into creating a relationship that would benefit all of them.[23]

Progress in peacemaking did not match this great vision. None the less, the peace treaty with Israel yielded a number of immediate benefits for Jordan. First and foremost, Jordan recovered its territory and water resources, and firmly marked its international frontier with Israel. By signing the treaty, Israel formally recognized Jordan's sovereignty, territorial integrity and political independence. Israel also undertook to refrain from the forcible transfer of population from the territory under its control into Jordan, thereby laying to rest the threat implicit in the slogan "Jordan is Palestine"—converting Jordan into an alternative homeland for the Palestinians. The Jordanian negotiators had deliberately inserted a clause prohibiting "transfer" because the treaty constituted a legal barrier against this threat.[24] The Israelis understood that "transfer" was a strategic concern about the very survival of the kingdom and were therefore willing to give the necessary commitment.[25] Peres explicitly acknowledged this when he stated that "Jordan is Jordan, and Palestine is Palestine." Significantly, Ariel Sharon, the most prominent advocate of the idea, abstained from voting rather than rejecting the treaty when it was placed before the Knesset. Evidently, he did not regard it as the definitive end of "Jordan is Palestine." However, after the treaty's ratification, the idea faded from the mainstream of Israeli political discourse.[26] The Knesset endorsed the peace treaty with Jordan by a majority of 105 to 3, with 6 abstentions. In December 1994 Binyamin Netanyahu, the leader of the Likud, visited Hussein in Amman. Hussein sought and received an assurance that the Likud did not support the "Jordan is Palestine" policy. Netanyahu assured Hussein that the Likud fully endorsed the peace treaty and were committed to the country's integrity and stability.[27]

Second, by moving fast to make peace with Israel ahead of progress on the Israeli–Palestinian track, Hussein restored Jordanian–American relations to their pre–Gulf War level. The material benefits, in terms of debt forgiveness and economic and military aid, were considerable. More generally, the peace partnership with Israel upgraded the importance of Jordan in American eyes. Because of its small size and limited resources Jordan was not regarded as a major strategic asset for America in the Middle East. The peace treaty with Israel made Jordan a more

valued ally for America and a model for peaceful coexistence and stability.[28] Clinton was the first American president to visit Jordan since
1974. Following the signing ceremony in the desert, Clinton appeared
before a joint session of the Jordanian parliament in Amman. He made
a stirring speech, promising that America would never let Jordan down,
that it would meet its military needs, and that it would contribute to the
development of the Rift Valley. He also paid homage to the Hashemite
dynasty and to its services to the Arab cause.

The peace treaty certainly served Hussein's dynastic interests. It
restored the alliance with a superpower; it revived the strategic understanding with Israel; and it underpinned the centrality of Jordan in
regional politics. Hussein had played for big stakes. He signed the
peace treaty not simply in order to recover territory and water resources
but to protect his kingdom against a takeover bid by his Palestinian
opponents and to forestall the emergence of an Israeli–Palestinian axis.
At one stroke he turned the tables on his radical Palestinian rivals and
reasserted the Hashemite dynasty's position as Israel's natural ally in
the region. The alliance with Israel could also serve as a deterrent to
aggression by Jordan's Arab neighbours, especially Syria. Most crucially, the peace with Israel went hand in hand with, and indeed made
possible, the alliance with the United States. By signing the peace
treaty Hussein in effect based the defence of the realm on two pillars,
Israel and the United States. It updated and brought into the open the
political strategy of Hussein's grandfather, Abdullah I, and was a dynastic move of momentous importance. There was, however, an internal
price to pay for this radical realignment of Jordan's foreign policy.

26. The King's Peace

The peace treaty profoundly affected Jordan's geopolitical position. Jordan shifted away from the Arab world, and especially from Iraq, and moved closer to America and Israel. The treaty, above all, offered an American and Israeli guarantee of the Hashemite regime's survival.[1] Jordan seemed set on carving out for itself a new regional role. It came to be seen by America as a linchpin of Middle East security and stability, and was declared by President Clinton to be one of America's "major non-NATO allies." This formal designation was expected to increase substantially the flow of American economic and military aid to the kingdom. Egypt felt marginalized, and Syria viewed Jordan's independent behaviour with growing suspicion. Hussein was accused in the Arab media of betraying the Palestinians and the Arab cause. By his own lights, however, he was still an Arab nationalist who was serving the Arab nation by making peace with Israel. In his speeches he often harked back to the historic role of the Hashemite dynasty in staging the Arab Revolt and in leading the Arab world towards independence. The treaty with Israel, he insisted, was not at the expense of any Arab party, but a step in the struggle for a comprehensive peace in the Middle East.

Hussein understood better than any other Arab leader the root causes of the Arab–Israeli conflict and the psychological barriers to its resolution. From this understanding sprang his determination to have a warm peace, and in this respect his model was unique. It was the only one that addressed the deep yearning of Israel's citizens to be accepted by their neighbours. It was precisely because the treaty with Jordan catered to this basic need that it enjoyed the support of all sectors of Israeli society and all major political parties. Jordan's peace with Israel was based on a strategic decision to foster a new atmosphere in the region, a climate conducive to cooperation and coexistence. Peace was expected to bring benefits not only to Jordan but to the entire Middle East, creating the conditions for stability, prosperity and interdependence.[2]

The main problem with this noble vision of peace was that it inspired only a minority of Hussein's citizens. From the outset, there was considerable opposition to the peace process, especially from the Islamic Action Front and anti-establishment circles. In May 1994 eight Islamist and left-wing parties established the Popular Arab-Jordanian Committee for Resisting Submission and Normalization. The leaders of this mass movement accused the government of ignoring the will of the people and of rushing ahead with a policy of "apostasy and defeatism" to sign a separate peace with Israel.[3] In the lower house, on 6 November 1994, 55 deputies voted to ratify the treaty, 23 voted against, and 2 abstained. Former prime minister Taher al-Masri, an establishment figure of Palestinian origins, was one of the two who abstained. Even after the treaty was ratified, the opposition continued to fight it tooth and nail, and some mainstream politicians, such as Ahmad Obeidat, joined the ranks of the anti-normalizers. Thus, from the beginning, Hussein was only too aware of the extent of the opposition to his peace policy. He firmly believed, however, that once the material benefits of peace began to trickle down to the people, they would come round to his way of thinking. In particular, he hoped that peace would alleviate two of the country's greatest social problems: poverty and unemployment. Everything thus hinged on the treaty delivering the much vaunted "peace dividend."

In the first year after the signature of the treaty, progress was achieved on a number of fronts. A series of bilateral agreements was signed for cooperation in tourism, energy, health, the environment, law enforcement and agriculture. A trade agreement was also concluded, but Jordanian manufacturers found it difficult to sell their products across the border because of the power of existing business interests. Jordanian businessmen were at a disadvantage because Israel's Gross National Product was ten times that of Jordan's. Israeli businessmen wanted all the benefits for themselves and without having to wait. This attitude did not allow the Jordanians to feel that they could achieve their aspirations in terms of economic development and growth through the peace process.[4] The economic benefits of the peace for Jordan remained marginal. There was some increase in tourism, trade and investment, but the overall impact on the economy was insubstantial.

A particularly sore point was Israeli protectionism in relation to the markets of the West Bank and Gaza. A basic idea of the peace process was to create a free-trade zone that encompassed Israel, Jordan and the Palestinian territories. In practice, Israel made it very difficult for Jordanian goods and services to get into the West Bank.[5] Resistance to normal relations with Israel ran much deeper than Hussein expected, and the new reality for which he yearned failed to materialize. The king had hoped to turn the peace with Israel into the people's peace, but it was widely perceived in Jordan as the king's peace. On the Israeli side, the peace with Jordan remained immensely popular, as did the king himself. It was often said, only half in jest, that if Hussein wanted to be the king of the Jews, he would be elected by popular acclaim. Both Rabin and Peres recognized the importance of delivering the economic dividends of peace. But the bureaucrats under them moved slowly and cautiously, and the promise presented by the treaty for ushering a new era of peace and prosperity remained largely unfulfilled.

Even when trade agreements were concluded, their implementation gave rise to a host of minor problems and to some friction between the two sides. Relations between the two countries came to depend to an unhealthy degree on two individuals, Hussein and Rabin. As a result, Hussein viewed relations between the two countries through the prism of this unique personal connection and tended to ignore other aspects of the relationship. He paid little attention to Peres or the different parties in Israel. For Rabin, similarly, the relationship with Hussein took precedence over everything else. So when parliament was critical of Israel's conduct or when the Jordanian government protested against Israeli actions, Rabin likewise did not pay much attention. He believed that he could solve any problem by talking directly to the king.[6] In effect, the two leaders became trouble-shooters in the peace process.

Marwan Muasher, Jordan's first ambassador to Israel, illustrated this general pattern with a concrete example. In April 1995 Rabin approved the expropriation of fifty-two hectares of Palestinian land in East Jerusalem for the building of a new Jewish neighbourhood. This move sparked a major uproar in Jordan and a threat by parliament to rescind the peace agreement. Muasher went to see Peres and several other officials. All of them told him that Rabin's mind was made up and that he would not reverse his decision. The king then sent a letter to the prime minister with Marwan Kasim, the chief of the royal court, urging him to stop. The letter stressed the sensitivity and the seriousness of the issue and the threat it posed to Jordanian–Israeli relations. The next morning, after reading the king's letter, Rabin reversed his decision.[7]

In 1995 Hussein completed his strategic move away from Iraq and into the American–Israeli orbit. In the 1980s he had cultivated the alliance with Iraq as an answer to the threat from an expansionist Israel. Iraq's invasion of Kuwait in 1990 destroyed that alliance. In the years after the Gulf War Hussein became increasingly outspoken in his criticism of Saddam Hussein and of his relentless grip on power. He spoke of the Iraqi people as deserving of democracy, and he floated ideas for reorganizing Iraq along federal lines. But he made his first open call for the overthrow of Saddam Hussein only in 1995. Such a risky move must have been made with at least the tacit backing of America and Israel. The call came after Hussein granted asylum to Saddam's two second cousins and sons-in-law. On 8 August, Lieutenant-General Hussein Kamel Hassan al-Majid and his brother, Colonel Saddam Kamel Hassan al-Majid, arrived in Amman and were accommodated with their wives and children in the Hashimiyya Palace. The younger brother had been the head of Saddam's personal bodyguard. Hussein Kamel had been the minister of military industries. Hussein gave Hussein Kamel not just asylum but a platform to vent his grievances against the Iraqi regime. With the Jordanian monarch standing by his side, Hussein Kamel declared his intention to overthrow the regime in Baghdad.

Hussein's own call for replacing the Ba'th regime in Baghdad came after one last try to persuade Saddam to mend his ways. Following the defection, the king sent a message to Saddam through Marwan Kasim, urging him to open a dialogue with the West, accept UN resolutions and "join in the region's march towards peace." Saddam's rejection of this advice prompted Hussein to advocate openly political change in Iraq. In a nationally televised speech, on 23 August, Hussein accused the Iraqi regime of endangering Jordan during the Gulf War by firing missiles across its airspace into Israel and of undermining its credibility in the Arab and international arenas. He charged that a few days before the defection, high-level discussions took place in Baghdad about attacking Kuwait and Saudi Arabia. Such a move, he claimed, would have inevitably exposed Iraq to dismemberment and fragmentation, and led to the destruction of "the eastern gate of the Arab homeland." The speech gave a hint of a personal ambition to rule Iraq by referring to the establishment of Iraq under the kings of the Hashemite monarchy until their demise in the coup of 1958. Hussein concluded with a promise to keep the Jordanian–Iraqi border open so as to "assist the people of Iraq until the long night of their suffering comes to an end."[8]

Hussein Kamel's real reason for leaving Iraq was not political disenchantment with the regime but a falling out with Saddam's ghastly son Uday. In Jordan, Kamel spoke with respect about Saddam but by calling for regime change in Iraq he burned his bridges. At first Hussein Kamel cooperated fully with Jordan's intelligence officers. He also gave CIA officers, British MI6 officers and UN arms inspectors a thorough briefing on Saddam's weapons of mass destruction. What he revealed was that in 1991, after the Gulf War, all Iraq's chemical and biological weapons had been destroyed on orders.[9] When the Anglo-American forces invaded Iraq in 2003 they discovered that everything that Kamel had told them back in 1995 was true: Iraq had no weapons of mass destruction.[10]

The two defectors were not the most gracious of house guests. Prince Talal bin Muhammad, Hussein's nephew and national security adviser, painted a particularly unflattering picture of Hussein Kamel:

He became increasingly truculent when he realized that the Americans were only interested in him for the information he could provide. He thought that the Americans would depose Saddam and have him as the head of Iraq. He also realized that the Iraqi opposition would not go anywhere near him because he stank of blood. He got increasingly disenchanted and stopped cooperating with us. He would sit up and play cards with the Jordanian guards at Al-Hashimiyya Palace and talk about his time at the top. He was semi-literate. He came with his brother Saddam Kamel, who was married to President Saddam's other daughter. There were about twelve children at different ages so we set up a school at Al-Hashimiyya Palace for them. The king's daughters, Alia and Zain, looked after the women. The men had lots of weapons and cash with them. They were not dependent on us. They would get drunk every night, and their guns would be lying around. They would make jokes about the massacres that they had committed against the Shia and Kurds. He was proud that he had killed 30,000 of his people in one day. This is the kind of scum that he was.[11]

After six months of increasingly exasperating behaviour, Hussein Kamel and his brother decided to go back to Iraq. His decision came as a relief to his Jordanian hosts, as he had long overstayed his welcome.

Forty-eight hours after their return to Iraq, the two brutal brothers were shot and dismembered on Saddam's orders. The women and children were spared. Relations between Iraq and Jordan remained tense and troubled, and rumours continued to circulate about Iraqi plans of attack. The challenge to the Iraqi regime reflected a more assertive and independent regional policy on the part of Jordan. It rang the alarm bells in Damascus and Cairo, and it prompted the presidents of both countries to rebuke Jordan for meddling in Iraq's internal affairs.

The Egyptians were also critical of Hussein for proceeding too fast towards normalization with Israel. This issue was aired at the second Middle East North Africa Summit (MENA) convened in Amman at the end of October 1995. Hundreds of government officials and business leaders from the region, North America, Europe and Asia attended this conference. Its goal was to facilitate the expansion of private sector investment in the region, to cement public–private partnership, and to work to enhance regional cooperation and development. The Jordanian hosts appeared in a confident mood, presenting 137 projects for which they sought foreign investment of $1.2 billion. From the Jordanian point of view, the summit was a success. Hussein hailed it as "a land-mark where we tried to present Jordan and Israel in a state of peace, and hopefully as a step towards comprehensive peace in the area to the world, and to call the world to come and be our partners . . . to benefit with us in the dividends of peace."[12] Amr Musa, the Egyptian foreign minister, struck a dissonant note in his opening speech. He warned against hurrying towards normalization before Israel accepted a Pales-tinian state, withdrew from Syrian and Lebanese territories, and removed the threat of weapons of mass destruction from the region. To Hussein this appeared like an attempt to undermine the summit, so he replied that they should not walk but run to peace. He also reminded Musa that Egypt was the country that had broken ranks and entered into full peace sixteen years earlier.[13]

Hussein's hopes for a better future suffered a shattering setback with the assassination of Itzhak Rabin. On Saturday evening, 4 November 1995, at a peace rally in Tel Aviv's largest square, a right-wing Jewish fanatic fired three bullets at the prime minister at close range. His aim was to derail the peace process and to put an end to the withdrawal from the Land of Israel. Rabin was rushed to hospital, where he died an hour later from his wounds. He was seventy-three years old. In his jacket pocket was found a neatly folded sheet of paper with the words of a song he had sung in the rally—"The Song of Peace." It was stained by his blood and pierced by one of the assassin's bullets.

The assassination of Israel's prime minister was a catastrophe for Hussein on every level. In a letter of condolence to Israel's president, Ezer Weizman, Hussein spoke of the loss of a true friend and a true champion of peace. "I shall always remember him," he wrote, "as my dedicated colleague and fellow shepherd of the Jordanian–Israeli peace process."[14] Rabin was buried with full military honours on Mount Herzl, Israel's national cemetery. Leaders from over eighty countries gathered in Jerusalem at a day's notice to pay homage to the fallen leader. Several Arab countries were represented: Egypt by President Mubarak; Jordan by King Hussein, Oman, Qatar, Tunisia and Morocco by their foreign ministers. Bill Clinton spoke at the graveside, ending his eulogy with two Hebrew words *Shalom, haver*, "Peace, friend." Hussein's words at the graveside resonated round the world. He mourned his friend with a eulogy that was both eloquent and rich in historical resonance. More than any of the other Arab guests, the king felt the poignancy of the moment. He was in Jerusalem for the first time since 1967 to pay homage to the commander who had led Israel's forces in the June War. "We are not ashamed," said the king, "nor are we afraid, nor are we anything but determined to continue the legacy for which my friend fell, as did my grandfather in this city when I was with him and but a boy."[15]

After the funeral, Hussein and his wife returned to the King David Hotel, where they met Randa Habib, a French journalist of Lebanese origins who had headed the office of the Agence France Presse in Jordan since 1987. She enjoyed privileged access to the king and was the only journalist who accompanied him in his private plane on the flight to the funeral. Seeing the tears rolling down his cheeks, she asked him about his feelings. Cigarette in hand, the king said to her, "I had to come to West Jerusalem for the first time in my life in order to bury a friend." There was a brief silence and then he added: "I have the impression that today I have also, in some way, buried the peace."[16]

Hussein had a private meeting after the funeral with Clinton, who was also staying in the King David Hotel. Just before Hussein came in, Clinton was briefed by Dennis Ross, who urged him to applaud the king's speech: "It was extraordinary, eloquent, emotional, and tinged with history. In contrast to Mubarak's, Hussein's showed what peace is

supposed to be about in terms of empathy and connecting as people."
The king, Ross went on, had some concern about Shimon Peres, fearing
that he was too partial towards Arafat. Hussein, suggested Ross, needed
to hear from the president that he understood that Jordan's interests
would be heavily affected by the permanent status talks, that America
would coordinate closely with the Jordanians as these progressed, perhaps even suggesting four-way talks between the Israelis, Palestinians,
Jordanians and themselves.

Clinton opened the meeting by telling the king that his speech had
deeply touched the Israelis and the Americans who were there. The
king remarked that he had hoped to find the right words and that he
had been unsure whether he was up to the task. Clinton assured him
that no one could have been more so. Clinton had heard that the king
had taken his delegation on to the terrace of the King David Hotel to
look over at the Old City. The king said this was the first time he had
seen Jerusalem since 1967, and that it was a magnificent and memo-
rable sight. Turning to business, Hussein said he could not figure out
why Asad was not moving on peace. Was it because Asad hoped to create a coalition with Iran and Iraq? He was not certain. Clinton thought
Asad wanted to move but found it difficult to act, that there were psychological barriers he had to overcome, and that they needed to push
him to overcome them. Dennis Ross added, "He sees himself as the last
Arab nationalist and he wants a process of reaching an agreement that
sets him apart from all others. Similarly, he also wants the substance of
his agreement to set him apart." The king concluded that movement
from Asad would benefit the entire region, but Jordan would press on
regardless.[17]

Clinton and Hussein both grossly underestimated the depth of Asad's
opposition to normalization with Israel. A month after their conversation, the CIA station chief in Amman handed the Jordanians an alarming document. It was three pages long and entitled "Jordan/Threat to
the Life of King Hussein." The plan to assassinate King Hussein and his
brother, Crown Prince Hassan, was said to be part of an overall Syrian
strategy. Asad had requested and received a new strategic situation
assessment, which included the following reasons for assassinating
Hussein:

a. The defection of Hussein Kamel and the role Jordan played by providing
him with political asylum, which was viewed by Syria as assistance to the

United States and Israel, and the beginning of a move to replace the regime in Iraq.

b. Hussein's deceiving of Asad, having promised not to sign a separate peace treaty with Israel, and in any event not to do so without Syria.

c. The inclusion of a clause in the peace treaty with Israel leasing it land in the Araba, which was a dangerous precedent from Syria's point of view.

d. Hussein's pushing for normalization between Arab countries, particularly the Gulf countries, and Israel.

e. The establishment of a new Syrian opposition organization called "17 April Organization" and the dissemination of anti-Syrian propaganda, particularly anti-Alawite, by Jordanian intelligence. This activity (so said the Syrians) was the straw that broke the camel's back.

According to the CIA report, President Asad had already given the go-ahead for the assassination of Hussein and his brother. The first phase of the plan, which had been put into effect, consisted of attacks on the king and his brother in the official Syrian media. On the assassination plan itself the CIA source did not have detailed information but nevertheless made the following assessments:

a. The assassination would probably be carried out in Jordan and not abroad, since Syrian intelligence was better able to do the job in Jordan than in a European or other country.

b. Syrian intelligence abroad (Amn al-Harijiyah) would be responsible for perpetrating the attack.

c. The attack would be carried out by someone close to the king, such as a bodyguard.

d. Officials in the Syrian Embassy in Amman probably knew of the plan but it was not clear if they were involved in any way.

Mention was also made by the informer of intentions to attack Arafat but he did not seem to be as major a target as Hussein or Hassan.[18] The CIA report was immediately shown to Hussein: he read it and reacted to it very calmly. Stricter security measures were adopted, and his bodyguards were subjected to routine checks every six months.[19] Later in the month the CIA station chief in Amman handed the authorities another secret report, this time on Iraqi plans against Jordan. Iraq was planning terrorist attacks against hostile Arab countries. To this end a group had been established and charged with the task of blowing up the United States Embassy in Amman and undermining the security and stability of Jordan. The group received training from intelligence officers, but the whole idea was postponed when one of the members of the group ran away. The CIA, however, had information that Iraq was continuing to train squads to carry out terrorist attacks against Western and Jordanian interests because of the king's support for the Iraqi opposition and his supposed plan to change the regime in Baghdad.[20]

Syrian and Iraqi threats did not deter Hussein from rushing forward towards normalization but a change did occur when Peres succeeded Rabin as Labour Party leader and prime minister. Hussein believed that the fact that Peres had been excluded from the negotiations of the peace treaty had alienated him to a degree. Hussein recognized that Peres had served his country, that he had always been a believer in peace, and that he was a fertile source of ideas for progress in every field, "but the relationship was different and it cooled down constantly."[21] Hussein suspected that Peres had a preference for progress on the Palestinian track and that Jordan's interests would suffer as a result. Peres continued to promote his vision of peace as the dawn of a new age in the region. Variations on a theme continued to flow from Peres's inventive political mind. The New Middle East, in a standard Peres utterance, would be "dominated by banks, not tanks, ballots, not bullets, and where the only generals would be General Motors and General Electric."

Challenges to Israel's security almost immediately distracted Peres from pursuing his vision of the New Middle East. Having reached the pinnacle of power, he tried to recast himself from Mr. Peace to Mr. Security. One serious mistake he made was to give the go-ahead for the assassination of Yahya Ayyash, the Hamas master bomb-maker. The so-called "Engineer" was killed in Gaza on 5 January 1996 by means of a booby-trapped cellular phone. Hamas retaliated with a series of devastating suicide bombs that claimed the lives of sixty Israelis. Peres made an even more serious mistake by ordering a major military operation in Lebanon. Operation Grapes of Wrath was launched on 11 April; its aim was to bring security to the Galilee by bombing the Hizbullah guerrillas in southern Lebanon. But the ultimate target of the operation was Syria. The idea was to put pressure on the civilians of southern Lebanon, for them to put pressure on the government of Lebanon, for it to put pressure on the Syrian government, and, finally, for the Syrian government to curb Hizbullah and grant immunity to the IDF in southern Lebanon. In short, the plan was to compel Syria to act as an Israeli *gendarme* in Lebanon.

Operation Grapes of Wrath involved the deliberate targeting of civilians. Nearly 400,000 civilians were driven by the IDF from their homes and villages in southern Lebanon and turned into refugees. Israeli brutality was condemned by the entire Arab world. Shortly after the invasion, 2,500 Jordanians took to the streets to demonstrate against Israel's aggression. The crisis provoked the strongest anti-Israeli sentiments since the signature of the peace treaty. Hussein sent Prime Minister Abdul Karim Kabariti to Israel on 16 April with two letters, one to Peres and one to President Ezer Weizman, urging them to end their military incursion and resume diplomacy. He pointed out that Israel's actions were undermining popular support for peace.[22] One day after Kabariti's visit, Israeli shells killed 102 refugees sheltering in a UN compound. The massacre in Qana drew fierce international condemnation and brought Operation Grapes of Wrath to its inglorious end on 27 April.

In the lead-up to the 26 May elections Binyamin Netanyahu, the aggressively right-wing leader of the Likud, went on the offensive. He charged that Labour brought peace without security and promised that the Likud would bring peace with security. Because of his immense popularity in Israel, Hussein could influence the outcome, and both candidates competed for his endorsement. Hussein misjudged both of them: he was unreasonably suspicious of Peres and rather naive about Netanyahu. He did not believe that the election of Netanyahu would necessarily herald the end of the peace process in the Middle East. He thought that what had been achieved was irreversible: "When the peace treaty with Jordan passed through the Knesset it had an overwhelming majority that we have never had on any other issue. And so it wasn't a peace between Jordan and Labour, it was a peace with Israel. I respected that and that is why I did not interfere in the elections in any form or way."[23]

In fact Hussein did knowingly display a bias in favour of Netanyahu by inviting him to Amman on the eve of the elections while declining to extend an invitation to Peres. Hussein was concerned that a victorious Peres would proceed swiftly to a sweeping agreement with Syria. Netanyahu managed to convince Hussein that he would keep the peace process going at a level and pace suitable to Jordan's political needs.[24] After his visit to Amman, Netanyahu was able to tell the Israeli public that although he headed a right-wing party, he was acceptable as a partner to their favourite Arab leader. Ali Shukri has confirmed that Hussein was not as neutral during the lead-up to the election as he pretended to be: "Privately, His Majesty wanted Netanyahu to win because he thought this was a man he could deal with. Netanyahu was young and Hussein did not believe for a moment that he would set out to destroy the peace. At the time everybody was saying that Netanyahu and his party were extremists, that they would reverse the Labour Party's peace policy. His Majesty wanted to give Netanyahu a chance."[25]

Hussein seriously misjudged the Jordanian stake in the Israeli elections because he attached too much importance to personalities and too little to political parties, their ideologies and their foreign policies. Marwan Muasher understood that whereas Labour leaders preferred to deal with Jordan as a way of escaping the hard choices they had to make with the Palestinians, the Likud had more sinister objectives. The Likud, he believed, wanted to collude with Jordan to prevent the establishment of a Palestinian state, which was implicit in the Oslo Accord. In the summer of 1995 Muasher had a conversation with Netanyahu, then leader of the opposition, in the cafeteria of the Knesset. Netanyahu said to him: "We have a joint interest. We have Palestinians in Israel, and you have Palestinians in Jordan. A Palestinian state on the West Bank would serve to radicalize the Palestinians in Israel and Jordan. That is not in our interests. We therefore have to work together to prevent the establishment of a Palestinian state." Muasher countered this argument by saying, "We look at things differently. We believe that the establishment of a Palestinian state in the West Bank and Gaza will help our own political identity because we have Jordanians of Palestinian origin who are reluctant to say that they are Jordanians so as not to appear to betray the Palestinian cause. But if they feel that the Palestinian political identity has evolved in the West Bank, they will no longer be reluctant to acknowledge their Jordanian identity. This is exactly like the Palestinians in Israel. None of them would want to leave Israel to live in a Palestinian state. But they want equal rights within Israel and they support the establishment of a Palestinian state for the sake of the other Palestinians, not in order to be radicalized." Netanyahu looked at Muasher and said, "Mr. Ambassador, I think I understand the

Jordanian position better than you do!" This encounter told Muasher two things. First, it demonstrated Netanyahu's arrogance. Second, it showed a refusal to accept that the establishment of an independent and viable Palestinian state was in Jordan's long-term interests.[26]

Peres fought a lacklustre campaign, leaving it to Netanyahu to do all the running. It was said that Peres behaved like the Jew in the Jewish joke who was challenged to a duel and sent a telegram to his opponent saying, "I am going to be late: start shooting without me." In the opinion polls they were running neck and neck, but when the results were out Netanyahu had won by a margin of 30,000 votes, with 50.4 percent of the vote to Peres's 49.6 percent. Labour won 34 seats in the Knesset, whereas the Likud won only 32. But under the new electoral law for the direct election of the prime minister, the task of forming the next government had to be assigned to Netanyahu. Hussein's not-so-subtle support for Netanyahu probably tipped the balance in his favour. A new chapter was opened in the complex relations between Jordan and the Jewish state.

27. Collision Course

The rise to power of Binyamin Netanyahu in May 1996 marked a break with the pragmatism that characterized Labour's approach towards the Arab world and the reassertion of an ideological hard line. It was back to the iron-wall strategy, and with a vengeance.[1] Netanyahu viewed Israel's relations with the Arab world as one of permanent conflict, as a never-ending struggle between the forces of light and the forces of darkness. His image of the Arabs was consistently and comprehensively negative, and it did not admit the possibility of diversity or change. Much of Netanyahu's vehemence and venom was reserved for the Palestinians. He launched a fierce assault on the notion that the Palestinian problem constituted the core and heart of the Middle East conflict. For him the Palestinian problem was not a genuine problem but an artificially manufactured one. He denied that the Palestinians had a right to national self-determination and argued that the primary cause of tension in the Middle East was inter-Arab rivalry.

Netanyahu denounced the Oslo Accord as incompatible with Israel's security and with the historic right of the Jewish people to the whole Land of Israel. He had led the right-wing opposition to the agreement that was signed on 28 September 1995, popularly known as Oslo II. It provided for further Israeli troop withdrawal beyond the Gaza and Jericho areas and the transfer of legislative authority to a democratically elected Palestinian Council. As soon as he got the chance, Netanyahu set about arresting and derailing the process that the Oslo Accords had set in motion. By making it clear that he remained absolutely opposed to Palestinian statehood, he all but pulled the keystone from the arch of peace. His aim was to preserve direct and indirect Israeli rule over the Palestinian areas by every means at his disposal. The main elements of his strategy were to lower Palestinian expectations, to weaken Yasser Arafat and his Palestinian Authority, to suspend the further redeployments stipulated in the Oslo Accords, and to order the construction of 2,000 new homes in the Jordan Valley.

In relation to the Arab states, and especially Syria, Netanyahu was similarly determined not to proceed any further down the path of land for peace. He believed that his tough position would compel the Arab states themselves to compromise further on their rights. He stated openly that he was going to change the rules of the game. But his strategy was fraught with danger because he had no experience in policy-making and no understanding of the limits of military power. The assumption that the Arabs would suddenly abandon their long struggle for the recovery of occupied land was not simply naive but also provocative. It created a dangerous tide in the relations between Israel and the Arab world. The programme of his government, and especially the building of new settlements on the West Bank, was widely interpreted in the Arab world as a declaration of war on the peace process.

Netanyahu did not command much respect even inside his own party. Senior members of the Likud regarded him as an intellectual lightweight, as glib and superficial, as little more than a purveyor of sound bites for American television. Netanyahu had been Israel's representative to the UN and deputy foreign minister, but in both posts he was more of a PR man than a policy-maker. He was that very rare thing—a genuine charlatan. As prime minister Netanyahu was not as bad as people thought he would be when he was competing for the top post—he was much, much worse. Within a very short time he succeeded in alienating most of his countrymen and all of Israel's allies abroad. Relations with Jordan became strained soon after his accession to power. At first criticism of the new Israeli prime minister was much more muted in the Jordanian media than in the rest of the Arab world. Hussein counselled his fellow Arabs against pessimism and against pushing Israel into a siege mentality. A flare-up of Israeli–Palestinian violence, he feared, could spill over into the kingdom or even revive the dreaded theory that "Jordan is Palestine." On the other hand, Netanyahu's reluctance to negotiate with Arafat inspired speculation about a Likud-sponsored "Jordanian option." Hussein tried to scotch these speculations by stating plainly that Jordan would "never be an alternative for the Palestinian leadership under any conditions." He wanted consultation and coordination with both Israel and the Palestinian Authority to protect Jordan's interest in the West Bank; he was not interested in negotiating instead of the Palestinians or in assuming responsibility for settling the Palestinian problem.[2]

Netanyahu tried to play off the Jordanians and the Palestinians against one another until one of his moves seriously backfired. The spark that set off the explosion was the opening, on the night of 25 September 1996, of an ancient tunnel close to the Al-Aqsa Mosque in the Old City of Jerusalem. Of no great import in itself, the new gate to the second century BC tunnel constituted a symbolic and psychological affront to the Palestinians and a blatant Israeli violation of the pledge to resolve the dispute over Jerusalem through negotiations, not via the fait accompli.[3] By giving the order to blast open a new entrance to the 2,000-year-old tunnel, Netanyahu also blasted away the last faint hopes of a peaceful dialogue with the Palestinians. The action set off a massive outburst of Palestinian anger and ignited the flames of confrontation. There was large-scale protest and rioting that got out of hand and provoked the Palestinian police to turn their guns on the Israeli soldiers. The violence intensified and engulfed the entire West Bank and Gaza. In three days of bloody clashes 14 Israeli solders and 54 Palestinians died. It was the most violent confrontation since the worst days of the intifada. The Israeli public was shocked by the scenes of Palestinian policemen opening fire on their Israeli counterparts. But most outside observers regarded Netanyahu's policy of blocking the peace process as the underlying cause of this costly and bloody conflict.

Hussein was furious. Netanyahu's action contravened Article 9 of the Israel–Jordan peace treaty, which says that "in accordance with the Washington Declaration, Israel respects the present special role of the Hashemite Kingdom of Jordan in Muslim holy shrines in Jerusalem." The injury was compounded by the fact that, only a few days before, Dore Gold, a senior aide to Netanyahu, had met with Hussein in Amman but said not a word about the tunnel. As a result of the meeting, rumours spread that Hussein had been privy to the plan and had approved it. Hussein followed the recommendation of his advisers and adopted a very tough line with Netanyahu over this issue.[4] Attempts by Netanyahu to renew contact were rebuffed by the king. Efraim Halevy was serving at that time as Israel's ambassador to the European Union in Brussels. At Netanyahu's request, Halevy paid a secret visit to the Jordanian capital and was able to obtain the consent of the king to receive two envoys of Netanyahu and thus to reactivate the connection between the two principals.[5]

A summit meeting in Washington was hastily called by President

Clinton on 2 October in an effort to calm the situation and to prevent the complete unravelling of the peace process. President Mubarak declined the invitation. Hussein, Arafat and Netanyahu all responded to the call, but the meeting ended without any agreement being reached. All the Arab leaders expressed their disappointment with the Israeli prime minister, but Hussein's disappointment was the most poignant because he was the only Arab who had not joined in the chorus of denunciation following Netanyahu's victory at the polls. There was a personal and a political aspect to the king's disappointment. His relations with Rabin had been based on mutual trust, and he had hoped to develop a similar relationship with Netanyahu. But he discovered the hard way that Netanyahu was devious, dishonest and completely unreliable. Netanyahu posed a serious threat to the king's plan to proceed step by step towards comprehensive peace in the Middle East. The king therefore spoke very sternly to Netanyahu at the White House, as the press reported at the time and as he confirmed later: "I spoke of the arrogance of power. I spoke of the need to treat people equally. I spoke of the need to make progress." Netanyahu said nothing, but, as they were leaving, he went up to Hussein and said: "I am determined to surprise you."[6]

Hussein's list of Israeli transgressions was leaked to Thomas Friedman at the *New York Times*: the illegal expropriation of Palestinian land for Jewish settlements; Israeli-imposed curfews on Palestinians that made it nearly impossible for them to work; the lack of a timetable for withdrawing Israeli troops from Hebron and starting negotiations on final status; the travesty of the tunnel; the persistence of Israel's fortress mentality when the only real security could come from mutual respect. "I speak for myself, for Itzhak Rabin, a man whom I had the great pride to call my friend, and for all peoples who benefit from peace," Hussein said to Netanyahu. "All this good will is being lost. We are at the edge of the abyss, and regardless of our best efforts, we might be just about to fall into it—all of us."[7]

It was heartbreaking for Hussein to watch all that he had built disintegrate so quickly. He was less ready to stick his neck out in defence of normalization with Israel in the aftermath of the bloody clashes in Jerusalem and the unproductive summit meeting in Washington. In Jordan the middle classes joined the Islamists and the Palestinian radicals in opposition to normalization. Thirty-eight groups, representing a wide range of political parties, professional associations and non-governmental organizations, signed a statement calling for resistance to "all forms of normalization with the Zionist enemy." Opinion polls reflected the deepening disillusion with the peace treaty at all levels of Jordanian society, and not just because of Netanyahu's actions. In one taken shortly after the Washington Declaration in July 1994, 82 percent of Jordanians polled believed that the economy would benefit from peace. In another, in January 1996, 47 percent of those polled felt that the economy had actually deteriorated in the first year of peace.[8]

Feeling against Israel was running high throughout the Arab world, from North Africa to the Persian Gulf. The third Middle East and North Africa Economic Conference, MENA III, was scheduled to open in Cairo in November. For a while it looked as if the conference would not convene at all. President Mubarak threatened to cancel it if Israel continued to renege on its commitments. He relented only under intense US pressure. MENA III opened in Cairo on 13 November in a climate of palpable hostility to the *muharwaluun*. The *muharwaluun*—those who "rush" or "scurry"—had become a key concept in Arab political discourse. The Syrian poet Nizar Qabbani coined the term after the handshake on the White House lawn between Rabin and Arafat that he interpreted as a humiliating act of surrender by the entire Arab nation. Qabbani poured his anger into a poem that he called *Al-Muharwaluun*:

> We stood in columns
> like sheep before slaughter
> we ran, breathless
> We scrambled to kiss
> the shoes of the killers.

The rush to normalize relations with the Zionist enemy was now widely derided by those who saw it as a mark of Arab weakness. Business was at the heart of this normalization, as was evident from these annual conferences. The original aim was to forge a regional economic order of which Israel would be an integral part and economic cooperation was expected to consolidate Middle East peace. At the first two MENA conferences, Israel had led the way in fostering Peres's vision of a new Middle East that incorporated the Jewish state. Hussein repeatedly promised his people that normalization would produce prosperity. Arafat used to say that, given the right economic climate, he would turn Palestine into a new Singapore. Another major argument advanced by the "scurriers" was that Arab conciliation would encourage Israel to complete the peace process on the Palestinian, Syrian and Lebanese fronts. Arab countries not involved directly in the conflict also accepted this logic. Morocco, Tunisia and Qatar decided to open liaison bureaus in Israel. Qatar even agreed to supply Israel with natural gas.

The critics of the "scurriers," on the other hand, argued that the Arabs should withhold the economic rewards of normalization as their last remaining means of pressure. Saudi Arabia refused to lift the boycott of Israel until a comprehensive peace had been achieved. Netanyahu's election tilted the balance in favour of the critics. He was held up as the embodiment of just how wrong the "scurriers" had been. The critics asked: "Why should we take part in an international economic gathering supposedly designed to underpin regional peace and security with economic cooperation when Israel rejects peace?" Jordan and the Palestinian Authority only sent medium-level delegations. Qatar delayed the opening of its liaison office in Tel Aviv and suspended her natural gas deal. Other governments told their delegations to make no deals with the Israelis. The Egyptians made it plain that since Israel was going back on the peace process, the Arabs would go back on the basic objectives of MENA I and II, and turn MENA III into a forum for inter-Arab business alone.[9]

Bilateral relations between Jordan and Israel fell after the tunnel crisis to their lowest ebb since the treaty was signed. At the popular level, passive scepticism turned into active opposition. At the official level, patience with Israel gave way to a more assertive articulation of Arab and Palestinian positions. Strong American and Arab reaction to "the tunnel uprising" compelled Netanyahu to give way on Hebron, the West Bank city where a small community of militant Jewish settlers ensconced themselves in the middle of a large Palestinian population. Hussein played a modest role in bringing the two warring sides to an agreement. He shuttled between Netanyahu in Tel Aviv and Arafat in Gaza until a compromise was reached. The Hebron Protocol was signed on 15 January 1997. It was a significant step in the Middle East peace process, the first agreement signed by the Likud government and the Palestinians. The protocol divided Hebron into two zones to be governed by different security arrangements. The Palestinian zone covered about 80 percent of Hebron, while the Jewish zone covered the other 20 percent. Palestinian critics pointed out that this formula for coexistence gave the 450 Jewish settlers (who constituted 0.3 percent of the population) the choicest 20 percent of the town's commercial centre, whereas the 160,000 Palestinians got 80 percent subject to numerous restrictions and limitations. The Hebron Protocol, however, also committed Israel to three further redeployments on the West Bank over the next eighteen months.

The Hebron Protocol averted the complete collapse of the Oslo peace process, but the mild optimism it generated was short-lived. Having been compelled to take a relatively conciliatory line over Hebron, Netanyahu adopted a confrontational approach to Jerusalem. By signing the protocol, Netanyahu had broken the Likud taboo on handing over land for peace. So he vowed to strengthen Israel's hold over Jerusalem and to resist any compromise or even meaningful negotiations with the Palestinians over the future of the holy city. He knew that no Arab could accept less than Arafat was demanding: shared sovereignty. But he believed that a forceful unilateral Israeli assertion of control over the city would dispel Arab illusions of recovering the eastern part, illusions that he claimed his Labour predecessors had encouraged. Netanyahu fired the opening shot in the battle for Jerusalem on 19 February with a plan for the construction of 6,500 housing units for 30,000 Israelis at Har Homa in annexed East Jerusalem. Har Homa was a pine-forested hill, south of the city proper, on the road to Bethlehem. Its Arabic name is Jabal Abu Ghunaym. The site was chosen in order to complete the chain of Jewish settlements around Jerusalem and cut off contact between the Arab side of the city and its hinterland in the West Bank. It was a blatant example of the Zionist tactic of creating facts on the ground to pre-empt negotiations. Consequently, every day the Palestinians had less land and Israel had less peace. Jordan joined in the angry Arab chorus of protest at Israel's actions.

In less than a year as prime minister, Netanyahu had destroyed Hussein's trust and driven him to the verge of despair by his arrogance, blatant disregard for written agreements and ceaseless expansionism. At a deeper level, Hussein felt that he could no longer rely on Israel to act as a strategic ally and as a partner on the road to peace. In an unusually strongly worded three-page letter to Netanyahu, Hussein expressed both his concern over the consequences of Israeli actions and his bitter personal disappointment with the man he helped to get elected. The letter is worth quoting at length for the light it sheds on Hussein's state of mind:

Prime Minister,

My distress is genuine and deep over the accumulating tragic actions which you have initiated at the head of the government of Israel, making peace—the worthiest objective of my life—appear more and more like a distant elusive mirage. I could remain aloof if the very lives of all Arabs and Israelis and their future were not fast sliding towards an abyss of bloodshed and disaster, brought about by fear and despair. I frankly cannot accept your repeated excuse of having to act the way you do under great duress and pressure. I cannot believe that the people of Israel seek bloodshed and disaster and oppose peace. Nor can I believe that the most constitutionally powerful prime minister in Israeli history would act on other than his total convictions. The saddest reality that has been dawning on me is that I do not find you by my side in working to fulfil God's will for the final reconciliation of all the descendants of the children of Abraham. Your course of action seems bent on destroying all I believe in or have striven to achieve with the Hashemite family since Faisal the First and Abdullah to the present times . . .

Mr. Prime Minister, if it is your intention to manoeuvre our Palestinian brethren into inevitable violent resistance, then order your bulldozers into the proposed settlement site . . .

Why the apparent continued deliberate humiliation of your so called Palestinian partners? Can any worthwhile relationship thrive in the absence of mutual respect and trust? Why are Palestinians confirming that their agricultural products still rot awaiting entry into Israel and export? Why the delay when it is known that unless work is authorized to commence on the Gaza port, before the end of this month, the complete project will suffer a year's delay? Finally, the Gaza Airport—all of us have addressed the subject numerous times with a view to having a legitimate Palestinian need met and to giving their leaders and people their own free access to the world rather than their present confinement and need to exit and return through other sovereign territories . . .

How can I work with you as a partner and true friend in this confused and confusing atmosphere when I sense an intent to destroy all I worked to build between our peoples and states? Stubbornness over real issues is one thing, but for its own sake, I wonder. In any event I have discovered that you have your own mindset and appear in no need for any advice from a friend.

I deeply regret having to write you this personal message, but it is my sense of responsibility and concern which has prompted me for posterity to do so in the face of the unknown.

     Sincerely,

     Hussein[10]

Ali Shukri delivered the royal missive by hand to the prime minister in his office in Jerusalem. Dore Gold was with him. Netanyahu was unable or unwilling to understand the Jordanian perspective on the events surrounding Har Homa. He claimed that 75 percent of the land they wished to build on had already been bought from its Arab owners, but he offered no proof and Shukri did not believe him. Shukri tried to explain that even if some of the land was bought, the whole operation was seen by Arabs as arbitrary and aggressive. Netanyahu dismissed these arguments and refused to budge.[11] His reply to the king's heart-breaking letter was insensitive and impertinent. He refused to accept any share of the responsibility for the setbacks in the peace process. At the time of the last election, he asserted, the peace process was "in its death throes." He went even further and sought credit for his contribution: "Instead of letting the Oslo agreement die out after the election, I looked for a way to try to revive it."

Netanyahu expressed surprise at the personal tone of the attacks against him. All the specific transgressions listed by the king were brushed aside as the "inevitable difficulties that occasionally crop up in the peace process." Netanyahu made it clear that he remained committed to carrying out the housing construction plan in East Jerusalem. Finally, he urged the king not to allow setbacks on the Palestinian track to affect Jordanian–Israeli relations. "It is our duty to understand our joint historic role and not to allow the obstacles on the Palestinian track to overshadow the understandings reached back in the days of my predecessors," he wrote.[12] It was not clear which particular predecessors or understandings Netanyahu had in mind. But it was difficult to avoid the impression that he was telling the king to mind his own business and not to meddle in Israeli–Palestinian affairs. There was no sign of contrition, no concession to the king's point of view and no trace of a single constructive idea in Netanyahu's reply.

A most tragic event occurred on 13 March when a deranged Jordanian soldier shot and killed seven Israeli schoolgirls and wounded six others on the "Island of Peace" at the Naharayim crossing point in the north. This area had only recently been restored to Jordanian sovereignty under the terms of the peace treaty, and the girls were on a school outing. The king and the queen, who were in Madrid on an official visit, immediately cancelled their trip and turned back to Jordan. "I cannot offer enough condolences or express enough personal sorrow to the mothers, fathers and brothers of these children who fell today," he said when he arrived. He was extremely angry about the breakdown of discipline in the army that had allowed this incident to happen. For years he had been telling all the people around him, and especially the military, that their neighbours had a complex about security, that this had to be taken into account, that they needed constant reassurances. Now he felt let down by the army, and he reprimanded those responsible. Shooting children, he said, is something one must not do in wartime, let alone when they were at peace.[13]

Three days later Hussein made an unprecedented visit to the Israeli village of Beit Shemesh to offer his personal condolences to the families of the victims. At the homes of the stricken families, he went down on his knees and shared in their grief. Hussein's simple humanity was deeply appreciated not just by the families but by the entire Israeli nation. In the Arab world, however, Hussein's gesture was interpreted differently: going down on your knees symbolizes submission and surrender. Hussein insisted that each of his visits be shown on Jordanian television, despite the fury he knew this would arouse among the extremist groups in Jordan. He wanted everyone to take note of the price of violence. "If there is any purpose in my life it will be to make sure that all the children do not suffer the way our generation did," he said to one of the families.[14]

One expression of Hussein's anguish did not receive any publicity: the offer of compensation to the families of the victims. He wanted to help the families in a material way but in keeping with Jewish traditions and customs. So he asked Lord Mishcon for advice and was told to send the sum of money he wanted to give to the president of Israel. Accordingly, Hussein sent a million dollars to President Ezer Weizman. A year later he received a letter that said:

Your Majesty,
Recently we commemorated the year of the terrible tragedy in Naharayim when seven young girls were killed and others were injured.

The people of Israel were most impressed by your visit to the bereaved families in Beit Shemesh and also by your humanitarian gesture of a monetary grant.

I wish to inform you that I invited the families and distributed among them the entire sum you sent. They asked me to convey to you their sincerest thanks and appreciation.[15]

Meanwhile, relations between Israel and the Palestinians continued to deteriorate as the bulldozers moved in to level the hillside at Har Homa. The bulldozers had to be given armed guards. Israeli soldiers clashed constantly with stone-throwing Palestinian youths. The violence spread to other parts of the West Bank. Hamas and Islamic Jihad sent suicide bombers into Israel, and the Palestinian Authority was unable to stop them. Was there anything Israel could do to prevent, or at least to limit, the outburst of violence against its citizens? Was there any link between Israel's backsliding on the Oslo agreements and Yasser Arafat's reluctance to act more decisively against Hamas and Islamic Jihad? Both the head of the Israeli General Security Service and the director of military intelligence were of the opinion that Arafat had no incentive to cooperate with Israel in the fight against Islamic terror as long as he believed that Israel was not complying with the Oslo Accords. Netanyahu rejected their assessment.[16] He regarded terrorist attacks by extremist Palestinian fringe groups as a strategic threat to the State of Israel, and he used these attacks to justify the freezing of the political process.

Hussein's natural optimism was sorely tried. The strain of the faltering peace process was beginning to tell. He had difficulty sleeping at night. His wife explained: "The short-sighted approach of Netanyahu and the hardliners in his government had put terrific pressure on the King to reverse the peace process. Everything he had worked for all his life, every relationship he had painstakingly built on trust and respect, every dream of peace and prosperity he had had for Jordan's children, was turning into a nightmare. I really did not know how much more Hussein could take."[17]

Just as things looked as if they could not get any worse, they did. On Thursday, 25 September 1997, two Mossad agents, carrying forged Canadian passports, tried to assassinate a Jordanian citizen in broad daylight on the streets of the Jordanian capital. The target of the operation was Khalid Mishal, political bureau chief of Hamas in Amman.

Prior to the operation, Hamas claimed responsibility for two consecutive suicide bombs in Jerusalem. It was decided to assassinate Hamas leaders in retaliation, and Mishal was chosen as the first target. The high-tech method chosen was to inject a slow-acting poison into his ear as he entered his office in Amman. The drug used was a synthetic opiate called Fentanyl that leaves no traces in the blood stream. The plan went disastrously wrong. Mishal was injected but not killed, and his bodyguard captured the two Mossad agents. The IDF chief of staff and its director of military intelligence claimed they were unaware of the mission until they heard reports that two Mossad agents had been apprehended by the police and the Mossad station chief in Amman had apparently opposed the mission for fear of damaging relations between Israel and Jordan. But the prime minister gave the go-ahead for this egregious act of political folly regardless. A hit-team of no fewer than eight people had been sent to Amman: two were apprehended by the Jordanian authorities; four others took refuge in the Israeli Embassy after their mission was aborted; a woman doctor and another Mossad agent checked into the Inter-Continental Hotel as a married couple, which they were not.

Hussein, Israel's best friend in the Arab world, said after the failed assassination bid that he felt as if somebody "had spat in his face." His sense of betrayal was all the more acute because three days before the attempt Israeli and Jordanian officials had considered together the problem of Islamist terror. The meeting took place in Amman within the framework of regular security cooperation between the two sides. At the meeting the Jordanian representatives reiterated their commitment to work closely with Mossad in the fight against terror. The king intervened in the dialogue personally to report an offer of a truce from Hamas. The offer was for a thirty-year truce between Israel and the Palestinians that included Hamas. He requested that this offer should be conveyed directly to the prime minister. He was thus all the more surprised and angry when he learned about the bizarre operation in Jordan's capital.

Netanyahu called Hussein as soon as he heard of the failure of the mission. He had apparently not taken into account the possibility that something could go wrong. Netanyahu asked Hussein to receive General Danny Yatom, the head of the Mossad, as soon as possible. He did not indicate the reason for the meeting, and Hussein assumed that it was connected with the Hamas truce proposal. By the time Yatom arrived, Hussein had been fully briefed about the incident. Yatom went by himself in a private aircraft and received a very frosty reception. General Ali Shukri and General Samih Batikhi, the head of the General Intelligence Department, were also there. Yatom and his family had spent the weekend before the operation on holiday in Aqaba and had been entertained by the king in person. How someone he treated as a friend could be involved in such a dastardly act was beyond the king's comprehension. Yatom explained that the two men in police custody were in fact Mossad agents and that their unit was called "Caesaria." Hussein told him that this kind of behaviour could not be tolerated and walked out of the meeting. Batikhi proceeded to lambaste Yatom for betraying their trust. Yatom replied that Mishal was in charge of the terrorist operations of Hamas. The Jordanians retorted that even if this were true, Israel could not take such liberties in their country. Batikhi got very angry and walked out. Yatom had been roundly rebuked and was forced to leave without having obtained any access to, or information on, the perpetrators of the crime. It was one of the shortest meetings in the annals of Israeli–Jordanian relations.

The most urgent problem for the Jordanians was how to save the life of Khalid Mishal, who was in an intensive care unit in hospital. For this they needed the antidote to the poison that had been injected into his ear. Ali Shukri called Dr. Oded Eran, the Israeli ambassador, who had been at his post for only two weeks before the crisis erupted. Eran called the prime minister's office and then called back. Netanyahu was reported as saying that the antidote was a state asset and that he could not reveal it. Shukri threatened to tell the press that Israel, like Iraq, had chemical weapons and had used them against a Jordanian citizen. He also warned that if the antidote was not divulged, Jordan would storm the embassy to capture the four Mossad agents who were holed up there. Eran remonstrated that this would be a violation of the Geneva Convention. Shukri retorted sharply that the Geneva Convention does not authorize embassies to harbour terrorists. He was not bluffing. An army unit was readied to storm the Israeli Embassy. Colonel Abdullah bin Hussein, the king's eldest son and the commander of the special forces, was put in charge of the operation.

It took the intervention of President Clinton to force Israel to relent. Hussein called Clinton to inform him of the crisis and to tell him that the future of the peace treaty was linked to the life of the Jordanian citizen who had been poisoned. If Mishal died, said Hussein, he would go on television that same evening, expose the whole story, suspend the peace treaty and put the attackers on public trial in Jordan. Clinton was dumbfounded and exclaimed about Netanyahu: "This man is impossible!" He added that Netanyahu was harming not only Jordanian and American interests but also jeopardizing the entire peace process in the Middle East. Clinton listened sympathetically as Hussein vented his anger; he tried to calm him down and urged him not to break off relations with Israel. A while later Clinton called to say that Netanyahu had agreed to release the antidote. Shortly before midnight an Israeli doctor arrived in a small aircraft and was taken straight to the hospital. The doctors did not want to take any chances with the sample of the antidote brought by the Israelis. Mishal, who was by now on a respirator, was instead given the correct drug from a supply in the hospital's stores, and he recovered.[18]

Jordan suspended all security cooperation with Israel following the meeting with Yatom. All Israel's efforts to send high-level emissaries were rebuffed by the king. He felt personally betrayed and did not want to see any Israelis. He specifically asked that Halevy should not be involved: he valued the relationship with him and did not want it to be tarnished by this sordid episode. Halevy himself responded to Netanyahu's desperate call for help and left his post in Brussels in haste to present himself in Jerusalem. He did not want his involvement to be made public because he considered that the relationship he had developed with the Hashemite house was a national, and not merely a personal, asset. Halevy looked at the situation from the king's point of view. Hussein had taken the courageous step of leading his country to sign a peace treaty with Israel in the face of bitter opposition from the majority of his citizens. His relationship with the Muslim Brotherhood was a delicate one: it was allied to Hamas, and the attempt on Mishal's life could not have come at a worst time. Israel had placed him in an acutely embarrassing situation, and Israel had to solve his problem in order to solve its own problem. If the king released the eight Israeli agents, he would be seen by his own people as a collaborator with the Mossad. The specific idea that Halevy put forward was the release of Shaikh Ahmed Yassin, the paraplegic spiritual leader of Hamas who had been languishing in an Israeli prison. This would enable the king to release the six agents. There was little support for Halevy's idea, but Netanyahu allowed him to try it out on the king.

Halevy went to Amman on Sunday, 28 September. He was received by Prince Hassan and General Batikhi. After listening to a litany of complaints, he put forward his proposal regarding Shaikh Yassin. Hassan said it was worthy of consideration, but Batikhi took a different line. He was out to exact as much as he could and indicated that the price for resolving the crisis would have to be the release of more prisoners in Israeli hands. In the early afternoon Halevy was taken to see the king, who made no effort to conceal his bitter feelings over what had transpired. But he intimated that he could accept the offer of the release of Shaikh Yassin together with other prisoners yet to be specified. Halevy obtained two other concessions. First, the king allowed him, in the face of strong opposition from Batikhi, to collect the four Mossad operatives from the embassy and take them back to Israel with him. Second, the king agreed that Netanyahu should come over to Amman that very evening to solidify the understandings that were beginning to emerge.

Towards midnight a helicopter left Jerusalem with a large Israeli delegation that included the prime minister; Ariel Sharon, the minister of national infrastructure; Itzhak Mordechai, the minister of defence; Efraim Halevy; Elyakim Rubinstein, the attorney general; and several aides. The king did not want to meet Netanyahu, so he asked Hassan and Batikhi to handle the discussion. They drove a hard bargain. It soon became clear that the release of the two detainees was not imminent. An understanding was reached on the principles of the deal, but the detailed negotiations were left in the hands of first Elyakim Rubinstein and then Ariel Sharon. Halevy, having extricated his prime minister from an exceedingly awkward situation, returned to his post in Brussels.[19] Rubinstein's abiding memory of the meeting is that the king kept repeating, "Why, why, why?"[20]

Sharon was never slow to seize opportunities, and the Mishal Affair allowed him to consolidate his own power and influence at the expense of the prime minister. At the meeting with the king, Sharon dissociated himself from the botched operation, which he described as "a terrible mistake."[21] Sharon's adviser for Arab affairs was Mjali Wahbah, a Druze from Beit Jan in the north and a member of the Knesset who had previously been a lieutenant-colonel in the IDF. Wahbah relates that shortly after he had started to work for Sharon in 1996, Ali Shukri called him and invited him to meet with his king in Amman. Wahbah was probably the only Israeli official who spoke to the king in Arabic. At the meeting Wahbah said he was very moved because it was his first encounter with a king. The king said, "Feel at home, my son." Wahbah spoke about his grandfather, who had met Hussein's grandfather, King Abdullah. The king told Wahbah about his mistake in joining the war against Israel in 1967 and his warning in 1973 that no one had listened to. The meeting lasted five hours, and at the end it was agreed to set up a channel of communication between the palace and Sharon.[22]

After the assassination attempt on Khalid Mishal, the king reluctantly agreed to see Sharon. Shukri had advised the king that Sharon hated Netanyahu's guts and that he was waiting for an opportunity to overthrow him.[23] Sharon spoke in Hebrew to the king, and Wahbah translated into Arabic. Sharon, who had a large farm in the Negev, said, "Your Majesty, if you let me take the two Mossad agents, I'll tie them up like kids. Then, as a punishment for their blunder, I'll sit on them all the way back home and, as you can see, I am not a lightweight." The deal was clinched. Jordan freed all the remaining Mossad operatives in return for the release of Shaikh Ahmad Yassin, 23 Jordanians and 50 Palestinians held in Israeli jails. After the meeting Shukri took Wahbah on one side and said to him, "I have a piece of advice for you. His Majesty does not like your prime minister, to put it mildly. It would be better if from now on you and Sharon handle this matter."[24] Netanyahu trusted Sharon about as much as Sharon trusted him but after the Amman disaster the prime minister handed over to his powerful rival the unofficial "Jordanian portfolio," sidelining David Levy, the hapless foreign minister, in the process. In the past Hussein and his brother used to worry about whether Israel and the PLO would collaborate to overthrow the house of Hashem. Now it was the turn of the Palestinians to worry about whether Hussein and Ariel Sharon, of all people, were in cahoots against them. It was a curious twist to the ever-changing triangular relationship between the principal parties to the conflict over Palestine.

Jordanian officials linked the botched assassination attempt to the peace process. They recalled that Hamas had hitherto refrained from mounting terrorist attacks outside the borders of Israel and the occupied territories. They reasoned that by trying to assassinate Mishal outside these borders, Israel intended to create an intolerable provocation. This would have compelled Hamas to react and to extend the terrorist war to new areas. Israel would have blamed Arafat for the new wave of violence, and the peace process would have once again been put on hold.[25] In this context the Hamas offer of a thirty-year truce that Hussein communicated to Netanyahu assumes added significance. Netanyahu was later to claim that he did not receive the offer until after the operation was over. Nobody in Jordan believed him. The message was given by Hussein himself to David Silberg, a Mossad official for whom he had a particular liking, for urgent transmission to the prime minister. Silberg told his Jordanian colleagues that he made sure that his report was on the prime minister's desk as soon as he got back— three days before the attack on Mishal. Hussein's conclusion was simple: Netanyahu was out to destroy peace. Hussein thought that Netanyahu was sending him a message to say that the peace with Jordan was not important to him and that peace with the Palestinians mattered even less. The fact that Mishal was hit after getting Hamas's offer of a moratorium meant that this was the Israeli answer: that Israel was not interested. So Hamas carried on with its operations to the detriment of Jordan, the Palestinians and Israel.[26]

By ordering the operation in Amman, Netanyahu showed himself to be irresponsible and short-sighted. The respected British weekly the *Economist* featured Netanyahu on its 11 October 1997 cover with the caption "Serial Bungler." The consequences of this particular bungle were very grave. Jordan froze security cooperation with Israel, asked for the closure of the Mossad station in Amman, and sought the resignation of General Yatom.[27] The operation also weakened Hussein, whose peace treaty with Israel remained as unpopular among his own people as it was popular among Israelis. The release of Shaikh Yassin, and his triumphal return to Gaza via Amman, made it more difficult for Arafat to meet Israel's demands for a mass arrest of Hamas activists. The fact that Israel was forced to release Shaikh Yassin increased his prestige and that of the organization he had founded during the first intifada. Thus, by relentlessly concentrating on Hamas, Netanyahu ended up raising it to a position of pivotal importance. By his own actions he came close to destroying one of the central planks in his policy towards the Palestinians: the refusal to negotiate until the violence was halted. Just as his opening of the tunnel in the Old City of Jerusalem forced him to reverse his policy of not trading land for peace, so the Mishal fiasco undermined his case for refusing to implement the Oslo Accords until the Palestinian Authority uprooted the infrastructure of Hamas.

Following a visit to the United States, during which many American Jewish leaders had expressed to them their dismay over Netanyahu's approach, Hussein and his wife paid a visit to London and stayed in their house in Kensington. Netanyahu asked for an urgent meeting there, apparently having been urged by his US Jewish supporters to repair relations with Hussein. Queen Noor was in the shower the next evening when Netanyahu arrived. The protocol officers had agreed that he alone would be going to the house, so she was startled to be informed that Mrs. Netanyahu had unexpectedly arrived with him. Noor went down to the drawing room with her hair half dried, determined to be hospitable and entirely apolitical, but she unintentionally stepped into a minefield. She tried to stress the positive impact on both societies—Arab and Israeli—of the institutional, business and individual contacts that had developed in recent years. As part of the progress in the peace process, they had been very encouraged to see that Israeli and Arab historians and scholars were reviewing textbooks and historical accounts with a view to correcting the propaganda on both sides. Mrs. Netanyahu bristled. "What do you mean, propaganda?" she said. Noor replied that one example of a distorting myth was the description of Palestine as "a land without a people for people without a land," when in fact generations of Palestinians had been living in Palestine for thousands of years. Sarah Netanyahu bristled again. "What do you mean?" she said. "When the Jews came to this area, there were no Arabs here. They came to find work when we built cities. There was nothing here before that." "I am certain many of your own historians would agree that that is not accurate," Noor replied. The exchange was quite an insight for her. Binyamin Netanyahu was known for his conservative rigidity, but to hear an erroneous version of history stated so emphatically by his wife in private was truly alarming. Did they really believe myths like this one? Noor wondered. And if so, what other misconceptions might impede their working together for a lasting peace?[28]

Disillusion with the treaty and with Israel undermined the king's position. He reacted by adopting increasingly authoritarian measures to suppress dissent. Democracy in Jordan had never been a historic right of the people but something that was granted in small doses by the monarch. Democracy did not develop its own impetus but remained subordinate to the royal agenda. Peace and democracy were intended to go hand in hand, but in practice the reverse happened: setbacks in the peace process impeded progress towards democracy and in some respects even reversed it. The press law was amended to enable the government to take punitive measures against opposition newspapers and weeklies. The king, who had been an excellent listener in the past, stopped listening. The man who had been renowned for his patience became angry and irascible, and the vision of a constitutional monarchy that had inspired him in the late 1980s faded away.[29] He paid no attention to parliament, and even more than before acted as his own prime minister and foreign minister. He also became increasingly intolerant of criticism of his policies, treating opposition to normalization as illegitimate. Repression reached such a level that the main Islamic opposition parties, and some mainstream politicians such as former Prime Minister Ahmad Obeidat, decided to boycott the parliamentary elections of 4 November 1997, which robbed them of their legitimacy.

Towards the end of the year Hussein made the decision to re-engage as a major player in the negotiations between Israel and the Palestinian Authority. On 4 December he issued an open letter to Prime Minister Abdul Salam Majali on Jordan's position regarding all the items on the final-status agenda. The background was "what appears to be the continuous attempt on the part of the Israeli prime minister to demolish the Palestinian–Israeli Oslo agreements." The three main items were security, Jerusalem and sovereignty. There were Likud claims that Israel needed to retain the Jordan Valley for its own protection but also to protect Jordan against an irredentist Palestinian entity. Hussein made it clear that "these claims are baseless and they are categorically and unequivocally rejected." On the other hand, Hussein highlighted Israel's commitment to Jordan's special role in the Muslim holy places in the Old City of Jerusalem as mandated in the treaty. Jordan was in a weak position here because it had to rely on Israel to serve as its advocate when the Jerusalem issue arose in the final-status talks. Finally, Hussein announced his intention to play a direct role in the next phase of negotiations. Now that the final disposition of the Palestine question was being negotiated, he wanted to be deeply involved, every step of the way, though not actually present at the table.[30]

On the Israeli side, Ariel Sharon started to play a more important role in the conduct of relations with Jordan. As we have seen, Sharon had been one of the loudest trumpeters within the Likud of the clarion call that "Jordan is Palestine." When the peace treaty was submitted by the Labour government to the Knesset for ratification, Sharon had refused to vote for it; he would not support any agreement that required Israel to concede territory.³¹ Sharon, however, changed his tune when he saw how popular the peace with Jordan turned out to be with the Israeli public. He therefore reinvented himself as a reformed character and as an advocate of a strong Jordan. As minister of infrastructure he was directly responsible for the water aspects of the peace treaty. During his first visit to Jordan after taking up his post, he had a private conversation with the king. Sharon explained why in the past he used to say that "Jordan is Palestine." The king heard him out without making any comment. Sharon added philosophically that men grow older, circumstances change, and opinions are corrected. After that meeting Sharon demonstrated on every occasion his commitment to close relations with Jordan.³² His abandonment of the plan to turn Jordan into an alternative homeland for the Palestinians gave the regime much satisfaction. His known opposition to Arafat and to the idea of Palestinian statehood went down well with the Jordanian hardliners, who were sometimes referred to as the "Jordanian Likud."

Security cooperation between Jordan and Israel was resumed by early 1998, but the atmosphere remained chilly. Netanyahu's announcement that he had no intention of withdrawing from the Jordan Valley rekindled Hussein's wrath. Hussein sent Netanyahu a letter denouncing the statement as an insult to his kingdom and a violation of Israel's commitments. The replacement of General Danny Yatom by Efraim Halevy as head of the Mossad restored some of the old warmth to the relations between Amman and Jerusalem.³³ Netanyahu, however, wanted to demonstrate to hardline Republicans and to the conservative Jews in America that Israel under his leadership was a strategic asset, that he was delivering, that he was not following in the footsteps of Itzhak Rabin. Rabin had wanted to make peace with Iraq in order to surround Syria and place it in a tight spot. Syria would have been surrounded by Israel, Jordan, Iraq and Turkey. Netanyahu's message to the American right was that US interests, and the Israel lobby's interests, were his interests. He would not make peace with Iraq even if that would isolate Syria. Indeed, he was prepared to go to war with Iraq: he had both the political will and the means to launch an aerial strike. The Pentagon had delivered twenty special F-15s to Israel. These could fly fully armed all the way to Baghdad and back without refuelling. One day Netanyahu came up with a plan to attack Iraq. He claimed that Saddam was still developing weapons of mass destruction and long-range missiles. He therefore wanted to attack these sites, and his plans were leaked to the press.[34]

Hussein was worried. Should the IDF overfly Jordan to attack Iraq, Jordan would be accused of colluding with Israel over the air raid. The climate in Jordan was one of disappointment with the meagre fruits of peace, and an attack on Iraq through Jordanian airspace was bound to provoke renewed calls for the renunciation of the treaty. Hussein knew that the majority of Israel's military leaders were against the plan; that Netanyahu was pressing them as he had pressed Danny Yatom into the Mishal Affair. Hussein had a secure telephone line to Netanyahu, but he did not use it because he had given up on him. Instead Hussein invited Efraim Halevy to a meeting in Amman on 11 February 1998 to express his concerns. Hassan and Shukri were also present. Hussein said that Israel would be completely on its own if it decided to attack Iraq. He also noted that no progress had been achieved in the talks between Israel and the Palestinian Authority since the Hebron Protocol and that this indicated that Netanyahu had a different agenda. Granting Israel access to attack Iraq through Jordan was unthinkable because the Jordanian public still strongly identified with Iraq. Both Jordan and Israel would suffer from an unprovoked attack on Iraq; it would be a terrible mistake. Hassan insisted that Israel had to respect the treaty and all other understandings between them. Halevy was apparently convinced by these arguments. He understood very well that if Israel attacked Iraq through Jordanian airspace, Jordan would be accused of collusion. The conversation reverted to final-status issues. Hussein said that Netanyahu was deliberately driving a wedge between Jordan and the Palestinian Authority, and Hassan described him as *insan la'im jiddan*—"a very nasty person." Both Hussein and Hassan emphasized their commitment to the resumption of negotiations because the absence of a settlement between Israel and the Palestinians posed a threat to Jordan.[35]

Hussein's health suddenly deteriorated in 1998. Binyamin Netanyahu, his nemesis, was called Bibi for short, and in jest Queen Noor began to call her husband's malady the Bibi virus, alluding to the bio-terrorism episode in Amman the previous autumn.[36] In fact, as Queen Noor knew better than anyone, her husband's first brush with cancer happened back in 1992. Moreover, Bibi most probably would not have been elected in 1996 had it not been for her husband's catastrophic mis-calculation. By interfering in the Israeli elections, Hussein helped to inflict Bibi not just on the Palestinians, Jordanians and Arabs in general but on Israel as well.

During Hussein's annual check-up at the Mayo Clinic in Rochester, Minnesota, in May 1998, the medical staff came up with theories involving various obscure viruses, but they did not identify any other anomalies in his system. Hussein and his wife left the clinic and headed for Washington, D.C., where he met President Clinton and Sec-retary of State Madeleine Albright to talk about reviving the stalled peace process. Then they went on to England for a week, to celebrate their twentieth wedding anniversary at Buckhurst Park in Ascot. Hus-sein seemed to have shaken off the fevers, and was happy and relaxed. On their return to Jordan the fevers came back, this time fiercer and more debilitating. In July 1998 Hussein went again to the Mayo Clinic. This time he was diagnosed with non-Hodgkin's lymphoma, with abnormal cells in multiple locations.[37] He was to stay in the clinic until the end of the year. During his absence his younger brother Hassan, who had been crown prince and heir apparent since 1965, acted as regent.

28. The Last Journey

The Mayo Clinic in Rochester, Minnesota, was king Hussein's home during the second half of 1998, before his last journey home. The cancer in his lymph glands caused occasional fever, weight loss, fatigue and extreme exhaustion. To deal with it, the doctors prescribed six courses of chemotherapy over five months, followed by a bone marrow transplant. Hussein was given a VIP suite that included a kitchen, a dining room and a little room for Queen Noor to sleep in next to his. The rest of their family and entourage stayed in a nearby hotel connected to the hospital by a tunnel. All Hussein's children and various other family members came and went. Hamzah, his beloved eldest son with Noor, spent several months by his father's side during the break between graduation from Harrow and the beginning of his first term as an officer cadet at the Royal Military Academy at Sandhurst. In between cycles of chemotherapy Hussein and his wife would fly to River House outside Washington or go on day trips around Minnesota in a silver Volkswagen Beetle she had bought shortly after their arrival. Throughout his time at the clinic, Hussein put a brave face on his illness, and, at least outwardly, projected hope and optimism. He had a heavy workload, countless messages from well-wishers and an endless stream of visitors. The doctors insisted that he had to rest to conserve his energy and Noor became the gatekeeper who enforced the doctors' orders. In her book *Leap of Faith* she gives a moving description of her husband's battle against cancer, of the agony of his final days, and of their travels back and forth between the Mayo Clinic, London and Amman.[1]

Hussein was the most undemanding of patients, profusely apologetic for any inconvenience he may have caused and almost pathetically grateful for every little thing that was done for him. He bore his suffering stoically, retained his gracious manners in adversity, and radiated warmth and humanity. All the doctors, nurses and staff in the clinic fell under his spell. His kindness and courtesy extended to everyone, regardless of their status and position. When he heard that one of the cleaners had a birthday, for example, he organized a jolly party for her in his suite, with refreshments, cards and presents. The woman was so moved, she cried uncontrollably.

Throughout his stay in the Mayo, Hussein kept in close touch with affairs at home. The year 1998 was a difficult one for Jordan and not just because of the illness and absence of the monarch. Living standards were declining. The annual growth rate of the GDP had dropped from 10 percent in 1992–94 to 5.6 percent in 1995, and then to 1.5 percent during 1996–98. The population was now growing at a faster rate than the GDP, resulting in a fall in per capita income.[2] The general sense of frustration was exacerbated by bureaucratic lethargy and incompetence. A scandal involving the contamination of the water supply to the capital led to the dismissal of the government of Abdul Salam Majali. He was replaced by Fayez Tarawneh, the former ambassador to the United States and chief negotiator with Israel. The new government faced the daunting task of restoring the people's confidence by ensuring transparency as they contended with a stagnant economy and a bloated bureaucracy. Prince Hassan continued the "national dialogue" that his brother had initiated with all segments of the public, and especially with the opposition. This did not produce any significant policy changes or any dramatic improvements, but it did have a pacifying effect on the domestic scene.[3]

Prince Hassan performed his duties as regent with great dedication, energy and efficiency. But, though he won the respect of the intellectuals and the technocrats, he failed to gain the affection of the masses. He was said to be aloof and to lack the common touch. His relations with the army were rather strained in part because he was not a military man himself and, more seriously, because of his open criticism of the leaders of the army. Moreover, the army was rooted in the rural Bedouin population, and Hassan did not have this avenue to the tribes. The money that was given by the regime to the Bedouins to secure their support came from the army coffers. Because Hassan did not dispense subsidies to the Bedouins directly, he did not enjoy the power of patronage that went with them. Hassan did have close relations with some of the Bedouin tribes, but the relationship was personal rather than institutional. His relations with successive prime ministers were not trouble-free either, reaching rock bottom with Abdul Karim Kabariti, who had been appointed on 19 March 1997. It was probably true that Hassan micro-managed the government more than was wise, doing so even more after becoming regent, but that was his character. At no point before or during his regency did Hassan try to build a power base of his own. On the contrary, he alienated many potential supporters in the government and in the army by his call for accountability, by his promise to root out corruption and by his outspoken attacks on vested interests.

With a touch of hyperbole, Hassan once described his brother and himself as one mind and soul in two bodies.[4] He looked up to Hussein, he was devoted to him, and he was extremely hurt by the false rumours of disloyalty that his opponents put about. Unlike his brother, Hassan was a steady and systematic policy-maker and a meticulous record-keeper. Every Thursday he sent a full report to his brother at the Mayo on the events, discussions and decisions of the previous week.[5] Nevertheless, Kabariti, both as prime minister and as chief of the royal court, was much more devoted to Hussein than to Hassan, perhaps understandably. Like Hussein's other close aides, Kabariti enjoyed the kind of direct access and personal contact that was now beginning to be denied to the regent. None of these aides was particularly sympathetic to Hassan, and most were harshly critical of him.

Relations between Hassan and Noor were correct rather than cordial. Hassan did not like Noor's pillow-talk access to the king on policy matters, and Sarvath, Hassan's Pakistani wife, did not like the way her husband was treated by the strong-willed Noor. Hassan did not visit his brother at Mayo even once; not because he did not want to but because he was deflected, being told that, if he went to the Mayo, the people at home would conclude that the king was dying. Hassan was kept in the dark about his brother's real state of health. He never spoke directly to the king's American doctors. Consequently, the sudden deterioration in his brother's health in the autumn of 1998 took him by surprise. As the issue of succession came to the fore, the court of the ailing king in a foreign land became thick with rumours and intrigues. Family feuds were added to bitter political rivalries to produce a scene fit for a Shakespearean tragedy. The title of Hussein's autobiography, *Uneasy Lies the Head*, was in fact based on a line from Shakespeare. The actual line from *Henry IV, Part II* runs: "Uneasy lies the head that wears a crown."

One of the chief plotters against Hassan was General Samih Batikhi, the head of the General Intelligence Department, the Mukhabarat. Batikhi was widely rumoured to be using his position to line his own pockets, and five years later he was in fact charged with corruption and put in prison. He also had ideas above his station. The head of the Jordanian secret service is meant to be a soldier, not a politician, but Batikhi persistently dabbled in politics and accumulated in his own hands considerable power and influence. Not content with this, he aspired to become a king-maker, perhaps in order to preserve his power and ill-gotten wealth. It was clear that if Hassan became king, this would not be possible. Hassan's zealous campaign against corruption had won him few friends in high places. There was a strong anti-Hassan lobby in Amman, and Batikhi was at its head. Unlike Hassan, Batikhi knew the real state of the king's health, and, also unlike Hassan, he had regular access to the king. There is an old saying that "Near and sly beats fair and square who isn't there," and Batikhi was near and sly. Hussein's main source of information on the affairs of his kingdom was none other than General Batikhi. Batikhi used to fly to the Mayo at regular intervals and hold long sessions in private with Hussein. It is a fair guess that Batikhi made the most of this opportunity to drip poison in the king's ear about the regent. If Hussein's entourage began to resemble a Byzantine court, Batikhi was chiefly responsible for the transformation.

As his health began to fail, Hussein became more and more obsessed with the responsibilities of his Hashemite heritage inherited from his great-grandfather and grandfather, which he had tried to discharge throughout his life.[6] Now he was determined to secure the line of succession. Batikhi was aware of Hussein's anxieties and exploited them to further his own ends. Having discredited Hassan and planted doubts in the king's mind about his suitability for kingship, Batikhi began to promote his alternative candidate for the succession: Prince Abdullah, the king's eldest son. Batikhi told Hussein that Abdullah was a good soldier, that he was widely respected, and that he had the strong support of the army behind him. The message was clear, and it did not have to be stated in so many words: the house of Hashem would be safer in the hands of the soldier-prince than in the hands of the would-be philosopher-king.

Prince Abdullah was largely an unknown quantity. Within the army he was reputed to be a tough, capable and courageous soldier. Outside the army little was known about him. He was the eldest son of the king by his English wife, Princess Muna, and he had followed the family tradition by going to the Royal Military Academy at Sandhurst before joining the Jordanian Army. Having an English mother was not an advantage because, although she converted to Islam, her son was not considered to be a pure Arab. Moreover, because Abdullah spoke English at home and had received his training in Britain and America, his command of classical Arabic was less than perfect. On the other hand, a number of things worked in Abdullah's favour. First, he was a handsome young man and very like his father in many ways. Second, he fitted neatly into the Hashemite line of succession because he bore the name Abdullah and his first-born son was called Hussein. Third, Abdullah was not a complete stranger to the title of crown prince. He had been named as crown prince three days after his birth on 30 January 1962 in accordance with the 1952 constitution. But it was a turbulent era, with frequent assassination attempts against the king, and to have an infant crown prince would have been risky for the Hashemite dynasty in the event of regicide. Therefore, in 1965, when Hassan reached the age of eighteen, the constitution was amended to make it possible for any brother of the king to be a crown prince, and Hassan was appointed because he was considered a safer bet than the mentally unstable middle brother, Muhammad bin Talal. So the appointment of Abdullah as crown prince could be seen as simply the restoration of his birthright. Fourth, Abdullah's beautiful wife, Rania, was a Palestinian with the potential to draw the support of the Palestinian segment of the population. Last but not least, as an officer in the army, Abdullah had a natural avenue to the tribes and hence the potential to build a strong power base in the rural parts of the country.

Abdullah had not been groomed to be king and his father had not spoken about him as a possible successor, but from early 1998 he was accorded a steadily higher public profile. He was given an office in the royal court, and he was seen more often at his father's side. In March, Abdullah accompanied his father on a visit to the United States and took part in some of his meetings. In May, on the forty-fifth anniversary of Hussein's ascent to the throne, Abdullah, who was the officer commanding the Special Forces, was promoted from the rank of colonel to that of major-general. His promotion combined with his popularity, not to mention his pedigree, made him a credible candidate for the post of deputy chief of staff and eventually chief of staff.[7]

Hussein's own attitude towards the Hashemite succession was constantly evolving and essentially equivocal. For Hussein, thoughts about changing the succession were nothing new. After his first brush with cancer in 1992, he had begun to think aloud about the subject in the presence of his close aides. Adnan Abu-Odeh recalls a flight to Brunei with the king and his favourite nephew, Prince Talal bin Muhammad. The king sought Abu-Odeh's reaction to some new ideas about the future of the family (Talal was not sitting with them during this conversation). He was vague but did say the following: "My brother Muhammad, because of his illness, was excluded and I chose my younger brother. Who is to come after my brother?" The king was not talking about replacing Prince Hassan but wondering who should come after him. He wanted to see justice achieved in the family after Hassan. The king had expressed his love, affection and respect for Talal on many occasions. He now asked Abu-Odeh to educate him in the affairs of state. The king thought highly of Talal but the context was one of being fair, of not excluding his other brother, Prince Muhammad, from being a successor to King Abdullah I through his children.[8]

Hussein's chequered private life complicated the question of the succession. He had five sons: Abdullah and Faisal from his second marriage; Ali from his third marriage; Hamzah and Hashim from his fourth marriage. Hamzah was said to be his favourite son. He closely resembled his father in physical appearance and in manner; he was also brought up bilingually, with a very impressive command of classical Arabic and a knowledge of the Koran. Queen Noor, who had converted to Islam just before her marriage, brought up her eldest son to be an Arab king. She was rumoured to be lobbying her husband to replace his brother with their son as crown prince and heir-apparent. On Hamzah's eighteenth birthday Hussein sent him an open letter stating that the prince was destined for "great achievements" and pointing out that he himself had been eighteen when he ascended the throne. The letter indicated that Hamzah was being groomed for bigger and better things. Hussein's transparent attempt to advance his favourite son's fortunes was assumed to reflect Queen Noor's growing influence behind the scenes, but it was done without her knowledge.[9]

Marwan Kasim, as chief of the royal court in 1995–6, also heard the king talk about the young generation of Hashemite princes, with particular reference to Hamzah. Before Hamzah could become heir to the throne, a constitutional amendment would be necessary, as the constitution stipulated that the crown prince could be only one of the king's brothers or his eldest son. On one occasion the king told Kasim that he wanted to introduce the following article into the constitution: "The crown prince of my crown prince will be Hamzah bin Hussein." Kasim took legal advice, which confirmed that such a change would be possible; but he feared that it would be fraught with political risks, so he told the king that this was a matter between himself and his brother.[10] Hussein also periodically raised the idea of a Hashemite family council, whose main task would be to choose a successor to Hassan from the pool of young princes. As his sister Basma understood it at the time, he was looking for ways and means of modernizing and invigorating the monarchy by drawing on the talents of its younger members.[11]

Speculation about Hassan's future refused to die down. At first Hussein tried to scotch it. In mid August he dismissed rumours concerning the succession to the throne as "nonsensical": he stressed that the succession was firmly in the hands of HRH Crown Prince El Hassan, and that speculation to the contrary was "out of line." When an Israeli paper reported American doubts about Hassan, Secretary of State Madeleine Albright called Hassan and assured him that the report was untrue. Hussein subsequently reiterated his "unwavering" confidence in his brother, "who has shouldered his responsibilities and performed his duties fully. As for what may transpire after that in the future . . . there is no justification at all for raising the subject now."[12]

One of the most difficult duties that Hassan had to perform as regent was to stand in for his brother as a facilitator in the Israeli–Palestinian negotiations on final status. Yet he discharged this role with distinction. Jordan was not a participant in the final-status talks, but it expected to play a pivotal role. As Prince Hassan put it, Jordan "would endeavour to be a centre of gravity." Jordan had a vital interest in these negotiations: it could not afford to shoulder the political costs of a collapsing peace process. The person chiefly responsible for the impasse was, predictably, the Israeli prime minister Binyamin Netanyahu. To break the impasse President Clinton convened a summit meeting at the Wye Plantation with Netanyahu and Arafat. Wye is a conference centre on the Chesapeake about an hour and a half's drive from Washington, D.C. The Wye summit opened on 17 October 1998 and lasted five days. Deadlock was reached after a few days of bad-tempered talks, and Netanyahu threatened to pack his bags and leave. Clinton called Hussein at the Mayo Clinic, where preparations were being made for his upcoming bone-marrow transplant, and asked for his advice on the stalled peace talks. Hussein immediately offered to go to the Plantation to help, no matter what the doctors said. Clinton accepted the offer.

By this time Netanyahu had become just about everybody's pet hate at the Mayo. The doctors and nurses shared the joke that their royal patient was afflicted by the Bibi bug. Few people, however, realized how seriously ill Hussein was when he again volunteered his services as a peacemaker. He was feeling frail and physically exhausted. Queen Noor accompanied him to Wye almost literally in a nursing capacity. They went to River House, their home on the Potomac, for a rest and the next day travelled on to Wye Mills on the president's helicopter, *Marine 1.* On landing, they were taken to Houghton House, a lovely private home in the grounds overlooking the Wye River. First the American negotiators and then the Palestinians arrived to brief the visitor. "Clinton looks totally exhausted and fed up," Noor noted in her journal. "The Palestinians are shocked, some to tears, by their first sight of Hussein since his illness began."[13] Dennis Ross, the chief peace processor, detailed the preparations for Hussein's arrival as well as his contribution to the proceedings:

The King's lymphoma was advanced and he was highly susceptible to infection; the Secretary announced to all of us that we needed to rub a special disinfectant soap on our hands shortly before greeting him. The State Department's Chief of Protocol walked around the table squeezing the soap from a bottle onto the hands of President Clinton, Arafat, Netanyahu, and the rest of us. This act and the gravity of the King's physical appearance—bald, gaunt, and gray—made the moment extremely poignant.

After the King greeted everyone, the President summarized where we were, going over each of the issues . . . When the President finished, the King spoke movingly of his being with us, the importance of the progress that was now being made, his expectation that we would finish this evening, and the need to put the remaining differences in perspective: "These differences pale in comparison to what is at stake. After agreement both sides will look back and not even recall these issues. It is now time to finish, bearing in mind the responsibility that both leaders have to their people and especially the children."

When he concluded, he again walked slowly around the table shaking hands. Arafat refrained from giving him his customary kiss on both cheeks, instead kissing his shoulder in order to avoid making contact with his skin.

The King's appearance and words moved us all. A pall hung over the table, and for ten minutes or so Bibi and Arafat spoke about the King's humanity and dedication and commitment to peace.[14]

Hussein's emotional appeal to the parties to rise above politics and work towards a better future for their children changed the tone of the talks but not for long. Hussein and his wife left Wye that evening to go home to River House so he could sleep in his own bed. When the negotiators resumed work on the specific issues at hand, Netanyahu dug in his heels again, citing domestic politics as his excuse. Even on a minor issue, the number of Palestinian prisoners to be released by Israel, his behaviour was erratic and baffling. Clinton was irate; he paced back and forth and told his aides: "That SOB doesn't want a deal. He is trying to humiliate Arafat and me in the process. What the hell does he expect Arafat to do in that situation?"[15]

Late that night Clinton called Hussein at River House and told him that they had again reached a dead end and that Netanyahu's plane was being readied for departure. Hussein convinced Clinton to hold firm and not to give in to Netanyahu's demands. If Netanyahu carried out his threat to leave, Hussein suggested that he and Clinton should hold a press conference to tell the world what had happened and to pin the responsibility for failure on Netanyahu. Hussein went to bed that night not knowing what the morning would bring, but Netanyahu turned out to be bluffing. In the morning the Israeli was still around, and the rollercoaster continued. Clinton asked Hussein to return to Wye for last-minute trouble-shooting, and back he went. "You cannot afford to fail," Hussein told the two Middle Eastern leaders and their aides. "You owe this to your people, to your children, to future generations." The two sides kept working all that day and all that night, until, at dawn, they had a deal. It was a modest one but better than failure. Israel agreed to return in stages 13 percent of the West Bank to the Palestinians and to release some Palestinian prisoners. The peace process was still alive, and Clinton invited the king and the queen to participate in the signing ceremony at the White House on 23 October.[16]

This was a high-profile media event, with the president acting as an accomplished master of ceremonies. People who saw Hussein on television screens round the world were shocked by his loss of hair and weight. But he sounded forceful as he presented his case for peace between long-standing enemies. "We quarrel, we agree. We are friendly, we are not friendly," he said. "But we have no right to dictate through irresponsible action or narrow-mindedness the future of our children and their children's children. There has been enough destruction. Enough death. Enough waste. It is time that, together, we occupy a place beyond ourselves, our peoples, that is worthy of them under the sun, the descendants of the children of Abraham."[17] Hussein received many accolades for his contribution to the successful outcome of the summit. President Clinton remarked that the king was physically the weakest and the most fragile among them but morally the strongest.[18]

The Jordanians portrayed the summit as a service to vital Jordanian interests and as an illustration of their country's indispensable regional role. They also saw the king's participation as an expression of international recognition of his personal stature and prestige.[19] In retrospect, Hussein's departure from his sickbed to support and guide the negotiators at Wye may be seen as his last practical contribution to the cause of peace. Hussein would be nominated for a Nobel Prize in 1998 for all his years of effort towards peace in the Middle East. The prize was ultimately awarded to the political leaders of Northern Ireland, but he was honoured by the nomination.

Hussein had a bone marrow tap when they returned to the Mayo, his fifth or sixth, but this one was particularly agonizing to watch. He was under a general anaesthetic and did not feel anything, but watching them wrench his body around and then violently break through the bone was so disturbing that a new nurse observing the procedure fainted. Noor empathized with her, as she was herself shaken by the brutal torment that her husband's body had to endure. The bone marrow was donated by Hussein's sister Basma and his brother Muhammad, the only members of his family whose blood was compatible for harvesting cells for a transplant. Hassan offered to help, but his blood was of a different type. Hussein gave an interview to Jordan Television, telling his people that the latest test showed no trace of lymphoma. "Thank God that everything is proceeding in a good manner," he said. "By God's will, this will be the final stage of treatment, after which I will return home." The Mayo Clinic issued its own statement. "His Majesty is in complete remission from lymphoma," the clinic said, and went on to explain that he would have an auto-transplant of his own healthy stem cells, a standard procedure to ensure a permanent remission.[20]

At about this time an incident occurred that may have affected Hussein's attitude towards his brother and heir-apparent. The Israeli newspaper *Yediot Aharonot* published an article that reported American sources as saying that Hussein had only three months to live. Randa Habib inadvertently became a player as well as a reporter in the events that unfolded subsequently. Habib was a French journalist of Lebanese origins who had headed the office of the Agence France Presse in Jordan since 1987 and enjoyed privileged access to the king. The agency's Jerusalem office called her that morning because they wanted to pick up the story, but she told them to wait until she got a reaction from the palace. She expected a prompt official denial. Yet all her efforts in the course of the next four hours to get a comment from the regent's office were in vain. She asked Prime Minister Tarawneh whether the king was dying, and he vigorously disputed this assessment. When she asked him why he was not issuing an official denial, he looked embarrassed. She then called Foreign Minister Abdul Ilah al-Khatib and asked him the same question. He replied that they had instructions not to comment. Habib concluded that Hassan had a hidden agenda—that he wanted Jordanians to hear the story and get used to the idea that their king was dying. She did not know how the king found out, but the next day he called her and said, "Thank you for what you have done. I always knew I could count on you. Always follow your gut feeling." Habib found out later that Hussein was very hurt when he learned that his brother would not deny the rumour about his imminent death. In her judgement, this incident was instrumental in sealing Hassan's fate.[21]

The Jordanian constitution states that an absence of the monarch from the country for over four months, while parliament is in recess, requires the convening of parliament for a special session. Parliament was duly convened on 22 November for a session that was no more than a mere formality. Prime Minister Fayez Tarawneh made a statement on the monarch's health, claiming that he had fully recovered and was to return home in the near future. Six days later Prince Hassan opened the regular session of parliament with the traditional speech from the throne. Despite these official announcements, all kinds of rumours continued to circulate about plans to change the succession. Some journalists reported that Queen Noor was tirelessly campaigning for her son Hamzah to replace her brother-in-law as crown prince, while others suggested that Hussein's second wife, Princess Muna, was lobbying on behalf of her son Abdullah. Abdullah himself told a journalist that he was proud of the fact that his father was called Abu Abdullah and that, constitutionally, there was nothing to prevent him from becoming king. Assuming the posture of a senior sibling, he contended that speculation was placing unnecessary pressure on Hamzah and that he should be allowed to grow up in peace. When asked whether he himself wanted to be king, Abdullah evaded the question, arguing that whatever he might say could be misinterpreted.[22]

Anyone could speculate about the future of Prince Hassan and the chances of the other candidates for the Hashemite throne, and journalists had a field day. Only one man, however, had the power to make changes. A major reason for the uncertainty surrounding the succession was that Hussein rarely spoke, even in private, about the subject. In the past he had often acted decisively and even impulsively, but on this matter he experienced great difficulty in making up his mind. Hussein was torn between his sense of duty towards his younger brother, who had served him so loyally for the past thirty-four years, and his love for two of his sons, Abdullah and Hamzah. Hussein faced a complex choice between demoting his brother there and then or allowing his brother to succeed but arranging for the succession to return to his line of the family after Hassan's reign. Hassan's son Rashid was nineteen years old, and, if matters were allowed to follow their natural constitutional course, Rashid would succeed upon his father's death. Hussein was isolated in the Mayo and cut off from contact with his brother. His illness, the chemotherapy and the gruelling treatment that he had to undergo made it all the more difficult for him to think clearly and to reach a final conclusion. It is a natural human tendency to put off unpleasant choices, and Hussein was not immune to this. He procrastinated and procrastinated until his own imminent death forced him to make a decision.

After Queen Noor, the person who spent most time with Hussein in his last months was his ADC, Colonel Hussein al-Majali. He was the son of Hazza' al-Majali, the prime minister who had been assassinated by Syrian agents on 29 August 1960. Hussein Majali was seven months old when his father was assassinated. Hussein became his guardian, mentor, idol and, eventually, his friend. Majali reciprocated the king's kindness with fierce loyalty and boundless devotion. He was at the king's side throughout the last seven months of his life, attending to his every need. Majali's brother Ayman was the king's chief of protocol, and he too spent long stretches of time in attendance at the Mayo. Hussein Majali, however, was the only Jordanian official to accompany the king on the last, desperate leg of his journey. He was the ultimate courtier, privy to his master's thoughts, feelings and suffering. Although Majali claimed that he was completely neutral in the matter of the succession, there were family loyalties at play. His sister was the second wife of Prince Muhammad bin Talal, the king's middle brother, who was said to harbour some lingering ill feelings towards Hassan for upstaging him as crown prince. Nevertheless, Majali is more important as a witness than as an actor in the drama that unfolded during the last seven months of the king's life.

According to Majali, in the first month at the Mayo in July 1998 the subject of the succession was not talked about because everybody wanted to believe that the king would make a complete recovery. It was not exactly taboo, but those close to the king did not feel like talking about it. It was only in October/November, as a result of the serious deterioration in the king's health, that the subject began to feature more prominently in their thoughts and discussions. The only official with whom the king discussed the matter directly was General Batikhi. Batikhi would go to Rochester for two days at a time to report to the king, and every meeting would last an hour or two, longer than any of the king's other appointments. Majali's guess is that the decision to remove Hassan began to take shape in the king's mind in October or November, but he did not hear that from the king himself. Even as he was moving towards a decision, the king preferred to keep all his options open. Rather than tell Majali directly, the king would say to him, "Has General Batikhi told you and Ayman?" without specifying what the general was meant to have said. The Majali brothers surmised that their master was planning to change the succession, but they could not be absolutely certain.[23]

Hussein's decision not to allow matters to take their natural course appears to have been reached in two stages. In the first Hussein made up his mind that Hassan should not succeed but had not yet determined the structure of the succession. In the second he settled on the final disposition, namely, that Abdullah was to replace Hassan. Abdullah made no move of his own to unseat his uncle. But when the first signs appeared that his uncle's fate was sealed, he saw no reason to rule himself out as a possible successor.[24] In November, Abdullah paid a visit to his father at the Mayo. Six months previously Abdullah had commanded a daring attack on Iraqi terrorists in Sahab and won his father's respect. At that time he told his father that he needed to know whether he had a career path in the army because, if so, he wanted to go on a course in Monterrey. Hussein advised him to go and held out the prospect of promotion to deputy chief of staff afterwards. In the Mayo, the two men had a breakfast that lasted about three hours. Abdullah recalls:

The first time was when he said, "I have great things in mind for you. I think you kind of learned it the hard way. I think I've let you down. You never asked for help and I never gave it to you. And I feel as a father looking back that I've let you down." I said, "A couple of years ago I would have said yes, but looking back at things, if I hadn't gone through the hardship that I did, I don't think I would have the experience and the knowledge that I have now. So, I am actually grateful." He said, "How is Sidi Hassan doing?" And I said, "You know it is very difficult. You're away and everybody's terrified. In all honesty, people don't think that there's going to be a Jordan without you there. God forbid if something happens to you."

He said, "I'm happy that when we get back you and I are going to have some talks. I need you to help me out on certain issues." I still didn't connect it with . . . I mean, I always thought great people like my father were not going to succumb to such a thing as cancer. So I expected that what he meant was again chief of staff. But then he said, "I want reforms as well as a lot of change and I want you there to assist me to change those things." So I thought: he's going to listen to what I've been saying on certain social issues and some of the army issues.[25]

Hussein and his wife spent Christmas in the hospital with their children. They marked the occasion with their extended family of nurses, doctors and the rest of the medical staff. Their time at the Mayo finally came to an end. They issued another press release, saying that they were leaving the hospital with the king's cancer in remission, but that it would take five years for this to be considered permanent. They greeted the New Year 1999 at River House with six of their children. Hussein was still very weak and took only occasional walks in the garden with

Noor and their daughter Iman—wearing his English shooting cap to keep his head warm and his mask against infection. He had also taken to using a cane again, partly because of his weakness and partly because of an enduring fondness for walking sticks, which he collected. With a profusion of apologies he admitted to his family that he had started smoking again. All in all, he was showing more signs of his old self.[26]

Despite all the meticulous care and attention that Hussein received at the Mayo Clinic, it is possible that the doctors underestimated the seriousness of his illness. They diagnosed a low grade of lymphoma when he might have been suffering from a higher one that was basically incurable. Whatever the grade, Hussein clearly needed a long period of time for convalescence. The doctors advised him to stop off for a week in London on his way back home because they knew he would be swamped once he arrived in Amman. On 5 January 1999 Hussein himself flew his plane to London, where, on 9 January, he received a surprise visit from his younger brother. The fact that Hassan had not visited Hussein at the Mayo even once was used by enemies as evidence of callousness and even disloyalty, but each time he had proposed a visit he had been discouraged. Hussein told Hassan that it was imperative that he stay put in Jordan, as he felt that a visit would feed the rumours that he was critically ill. He also felt the political situation was too uncertain to have them both out of the country at the same time. He was effusive in his praise for his younger brother, frequently referring to Hassan as the cornerstone of the Hashemites and the tree trunk that supported them all. Hassan for his part was now seriously troubled by the rumours that his brother was contemplating changes to the succession and had made the trip to London without clearing it in advance with his brother. Princess Sarvath, Hassan's wife, made three attempts to see the king, all of which were thwarted. On one occasion, she waited for several days in the United States but even then was not allowed to visit him.

Hussein and Hassan spent a couple of hours on their own in the king's house in London. When the two brothers met, they fell into each other's arms. According to Sarvath, it was a most moving reunion, and the conversation was conducted in a completely cordial atmosphere. Hussein laughed and joked, but he also confided that he was still not at all strong, that he hoped to stay longer in England, and that he wanted

Hassan to stay in charge after he returned home. The question of the constitutional arrangements governing the succession was not even raised on this occasion. In the past Hussein had made various suggestions for change, notably the setting up of a family council, but Hassan had had his doubts. He was of the opinion that if the Pandora's Box of constitutional change was opened, there were many detractors of the Hashemite monarchy who might take the opportunity to make other, more serious moves. He therefore preferred to leave things open, and Hussein knew this. As the brothers were chatting, Queen Noor and Prince Abdullah Hassan was not particularly pleased to see them as he did not fully trust them. He got up and said that perhaps he ought to be on his way. He got into his car and drove to the airport.[27]

The private meeting between Hussein and Hassan in London prompted a fresh round of press speculation. So did the meeting between Hussein and Prince Abdullah. Abdullah was already in London, and Hussein asked him through Majali to stay there for another day or two so they could meet and talk. Majali believes that it was at this meeting the king first intimated to his son that he had him in mind as his successor.[28] Abdullah himself was not entirely certain, but he could tell that his father was very tense after the meeting with Prince Hassan. Abdullah said that he had to go back to Jordan because, as the commander of Special Operations, he was directly responsible for the security arrangements and for the motorcade on Hussein's return. Hussein was sorry that they did not get a chance for a serious talk. He made comments on some members of the family with whom he was displeased and added cryptically: "I have issues with these people that I want dealt with together with you when I get back."[29] Abdullah's account suggests that Hussein was planning to return home sooner than he told Hassan.

Hussein's unexpected meeting with Hassan in London remains something of a puzzle and reveals the evident complexity in Hussein's attitude towards his brother. On the one hand, Hussein conveyed confidence in his brother and even gratitude for sharing the burdens of kingship. He spoke of him to the prime minister, for his report to parliament, as *qurrat al-'ein*, "the apple of his eye," something precious and indispensable. On the other hand, the possibility of dropping Hassan was present in his mind, although he did not breathe a word about it. Was it kindness, the emotion of reunion or calculated ruthlessness that led Hussein to dissemble so comprehensively with his brother? Could he just not bring himself to tell him the truth to his face and so thought it kinder to indulge him with talk of plans for the future that would never be realized? Was Hussein afraid that Hassan would take steps to forestall a change in the succession and therefore cunningly lulled him into a false sense of security? Was Hussein a ruthless dissembler and the master of the multiple agenda? Or had his illness so confused him by this point that he could not maintain a clear strategy? We shall probably never have a clear-cut answer to these questions.

A few days before his departure to Jordan, Hussein taped a televised address to announce his imminent arrival. The next day he became slightly feverish. A doctor from the Mayo Clinic who was travelling with them recommended that, at the last scheduled visit to St. Bartholomew's Hospital, the king should be given not only the usual blood transfusion but also a bone-marrow tap. The suggestion had a depressing effect. "Hussein's spirits and demeanor plummeted," Noor wrote in her journal. "He seemed to sink into himself with dread, especially after having publicly announced his arrival home."[30] The succession was constantly on her husband's mind. "One of the most burdensome tasks he had set for himself," she writes, "was to put the family and the country's future on a confident path. He had been thinking aloud about the subject for years, and naturally it became a paramount concern at Mayo. He wished that his brother, Crown Prince Hassan, had supported his idea for a Hashemite family council to recommend Hussein's successor on the basis of merit, a change that would have required an amendment to the Constitution, which at the time provided for the eldest son or, since 1965, a brother, to succeed the King."[31]

On 19 January the royal party left England aboard a Jordanian Gulf-stream 4. On the way they were picked up by RAF, French and Italian fighter escorts. Despite his immense fatigue, Hussein piloted for the entire trip, with a break for lunch. In Amman a hero's welcome awaited him. He descended from the aircraft unaided, and on touching Jordanian soil knelt down and prayed. Noor was by his side and joined him in reciting the Muslim prayer known as the "Fatiha" to thank God for his safe return home. They were greeted by their relatives, courtiers and Arab VIPs waiting on the tarmac and then moved on to a hangar reception for government officials, the press and other guests. Adnan Abu-

Odeh, the long-time political adviser, was one of the officials waiting on the tarmac. He had been a communist in his youth, but his feelings towards his monarch verged on hero-worship—just one example of the deep affection and loyalty that Hussein inspired in so many of the people who worked for him. Abu-Odeh's description of the encounter on the tarmac is therefore worth quoting in full:

On arrival at the airport in Amman Hussein looked very frail. We were all instructed not to kiss him and not to talk to him because his body was so weak. We obeyed. But he held my hand. In November 1998 I had left a happy birthday message at his home in Washington. At Amman airport, he said, "Abu Sa'id, I am sorry I was not at home when you called on my birthday. How is Umm Sa'id and how are the kids?" I replied, "We are all well and thinking of you and hope you get better soon." This was the sincere, the humane King Hussein, a man with the most wonderful manners. He was so kind, so considerate and so noble. He was dying and yet he was the one who was giving sympathy instead of being the one to receive sympathy. He was a great man. That was Hussein—sympathetic, truly sympathetic.[32]

The ride from the airport to the royal residence at Bab al-Salam was euphoric but foolhardy, given Hussein's frailty. Hundreds of thousands of people came out to greet their king in spite of the driving rain and wind. Hussein asked that the sun roof of the car be opened so that he could wave to the crowds that lined the streets. Noor tried to dissuade him, but he was adamant: if his people were going to stand in the bitter rain, so would he. Noor braced his legs inside the car to give him support. By the time they got home he was completely soaked, and Noor's orders made the nightly news: "*Yella, Hamaam,*" meaning "Time for a hot bath."[33]

The next day Hussein gave an interview to Christiane Amanpour, who was covering his return home for CNN. She asked him about his plans, and he replied that he had always been a fatalist, that he always knew that there was a beginning and an end to life, and now he felt it more than at any time in the past. His concern, he said, was not for himself but for Jordan and its people, for its stability and progress. Amanpour asked whether this meant a change in the current plan for crown prince Hassan to be his successor. Hussein was evasive. He said that Hassan had done much good during the years spent by his side, but he also implied, in a very convoluted way, that Hassan was perhaps not the most suitable member of their family to succeed him. "So, sir," persisted Amanpour, "is that a yes or a no? Are you going to change the line of succession?" King Hussein: "I'm not prepared to say anything, so please don't commit me to anything whatsoever because I really haven't come up with anything—I have only thoughts and ideas, and I've always had to take the final decisions and, although this has been contested at times, it is my responsibility and I will come to it at an appropriate time."[34]

Significantly, Hussein did not give any clues as to other possible candidates for the succession. He did not mention even indirectly any of his sons. He could have been thinking of either Abdullah or Hamzah, but he kept all his options open. Hassan was feeling less and less secure in his position as crown prince by the hour. He wanted to see his brother as soon as possible, but he was kept waiting either by his brother or by his brother's entourage for three days. On 21 January, Hassan sent a letter to his brother that, without saying so in so many words, sought confirmation of his position as heir-apparent. The letter was written in the flowery classical Arabic of which Hassan was a master and ended with the following words: "O father, brother, and friend, and venerable king, after having served as crown prince of your auspicious reign since my early youth and until now, which brought grey streaks to my hair, I find myself in this position, and I place myself in your hands and abide by your sublime and noble order."[35]

Hassan was summoned to Bab al-Salam to see the king the following day, Friday, 22 January. Three days later a royal decree removed him from his position as crown prince. Most observers assumed this was the meeting at which the king informed Hassan for the first time of his decision to designate Abdullah as crown prince. This was not the case. A letter written by Hassan to Hussein three days after his dismissal is the only first-hand account we have of what actually transpired at the meeting. The letter describes Hassan's joy at Hussein's return to Jordan on 19 January, which was the second day of Eid al-Fitr, when the fast is broken at the end of Ramadan:

Subsequent to this joyous event, three days passed without us meeting. During that time, the media spoke of an impending decision by Your Majesty to relieve me from my responsibilities as Crown Prince, levelling all sorts of allegations and accusations against me, and attributing those allegations to both official and unofficial sources. On Friday evening, 22nd January 1999, I had the honour of meeting with Your Majesty. It was a brotherly and frank conversation and I recollect mentioning the media reports to Your Majesty. Your Majesty directed me not to pay any attention to such news. I also asked Your Majesty what I should do with respect to my duties as Crown Prince. Your Majesty instructed that I should proceed with my duties as normal, reiterating your unwavering confidence and trust in my loyalty and faithfulness. In spite of that, I handed Your Majesty a letter in which I put myself at your disposal; a letter which you subsequently ordered published.

A few days later, on 25th January, Your Majesty's decree to relieve me from my duties as Crown Prince was announced. On that same evening, I received a Royal letter from Your Majesty.[36]

All the evasions and equivocations of the previous year had suddenly come to an end. Prime Minister Fayez Tarawneh was summoned and informed of Hussein's decision to replace Hassan with Abdullah as crown prince. Hussein also showed the prime minister a draft of the letter he had written to Hassan. It was a brief and friendly letter, thanking Hassan for his services. Despite the devastating impact that the decision to replace him must have had, Hassan accepted it calmly and with good grace. He told the king that he was his humble servant and that he would abide by his decision. Hassan's options were: to try to foil the change in the succession, to go into exile in London, or to stay at home and maintain a dignified silence. From the very start he opted for the last. To stage a counter-coup went against his nature, and he never even considered it.[37] Throughout the crisis, Hassan behaved in a calm, measured and statesmanlike manner. He even offered his help in smoothing over the process of transition. Both the king's ADC and the prime minister were impressed by the manner in which Hassan conducted himself following this cruel reversal in his fortunes.[38] Eventually, after the meetings with Hassan and Tarawneh, Hussein called his son over. It was an emotional and poignant encounter, as Abdullah recalled:

My father wasn't looking very well and he said, "Look, for many reasons I have been wanting to say this for a while. What I want to say to you is all I am doing is rewriting, as opposed to writing, history. You were crown prince when you were born and I want you to become crown prince again. And there are two reasons." I said, "Sidi, this is something that I have never wanted. I don't want this job." He said, "That is one of the reasons why I want you to have it. The other reason is because I know that out of all the members of the family you can keep the balance." When I was a young child growing up, I was the eldest, so I treated everybody fairly and I looked after everybody. I had a good relationship with all my siblings and cousins. For him, that was very important.

I said, "What about Prince Hassan?" He said, "Look, I'm not doing well . . . I am going back." I said, "And so what happens if something happens to you? If you want me to become crown prince, then I have got to make a decision on who is going to work with me." It was very hard for him at that time and I said, "I guess what you are saying to me, Father, is that you don't think that you are going to make it." And so there was a bit of silence there as we tried to come to grips with the reality of the situation that he was facing. And he said, "He is my brother and he is your uncle, so try to do the best you can." He wasn't proud . . . he said, "You are my son. I have had a lot of faith all these years and I want you to step into these shoes." But I kind of had a feeling that he wished that things had continued . . . I don't know if it is fair for me to say that I think it was a tremendous disappointment that his right-hand man for thirty-four years . . . It's his brother at the end of the day. And to make a decision that somebody who has been with you for so many years is not the man that you want.

He said, "I am feeling very tired." So I had another five minutes to ask a lot more questions. I needed six months really of questions to ask him. I just ticked off what I thought was the most important. The sadness of that conversation was not my being crown prince, it was him saying: I am not going to make it. That was a shock. I didn't care about the position. I told my father: "I care about you." And the conversation was more about: let us put the emotion aside and deal with some practical aspects. I was not ready for that.

The last two weeks I pretty much knew what he was going to say, but it was still a shock when he said it. And the biggest shock was not that I was becoming crown prince but that he was dying and the implications of that for me. I could have done with four or five years of tutoring under him to get comfortable and all of a sudden I was being thrown in at the deep end of this. I lost twelve kilos in a week. My father was going back. I could see in his eyes that he didn't think he was going to make it. It was pretty tough between the father and the son.[39]

While Hassan and Abdullah changed places, the position of young Prince Hamzah remained uncertain. Contrary to media reports, Noor had been advocating all along that Hamzah should have an opportunity to attend university and develop his intellectual interests and talents. She quotes her husband telling her: "I want Hamzah to finish what I was not able to do in terms of schooling, and let him be the critical partner with Abdullah," and that she fully supported his decision. After Abdullah had the meeting with his father, he asked to see her. He was completely surprised by the sudden turn of events, he said. Hassan had been Crown Prince since 1965, and Abdullah said that he had assumed that after Hassan his father's choice would be Hamzah, and he had been willing to support that choice. Noor told her stepson that it was important for her that he knew that she fully supported his father's choice and had complete confidence in him. "I will be here for you, and honour my father's wishes toward Hamzah," Abdullah told her. She said she would wholeheartedly support him in every way she could, and do everything in her power to ensure that he and his father had as much time to work together as possible. She hugged him as he left, still stunned, to return home and inform his wife, Rania.[40]

Prince Talal bin Muhammad justified his uncle's decision to replace Hassan with Abdullah as crown prince and as the head of the Hashemite clan. Talal and Abdullah belonged to the younger generation of Hashemite princes on whom Hussein pinned his hopes. They were not just cousins but friends who had served together in the army in some very testing conditions. According to Talal, of all Hussein's children Abdullah was most like the current head of the family: very open, strong, assertive and courageous. He was therefore the best choice to rule Jordan; he was the family's great hope. In Talal's judgement, Abdullah was much better suited to rule than their uncle Hassan. Dynastic considerations were paramount. Talal's gloss on the critical meeting in Amman was that Hussein said to Abdullah: "If Hassan becomes king, that would be the end of the Husseins and the bin Muhammads. But if you become king, the Husseins, the Muhammads, and the Hassans will all go on." Talal elaborated: "The implication was that under Hassan the family would no longer be a unified family. The family would disintegrate. Hassan's behaviour would exclude the rest of the family and cost us the throne."[41]

In the midst of this family drama, Hussein's health took a sharp turn for the worse. Exposure to the elements during his triumphal ride home did not do him any good. He developed a new ailment: unrelenting hiccups. Hussein had blood and plasma transfusions on an almost daily basis, but his condition did not improve. His physicians decided to perform another CT scan and yet another bone-marrow tap. The scan confirmed that his cancer had already returned. The king and the queen were presented with three options: to keep the king comfortable and stay in Amman; to stay at home but have another course of chemotherapy; or to return to the Mayo to try another transplant. The last option was the most dangerous but it was his only chance for remission. Neither hesitated. "We're going back," the king told the doctors.[42]

It was Monday, 25 January. The king asked for seventy-two hours to attend to some important matters but was told by Hussein Majali, his ADC, that they had to leave for the Mayo the following day at noon. He had only the rest of the day to complete all his unfinished business. The king still had the draft of his original, polite "thank you" letter to his brother, but he now threw it into the fire. Instead he settled down to write the now infamous, fourteen-page-long letter that took six hours to complete. This was the king's last letter and, in a sense, his last will and testament. It was a rambling, polemical and politically explosive letter, laced with insults and unsubstantiated charges against his younger brother. Majali described in graphic detail the process by which this controversial letter came to be written at Bab al-Salam, the "Gate of Peace":

His Majesty looked at me and told me to bring two yellow pads and a bunch of pencils. He used to love writing on yellow pads. He sat in his sitting room by the coffee table and started writing the letter in the early afternoon. Once he started writing, he did not want to be disturbed. Queen Noor would go to him every hour or so to massage his back because it became very stiff. He was weak and frail at that time . . . The fourteen-page letter was finished and typed around nine o'clock in the evening. The change of the succession was announced on the news at 11:00. Before the announcement, His Majesty met with Prince Hassan, Prince Abdullah, the family elders and all the chiefs of all the main institutions in Jordan. There were many people whom His Majesty wanted to inform about his decision before making it public, and they were all invited to the palace.[43]

Although it touched on a whole host of irrelevant issues ranging from weapons of mass destruction to environmental pollution, most of the letter was self-justifying and revolved round the issue of the succession. Hussein claimed, implausibly, that he returned to the homeland with the intention of abdicating in Hassan's favour, but "I and my immediate family were hurt by the backbiting and slander." An impassioned but slightly strange defence of Noor follows: "She is a Jordanian who belongs with all her senses to this homeland and raises her head high when she defends it and its causes." There is also a detailed account of Hussein's proposal to set up a family council in his own lifetime, which Hassan had declined because he regarded it as tantamount to the opening of a Pandora's box. This is followed by the cruellest cut of all: the reference to parasites and opportunists who thought that his illness gave them their chance. To be sure, there was no shortage of opportunists and time-servers in the Hashemite court, but Hassan was not one of them. Hassan was the victim, not the perpetrator, of the plots that were hatched in the twilight of Hussein's reign. Hassan is further accused of exceeding his authority, of acting in an arbitrary manner and of settling scores during the six months that he was regent. Another charge is that he meddled in the affairs of the army, tried to politicize it and impugned the good name of the chief of staff. In addition, Hassan is criticized for disloyalty and for all manner of presumption to kingship. Finally, Hussein refers to Hassan's letter in which he left it to him to settle the issue of the succession and coldly announces his decision "to name His Royal Highness Prince Abdullah bin Hussein to assume the powers and responsibilities of the crown prince of the Hashemite Kingdom of Jordan immediately."[44]

Majali remarked to the author, in a moment of startling candour, that 90 percent of the letter was untrue. Prince Hassan himself refuted the allegations against him point by point in his twelve-page letter of 28 January, which was never published.[45] The question therefore arises: why did Hussein write such a damning and wildly inaccurate letter to the younger brother who had served him so faithfully and so ably for over a third of a century? One answer might be that the pain and the pain-killers clouded Hussein's judgement and prevented him from reflecting on and editing what he was writing. But the more likely explanation is that Hussein acted deliberately to disqualify Hassan and to discourage him from taking any counter-measures he might contemplate to defend his position. In the words of Marwan Kasim: "The purpose of the king's letter was to discredit Prince Hassan in the eyes of the bureaucracy and the military and to give his son a breathing space to consolidate his power."[46] Talal bin Muhammad had no doubt whatever that this was indeed the king's motive:

The letter to Hassan was out of character and very harsh. The reason His Majesty did it was to make the way clear for Abdullah. It was very cruel but it had to be done. He had to break Hassan in public completely and utterly so he could offer no resistance to Abdullah. He did not have time to consolidate Abdullah as crown prince, as his anointed heir. He died a week later.

He wrote the letter the day before he returned to the Mayo. He wrote it so there would be no ambiguity as to where loyalty should lie after him. Loyalty should be to Abdullah. This came as a relief to many people. People breathed a sigh of relief. There was no Hassan camp and Abdullah camp. There was a smooth transition. The only resentment was from Hassan and his immediate circle. Most Jordanians were happy to change allegiance.

His Majesty wanted to make a change in the succession. So he procrastinated and procrastinated almost literally until his last day. The ruthlessness of his last letter to Hassan was justified. He worried that Hussan would create trouble for Abdullah and he was determined to prevent him. It was an exercise in pure power-politics.[47]

Having deposed his brother and anointed his eldest son as his heir, the ailing monarch returned immediately to the Mayo Clinic. On Tuesday, 26 January, after exactly a week in his capital, he boarded a TriStar plane that took him to the United States. He was tired and frail, but he shook hands and said something to each of the dignitaries who stood in line to bid him farewell. To Zaid Rifa'i, the crafty old courtier, he said, "Don't play any of your tricks with my son." To his nephew Talal bin Muhammad he said only one word: *Ashkorak*, "I thank you."[48]

Back at the Mayo Clinic, Hussein was given another bout of chemotherapy and a bone-marrow transplant. Because of the perils involved, he was placed in the Intensive Care Unit so he could be closely monitored around the clock. As soon as his condition improved slightly, he was moved back into his old room, but little by little he became confused and quiet. He was visibly losing the battle against cancer and his wife made the decision to take him back home to die. His human decency, kindness and generosity, however, were in evidence until the end. Majali recalled one particularly moving example of his humanity. It was the morning of 4 February, the day of their departure. Hussein was a little disoriented. He was watching CNN news in English but commenting on it in Arabic. Majali, Noor, Hamzah and a nurse were with him. They massaged his leg in order to get the blood circulation going. Hussein suddenly looked at the nurse and said to her in Arabic: "My daughter, do you have a family, are they OK, do you have a nice house, do you have heating in your house?" Hussein then turned to Hamzah and asked him to tell his ADC to take care of this woman. The nurse was American, and had not understood a word of what the patient was saying. This little episode confirmed what the people around Hussein always knew: he was a genuinely caring and an exceptionally kind man.[49]

On the last journey home Hussein was accompanied by his wife, a medical team, a flight nurse, a respiratory therapist and all the equipment and medication he could possibly need. Once again they had fighter escorts, but this time no one paid attention to them. From the airport the patient, who had lost consciousness during the flight, was taken directly to the King Hussein Medical Centre. Outside the hospital thousands of Jordanians kept up a vigil in the rain. Inside the hospital Hussein's family gathered to say their final farewells. Noor could not help feeling that having his family together gave him peace at the end.

Hussein died on Sunday, 7 February. He was sixty-three years old. He was facing Mecca when his heart stopped beating. At the moment of his death, Noor was standing next to his bed holding his hand, surrounded by their children and other relatives. Noor turned to Abdullah, gave him a big hug and said, "The king is dead; long live the king."[50] Abdullah's first act as king was to issue a royal decree appointing his half-brother Hamzah bin Al Hussein crown prince of the Hashemite Kingdom of Jordan with immediate effect.

The funeral, in accordance with Muslim custom, was held the following day. Despite the short notice, it brought to the Jordanian capital an extraordinary galaxy of international luminaries to pay their respects: kings and queens, presidents and prime ministers, soldiers and statesmen, friends and foes. A delegation of four American presidents was led by Bill Clinton, who called the king "a partner and friend." There were delegations from all the Arab countries from North Africa to the Gulf, including two former foes—Asad and Arafat. By far the largest foreign delegation came from Israel, with President Ezer Weizman at its head. By their very presence at the funeral, these leaders expressed the appreciation of the whole international community for the critical role that the king had played in the struggle for peace in the Middle East. Hussein bin Talal was a titanic figure, an outstanding Hashemite ruler and, above all else, a peacemaker. He was also a popular monarch. His coffin was placed on a funeral bier for the long procession through the capital to the Raghdan Palace and then to the royal cemetery for burial. The rain was unremitting, and the fog was thick. "*Hatta al samaa tabki 'ala Al Hussein,*" the people in the streets said to one another: "Even the sky is crying over Al Hussein."

Epilogue: The Life and Legacy

An Israeli intelligence report written in the early 1980s described Jordan's King Hussein as a man trapped on a bridge burning at both ends, with crocodiles in the river beneath him: he cannot go forward, he cannot retreat, he cannot jump. He is a slave of the status quo. This uncharacteristically flowery intelligence assessment rightly stresses the extraordinarily severe constraints under which Hussein had to operate throughout his political career. What it leaves out of account are the personal qualities of charisma, courage, determination and far-sightedness that enabled Hussein to cope with these constraints and to survive in the face of overwhelming odds.

Hussein was a full-blooded Hashemite king. He was a direct descendant of the Prophet Muhammad and the great-grandson of Hussein the Sharif of Mecca, the leader of the Arab struggle for independence during the First World War. But it was his grandfather Abdullah, the founder of the Emirate of Transjordan, who had the most profound influence on his political thinking. It was Abdullah who educated Hussein, who taught him what it meant to be a Hashemite, and who enjoined him to preserve and develop the kingdom that he had created. The assassination of his grandfather and mentor at the Al-Aqsa Mosque in Jerusalem in 1951 was the most formative influence in Hussein's early life. He was only fifteen years old at the time, and the hopes of his family, and especially of his formidable mother, were pinned on him. Thus, from a very young age, Hussein carried on his shoulders a heavy sense of responsibility for the Hashemite heritage. Above all, this meant preserving Jordan as an independent state under the rule of the Hashemite dynasty. It also meant making Jordan a major player in regional and international politics.

From the beginning there was a huge disparity between these lofty ambitions and the paucity of the means available for achieving them. The Hashemite rulers of Jordan were dealt a weak hand. When Hussein ascended the throne he inherited a poor desert kingdom, with no oil and limited industrial capacity, surrounded by enemies who questioned its very right to exist. Hussein's principal legacy was one of success in defying the obituarists and transcending the in-built limitations of his kingdom. He was able to give Jordan political weight in regional affairs and even at the global level that went a long way beyond its small population, limited economy and proud but modest army. This is the legacy that King Abdullah II inherited from his father in 1999 and one that, despite being unprepared for the job, he has succeeded in perpetuating.

But though Hussein succeeded in building Jordan as a polity, as a political entity with a significant role in regional affairs and in international diplomacy, he never had a vision of a self-sustaining economy for Jordan. He had no understanding and virtually no interest in economic matters. Instead he used his international connections to maintain a steady stream of funds from abroad to keep his country afloat. His talents as the fundraiser-in-chief were stretched to the limit in finding new sources of supply as the international political situation kept changing. The main sources of economic aid were Britain in the early 1950s, America from 1957 onwards, the Gulf states in the 1960s and 1970s, the Arab League after the expulsion of Egypt over its separate peace with Israel in the late 1970s, Iraq in the 1980s until the Gulf War of 1991, and America again after the conclusion of the peace treaty with Israel in 1994. At the end of Hussein's reign Jordan was still crucially dependent on external sources of funding. This was another legacy that he bequeathed to his son and successor: the never ending struggle for solvency.

No problem that Hussein had to confront during his reign was more taxing or more persistent than the problem of Palestine, the roots of which went back to the emergence of Zionism as a political movement at the end of the nineteenth century. The result was a clash between two peoples and two national movements over the same land. In the 1948 war for Palestine, the real losers were the Palestinians. The State of Israel was established, Jordan occupied and later annexed the West Bank, and the Palestinians were left out in the cold. Abdullah pursued a policy of absorbing the Palestinians into his enlarged kingdom but met with only limited success. Palestinians accounted for roughly half of Jordan's population, but most of them did not want to be loyal subjects of the Hashemites; they wanted their own independent state, flag and anthem. King Abdullah was assassinated by Palestinian nationalists in 1951 because they considered that he had betrayed their national cause. The Palestinian problem, from their perspective, was the product of a conspiracy between Hashemites and Zionists.

As I hope this book has shown, Hussein never underestimated the seriousness of the Palestinian challenge. In his speeches he repeatedly referred to the Palestine question as a question of life and death for the Hashemite Kingdom of Jordan. He knew that there was a great deal of Arab and international sympathy and support for the Palestinians. He therefore posed as, and gradually made himself, in his own eyes, the champion of the Palestinians so that this support would be to the benefit and not to the detriment of his country. With the emergence of the Palestine Liberation Organization in the mid 1960s it became increasingly difficult to maintain the idea that Jordan was one united family. Hussein and the PLO were competitors for the allegiance of the Palestinians living in Jordan. True, the PLO had been created to liberate Palestine from Israel, but its struggle against Israel had far-reaching consequences for Jordan.

The difference between Hussein and the PLO leaders was that they believed in the armed struggle for the liberation of Palestine and he did not. Like his grandfather, he was the king of realism. In 1948 King Abdullah was the only Arab leader with a realistic appreciation of the military balance between the two sides. Abdullah may not have understood fully the ideological forces that drove the Jews to strive so relentlessly for a state of their own, but he could tell a going concern when he saw one.

Hussein, similarly, faced up to facts. He realized that Israel was a strong neighbour which was there to stay. He never harboured any illusions that Israel could be defeated on the battlefield or of fighting Israel for the sake of eliminating it. The issue for him was how to resolve the Arab–Israeli dispute peacefully, how to end the conflict, how to reach an accommodation with the State of Israel and to close this war-filled chapter in the history of the region. These aims could only be achieved, he concluded, by means of a direct dialogue with the enemy which, in view of the Arab taboo, had to be secret. Moreover, Hussein did not want to have this dialogue second-hand; he wanted to meet the enemy face-to-face to see what they were about and to work out together a way forward. Significantly, it was not the Israelis but Hussein himself who took the initiative, in 1963, in establishing the covert dialogue across the battle lines that continued, with some intervals, until the peace treaty was concluded three decades later.

A great deal changed in the Middle East in the intervening years, most notably as a result of the June War of 1967. Hussein always maintained that he had no choice but to join the other Arab countries in the war against Israel, but his explanations were unconvincing. Joining in the war was a catastrophic miscalculation and one that cost him half his kingdom. In six fateful days he lost East Jerusalem and the West Bank, which his grandfather had succeeded in salvaging from the dismal wreck of Arab Palestine in 1948. He felt an acute sense of personal responsibility to recover the lost territory, and especially the old city of Jerusalem, because of its importance not just to Jordanians but to Arabs and Muslims everywhere. While other Arab leaders indulged in mutual recriminations, Hussein dealt in a practical way with the bitter consequences of defeat. He understood better than any other leader the new rules of the game.

First of all, Jordan accepted UN Resolution 242 of November 1967 and the principle of land for peace, which became the cornerstone of Jordanian diplomacy. At a deeper level, however, Hussein understood the importance of giving Israel the sense of security needed to make concessions for the sake of peace. In the aftermath of defeat, the dialogue across the battle lines was resumed and intensified. Hussein's terms never changed. From the beginning he offered his Israeli interlocutors full, contractual peace in exchange for the occupied territories with only minor border modifications. His aim was not a separate peace with Israel but a comprehensive peace in the Middle East. Nor was he alone in striving for peace on the Arab side. After the war, he and Gamal Abdel Nasser emerged as the leading moderates in the Arab camp. Abdel Nasser knew and approved of Hussein's secret talks with the enemy, provided they did not lead to a separate peace. Despite Abdel Nasser's tacit support, it took a great deal of courage on Hussein's part to pursue this solo diplomacy.

The quest for a land-for-peace deal was frustrated not by Arab intransigence but by Israeli intransigence. By its actions Israel revealed that it preferred land to peace with its neighbours. Soon after the end of the 1967 war it began to build settlements in the occupied territories.

Building civilian settlements on occupied territory was not just illegal under international law but a major obstacle to peace. There were some early signs of flexibility on the part of the Israeli cabinet in relation to the Sinai Peninsula and the Golan Heights but none towards the West Bank. All the major parties in the 1967–70 national unity government were united in their determination to keep at least a substantial part of the West Bank in perpetuity. There were proponents of the "Palestinian option" and proponents of the "Jordanian option," but in practical terms the debate was between those who did not want to return the West Bank to Jordan and those who did not want to return it to the Palestinians who lived there. Despite Hussein's best efforts, the diplomatic deadlock persisted for another decade, until Anwar Sadat's visit to Jerusalem in 1977. Sadat did what Hussein had studiously avoided, namely, a bilateral deal with Israel that left the Palestinian problem unresolved. The two countries changed places: Egypt was drummed out of the Arab League while Jordan joined the Arab mainstream.

In the aftermath of the Lebanon War of 1982 Ronald Reagan launched a peace plan that called for the creation of a Palestinian homeland in association with Jordan. The Likud government headed by Menachem Begin flatly rejected this plan. In the mid 1980s Hussein tried a new tack. He wanted to "repackage" the PLO in a way that would make it acceptable to America so that America would put pressure on Israel to negotiate. The result was the Jordan–PLO accord of 11 February 1985. But the PLO turned out to be evasive and unreliable and the peace partnership broke down the following year. In April 1987 Hussein reached an agreement with Foreign Minister Shimon Peres on an international conference to which all the parties to the conflict would be invited and which would then divide up into bilateral working groups. But Itzhak Shamir, the Likud leader and prime minister, scuppered this "London Agreement." Later that year the first intifada broke out. It was a full-scale revolt against Israeli rule in Gaza and the West Bank, a non-violent Palestinian war of independence. Fearing that the intifada would spread from the West Bank to the East Bank, on 31 July 1988 Hussein severed the legal and administrative links between his kingdom and the West Bank. Belatedly and reluctantly, he acknowledged that the PLO was the sole legitimate representative of the Palestinian people.

Following this disengagement from the West Bank, and in a sense from the Palestine problem, Hussein concentrated his efforts on building a liberal, moderate Arab order. He wanted the moderates rather than the PLO and the radicals to set the tone in the Arab world and to build a pro-Western Arab coalition that would promote stability and prosperity in the region. The main achievement of this phase was the creation of the Arab Cooperation Council, consisting of Jordan, Iraq, Egypt and Yemen. A second important aspect of Hussein's foreign policy during the 1980s was the cultivation of an alliance with Saddam Hussein's Iraq. The alliance constituted some sort of a strategic counterweight to Israel and it brought rich economic rewards, but because of Saddam's unpredictability it also carried risks. Iraq's invasion of Kuwait in 1990 destroyed the emerging moderate Arab order and split the Arabs down the middle. Hussein tried to work out an Arab solution to the crisis, but he was not given a chance. He came under strong pressure to join the American-led war against Iraq but he resisted all the pressures and the blandishments. It was a difficult period in Jordan's history, fraught with perils and uncertainties. There was a real danger that Jordan would become a battleground between Iraq and Israel and that the hard-liners on the Israeli right would seize the opportunity to realize their programme of turning the Hashemite Kingdom of Jordan into a Palestinian state. Hussein forestalled the danger by secretly meeting Itzhak Shamir in England and getting him to agree to respect Jordan's neutrality when the bombs started falling. This was a striking example of the use made by Hussein of his back channel to Tel Aviv to protect the security of his country.

Jordan was an enthusiastic participant in the American-led peace process that got under way after the Gulf War, and provided an umbrella for non-PLO Palestinian participation in the Madrid peace conference. But little progress was made in the subsequent bilateral negotiations in Washington under American auspices. The Oslo Accord between the PLO and Israel in September 1993 took Jordan and the other Arab states by complete surprise. Hussein's initial reaction was anger at the PLO for breaking rank and suspicion that Israel intended to drop him in favour of a partnership with the PLO. But Itzhak Rabin succeeded in reassuring him that his government remained committed to the survival of the monarchy in Amman and that Jordan's interests would be taken into account in all future negotiations with the PLO. The Oslo Accord involved not just a risk but also an opportunity for Jordan. Once the PLO had made its peace with the Jewish state, there was no longer any reason for Jordan to hold back from doing so too. The Arab taboo had been broken, and the road was clear to the direct negotiations that culminated in the signature of a peace treaty between Jordan and Israel on 26 October 1994.

Hussein viewed the peace treaty with Israel as the crowning achievement of his reign. It clearly served his dynastic interests but he firmly believed that it also served Jordan's national interests. It restored the alliance with America which had been badly damaged by Jordan's stand during the Gulf War; it restored lost territory and water resources; it revived the strategic understanding with the State of Israel; and it underpinned the centrality of Jordan in regional politics. Crucially, it also protected his kingdom from a takeover bid by his Palestinian opponents and forestalled the emergence of an Israeli–Palestinian axis. By concluding his own pact with Israel, Hussein turned the tables on his radical Palestinian rivals and reasserted the Hashemite dynasty's position as Israel's natural ally in the region. Most of all, the peace agreement provided a lasting defence against the dreaded policy of the Israeli right of toppling the monarchy in Amman and transforming the Hashemite Kingdom of Jordan into the Republic of Palestine. The spectre of Jordan becoming an alternative homeland for the Palestinians was finally laid to rest. A comprehensive peace settlement for the Middle East was beyond Hussein's reach, but he successfully stopped Jordan from becoming the solution to the Palestinian problem.

There was, however, an internal price to pay for the peace with Israel. Peace and democracy usually go hand in hand, but they did not do so in this case. There was strong popular opposition to peace and normalization with Israel, and many prominent Jordanian politicians thought that Hussein was in too much of a hurry, that he was conceding too much in his dealings with the Israelis. Hussein realized the depth of the opposition to his peace policy but he counted on the material benefits of peace to bring about a change in attitudes. The much vaunted "peace dividend," however, failed to materialize, and the opposition to his policy persisted and gathered momentum. Hussein had never been particularly tolerant of political opposition but, feeling increasingly isolated and embattled, he resorted to draconian measures, including the arrest and imprisonment of his opponents. Even when elections were allowed, the electoral law was manipulated to produce results that favoured the king. Neither parliament nor the constitution could limit his decision-making power. The freedom of the press was curtailed, dissident parliamentarians were subjected to pressure from the palace, and the power of the secret police grew at an alarming rate. Far from paving the way to greater freedom and democracy, the peace treaty with Israel ushered in an era of political repression and authoritarianism. This too was part of the legacy that Hussein bequeathed to his successor. Hussein's legacy is thus a mixed one: there were shadows as well as light; failures as well as some remarkable successes.

In the West, King Hussein enjoyed a degree of respect and admiration that no other Arab leader could match. Just one example of it was the memorial service held in St. Paul's Cathedral in London on 5 July 1999, the first occasion since before the First World War that a foreign monarch had been honoured in this way. The Christian service to a Muslim leader of "extraordinary dignity and exceptional modesty" was also the first occasion on which the Koran was read from at St. Paul's. King Abdullah II and his family were joined by European royal families, prime ministers and representatives from almost every country in the world and 2,000 friends of the "Lion of Jordan." The steps of the cathedral were lined by a Guard of Honour from the Royal Military Academy, Sandhurst. The Prince of Wales paid tribute in his address to his old friend as "a man amongst men and a king amongst kings." The second reading was from Matthew 5—"Blessed be the peacemakers, for they will be called the children of God." That was probably how Hussein bin Talal himself would have wanted to be remembered most of all, and that was his most enduring legacy—the possibility, at least, of peace in the Middle East.

Notes

CHAPTER 1: THE HASHEMITE HERITAGE

1. Timothy J. Paris, *Britain, the Hashemites and Arab Rule 1920–1925: The Sherifian Solution* (London: Frank Cass, 2003).
2. Elie Kedourie, *In the Anglo-Arab Labyrinth: The McMahon–Husayn Correspondence and Its Interpretations 1914–1939* (Cambridge: Cambridge University Press, 1976).
3. Adeed Dawisha, *Arab Nationalism in the Twentieth Century: From Triumph to Despair* (Princeton, NJ: Princeton University Press, 2003), 34.
4. Quoted in ibid.
5. Kathryn Tidrick, *Heart-beguiling Araby*, 2nd ed. (London: I. B. Tauris, 1989).
6. Kedourie, *In the Anglo-Arab Labyrinth*.
7. T. E. Lawrence, *Revolt in the Desert* (London: Jonathan Cape, 1927), 12.
8. Isaiah Friedman, *Palestine: A Twice-promised Land?* (New Brunswick, NJ: Transaction Publishers, 2000).
9. Elizabeth Monroe, *Britain's Moment in the Middle East 1914–1971*, new and rev. 2nd ed. (London: Chatto and Windus, 1981).
10. Paris, *Britain, the Hashemites and Arab Rule*, 44.
11. George Antonius, *The Arab Awakening: The Story of the Arab National Movement*, 1965 ed. (New York: Capricorn Books, 1938), 267–9, 331–2.
12. Avi Shlaim, "The Balfour Declaration and Its Consequences" in *More Adventures with Britannia: Personalities, Politics and Culture in Britain*, ed. Wm. Roger Louis (London: I. B. Tauris, 2005).
13. James Morris, *The Hashemite Kings* (London: Faber and Faber, 1959), 63–65.
14. David Fromkin, *A Peace to End All Peace: Creating the Modern Middle East 1914–1922* (London: Penguin, 1991).
15. Ibid., 440.
16. Alec Seath Kirkbride, *A Crackle of Thorns: Experiences in the Middle East* (London: John Murray, 1956), 27.
17. Martin Gilbert, *Winston S. Churchill. Volume IV: The Stricken World 1916–1922* (London: Heinemann, 1975), 553.
18. Kirkbride, *A Crackle of Thorns*, 19–20.

19. Gilbert, *Churchill, Volume IV,* 545.
20. Mary C. Wilson, *King Abdullah, Britain and the Making of Jordan* (Cambridge: Cambridge University Press, 1987), 36–7.
21. For a detailed account see Avi Shlaim, *Collusion Across the Jordan: King Abdullah, the Zionist Movement, and the Partition of Palestine* (Oxford: Clarendon Press, 1988). An abridged and revised paperback edition of this book appeared as Avi Shlaim, *The Politics of Partition: King Abdullah, the Zionists, and Palestine 1921–1951* (Oxford: Oxford University Press, 1990). It was reissued with a new preface in 1998. I have drawn heavily on these books in the writing of this chapter.
22. Ezra Danin, "Talk with Abdullah, 17 Nov. 1947," S25/4004, and Elias Sasson to Moshe Shertok, 20 November 1947, S25/1699, Central Zionist Archives (CZA), Jerusalem. See also Shlaim, *Collusion Across the Jordan,* 110–17.
23. Iraqi Parliament, *Taqrir Lajnat al-Tahqiq al-Niyabiyya fi Qadiyyat Filastin* [Report of the Parliamentary Committee of Inquiry into the Palestine Question], in Arabic (Baghdad: 1949).
24. Golda Meir's verbal report to the thirteen-member Provisional State Council, Israel State Archives, *Provisional State Council: Protocols 18 April–13 May 1948,* in Hebrew (Jerusalem: Israel State Archives, 1978), 40–44.
25. Golda Meir, *My Life* (London: Weidenfeld and Nicolson, 1975), 176–80.
26. For a comprehensive review of the literature and the debate see Avraham Sela, "Transjordan, Israel and the 1948 War: Myth, Historiography and Reality," *Middle Eastern Studies,* 24: 4 (October 1992).
27. Eugene L. Rogan, "Jordan and 1948: The Persistence of an Official History" in *The War for Palestine: Rewriting the History of 1948,* eds. Eugene L. Rogan and Avi Shlaim (Cambridge: Cambridge University Press, 2001).
28. See in particular Sela, "Transjordan, Israel and the 1948 War: Myth, Historiography and Reality." My reply to my Israeli critics on this and other issues is contained in Avi Shlaim, "The Debate about 1948," *International Journal of Middle East Studies,* 27: 3 (1995).
29. Interview with Yaacov Shimoni. Also in Shlaim, *Collusion Across the Jordan,* 142.
30. For part of the story see Joshua Landis, "Syria and the Palestine War: Fighting King Abdullah's 'Greater Syria Plan' " in *The War for Palestine: Rewriting the History of 1948,* eds. Eugene L. Rogan and Avi Shlaim (Cambridge: Cambridge University Press, 2001).
31. Benny Morris, *The Birth of the Palestinian Refugee Problem Revisited,* 2nd ed. (Cambridge: Cambridge University Press, 2004), Appendix 1.
32. Yoav Gelber, *Jewish–Transjordanian Relations 1921–1948* (London: Frank Cass, 1997).
33. David Ben-Gurion's diary, 18 July 1949, Ben-Gurion Archive, Sede-Boker.

34. Ben-Gurion's diary, 13 February 1951. See also Avi Shlaim, *The Iron Wall: Israel and the Arab World* (New York: W. W. Norton, 2000), 66–67.
35. Ibid., 67–68.

CHAPTER 2: MURDER OF A MENTOR

1. Hussein bin Talal, *Uneasy Lies the Head: An Autobiography* (London: Heinemann, 1962), 10.
2. Ibid., 14.
3. John Bagot Glubb, *A Soldier with the Arabs* (London: Hodder and Stoughton, 1957), 281, 293.
4. Alec Kirkbride, *From the Wings: Amman Memoirs 1947–1951* (London: Frank Cass, 1976), 121.
5. Quoted in Mary C. Wilson, *King Abdullah, Britain and the Making of Jordan* (Cambridge: Cambridge University Press, 1987), 132.
6. Interview with Prince Raad bin Zaid.
7. Hussein bin Talal, *Uneasy Lies the Head*, 12.
8. Ibid., 12–13.
9. Interview with Sharif Zaid bin Shaker.
10. Interview with Marwan Kasim.
11. Hussein bin Talal, *Uneasy Lies the Head*, 13–17.
12. Philip Geyelin's interview with Hussein, October 1991, "The Papers of Philip Geyelin," Middle East Centre Archive, St. Antony's College, Oxford. Philip Geyelin, a senior American journalist who worked for the *Washington Post*, conducted this interview and many others for a biography of King Hussein that he never completed.
13. Jordanian government text of 5 November 1992, address by King Hussein, quoted in Philip Geyelin, "Hashemite: The Story of King Hussein of Jordan," unpublished manuscript, "The Papers of Philip Geyelin," Middle East Centre Archive, St. Antony's College, Oxford.
14. Hussein bin Talal, *Uneasy Lies the Head*, 7–9, 19.
15. Ibid., 8.
16. Ibid., 9.
17. Interview with Moshe Sasson, Jerusalem, 8 September 1982. See also Avi Shlaim, *Collusion Across the Jordan: King Abdullah, the Zionist Movement, and the Partition of Palestine* (Oxford: Clarendon Press, 1988), 584–606.
18. Elias Sasson to Walter Eytan, 21 July 1951, 2408/11, Israel State Archives (ISA), Jerusalem.
19. Israel and the Arab States, a consultation in the prime minister's office, 1 October 1952, 2446/7, ISA.
20. Avi Shlaim, "Husni Za'im and the Plan to Resettle Palestinian Refugees in Syria," *Journal of Palestine Studies*, 15:4 (Summer 1986).

21. Mendel Cohen, *Behatzero shel hamelech Abdullah [At the Court of King Abdullah]*, in Hebrew (Tel Aviv: Am Oved, 1980), 84–91.
22. Ibid., 91–6.
23. Kirkbride, *From the Wings*, 140–41.
24. Quoted in Wilson, *King Abdullah, Britain and the Making of Jordan*, 132.
25. Kirkbride, *From the Wings*, 141.
26. Ibid., 142.
27. Hazza' al-Majali, *Mudhakkarati [My Memoirs]*, in Arabic (Beirut: Dar al-'Ilm lil-Malayeen, 1960).
28. Kirkbride, *From the Wings*, 142–43.
29. Interview with Prince Talal bin Muhammad.
30. Kirkbride, *From the Wings*, 143–44.
31. Robert B. Satloff, *From Abdullah to Hussein: Jordan in Transition* (New York: Oxford University Press, 1993), 41.
32. Hussein bin Talal, *Uneasy Lies the Head*, 22–29.
33. Quoted in Peter Snow, *Hussein: A Biography* (London: Barrie and Jenkins, 1972), 40–41.
34. Hussein bin Talal, *Uneasy Lies the Head*, 29–32.
35. Interview with Prince El Hassan bin Talal.
36. Hussein bin Talal, *Uneasy Lies the Head*, 33–34.
37. Satloff, *From Abdullah to Hussein*, 73.
38. Quoted in James Lunt, *Hussein of Jordan* (London: Fontana/Collins, 1990), 25.
39. Snow, *Hussein*, 51.

CHAPTER 3: THE MAKING OF A KING

1. Hussein bin Talal, *Uneasy Lies the Head: An Autobiography* (London: Heinemann, 1962), 48–49.
2. Interview with Princess Basma bint Talal.
3. Interview with Prince Talal bin Muhammad; and Lawrence Tal, *Politics, the Military, and National Security in Jordan 1955–1967* (Basingstoke: Palgrave Macmillan, 2002), 32, 134.
4. Philip Geyelin's interview with King Hussein, October 1991, "The Papers of Philip Geyelin," Middle East Centre Archive, St. Antony's College, Oxford.
5. Joseph A. Massad, *Colonial Effects: The Making of National Identity in Jordan* (New York: Columbia University Press, 2001), 169–71.
6. Ibid., 172–73.
7. Geoffrey Furlonge, "Political Review of Jordan for 1953," 25 January 1954, FO 371/119873, Public Record Office (PRO).
8. Interview with Sharif Zaid bin Shaker.
9. Philip Geyelin's interview with King Hussein, October 1991, "The Papers of Philip Geyelin."

10. Robert B. Satloff, *From Abdullah to Hussein: Jordan in Transition* (New York: Oxford University Press, 1993), 75–76.
11. Interview with Prince Talal bin Muhammad.
12. Avi Plascov, *The Palestinian Refugees in Jordan 1948–1957* (London: Frank Cass, 1981).
13. Amnon Cohen, *Political Parties in the West Bank under the Jordanian Regime 1949–1967* (Ithaca: Cornell University Press, 1982), 71.
14. Benny Morris, *Israel's Border Wars 1949–1956: Arab Infiltration, Israeli Retaliation, and the Countdown to the Suez War* (Oxford: Clarendon Press, 1993).
15. King Abdullah, *My Memoirs Completed: "Al Takmilah"* (London: Longman, 1978), xvi.
16. Interview with King Hussein bin Talal, 3 December 1996, Buckhurst Park, Ascot. An abridged version of this interview was published after the king's death under the title "His Royal Shyness: King Hussein and Israel," *New York Review of Books*, 15 July 1999.
17. Protocol of a meeting held with district commanders on 2 July 1952 and chaired by Ahmed Sidqi al-Jundi, collection of Jordanian records of the General Investigations, General Security and Military Intelligence departments captured by the IDF during the June War. Classified papers deposited in the Ben-Gurion Archive, Sede–Boker.
18. E. H. Hutchison, *Violent Truce: A Military Observer Looks at the Arab–Israeli Conflict 1951–1955* (New York: Devin-Adiar, 1956), 44.
19. John Bagot Glubb, *A Soldier with the Arabs* (London: Hodder and Stoughton, 1957), 310.
20. Ariel Sharon, *Warrior: The Autobiography of Ariel Sharon* (London: Macdonald, 1989), 90–91.
21. Yemima Rosenthal, ed., *Documents on the Foreign Policy of Israel.* Volume XIII: *1953* (Jerusalem: Israel State Archives, 1995), introduction and editorial note, 769–71.
22. Arye Eilan to Gideon Rafael, 4 January 1954, FM 2474/13A, Israel State Archives (ISA), quoted in Morris, *Israel's Border Wars*, 67.
23. Interview with Natheer Rasheed.
24. Philip Geyelin, "Hashemite: The Story of King Hussein of Jordan," unpublished manuscript, "The Papers of Philips Geyelin," Middle East Centre Archive, St. Antony's College, Oxford, Chapter 14, 13.
25. Satloff, *From Abdullah to Hussein*, 86–87.
26. Ann Dearden, *Jordan* (London: Robert Hale, 1958), 107.
27. Satloff, *From Abdullah to Hussein*, 87.

CHAPTER 4: THE BAGHDAD PACT FIASCO

1. Fawaz A. Gerges, *The Superpowers and the Middle East: Regional and International Politics 1955–1967* (Boulder, CO: Westview Press, 1994), 26.

2. Uriel Dann, "The Foreign Office, the Baghdad Pact and Jordan," *Asian and African Studies,* 21 (1987).
3. Humphroy Trevelyan, *The Middle East in Revolution* (London: Macmillan, 1970), 56.
4. Gerges, *The Superpowers and the Middle East,* 25.
5. Charles Duke, "Jordan: Annual Review for 1955," 27 July 1956, FO 371/121461, Public Record Office (PRO).
6. Hussein bin Talal, *Uneasy Lies the Head: An Autobiography* (London: Heinemann, 1962), 83.
7. Ibid., 87.
8. Interview with Prince Talal bin Muhammad.
9. Hussein bin Talal, *Uneasy Lies the Head,* 86.
10. Ibid., 86–87.
11. Nutting to Eden, 18 June 1955, cited in Robert B. Satloff, *From Abdullah to Hussein: Jordan in Transition* (New York: Oxford University Press, 1993), 111.
12. Hussein bin Talal, *Uneasy Lies the Head,* 88.
13. Satloff, *From Abdullah to Hussein,* 110.
14. Elie Podeh, *The Quest for Hegemony in the Arab World: The Struggle over the Baghdad Pact* (Leiden: Brill, 1995), 175–77.
15. Ibid., 176–83.
16. Dann, "The Foreign Office, the Baghdad Pact and Jordan."
17. Charles Duke, "Jordan: Annual Review for 1955," 27 July 1956, FO 371/121461, PRO.
18. Hussein bin Talal, *Uneasy Lies the Head,* 93.
19. Trevelyan, *The Middle East in Revolution,* 57.
20. John Bagot Glubb, *A Soldier with the Arabs* (London: Hodder and Stoughton, 1957), 393–97.
21. Lawrence Tal, *Politics, the Military, and National Security in Jordan 1955–1967* (Basingstoke: Palgrave Macmillan, 2002), 22.
22. Interview with Mreiwad al-Tall.
23. Hazza' al-Majali, *Mudhakkarati [My Memoirs],* in Arabic (Beirut: Dar al-Ilm lil-Malayeen, 1960), 72.
24. Glubb, *A Soldier with the Arabs,* 407.
25. Hussein bin Talal, *Uneasy Lies the Head,* 92–93.
26. E. Schneorson to E. Elath, 4 January 1956, 3745/1, ISA.
27. Quoted in Uriel Dann, "Glubb and the Politicization of the Arab Legion: An Annotated Document," *Asian and African Studies,* 21 (1987).
28. Anthony Eden, *Full Circle: The Memoirs of the Rt. Hon. Sir Anthony Eden* (London: Cassell, 1960), 345–46.
29. Satloff, *From Abdullah to Hussein,* 131–32.
30. Interview with Prince El Hassan bin Talal.
31. Peter Snow, *Hussein: A Biography* (London: Barrie and Jenkins, 1972), 65.
32. James Morris, *The Hashemite Kings* (London: Faber and Faber, 1959), 205.

33. Charles Duke, "Jordan: Annual Review for 1955," 27 July 1956, FO 371/121461, PRO.
34. Hussein bin Talal, *Uneasy Lies the Head*, 57.
35. Amalia and Aharon Barnea, *Mine Enemy* (London: Halban, 1989).
36. Ibid., Chapter 5.

CHAPTER 5: THE DISMISSAL OF GLUBB

1. James Morris, *The Hashemite Kings* (London: Faber and Faber, 1959), 206–7.
2. Evelyn Shuckburgh, *Descent to Suez: Diaries 1951–1956* (London: Weidenfeld and Nicolson, 1986), 292.
3. C. H. Johnston, "Jordan: Annual Review for 1956," 19 March 1957, FO 371/127876, Public Record Office (PRO).
4. Hussein bin Talal, *Uneasy Lies the Head: An Autobiography* (London: Heinemann, 1962), 107–12.
5. Morris, *The Hashemite Kings*, 209.
6. Interview with Marwan Kasim.
7. Hussein bin Talal, *Uneasy Lies the Head*, 116.
8. Interview with Marwan Kasim; interview with Natheer Rasheed.
9. Interview with Prince Talal bin Muhammad.
10. Hussein bin Talal, *Uneasy Lies the Head*, 117–18.
11. Interview with Marwan Kasim.
12. Morris, *The Hashemite Kings*, 211.
13. Anthony Eden, *Full Circle: The Memories of the Rt. Hon. Sir Anthony Eden* (London: Cassell, 1960), 347–48.
14. Ibid., 348–49.
15. Hussein bin Talal, *Uneasy Lies the Head*, 119–20.
16. Interview with Ahmad al-Lozi.
17. Eden, *Full Circle*, 349.
18. Anthony Nutting, *No End of a Lesson: The Story of Suez* (London: Constable, 1967), 18.
19. Mohamed H. Heikal, *Cutting the Lion's Tail: Suez through Egyptian Eyes* (London: André Deutsch, 1986), 96–98.
20. Lester Mallory to DOS, 16 March 1956, *Foreign Relations of the United States 1955–1957*. Volume XIII. *Near East: Jordan—Yemen* (Washington, DC: United States Government Printing House, 1988), 33.
21. Ann Dearden, *Jordan* (London: Robert Hale, 1958), 119.
22. Morris, *The Hashemite Kings*, 211.
23. P. J. Vatikiotis, *Politics and the Military in Jordan: A Study of the Arab Legion 1921–1957* (London: Frank Cass, 1967), 124.
24. C. H. Johnston, "Jordan: Annual Review for 1956," 19 March 1957, FO 371/127876, PRO.
25. Ibid.
26. Captain Aluf Hareven, Military Intelligence, to Foreign Ministry, 14 May

1956, "The Establishment of a Fedayeen Organisation in Jordan," 3745/1, Israel State Archive (ISA), Jerusalem.

27. Zeid Raad, "A Nightmare Avoided: Jordan and Suez 1956," *Israel Affairs*, 1:2 (Winter 1994).

28. S. B. Yeshaya to the director-general of the Foreign Ministry, 15 October 1956, 3745/1, ISA.

29. Research Department, Foreign Ministry, 18 October 1956, "Israel and the Entry of an Iraqi Army into Jordan," 3745/1, ISA.

30. Research Department, Foreign Ministry, 24 October 1956, "The New Jordanian Parliament," 3745/1, ISA.

31. S. Divon to Foreign Minister, 15 October 1956, 3745/1, ISA.

32. Eliahu Elath, London, to the Foreign Ministry, 13 December 1956, 3745/1, ISA.

CHAPTER 6: THE LIBERAL EXPERIMENT

1. Hussein bin Talal, *Uneasy Lies the Head: An Autobiography* (London: Heinemann, 1962), 127.

2. Ibid., 128.

3. Interview with Marwan Kasim.

4. Robin Bidwell, *Dictionary of Modern Arab History* (London: Kegan Paul, 1998), 292.

5. Moshe Dayan, *Diary of the Sinai Campaign* (London: Sphere Books, 1967), 89.

6. David Ben-Gurion's diary, 17 October 1956, the Ben-Gurion Archive, Sede-Boker. For an English version see "Ben-Gurion's Diary: The Suez–Sinai Campaign" in *The Suez–Sinai Crisis 1956: Retrospective and Reappraisal*, eds. Selwyn Ilan Troen and Moshe Shemesh (London: Frank Cass, 1990), 303.

7. Avi Shlaim, "The Protocol of Sèvres, 1956: Anatomy of a War Plot," *International Affairs*, 73:3 (July 1997).

8. Appendix in ibid. The text of "The Protocol of Sèvres, 24 October 1956" was first published as Appendix A in Keith Kyle, *Suez* (London: Weidenfeld and Nicolson, 1991).

9. Zeid Raad, "A Nightmare Avoided: Jordan and Suez 1956," *Israel Affairs*, 1:2 (Winter 1994).

10. Hazza' al-Majali, *Mudhakkarati [My Memoirs]*, in Arabic (Beirut: Dar al-Ilm lil-Malayeen, 1960).

11. Anwar al-Khatib al-Tamimi, *Ma'a Salah al-Din fi al-Quds: Ta'ammulat wa-Dhikrayat [With Salah al-Din in Jerusalem: Contemplations and Memoirs]*, in Arabic (Jerusalem: Dar al-Tibaah al-Arabiyah, 1989), 105–11.

12. Charles Johnston, *The Brink of Jordan* (London: Hamish Hamilton, 1972), 27.

13. Peter Snow, *Hussein: A Biography* (London: Barrie and Jenkins, 1972), 100.

14. Quoted in Kennett Love, *Suez—The Twice-fought War: A History* (New York: McGraw-Hill, 1969), 532–33.
15. Khatib, *Ma'a Salah al-Din fi al-Quds*, 111.
16. Dayan, *Diary of the Sinai Campaign*, 89–90.
17. Philip Geyelin's interview with Ali Abu Nuwar, 20 June 1990, "The Papers of Philip Geyelin," Middle East Centre Archive, St. Antony's College, Oxford.
18. Interview with Prince El Hassan bin Talal.
19. James Morris, *The Hashemite Kings* (London: Faber and Faber, 1959), 213.
20. Snow, *Hussein*, 100–1.
21. C. H. Johnston, "Jordan: Annual Review for 1956," 19 March 1957, FO 371/127876, PRO.
22. John Bagot Glubb, *A Soldier with the Arabs* (London: Hodder and Stoughton, 1957), 432.
23. Johnston, *The Brink of Jordan*, 81.
24. Munib al-Madi and Suleiman Musa, *Tarikh al-urdunn fi al-qarn al-'ishreen* [*The History of Jordan in the Twentieth Century*], in Arabic, 2nd ed., Volume I (Amman: Maktaba al-Muhtasab, 1988), 648.
25. Lester Mallory to the DOS, 9 November 1956, *Foreign Relations of the United States 1955–1957*. Volume XIII. *Near East: Jordan–Yemen* (Washington, DC: United States Government Printing House, 1988), 59.
26. Ibid., 64.
27. Interview with Sir Roger Tomkys.
28. "Memorandum of a Conversation," 10 December 1956, *Foreign Relations of the United States*. Volume XIII, 74.
29. Sir Harold Caccia to FO, 25 December 1956, FO 371/121525, PRO.
30. "Memorandum of a Conversation," 17 January 1957, *Foreign Relations of the United States*. Volume XIII, 81–83.
31. Gideon Rafael to Foreign Ministry, 22 January 1957, 3745/1, ISA.
32. Morris, *The Hashemite Kings*, 214.
33. Johnston, *The Brink of Jordan*, 27.
34. Shimshon Arad, Washington, "The Situation in Jordan," 29 April 1957, 3745/1, ISA.
35. Robert B. Satloff, *From Abdullah to Hussein: Jordan in Transition* (New York: Oxford University Press, 1993), 161.
36. Ibid., 154.
37. Hussein bin Talal, *Uneasy Lies the Head*, 133–34.
38. Mallory to DOS, 13 February 1957, *Foreign Relations of the United States*. Volume XIII, 84–86.
39. Johnston, *The Brink of Jordan*, 163.
40. Ibid., 47–48.
41. Hussein bin Talal, *Uneasy Lies the Head*, 128–31.

CHAPTER 7: A ROYAL COUP

1. Lester Mallory to the DOS, 29 March 1957, *Foreign Relations of the United States 1955–1957*. Volume XIII. *Near East: Jordan–Yemen* (Washington, DC: United States Government Printing House, 1988), 88–89.
2. C. H. Johnston, "Jordan: Annual Review for 1956," 19 March 1957, FO 371/127876, Public Record Office (PRO).
3. Interview with Natheer Rasheed; and Joseph A. Massad, *Colonial Effects: The Making of National Identity in Jordan* (New York: Columbia University Press, 2001), 193.
4. Hussein bin Talal, *Uneasy Lies the Head: An Autobiography* (London: Heinemann, 1962), 135.
5. C. H. Johnston, "Jordan: Annual Review for 1956," 19 March 1957, FO 371/127876, PRO.
6. Hussein bin Talal, *Uneasy Lies the Head*, 135.
7. Uriel Dann, *King Hussein and the Challenge of Arab Radicalism: Jordan 1955–1967* (New York: Oxford University Press, 1989), 56.
8. James Morris, *The Hashemite Kings* (London: Faber and Faber, 1959), 216.
9. Hussein bin Talal, *Uneasy Lies the Head*, 136.
10. Elie Podeh, "The Struggle for Arab Hegemony after the Suez Crisis," *Middle Eastern Studies*, 29:1 (January 1993).
11. Hussein bin Talal, *Uneasy Lies the Head*, 137–51.
12. Peter Snow, *Hussein: A Biography* (London: Barrie and Jenkins, 1972), 108–13.
13. Miles Copeland, *The Game of Nations: The Amorality of Power Politics* (London: Weidenfeld and Nicolson, 1969), 189.
14. Interview with Natheer Rasheed.
15. Johnston to Lloyd, 14 May 1957, FO 371.127880/VJ 1015/118. Cited in Robert B. Satloff, *From Abdullah to Hussein: Jordan in Transition* (New York: Oxford University Press, 1993), 168.
16. *Foreign Relations of the United States*. Volume XIII, 94–97.
17. Erskine B. Childers, *The Road to Suez: A Study of Western–Arab Relations* (London: MacGibbon and Kee, 1962), Appendix B, 397–401.
18. Lawrence Tal, *Politics, the Military, and National Security in Jordan 1955–1967* (Basingstoke: Palgrave Macmillan, 2002), 45.
19. Satloff, *From Abdullah to Hussein*, 167.
20. P. J. Vatikiotis, *Politics and the Military in Jordan: A Study of the Arab Legion 1921–1957* (London: Frank Cass, 1967), 130–35.
21. Childers, *The Road to Suez*, 398.
22. Tal, *Politics, the Military, and National Security in Jordan*, 49.
23. Dann, *King Hussein and the Challenge of Arab Radicalism*, 60.
24. *Foreign Relations of the United States*. Volume XIII, 100–9.
25. Charles Johnston, *The Brink of Jordan* (London: Hamish Hamilton, 1972), 61; and Satloff, *From Abdullah to Hussein*, 171–72.

26. Dann, *King Hussein and the Challenge of Arab Radicalism*, 64.
27. Johnston, *The Brink of Jordan*, 62.
28. C. H. Johnston, "Jordan: Annual Review for 1957," 28 January 1958, FO 371/134006, PRO.
29. Johnston, *The Brink of Jordan*, 62.
30. Ibid, 79–81.
31. *Foreign Relations of the United States.* Volume XIII, 109.
32. C. H. Johnston, "Jordan: Annual Review for 1957," 28 January 1958, FO 371/134006, PRO.
33. Wilbur Crane Eveland, *Ropes of Sand: America's Failure in the Middle East* (New York: W. W. Norton, 1980), 183–84.
34. Ibid., 188.
35. Ibid., 189–91.
36. Bob Woodward, "CIA Paid Millions to Jordan's King Hussein," *Washington Post*, 18 February 1977; Bob Woodward, *Veil: The Secret Wars of the CIA 1981–1987* (New York: Simon and Schuster, 1987), 238.
37. Philip Geyelin, "Hashemite: The Story of King Hussein of Jordan," unpublished manuscript, "The Papers of Philip Geyelin," Middle East Centre Archive, St. Antony's College, Oxford, Chapter 30, 9–10.
38. Interview with a former CIA official who wished to remain anonymous.
39. Interview with Mreiwad al-Tall.
40. Satloff, *From Abdullah to Hussein*, 174–75.
41. C. H. Johnston, "Jordan: Annual Review for 1957," 28 January 1958, FO 371/134006, PRO.
42. Ibid.

CHAPTER 8: THE YEAR OF REVOLUTION

1. Malcolm H. Kerr, *The Arab Cold War: Gamal Abd al-Nasir and His Rivals 1958–1970*, 3rd ed. (London: Oxford University Press, 1971).
2. Elie Podeh, *The Decline of Arab Unity: The Rise and Fall of the United Arabic Republic* (Brighton: Sussex Academic Press, 1999), 39–48. See also Patrick Seale, *The Struggle for Syria: A Study in Post-war Arab Politics 1945–1958* (London: Oxford University Press, 1965), 321.
3. Podeh, *The Decline of Arab Unity*, 47.
4. Charles Johnston, *The Brink of Jordan* (London: Hamish Hamilton, 1972), 88.
5. James Lunt, *Hussein of Jordan* (London: Fontana/Collins, 1990), 70.
6. I am grateful to Foulath Hadid for sharing with me his knowledge of Iraqi history during this period.
7. Hussein bin Talal, *Mihnati ka-malik [My Profession as King]*, in Arabic, (Amman: Al-Ahliyya Publishing House, [n.d.]), 140–46.
8. Douglas Little, "A Puppet in Search of a Puppeteer? The United States,

King Hussein and Jordan 1953–1970," *International History Review*, 18:3 (August 1995).

9. Harold Macmillan, *Riding the Storm 1956–1959* (London: Macmillan, 1971), 503.

10. Lawrence Tal, *Politics, the Military, and National Security in Jordan 1955–1967* (Basingstoke: Palgrave Macmillan, 2002), 56.

11. Mouayad Ibrahim K. al-Windawi, "Anglo-Iraqi Relations 1945–1958" (unpublished Ph.D. thesis, University of Reading, 1989), 321.

12. Michael Ionides, *Divide and Lose: The Arab Revolt of 1955–1958* (London: Geoffrey Bles, 1960), 246.

13. Yossi Melman and Dan Raviv, *Behind the Uprising: Israelis, Jordanians, and Palestinians* (New York: Greenwood Press, 1989), 55–56.

14. Uriel Dann, *King Hussein and the Challenge of Arab Radicalism: Jordan 1955–1967* (New York: Oxford University Press, 1989), 86–87.

15. Little, "A Puppet in Search of a Puppeteer? The United States, King Hussein and Jordan 1953–1970."

16. Hussein bin Talal, *Uneasy Lies the Head: An Autobiography* (London: Heinemann, 1962), 160–61.

17. Interview with King Hussein bin Talal.

18. Al-Windawi, "Anglo-Iraqi Relations 1945–1958," 330.

19. Hussein bin Talal, *Uneasy Lies the Head*, 155.

20. Interview with Ali Shukri.

21. Philip Geyelin, "Hashemite: The Story of King Hussein of Jordan," unpublished manuscript, "The Papers of Philip Geyelin," Middle East Centre Archive, St. Antony's College, Oxford, Chapter 29, 15.

22. Eliezer Be'eri, *Army Officers in Arab Politics and Society* (New York: Praeger, 1970), 176.

23. Humphrey Trevelyan, *The Middle East in Revolution* (London: Macmillan, 1970), 135–37.

24. For an analysis of a first-hand account of the massacre see Elie Kedourie, *Arabic Political Memoirs and Other Studies* (London: Frank Cass, 1974), 179–82.

25. Al-Windawi, "Anglo-Iraqi Relations 1945–1958," 327–28.

26. Little, "A Puppet in Search of a Puppeteer? The United States, King Hussein and Jordan 1953–1970."

27. Heath Mason to FO, 16 July 1958, FO 371/134038/30190, Public Record Office (PRO).

28. Macmillan, *Riding the Storm 1956–1959*, 518.

29. Geyelin, "Hashemite: The Story of King Hussein of Jordan," Chapter 29, 15.

30. Macmillan, *Riding the Storm 1956–1959*, 518.

31. Avi Shlaim, "Israel, the Great Powers, and the Middle East Crisis of 1958," *Journal of Imperial and Commonwealth History*, 27:2 (May 1999).

32. David Ben-Gurion's diary, 14 July 1958, Ben-Gurion Archive, Sede-Boker.

33. Lord Hood to Sir William Hayter, 9 September 1958, FO 371/134279, PRO.
34. Minutes by C. A. E. Shuckburgh, 28 July 1958, FO 371/134289/30190, PRO.
35. Interview with King Hussein bin Talal.
36. Hussein bin Talal, *Uneasy Lies the Head*, 168.
37. Ibid., 167.
38. Interview with Prince Talal bin Muhammad.
39. Ibid.
40. Johnston, *The Brink of Jordan*, 104.
41. James Morris, *The Hashemite Kings* (London: Faber and Faber, 1959), 220.
42. Ibid., 222.
43. Johnston, *The Brink of Jordan*, 106.
44. Robert B. Satloff, "The Jekyll-and-Hyde Origins of the US–Jordanian Strategic Relationship" in *The Middle East and the United States: A Historical and Political Reassessment*, ed. David W. Lesch (Boulder, CO: Westview, 2003), 128.
45. *Foreign Relations of the United States 1955–1957*. Volume XIII. *Near East: Jordan–Yemen* (Washington, DC: United States Government Printing House, 1988), 74–77.
46. Dann, *King Hussein and the Challenge of Arab Radicalism*, 91.
47. Johnston, *The Brink of Jordan*, 107.
48. Macmillan, *Riding the Storm 1956–1959*, 524.
49. Johnston, *The Brink of Jordan*, 108–11.
50. Ibid., 109, 112.
51. Hussein bin Talal, *Uneasy Lies the Head*, 172.
52. Ibid., 179–85.
53. Tal, *Politics, the Military, and National Security in Jordan*, 65.
54. R. Levi to Foreign Ministry, 14 November 1958, "Jordan," 3745/4, Israel State Archive (ISA).
55. Quoted in Tal, *Politics, the Military, and National Security in Jordan*, 153.

CHAPTER 9: ARAB FOES AND JEWISH FRIENDS

1. Lawrence Tal, *Politics, the Military, and National Security in Jordan 1955–1967* (Basingstoke: Palgrave Macmillan, 2002), 69.
2. Interview with Ahmad al-Lozi.
3. Tal, *Politics, the Military, and National Security in Jordan*, 67–69.
4. Hussein bin Talal, *Uneasy Lies the Head: An Autobiography* (London: Heinemann, 1962), 196.
5. Interview with Jamal Sha'er; and Peter Snow, *Hussein: A Biography* (London: Barrie and Jenkins, 1972), 134.

6. Tal, *Politics, the Military, and National Security in Jordan*, 73–74.
7. C. H. Johnston, "Jordan: Annual Review for 1959," 16 January 1960, FO 371/151040, Public Record Office (PRO).
8. Yossi Melman and Dan Raviv, *Behind the Uprising: Israelis, Jordanians, and Palestinians* (New York: Greenwood Press, 1989), 56–57.
9. Charles Johnston, *The Brink of Jordan* (London: Hamish Hamilton, 1972), 156.
10. Malik Mufti, "The United States and Nasserist Pan-Arabism" in *The Middle East and the United States: A Historical and Political Reassessment,* ed. David W. Lesch (Boulder, CO: Westview Press, 1996), 168.
11. Hussein bin Talal, *Uneasy Lies the Head,* 186–94.
12. *Foreign Relations of the United States 1961–1963.* Volume XVII. *Near East: 1961–1962,* Department of State (Washington, DC: United States Government Printing House, 1994), 273–76.
13. Interview with Sir Roger Tomkys.
14. J. P. C. E. Henniker-Major, "Annual Political Review for Jordan for 1961," FO 371/164080, PRO.
15. Hussein bin Talal, *Uneasy Lies the Head,* 220–21.
16. Ibid, 222–28.
17. John Henniker, *Painful Extractions: Looking Back at a Personal Journey* (Eye, Suffolk: Thornham Books, 2002), 128–29.
18. J. P. C. E. Henniker-Major, "Annual Political Review for Jordan for 1961," FO 371/164080, PRO.
19. Uriel Dann, *King Hussein and the Challenge of Arab Radicalism: Jordan 1955–1967* (New York: Oxford University Press, 1989), 116–17.
20. Interview with Princess Basma bint Talal.
21. Dann, *King Hussein and the Challenge of Arab Radicalism,* 120.
22. Philip Robins, *A History of Jordan* (Cambridge: Cambridge University Press, 2003), 106–7.
23. Interview with Tariq al-Tall.
24. Interview with Mreiwad al-Tall.
25. Asher Susser, *On Both Banks of the Jordan: A Political Biography of Wasfi al-Tall* (London: Frank Cass, 1994), 51–55; and Tal, *Politics, the Military, and National Security in Jordan,* 88–89.
26. Roderick Parkes, "Annual Political Review for Jordan, 1962," FO 371/164080, PRO.
27. Interview with Ali Shukri.
28. Roderick Parkes, "Annual Political Review for Jordan, 1962," FO 371/164080, PRO.
29. Kamal S. Salibi, *The Modern History of Jordan* (London: I. B. Tauris, 1993), 206–7.
30. Roderick Parkes, "Annual Political Review for Jordan, 1962," FO 371/164080, PRO.
31. Ibid.

32. Roderick Parkes, "Jordan: Annual Review for 1963," FO 371/175645, PRO.

33. Snow, *Hussein,* 154–55.

34. Roderick Parkes, "Jordan: Annual Review for 1963," FO 371/175645, PRO.

35. Ibid.

36. Interview with King Hussein bin Talal.

37. Melman and Raviv, *Behind the Uprising,* 59–62.

38. Gideon Shomron to the Foreign Ministry, 10 August 1960, 3782/16, Israel State Archives (ISA).

39. Gideon Shomron to Avraham Cohen, the Foreign Ministry, 27 September 1960, 3782/16, ISA.

40. Gideon Shomron to Avraham Cohen, the Foreign Ministry, 20 October 1960, 3782/16, ISA.

41. Avraham Cohen to Gideon Shomron, London, 24 October 1960, 3782/16, ISA.

42. Gideon Shomron to Avraham Cohen, the Foreign Ministry, 20 December 1961, 3782/16, ISA.

43. Avi Shlaim, *Collusion Across the Jordan: King Abdullah, the Zionist Movement, and the Partition of Palestine* (Oxford: Clarendon Press, 1988), 141. The Jewish Agency made payments to King Abdullah in the 1930s for the option of a lease on his land in Ghaur al-Kibd—an option that was never exercised. This provided a veneer of legitimacy for what could otherwise be construed as the payment of a political subsidy or bribe. Modest sums of money were also given by Jewish Agency officials to Abdullah in 1946 and 1947 to consolidate the covert relationship with him. Some of Abdullah's courtiers also received money from the Jewish Agency. Shlaim, Collusion across the Jordan, 50–54, 78–82, 616–17.

44. Moshe Zak, *Hussein oseh shalom [Hussein Makes Peace],* in Hebrew (Ramat-Gan: Bar-Ilan University Press, 1996), 63.

45. Selwyn Lloyd to Sir Francis Rundall (Tel Aviv), 12 August 1958, FO 371/134285, PRO.

46. Zaki Shalom, *The Superpowers, Israel and the Future of Jordan 1960–1963: The Perils of the Pro-Nasser Policy* (Brighton: Sussex Academic Press, 1999), Chapter 8.

47. Yaacov Herzog's papers at the Israel State Archives in Jerusalem have not been declassified under the thirty-year rule because of their special sensitivity. So I am particularly grateful to his daughter, Shira Herzog, for giving me unrestricted access to her father's private papers.

48. "Meeting with Charles," 24 September 1963, "The Private Papers of Yaacov Herzog," Jerusalem. "Charles" was the code name the Israelis gave to Hussein.

49. Ibid.

50. This is one of the main arguments of Shalom, *The Superpowers, Israel and the Future of Jordan.*
51. Interview with Major-General Meir Amit.
52. Interview with Adnan Abu-Odeh.

CHAPTER 10: THE PALESTINIAN CHALLENGE

1. J. F. S. Phillips, "Jordan 1964: Arma Virumque," FO 371/180728, Public Record Office (PRO).
2. Malcolm H. Kerr, *The Arab Cold War: Gamal Abd al-Nasir and His Rivals 1958–1970*, 3rd ed. (London: Oxford University Press, 1971), Chapter 4.
3. Avraham Sela, *Ahdut betokh perud ba-ma'arekhet habein-arvit: ve'idot ha-pisgah ha-arviyot 1964–1982 [Unity within Disunity in the Inter-Arab System: The Arab Summit Conferences 1964–1982],* in Hebrew (Jerusalem: Magnes Press, 1982), 1.
4. Moshe Shemesh, *The Palestinian Entity 1959–1974: Arab Politics and the PLO*, 2nd ed. (London: Frank Cass, 1996), Chapter 1.
5. Asher Susser, *On Both Banks of the Jordan: A Political Biography of Wasfi al-Tall* (London: Frank Cass, 1994), 80.
6. George Ball, acting secretary of state, "Memorandum for the President: Your Meeting with King Hussein," 10 April 1964, NSF Country File, Box 148, Lyndon B. Johnson Library, Austin, Texas (LBJL).
7. R. W. Komer, "Memorandum for the President," 13 April 1964, NSF Country File, Box 148, LBJL.
8. "Memorandum of Conversation," 14 and 15 April 1964, NSF Country File, Box 148, LBJL.
9. "Second meeting with Charles," Part 1, 2 May 1964, "The Private Papers of Yaacov Herzog," Jerusalem.
10. "Impressions," ibid.
11. R. W. Komer, "Memorandum for the President," 9 August 1964 and 1 February 1965, NSF Country File, Box 146, LBJL.
12. The Central Intelligence Agency, "Special Report: The Jordan Waters Issue," NSF Country File, Box 146, LBJL.
13. "General Comments of King Husayn on Arab Summit Conference," NSF Country File, Box 146, LBJL.
14. "Third Meeting with Charles," 19 December 1964, "The Private Papers of Yaacov Herzog." Herzog was an observant Jew and as such he did not permit himself to write on Sabbath because writing constituted work. The notes for his eight-page report on the meeting were made on Saturday night with the help of the host.
15. R. W. Komer, "Memorandum for the President," 3 February 1965, NSF Country File, Box 146, LBJL. Emphasis in the original.
16. R. W. Komer, "Memorandum for the President," 26 January 1965, NSF Country File, Box 146, LBJL. Emphasis in the original.

17. Talbot to Department of State, 8 February 1965, NSF Country File, Box 146, LBJL.
18. Talbot to Department of State, 9 February 1965, NSF Country File, Box 146, LBJL.
19. Yitzhak Rabin, *The Rabin Memoirs* (London: Weidenfeld and Nicolson, 1979), 50–51.
20. R. W. Parkes, "Jordan: Annual Review for 1965," FO 371/186547, PRO.
21. Interview with Mreiwad al-Tall.
22. Interview with Dr. Hazem Nusseibeh.
23. Susser, *On Both Banks of the Jordan,* 82.
24. Dr. Yaacov Herzog was not present at the meeting because he was in the throes of a deep psychological crisis triggered by the invitation to become the Chief Rabbi of Britain. When the crisis was over, Levi Eshkol appointed Herzog as a political adviser and later as the director general of his office.
25. Moshe Zak, *Hussein oseh shalom [Hussein Makes Peace],* in Hebrew (Ramat-Gan: Bar-Ilan University Press, 1996), 79–80.
26. Interview with King Hussein bin Talal.
27. Zak, *Hussein oseh shalom,* 79–81.
28. David Shaham, *Israel—40 ha-Shanim [Israel—The 40 Years],* in Hebrew (Tel Aviv: Am Oved, 1991), 215.
29. Interview with King Hussein bin Talal.

CHAPTER 11: THE ROAD TO WAR

1. Interview with King Hussein bin Talal.
2. Interview with Lieutenant-General Itzhak Rabin, Tel Aviv, 22 August 1982.
3. Interview with Miriam Eshkol, London, 12 December 2002.
4. Ze'ev Bar-Lavie, *Hamishtar ha-hashemi 1949–1967 ve-ma'amado ba-gada ha-ma'aravit [The Hashemite Regime 1949–1967, and Its Status in the West Bank],* in Hebrew (Tel Aviv: The Shiloah Center, 1981), 45–46.
5. Interview with Mreiwad al-Tall.
6. Moshe Shemesh, "The IDF Raid on Samu': The Turning-Point in Jordan's Relations with Israel and the West Bank Palestinians," *Israel Studies,* 7:1 (Spring 2002).
7. Ibid.
8. Undated and unsigned letter, "The Private Papers of Yaacov Herzog," Jerusalem.
9. Ambassador in London to Foreign Ministry, 24 November 1966, ibid.
10. Subject: "Jordan," 12 December 1966, 4094/10, Israel State Archives (ISA).
11. Cable from Ambassador Burns, 13 December 1966, NSF Country File, Box 146, Lyndon B. Johnson Library, Austin, Texas (LBJL).

12. Interview with Richard Viets.
13. Message to King Hussein of Jordan, 23 November 1966, NSF Country File, Box 146, LBJL.
14. Burns to secretary of state with copy to the White House, 11 December 1966, NSF Country File, Box 146, LBJL.
15. Burns to secretary of state, 11 December 1966, NSF Country File, Box 146, LBJL.
16. CIA, "The Jordanian Regime: Its Prospects and the Consequences of its Demise," 13 December 1966, NSF Country File, Box 146, LBJL.
17. Douglas Little, "A Puppet in Search of a Puppeteer? The United States, King Hussein and Jordan, 1953–1970," *International History Review*, 18:3 (August 1995).
18. Walt Rostow to the president, 22 December 1966, NSF Country File, Box 146, LBJL.
19. Vick Vance and Pierre Lauer, *Hussein of Jordan: My "War" with Israel* (New York: William Morrow, 1969), 43–53.
20. Samir A. Mutawi, *Jordan in the 1967 War* (Cambridge: Cambridge University Press, 1987), 108–11.
21. Interview with King Hussein bin Talal.
22. Quoted in Roland Dallas, *King Hussein: A Life on the Edge* (London: Profile Books, 1999), 105.
23. Quoted in Jeremy Bowen, *Six Days: How the 1967 War Shaped the Middle East* (London: Simon and Schuster, 2003), 66.
24. Odd Bull, *War and Peace in the Middle East: The Experiences and Views of a UN Observer* (London: Leo Cooper, 1976), 113.
25. Interview with King Hussein bin Talal.
26. Dean Rusk, *As I Saw It: A Secretary of State's Memoirs* (London: I. B. Tauris, 1991), 331.
27. Abba Eban, *An Autobiography* (London: Weidenfeld and Nicolson, 1978), 408.
28. Vance and Lauer, *Hussein of Jordan: My "War" with Israel*, 68–70. Hussein refused to discuss this incident in his extensive interviews with Vance and Lauer.
29. Richard Helms, *A Look Over My Shoulder: A Life in the Central Intelligence Agency* (New York: Random House, 2003), 303–4.
30. Ezer Weizman, *On Eagles' Wings: The Personal Story of the Leading Commander of the Israeli Air Force* (London: Weidenfeld and Nicolson, 1976), 242–43.
31. Interview with Moshe Sasson.
32. Vance and Lauer, *Hussein of Jordan: My "War" with Israel*, 95–96. The main reason Hussein believed this charge was because, as he later admitted, the technical side of Jordanian intelligence during the war was very poor.
33. Ibid., 88–93.

34. Moshe Zak, *Hussein oseh shalom [Hussein Makes Peace]*, in Hebrew (Ramat-Gan: Bar-Ilan University Press, 1996), 117–18.
35. Mutawi, *Jordan in the 1967 War*, 139–40; Vance and Lauer, *Hussein of Jordan: My "War" with Israel*, 95–96.
36. Tom Segev, *1967: ve-ha'aretz shinta et paneha [1967: And the Land was Transformed]* in Hebrew (Jerusalem: Keter, 2005), 377–78.
37. Zak, *Hussein oseh shalom*, 118.
38. Segev, *1967*, 378.
39. Vance and Lauer, *Hussein of Jordan: My "War" with Israel*, 65.
40. Remez to Levavi, 7 June 1967, "Hussein," "The Private Papers of Yaacov Herzog," Jerusalem.
41. Remez and Admoni to Levavi, 7 June 1967, ibid.
42. "A Conversation between Jock Smith and Naftali Kenan," 7 June 1967, 5.30, ibid.
43. Vance and Lauer, *Hussein of Jordan: My "War" with Israel*, 97.

CHAPTER 12: PICKING UP THE PIECES

1. Samir A. Mutawi, *Jordan in the 1967 War* (Cambridge: Cambridge University Press, 1987), 164.
2. Amman to FO, 17 July 1967, PREM, 13/1622, Public Record Office (PRO).
3. Lawrence Tal, *Politics, the Military, and National Security in Jordan 1955–1967* (Basingstoke: Palgrave Macmillan, 2002), 120–21.
4. Mahmoud Riad, *The Struggle for Peace in the Middle East* (London: Quartet, 1981), 46.
5. Reuven Pedatzur, "Coming Back Full Circle: The Palestinian Option in 1967," *Middle East Journal*, 49:2 (Spring 1995).
6. Oxford doctoral thesis in progress by Avi Raz, "The Palestinian Option: Israel and the West Bank Leadership 1967–1969." I am grateful to Mr. Raz for sharing with me some of his primary sources for the thesis.
7. Yaacov Herzog's diary, 15 June 1967, 4511A/3, Israel State Archives (ISA).
8. Avi Shlaim, *The Iron Wall: Israel and the Arab World* (New York: W. W. Norton, 2000), 253–55.
9. Reuven Pedatzur, "The June Decision was Cancelled in October," *Ha'aretz*, 12 May 1995.
10. *Foreign Relations of the United States 1964–1968*. Volume XIX. *Arab–Israeli Crisis and War 1967* (Washington, DC: United States Government Printing House, 2004), 577–80.
11. Ibid., 583–85.
12. Yaacov Herzog's diary, 2 July 1967, 4511A/3, ISA.
13. "Meeting with Charles on Sunday, July 2nd, from 8:10 p.m. to 9:45 p.m.," "The Private Papers of Yaacov Herzog," Jerusalem.
14. Michael Bar-Zohar, *Khayav ve-moto shel nasikh yehudi: biographia shel*

Yaacov Herzog [The Life and Times of a Jewish Prince: A Biography of Yaacov Herzog], in Hebrew (Tel Aviv: Yediot Aharonot, 2003), 283–84. Tom Segev, *1967: ve-ha'aretz shinta et paneha [1967: And the Land was Transformed]*, in Hebrew (Jerusalem: Keter, 2005), 536.

15. Yaacov Herzog's diary, 7 July 1967, 4511A/3, ISA.
16. Foreign Office, 30 June 1967, "Visit of King Hussein: Brief for Prime Minister and Secretary of State," FCO 17/240, PRO.
17. "Record of Conversation between the Prime Minister and the King of Jordan at No. 10 Downing Street at 2:30 p.m. on Monday, July 3, 1967," FCO 17/240, PRO.
18. Addendum to "Meeting with Charles on Sunday, July 2nd, from 8:10 p.m. to 9:45 p.m.," "The Private Papers of Yaacov Herzog," Jerusalem.
19. Amman to FO, 17 July 1967, PREM, 13/1622, PRO.
20. Dean Rusk, "Memorandum for the President," 20 July 1967, NSF Country File, Middle East, Box 113, Lyndon B. Johnson Library, Austin, Texas (LBJL); London to secretary of state, 22 July 1967, and Amman to secretary of state, 4 August 1967, POL 27–14 ARAB-ISR, United States National Archives, Washington, DC (USNA).
21. Amman to secretary of state, 26 July 1967, NSF Country File, Middle East, Box 113, LBJL.
22. Abdel Majid Farid, *Nasser: The Final Years* (Reading: Ithaca Press, 1994), 51–67.
23. Yoram Meital, "The Khartoum Conference and Egyptian Policy after the 1967 War: A Re-examination," *Middle East Journal*, 54:1 (Winter 2000).
24. Interview with King Hussein bin Talal.
25. Meital, "The Khartoum Conference and Egyptian Policy after the 1967 War: A Re-examination."
26. Robert Stephens, *Nasser: A Political Biography* (London: Allen Lane, 1971), 523.
27. Amman to FO, 8 September 1967, PREM, 13/1623, PRO; and undated report on plain paper "Highlights of the Khartoum Conference from King Husayn on 2 September." The name of the author is not given but it was most probably Jack O'Connell, the CIA station chief in Amman. NSF Country File, Middle East, Box 113, LBJL.
28. Amman to secretary of state, 4 September 1967, POL 27–14 ARAB-ISR, USNA.
29. Baruch Gilead to Foreign Ministry, 16 October 1967, 3835/5, ISA.
30. Amman to FO, 7 October 1967, FCO 17/550, PRO.
31. King Hussein to President Johnson, 7 October 1967, NSF Special Heads of State Correspondence, Box 31, LBJL.
32. *Foreign Relations of the United States 1964–1968*. Volume XIX. *Arab–Israeli Crisis and War 1967*, 1004–6, 1012–16.

33. Interview with King Hussein bin Talal.
34. "A Special Chapter on Charles, dictated on 3.11.67," "The Private Papers of Yaacov Herzog," Jerusalem.
35. "Two Meetings with Charles (on the morning of November 19th and on the morning of November 20th respectively)," ibid.
36. Herzog to prime minister, 21 November 1967, ibid.
37. Avi Shlaim, "Interview with Abba Eban, 11 March 1976," *Israel Studies*, 8:1 (Spring 2003).
38. Helena Cobban, *The Palestinian Liberation Organisation: People, Power and Politics* (Cambridge: Cambridge University Press, 1984), 38–39.
39. CIA, "Jordanian Ex-prime minister Wasfi Tal's Policy Proposals for Countering the Arab Defeat and Its Consequences in Jordan," 13 September 1967, NSF Country File, Box 147, LBJL.
40. Douglas Little, "A Puppet in Search of a Puppeteer? The United States, King Hussein and Jordan 1953–1970," *International History Review*, 18:3 (August 1995).
41. "Jordan and the Fedayeen," 5 December 1967, 3835/5, ISA.
42. Cobban, *The Palestinian Liberation Organisation*, 41–42.
43. Interview with King Hussein bin Talal.

CHAPTER 13: DIALOGUE ACROSS THE BATTLE LINES

1. Interview with Zaid Rifa'i.
2. "Record of Meeting held on 3.5.68," "The Private Papers of Yaacov Herzog," Jerusalem.
3. "Two talks with Z.R., 5 and 6 May 1968" and "Protocol of the Ministerial Defence Committee with the participation of all the members of the cabinet, 8 May 1968," Ibid.
4. "Protocol of the Ministerial Defence Committee with the participation of all the members of the cabinet, 8 May 1968," ibid.
5. Herzog to Eban, 19 June 1968, ibid.
6. The proposed procedure reflected the Israeli diplomat's penchant for precision and his love of cloak-and-dagger operations. The Israeli boat, using beams, was to signal in Morse code the word "Musa"—the code for Jordan. Musa was to reply "Davis"—the code for Herzog. The signals were to be repeated until the boats joined. Musa was then to follow the instructions given by Davis in English. This was Arrangement A. Arrangement B was to meet in London at a date to be confirmed. Paper headed "Arrangement A, Arrangement B," ibid.
7. "Conversations with Charles and his adviser on 22nd and 24th August [1968]," ibid.
8. Abba Eban, *Personal Witness: Israel through My Eyes* (New York: Putnam's, 1992), 496–98.
9. Harrison M. Symmes to secretary of state, 20 March 1968, NSF Country File, Box 147, Lyndon B. Johnson Library, Austin, Texas (LBJL).

10. Walt Rostow to President Johnson, 31 May 1968, NSF Country File, Box 148, LBJL.
11. Interview with Zaid Rifa'i.
12. Reuven Pedatzur, "The Circle Closes," *Ha'aretz*, 10 November 1995.
13. "Memorandum of Conversation," 4 June 1968, POL 27–14 ARAB-ISR, United States National Archives, Washington, DC (USNA).
14. Amman to secretary of state, 20 July 1968, NSF Country File, Box 147, LBJL.
15. Moshe Zak, *Hussein oseh shalom [Hussein Makes Peace],* in Hebrew (Ramat-Gan: Bar-Ilan University Press, 1996), 44.
16. Yaacov Herzog's diary, 10 July 1968, A4511/4, Israel State Archives (ISA).
17. Zak, *Hussein oseh shalom,* 155.
18. Thomas Friedman, *From Beirut to Jerusalem* (London: Fontana Books, 1990), 261.
19. Interview with Moshe Sasson.
20. "General Objectives and Atmosphere" [n.d.], "The Private Papers of Yaacov Herzog," Jerusalem.
21. Yaacov Herzog's report to the cabinet, 6 October 1968, ibid.
22. Abba Eban, *An Autobiography* (London: Weidenfeld and Nicolson, 1978), 446.
23. Eban to Eshkol, 29 September 1968, "The Private Papers of Yaacov Herzog," Jerusalem.
24. Interview with King Hussein bin Talal.
25. The above account is based on five documents written by Dr. Yaacov Herzog, and especially his notes on the cabinet meeting of 27 October 1968, "The Private Papers of Yaacov Herzog," Jerusalem.
26. "Speaking Notes for Use with Mr. Rusk on 4 November 1968" [no author], NSF Country File, Box 148, LBJL.
27. Reuven Pedatzur, "And This Is the History of Gaza since '67," *Ha'aretz,* 7 November 2003.
28. "Meeting Held on November 19, 1968," "The Private Papers of Yaacov Herzog," Jerusalem.
29. Harrison M. Symmes to secretary of state, 17 September 1968, NSF Country File, Box 147, LBJL.
30. Harrison M. Symmes to secretary of state, 9 December 1968, NSF Country File, Box 148, LBJL.
31. Harrison M. Symmes to secretary of state, 20 December 1968, POL 27–14 ARAB-ISR/Sandstorm, Box 1841, USNA. Emphasis in the original.
32. "Charles—from December 1968 to the end of August 1969," "The Private Papers of Yaacov Herzog," Jerusalem.
33. Ibid.
34. Ibid.; and Remez to the Foreign Ministry, 27 January 1969, ibid.
35. "Charles—from December 1968 to the end of August 1969," ibid.
36. Ibid. Not wanting Allon to feel left out, Hussein looked around, found a rifle, and gave it to him as a present.

37. Barbour to secretary of state, 18 April 1969, POL 27–14 ARAB-ISR/Sandstorm, Box 1841, USNA.
38. Rogers to Tel Aviv, 19 April 1969, POL 27–14 ARAB-ISR/Sandstorm, Box 1841, USNA.
39. Golda Meir, *My Life* (London: Weidenfeld and Nicolson, 1975), 312.
40. Interview with Simha Dinitz.
41. Philip Adams, "Jordan: Annual Review for 1969," FCO 17/1039, Public Record Office (PRO).
42. "Charles—from December 1968 to the end of August 1969"; and Remez to prime minister, 24 April 1969, "The Private Papers of Yaacov Herzog," Jerusalem.
43. Raad Alkadiri, "Strategy and Tactics in Jordanian Foreign Policy 1967–1988" (unpublished D.Phil. thesis, University of Oxford, 1995), 36–37.
44. "Charles—from December 1968 to the end of August 1969"; and Remez to prime minister, 25 April 1969, "The Private Papers of Yaacov Herzog," Jerusalem.
45. "Charles—from December 1968 to the end of August 1969," ibid.
46. Philip Adams, "Jordan: Annual Review for 1969," FCO 17/1039, PRO.
47. "Charles—from December 1968 to the end of August 1969," "The Private Papers of Yaacov Herzog," Jerusalem.
48. Philip Adams, "Jordan: Annual Review for 1968." This document was missing from the Public Record Office. I am grateful to Ms. Penny Prior of the Records and Historical Department of the Foreign and Commonwealth Office for sending me a copy of their last copy.
49. Philip Adams, "Jordan: Annual Review for 1969," FCO 17/1039, PRO.
50. "Sharif NASIR bin Jamil" [n.d.], NSF Country File, Box 147, LBJL.
51. Private information.
52. Philip Adams, "Jordan: Annual Review for 1969," FCO 17/1039, PRO.
53. London to prime minister, 18 September 1969, "The Private Papers of Yaacov Herzog," Jerusalem.
54. Odell to secretary of state, 30 August 1969, POL 27–14 ARAB-ISR/Sandstorm, Box 1841, USNA.
55. "Jordanian–Israeli Settlement" [no author and n.d.], POL 27–14 ARAB-ISR/Sandstorm, Box 1841, USNA.
56. "Meeting with the colleague of Chaim and the adviser on 28.9.69"; and "Report on Jordan following the talk on 28.9.69 with the colleague of Chaim and the adviser," "The Private Papers of Yaacov Herzog," Jerusalem.
57. "Report on Jordan following the talk on 28.9.69 with the colleague of Chaim and the adviser," ibid.
58. Mahmoud Riad, *The Struggle for Peace in the Middle East* (London: Quartet, 1981), 117.

CHAPTER 14: CIVIL WAR

1. J. F. S. Phillips, "Jordan: Annual Review for 1970," FCO 17/1411, Public Record Office (PRO).
2. Yezid Sayigh, *Armed Struggle and the Search for State: The Palestinian National Movement, 1949–1993* (Oxford: Clarendon Press, 1997).
3. Helena Cobban, *The Palestinian Liberation Organisation: People, Power and Politics* (Cambridge: Cambridge University Press, 1984), 48–49.
4. Malcolm H. Kerr, *The Arab Cold War: Gamal Abd al-Nasir and His Rivals 1958–1970*, 3rd ed. (London: Oxford University Press, 1971), 142.
5. Kamal S. Salibi, *The Modern History of Jordan* (London: I. B. Tauris, 1993), 233.
6. Moshe Zak, "Israeli–Jordanian Negotiations," *Washington Quarterly*, 8:1 (Winter 1985).
7. J. F. S. Phillips, "Jordan: Annual Review for 1970," FCO 17/1411, PRO.
8. "Message transmitted by Zurhellen 0245 A. M. 4 June," "The Private Papers of Yaacov Herzog," Jerusalem.
9. Barnes (Tel Aviv) to FCO, 5 June 1970, FCO 17/1066, PRO.
10. Interview with Marwan Kasim.
11. Interview with King Hussein bin Talal.
12. Salibi, *The Modern History of Jordan*, 233.
13. "No. 146, 9 June 1970," "The Private Papers of Yaacov Herzog," Jerusalem.
14. Barnes (Tel Aviv) to FCO, 12 June 1970, FCO 17/1066, PRO.
15. "Protocol of the Meeting of the IDF General Staff, 15 June 1970."
16. J. F. S. Phillips, "Jordan: Annual Review for 1970," FCO 17/1411, PRO.
17. Major-General Aharon Yariv's report, "Protocol of the Meeting of the IDF General Staff, 22 June 1970."
18. Roland Dallas, *King Hussein: A Life on the Edge* (London: Profile Books, 1999), 133.
19. Henry Kissinger, *White House Years* (Boston: Little Brown, 1979), 595–96.
20. Ibid., 597.
21. Interview Natheer Rasheed.
22. Interview with King Abdullah bin Hussein.
23. One story that Sharif Nasser's subordinates liked to repeat was of a trip to the northern front to plan a strategy to repel a Syrian invasion. One staff officer raised his hand and said, "How do we retreat?" Sharif Nasser pulled out a Sten gun and emptied the magazine over the heads of his staff. Everybody took to the ground and he shouted, "Next time I hear someone mention retreat, I won't miss!" Interview with Prince Talal bin Muhammad.
24. Oriana Fallaci, "An Interview with King Hussein: 'I am prepared to confront anyone who tries to expel me,' " *Ma'ariv*, 12 June 1970.

25. Interview with Prince Raad bin Zaid.
26. Salibi, *The Modern History of Jordan*, 234.
27. Chronology, "Jordan: Annual Review for 1970," FCO 17/1411, PRO.
28. Sayigh, *Armed Struggle and the Search for State*, 263.
29. Interview with Ali Shukri.
30. Kissinger, *White House Years*, 599.
31. Interview with Natheer Rasheed.
32. Philip Geyelin's interview with Adnan Abu-Odeh, 20 July 1988, "The Papers of Philip Geyelin," Middle East Centre Archive, St. Antony's College, Oxford.
33. Patrick Seale, *Asad of Syria: The Struggle for the Middle East* (London: I. B. Tauris, 1988), 158.
34. Interview with Adnan Abu-Odeh.
35. Peter Tripp in interview for the BBC2 historical documentary programme *UK Confidential*, broadcast on 1 January 2000.
36. Secretary of state to prime minister, 21 September 1970, PREM 15/124, PRO.
37. CM (70), 20th Conclusions. "Conclusions of a Meeting the Cabinet held at 10 Downing Street, S.W. 1, on Monday, 21 September, 1970, at 10:30 a.m.," PRO.
38. Ibid.
39. Richard M. Nixon, *The Memoirs of Richard Nixon* (London: Sidgwick and Jackson, 1978), 483.
40. Mahmoud Riad, *The Struggle for Peace in the Middle East* (London: Quartet, 1981), 162.
41. Kissinger, *White House Years*, 614.
42. Ibid., 621–24.
43. Moshe Zak, *Hussein oseh shalom [Hussein Makes Peace]*, in Hebrew (Ramat-Gan: Bar-Ilan University Press, 1996), 125.
44. Yaacov Herzog to Golda Meir, 25 September 1970, "Memo on US–Israel Contacts on Syrian–Jordan Situation," "The Private Papers of Yaacov Herzog," Jerusalem.
45. "Protocol of the Meeting of the IDF General Staff, 21 September 1970."
46. "The Private Papers of Yaacov Herzog," Jerusalem.
47. Oral History Project, Leonard Davis Institute for International Relations, Jerusalem. Fifth interview with Yigal Allon, 4 June 1979, 5001/19, Israel State Archives (ISA), Jerusalem.
48. Quoted in Yaacov Herzog to Golda Meir, 25 September 1970, "Memo on US–Israel Contacts on Syrian–Jordan Situation," "The Private Papers of Yaacov Herzog," Jerusalem.
49. Interview with Zaid Rifa'i.
50. Kissinger, *White House Years*, 628.
51. *The 50 Years War*, transcript of interview for the six-part BBC television series, Middle East Centre Archive, St. Antony's College, Oxford (1998), Mordechai Hod, commander of the IAF, 21 January 1997.

52. Interview with Natheer Rasheed.
53. Interview with Prince Raad bin Zaid.
54. Sayigh, *Armed Struggle and the Search for State*, 264.
55. Israeli intelligence thought that the man to watch in the Iraqi Ba'th Party was another member of the Takriti clan: Saddam Hussein. "Protocol of the Meeting of the IDF General Staff, 26 October 1970."
56. Sayigh, *Armed Struggle and the Search for State*, 268.
57. "Middle East: A Secret Rendezvous," *Time*, 23 November 1970.
58. "Meeting on the initiative of Charles and the adviser with Allon and Herzog, Saturday evening, 3.10.70," "The Private Papers of Yaacov Herzog," Jerusalem.
59. Oral History Project, Leonard Davis Institute for International Relations, Jerusalem. Fifth interview with Yigal Allon, 4 June 1979, 5001/19, ISA.
60. Raad Alkadiri, "Strategy and Tactics in Jordanian Foreign Policy 1967–1988" (unpublished D.Phil. thesis, University of Oxford, 1995), 55–56.
61. Interview with Mreiwad al-Tall.
62. Asher Susser, *On Both Banks of the Jordan: A Political Biography of Wasfi al-Tall* (London: Frank Cass, 1994), 154.
63. Interview with Abdullah Salah. Salah was at the scene of the murder and suffered a minor injury.
64. Susser, *On Both Banks of the Jordan*, 168–69.

CHAPTER 15: THE UNITED ARAB KINGDOM PLAN

1. B. L. Strachan to R. M. Evans, 4 December 1970, FCO 17/1201, Public Record Office (PRO).
2. Interview with Zaid Rifa'i.
3. J. F. S. Phillips to A. D. Parsons, 11 November 1971, FCO 17/1504, PRO.
4. J. A. Fortescue, "Record of Conversation between King Hussein of Jordan and His Majesty's Ambassador, Paris, on 15 December 1970." FCO 17/1101, PRO.
5. The text of King Hussein's speech is reproduced in *Journal of Palestine Studies*, 1:4 (Summer 1972).
6. The text of the PLO statement is reproduced in ibid.
7. Newspaper cutting [no title, n.d.], FCO 17/1687, PRO.
8. Summary of the Arabic language press comments on the Hussein plan, 12 April 1972, FCO 17/1687, PRO.
9. Barnes to FCO, 16 March 1972, FCO 17/1687, PRO.
10. Mohamed Heikal, *The Road to Ramadan* (London: Collins, 1975), 120–21.
11. Algiers to London, 17 March 1972, FCO 17/1687, PRO.
12. Kamal S. Salibi, *The Modern History of Jordan* (London: I. B. Tauris, 1993), 254.
13. Alan Hart, *Arafat: A Political Biography*, rev. ed. (London: Sidgwick and Jackson, 1994), 219–20.

14. *Sunday Times*, 15 June 1969, as quoted in David Hirst, *The Gun and the Olive Branch: The Roots of Violence in the Middle East* (London: Faber and Faber, 1977), 264.

15. Interview with Simha Dinitz.

16. Moshe Zak, *Hussein oseh shalom [Hussein Makes Peace]*, in Hebrew (Ramat-Gan: Bar-Ilan University Press, 1996), 192–93.

17. Interview with King Hussein bin Talal.

18. Phillips to FCO, 23 November 1970, FCO 17/1066, PRO.

19. Zak, *Hussein oseh shalom*, 46, 161–63, 179–80.

20. Ibid., 16, 35, 46, 162–63, 227; and Moshe Zak's handwritten notes on the protocol of the meeting of 21 March 1972 in "The Private Papers of Moshe Zak," Ramat Aviv. I am grateful to Sarah Zak for giving me access to the papers of her late husband.

21. Zak, *Hussein oseh shalom*, 162.

22. H. G. Balfour-Paul to A. D. Parsons, 2 October 1972, FCO 17/1693, PRO.

23. John Phillips to Sir Alec Douglas-Home, 3 July, 1972, FCO 17/1689, PRO.

24. H. G. Balfour-Paul to the secretary of state for foreign and commonwealth affairs, "Jordan: First Impressions," 26 September 1972, FCO 17/1690, PRO.

CHAPTER 16: THE OCTOBER WAR

1. Yehuda Lukacs, *Israel, Jordan, and the Peace Process* (New York: Syracuse University Press, 1999), 3.

2. Henry Kissinger, *Years of Upheaval* (London: Weidenfeld and Nicolson, 1982), 218–19. Emphasis in the original.

3. Ibid., 219–20.

4. Ibid., 461.

5. Moshe Zak, *Hussein oseh shalom [Hussein Makes Peace]*, in Hebrew (Ramat-Gan: Bar-Ilan University Press, 1996), 46–47, 163.

6. Samir Al-Rifa'i, "The 1974 Rabat Conference: A Crucial Arab Summit" (unpublished M.Phil. thesis, University of Cambridge, 1989), 38–41.

7. Ibid., 41–42.

8. Ibid., 42–43.

9. Abu Iyad and Eric Rouleau, *My Home, My Land: A Narrative of the Palestinian Struggle* (New York: Times Books, 1978), 121–22.

10. Interview with Sharif Zaid bin Shaker.

11. General Fathi Abu Taleb confirmed to Adiba Mango, my research assistant, on 15 December 2002 that he had accompanied King Hussein and Zaid Rifa'i to the meeting in Israel on 25 September 1973 but he refused to talk about it and he declined my request for an interview.

12. Gai Gavra, "The Hussein–Golda Meeting on the Eve of the Yom Kippur War," in Hebrew (unpublished BA thesis, Tel Aviv University, 2000). I am

grateful to Gai Gavra for giving me a copy of his well-researched and highly informative 116-page paper.

13. Ibid., 47.

14. Ahron Bregman, *Israel's Wars 1947–1993* (London: Routledge, 2000), 77.

15. Gavra, "The Hussein–Golda Meeting on the Eve of the Yom Kippur War (Hebrew)," 62.

16. Conversation with Shlomo Gazit, former director of military intelligence, Oxford, 25 September 1999.

17. Interview with King Hussein bin Talal.

18. Interview with Zaid Rifa'i.

19. Eli Zeira, *Milchemet Yom ha-Kippurim: Mytos mul Metsiut [The Yom Kippur War: Myth against Reality]*, in Hebrew (Tel Aviv: Yediot Aharonot, 1993), 95–99.

20. Interview with Mordechai Gazit. Gazit elaborated on some of these points in an unpublished paper entitled "The Yom Kippur War: A Critical Look at Commonly Accepted Assumptions." I am grateful to Mordechai Gazit for putting at my disposal a copy of this paper.

21. Raad Alkadiri, "Strategy and Tactics in Jordanian Foreign Policy 1967–1988" (unpublished D.Phil. thesis, University of Oxford, 1995), 78–79.

22. Kissinger, *Years of Upheaval*, 500.

23. Zak, *Hussein oseh shalom*, 135.

24. Mohamed Heikal, *The Road to Ramadan* (London: Collins, 1975), 221–22.

25. Kissinger, *Years of Upheaval*, 506.

26. Interview with Prince Talal bin Muhammad.

27. Moshe Dayan, *Avnei Derekh: Otobiographia [Milestones: An Autobiography]*, in Hebrew (Tel Aviv: Yediot Aharonot, 1976), 542.

28. Zak, *Hussein oseh shalom*, 136–37.

29. Chaim Herzog, *The Arab–Israeli Wars: War and Peace in the Middle East* (New York: Vintage Books, 1982), 303.

30. Yossi Melman and Dan Raviv, *Behind the Uprising: Israelis, Jordanians, and Palestinians* (New York: Greenwood Press, 1989), 121–22.

31. Heikal, *The Road to Ramadan*, 236.

32. Kissinger, *Years of Upheaval*, 540.

CHAPTER 17: THE ROAD TO RABAT

1. Interview with King Hussein bin Talal.

2. Henry Kissinger, *Years of Upheaval* (London: Weidenfeld and Nicolson, 1982), 655.

3. Samir Al-Rifa'i, "The 1974 Rabat Conference: A Crucial Arab Summit" (unpublished M.Phil. thesis, University of Cambridge, 1989), 54–57.

4. Kissinger, *Years of Upheaval*, 846–48.

5. Oral History Project, Leonard Davis Institute for International Relations, Jerusalem. Fifth interview with Yigal Allon, 4 June 1979, 5001/19, Israel State Archives (ISA).

6. Kissinger, *Years of Upheaval*, 848.

7. Zaid Rifa'i told me that after every meeting with the Israelis, he would give His Majesty a typed report in English and that the king kept these reports with his private papers at home rather than in the royal court. When I interviewed King Hussein at Buckhurst Park, on 3 December 1996, he said he had all his notes back home in Amman and that he would be more than happy to check them for me. Unfortunately, I was too slow and by the time I was ready to follow up, the king was seriously ill with cancer. After the king's death, I did my best to gain access to his notes and reports about the secret meetings but without any success. No one seemed to know where these papers were and indeed whether they had survived at all. The people I approached included half a dozen court officials as well as Zaid Rifa'i, Queen Noor and King Abdullah bin Hussein.

8. Interview with Mordechai Gazit.

9. Interview with Adnan Abu-Odeh.

10. Moshe Zak, "Fruitless Bargaining with King Hussein," *Jerusalem Post*, 27 September 1991.

11. Extracts from the record of the meeting with King Hussein on 7 March 1974, "The Private Papers of Moshe Zak," Ramat Aviv, Israel. Moshe Zak was given access to the classified protocols of all the secret meetings between Israeli officials and King Hussein. As the talks were in English, the protocols are also in English. Zak, however, made notes on these protocols in Hebrew. I retranslated the above extracts from Hebrew into English because I had no access to the original English version.

12. Interview with Mordechai Gazit.

13. Kissinger, *Years of Upheaval*, 1,037.

14. Ibid., 1,038.

15. Shimon Peres, *David's Sling* (London: Weidenfeld and Nicolson, 1970), 259.

16. Ibid., 976.

17. Interview with Dan Patir.

18. Yossi Melman and Dan Raviv, *Behind the Uprising: Israelis, Jordanians, and Palestinians* (New York: Greenwood Press, 1989), 127–29.

19. Ibid., 129–30; and Shimon Peres, *Battling for Peace: Memoirs* (London: Weidenfeld and Nicolson, 1995), 165, 301.

20. Matti Golan, *Shimon Peres: A Biography* (London: Weidenfeld and Nicolson, 1982), 153–54.

21. Interviews with Zaid Rifa'i and Mreiwad al-Tall.

22. Al-Rifa'i, "The 1974 Rabat Conference: A Crucial Arab Summit," 68–77.

23. Interview with Zaid Rifa'i.

24. Madiha Rashid Al Madfai, *Jordan, the United States and the Middle East Peace Process 1974–1991* (Cambridge: Cambridge University Press, 1993), 21.
25. Interview with King Hussein bin Talal.
26. Interview with Prince Talal bin Muhammad.
27. Interview with Dr. Kamel Abu Jaber.
28. Yehuda Lukacs, *Israel, Jordan, and the Peace Process* (New York: Syracuse University Press, 1999), 140.
29. Dan Raviv and Yossi Melman, *Every Spy a Prince: The Complete History of Israel's Intelligence Community* (Boston: Houghton Mifflin, 1990), 213–14.
30. Moshe Zak, "Israeli–Jordanian Negotiations," *Washington Quarterly*, 8:1 (Winter 1985).
31. Interview with Adnan Abu-Odeh.
32. Gideon Rafael, *Destination Peace: Three Decades of Israeli Foreign Policy* (New York: Stein and Day, 1981), 363; and Yossi Melman, "Talks Amidst Hostility," *Ha'aretz*, 2 August 1991.
33. Melman and Raviv, *Behind the Uprising*, 130–34.
34. Oral History Project, Leonard Davis Institute for International Relations, Jerusalem. Fifth interview with Yigal Allon, 4 June 1979, 5001/19, Israel State Archives (ISA).
35. Zak, "Israeli–Jordanian Negotiations."
36. Interview with King Hussein bin Talal.

CHAPTER 18: THE CAMP DAVID ACCORDS

1. Jimmy Carter, *Keeping Faith: Memoirs of a President* (London: Collins, 1982), 285.
2. Interview with Prince Talal bin Muhammad.
3. Interview with Sharif Zaid bin Shaker.
4. Moshe Dayan, *Breakthrough: A Personal Account of the Egypt–Israel Peace Negotiations* (London: Weidenfeld and Nicolson, 1981), 35–37.
5. Interview with King Hussein bin Talal.
6. Eliahu Ben Elissar, *Lo Od Milhama [No More War]*, in Hebrew (Jerusalem: Ma'ariv, 1995), 33–36.
7. Interview with King Hussein bin Talal.
8. "King Hussein Calls on Arabs to Heal Splits, Not to Aggravate Them," *Jordan Times*, 29 November 1977.
9. Interview with Laila Sharaf.
10. Raad Alkadiri, "Strategy and Tactics in Jordanian Foreign Policy 1967–1988" (unpublished D.Phil. thesis, University of Oxford, 1995), 104.
11. Letter from Jimmy Carter to King Hussein, 16 August 1978, Box 13, "The Papers of Philip Geyelin," Middle East Centre Archive, St. Antony's College, Oxford.

12. Letter from King Hussein to Jimmy Carter, 27 August 1978, ibid.
13. Interview with Dan Patir.
14. Interviews with King Hussein bin Talal, Prince Raad bin Zaid and Nicholas Veliotis.
15. Carter, *Keeping Faith*, 397.
16. Zbigniew Brzezinski, *Power and Principle: Memoirs of a National Security Adviser 1977–1981* (London: Weidenfeld and Nicolson, 1983), 261.
17. Carter, *Keeping Faith*, 404.
18. Obituary of Cyrus Vance by Harold Jackson, *Guardian*, 14 January 2002.
19. Cyrus Vance, *Hard Choices: Critical Years in America's Foreign Policy* (New York: Simon and Schuster, 1983), 229–30.
20. Interviews with King Hussein bin Talal, Laila Sharaf and Marwan Kasim. For the text of the Questions and Answers see Appendix B in Madiha Rashid Al Madfai, *Jordan, the United States and the Middle East Peace Process 1974–1991* (Cambridge: Cambridge University Press, 1993), 222–30.
21. Interview with Nicholas Veliotis.
22. Carter, *Keeping Faith*, 409.
23. Interview with Ali Shukri.
24. Robert Fisk, *The Great War for Civilisation: The Conquest of the Middle East* (London: Fourth Estate, 2005), 183.
25. Mahmoud Riad, *The Struggle for Peace in the Middle East* (London: Quartet, 1981), 330–34.
26. Interview with Prince Talal bin Muhammad.
27. Al Madfai, *Jordan, the United States and the Middle East Peace Process 1974–1991*, 64.
28. Ibid., 54–56, 80.

CHAPTER 19: LEBANON AND THE REAGAN PLAN

1. Queen Noor, *Leap of Faith: Memoirs of an Unexpected Life* (London: Weidenfeld and Nicolson, 2003), 81.
2. Ibid., 2.
3. Ibid., 258–59.
4. Interview with Prince Talal bin Muhammad.
5. Interview with Ali Shukri.
6. Interview with Cranwell G. Montgomery.
7. Interview with King Abdullah bin Hussein.
8. Interview with Prince Talal bin Muhammad.
9. Ronald Reagan, *An American Life* (London: Hutchinson, 1990), 410.
10. Interview with Richard Viets. On that first visit the Reagans invited the king and Queen Noor to lunch in their private quarters. Viets was also invited. In the middle of this small affair, Reagan suddenly said, "I understand that the Dead Sea is so salty that no fish can survive in it." The comment was not germane to anything that went on before. Hussein

said, "That's correct. No fish can survive there." Reagan: "I think we can help you out. We have special fish in California and I think they would love to live in the Dead Sea." Hussein's eyes went almost into the dome of his head; he could hardly believe that this conversation was taking place. After lunch Reagan took Viets aside and said he was going to have members of his staff contact him to arrange the shipment of the fish. The two of them, Reagan said, were going to sort out this problem for Jordan. Viets was embarrassed but the king was characteristically good-humoured. When they met on future occasions, he would often rib Viets by saying, "When are you going to bring the fish?!"

11. "King Appeals for Decisive Arab Action on Lebanon Situation," *Jordan Times*, 18 March 1978.
12. Interview with Adnan Abu-Odeh.
13. Ze'ev Schiff and Ehud Yaari, *Israel's Lebanon War* (London: Allen and Unwin, 1985), 39–44.
14. Arye Naor, *Memshalah be-milhamah: tifkud memshelet yisrael be-milhemet levanon, 1982 [Cabinet at War: The Functioning of the Israeli Cabinet during the Lebanon War 1982]*, in Hebrew (Tel Aviv: Lahav, 1986), 119–20.
15. Interview with Prince Talal bin Muhammad.
16. Interview with Sharif Zaid bin Shaker.
17. George P. Shultz, *Turmoil and Triumph: My Years as Secretary of State* (New York: Scribner's, 1993), 87.
18. Mohamed Heikal, *Secret Channels: The Inside Story of Arab–Israeli Peace Negotiations* (London: HarperCollins, 1996), 356.
19. Caspar Weinberger, *Fighting for Peace: Seven Critical Years at the Pentagon* (London: Michael Joseph, 1990), 101.
20. Interview with Nicholas Veliotis.
21. Noor, *Leap of Faith*, 215.
22. William B. Quandt, *Peace Process: American Diplomacy and the Arab–Israeli Conflict since 1967* (Berkeley: University of California Press, 2001), 256–57.
23. Raad Alkadiri, "Strategy and Tactics in Jordanian Foreign Policy 1967–1988" (unpublished D.Phil. thesis, University of Oxford, 1995), 138–39; and John Newhouse, "Profiles: Monarch," *New Yorker*, 19 September 1983.
24. Quandt, *Peace Process*, 257.
25. Interview with Nicholas Veliotis.
26. Reagan, *An American Life*, 431.

CHAPTER 20: PEACE PARTNERSHIP WITH THE PLO

1. Raad Alkadiri, "Strategy and Tactics in Jordanian Foreign Policy 1967–1988" (unpublished D.Phil. thesis, University of Oxford, 1995), 175.

2. Interview with Shimon Peres.
3. "Address by His Majesty King Hussein I to the Nation, Wednesday, 19 February 1986" (Hashemite Kingdom of Jordan, Ministry of Information), 45.
4. Interview with Taher al-Masri.
5. Ibid.
6. George P. Shultz, *Turmoil and Triumph: My Years as Secretary of State* (New York: Scribner's, 1993), 457.
7. Ibid., 445.
8. Ibid., 447.
9. Madiha Rashid Al Madfai, *Jordan, the United States and the Middle East Peace Process 1974–1991* (Cambridge: Cambridge University Press, 1993), 169.
10. Shultz, *Turmoil and Triumph*, 451.
11. Ibid., 451.
12. Interview with Shimon Peres.
13. Moshe Zak, *Hussein oseh shalom [Hussein Makes Peace]*, in Hebrew (Ramat-Gan: Bar-Ilan University Press, 1996), 201–2, 263–64.
14. Shultz, *Turmoil and Triumph*, 452–55.
15. Adam Garfinkle, *Israel and Jordan in the Shadow of War: Functional Ties and Futile Diplomacy in a Small Place* (London: Macmillan, 1992), 113.
16. Alan Hart, *Arafat: A Political Biography*, rev. ed. (London: Sidgwick and Jackson, 1994), 444–46.
17. Yossi Melman and Dan Raviv, *Behind the Uprising: Israelis, Jordanians, and Palestinians* (New York: Greenwood Press, 1989), 173.
18. Interview with Shimon Peres.
19. Lady Mishcon always laid on a lavish lunch for her distinguished guests and the atmosphere was usually relaxed, with a great deal of small talk and a mixture of Jewish and Arab humour. Beilin described the king as "smiley, very nice, very friendly, very outgoing, and surprisingly modest." Interview with Dr. Yossi Beilin.
20. Melman and Raviv, *Behind the Uprising*, 166–67.
21. Andrew Gowers and Tony Walker, *Behind the Myth: Yasser Arafat and the Palestinian Revolution* (London: W. H. Allen, 1990), 261.
22. Shultz, *Turmoil and Triumph*, 460.
23. "Address by His Majesty King Hussein I to the Nation, Wednesday, 19 February 1986" (Hashemite Kingdom of Jordan, Ministry of Information), 85.
24. Interview with Dr. Taher Kanaan.
25. Yehuda Lukacs, *Israel, Jordan, and the Peace Process* (New York: Syracuse University Press, 1999), 164.
26. Melman and Raviv, *Behind the Uprising*, 175; and Zak, *Hussein oseh shalom*, 204–5.
27. Shultz, *Turmoil and Triumph*, 790.

28. Queen Noor, *Leap of Faith: Memoirs of an Unexpected Life* (London: Weidenfeld and Nicolson, 2003), 271.
29. Shultz, *Turmoil and Triumph*, 844.
30. Interview with Adnan Abu-Odeh.
31. Interviews with Taher al-Masri and Dr. Samir Mutawi.
32. Alan Friedman, *Spider's Web: Bush, Saddam, Thatcher and the Decade of Deceit* (London: Faber and Faber, 1993), 26–27.
33. David Schenker, *Dancing with Saddam: The Strategic Tango of Jordanian–Iraqi Relations* (Lanham: Lexington Books, 2003), 37.
34. For data on Jordan's finances in general see Laurie A. Brand, *Jordan's Inter-Arab Relations: The Political Economy of Alliance Making* (New York: Columbia University Press, 1994).
35. Interview with Prince Talal bin Muhammad.
36. Interview with Ali Shukri.

CHAPTER 21: THE LONDON AGREEMENT

1. Ali Mahafza, *'Ashrat a'awam min al-kifah wa al-bina: majmuat khutub jalalat al-malik Hussein bin Talal 1977–1987 [Ten Years of Struggle and Building: The Collected Speeches of His Majesty King Hussein bin Talal 1977–1987]*, in Arabic (Amman: Markaz al-Kitab al-Urduni, 1988), 894–916.
2. Shayke Ben-Porat, *Sikhot im Yossi Beilin [Talks with Yossi Beilin]*, in Hebrew (Tel Aviv: Hakibbutz Hameuhad Publishing House, 1996), 89–94.
3. Shimon Peres, *Battling for Peace: Memoirs* (London: Weidenfeld and Nicolson, 1995), 305–9.
4. *The Peres–Hussein London Agreement*, 11 April 1987, ibid., Appendix 2, 361–62.
5. Ibid., 308–9; and Yitzhak Shamir, *Summing Up: An Autobiography* (London: Weidenfeld and Nicolson, 1994), 169.
6. George P. Shultz, *Turmoil and Triumph: My Years as Secretary of State* (New York: Scribner's, 1993), 938–39.
7. Ibid., 940–41.
8. Arye Naor, *Ktovet al ha-kir: le'an molikh ha-Likud [Writing on the Wall: Where Is the Likud Leading?]*, in Hebrew (Tel Aviv: Edanim, 1988), 177–79.
9. *New York Times,* 13 May 1987, quoted in Andrew Gowers and Tony Walker, *Behind the Myth: Yasser Arafat and the Palestinian Revolution* (London: W. H. Allen, 1990), 266.
10. Interview with Shimon Peres.
11. Interview with King Hussein bin Talal.
12. Interview with Ali Shukri.
13. Interview with Yossi Beilin.
14. Shamir, *Summing Up*, 257.

15. Efraim Halevy, *Man in the Shadows: Inside the Middle East Crisis with the Man Who Led the Mossad* (London: Weidenfeld and Nicolson, 2006), Chapter 1.
16. Interview with Dan Meridor.
17. Yediot Aharonot, 4 February 1994, quoted in Yehuda Lukacs, *Israel, Jordan, and the Peace Process* (New York: Syracuse University Press, 1999), 173.
18. Queen Noor, *Leap of Faith: Memoirs of an Unexpected Life* (London: Weidenfeld and Nicolson, 2003), 276.
19. Interview with Marwan Kasim.
20. *The 50 Years War,* transcript of interview for six-part BBC television series, Middle East Centre Archive, St. Antony's College, Oxford (1998), King Hussein, 2 March 1997.
21. Interview with King Abdullah bin Hussein.
22. Interview with Dan Meridor.
23. Shultz, *Turmoil and Triumph,* 942–43.
24. Ibid., 944–47.
25. Noor, *Leap of Faith,* 277.
26. Interview with Taher al-Masri.
27. "Talking Points: Hussein—First Meeting" [n.d.], Box 28, "The Papers of Philip Geyelin," Middle East Centre Archive, St. Antony's College, Oxford.
28. Shultz, *Turmoil and Triumph,* 947–48.
29. Interview with Taher al-Masri.
30. Address by King Hussein to the Arab League Summit Conference, Amman, 8 November 1987, Mahafza, *'Ashrat a'awam min al-kifah wa al-bina,* 1,058–60.
31. The 50 Years War, King Hussein, 2 March 1997.

CHAPTER 22: INTIFADA AND DISENGAGEMENT

1. Don Peretz, *Intifada: The Palestinian Uprising* (Boulder, CO: Westview Press, 1990), 167.
2. George P. Shultz, *Turmoil and Triumph: My Years as Secretary of State* (New York: Scribner's, 1993), 1, 018–26.
3. *The 50 Years War,* transcript of interview for six-part BBC television series, Middle East Centre Archive, St. Antony's College, Oxford (1998), Zaid Rifa'i, 6 March 1997.
4. Ze'ev Schiff and Ehud Yaari, *Intifada: The Palestinian Uprising—Israel's Third Front* (New York: Simon and Schuster, 1990), 297–99.
5. Interview with Richard Viets.
6. Raad Alkadiri, "Strategy and Tactics in Jordanian Foreign Policy 1967–1988" (unpublished D.Phil. thesis, University of Oxford, 1995), 194–95.

7. Shultz, *Turmoil and Triumph*, 1,025–7.
8. Adnan Abu-Odeh, *Jordanians, Palestinians, and the Hashemite Kingdom in the Middle East Peace Process* (Washington, DC: United States Institute of Peace Press, 1999), 224–25.
9. Interview with Adnan Abu-Odeh.
10. Ibid.
11. Interview with Taher al-Masri.
12. Asher Susser, *In through the Out Door: Jordan's Disengagement and the Middle East Peace Process* (Washington, DC: Washington Institute for Near East Policy, 1990), 13.
13. Shultz, *Turmoil and Triumph*, 1, 030–31.
14. *Jordan Times*, 9 April 1988.
15. Shimon Peres to King Hussein, 26 July 1988, "The Private Papers of Moshe Zak," Ramat Aviv.
16. King Hussein to Shimon Peres, 27 July 1988, ibid.
17. Interview with Adnan Abu-Odeh.
18. Interview with King Hussein bin Talal.
19. Address by King Hussein on Jordan's Disengagement from the West Bank, 31 July 1988, in *The Israeli–Palestinian Conflict: A Documentary Record 1967–1990*, ed. Yehuda Lukacs (Cambridge: Cambridge University Press, 1992), 520–25.
20. Queen Noor, *Leap of Faith: Memoirs of an Unexpected Life* (London: Weidenfeld and Nicolson, 2003), 280.
21. Interview with Dr. Taher Kanaan.
22. Interview with Taher al-Masri.
23. Shultz, *Turmoil and Triumph*, 1, 033.
24. Schiff and Yaari, *Intifada*, 271–72.
25. Susser, *In through the Out Door*, 37.
26. Adiba Mango, "Jordan on the Road to Peace 1988–1999" (unpublished D.Phil. thesis, University of Oxford, 2002), 45.
27. Philip Robins, *A History of Jordan* (Cambridge: Cambridge University Press, 2003), 177.
28. Interview with Ali Shukri.
29. Laurie A. Brand, *Jordan's Inter-Arab Relations: The Political Economy of Alliance Making* (New York: Columbia University Press, 1994), 95.
30. Interviews with Ali Shukri, Prince Talal bin Muhammad and Prince Raad bin Zaid.
31. Philip Geyelin, draft of "Chapter 1: 1988/1989: The Bush Connection," unfinished book manuscript, Box 27, "The Papers of Philip Geyelin," Middle East Centre Archive, St. Antony's College, Oxford.
32. Personal memorandum from King Hussein to President Bush, February 1989, Box 13, ibid.
33. Interview with Marwan Kasim.
34. Interview with Prince El Hassan bin Talal.

35. Mango, "Jordan on the Road to Peace 1988–1999," 45–53.
36. Interview with Marwan Kasim.
37. Interview with Samir Mutawi.
38. Interview with Prince Raad bin Zaid.
39. Interview with Sharif Zaid bin Shaker.
40. Robins, *A History of Jordan*, 101.
41. Noor, *Leap of Faith*, 296.
42. Robins, *A History of Jordan*, 174.
43. Interview with Prince Raad bin Zaid.

CHAPTER 23: THE GULF CRISIS AND WAR

1. Government of the Hashemite Kingdom of Jordan, White Paper, *Jordan and the Gulf Crisis: August 1990–March 1991* (Amman: August 1991), 4.
2. Interview with Ihsan Shurdom.
3. George Bush and Brent Scowcroft, *A World Transformed*, 1st ed. (New York: Vintage, 1998), 318.
4. Jordan, White Paper, 4–5.
5. Bush and Scowcroft, *A World Transformed*, 319.
6. Interview with Wesley Egan. Egan served in the American Embassy in Cairo during the Gulf crisis.
7. James A. Baker III, *The Politics of Diplomacy: Revolution, War and Peace 1989–1992* (New York: Putnam's, 1995), 290.
8. Queen Noor, *Leap of Faith: Memoirs of an Unexpected Life* (London: Weidenfeld and Nicolson, 2003), 307–8.
9. *Washington Post*, 15 August 1990.
10. Mohamed Heikal, *Illusions of Triumph: An Arab View of the Gulf War* (London: Fontana, 1992), 273–75.
11. J. O'C [Jack O'Connell], "The Persian Gulf Crisis," Box 17, "The Papers of Philip Geyelin," Middle East Centre Archive, St. Antony's College, Oxford. Jack O'Connell was the CIA station chief in Amman from 1967 to 1971, and, after retiring from government service in 1972, an adviser and representative of the Jordanian government in Washington.
12. Heikal, *Illusions of Triumph*, 288.
13. Noor, *Leap of Faith*, 310.
14. Lawrence Tal, "Jordan" in *The Cold War and the Middle East*, eds. Yezid Sayigh and Avi Shlaim (Oxford: Oxford University Press, 1997), 121.
15. Interviews with Christopher Prentice and Sir Mark Allen. Christopher Prentice was Britain's ambassador to Jordan 2002–6. Mark Allen was counsellor (political) at the British Embassy in Amman 1990–94.
16. According to one friend, a wealthy Arab businessman, Hussein deeply yearned for the restoration of the Hashemite monarchy in Iraq. The friend was Hany Salaam, the father-in-law of Prince Talal bin Muhammad, Hussein's favourite nephew and national security adviser. Talal was

married to Ghida, and both were close to Hussein and to Queen Noor. According to Salaam, Hussein and Saddam were very close, and Hussein hoped to become the dominant figure in the relationship. A long-term ambition that Hussein very rarely talked about was to regain Iraq for the Hashemite dynasty. He also had a candidate in mind for the Iraqi throne: Talal bin Muhammad, although Hussein did not broach the subject with Talal. Salaam further relates that Hussein was not altogether surprised by Saddam's invasion of Kuwait. Hussein thought he could deter Saddam from resorting to force, but he overestimated his influence over him. Even after the invasion, Hussein continued to think that the Americans would not act and that Saddam would be the winner in the end. Hussein thought that Iraq would emerge from the conflict as the dominant power in the Gulf and that Jordan would benefit from the change in the regional balance of power. This is why he did not break with Saddam in the early phase of the crisis. Salaam himself considered all these ideas to be unrealistic. But he had no doubt that Hussein was serious about his secret agenda of preparing the ground for a Jordanian takeover of Iraq. Conversation with Hany Salaam, London, 26 November 2002. I have no firm evidence either to confirm or to contradict this account of what went on in Hussein's mind during the Gulf conflict. I simply report it here for what it is worth.

17. Interview with Prince El Hassan bin Talal. In retrospect, Prince Hassan rather wished that his brother had sacked him over this policy issue then and there and spared him the hurt and humiliation of the final dismissal as crown prince.
18. Jordan, White Paper, 6.
19. Heikal, *Illusions of Triumph*, 291.
20. Bush and Scowcroft, *A World Transformed*, 348–49.
21. Interview with Sharif Zaid bin Shaker.
22. Bush and Scowcroft, *A World Transformed*, 340, 347–48.
23. Heikal, *Illusions of Triumph*, 320.
24. Adiba Mango, "Jordan on the Road to Peace 1988–1999" (unpublished D.Phil. thesis, University of Oxford, 2002), 68–69.
25. "Documents from PLG's trip to Jordan in January 1991," "The Papers of Philip Geyelin."
26. Interview with Sir Roger Tomkys.
27. Heikal, *Illusions of Triumph*, 321.
28. Interview with Adnam Abu-Odeh. Of course, Queen Victoria would have treated an Indian maharaja with exemplary courtesy.
29. Efraim Halevy, *Man in the Shadows: Inside the Middle East Crisis with the Man Who Led the Mossad* (London: Weidenfeld and Nicolson, 2006), 27.
30. Ibid., 27–28.
31. Noor, *Leap of Faith*, 312–13.

32. Jordan, White Paper.
33. Interview with Sharif Zaid bin Shaker.
34. Interview with Hasan Abu-Nimah.
35. Interview with King Hussein bin Talal.
36. Ibid.
37. Interview with Adnan Abu-Odeh.
38. Interview with King Abdullah bin Hussein.
39. Khaled bin Sultan and Patrick Seale, *Desert Warrior: A Personal View of the Gulf War by the Joint Forces Commander* (London: HarperCollins, 1995), 181.
40. Ibid., 210.
41. Interview with King Hussein bin Talal. The 400,000 refugees from Kuwait included Palestinians and other Arabs, mainly Syrian and Iraqi Bedouins, who had no citizenship rights. *Bidun* literally means "without." The actual number of refugees was closer to 300,000 then to 400,000.
42. Adam Garfinkle, *Israel and Jordan in the Shadow of War: Functional Ties and Futile Diplomacy in a Small Place* (London: Macmillan, 1992), 173.
43. Yitzhak Shamir, *Summing Up: An Autobiography* (London: Weidenfeld and Nicolson, 1994), 218–19.
44. Halevy, *Man in the Shadows*, 29–30.
45. Interview with Adnan Abu-Odeh.
46. Interview with Ali Shukri.
47. Moshe Zak, *Hussein oseh shalom [Hussein Makes Peace],* in Hebrew (Ramat-Gan: Bar-Ilan University Press, 1996), 35–36, 47–50, 227–28.
48. Interview with King Hussein bin Talal.
49. Interview with Sharif Zaid bin Shaker.
50. Noor, *Leap of Faith*, 324.
51. Halevy, *Man in the Shadows*, 31–32.
52. Interview with Dan Meridor.
53. Interview with Ali Shukri.
54. *The 50 Years War*, transcript of interview for six-part BBC television series, Middle East Centre Archive, St. Antony's College, Oxford (1998), King Hussein, 2 March 1997.
55. Interview with Dan Meridor.
56. Interview with King Abdullah bin Hussein.
57. Interview with Sharif Zaid bin Shaker.
58. Interview with King Abdullah bin Hussein.
59. Uri Avnery, "In Israel, Reckless Talk about Jordan," *International Herald Tribune*, 7 September 1990; and Ze'ev Schiff, *Ha'aretz*, 3 March 1991.
60. Jordan, White Paper, 61–66.

CHAPTER 24: FROM MADRID TO OSLO

1. Queen Noor, *Leap of Faith: Memoirs of an Unexpected Life* (London: Weidenfeld and Nicolson, 2003), 341.
2. Adiba Mango, "Jordan on the Road to Peace 1988–1999" (unpublished D.Phil. thesis, University of Oxford, 2002), 94.
3. James A. Baker III, *The Politics of Diplomacy: Revolution, War and Peace, 1989–1992* (New York: Putnam's, 1995), 450–51.
4. Mango, "Jordan on the Road to Peace 1988–1999," 102.
5. Baker III, *The Politics of Diplomacy*, 451.
6. Ibid., 464–65.
7. Interview with King Hussein bin Talal.
8. Baker III, *The Politics of Diplomacy*, 423–25.
9. Interview with Dr. Musa al-Keilani.
10. Interview with Dan Meridor.
11. Mango, "Jordan on the Road to Peace 1988–1999," 105.
12. Baker III, *The Politics of Diplomacy*, 469.
13. Interview with Taher al-Masri.
14. Interview with Dr. Musa Braizat.
15. Hanan Ashrawi, *This Side of Peace: A Personal Account* (New York: Simon and Schuster, 1995), 122–24.
16. Interviews with Musa Braizat and Awn Khasawneh.
17. Chris Hedges, "For King Hussein, a Last Shot at Peace," *International Herald Tribune*, 31 October 1991.
18. Interview with Adnan Abu-Odeh.
19. Mango, "Jordan on the Road to Peace 1988–1999," 118–19.
20. Interview with Taher al-Masri.
21. Elyakim Rubinstein, lecture, 12 October 2001, "The Peace between Israel and Jordan—Chapters in its Making," in Hebrew. I am grateful to Supreme Court Judge Elyakim Rubinstein for putting the text of his lecture at my disposal.
22. Mango, "Jordan on the Road to Peace 1988–1999," 153.
23. Interview with Kamel Abu Jaber.
24. Noor, *Leap of Faith*, 351–53. "Sidi" is a term of respect that is much less formal than "His Majesty." Hussein was usually called "Sayidna," or "our master," by those who were close to him, and he himself always referred to his younger brother respectfully as "Sidi Hassan."
25. Mahmoud Abbas, *Through Secret Channels* (Reading: Garnet, 1995), 187.
26. Interview with Wesley Egan.
27. Nora Boustany, "King Hussein Fears Prospects for Peace Could Raise Premature Hope in Jordan," *International Herald Tribune*, 18–19 September 1993.
28. Efraim Halevy, *Man in the Shadows: Inside the Middle East Crisis with the Man Who Led the Mossad* (London: Weidenfeld and Nicolson, 2006), 49.

29. Interview with King Hussein bin Talal.
30. Noor, *Leap of Faith*, 361.
31. *The 50 Years War*, transcript of interview for six-part BBC television series, Middle East Centre Archive, St. Antony's College, Oxford (1998), King Hussein, 2 March 1997, 80.
32. Interviews with Fayez Tarawneh and Marwan Muasher.
33. Interview with Adnan Abu-Odeh.
34. Jerrold Kessel, "Rabin Soothes King at Secret Meeting," *Guardian*, 29 September 1993.
35. Noor, *Leap of Faith*, 364.
36. Jerrold Kessel, "Rabin Soothes King at Secret Meeting," *Guardian*, 29 September 1993.
37. Interview with Ali Shukri.
38. Elyakim Rubinstein, "The Peace Treaty with Jordan," in Hebrew, *Hamishpat*, 6 (December 1995).
39. Interview with Taher al-Masri.
40. Interview with Shimon Peres.
41. Interview with King Hussein bin Talal.
42. Interview with Prince El Hassan bin Talal.
43. Uri Savir, *The Process: 1,100 Days that Changed the Middle East* (New York: Random House, 1998), 84.
44. Shalom Yerushalmi, "Jordan: Before the Peace," *Ma'ariv*, 10 November 1993.
45. Interview with Shimon Peres.
46. Interview with Eitan Haber; and Halevy, *Man in the Shadows*, 50–51.
47. Under the old system, each voter could cast the number of votes corresponding to the deputies to be returned from the country's multi-member constituencies. Under the amended system, each voter could cast only a single vote.

CHAPTER 25: PEACE TREATY

1. Ari Shavit, "Smiley Stopped Smiling: An Interview with Efraim Halevy," *Ha'aretz*, 5 September 2003.
2. Moshe Zak, *Hussein oseh shalom [Hussein Makes Peace]*, in Hebrew (Ramat-Gan: Bar-Ilan University Press, 1996), 293–94.
3. Interview with King Hussein bin Talal.
4. Interview with Professor Itamar Rabinovich.
5. Efraim Halevy, *Man in the Shadows: Inside the Middle East Crisis with the Man Who Led the Mossad* (London: Weidenfeld and Nicolson, 2006), 87–88.
6. Dennis Ross, *The Missing Peace: The Inside Story of the Fight for Middle East Peace* (New York: Farrar, Straus and Giroux, 2004), 174–77.
7. Interview with King Hussein bin Talal.

8. Queen Noor, *Leap of Faith: Memoirs of an Unexpected Life* (London: Weidenfeld and Nicolson, 2003), 368–69.
9. Interview with Taher al-Masri.
10. Ibid.
11. Ibid.
12. Interview with Adnan Abu-Odeh.
13. Interview with Professor Itamar Rabinovich; and Halevy, *Man in the Shadows*, 101.
14. Noor, *Leap of Faith*, 374–77.
15. Interview with Awn Khasawneh.
16. Halevy, *Man in the Shadows*, 111.
17. Munther J. Haddadin, *Diplomacy on the Jordan: International Conflict and Negotiated Resolution* (Boston: Kluwer Academic, 2002), 379.
18. Interview with Dr. Munther Haddadin.
19. David Horovitz, ed., *Yitzhak Rabin: Soldier of Peace* (London: Peter Halban, 1996), 129; and David Makovsky, *Making Peace with the PLO: The Rabin Government's Road to the Oslo Accord* (Boulder, CO: Westview Press, 1996), 158–60.
20. Interview with Awn Khasawneh.
21. Interview with Hasan Abu-Nimah.
22. Shimon Shamir, "Three Years after the Signature of the Peace Treaty with Jordan: The Desert Is Still Arid," *Ha'aretz*, 22 October 1997.
23. Interview with King Hussein bin Talal.
24. Interview with Awn Khasawneh.
25. Elyakim Rubinstein, lecture, 12 October 2001, "The Peace between Israel and Jordan—Chapters in Its Making," in Hebrew. I am grateful to Supreme Court Judge Elyakim Rubinstein for putting the text of his lecture at my disposal.
26. Marc Lynch, *State Interests and Public Spheres: The International Politics of Jordan's Identity* (New York: Columbia University Press, 1999), 184.
27. Asher Susser, *The Jordanian–Israeli Peace Negotiations: The Geopolitical Rationale of a Bilateral Relationship*. Davis Occasional Papers, No. 73 (Jerusalem: Leonard Davis Institute for International Relations, Hebrew University of Jerusalem, 1999), 22–23.
28. Interview with Marwan Muasher.

CHAPTER 26: THE KING'S PEACE

1. Marc Lynch, *State Interests and Public Spheres: The International Politics of Jordan's Identity* (New York: Columbia University Press, 1999), 180.
2. Marwan Muasher, "Jordan and the Peace Process," *Peacewatch*, 99, (Washington Institute for Near East Policy, 19 June 1996).

3. Ami Ayalon and Bruce Maddy-Weitzman, eds., *Middle East Contemporary Survey.* Volume XVIII: *1994* (Boulder, CO: Westview Press, 1996), 439.
4. Interview with Dr. Hani Mulki.
5. Interview with Rajai Muasher.
6. Interview with Marwan Muasher.
7. Ibid.
8. Bruce Maddy-Weitzman, ed., *Middle East Contemporary Survey.* Volume XIX: *1995* (Boulder, CO: Westview Press, 1997), 74–75.
9. Hans Blix, *Disarming Iraq: The Search for Weapons of Mass Destruction* (London: Bloomsbury, 2004), 29, 71, 240.
10. Interview with Ali Shukri.
11. Interview with Prince Talal bin Muhammad.
12. Adiba Mango, "Jordan on the Road to Peace 1988–1999" (unpublished D.Phil. thesis, University of Oxford, 2002), 213–14.
13. Ibid.
14. King Hussein to Ezer Weizman, 5 November 1995, "The Private Papers of General Ali Shukri," Amman.
15. Fouad Ajami, *The Dream Palace of the Arabs: A Generation's Odyssey* (New York: Pantheon Books, 1998), 294–95.
16. Randa Habib, "La Mort de Hussein, Celle de Rabin: Enterre-t-on la Paix?" Unpublished manuscript. I am grateful to Randa Habib for allowing me to quote from the manuscript of her forthcoming book.
17. Dennis Ross, *The Missing Peace: The Inside Story of the Fight for Middle East Peace* (New York: Farrar, Straus and Giroux, 2004), 214–15.
18. Secret—Immediate, Report No. 8592, 4 December 1995, "Jordan/Threat to the Life of King Hussein," "The Private papers of General Ali Shukri."
19. Interview with Ali Shukri.
20. Secret—Immediate, Report No. 9101, 20 December 1995, "Iraq/ Attack Intentions in Jordan," "The Private Papers of General Ali Shukri."
21. Interview with King Hussein bin Talal.
22. Mango, "Jordan on the Road to Peace 1988–1999," 218–19.
23. Interview with King Hussein bin Talal.
24. Itamar Rabinovich, *Waging Peace: Israel and the Arabs at the End of the Century* (New York: Farrar, Straus and Giroux, 1999), 99.
25. Interview with Ali Shukri.
26. Interview with Marwan Muasher.

CHAPTER 27: COLLISION COURSE

1. Avi Shlaim, *The Iron Wall: Israel and the Arab World* (New York: W. W. Norton, 2000), Chapter 15.
2. Bruce Maddy-Weitzman, ed., *Middle East Contemporary Survey.* Volume XX: *1996* (Boulder, CO: Westview Press, 1998), 437–38.

3. Laura Zittrain Eisenberg and Neil Caplan, *Negotiating Arab–Israeli Peace: Patterns, Problems, Possibilities* (Bloomington: Indiana University Press, 1998), 149.
4. Briefing notes of Ali Shukri, 20.45, 28 September 1996, "The Private Papers of General Ali Shukri," Amman.
5. Efraim Halevy, *Man in the Shadows: Inside the Middle East Crisis with the Man Who Led the Mossad* (London: Weidenfeld and Nicolson, 2006), 147–48.
6. Interview with King Hussein bin Talal.
7. Queen Noor, *Leap of Faith: Memoirs of an Unexpected Life* (London: Weidenfeld and Nicolson, 2003), 392–93.
8. Roland Dallas, *King Hussein: A Life on the Edge* (London: Profile Books, 1999), 232.
9. David Hirst, "Arabs to Shun Israel at Economic Summit," *Guardian*, 13 November 1996.
10. King Hussein to Prime Minister Binyamin Netanyahu, 9 March 1997, "The Private Papers of General Ali Shukri."
11. Interview with Ali Shukri.
12. *Jordan Times*, 13 March 1997.
13. Interview with Ihsan Shurdom.
14. Noor, *Leap of Faith*, 396.
15. President Ezer Weizman to His Majesty, King Hussein bin Talal, 27 April 1998, "The Private Papers of General Ali Shukri."
16. Ze'ev Schiff, "The Government against the Intelligence," *Ha'aretz*, 26 September 1997.
17. Noor, *Leap of Faith*, 397.
18. Halevy, *Man in the Shadows*, 164–75; Patrick Cockburn, "Bibi Netanyahu's failed bid to emulate King Claudius," *Independent*, 10 October 1997; Interview with Ali Shukri.
19. Halevy, *Man in the Shadows*, 164–75.
20. Elyakim Rubinstein, unpublished text of a lecture, 12 October 2001, "The Peace between Israel and Jordan—Chapters in Its Making," in Hebrew.
21. Ali Shukri's notes, 28 September 1997, "The Private Papers of General Ali Shukri."
22. Carmel, "Arik Sent Me."
23. Ali Shukri's notes, 28 September 1997, "The Private Papers of General Ali Shukri."
24. Carmel, "Arik Sent Me."
25. Ze'ev Schiff, "A Flaw in Strategic Thinking," *Ha'aretz*, 14 November 1997.
26. Interview with Ali Shukri.
27. Bruce Maddy-Weitzman, ed., *Middle East Contemporary Survey*. Volume XXI: *1997* (Boulder, CO: Westview Press, 2000), 94.
28. Noor, *Leap of Faith*, 393–94.

29. Interview with Dr. Mustafa Hamarneh.
30. Robert Satloff, "The King is Back . . . and 'Final Status' Talks May Be Just Round the Corner," 10 December 1997, *Peacewatch/Policywatch: Anthology 1997*, compiled and edited by Elyse Aronson and Monica Neal (Washington, DC: Washington Institute for Near East Policy, 1998), 283–85.
31. Doron Rosenblum, "A Little Anthology of Blindness and Eye-opening," *Ha'aretz*, 12 February 2004.
32. Smadar Peri, "The King and I: An Exclusive Interview with Ali Shukri," *Yediot Aharonot*, 1 October 1999.
33. Bruce Maddy-Weitzman, ed., *Middle East Contemporary Survey*. Volume XXII: *1998* (Boulder, CO: Westview Press, 2001), 77.
34. Interview with Ali Shukri.
35. Ali Shukri's notes, 11 February 1998, "The Private Papers of General Ali Shukri." The conversation was in English and Ali Shukri's notes are also in English except for three words—"very nasty person"—which are written in Arabic in brackets.
36. Noor, *Leap of Faith*, 400.
37. Ibid.

CHAPTER 28: THE LAST JOURNEY

1. Queen Noor, *Leap of Faith: Memoirs of an Unexpected Life* (London: Weidenfeld and Nicolson, 2003), 424.
2. Adiba Mango, "Jordan on the Road to Peace 1988–1999" (unpublished D.Phil. thesis, University of Oxford, 2002), 236–37.
3. Bruce Maddy-Weitzman, ed., *Middle East Contemporary Survey*. Volume XXII: *1998* (Boulder, CO: Westview Press, 2001), 362–68.
4. Interview with Prince El Hassan bin Talal.
5. Ibid.
6. Samir A. Mutawi, *Jordan in the 1967 War* (Cambridge: Cambridge University Press, 1987), 19–20.
7. Maddy-Weitzman, ed., *Middle East Contemporary Survey*. Volume XXII: *1998*, 366.
8. Interview with Adnan Abu-Odeh.
9. Philip Robins, *A History of Jordan* (Cambridge: Cambridge University Press, 2003), 196. Queen Noor denied that she influenced her husband to change the succession. Her main mission throughout their time in Mayo was to save her husband, and the situation did not seem hopeless until the very end. She kept hoping that the treatment would work and that he would recover. She is emphatic that she did not discuss the succession with her husband until he was about to tell Abdullah. Whenever relatives raised the issue, she replied it was the will of God and the judgement of Hussein. Whenever Abdul Karim Kabariti referred to the matter,

she changed the subject. She had very little contact with General Samih Batikhi, and she certainly did not conspire with him against Hassan. Nor did she lobby for her son Hamzah, who was only eighteen at the time. Once the decision was made, she gave Abdullah all her support. All the rumours surrounding her role in the crisis emanated from Amman, and they were baseless. As for the letter that Hussein sent to Hamzah on his eighteenth birthday, it was written without Noor's knowledge. When she read the letter in the press, she thought it was unfortunate and pointed out to her husband that it may not be well received by Hassan. She did not push her son forward because there was an incumbent crown prince. Besides, Hussein and Hamzah had an excellent relationship; they were the best of friends. Hussein could talk to Hamzah directly about this or any other matter if he wanted to. Conversation with Queen Noor, Oxford, 12 November 2006.

10. Interview with Marwan Kasim.
11. Interview with Princess Basma bint Talal.
12. Maddy-Weitzman, ed., *Middle East Contemporary Survey.* Volume XXII: *1998*, 365.
13. Noor, *Leap of Faith*, 413.
14. Dennis Ross, *The Missing Peace: The Inside Story of the Fight for Middle East Peace* (New York: Farrar, Straus and Giroux, 2004), 448–49.
15. Ibid., 450.
16. Noor, *Leap of Faith*, 415.
17. Ibid., 416.
18. Interview with Ihsan Shurdom.
19. Maddy-Weitzman, ed., *Middle East Contemporary Survey,* Volume XXII: *1998*, 381–82.
20. Noor, *Leap of Faith*, 416–18.
21. Randa Habib email to Avi Shlaim, 12 December 2006.
22. Maddy-Weitzman, ed., *Middle East Contemporary Survey.* Volume XXII: *1998*, 364–66.
23. Interview with Hussein Majali.
24. Interview with Christopher Prentice, Oxford, 7 November 2006. Mr. Prentice was the British ambassador to Amman, 2002–6.
25. Interview with King Abdullah bin Hussein.
26. Noor, *Leap of Faith*, 419–20.
27. Interview with Prince El Hassan bin Talal and Princess Sarvath, London, 11 January 2007.
28. Interview with Hussein Majali.
29. Interview with King Abdullah bin Hussein.
30. Noor, *Leap of Faith*, 420–21.
31. Ibid., 420.
32. Interview with Adnan Abu-Odeh.
33. Noor, *Leap of Faith*, 424.

34. CNN transcript of 20 January 1999 interview with His Majesty King Hussein conducted by CNN Chief International Correspondent Christiane Amanpour in Amman. King Hussein's interviews and press conferences, www.kinghussein.gov.jo.

35. Prince Hassan to King Hussein, 21 January 1999, reproduced in *Journal of Palestine Studies*, 28:3 (Spring 1999).

36. Twelve-page letter from El Hassan bin Talal to HM King Hussein, Amman, 28 January 1999. I am grateful to Prince Hassan for placing a copy of this letter, in its original Arabic and in its English version, at my disposal. Prince Hassan expected this letter to be published because it was a reply to the king's letter of 25 January 1999, which was released to the media immediately. But the king's aides did not release the reply. General Samir Batikhi instructed Prince Hassan not to make any statements to the media following his dismissal. The lengths to which General Batikhi went to silence and neutralize Hassan suggest that he was afraid that Hassan might mount a counter-coup.

37. Interview with Prince El Hassan bin Talal.

38. Interviews with Hussein Majali and Fayez Tarawneh.

39. Interview with King Abdullah bin Hussein.

40. Noor, *Leap of Faith*, 426.

41. Interview with Prince Talal bin Muhammad.

42. Noor, *Leap of Faith*, 427.

43. Interview with Hussein Majali.

44. King Hussein to Prince Hassan, 25 January 1999, text reproduced in *Journal of Palestine Studies*, 28:3 (Spring 1999).

45. El Hassan bin Talal to King Hussein, Amman, 28 January 1999. See Note 36.

46. Interview with Marwan Kasim.

47. Interview with Prince Talal bin Muhammad.

48. Ibid.

49. Interview with Hussein Majali. At St. John's Eye Hospital in Jerusalem there is a photograph of King Hussein taken in 1961 signing a piece of paper that declared that on his death his eyes were to be removed and used to give sight to someone. He was the first person ever to issue such an instruction at the hospital, but for medical reasons when he died his eyes could not be used. I am grateful to Jill, Duchess of Hamilton, for this piece of information.

50. Noor, *Leap of Faith*, 431–32.

Jordanian Secret Meetings with Israeli Officials

DATE	PLACE	PARTICIPANTS
24 Sept. 1963	London	King Hussein, Dr. Yaacov Herzog
2 May 1964	London	Hussein, Herzog
19 Dec. 1964	London	Hussein, Herzog
19 Sept. 1965	Paris	Hussein, Golda Meir
2 July 1967	London	Hussein, Herzog
19 Nov. 1967	London	Hussein, Herzog
20 Nov. 1967	London	Hussein, Herzog
3 May 1968	London	Hussein, Zaid Rifa'i, Abba Eban, Herzog
5 May 1968	London	Rifa'i, Herzog
6 May 1968	London	Rifa'i, Herzog
19 June 1968	London	Rifa'i, Herzog
20 June 1968	London	Rifa'i, Herzog
22 Aug. 1968	London	Hussein, Rifa'i, Herzog
24 Aug. 1968	London	Hussein, Rifa'i, Herzog
27 Sept. 1968	London	Hussein, Rifa'i, Yigal Allon, Eban, Herzog
29 Sept. 1968	London	Rifa'i, Herzog
16 Oct. 1968	London	Rifa'i, Gen. Amer Khammash, Gen. Chaim Bar-Lev, Herzog
18 Oct. 1968	London	Hussein, Rifa'i, Khammash, Bar-Lev, Herzog
19 Nov. 1968	Aqaba Bay	Hussein, Rifa'i, Sharif Nasser bin Jamil, Allon, Eban, Herzog
19 Dec. 1968	London	Rifa'i, Herzog
26 Jan. 1969	London	Rifa'i, Herzog
28 Jan. 1969	London	Hussein, Rifa'i, Herzog
20 Feb. 1969	Aqaba Bay	Hussein, Rifa'i, Allon, Eban, Herzog
23 Apr. 1969	London	Rifa'i, Herzog
25 Apr. 1969	London	Hussein, Rifa'i, Herzog
27 Apr. 1969	London	Rifa'i, Herzog
25 May 1969	Coral Island	Hussein, Rifa'i, Eban, Allon, Herzog
26 July 1969	London	Rifa'i, Herzog
17 Sept. 1969	London	Rifa'i, Herzog
28 Sept. 1969	London	Rifa'i, Sharif Nasser, Bar-Lev, Herzog

DATE	PLACE	PARTICIPANTS
3 Oct. 70	Wadi Araba	Hussein, Rifa'i, Allon, Herzog
21 Mar. 1972	Wadi Araba	Hussein, Meir
29 June 1972	Wadi Araba	Hussein, Rifa'i, Meir, Moshe Dayan
19 Nov. 1972	Wadi Araba	Hussein, Rifa'i, Meir, Dayan
9 May 1973	Wadi Araba	Hussein, Meir
6 Aug. 1973	Wadi Araba	Hussein, Meir
25 Sept. 1973	Tel Aviv	Hussein, Rifa'i, Meir, Mordechai Gazit
26 Jan. 1974	Wadi Araba	Hussein, Rifa'i, Meir, Dayan, Gazit
7 Mar. 1974	Wadi Araba	Hussein, Rifa'i, Meir, Dayan, Gazit
28 Aug. 1974	Wadi Araba	Hussein, Rifa'i, Itzhak Rabin, Allon, Shimon Peres, Gazit
19 Oct. 1974	Wadi Araba	Hussein, Rifa'i, Rabin, Allon, Peres
28 May 1975	Wadi Araba	Hussein, Rifa'i, Rabin, Allon, Peres
March 1977	Tel Aviv	Hussein, Rifa'i, Rabin, Allon, Peres
22 Aug. 1977	London	Hussein, Dayan
19 July 1985	London	Hussein, Rifa'i, Peres
5 Oct. 1985	London	Hussein, Rifa'i, Peres, Yossi Beilin
March 1986	Strasbourg	Hussein, Rabin
July 1986	Aqaba	Hussein, Rifa'i, Rabin, Peres, Gen. Moshe Levy
11 Apr. 1987	London	Hussein, Rifa'i, Peres, Beilin, Efraim Halevy, Nahum Admoni
18 July 1987	Sussex	Hussein, Itzhak Shamir, Elyakim Rubinstein, Yossi Ben-Aharon, Halevy, Brig. Gen. Azriel Nevo
4–5 Jan. 1991	Ascot	Hussein, Sharif Zaid bin Shaker, Adnan Abu-Odeh, Brig. Gen. Ali Shukri, Shamir, Rubinstein, Ben-Aharon, Maj. Gen. Ehud Barak
26 Sept. 1993	Aqaba	Hussein, Prince Hassan, Shaker, Shukri, Rabin, Rubinstein, Eitan Haber, Halevy
2 Nov. 1993	Amman	Hussein, Hassan, Abdul Salam Majali, Peres, Avi Gil, Halevy
19 May 1994	London	Hussein, Hassan, Rabin, Rubinstein, Halevy
25 July 1994	Washington	Hussein, Majali, Rabin, Peres, Itamer Rabinovich
29 Sept. 1994	Aqaba	Hussein, Hassan, Fayez Tarawneh, Rabin, Rubinstein, Halevy
12 Oct. 1994	Amman	Hussein, Hassan, Awn Khasawneh, Rabin, Rubinstein, Halevy
16–17 Oct. 1994	Amman	Hussein, Hassan, Majali, Khasawneh, Munther Haddadin, Rabin, Peres, Rubinstein, Halevy

The Hashemite Dynasty

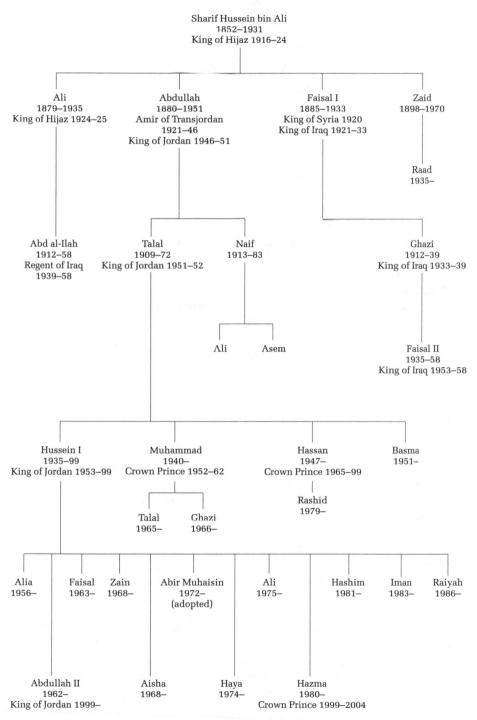

Chronology

14 Nov. 1935	Hussein bin Talal born in Amman.
22 Mar. 1946	Anglo-Jordanian treaty signed, granting Transjordan independence.
15 May 1946	Amirate of Transjordan renamed the Hashemite Kingdom of Jordan.
29 Nov. 1947	UN resolution for the partition of Palestine.
15 Mar. 1948	Anglo-Jordanian treaty of alliance signed.
14 May 1948	Proclamation of the State of Israel.
15 May 1948– 7 Jan. 1949	First Arab–Israeli War.
1 Dec. 1948	Palestinian Congress in Jericho votes for the absorption of the West Bank into Jordan.
3 Apr. 1949	Jordanian–Israeli armistice agreement signed.
24 Apr. 1950	Parliament approves unification of East and West banks.
20 July 1951	King Abdullah I assassinated in Jerusalem.
6 Sept. 1951	King Talal's formal accession to the throne.
9 Sept. 1951	Hussein bin Talal named crown prince.
1 Jan. 1952	New Jordanian constitution promulgated.
23 July 1952	Free Officers' Revolution in Egypt.
11 Aug. 1952	King Talal abdicates; Hussein bin Talal proclaimed king.
2 May 1953	King Hussein's formal accession to the throne.
14–15 Oct. 1953	The Qibya raid.
24 Feb. 1955	Iraq and Turkey sign the Baghdad Pact.
5 Apr. 1955	Britain joins the Baghdad Pact.
16 Apr. 1955	King Hussein marries Princess Dina (Dina Abdul Hamid).
27 Sept. 1955	Nasser announces the "Czech" arms deal.
20 Oct. 1955	Egypt, Syria and Saudi Arabia sign defence pact.
15 Dec. 1955	Jordan prepares to join the Baghdad Pact.
16–19 Dec. 1955	Anti–Baghdad Pact riots in Jordan.
7–9 Jan. 1956	Second wave of anti–Baghdad Pact riots.
1 Mar. 1956	King Hussein dismisses Glubb Pasha.
12 Mar. 1956	Egypt, Syria and Saudi Arabia offer to replace the British subsidy.
24 May 1956	Ali Abu Nuwar appointed chief of staff.
26 July 1956	Egypt nationalizes the Suez Canal Company.

10 Oct. 1956	IDF raid on Qalqilyah.
21 Oct. 1956	National Socialist Party wins election to the lower house.
22–4 Oct. 1956	Protocol of Sèvres.
24 Oct. 1956	Defence pact signed by Jordan, Egypt and Syria.
27 Oct. 1956	Suleiman Nabulsi appointed prime minister.
29 Oct.– 7 Nov. 1956	The Suez War.
5 Jan. 1957	Anti-communist Eisenhower Doctrine proclaimed.
19 Jan. 1957	King Hussein signs Arab solidarity agreement.
13 Mar. 1957	Anglo-Jordanian treaty abrogated.
8 Apr. 1957	First Armoured Car Regiment surrounds Amman.
10 Apr. 1957	King Hussein dismisses Prime Minister Nabulsi.
13 Apr. 1957	Ali Abu Nuwar's coup and Hussein's counter-coup.
22 Apr. 1957	A National Congress of left-wing parties is held in Nablus.
23 Apr. 1957	Demonstrations against the Eisenhower Doctrine and the government of Fakhri al-Khalidi.
24 Apr. 1957	Washington offers Jordan financial help under the Eisenhower Doctrine.
25 Apr. 1957	Ibrahim Hashem forms new government, martial law imposed and political parties banned.
29 Apr. 1957	US approves an annual grant to Jordan of $10 million.
24 June 1957	King Hussein divorces Princess Dina.
1 Feb. 1958	Syria and Egypt merge to form the United Arab Republic (UAR).
14 Feb. 1958	Arab Union is formed by a merger of Jordan and Iraq.
14 July 1958	Revolution in Iraq and assassination of royal family.
16 July 1958	King Hussein requests military assistance from Britain and America.
17 July 1958	British troops arrive in Jordan for "Operation Fortitude."
29 Oct. 1958	British troops are withdrawn from Jordan.
Mar. 1959	King Hussein's visit to Washington.
5 May 1959	Hazza' al-Majali succeeds Samir Rifa'i as prime minister.
17 May 1959	Arrest and conviction of General Sadiq al-Shar'a.
29 Aug. 1960	Prime Minister Hazza' al-Majali assassinated in Amman.
25 May 1961	Hussein marries Princess Muna (Antoinette Gardiner).
28 Sept. 1961	Syrian coup leads to dissolution of UAR.
28 Jan. 1962	Wasfi al-Tall forms his first government.
30 Jan. 1962	Birth of Crown Prince Abdullah.
2 July 1962	Wasfi al-Tall presents his White Paper on Palestine.
Sept. 1962	Outbreak of war in Yemen.
8 Feb. 1963	Ba'thist coup in Iraq.

8 Mar. 1963	Ba'thist coup in Syria.
17 Apr. 1963	New United Arab Republic proclaimed by Egypt, Syria and Iraq. Pro-Arab unity demonstrations in Jordan.
21 Aug. 1963	Establishment of diplomatic relations between Jordan and the Soviet Union.
13–17 Jan. 1964	First Arab summit meeting, in Cairo, decides on Jordan River diversion, Unified Arab Command and Palestinian entity.
14 Apr. 1964	King Hussein meets President Johnson in the White House.
5–11 Sept. 1964	Second Arab Summit, in Alexandria.
1 Apr. 1965	Hassan bin Talal appointed crown prince.
13–17 Sept. 1965	Third Arab summit, in Casablanca.
23 Feb. 1966	Left-wing coup in Syria followed by increased PLO activity against Israel.
7 Nov. 1966	Syria and Egypt sign mutual defence treaty.
13 Nov. 1966	Israeli raid on West Bank village of Samu'.
Nov.–Dec. 1966	Mass demonstrations and riots following Samu' raid. PLO intensifies propaganda campaign against Jordan.
4 Jan. 1967	Jordan closes PLO offices in Jerusalem.
23 Feb. 1967	Jordan recalls its ambassador from Egypt.
7 Apr. 1967	Israeli aircraft shoot down seven Syrian MiGs.
16 May 1967	Nasser deploys troops in Sinai.
19 May 1967	Nasser requests withdrawal of UN Emergency Force from Sinai.
22 May 1967	Nasser closes the Straits of Tiran to Israeli shipping.
30 May 1967	King Hussein signs mutual defence pact with Egypt placing Jordanian Army under Egyptian command.
4 June 1967	Mutual defence pact signed between Egypt and Iraq.
5–10 June 1967	The June War.
26 June 1967	King Hussein addresses UN General Assembly.
27 June 1967	Israel annexes East Jerusalem.
28 June 1967	King Hussein meets President Johnson in Washington.
10 July 1967	King Hussein meets President Nasser in Cairo.
28 Aug.– 1 Sept. 1967	Fourth Arab League summit, in Khartoum.
30 Sept. 1967	King Hussein visits Cairo.
2–5 Oct. 1967	King Hussein's first official visit to Moscow.
3–12 Nov. 1967	King Hussein in the United States.
22 Nov. 1967	UN Security Council passes Resolution 242.
21 Mar. 1968	Battle of Karameh.
3 Feb. 1969	Yasser Arafat elected chairman of the PLO.
Mar. 1969– Aug. 1970	Israeli–Egyptian "War of Attrition."

26 Apr. 1969	King Hussein presents joint Jordanian–Egyptian peace plan to President Nixon.
9 Dec. 1969	The Rogers Plan is announced.
15 Dec. 1969	Israel rejects the Rogers Plan.
21 Dec. 1969	Fifth Arab League summit, in Rabat.
10 Feb. 1970	Jordan announces new measures aimed at curbing fedayeen activity and restoring order in the country.
9 June 1970	King Hussein's motorcade ambushed by fedayeen and PFLP abducts sixty-eight foreign hostages in Amman.
10 June 1970	King Hussein and Arafat agree on a ceasefire.
11 June 1970	Sharif Nasser bin Jamil, commander-in-chief of the army, and Sharif Zaid bin Shaker, commander of the Third Armoured Division, resign.
19 June 1970	The second Rogers Plan.
10 July 1970	Jordan and the PLO sign an agreement brokered by the Arab Reconciliation Committee.
26 July 1970	Jordan accepts the second Rogers Plan.
Aug. 1970	Sharif Zaid bin Shaker reinstated, promoted to deputy chief of staff.
7 Aug. 1970	Israeli–Egyptian ceasefire under the Rogers Plan.
1 Sept. 1970	King Hussein's motorcade ambushed by fedayeen.
6–12 Sept. 1970	Three airliners hijacked by the PFLP in Amman.
16 Sept. 1970	Military government appointed under Brigadier Muhammad Daoud.
17–27 Sept. 1970	Showdown between Jordanian Army and fedayeen.
19–22 Sept. 1970	Syrian military incursion into Jordan.
26 Sept. 1970	Arab summit meeting in Cairo to resolve the crisis in Jordan.
27 Sept. 1970	King Hussein signs ceasefire agreement with PLO.
28 Sept. 1970	President Nasser dies and Anwar Sadat succeeds him.
13 Oct. 1970	The Amman Agreement signed between Jordan and the PLO.
Mar.–Apr. 1971	Jordan resumes offensive against fedayeen.
13–17 July 1971	Final assault on fedayeen in Jerash–Ajlun.
4 Oct. 1971	The third Rogers Plan.
28 Nov. 1971	Prime Minister Wasfi al-Tall assassinated in Cairo.
29 Feb. 1972	Anwar Sadat releases Wasfi al-Tall's assassins from prison.
15 Mar. 1972	King Hussein unveils the United Arab Kingdom (UAK) Plan.
16 Mar. 1972	The PLO rejects the UAK Plan.
21 Dec. 1972	King Hussein divorces Princess Muna.
24 Dec. 1972	King Hussein marries Queen Alia (Alia Toukan).
10–12 Sept. 1973	Tripartite Jordanian–Syrian–Egyptian summit in Cairo.
6–26 Oct. 1973	The October War.

22 Oct. 1973	UN Security Council Resolution 338 calls for direct negotiations to implement 242.
21 Dec. 1973	The Geneva peace conference.
18 Jan. 1974	The Israeli–Egyptian disengagement agreement is signed.
31 May 1974	The Israeli–Syrian disengagement agreement is signed.
26–9 Oct. 1974	Arab League summit at Rabat recognizes the PLO as "the sole legitimate representative of the Palestinian people."
13 Apr. 1975	Outbreak of the Lebanese Civil War.
1 Sept. 1975	Israeli–Egyptian interim agreement, Sinai II.
1 June 1976	Syrian military intervention in Lebanon.
9 Feb. 1977	Queen Alia dies in a helicopter accident.
17 May 1977	Rise to power in Israel of right-wing Likud Party.
1 Oct. 1977	Joint statement by the US and USSR for reconvening the Geneva peace conference.
19–21 Nov. 1977	Sadat's visit to Jerusalem.
14 Mar. 1978	IDF launches Operation Litani in southern Lebanon.
15 June 1978	King Hussein marries Queen Noor (Lisa Halaby).
5–17 Sept. 1978	The Camp David Conference.
17 Sept. 1978	Israel and Egypt sign the Camp David Accords.
2–5 Nov. 1978	Arab League summit in Baghdad denounces the Camp David Accords.
1 Feb. 1979	The Islamic Revolution in Iran.
26 Mar. 1979	Israel–Egypt peace treaty is signed at the White House.
1 Apr. 1979	Jordan severs diplomatic relations with Egypt.
17 Sept. 1980	Outbreak of war between Iraq and Iran.
7 June 1981	Israel bombs the Iraqi nuclear reactor near Baghdad.
6 Oct. 1981	Anwar Sadat is assassinated and Husni Mubarak succeeds.
14 Dec. 1981	Israeli annexation of the Golan Heights.
6 June 1982	Israeli invasion of Lebanon.
4 July 1982	IDF begins siege of West Beirut.
21 Aug. 1982	PLO fighters are evacuated from Beirut.
1 Sept. 1982	President Reagan announces his Middle East peace plan.
9 Sept. 1982	Arab League summit in Fez.
4 Apr. 1983	King Hussein and Arafat reach a draft agreement.
10 Apr. 1983	Jordan abandons initiative with the PLO.
Feb. 1984	Jordan reopens dialogue with the PLO.
25 Sept. 1984	Jordan re-establishes diplomatic relations with Egypt.
22 Nov. 1984	King Hussein opens the Seventeenth PNC session in Amman.
11 Feb. 1985	The Jordanian–PLO accord is signed.
1 Oct. 1985	Israel bombs PLO headquarters in Tunis.
19 Feb. 1986	The Jordanian–PLO accord is abrogated.
July 1986	Closure of PLO and Fatah offices in Amman.

Aug. 1986	Jordan unveils the West Bank Development Plan.
11 Apr. 1987	The Hussein–Peres London Agreement.
19 Oct. 1987	Hussein–Shultz meeting in London.
8–11 Nov. 1987	Arab League summit in Amman.
9 Dec. 1987	Outbreak of the first Palestinian intifada.
27 Jan. 1988	George Shultz launches his peace initiative.
7–9 June 1988	Arab League summit in Algiers.
18 July 1988	End of the Iran–Iraq War.
28 July 1988	Jordan terminates West Bank Development Plan.
31 July 1988	Jordan disengages from the West Bank.
15 Nov. 1988	PNC meeting in Algiers recognizes Israel and accepts UN resolutions on Palestine.
14 Dec. 1988	Arafat accepts US terms for talks with the PLO.
16 Feb. 1989	The Arab Cooperation Council is formed.
18 Apr. 1989	Outbreak of riots in Ma'an.
8 Nov. 1989	Parliamentary elections are held.
Apr. 1990	King Hussein appoints a sixty-member royal commission to draft a national charter.
2 Aug. 1990	Iraq invades Kuwait.
3 Aug. 1990	Arab League condemns the Iraqi invasion of Kuwait.
10 Aug. 1990	Arab League approves military intervention against Iraq.
24 Dec. 1990	The Jordanian National Charter is announced.
16 Jan.–28 Feb. 1991	The Gulf War.
Mar. 1991	President Bush announces major new Middle East peace initiative.
9 June 1991	The Jordanian National Charter is adopted at a national conference.
30–31 Oct. 1991	Middle East peace conference convenes in Madrid.
14 Dec. 1991	Bilateral Arab–Israeli peace talks begin in Washington.
5 July 1992	Political parties are legalized.
Aug. 1992	King Hussein undergoes cancer surgery in the United States.
13 Sept. 1993	Israel–PLO Declaration of Principles on Interim Self-government is signed in the White House (Oslo Accord).
14 Sept. 1993	Jordan and Israel sign a common agenda in Washington.
1 Oct. 1993	Prince Hassan and Shimon Peres launch the Jordanian–US–Israeli Economic Committee in Washington.
8 Nov. 1993	Parliamentary elections.
4 May 1994	Israel and PLO reach agreement in Cairo on the application of the Declaration of Principles.

18 July 1994	Jordanian–Israeli negotiations move to the region.
25 July 1994	Washington Declaration is signed, ending state of war between Jordan and Israel.
26 July 1994	Hussein and Rabin address a joint session of Congress.
26 Oct. 1994	Jordan and Israel sign a peace treaty.
28 Sept. 1995	Israeli–Palestinian Interim Agreement on the West Bank and the Gaza Strip (Oslo II) is signed.
29–31 Oct. 1995	Second MENA economic summit held in Amman.
4 Nov. 1995	Rabin is assassinated and Peres succeeds him.
5 Jan. 1996	Hamas master bomb-maker Yahya Ayyash ("The Engineer") is assassinated by Israel.
11 Apr. 1996	Israel launches Operation Grapes of Wrath in south Lebanon.
29 May 1996	Binyamin Netanyahu defeats Peres in Israeli elections.
25 Sept. 1996	Clashes following opening of tunnel in the Old City of Jerusalem.
2 Oct. 1996	Summit meeting in Washington, D.C., with Clinton, Hussein and Netanyahu.
13 Nov. 1996	Third MENA economic summit opens in Cairo.
15 Jan. 1997	The Hebron Protocol is signed.
9 Mar. 1997	Hussein sends strongly worded letter to Netanyahu.
13 Mar. 1997	Six Israeli schoolgirls killed by a Jordanian soldier at Naharayim crossing.
18 Mar. 1997	Construction begins of Jewish housing at Har Homa in East Jerusalem.
25 Sept. 1997	The Khalid Mishal Affair.
14 July 1998	King Hussein leaves Jordan for medical treatment in the United States.
23 Oct. 1998	The signing of the Wye River Memorandum.
19 Jan. 1999	King Hussein returns to Jordan from the United States after treatment for cancer.
25 Jan. 1999	Crown Prince Hassan dismissed and Prince Abdullah bin Hussein named crown prince.
26 Jan. 1999	King Hussein leaves for the United States for emergency medical treatment.
5 Feb. 1999	King Hussein's final return to Jordan.
7 Feb. 1999	King Hussein dies, King Abdullah II proclaimed king and Prince Hamzah appointed crown prince.
8 Feb. 1999	King Hussein's funeral.

Interviews

JORDANIAN OFFICIALS
(With very few exceptions, interviews were held in Amman.)

NAME	DATE	PRINCIPAL POSITION
Abdullah bin Hussein	19 December 2002	King
Dr. Kamel Abu Jaber	13 September 2001	Foreign Minister
Hasan Abu-Nimah	7 March 2002	Ambassador
Adnan Abu-Odeh	16 September 2001 17 September 2002	Political Adviser
Jawad al-Anani	19 September 2002	Foreign Minister
Fouad Ayoub	15 March 2002	Ambassador
Princess Basma bint Talal	21 December 2002	Sister of Hussein
Dr. Musa Braizat	21 December 2002	Ambassador
Dr. Munther Haddadin	15 September 2002 17 September 2002	Minister of Water and Irrigation
Dr. Mustafa Hamarneh	14 March 2002	Academic
Prince El Hassan bin Talal	19 September 2001 17 September 2002 11 January 2007	Crown Prince
Hussein bin Tala	3 December 1996	King
Dr. Taher Kanaan	11 September 2002	Minister of Planning
Marwan Kasim	17 September 2001 15 September 2002 19 September 2002 16 December 2002 18 December 2002	Deputy Prime Minister

NAME	DATE	PRINCIPAL POSITION
General Muhammad Rasoul al-Keilani	20 December 2002	Director of General Intelligence
Dr. Musa al-Keilani	20 December 2002	Journalist
Awn Khasawneh	22 December 2002	Chief of the Royal Court
Abdul Ilah al-Khatib	13 March 2002	Foreign Minister
Ahmad al-Lozi	15 December 2002	Prime Minister
Dr. Abdul Salam Majali	18 September 2001 19 September 2001	Prime Minister
General Hussein Majali	21 December 2002	Chief Security Officer to Hussein
Taher al-Masri	21 September 2001 6 March 2002 10 March 2002 11 March 2002 14 September 2002	Prime Minister
Marwan Muasher	13 March 2002	Foreign Minister
Rajai Muasher	21 December 2002	Minister of Industry and Trade
Dr. Hani Mulki	17 September 2001	Minister of Trade
Dr. Samir Mutawi	18 September 2001 6 March 2002	Minister of Information
Omar Nabulsi	20 September 2002	Minister of National Economy
Dr. Hazem Nusseibeh	18 September 2002	Foreign Minister
Prince Raad bin Zaid	6 September 2002	Lord Chamberlain
General Natheer Rasheed	20 September 2002	Director of Intelligence
Zaid Rifa'i	19 September 2002 20 December 2002	Prime Minister
Abdullah Salah	12 December 2002	Ambassador
Princess Sarvath	11 January 2007	Wife of Prince Hassan
Dr. Jamal Sha'er	20 September 2001	Minister of Local Government

NAME	DATE	PRINCIPAL POSITION
Sharif Zaid bin Shaker	12 March 2002	Prime Minister
Laila Sharaf	18 September 2002 22 December 2002	Minister of Information
General Ali Shukri	16 September 2001 17 September 2001 18 September 2001 11 September 2002 13 September 2002 11 December 2002 13 December 2002 14 December 2002 15 December 2002 16 December 2002 19 December 2002 22 December 2002 24 February 2003 26 March 2003 9 June 2003 12 June 2003	Director of Hussein's Private Office
General Ihsan Shurdom	12 March 2002	Commander of the Air Force
General Tahseen Shurdom	16 September 2002	Director of Public Security
Prince Talal bin Muhammad	11 September 2002 12 September 2002 24 September 2002	National Security Adviser to Hussein
Mreiwad al-Tall	12 September 2001	Court Official
Tariq al-Tall	11 August 2001	Academic
Dr. Fayez Tarawneh	18 December 2002	Prime Minister

ISRAELI OFFICIALS
(Interviews were held in Tel Aviv and Jerusalem.)

Major-General Meir Amit	21 March 2002	Director of the Mossad
Dr. Yossi Beilin	23 June 2004	Minister of Justice
Simha Dinitz	21 July 1982	Director-General of PM's office

NAME	DATE	PRINCIPAL POSITION
Miriam Eshkol	12 December 2002	Librarian of the Knesset
Mordechai Gazit	22 June 2004	Director-General of PM's office
General Shlomo Gazit	23 June 2004	Director of Military Intelligence
Eitan Haber	24 June 2004	Director-General of PM's office
Dan Meridor	21 June 2004	Minister of Justice
Dan Patir	20 June 2004	Press Secretary to PM
Shimon Peres	22 June 2004 24 June 2004	Prime Minister
Itzhak Rabin	22 August 1982	Prime Minister
Professor Itamar Rabinovich	23 June 2004	Ambassador to United States
Moshe Sasson	8 September 1982 21 March 2002	Ambassador to Egypt
Yaacov Shimoni	26 September 1982	Foreign Ministry Official

AMERICAN OFFICIALS
(Interviews held in Washington, D.C.)

Wesley Egan	2 December 2003	Ambassador to Jordan
Cranwell G. Montgomery	3 December 2003	Ambassador to Oman
Nicholas Veliotis	3 December 2003	Ambassador to Jordan
Richard Viets	1 December 2003	Ambassador to Jordan

BRITISH OFFICIALS

Sir Mark Allen	23 February 2007 (Oxford)	Political Counsellor, Amman
Christopher Prentice	7 November 2006 (Oxford)	Ambassador to Jordan
Sir Roger Tomkys	29 September 2001 (Cambridge)	Ambassador to Syria

Bibliography

ARCHIVES

Ben-Gurion Archive, Sede-Boker
Central Zionist Archives, Jerusalem (CZA)
Israel State Archives, Jerusalem (ISA)
Lyndon B. Johnson Library, Austin, Texas (LBJL)
Middle East Centre Archive, St. Antony's College, Oxford
Public Record Office, London (PRO)
United States National Archives, Washington, DC (USNA)

PRIVATE PAPERS

David Ben-Gurion's diary, Ben-Gurion Archive, Sede-Boker
Philip Geyelin, Middle East Centre Archive, St. Antony's College, Oxford
Dr. Yaacov Herzog, Jerusalem
Jordanian records of the General Investigations, General Security and Military
    Intelligence departments captured by the IDF during the June War of 1967.
    Classified papers deposited in the Ben-Gurion Archive, Sede-Boker
General Ali Shukri, Amman
Moshe Zak, Ramat Aviv

ORAL HISTORY

Oral History Project, Leonard Davis Institute for International Relations, Jeru-
    salem. Twenty-three interviews with Yigal Allon, ISA
The 50 Years War. Transcripts of interviews for the six-part BBC television
    series, 1998. Middle East Centre Archive, St. Antony's College, Oxford

PERIODICALS

The Guardian
Ha'aretz

International Herald Tribune
Jerusalem Post
Jordan Times
Ma'ariv
The New Yorker
Time
Washington Post
Yediot Aharonot

DOCUMENTS AND OFFICIAL PUBLICATIONS

Foreign Relations of the United States. Washington, DC: United States Government Printing House, various dates of publication. Volumes on the Middle East 1955–68.

Government of the Hashemite Kingdom of Jordan. White Paper, *Jordan and the Gulf Crisis August 1990–March 1991.* Amman, August 1991.

Iraqi Parliament. *Taqrir Lajnat at-Tahqiq al-Niyabiyya fi Qadiyyat Filastin* [*Report of the Parliamentary Committee of Inquiry into the Palestine Question*], in Arabic (Baghdad, 1949).

Israel State Archives. *Provisional State Council: Protocols 18 April–13 May 1948,* in Hebrew (Jerusalem, 1978).

Rosenthal, Yemima, ed. *Documents on the Foreign Policy of Israel.* Volume VIII: 1953. Jerusalem: Israel State Archives, 1995.

WORKS CITED

Abbas, Mahmoud. *Through Secret Channels.* Reading: Garnet, 1995.

Abdullah, King. *My Memoirs Completed: "Al Takmilah."* London: Longman, 1978.

Abu-Odeh, Adnan. *Jordanians, Palestinians, and the Hashemite Kingdom in the Middle East Peace Process.* Washington, DC: United States Institute of Peace Press, 1999.

Ajami, Fouad. *The Dream Palace of the Arabs: A Generation's Odyssey.* New York: Pantheon Books, 1998.

Alkadiri, Raad. "Strategy and Tactics in Jordanian Foreign Policy 1967–1988." Unpublished D.Phil. thesis, University of Oxford, 1995.

al-Khatib al-Tamimi, Anwar. *Ma'a Salah al-Din fi al-Quds: ta'ammulat wa-dhikrayat* [*With Salah al-Din in Jerusalem: Contemplations and Memoirs*], in Arabic. Jerusalem: Dar al-Tibaah al-Arabiyah, 1989.

Al Madfai, Madiha Rashid. *Jordan, the United States and the Middle East Peace Process 1974–1991.* Cambridge: Cambridge University Press, 1993.

al-Madi, Munib, and Suleiman Musa. *Tarikh al-urdunn fi al-qarn al-'ishreen*

[The History of Jordan in the Twentieth Century], in Arabic. Volume I. 2nd ed. Amman: Maktabat al-Muhtasab, 1988.

al-Majali, Hazza'. *Mudhakkarati [My Memoirs]*, in Arabic. Beirut: Dar al-Ilm lil-Malayeen, 1960.

Al-Rifa'i, Samir. "The 1974 Rabat Conference: A Crucial Arab Summit." Unpublished M.Phil. thesis, University of Cambridge, 1989.

al-Windawi, Mouayad Ibrahim K. "Anglo-Iraqi Relations 1945–1958." Unpublished Ph.D. thesis, University of Reading, 1989.

Antonius, George. *The Arab Awakening: The Story of the Arab National Movement*. 1965 ed. New York: Capricorn Books, 1938.

Ashrawi, Hanan. *This Side of Peace: A Personal Account*. New York: Simon and Schuster, 1995.

Ayalon, Ami, and Bruce Maddy-Weitzman, eds., *Middle East Contemporary Survey. Volume XVIII: 1994*. Boulder, CO: Westview Press, 1996.

Baker III, James A. *The Politics of Diplomacy: Revolution, War and Peace 1989–1992*. New York: Putnam's, 1995.

Bar-Lavie, Ze'ev. *Hamishtar ha-hashemi 1949–1967, ve-ma'amado ba-gada ha-ma'aravit [The Hashemite Regime 1949–1967, and Its Status in the West Bank]*, in Hebrew. Tel Aviv: The Shiloah Center, 1981.

Barnea, Amalia and Aharon. *Mine Enemy*. London: Halban, 1989.

Bar-Zohar, Michael. *Khayav ve-moto shel nasikh yehudi: biographia shel Yaacov Herzog [The Life and Times of a Jewish Prince: A Biography of Yaacov Herzog]*, in Hebrew. Tel Aviv: Yediot Aharonot, 2003.

Be'eri, Eliezer. *Army Officers in Arab Politics and Society*. New York: Praeger, 1970.

Ben Elissar, Eliahu. *Lo od milhama [No More War]*, in Hebrew. Jerusalem: Ma'ariv, 1995.

Ben-Porat, Shayke. *Sikhot im Yossi Beilin [Talks with Yossi Beilin]*, in Hebrew. Tel Aviv: Hakibbutz Hameuhad Publishing House, 1996.

Bidwell, Robin. *Dictionary of Modern Arab History*. London: Kegan Paul, 1998.

Blix, Hans. *Disarming Iraq: The Search for Weapons of Mass Destruction*. London: Bloomsbury, 2004.

Bowen, Jeremy. *Six Days: How the 1967 War Shaped the Middle East*. London: Simon and Schuster, 2003.

Brand, Laurie A. *Jordan's Inter-Arab Relations: The Political Economy of Alliance Making*. New York: Columbia University Press, 1994.

Bregman, Ahron. *Israel's Wars 1947–1993*. London: Routledge, 2000.

Brzezinski, Zbigniew. *Power and Principle: Memoirs of a National Security Adviser 1977–1981*. London: Weidenfeld and Nicolson, 1983.

Bull, Odd. *War and Peace in the Middle East: The Experiences and Views of a UN Observer*. London: Leo Cooper, 1976.

Bush, George, and Brent Scowcroft. *A World Transformed*. New York: Vintage, 1998.

Cartor, Jimmy. *Keeping Faith: Memoirs of a President*. London: Collins, 1982.

Childers, Erskine B. *The Road to Suez: A Study of Western–Arab Relations.* London: MacGibbon and Kee, 1962.

Cobban, Helena. *The Palestinian Liberation Organisation: People, Power, and Politics.* Cambridge: Cambridge University Press, 1984.

Cohen, Amnon. *Political Parties in the West Bank under the Jordanian Regime 1949–1967.* Ithaca: Cornell University Press, 1982.

Cohen, Mendel. *Behatzero shel hamelech Abdullah* [*At the Court of King Abdullah*], in Hebrew. Tel Aviv: Am Oved, 1980.

Copeland, Miles. *The Game of Nations: The Amorality of Power Politics.* London: Weidenfeld and Nicolson, 1969.

Dallas, Roland. *King Hussein: A Life on the Edge.* London: Profile Books, 1999.

Dann, Uriel. "Glubb and the Politicization of the Arab Legion: An Annotated Document." *Asian and African Studies,* 21 (1987).

——. "The Foreign Office, the Baghdad Pact and Jordan." *Asian and African Studies,* 21 (1987).

——. *King Hussein and the Challenge of Arab Radicalism: Jordan 1955–1967.* New York: Oxford University Press, 1989.

Dawisha, Adeed. *Arab Nationalism in the Twentieth Century: From Triumph to Despair.* Princeton, NJ: Princeton University Press, 2003.

Dayan, Moshe. *Diary of the Sinai Campaign.* London: Sphere Books, 1967.

——. *Avnei derekh: otobiographia* [*Milestones: An Autobiography*], in Hebrew. Tel Aviv: Yediot Aharonot, 1976.

——. *Breakthrough: A Personal Account of the Egypt–Israel Peace Negotiations.* London: Weidenfeld and Nicolson, 1981.

Dearden, Ann. *Jordan.* London: Robert Hale, 1958.

Eban, Abba. *An Autobiography.* London: Weidenfeld and Nicolson, 1978.

——. *Personal Witness: Israel Through My Eyes.* New York: Putnam's, 1992.

Eden, Anthony. *Full Circle: The Memoirs of the Rt. Hon. Sir Anthony Eden.* London: Cassell, 1960.

Eisenberg, Laura Zittrain, and Neil Caplan. *Negotiating Arab–Israeli Peace: Patterns, Problems, Possibilities.* Bloomington: Indiana University Press, 1998.

Eveland, Wilbur Crane. *Ropes of Sand: America's Failure in the Middle East.* New York: W. W. Norton, 1980.

Farid, Abdel Majid. *Nasser: The Final Years.* Reading: Ithaca Press, 1994.

Fisk, Robert. *The Great War for Civilisation: The Conquest of the Middle East.* London: Fourth Estate, 2005.

Friedman, Alan. *Spider's Web: Bush, Saddam, Thatcher and the Decade of Deceit.* London: Faber and Faber, 1993.

Friedman, Isaiah. *Palestine: A Twice-promised Land?* New Brunswick, NJ: Transaction Publishers, 2000.

Friedman, Thomas. *From Beirut to Jerusalem.* London: Fontana Books, 1990.

Fromkin, David. *A Peace to End All Peace: Creating the Modern Middle East 1914–1922.* London: Penguin, 1991.

Garfinkle, Adam. *Israel and Jordan in the Shadow of War: Functional Ties and Futile Diplomacy in a Small Place*. London: Macmillan, 1992.

Gavra, Gai. "The Hussein–Golda Meeting on the Eve of the Yom Kippur War," in Hebrew. Unpublished BA thesis, Tel Aviv University, 2000.

Gazit, Mordechai. "The Yom Kippur War: A Critical Look at Commonly Accepted Assumptions." Unpublished paper.

Gelber, Yoav. *Jewish–Transjordanian Relations 1921–48*. London: Frank Cass, 1997.

Gerges, Fawaz A. *The Superpowers and the Middle East: Regional and International Politics 1955–1967*. Boulder, CO: Westview Press, 1994.

Geyelin, Philip. "Hashemite: The Story of King Hussein of Jordan." Unfinished and unpublished manuscript. Middle East Centre Archive, St. Antony's College, Oxford.

Gilbert, Martin. *Winston S. Churchill. Volume IV: The Stricken World 1916–1922*. London: Heinemann, 1975.

Glubb, John Bagot. *A Soldier with the Arabs*. London: Hodder and Stoughton, 1957.

Golan, Matti. *Shimon Peres: A Biography*. London: Weidenfeld and Nicolson, 1982.

Gowers, Andrew, and Tony Walker. *Behind the Myth: Yasser Arafat and the Palestinian Revolution*. London: W. H. Allen, 1990.

Haddadin, Munther J. *Diplomacy on the Jordan: International Conflict and Negotiated Resolution*. Boston: Kluwer Academic, 2002.

Halevy, Efraim. *Man in the Shadows: Inside the Middle East Crisis with the Man Who Led the Mossad*. London: Weidenfeld and Nicolson, 2006.

Hart, Alan. *Arafat: A Political Biography*. Revised ed. London: Sidgwick and Jackson, 1994.

Heikal, Mohamed H. *The Road to Ramadan*. London: Collins, 1975.

——. *Cutting the Lion's Tail: Suez Through Egyptian Eyes*. London: André Deutsch, 1986.

——. *Illusions of Triumph: An Arab View of the Gulf War*. London: Fontana, 1992.

——. *Secret Channels: The Inside Story of Arab–Israeli Peace Negotiations*. London: HarperCollins, 1996.

Helms, Richard. *A Look Over My Shoulder: A Life in the Central Intelligence Agency*. New York: Random House, 2003.

Henniker, John. *Painful Extractions: Looking Back at a Personal Journey*. Eye, Suffolk: Thornham Books, 2002.

Herzog, Chaim. *The Arab–Israeli Wars: War and Peace in the Middle East*. New York: Vintage Books, 1982.

Hirst, David. *The Gun and the Olive Branch: The Roots of Violence in the Middle East*. London: Faber and Faber, 1977.

Horovitz, David, ed. *Yitzhak Rabin: Soldier of Peace*. London: Peter Halban, 1996.

Hussein bin Talal. *Uneasy Lies the Head: An Autobiography.* London: Heineman, 1962.

——. *Mihnati ka-malik* [*My Profession as King*], in Arabic. Amman: Al-Ahliyya Publishing House, [n.d.].

Hutchison, E. H. *Violent Truce: A Military Observer Looks at the Arab–Israeli Conflict 1951–1955.* New York: Devin-Adiar, 1956.

Ionides, Michael. *Divide and Lose: The Arab Revolt of 1955–1958.* London: Geoffrey Bles, 1960.

Iyad, Abu, and Eric Rouleau. *My Home, My Land: A Narrative of the Palestinian Struggle.* New York: Times Books, 1978.

Johnston, Charles. *The Brink of Jordan.* London: Hamish Hamilton, 1972.

Kedourie, Elie. *Arabic Political Memoirs and Other Studies.* London: Frank Cass, 1974.

——. *In the Anglo-Arab Labyrinth: The McMahon–Husayn Correspondence and Its Interpretations 1914–1939.* Cambridge: Cambridge University Press, 1976.

Kerr, Malcolm H. *The Arab Cold War: Gamal Abd al-Nasir and His Rivals 1958–1970.* 3rd ed. London: Oxford University Press, 1971.

Kirkbride, Alec Seath. *A Crackle of Thorns: Experiences in the Middle East.* London: John Murray, 1956.

——. *From the Wings: Amman Memoirs 1947–1951.* London: Frank Cass, 1976.

Kissinger, Henry. *White House Years.* Boston: Little Brown, 1979.

——. *Years of Upheaval.* London: Weidenfeld and Nicolson, 1982.

Kyle, Keith. *Suez.* London: Weidenfeld and Nicolson, 1991.

Landis, Joshua. "Syria and the Palestine War: Fighting King Abdullah's 'Greater Syria Plan.' " In *The War for Palestine: Rewriting the History of 1948*, Eugene L. Rogan and Avi Shlaim, eds. Cambridge: Cambridge University Press, 2001.

Lawrence, T. E. *Revolt in the Desert.* London: Jonathan Cape, 1927.

Little, Douglas. "A Puppet in Search of a Puppeteer? The United States, King Hussein, and Jordan 1953–1970." *International History Review*, 18:3 (August 1995).

Love, Kennett. *Suez—The Twice-fought War: A History.* New York: McGraw-Hill, 1969.

Lukacs, Yehuda, ed. *The Israeli–Palestinian Conflict: A Documentary Record 1967–1990.* Cambridge: Cambridge University Press, 1992.

——. *Israel, Jordan, and the Peace Process.* New York: Syracuse University Press, 1999.

Lunt, James. *Hussein of Jordan.* London: Fontana/Collins, 1990.

Lynch, Marc. *State Interests and Public Spheres: The International Politics of Jordan's Identity.* New York: Columbia University Press, 1999.

Macmillan, Harold. *Riding the Storm 1956–1959.* London: Macmillan, 1971.

Maddy-Weitzman, Bruce, ed. *Middle East Contemporary Survey.* Volume XIX: *1995.* Boulder, CO: Westview Press, 1997.

——. *Middle East Contemporary Survey.* Volume XX: *1996.* Boulder, CO: Westview Press, 1998.

——. *Middle East Contemporary Survey.* Volume XXI: *1997.* Boulder, CO: Westview Press, 2000.

——. *Middle East Contemporary Survey.* Volume XXII: *1998.* Boulder, CO: Westview Press, 2001.

Mahafza, Ali. *'Ashrat a'awam min al-kifah wa al-bina: majmuat khutub jalalat al-malik Hussein bin Talal 1977–1987 [Ten Years of Struggle and Building: The Collected Speeches of His Majesty King Hussein bin Talal 1977–1987],* in Arabic. Amman: Markaz al-Kitab al-Urduni, 1988.

Makovsky, David. *Making Peace with the PLO: The Rabin Government's Road to the Oslo Accord.* Boulder, CO: Westview Press, 1996.

Mango, Adiba. "Jordan on the Road to Peace 1988–1999," Unpublished D.Phil. thesis, University of Oxford, 2002.

Massad, Joseph A. *Colonial Effects: The Making of National Identity in Jordan.* New York: Columbia University Press, 2001.

Meir, Golda. *My Life.* London: Weidenfeld and Nicolson, 1975.

Meital, Yoram. "The Khartoum Conference and Egyptian Policy after the 1967 War: A Re-examination." *Middle East Journal,* 54:1 (Winter 2000).

Melman, Yossi, and Dan Raviv. *Behind the Uprising: Israelis, Jordanians, and Palestinians.* New York: Greenwood Press, 1989.

Monroe, Elizabeth. *Britain's Moment in the Middle East 1914–1971.* New and revised 2nd ed. London: Chatto and Windus, 1981.

Morris, Benny. *Israel's Border Wars 1949–1956: Arab Infiltration, Israeli Retaliation, and the Countdown to the Suez War.* Oxford: Clarendon Press, 1993.

——. *The Birth of the Palestinian Refugee Problem Revisited.* Cambridge: Cambridge University Press, 2004.

Morris, James. *The Hashemite Kings.* London: Faber and Faber, 1959.

Mufti, Malik. "The United States and Nasserist Pan-Arabism." In *The Middle East and the United States: A Historical and Political Reassessment,* David W. Lesch, ed. Boulder, CO: Westview Press, 1996.

Mutawi, Samir A. *Jordan in the 1967 War.* Cambridge: Cambridge University Press, 1987.

Naor, Arye, *Memshalah be-milhamah: tifkud memshelet yisrael bc-milhemet levanon, 1982 [Cabinet at War: The Functioning of the Israeli Cabinet during the Lebanon War, 1982],* in Hebrew. Tel Aviv: Lahav, 1986.

——. *Ktovet al ha-kir: le'an molikh ha-Likud [Writing on the Wall: Where Is the Likud Leading?],* in Hebrew. Tel Aviv: Edanim, 1988.

Nixon, Richard M. *The Memoirs of Richard Nixon.* London: Sidgwick and Jackson, 1978.

Noor, Queen. *Leap of Faith: Memoirs of an Unexpected Life.* London: Weidenfeld and Nicolson, 2003.

Nutting, Anthony. *No End of a Lesson: The Story of Suez.* London: Constable, 1967.

Paris, Timothy J. *Britain, the Hashemites and Arab Rule 1920–1925: The Sheri-fian Solution*. London: Frank Cass, 2003.

Pedatzur, Reuven. "Coming Back Full Circle: The Palestinian Option in 1967." *Middle East Journal*, 49:2 (Spring 1995).

Peres, Shimon. *David's Sling*. London: Weidenfeld and Nicolson, 1970.

———. *Battling for Peace: Memoirs*. London: Weidenfeld and Nicolson, 1995.

Peretz, Don. *Intifada: The Palestinian Uprising*. Boulder, CO: Westview Press, 1990.

Plascov, Avi. *The Palestinian Refugees in Jordan 1948–1957*. London: Frank Cass, 1981.

Podeh, Elie. "The Struggle for Arab Hegemony after the Suez Crisis." *Middle Eastern Studies*, 29:1 (January 1993).

———. *The Quest for Hegemony in the Arab World: The Struggle over the Bagh-dad Pact*. Leiden: Brill, 1995.

———. *The Decline of Arab Unity: The Rise and Fall of the United Arab Repub-lic*. Brighton: Sussex Academic Press, 1999.

Quandt, William B. *Peace Process: American Diplomacy and the Arab–Israeli Conflict since 1967*. Berkeley: University of California Press, 2001.

Raad, Zeid. "A Nightmare Avoided: Jordan and Suez 1956." *Israel Affairs*, 1:2 (Winter 1994).

Rabin, Yitzhak. *The Rabin Memoirs*. London: Weidenfeld and Nicolson, 1979.

Rabinovich, Itamar. *Waging Peace: Israel and the Arabs at the End of the Cen-tury*. New York: Farrar, Straus and Giroux, 1999.

Rafael, Gideon. *Destination Peace: Three Decades of Israeli Foreign Policy*. New York: Stein and Day, 1981.

Raviv, Dan, and Yossi Melman. *Every Spy a Prince: The Complete History of Israel's Intelligence Community*. Boston: Houghton Mifflin, 1990.

Raz, Avi. "The Palestinian Option: Israel and the West Bank Leadership 1967–1969." D.Phil. thesis in progress in 2007, University of Oxford.

Reagan, Ronald. *An American Life*. London: Hutchinson, 1990.

Riad, Mahmoud. *The Struggle for Peace in the Middle East*. London: Quartet, 1981.

Robins, Philip. *A History of Jordan*. Cambridge: Cambridge University Press, 2003.

Rogan, Eugene L. "Jordan and 1948: The Persistence of an Official History." In *The War for Palestine: Rewriting the History of 1948*, Eugene L. Rogan and Avi Shlaim, eds. Cambridge: Cambridge University Press, 2001.

Ross, Dennis. *The Missing Peace: The Inside Story of the Fight for Middle East Peace*. New York: Farrar, Straus and Giroux, 2004.

Rubinstein, Elyakim. "The Peace Treaty with Jordan," in Hebrew. *Hamishpat*, 6 (December 1995).

———. "The Peace Between Israel and Jordan—Chapters in Its Making," in Hebrew. Unpublished lecture, 12 October 2001.

Rusk, Dean. *As I Saw It: A Secretary of State's Memoirs*. London: I. B. Tauris, 1991.

Salibi, Kamal S. *The Modern History of Jordan*. London: I. B. Tauris, 1993.

Satloff, Robert B. *From Abdullah to Hussein: Jordan in Transition*. New York: Oxford University Press, 1993.

——. "The Jekyll-and-Hyde Origins of the US–Jordanian Strategic Relationship." In *The Middle East and the United States: A Historical and Political Reassessment*, David W. Lesch, ed. Boulder, CO: Westview, 2003.

Savir, Uri. *The Process: 1,100 Days that Changed the Middle East*. New York: Random House, 1998.

Sayigh, Yezid. *Armed Struggle and the Search for State: The Palestinian National Movement 1949–1993*. Oxford: Clarendon Press, 1997.

Schenker, David. *Dancing with Saddam: The Strategic Tango of Jordanian–Iraqi Relations*. Lanham: Lexington Books, 2003.

Schiff, Ze'ev, and Ehud Ya'ari. *Israel's Lebanon War*. London: Allen and Unwin, 1985.

——. *Intifada: The Palestinian Uprising—Israel's Third Front*. New York: Simon and Schuster, 1990.

Seale, Patrick. *The Struggle for Syria: A Study in Post-war Arab Politics 1945–1958*. London: Oxford University Press, 1965.

——. *Asad of Syria. The Struggle for the Middle East*. London: I. B. Tauris, 1988

Segev, Tom. *1967: ve-ha'aretz shinta et paneha [1967: And the Land Was Transformed]*, in Hebrew. Jerusalem: Keter, 2005.

Sela, Avraham. *Ahdut betokh perud ba-ma'arekhet habein-arvit: ve'idot ha-pisgah ha-arviyot 1964–1982 [Unity within Disunity in the Inter-Arab System: The Arab Summit Conferences 1964–1982]*, in Hebrew. Jerusalem: Magnes Press, 1982.

——. "Transjordan, Israel and the 1948 War: Myth, Historiography and Reality." *Middle Eastern Studies*, 24: 4 (October 1992).

Shaham, David. *Israel—40 ha-shanim [Israel—The 40 Years]*, in Hebrew. Tel Aviv: Am Oved, 1991.

Shalom, Zaki. *The Superpowers, Israel and the Future of Jordan 1960–1963: The Perils of the Pro-Nasser Policy*. Brighton: Sussex Academic Press, 1999.

Shamir, Yitzhak. *Summing Up: An Autobiography*. London: Weidenfeld and Nicolson, 1994.

Sharon, Ariel. *Warrior: The Autobiography of Ariel Sharon*. London: Macdonald, 1989.

Shemesh, Moshe. *The Palestinian Entity 1959–1974: Arab Politics and the PLO*. 2nd ed. London: Frank Cass, 1996.

——. "The IDF Raid on Samu: The Turning-Point in Jordan's Relations with Israel and the West Bank Palestinians." *Israel Studies*, 7:1 (Spring 2002).

Shlaim, Avi. "Husni Za'im and the Plan to Resettle Palestinian Refugees in Syria." *Journal of Palestine Studies*, 15:4 (Summer 1986).

——. *Collusion Across the Jordan: King Abdullah, the Zionist Movement, and the Partition of Palestine*. Oxford: Clarendon Press, 1988.

——. *The Politics of Partition: King Abdullah, the Zionists, and Palestine 1921–1951*. Oxford: Oxford University Press, 1990.

——. "The Debate About 1948." *International Journal of Middle East Studies*, 27:3 (1995).

——. "The Protocol of Sèvres 1956: Anatomy of a War Plot." *International Affairs*, 73:3 (July 1997).

——. "His Royal Shyness: King Hussein and Israel." *New York Review of Books*, 15 July 1999.

——. "Israel, the Great Powers, and the Middle East Crisis of 1958." *Journal of Imperial and Commonwealth History*, 27:2 (May 1999).

——. *The Iron Wall: Israel and the Arab World*. New York: W. W. Norton, 2000.

——. "Interview with Abba Eban, 11 March 1976." *Israel Studies*, 8:1 (Spring 2003).

——. "The Balfour Declaration and Its Consequences." In *More Adventures with Britannia: Personalities, Politics and Culture in Britain*, Wm. Roger Louis, ed. London: I. B. Tauris, 2005.

Shuckburgh, Evelyn. *Descent to Suez: Diaries 1951–1956*. London: Weidenfeld and Nicolson, 1986.

Shultz, George P. *Turmoil and Triumph: My Years as Secretary of State*. New York: Scribner's, 1993.

Snow, Peter. *Hussein: A Biography*. London: Barrie and Jenkins, 1972.

Stephens, Robert. *Nasser: A Political Biography*. London: Allen Lane, 1971.

Sultan, Khaled bin, and Patrick Seale. *Desert Warrior: A Personal View of the Gulf War by the Joint Forces Commander*. London: HarperCollins, 1995.

Susser, Asher. *In Through the Out Door: Jordan's Disengagement and the Middle East Peace Process*. Washington, DC: The Washington Institute for Near East Policy, 1990.

——. *On Both Banks of the Jordan: A Political Biography of Wasfi al-Tall*. London: Frank Cass, 1994.

——. *The Jordanian–Israeli Peace Negotiations: The Geopolitical Rationale of a Bilateral Relationship*. Davis Occasional Papers, No. 73. Jerusalem: Leonard Davis Institute for International Relations, Hebrew University of Jerusalem, 1999.

Tal, Lawrence. "Jordan." In *The Cold War and the Middle East*, Yezid Sayigh and Avi Shlaim, eds. Oxford: Oxford University Press, 1997.

——. *Politics, the Military, and National Security in Jordan 1955–1967*. Basingstoke: Palgrave Macmillan, 2002.

Tidrick, Kathryn. *Heart-beguiling Araby*. 2nd ed. London: I. B. Tauris, 1989.

Trevelyan, Humphrey. *The Middle East in Revolution*. London: Macmillan, 1970.

Troen, Selwyn Ilan, and Moshe Shemesh, eds., *The Suez–Sinai Crisis 1956: Retrospective and Reappraisal*. London: Frank Cass, 1990.

Vance, Cyrus. *Hard Choices: Critical Years in America's Foreign Policy*. New York: Simon and Schuster, 1983.

Vance, Vick, and Pierre Lauer. *Hussein of Jordan. My "War" with Israel*. New York: William Morrow, 1969.

Vatikiotis, P. J. *Politics and the Military in Jordan: A Study of the Arab Legion 1921–1957*. London: Frank Cass, 1967.

Weinberger, Caspar. *Fighting for Peace: Seven Critical Years at the Pentagon*. London: Michael Joseph, 1990.

Weizman, Ezer. *On Eagles' Wings: The Personal Story of the Leading Commander of the Israeli Air Force*. London: Weidenfeld and Nicolson, 1976.

Wilson, Mary C. *King Abdullah, Britain and the Making of Jordan*. Cambridge: Cambridge University Press, 1987.

Woodward, Bob. *Veil: The Secret Wars of the CIA 1981–1987*. New York: Simon and Schuster, 1987.

Zak, Moshe. "Israeli–Jordanian Negotiations." *Washington Quarterly*, 8:1 (Winter 1985).

——. *Hussein oseh shalom [Hussein Makes Peace]*, in Hebrew. Ramat-Gan: Bar-Ilan University Press, 1996.

Zeira, Eli. *Milchemet yom ha-kippurim: mytos mul metsiut [The Yom Kippur War: Myth against Reality]*, in Hebrew. Tel Aviv: Yediot Aharonot, 1993.

Index

Page numbers in *italics* refer to maps

A NOTE ABOUT THE AUTHOR

Avi Shlaim was born in Baghdad in 1945, grew up in Israel, and studied at Cambridge and the London School of Economics. He is a fellow
of St. Anthony's College and professor of international relations at the
University of Oxford. He was elected a fellow of the British Academy in
2006. His books include *Collusion Across the Jordan: King Abdullah,
the Zionist Movement, and the Partition of Palestine* (winner of the
Political Studies Association's W.J.M. Mackenzie Book Prize, 1988),
*The Politics of Partition: King Abdullah, the Zionists, and Palestine
1921–1951, War and Peace in the Middle East: A Concise History,* and
The Iron Wall: Israel and the Arab World. He lives in Oxford.

A NOTE ON THE TYPE

The text of this book was composed in Melior, a typeface designed
by Hermann Zapf and issued in 1952. Born in Nuremberg, Germany,
in 1918, Zapf has been a strong influence in printing since 1939.
Melior, like Times Roman (another popular twentieth-century typeface), was created specifically for use in newspaper composition.
With this functional end in mind, Zapf nonetheless chose to base the
proportions of his letter forms on those of the golden section. The
result is a typeface of unusual strength and surpassing subtlety.

COMPOSED BY

North Market Street Graphics, Lancaster, Pennsylvania

PRINTED AND BOUND BY

Berryville Graphics, Berryville, Virginia

DESIGNED BY

Iris Weinstein